Mao-chan

① 1

Story by
Ken Akamatsu

Art by
RAN

Translated and adapted
by Kathleen Westlake

Lettered by
North Market Street Graphics

BALLANTINE BOOKS * NEW YORK

A Del Rey Manga/Kodansha Trade Paperback Original

Mao-chan volume 1 copyright © 2002 by XEBEC, Riku-Mao Honbu
copyright © 2003 by Ken Akamatsu and RAN
Mao-chan volume 2 copyright © 2002 by XEBEC, Riku-Mao Honbu
copyright © 2003 by Ken Akamatsu and RAN
English translation copyright © 2008 by XEBEC, Riku-Mao Honbu
copyright © 2008 by Ken Akamatsu and RAN

All rights reserved.

Published in the United States by Del Rey, an imprint of The Random House Publishing Group, a division of Random House, Inc., New York.

DEL REY is a registered trademark and the Del Rey colophon is a trademark of Random House, Inc.

Publication rights arranged through Kodansha Ltd.

First published in Japan in 2002 by Kodansha Ltd., Tokyo as
Rikujo Boueitai Mao Chan volumes 1 and 2

ISBN 978-0-345-50181-3

Printed in the United States of America

www.delreymanga.com

2 4 6 8 9 7 5 3 1

Translator/adapter: Kathleen Westlake
Lettering: North Market Street Graphics

CONTENTS

HONORIFICS EXPLAINED

Throughout the Del Rey Manga books, you will find Japanese honorifics left intact in the translations. For those not familiar with how the Japanese use honorifics and, more important, how they differ from American honorifics, we present this brief overview.

Politeness has always been a critical facet of Japanese culture. Ever since the feudal era, when Japan was a highly stratified society, use of honorifics—which can be defined as polite speech that indicates relationship or status—has played an essential role in the Japanese language. When addressing someone in Japanese, an honorific usually takes the form of a suffix attached to one's name (example: "Asuna-san"), is used as a title at the end of one's name, or appears in place of the name itself (example: "Negi-sensei," or simply "Sensei!").

Honorifics can be expressions of respect or endearment. In the context of manga and anime, honorifics give insight into the nature of the relationship between characters. Many English translations leave out these important honorifics and therefore distort the feel of the original Japanese. Because Japanese honorifics contain nuances that English honorifics lack, it is our policy at Del Rey not to translate them. Here, instead, is a guide to some of the honorifics you may encounter in Del Rey Manga.

-san: This is the most common honorific and is equivalent to Mr., Miss, Ms., or Mrs. It is the all-purpose honorific and can be used in any situation where politeness is required.

-sama: This is one level higher than "-san" and is used to confer great respect.

-dono: This comes from the word "tono," which means "lord." It is an even higher level than "-sama" and confers utmost respect.

-kun: This suffix is used at the end of boys' names to express familiarity or endearment. It is also sometimes used by men among friends, or when addressing someone younger or of a lower station.

-chan: This is used to express endearment, mostly toward girls. It is also used for little boys, pets, and even among lovers. It gives a sense of childish cuteness.

Bozu: This is an informal way to refer to a boy, similar to the English terms "kid" and "squirt."

Sempai/
Senpai: This title suggests that the addressee is one's senior in a group or organization. It is most often used in a school setting, where underclassmen refer to their upperclassmen as "sempai." It can also be used in the workplace, such as when a newer employee addresses an employee who has seniority in the company.

Kohai: This is the opposite of "sempai" and is used toward underclassmen in school or newcomers in the workplace. It connotes that the addressee is of a lower station.

Sensei: Literally meaning "one who has come before," this title is used for teachers, doctors, or masters of any profession or art.

-[blank]: This is usually forgotten in these lists, but it is perhaps the most significant difference between Japanese and English. The lack of honorific means that the speaker has permission to address the person in a very intimate way. Usually, only family, spouses, or very close friends have this kind of permission. Known as *yobisute*, it can be gratifying when someone who has earned the intimacy starts to call one by one's name without an honorific. But when that intimacy hasn't been earned, it can be very insulting.

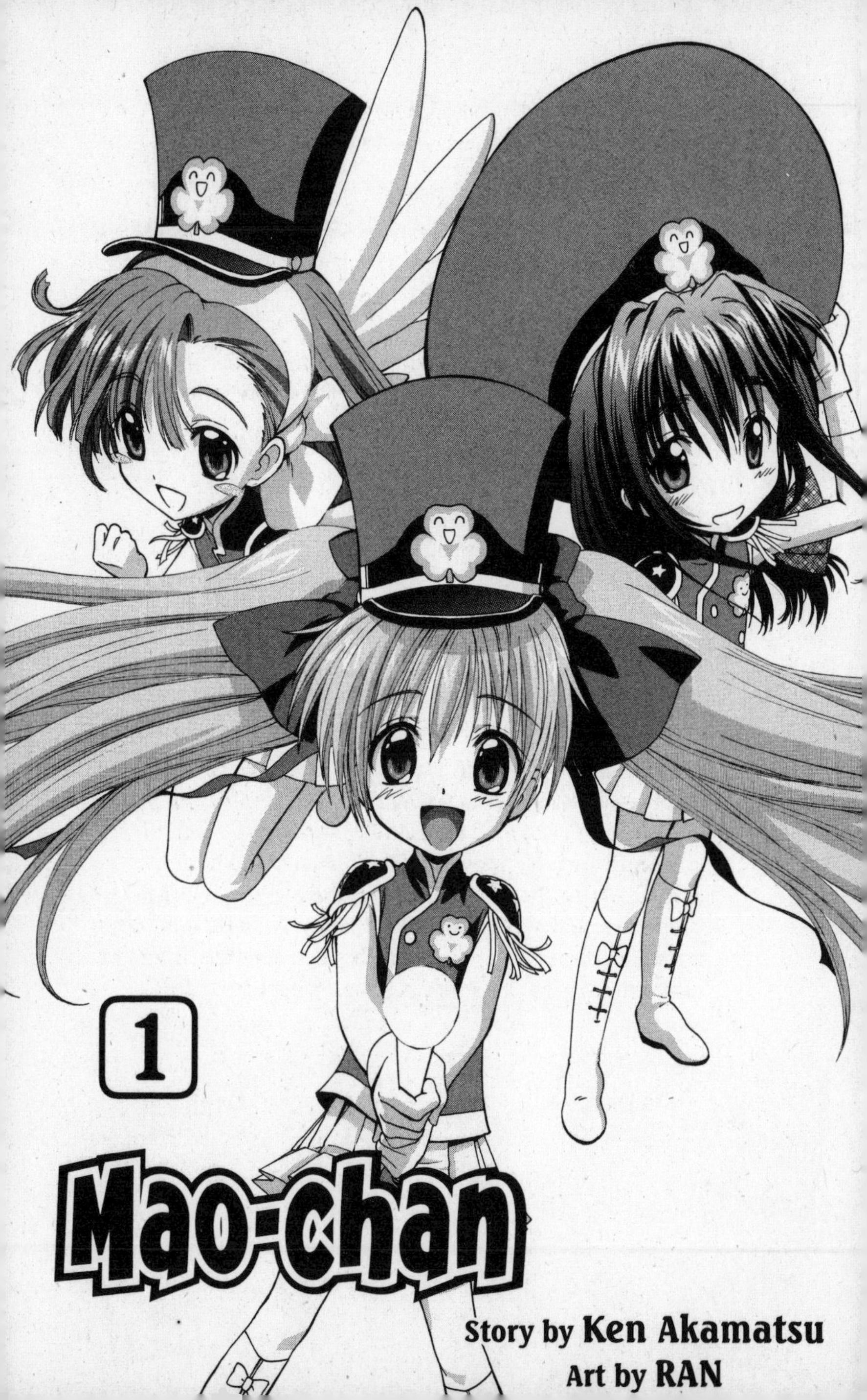

1

Mao-chan

Story by Ken Akamatsu

Art by RAN

CONTENTS

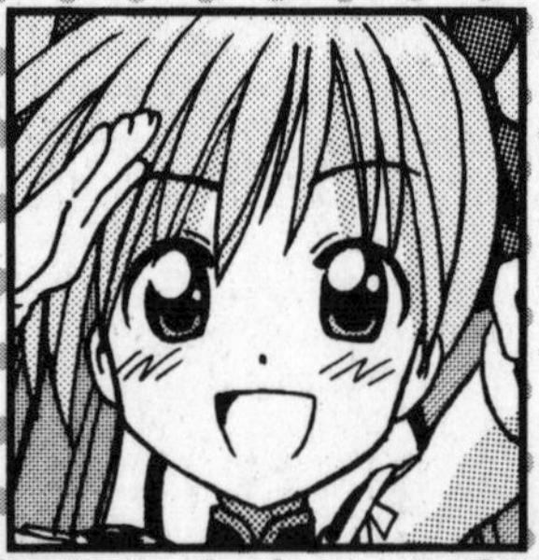

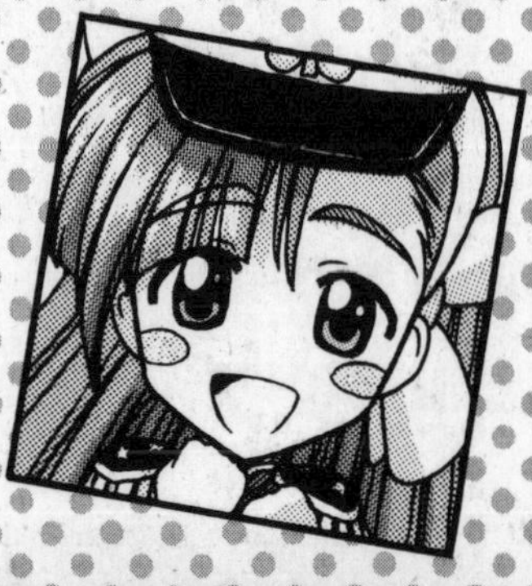

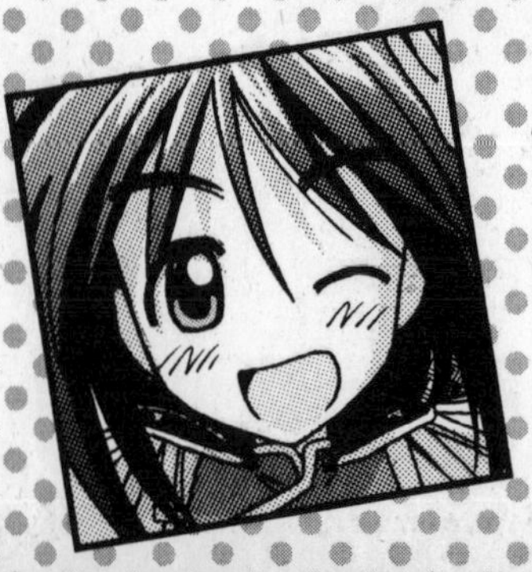

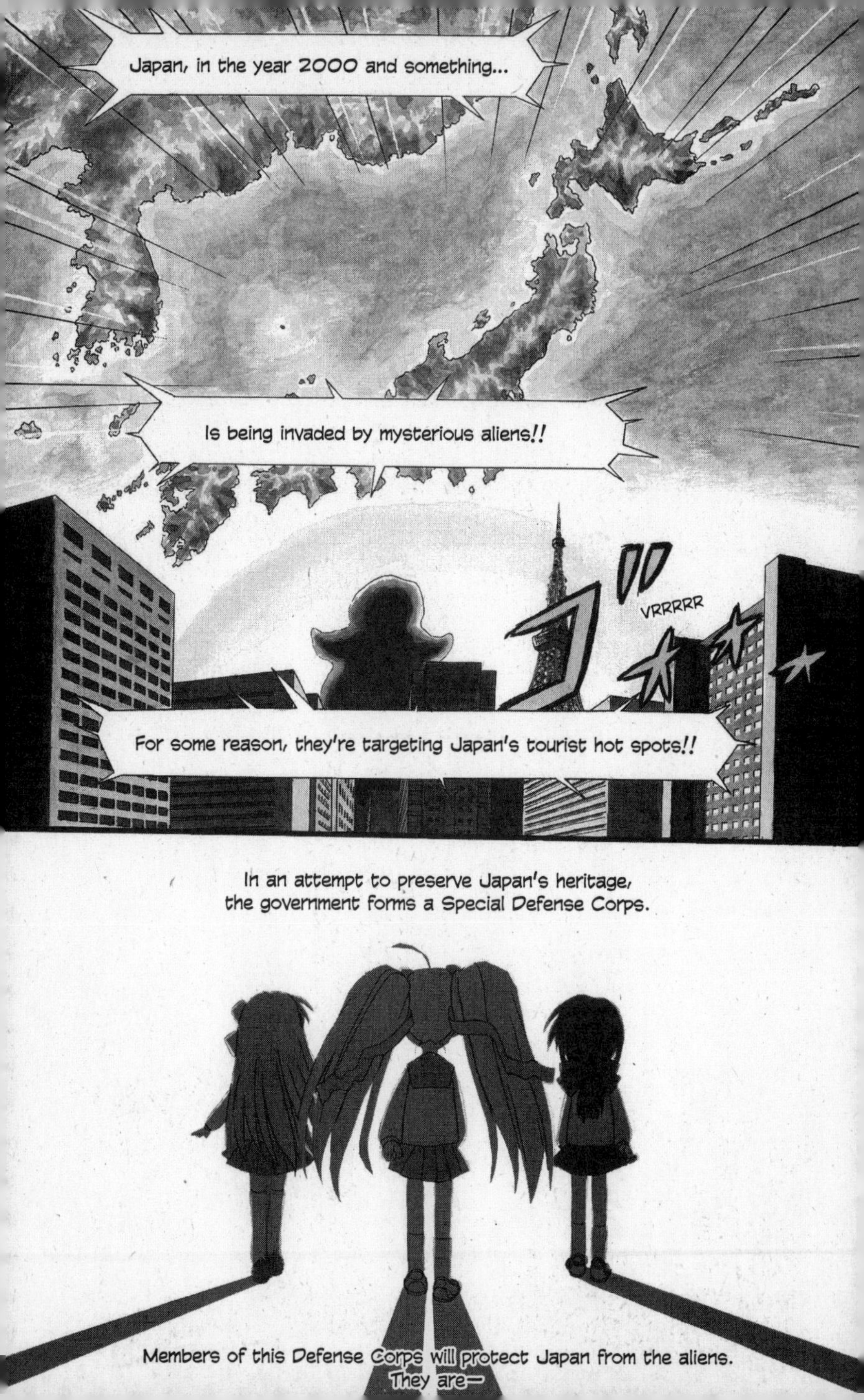
Japan, in the year 2000 and something...
Is being invaded by mysterious aliens!!
VRRRRR
For some reason, they're targeting Japan's tourist hot spots!!
In an attempt to preserve Japan's heritage, the government forms a Special Defense Corps.
Members of this Defense Corps will protect Japan from the aliens. They are—

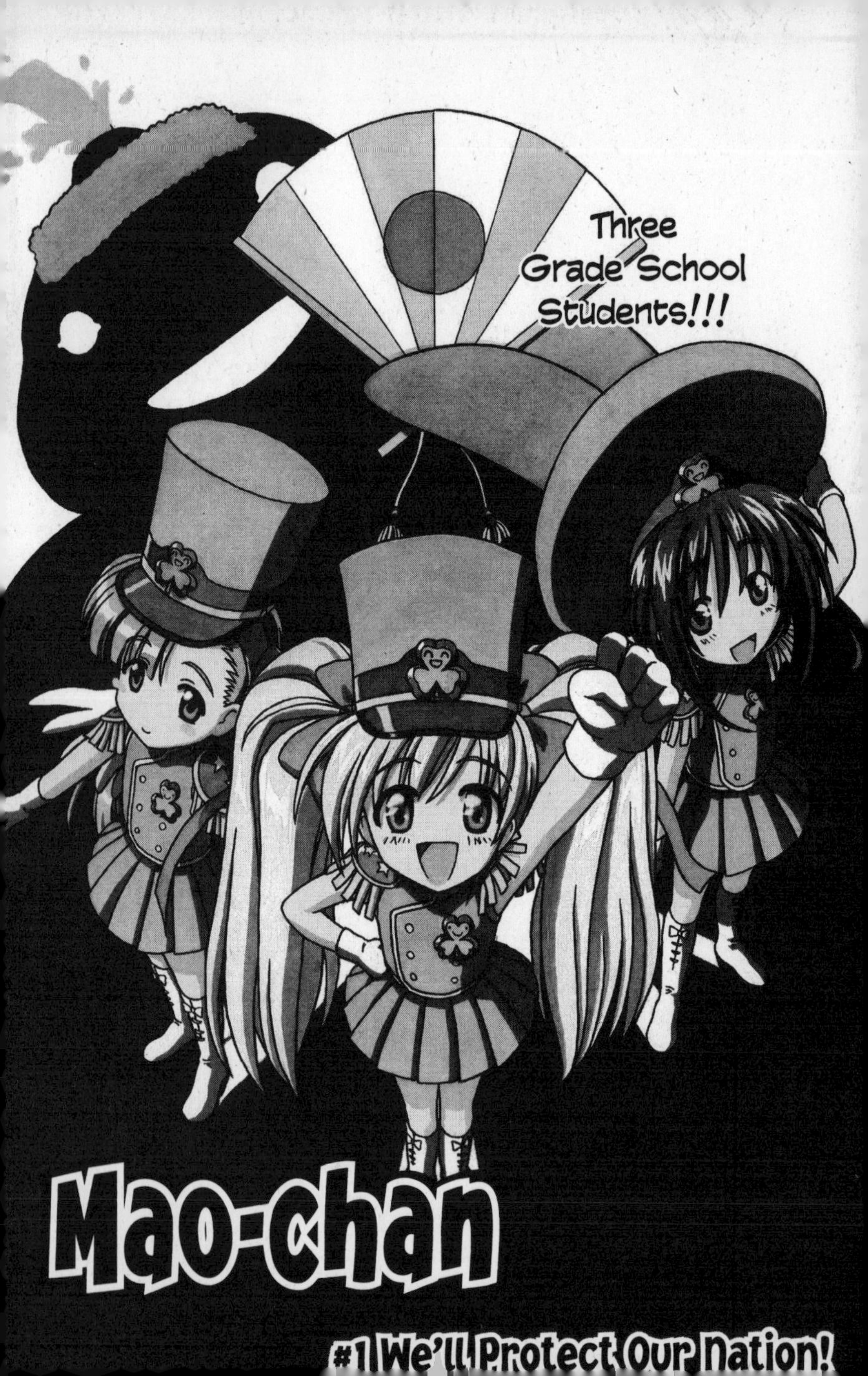
Three Grade School Students!!!
Mao-chan
#1 We'll Protect Our Nation!

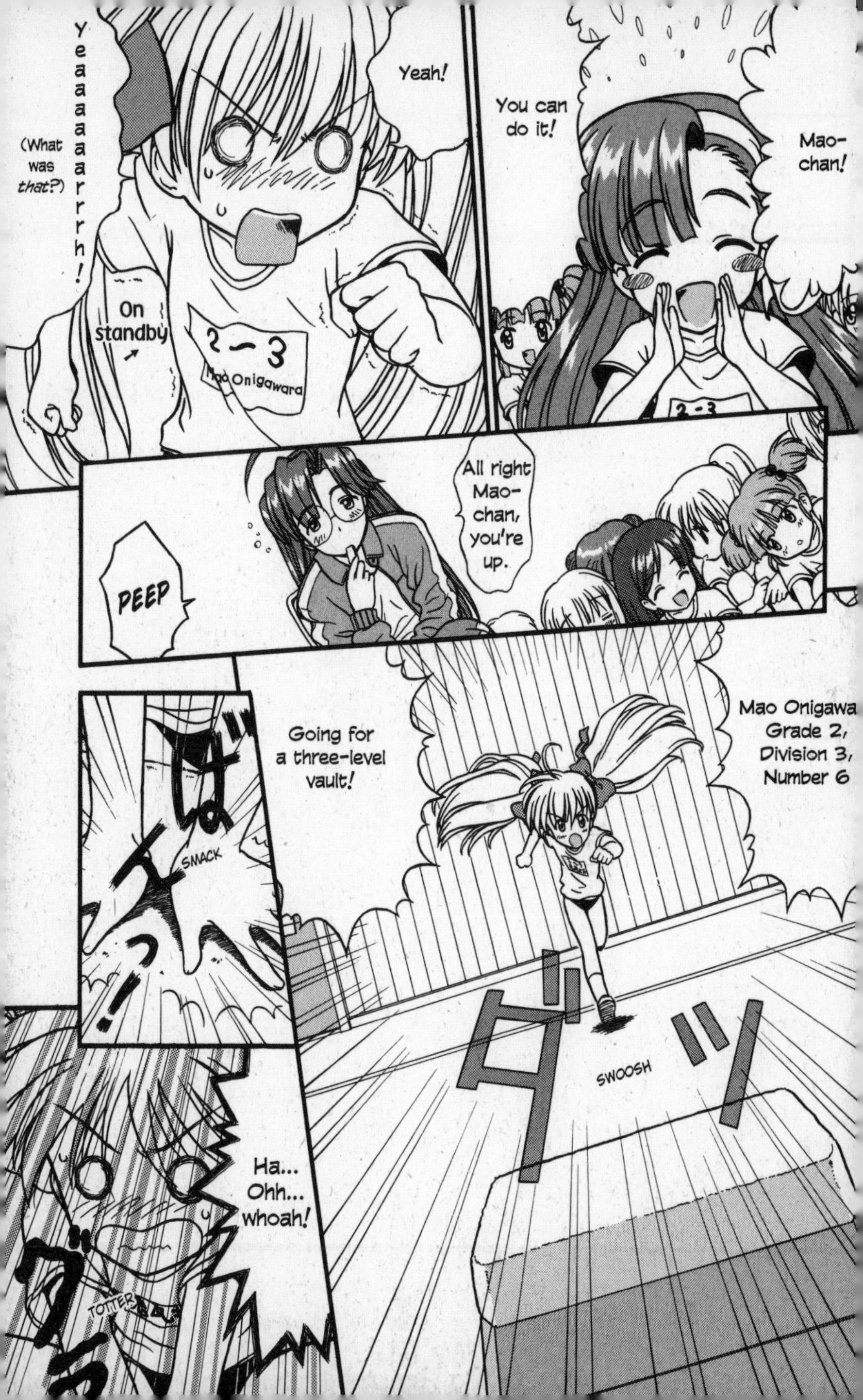
Mao-chan!
You can do it!
Yeah!
Yeaaaaaaarrrrh!
(What was *that?*)
On standby
2-3
Mao Onigawara
All right Mao-chan, you're up.
PEEP
Mao Onigawa
Grade 2, Division 3, Number 6
Going for a three-level vault!
SWOOSH
SMACK
Ha... Ohh... whoah!
TOTTER

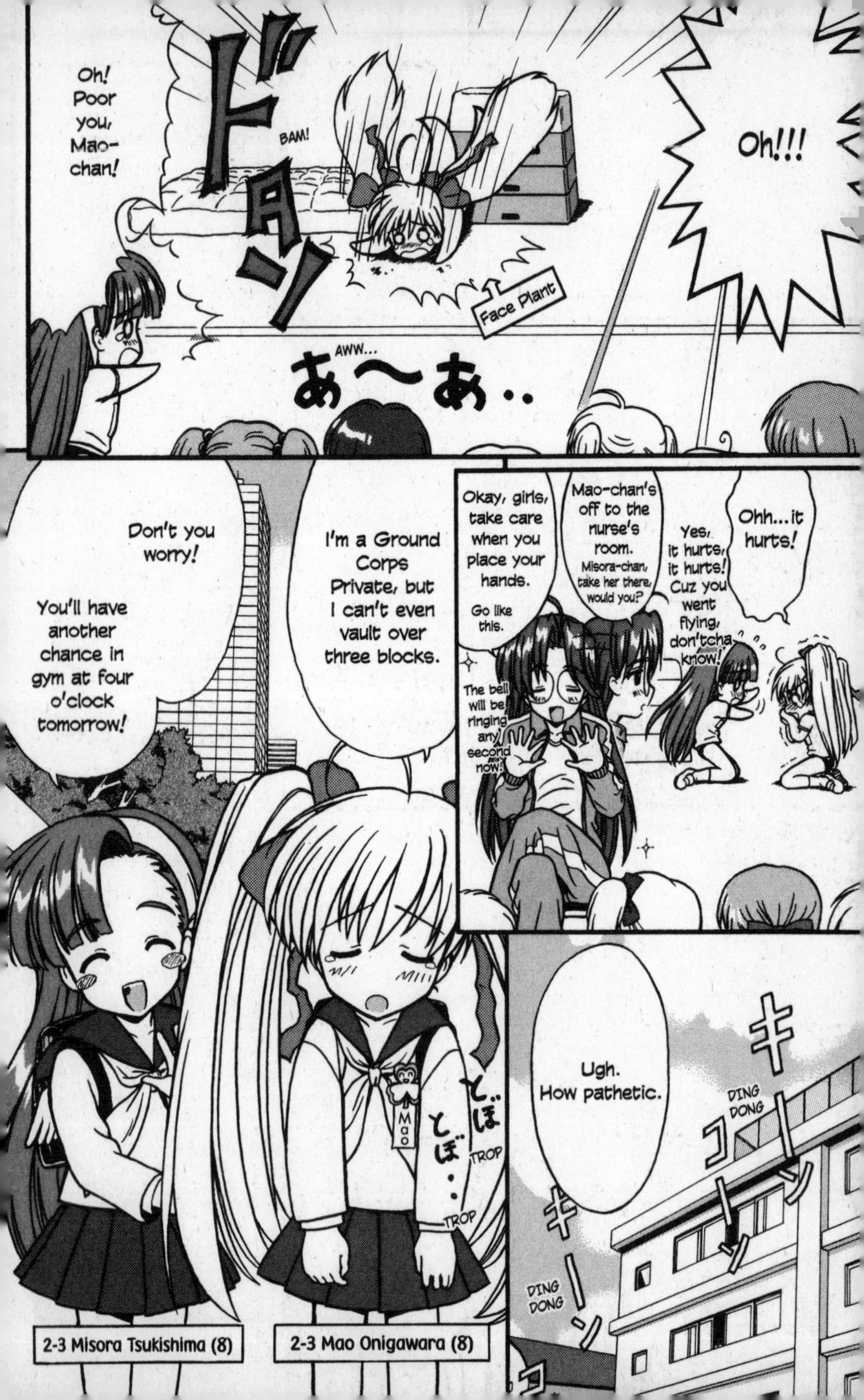
Oh!!!
ドダン!
BAM!
Oh! Poor you, Mao-chan!
Face Plant
あ〜あ..
AWW...
Ohh...it hurts!
Yes, it hurts, it hurts! Cuz you went flying, don'tcha know!
Mao-chan's off to the nurse's room. Misora-chan, take her there, would you?
Okay, girls, take care when you place your hands.
Go like this.
The bell will be ringing any second now!
キーンコーン
DING DONG
キーン
DING DONG
Ugh. How pathetic.
I'm a Ground Corps Private, but I can't even vault over three blocks.
Don't you worry!
You'll have another chance in gym at four o'clock tomorrow!
とぼとぼ..
TROP
TROP
Mao
2-3 Mao Onigawara (8)
2-3 Misora Tsukishima (8)

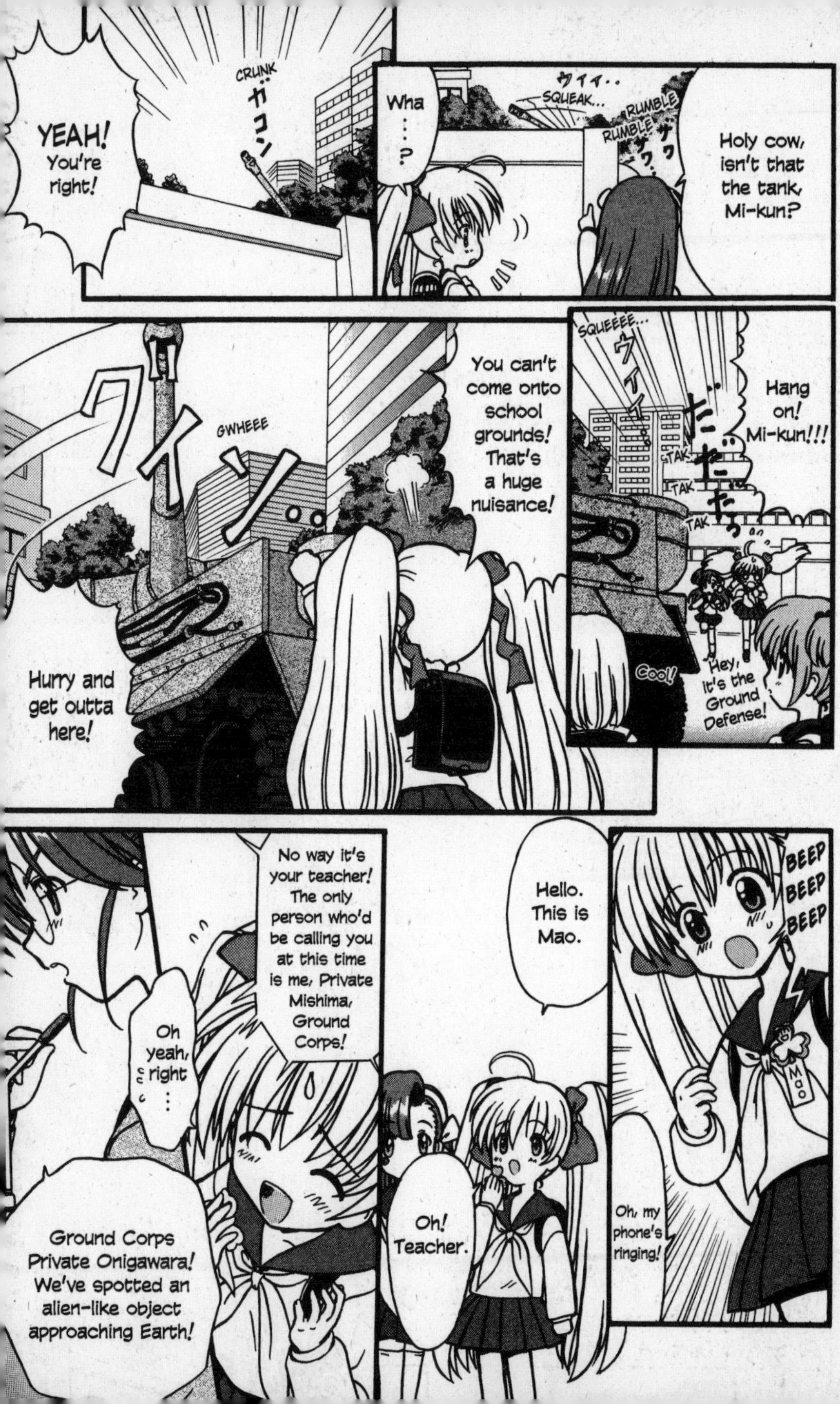
Holy cow, isn't that the tank, Mi-kun?
RUMBLE
RUMBLE
SQUEAK...
Wha...?
CRUNK
YEAH! You're right!
SQUEEEE...
Hang on! Mi-kun!!!
TAK
TAK
TAK
Cool!
Hey, it's the Ground Defense!
You can't come onto school grounds! That's a huge nuisance!
GWHEEE
Hurry and get outta here!
BEEP BEEP BEEP
Mao
Oh, my phone's ringing!
Hello. This is Mao.
Oh! Teacher.
No way it's your teacher! The only person who'd be calling you at this time is me, Private Mishima, Ground Corps!
Oh yeah, right...
Ground Corps Private Onigawara! We've spotted an alien-like object approaching Earth!

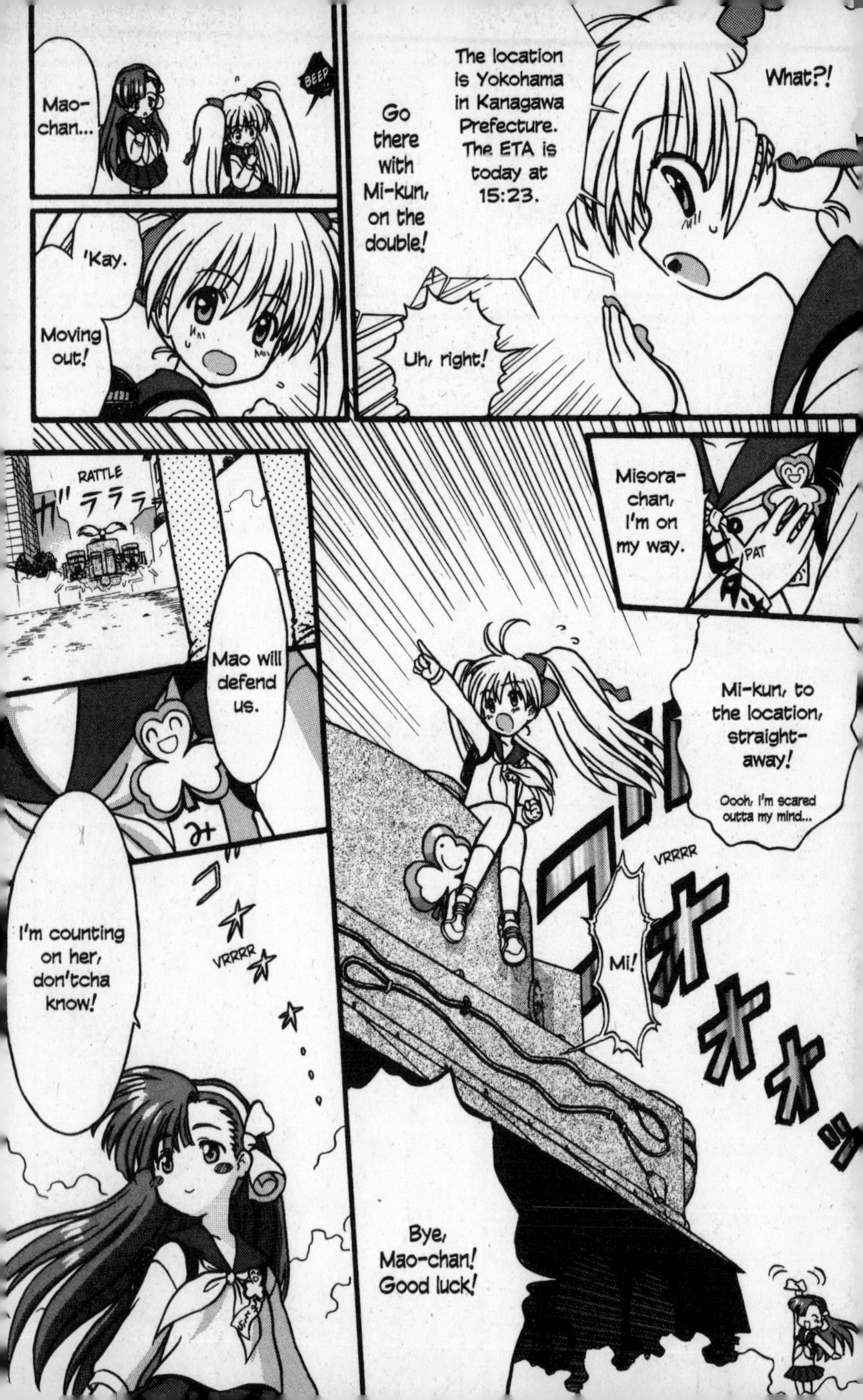
What?!
The location is Yokohama in Kanagawa Prefecture. The ETA is today at 15:23.
Go there with Mi-kun, on the double!
Uh, right!
BEEP
Mao-chan...
'Kay.
Moving out!
Misora-chan, I'm on my way.
PAT
Mi-kun, to the location, straight-away!
Oooh, I'm scared outta my mind...
VRRRR
Mi!
Bye, Mao-chan! Good luck!
RATTLE
Mao will defend us.
VRRRR
I'm counting on her, don'tcha know!

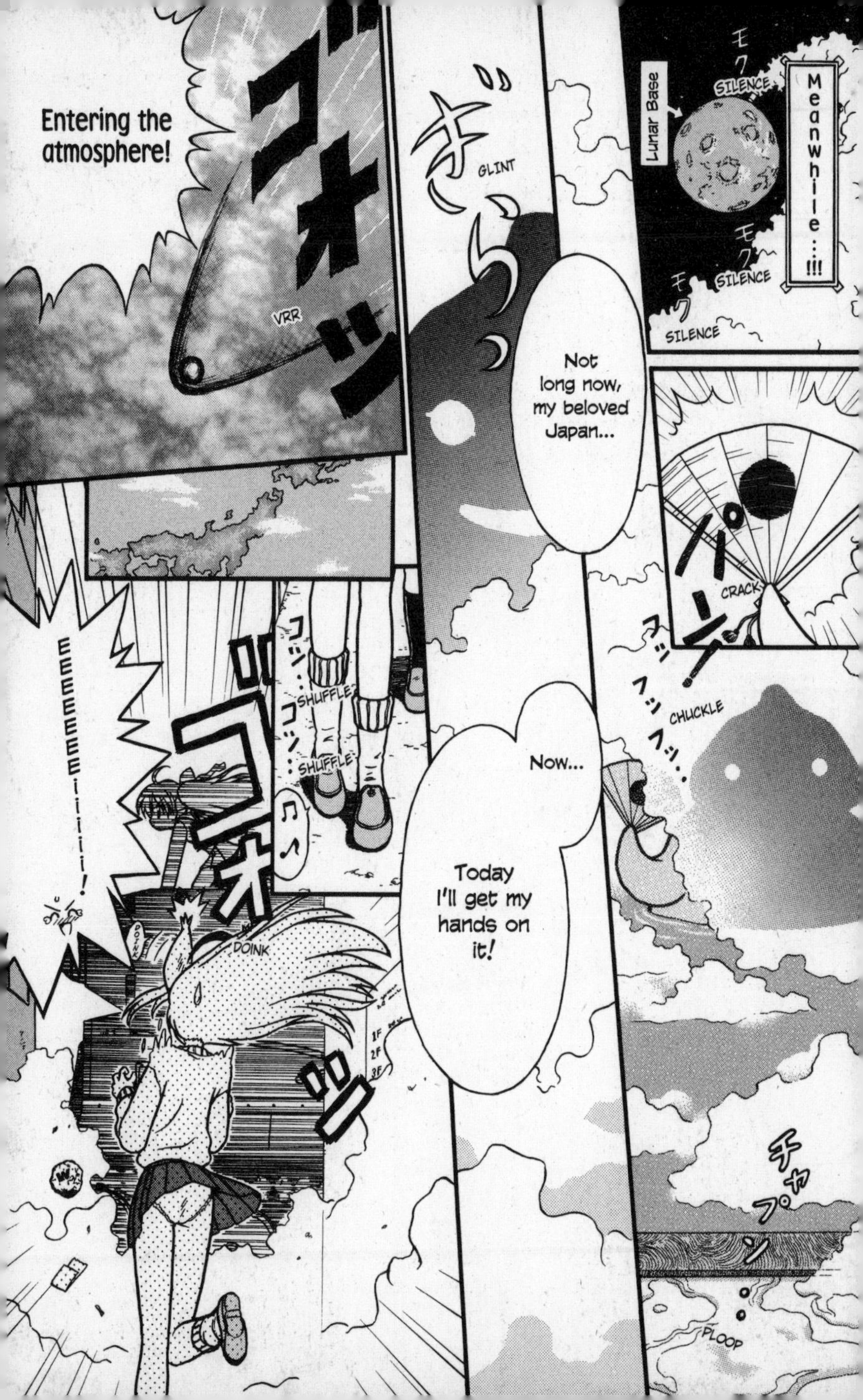

Meanwhile...!!!
Lunar Base
SILENCE
SILENCE
SILENCE
CRACK
CHUCKLE
PLOOP
Not long now, my beloved Japan...
GLINT
Now...
Today I'll get my hands on it!
Entering the atmosphere!
VRR
SHUFFLE
SHUFFLE
EEEEEEEEi i i i i i!
DOINK
DOINK
1F
2F
3F

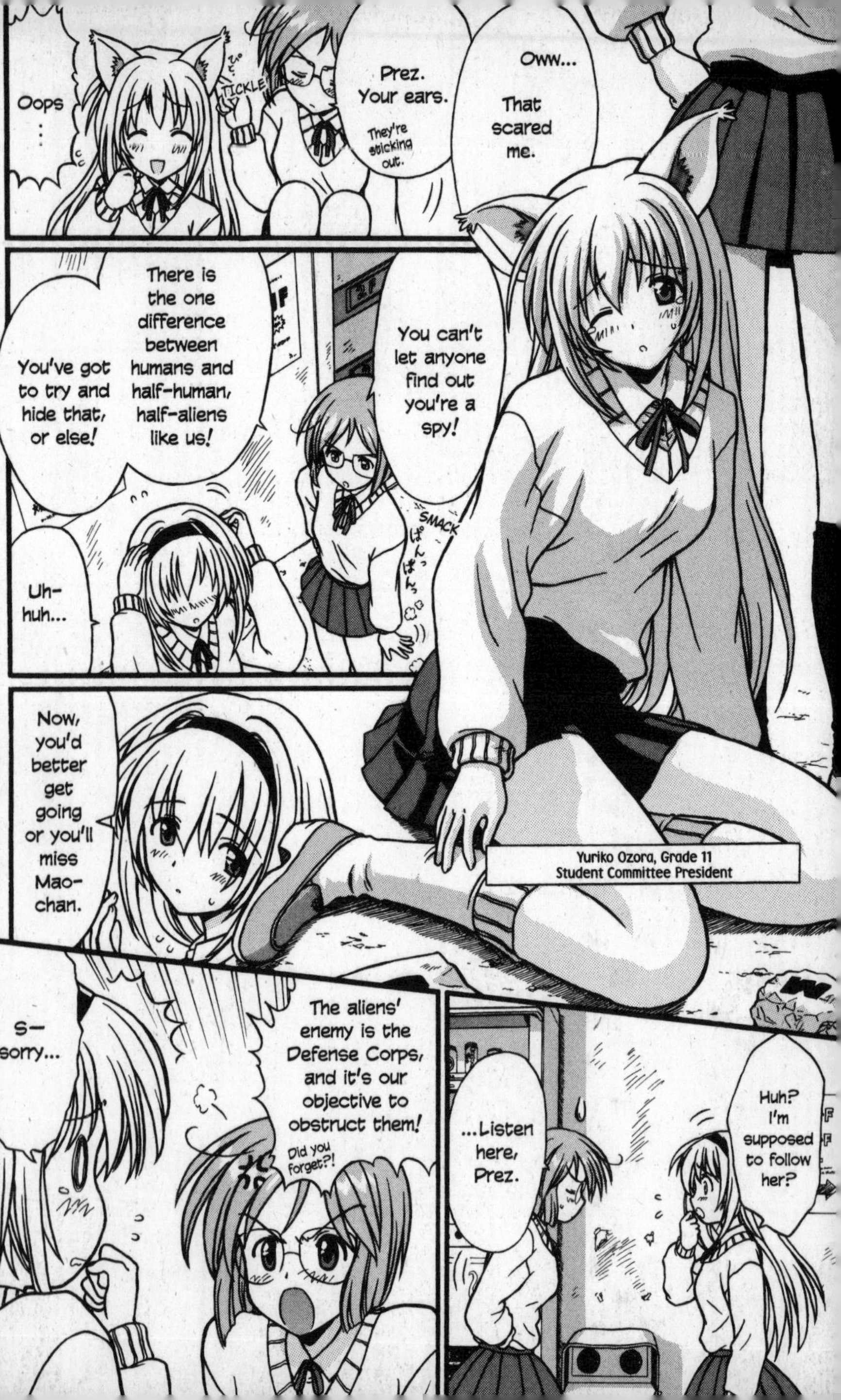
Oww...
That scared me.
Yuriko Ozora, Grade 11
Student Committee President
Prez. Your ears.
They're sticking out.
TICKLE
Oops...
You can't let anyone find out you're a spy!
There is the one difference between humans and half-human, half-aliens like us!
You've got to try and hide that, or else!
SMACK
Uh-huh...
Now, you'd better get going or you'll miss Mao-chan.
Huh? I'm supposed to follow her?
...Listen here, Prez.
The aliens' enemy is the Defense Corps, and it's our objective to obstruct them!
Did you forget?!
S—sorry...

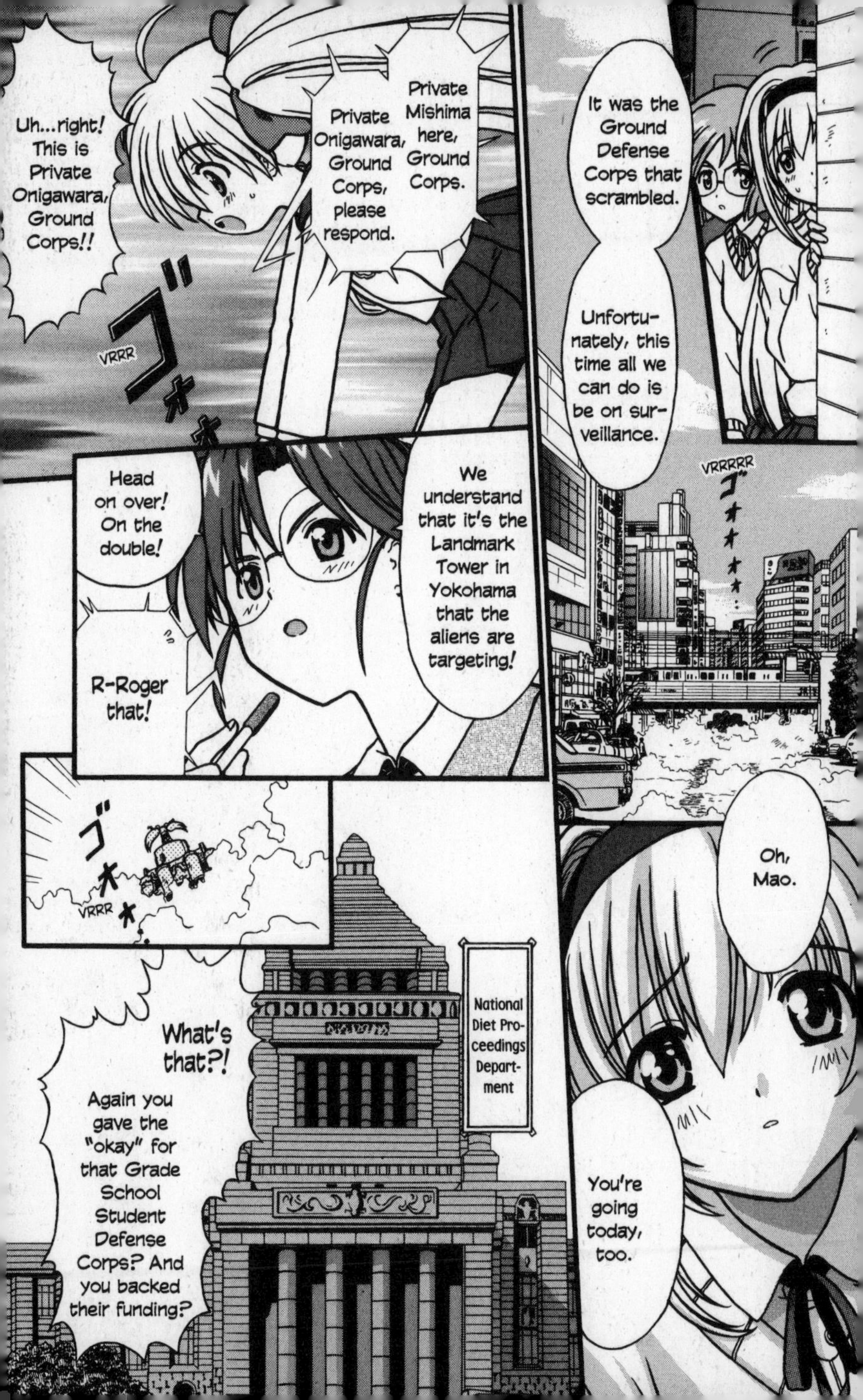
It was the Ground Defense Corps that scrambled.
Unfortunately, this time all we can do is be on surveillance.
Private Mishima here, Ground Corps.
Private Onigawara, Ground Corps, please respond.
Uh...right! This is Private Onigawara, Ground Corps!!
VRRR
VRRRRR
We understand that it's the Landmark Tower in Yokohama that the aliens are targeting!
Head on over! On the double!
R-Roger that!
Oh, Mao.
You're going today, too.
VRRR
National Diet Proceedings Department
What's that?!
Again you gave the "okay" for that Grade School Student Defense Corps? And you backed their funding?

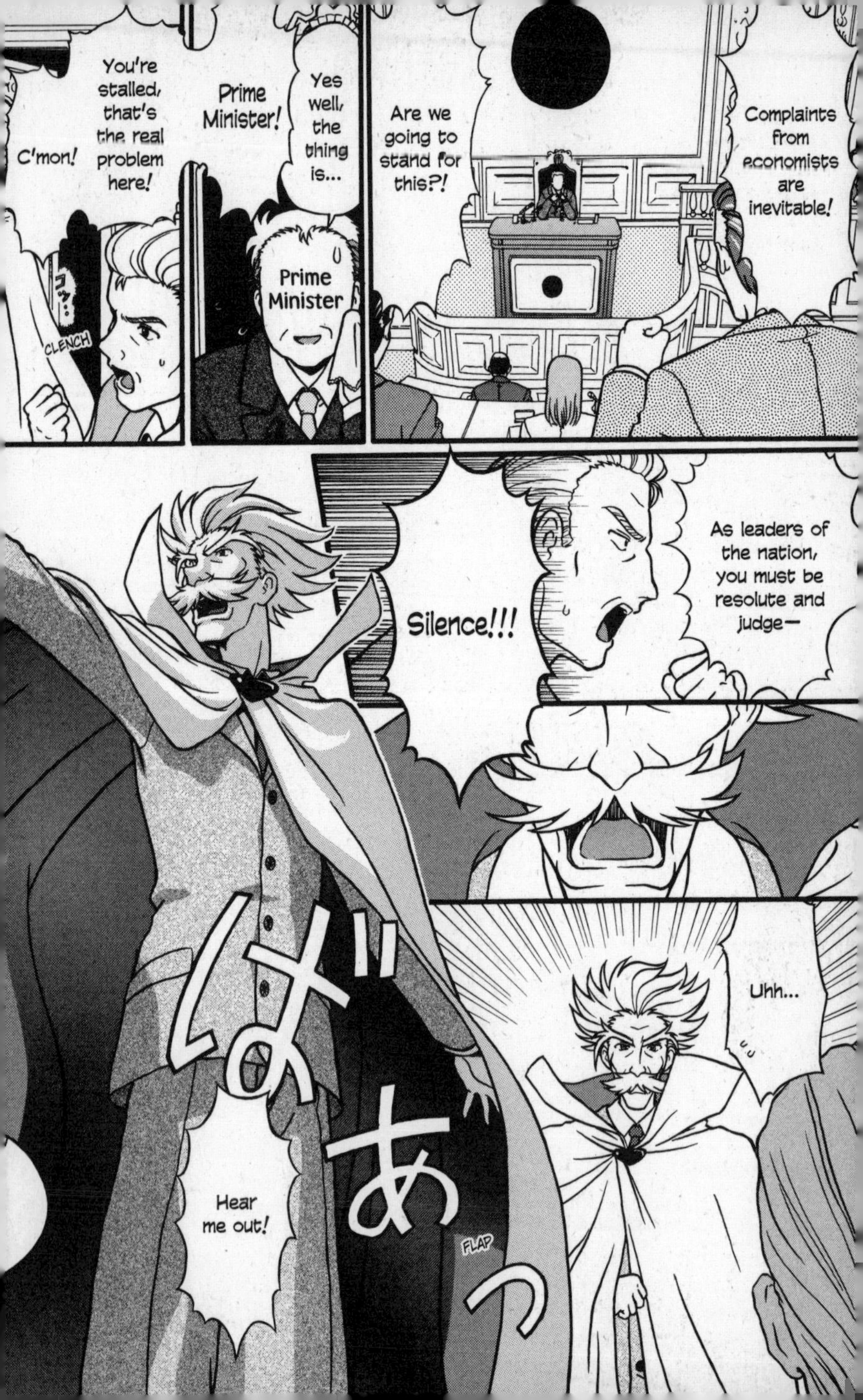
Complaints from economists are inevitable!
Are we going to stand for this?!
Yes well, the thing is...
Prime Minister
Prime Minister!
You're stalled, that's the real problem here!
C'mon!
ゴッ...
CLENCH
As leaders of the nation, you must be resolute and judge—
Silence!!!
Uhh...
ばあっ
Hear me out!
FLAP

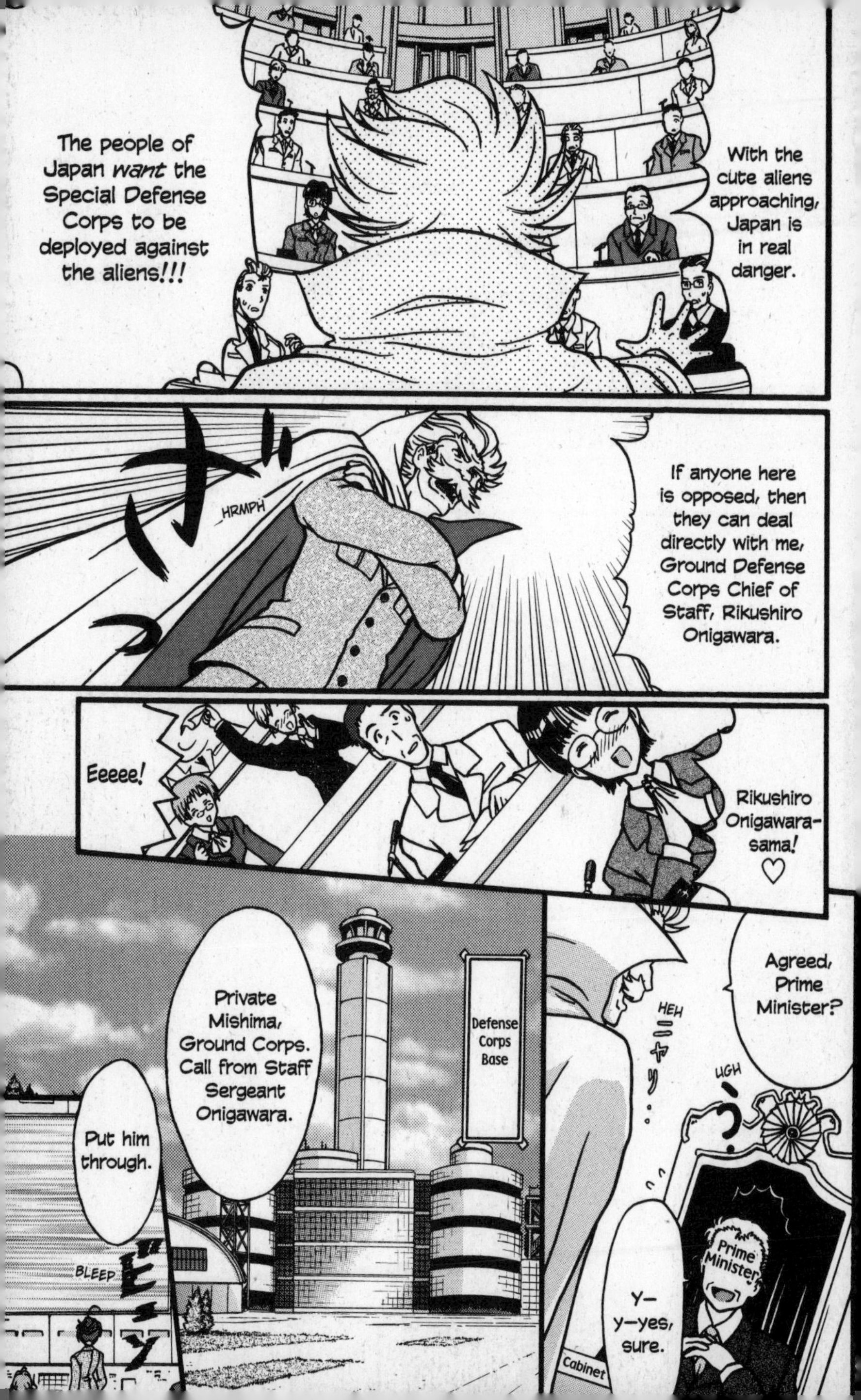
With the cute aliens approaching, Japan is in real danger.
The people of Japan *want* the Special Defense Corps to be deployed against the aliens!!!
If anyone here is opposed, then they can deal directly with me, Ground Defense Corps Chief of Staff, Rikushiro Onigawara.
HRMPH
Rikushiro Onigawara-sama! ♡
Eeeee!
Agreed, Prime Minister?
HEH
UGH
Prime Minister
Y— y—yes, sure.
Cabinet
Defense Corps Base
Private Mishima, Ground Corps. Call from Staff Sergeant Onigawara.
Put him through.
BLEEP

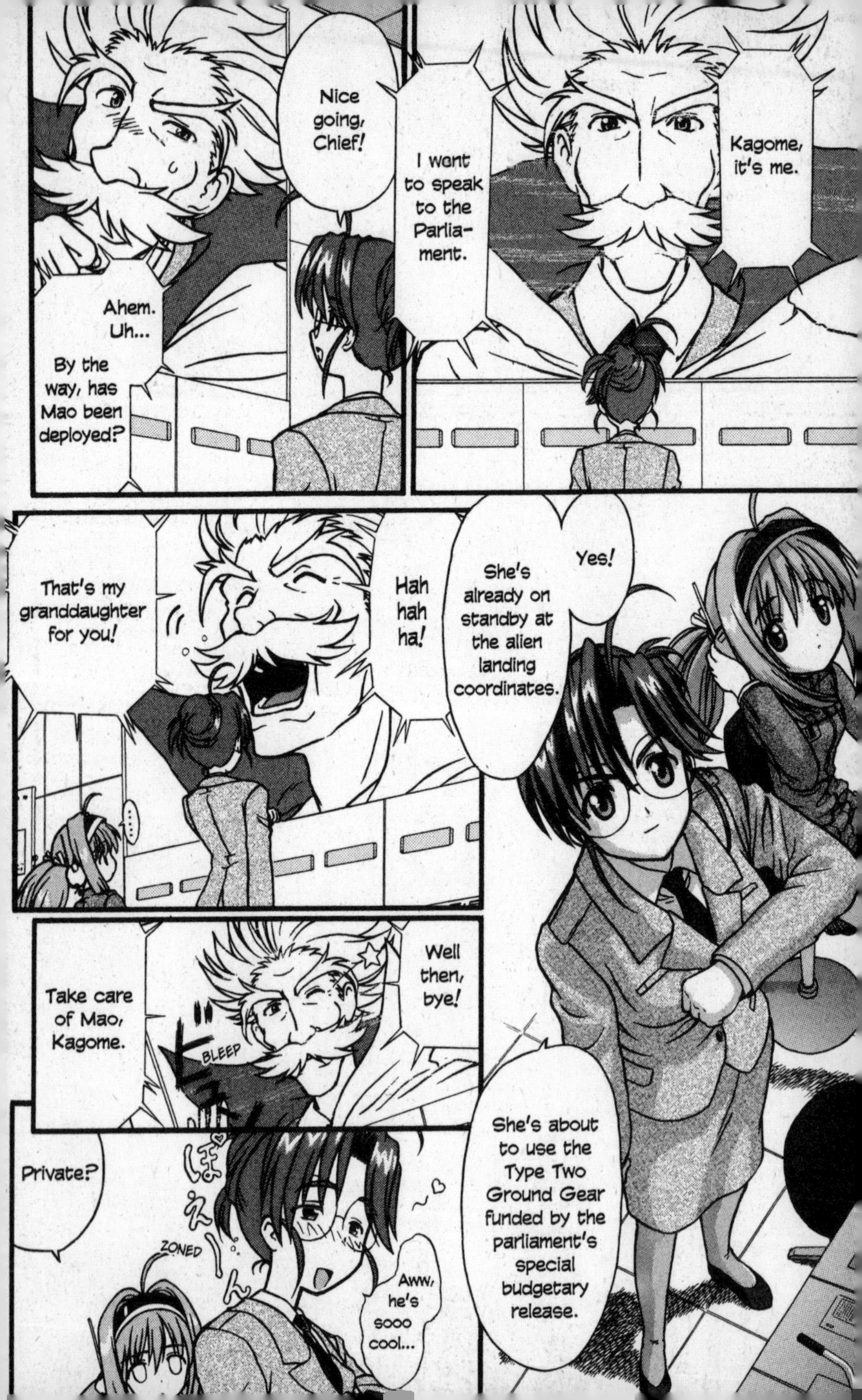
Kagome, it's me.
I want to speak to the Parlia-ment.
Nice going, Chief!
Ahem. Uh...
By the way, has Mao been deployed?
Yes!
She's already on standby at the alien landing coordinates.
She's about to use the Type Two Ground Gear funded by the parliament's special budgetary release.
Hah hah ha!
That's my granddaughter for you!
...
Well then, bye!
Take care of Mao, Kagome.
BLEEP
Aww, he's sooo cool...
ZONED
Private?

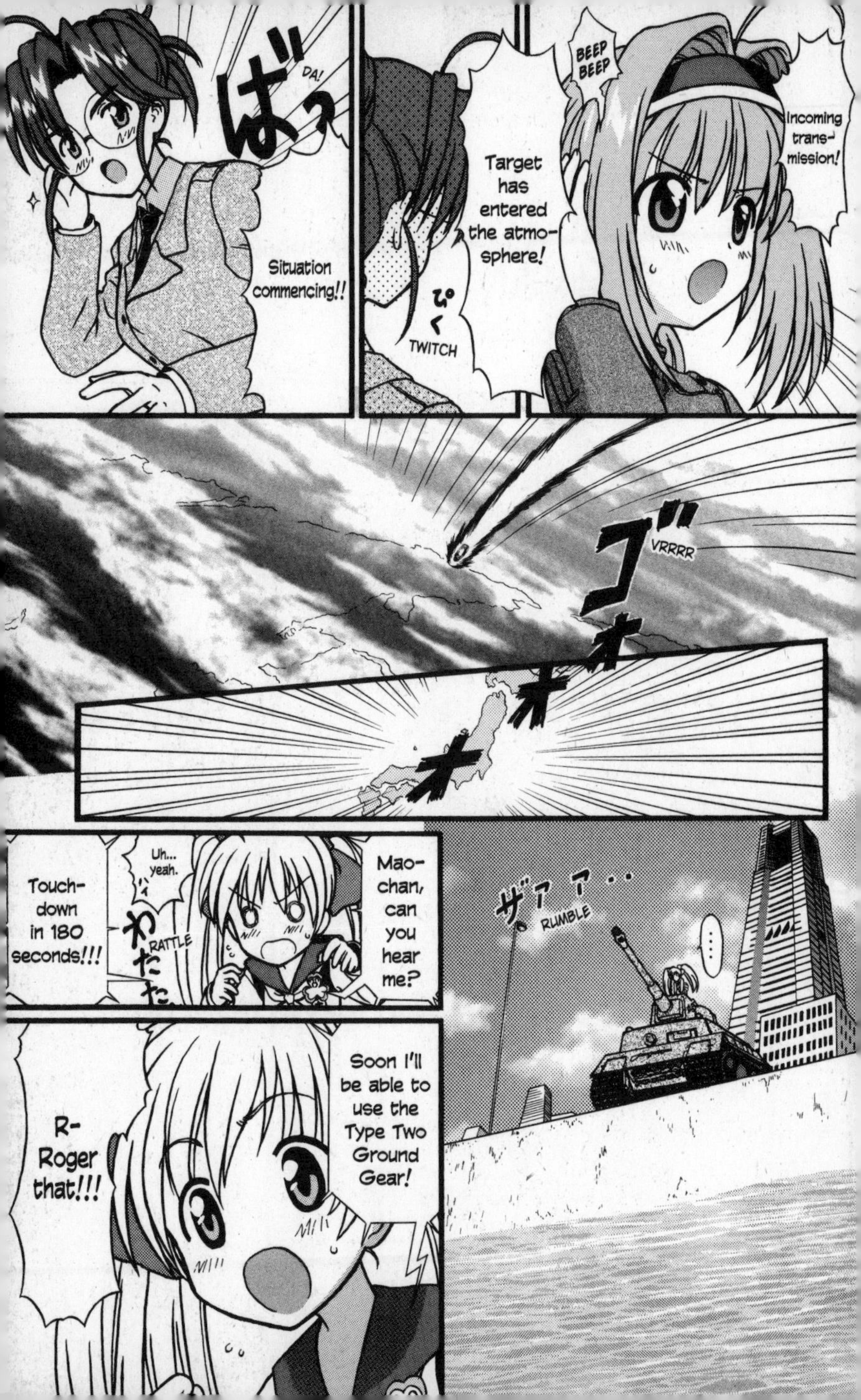
BEEP BEEP
Incoming trans-mission!
Target has entered the atmo-sphere!
ぴく
TWITCH
ばっ
DA!
Situation commencing!!
ゴオオ
VRRRR
ザァァ‥
RUMBLE
...
Mao-chan, can you hear me?
Uh... yeah.
わたた
RATTLE
Touch-down in 180 seconds!!!
Soon I'll be able to use the Type Two Ground Gear!
R-Roger that!!!

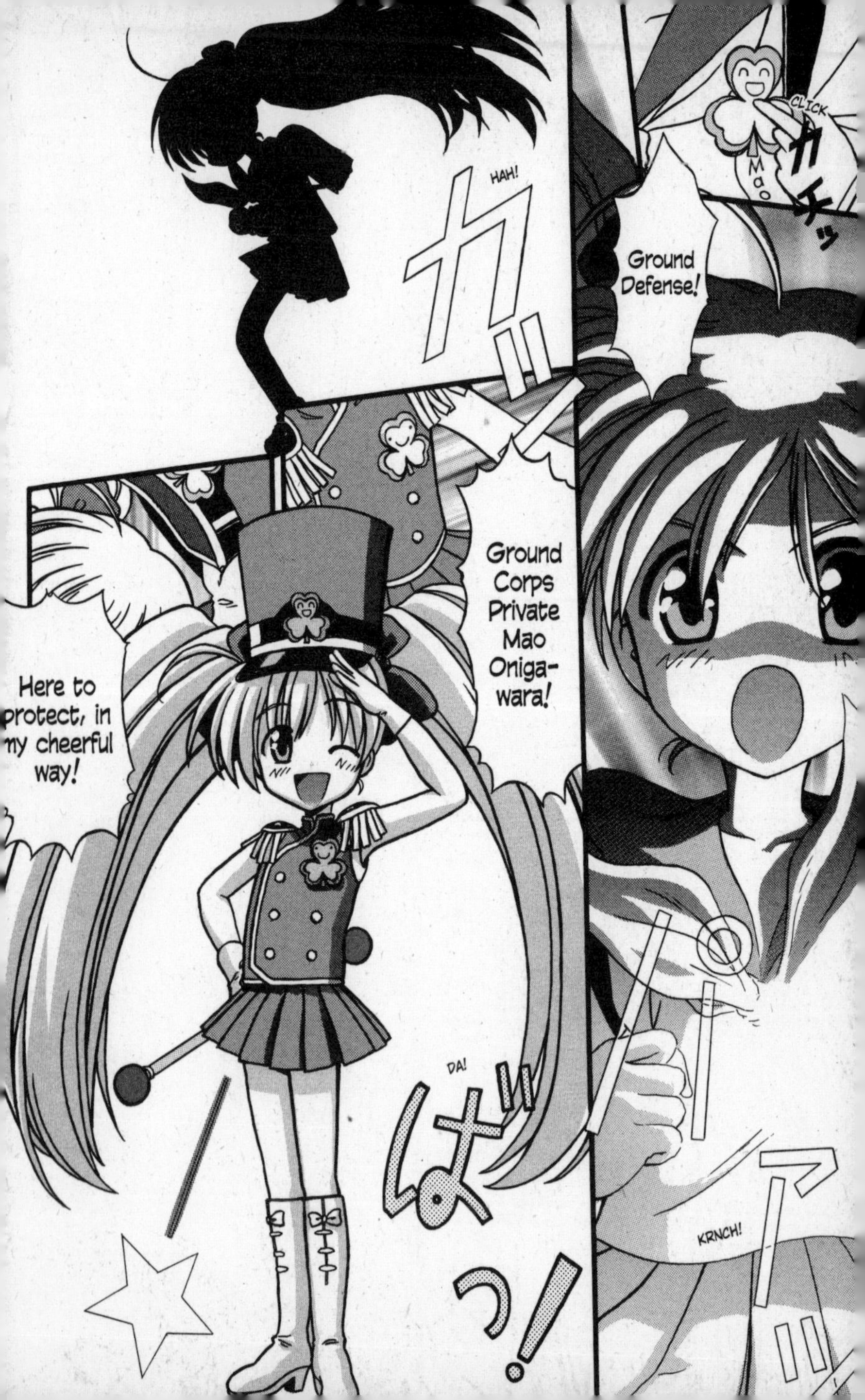
CLICK
Mao
Ground Defense!
HAH!
KRNCH!
Ground Corps Private Mao Oniga-wara!
Here to protect, in my cheerful way!
DA!

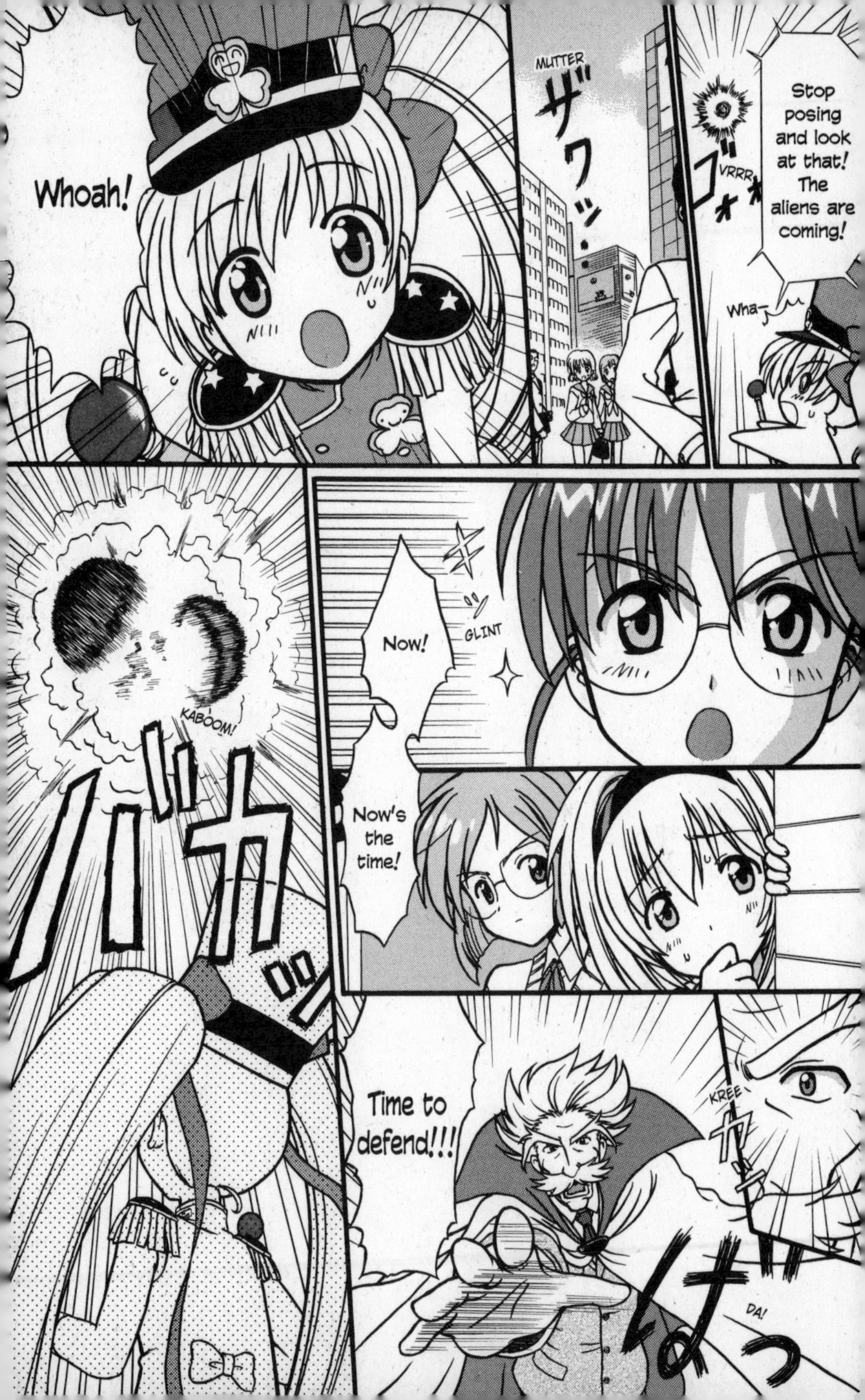

Stop posing and look at that! The aliens are coming!
VRRR
Wha-
MUTTER
Whoah!
Now!
GLINT
Now's the time!
KABOOM!
KREE
Time to defend!!!
DA!

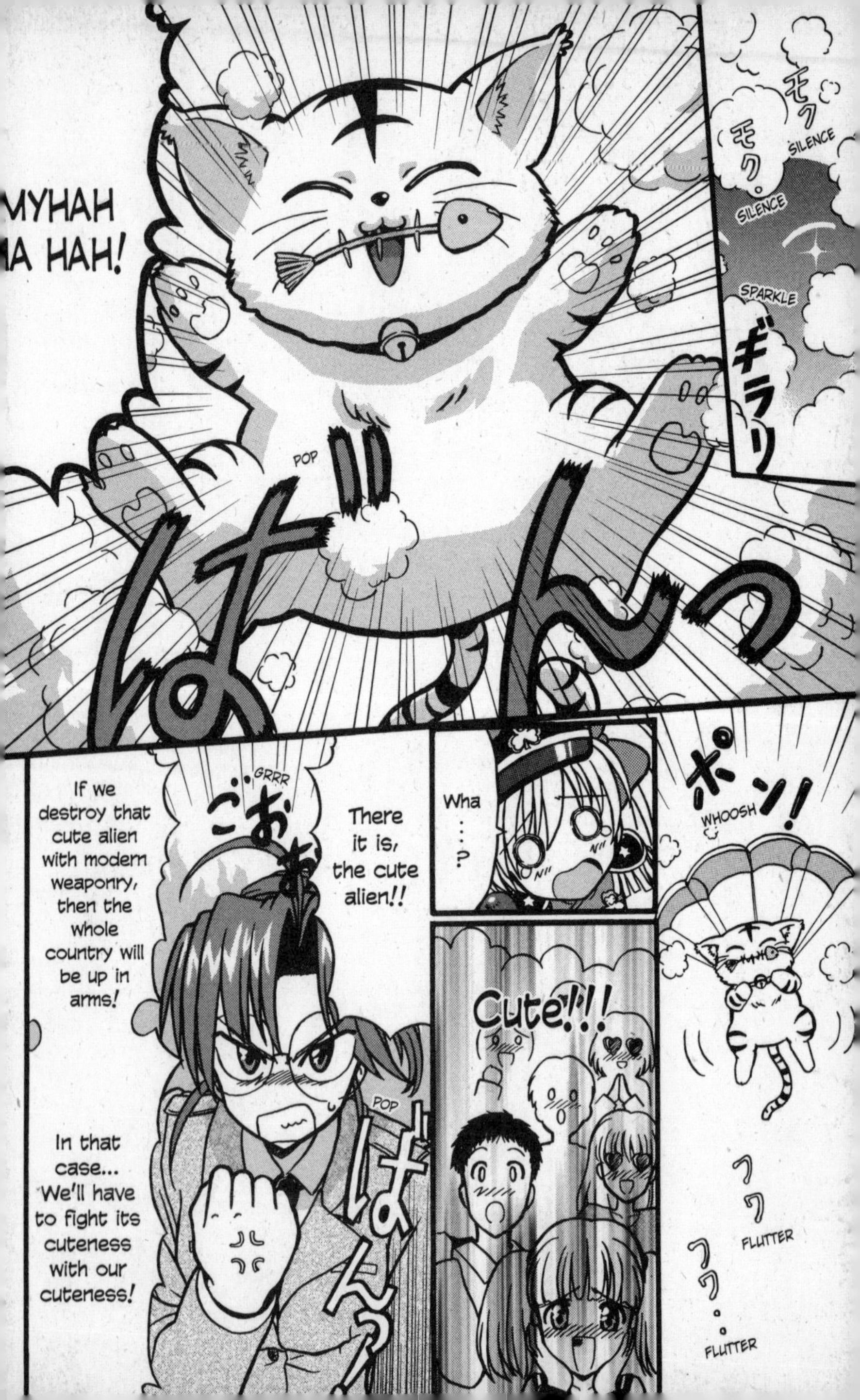
モクモク。
SILENCE
SILENCE
SPARKLE
ギラリ
MYHAH
A HAH!
POP
ばんっ
ポンッ!
WHOOSH
フワフワ
FLUTTER
フワ。。
FLUTTER
Wha...?
Cute!!!
There it is, the cute alien!!
ごお
GRRR
If we destroy that cute alien with modern weaponry, then the whole country will be up in arms!
In that case... We'll have to fight its cuteness with our cuteness!
POP
ばんっ

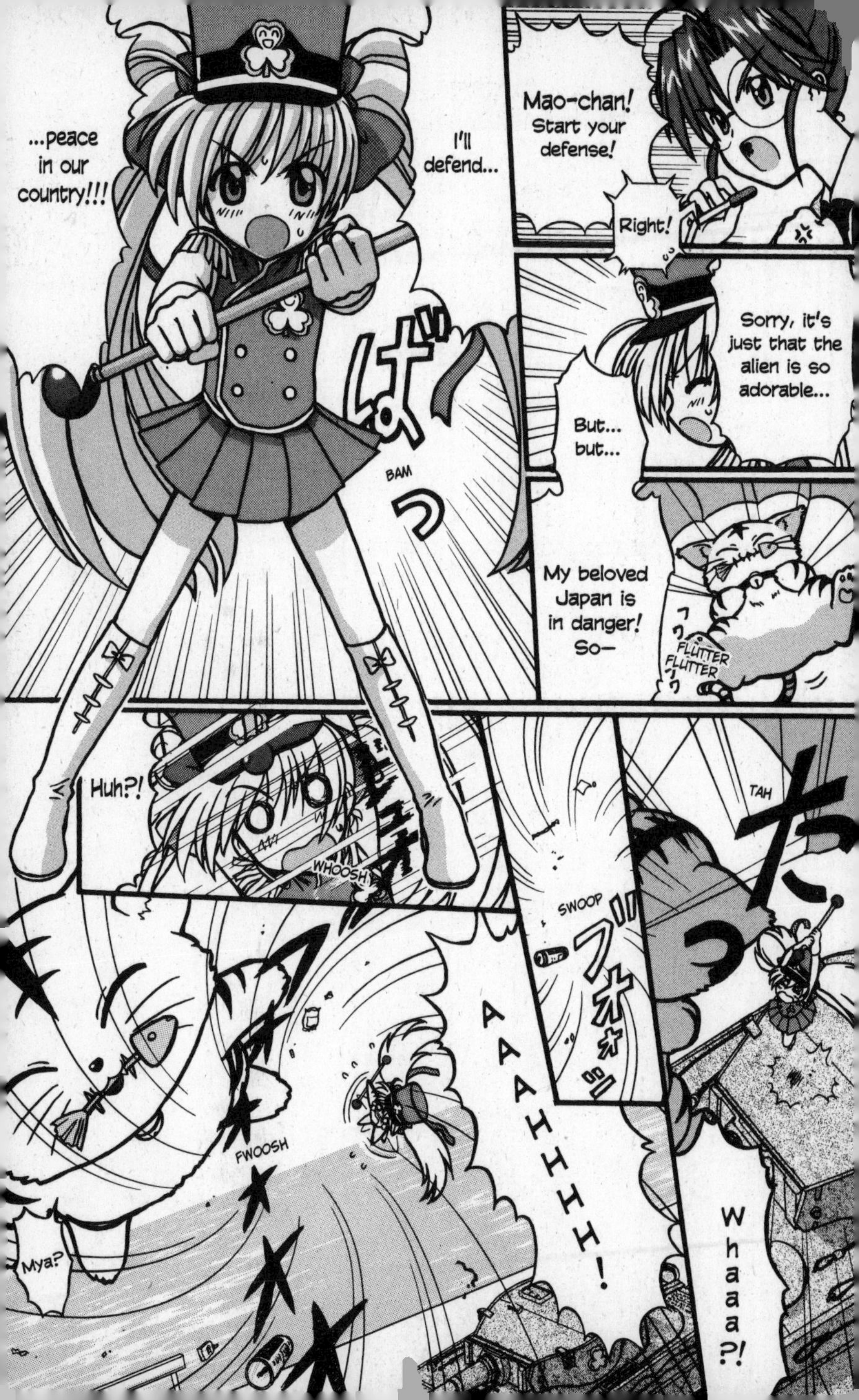
Mao-chan! Start your defense!
Right!
Sorry, it's just that the alien is so adorable...
But... but...
My beloved Japan is in danger! So—
FLUTTER FLUTTER
I'll defend...
...peace in our country!!!
BAM
TAH
Whaaa?!
Huh?!
WHOOSH
SWOOP
AAAHHHH!
FWOOSH
Mya?

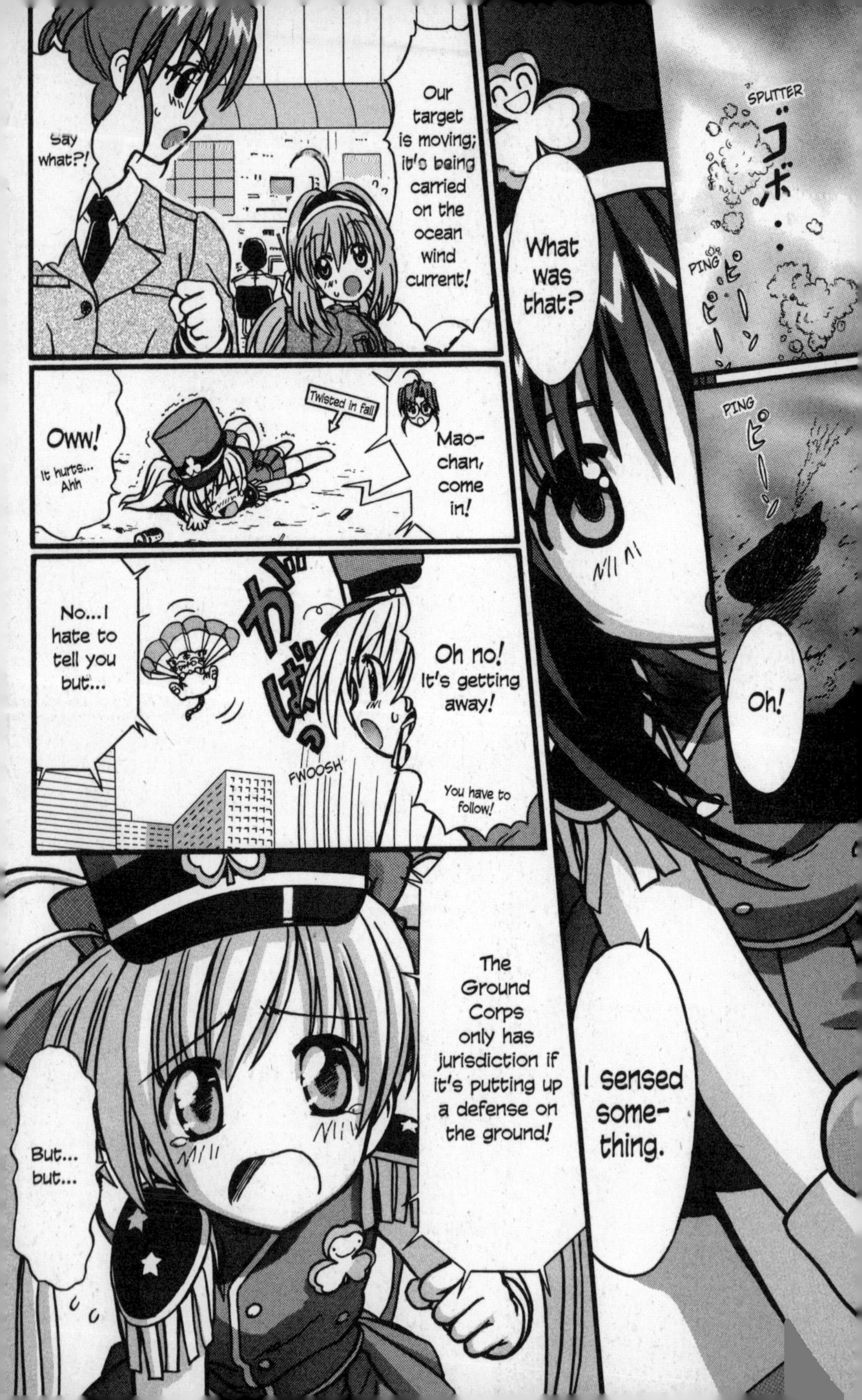
SPUTTER
ゴボ・・
PING
ピーー
PING
ピーー
Oh!
What was that?
I sensed something.
Our target is moving; it's being carried on the ocean wind current!
Say what?!
Mao-chan, come in!
Twisted in fall
Oww!
It hurts... Ahh
Oh no! It's getting away!
You have to follow!
FWOOSH
No...I hate to tell you but...
The Ground Corps only has jurisdiction if it's putting up a defense on the ground!
But... but...

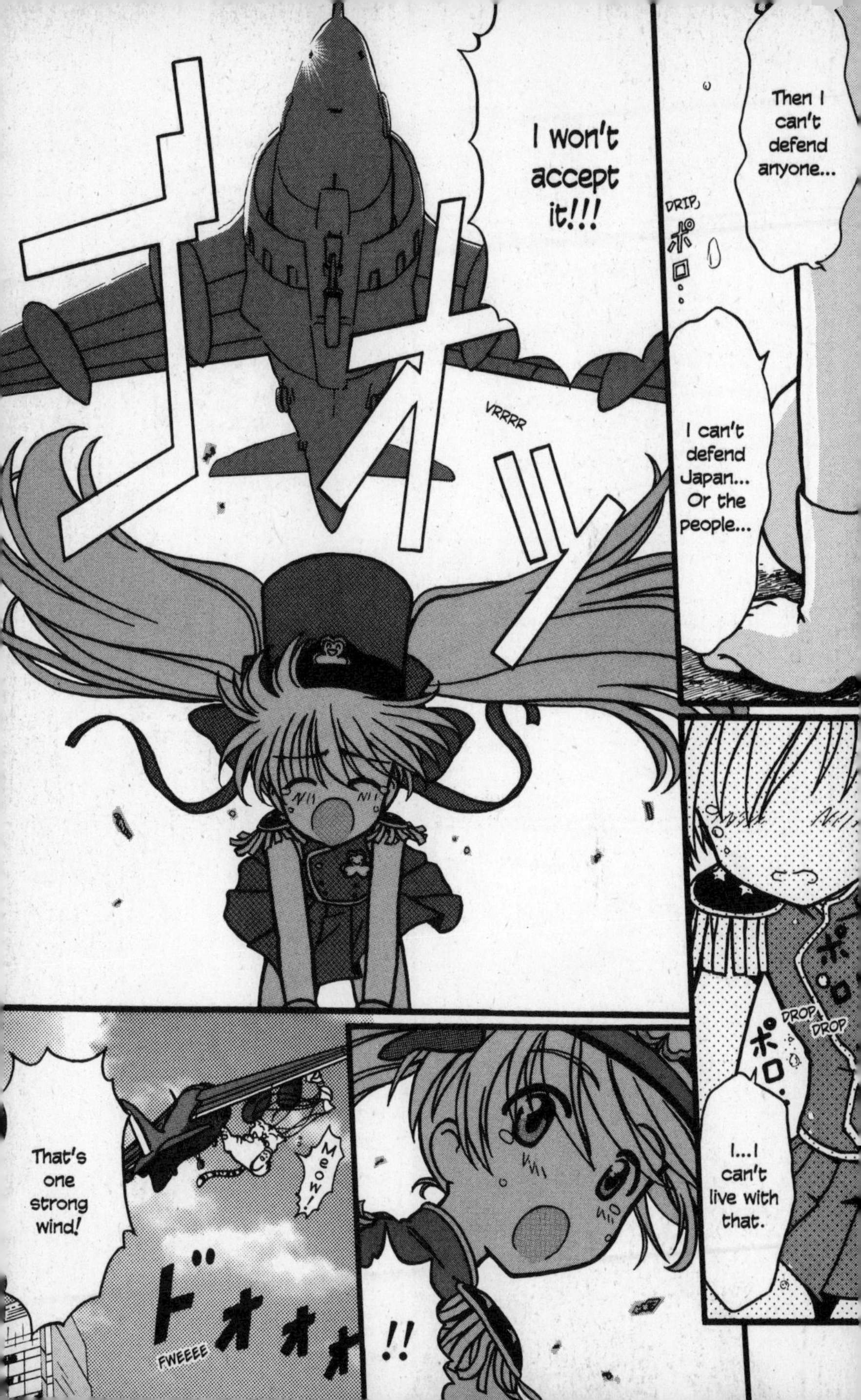
Then I can't defend anyone...
DRIP
ポロ
I can't defend Japan... Or the people...
ポロ
DROP
DROP
ポロ
I...I can't live with that.
I won't accept it!!!
ゴオッ
VRRRR
!!
That's one strong wind!
Meow!
ドオオオ
FWEEEE

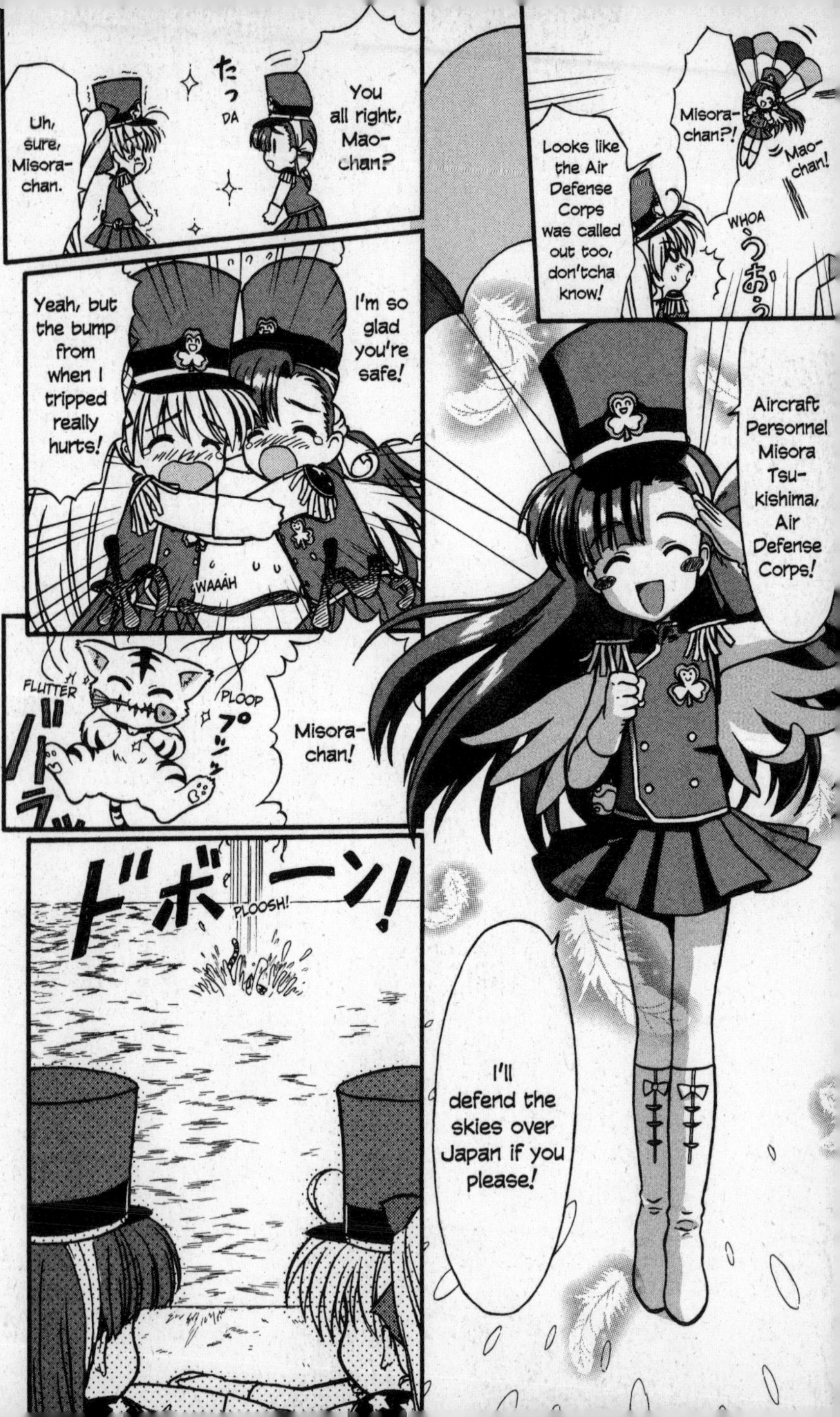
Mao-chan!
Misora-chan?!
WHOA
うおっ
Looks like the Air Defense Corps was called out too, don'tcha know!
Aircraft Personnel Misora Tsukishima, Air Defense Corps!
I'll defend the skies over Japan if you please!
You all right, Mao-chan?
たっ
DA
Uh, sure, Misora-chan.
I'm so glad you're safe!
Yeah, but the bump from when I tripped really hurts!
WAAAH
Misora-chan!
ポッ
PLOOP
FLUTTER
ドボーン!
PLOOSH!

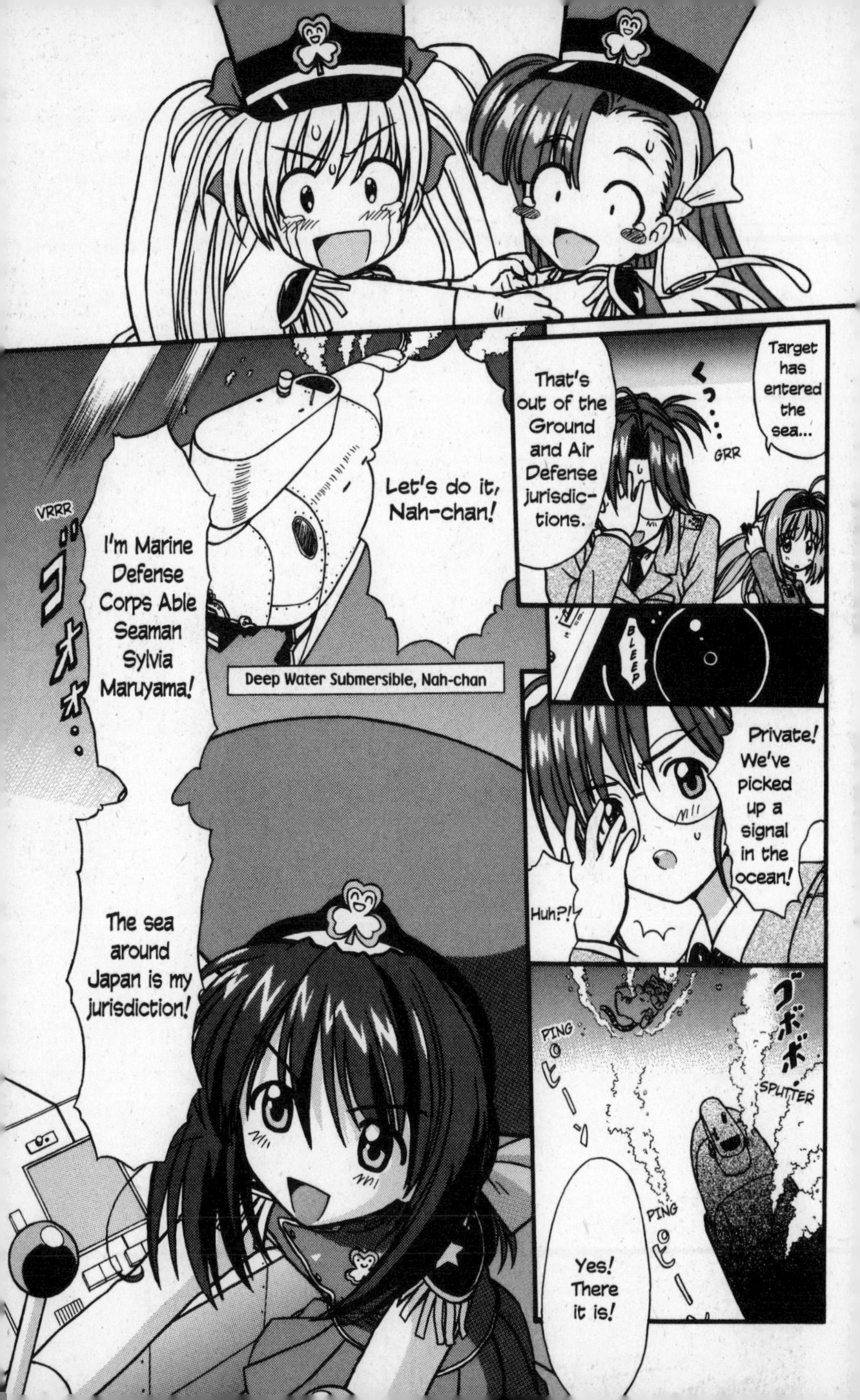
Target has entered the sea...
That's out of the Ground and Air Defense jurisdictions.
くっ…
GRR
BLEEP
Private! We've picked up a signal in the ocean!
Huh?!
ゴボボ
SPLUTTER
PING
ピー
PING
ピー
Yes! There it is!
Let's do it, Nah-chan!
I'm Marine Defense Corps Able Seaman Sylvia Maruyama!
VRRR
ゴオオ…
Deep Water Submersible, Nah-chan
The sea around Japan is my jurisdiction!

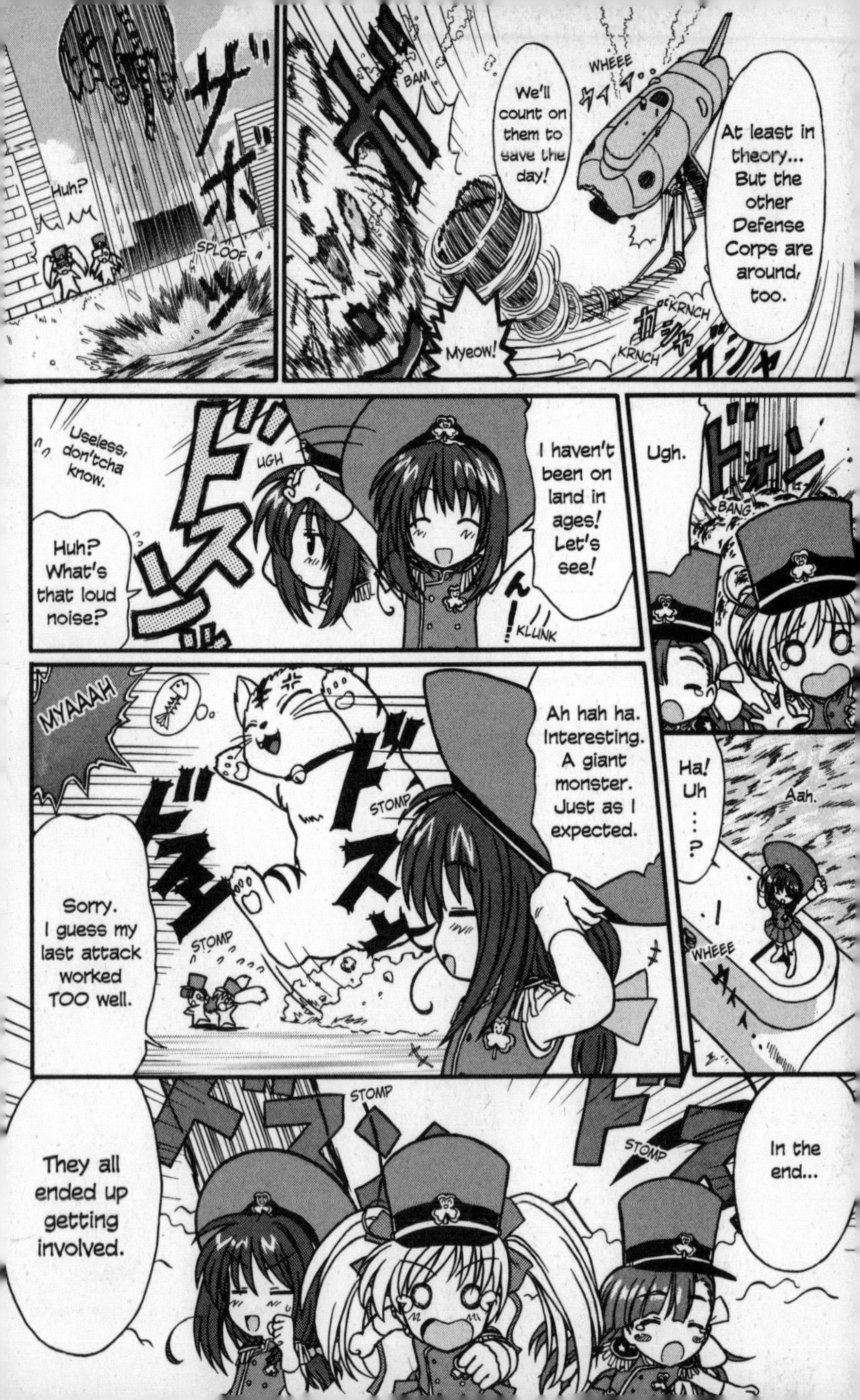
At least in theory... But the other Defense Corps are around, too.
WHEEE
We'll count on them to save the day!
BAM
KRNCH
KRNCH
Myeow!
SPLOOF
Huh?
Ugh.
BANG
I haven't been on land in ages! Let's see!
KLUNK
UGH
Useless, don'tcha know.
Huh? What's that loud noise?
Ah hah ha. Interesting. A giant monster. Just as I expected.
STOMP
MYAAAH
Sorry. I guess my last attack worked TOO well.
STOMP
Ha! Uh ...?
Aah.
WHEEE
In the end...
STOMP
STOMP
They all ended up getting involved.

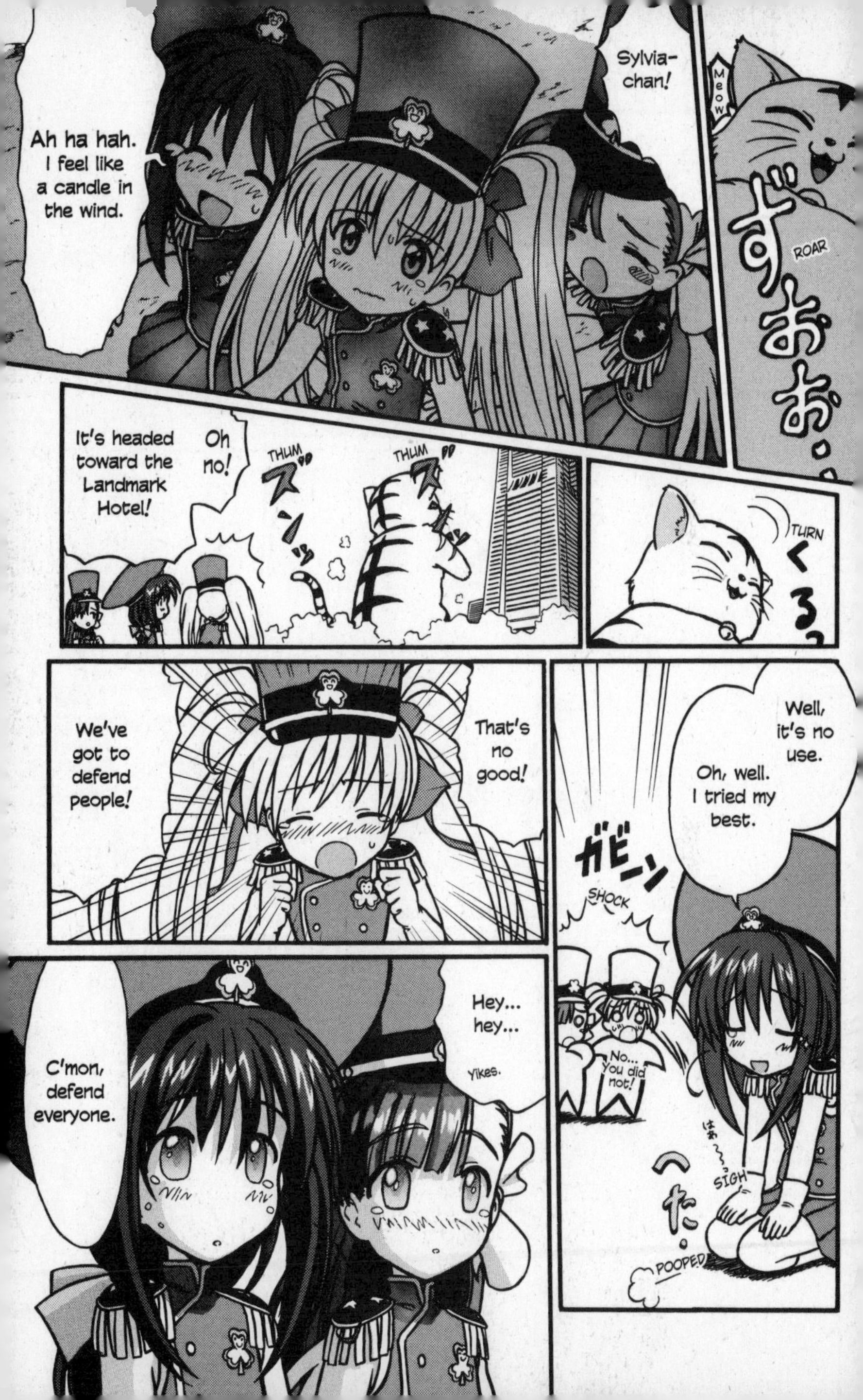

Meow
ずおお。
ROAR
Sylvia-chan!
Ah ha hah. I feel like a candle in the wind.
くるっ
TURN
Oh no!
It's headed toward the Landmark Hotel!
ズンッ
THUM
THUM
Well, it's no use.
Oh, well. I tried my best.
ガビーン
SHOCK
No... You did not!
はぁ〜〜
SIGH
へたっ
POOPED
That's no good!
We've got to defend people!
Hey... hey...
Yikes.
C'mon, defend everyone.

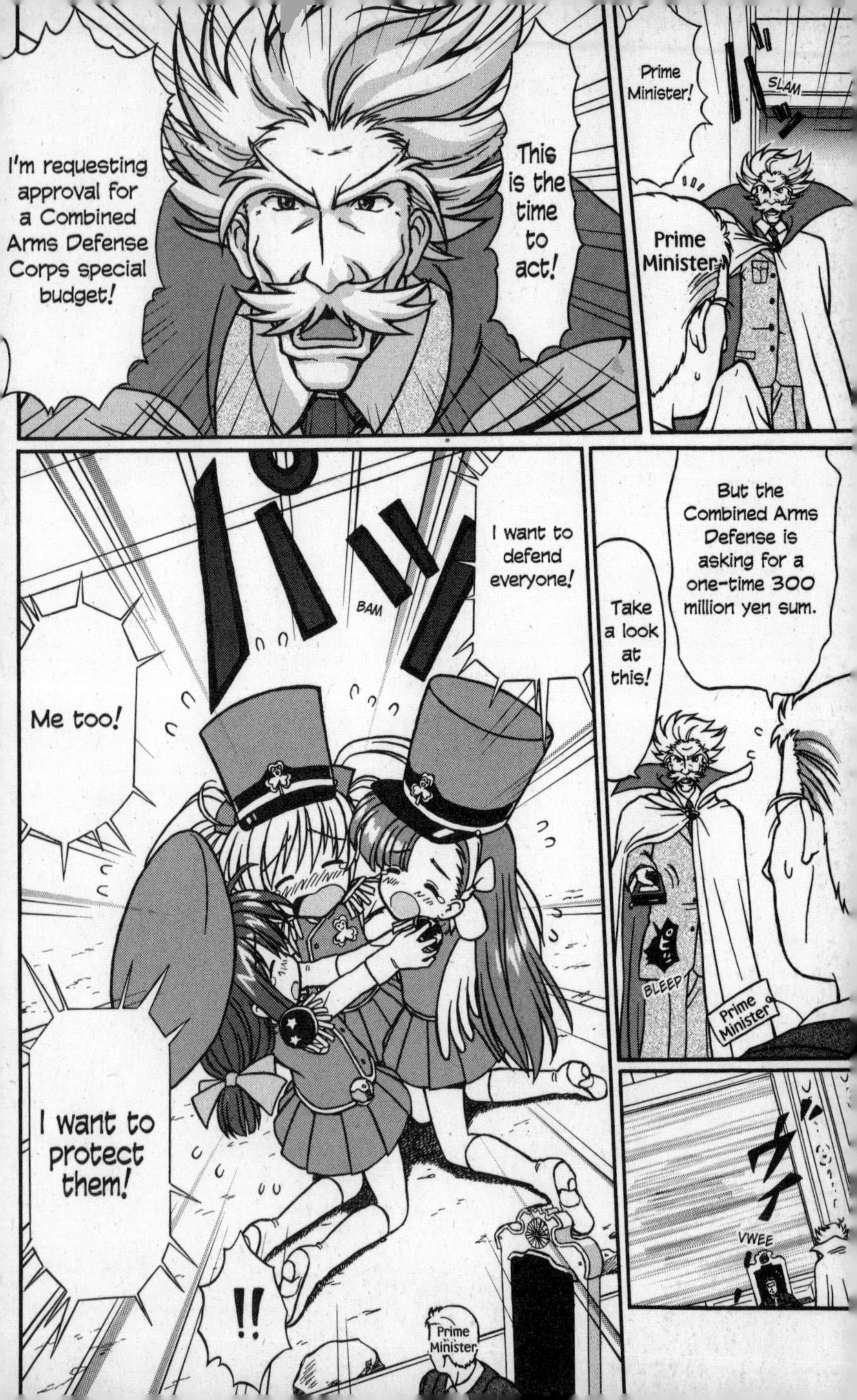

Prime Minister!
SLAM
Prime Minister
This is the time to act!
I'm requesting approval for a Combined Arms Defense Corps special budget!
But the Combined Arms Defense is asking for a one-time 300 million yen sum.
Take a look at this!
BLEEP
Prime Minister
VWEE
I want to defend everyone!
BAM
Me too!
I want to protect them!
!!
Prime Minister

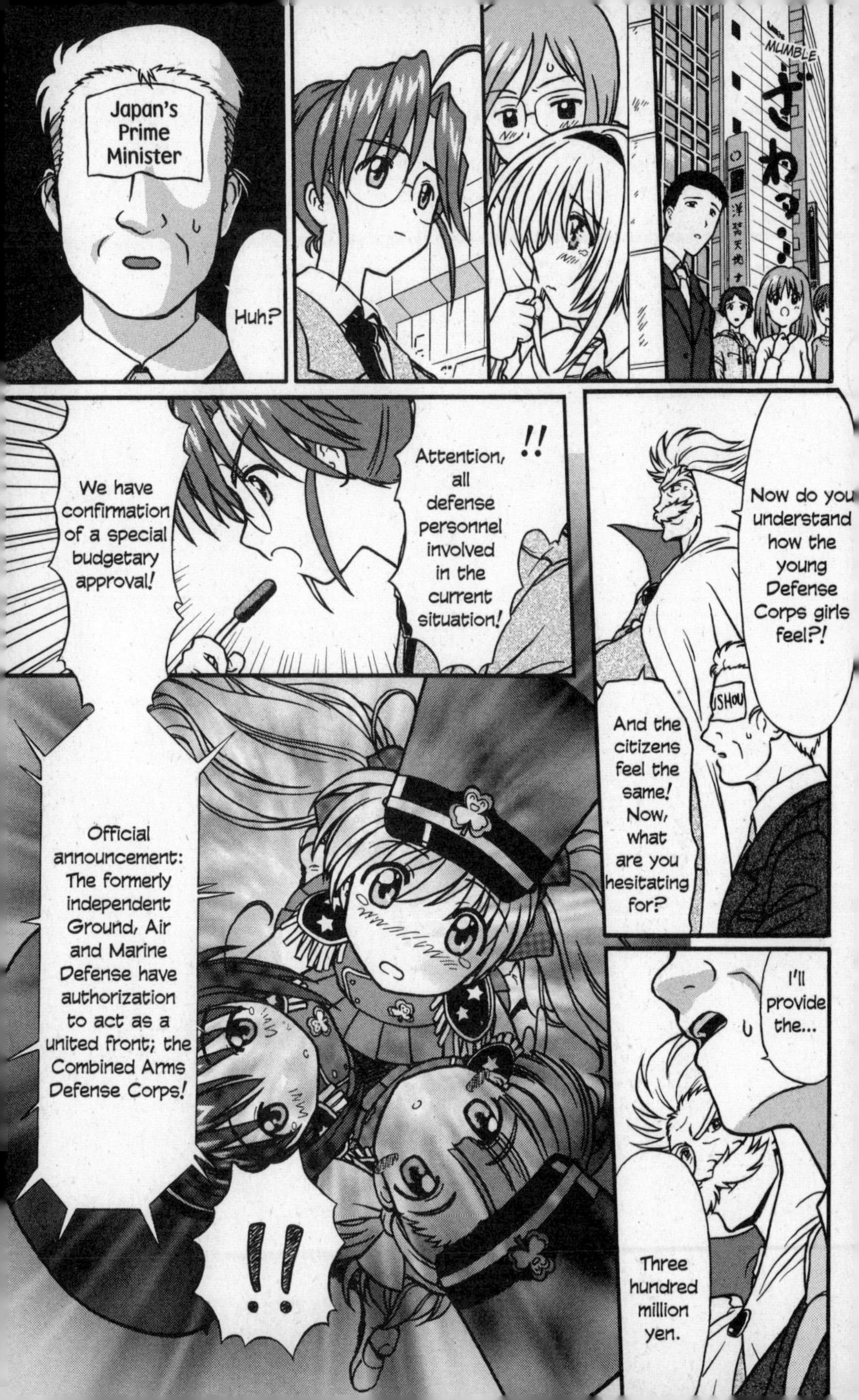

MUMBLE
ざわ…
Japan's Prime Minister
Huh?
Now do you understand how the young Defense Corps girls feel?!
!!
Attention, all defense personnel involved in the current situation!
We have confirmation of a special budgetary approval!
SHOU
And the citizens feel the same! Now, what are you hesitating for?
I'll provide the...
Three hundred million yen.
Official announcement: The formerly independent Ground, Air and Marine Defense have authorization to act as a united front; the Combined Arms Defense Corps!
!!

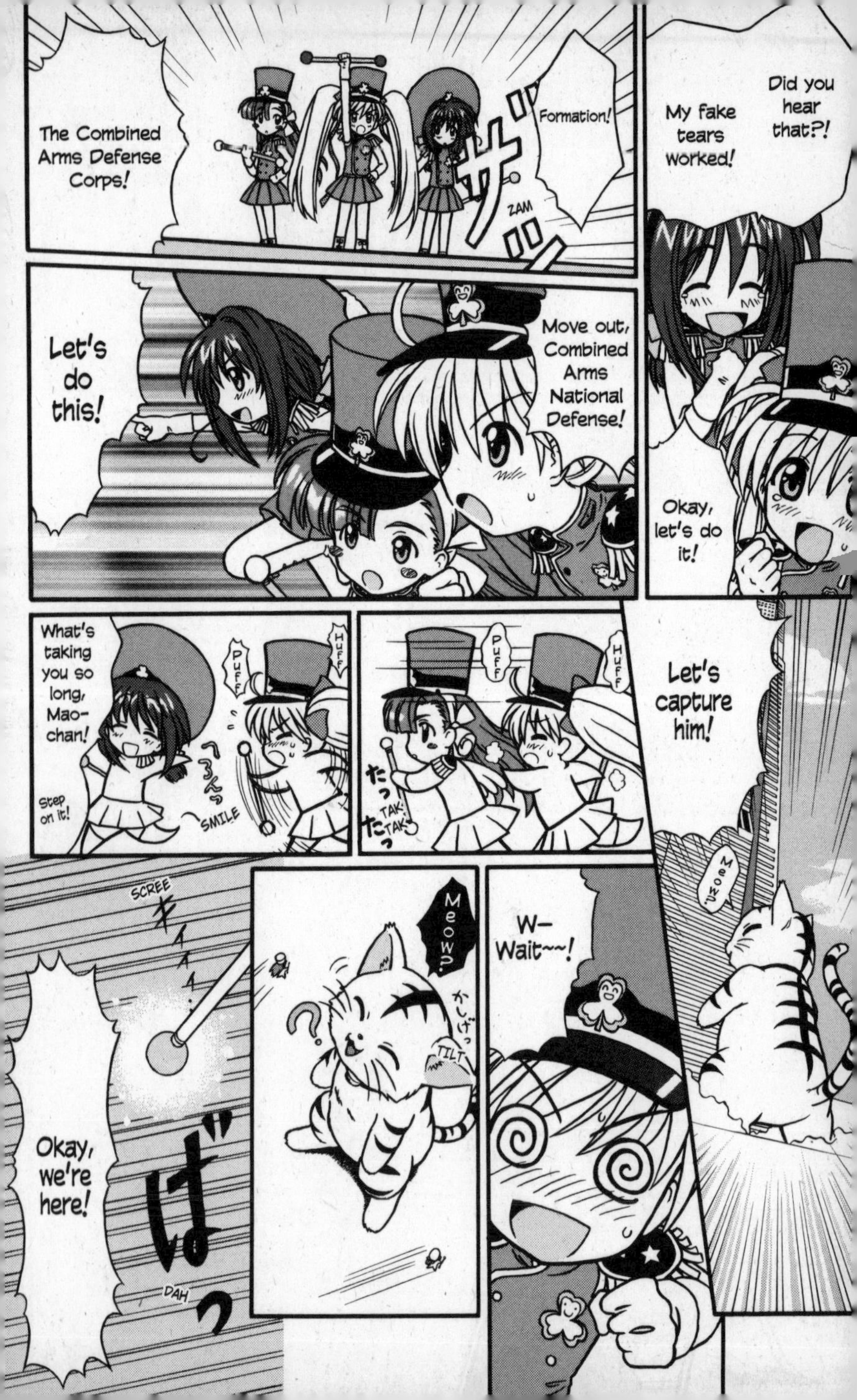

Did you hear that?!
My fake tears worked!
Okay, let's do it!
Formation!
ZAM
The Combined Arms Defense Corps!
Move out, Combined Arms National Defense!
Let's do this!
Let's capture him!
Meow?!
Huff
Puff
TAK TAK
Huff
Puff
What's taking you so long, Mao-chan!
SMILE
Step on it!
W-Wait~~!
Meow?!
TILT
SCREE
Okay, we're here!
DAH

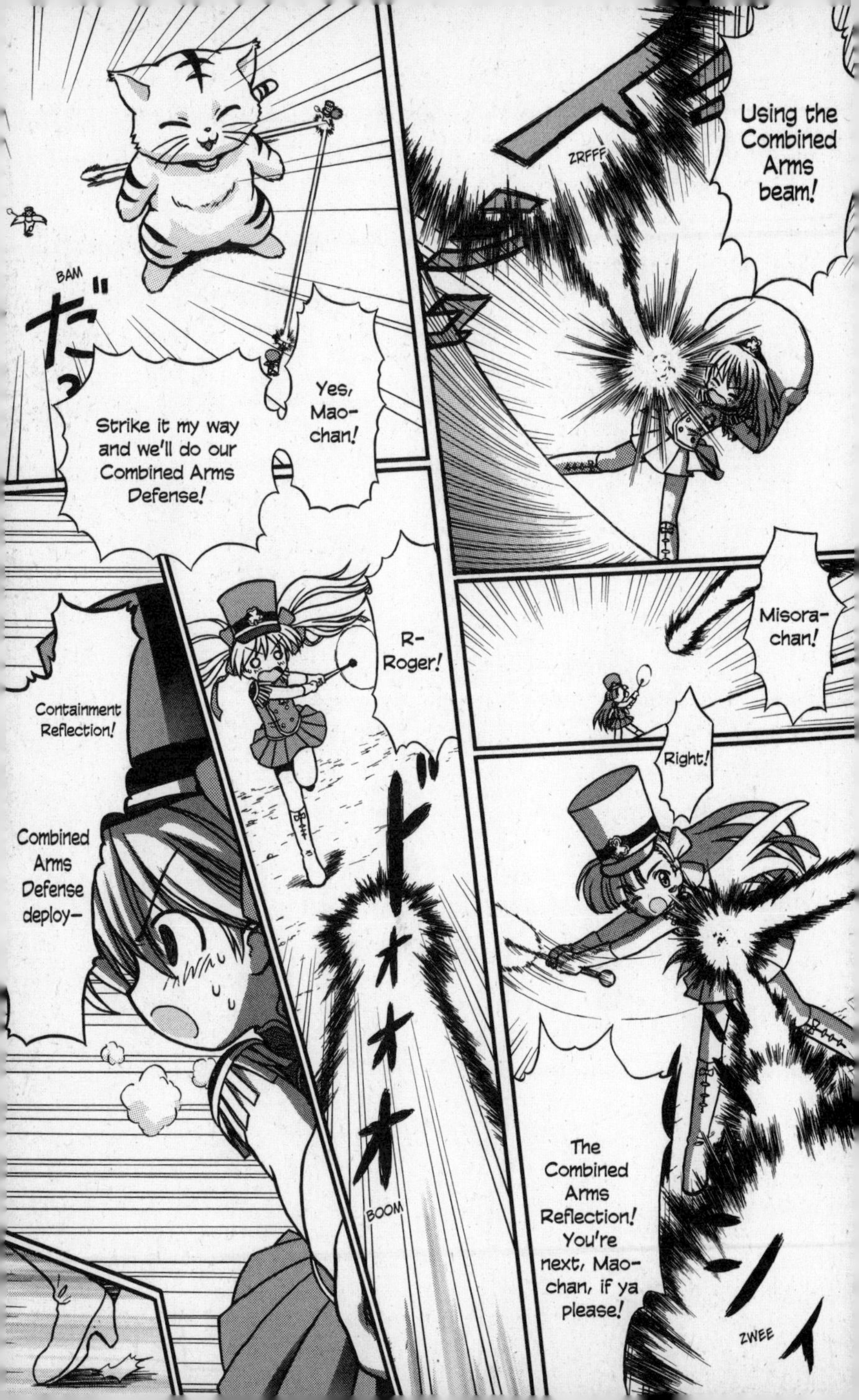

ZRFFF
Using the Combined Arms beam!
BAM
だっ
Strike it my way and we'll do our Combined Arms Defense!
Yes, Mao-chan!
Misora-chan!
Right!
The Combined Arms Reflection! You're next, Mao-chan, if ya please!
ZWEE
R-Roger!
BOOM
Containment Reflection!
Combined Arms Defense deploy–

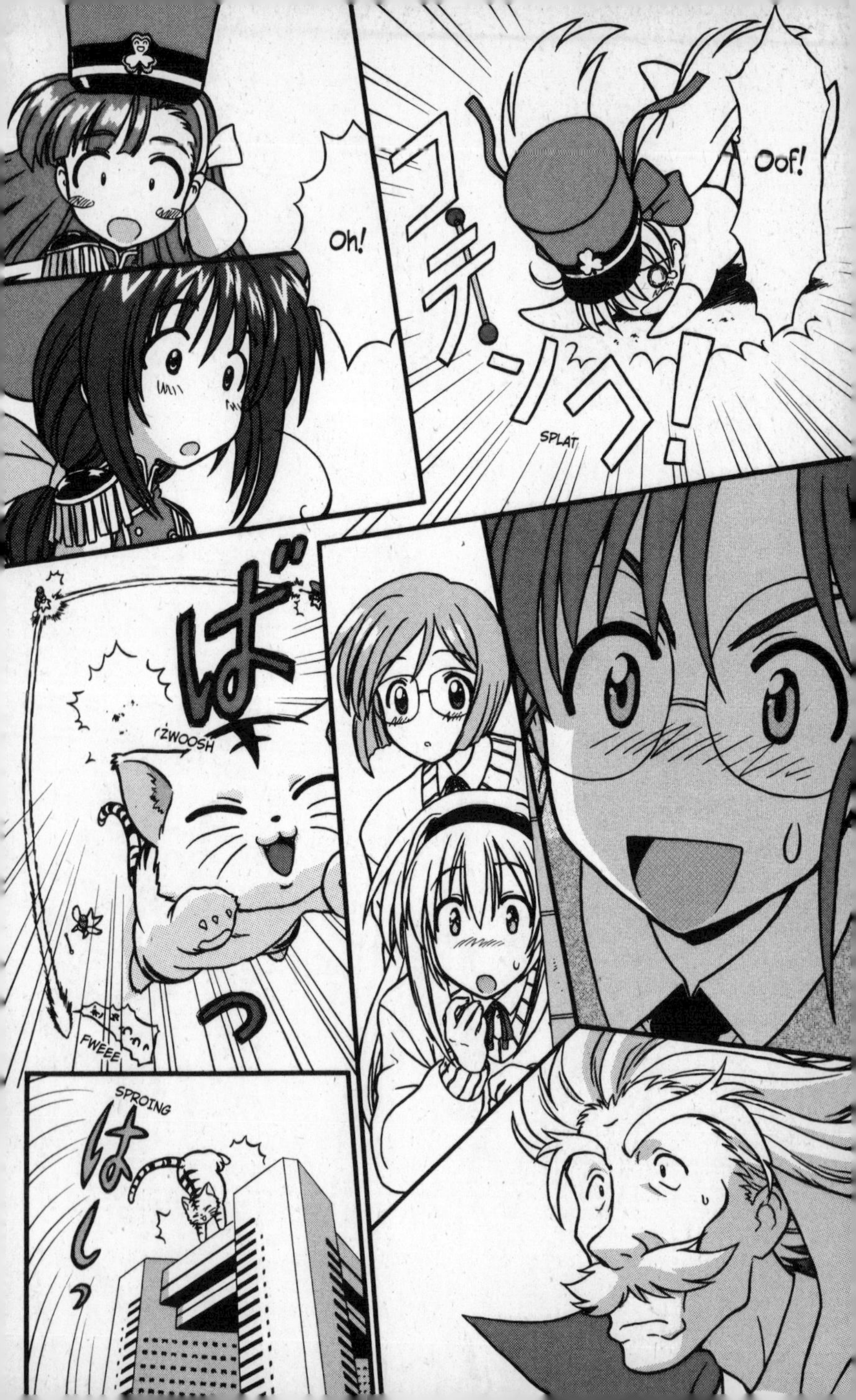
Oof!
SPLAT
Oh!
ばっ
ZWOOSH
FWEEE
SPROING
はしっ

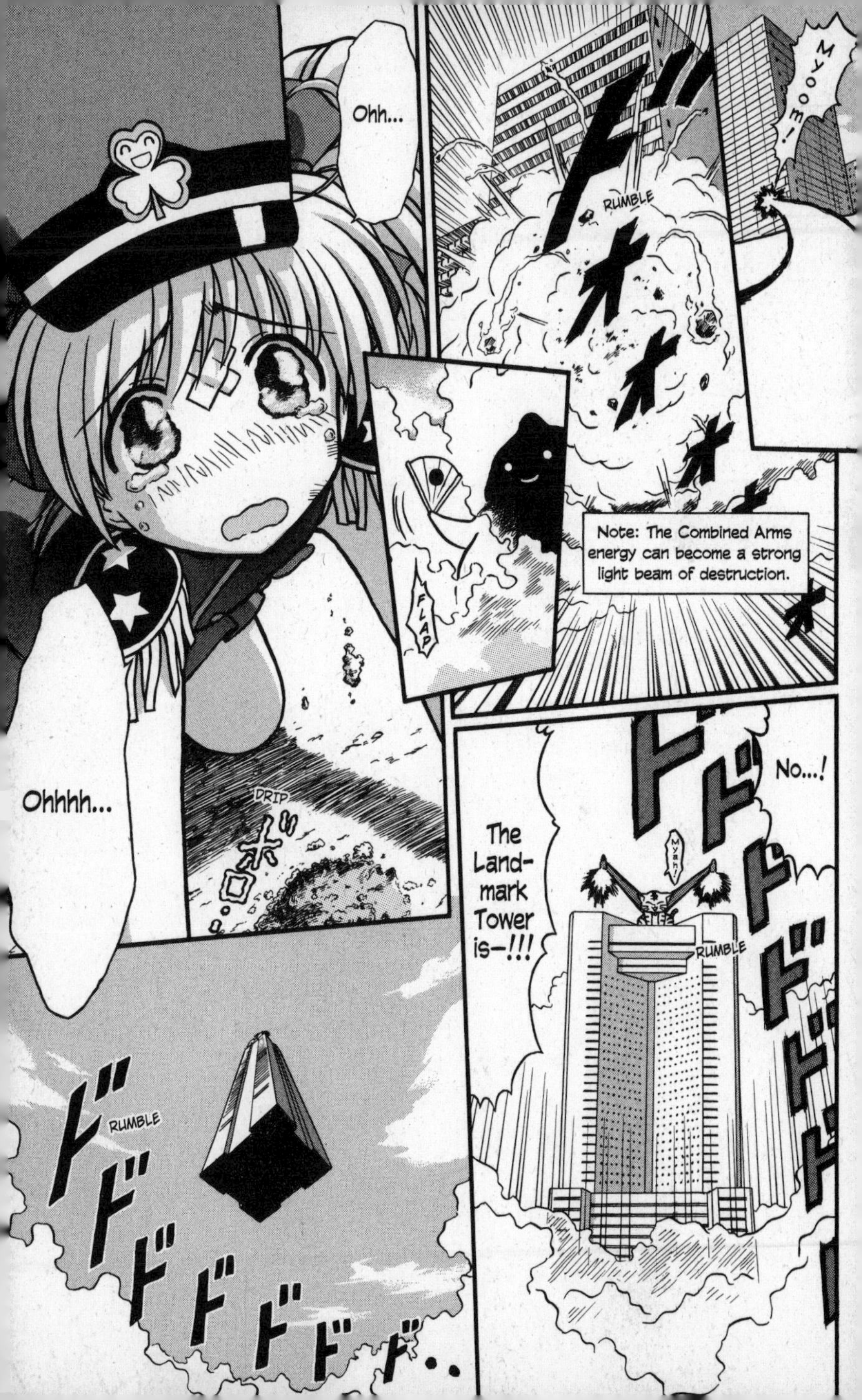
Myoom!
RUMBLE
Note: The Combined Arms energy can become a strong light beam of destruction.
FLAP
Ohh...
Ohhhh...
DRIP
No...!
Myah!
The Landmark Tower is—!!!
RUMBLE
RUMBLE

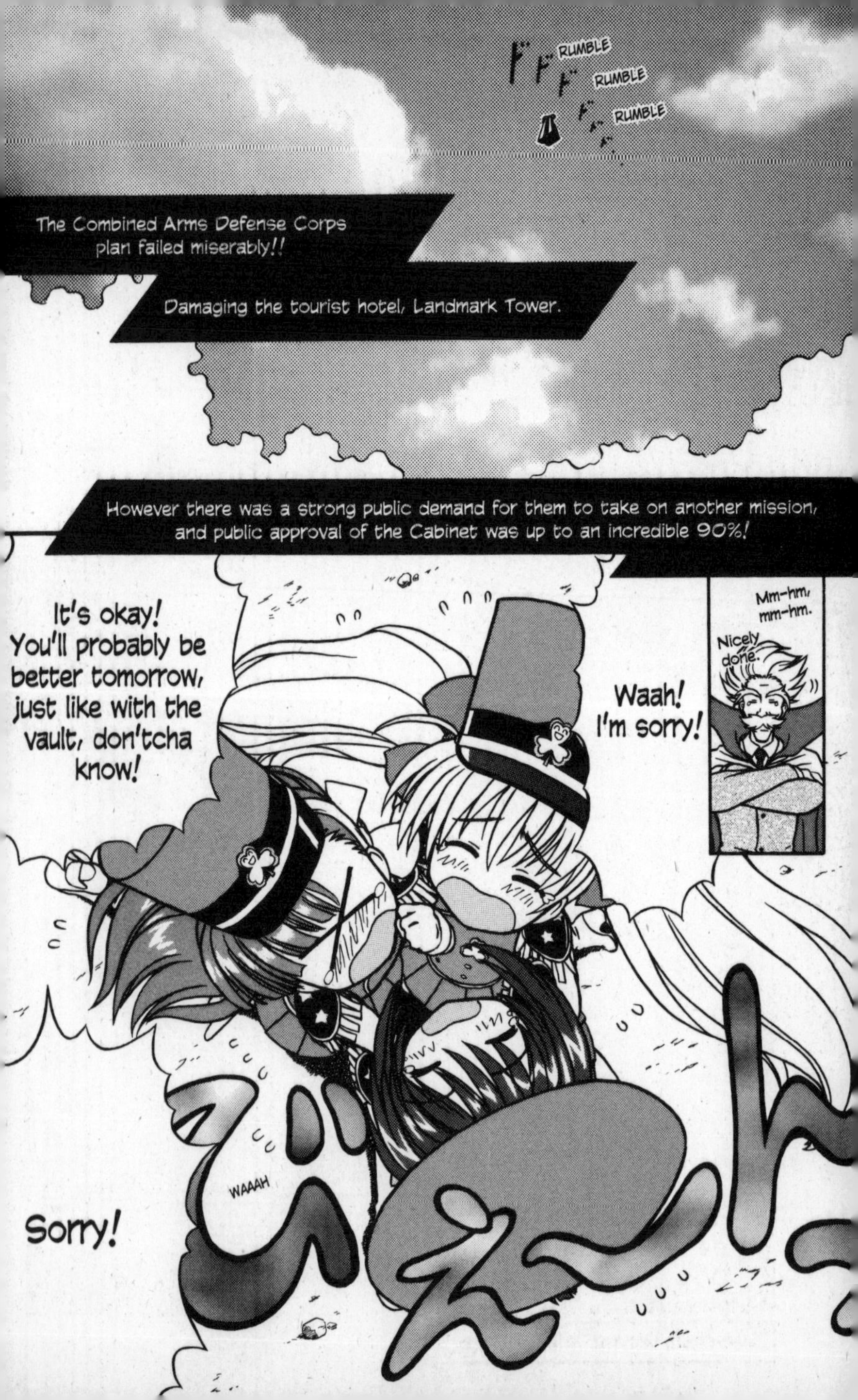
RUMBLE
RUMBLE
RUMBLE
The Combined Arms Defense Corps plan failed miserably!!
Damaging the tourist hotel, Landmark Tower.
However there was a strong public demand for them to take on another mission, and public approval of the Cabinet was up to an incredible 90%!
Mm-hm, mm-hm.
Nicely done.
Waah! I'm sorry!
It's okay! You'll probably be better tomorrow, just like with the vault, don'tcha know!
WAAAH
Sorry!

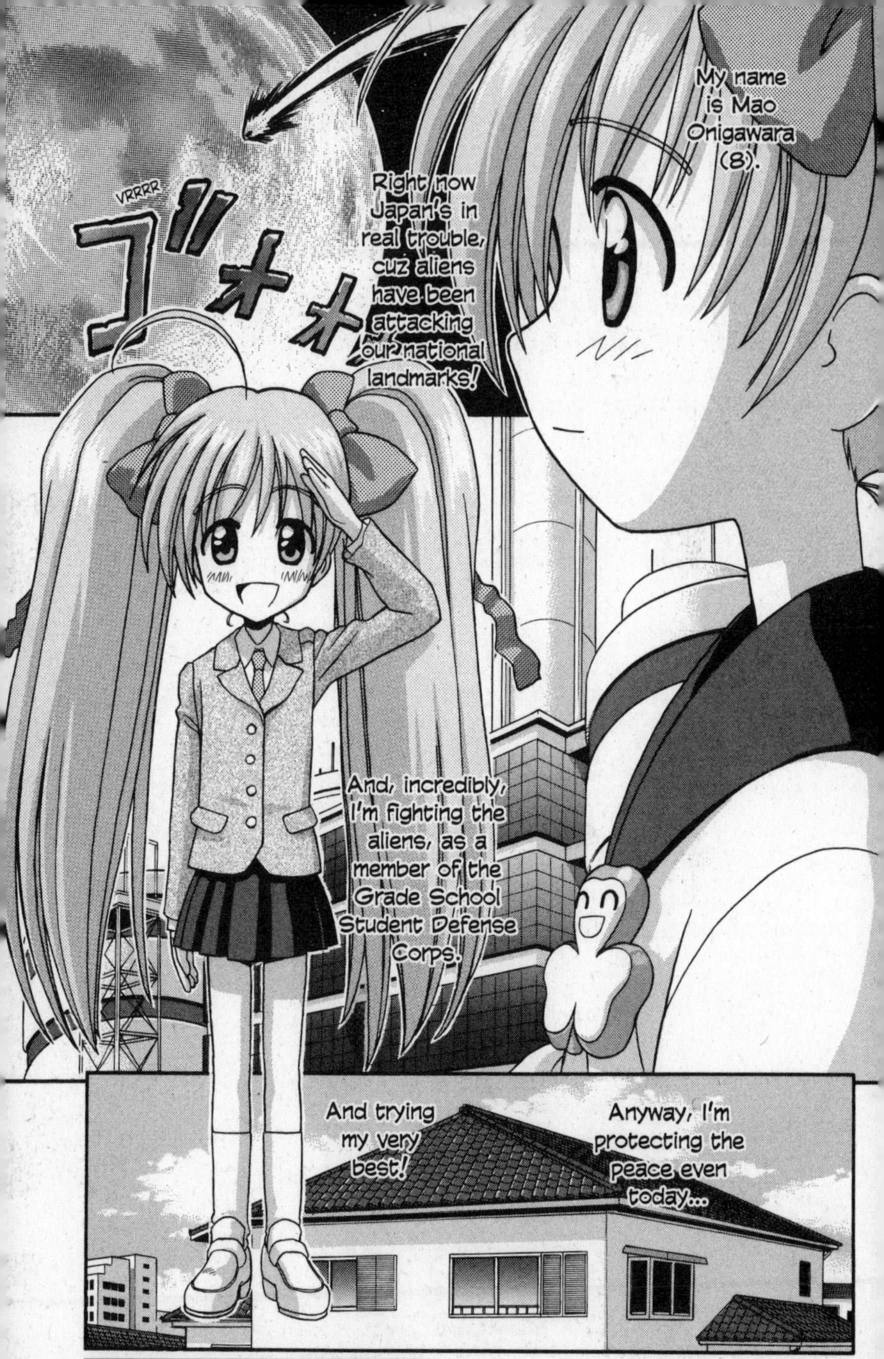
My name is Mao Onigawara (8).
Right now Japan's in real trouble, cuz aliens have been attacking our national landmarks!
VRRRR
And, incredibly, I'm fighting the aliens, as a member of the Grade School Student Defense Corps.
Anyway, I'm protecting the peace even today...
And trying my very best!

Mao-chan, Ground Defense Corps

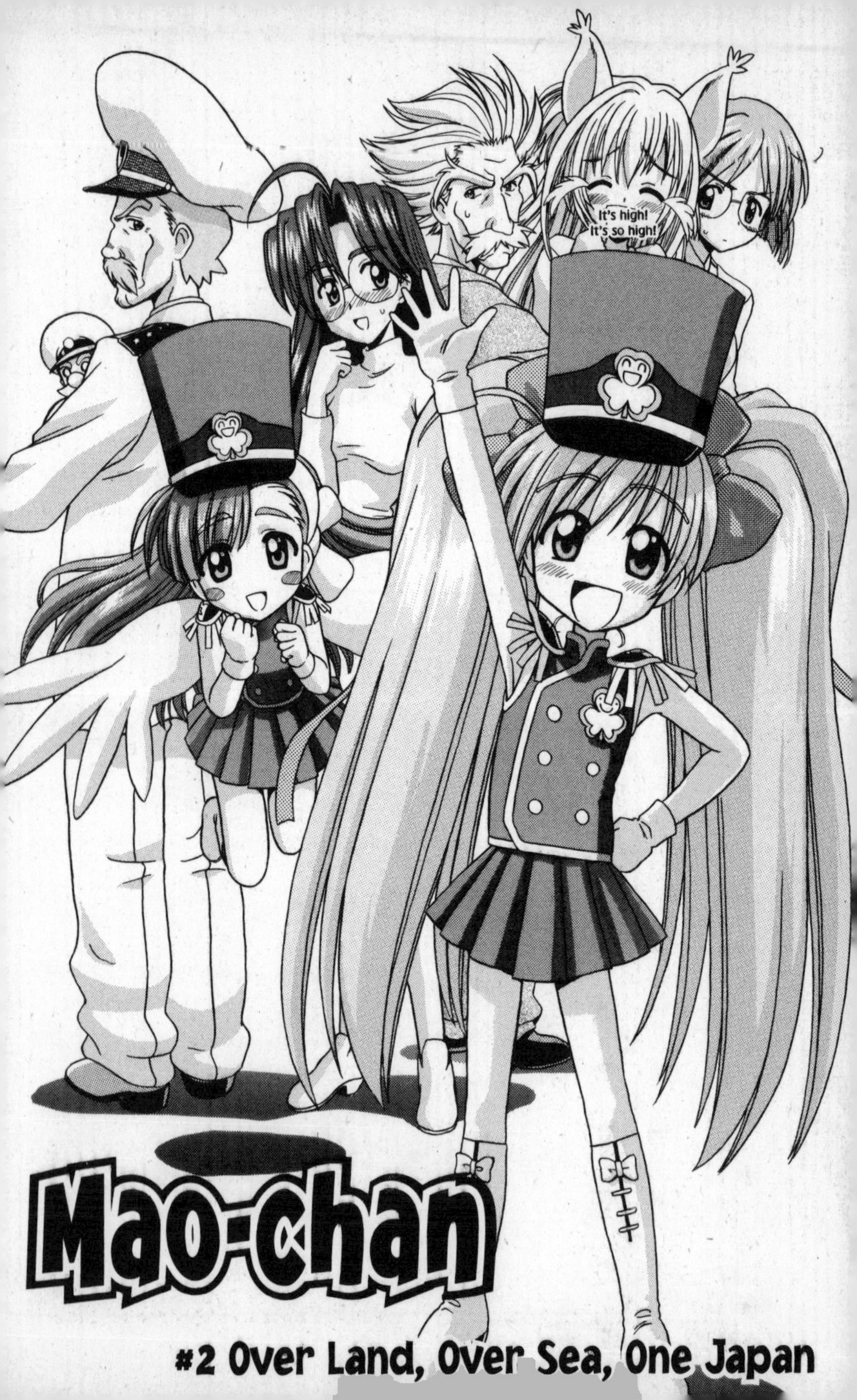
It's high! It's so high!

Mao-chan

#2 Over Land, Over Sea, One Japan

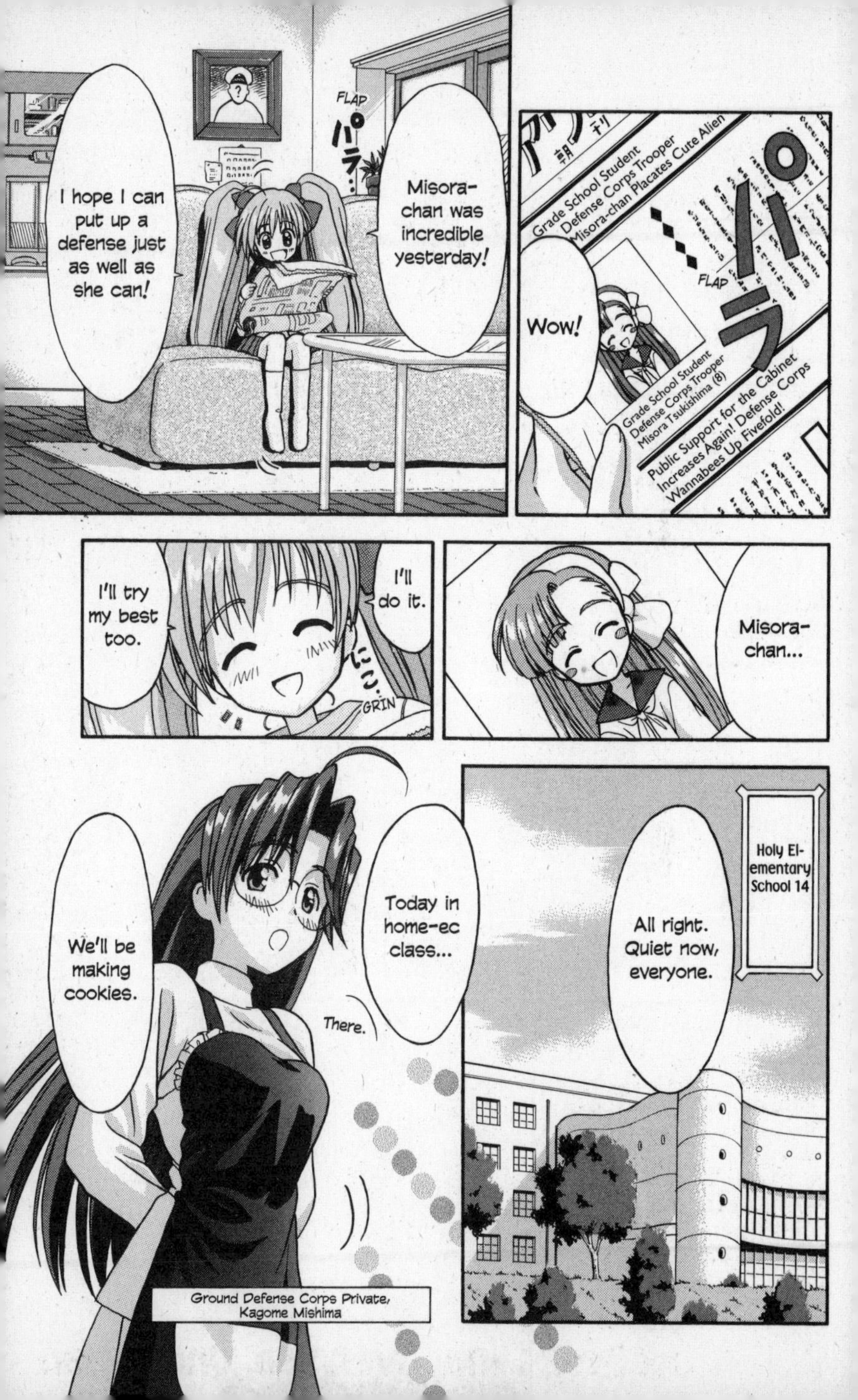
Grade School Student Defense Corps Trooper Misora-chan Placates Cute Alien
FLAP
Wow!
Grade School Student Defense Corps Trooper Misora Tsukishima (8)
Public Support for the Cabinet Increases Again! Defense Corps Wannabees Up Fivefold!
FLAP
Misora-chan was incredible yesterday!
I hope I can put up a defense just as well as she can!
Misora-chan...
I'll do it.
GRIN
I'll try my best too.
Holy Elementary School 14
All right. Quiet now, everyone.
Today in home-ec class...
There.
We'll be making cookies.
Ground Defense Corps Private, Kagome Mishima

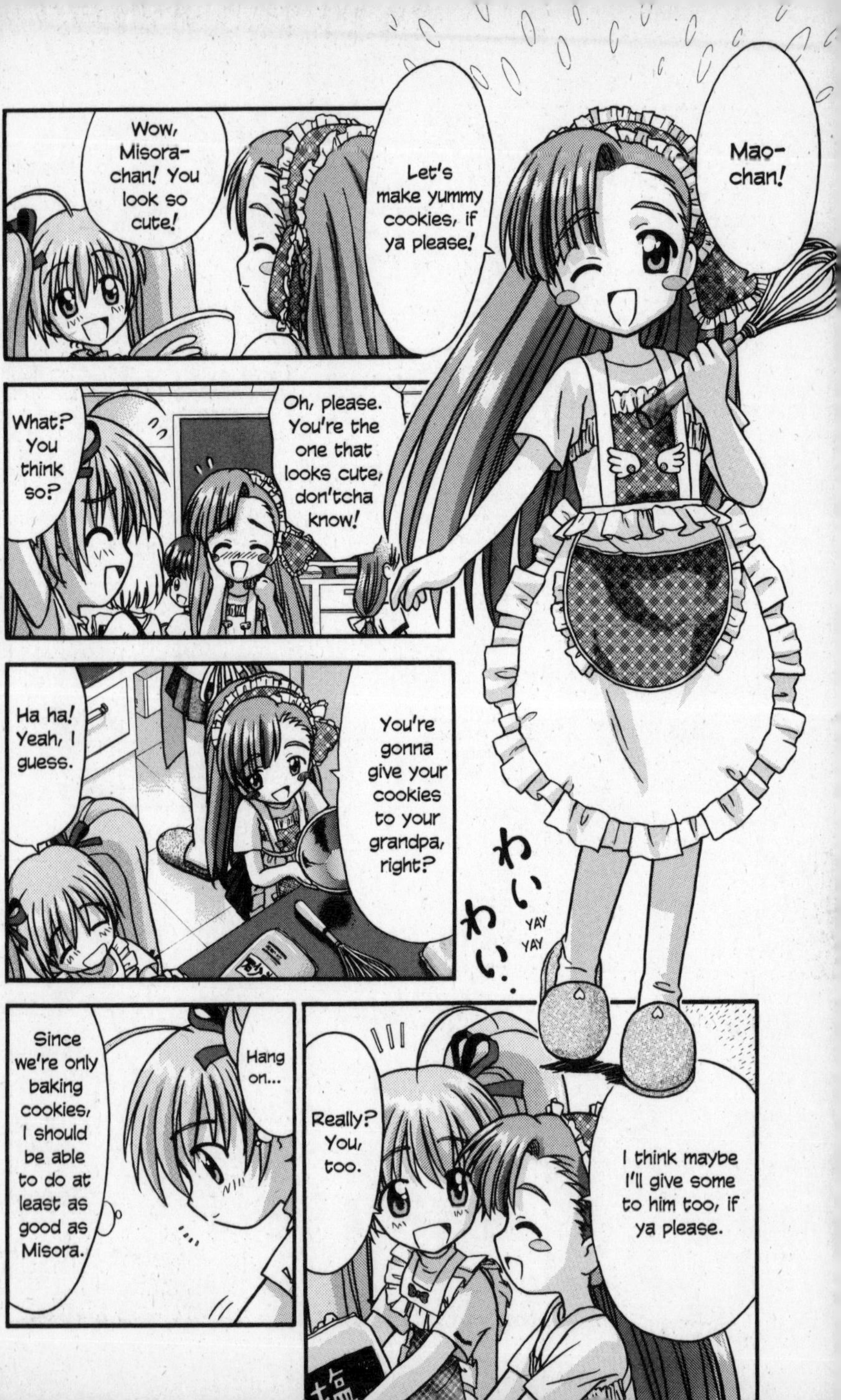
Mao-chan!
Let's make yummy cookies, if ya please!
わいわい
YAY YAY
Wow, Misora-chan! You look so cute!
Oh, please. You're the one that looks cute, don'tcha know!
What? You think so?
You're gonna give your cookies to your grandpa, right?
Ha ha! Yeah, I guess.
I think maybe I'll give some to him too, if ya please.
Really? You, too.
Hang on...
Since we're only baking cookies, I should be able to do at least as good as Misora.

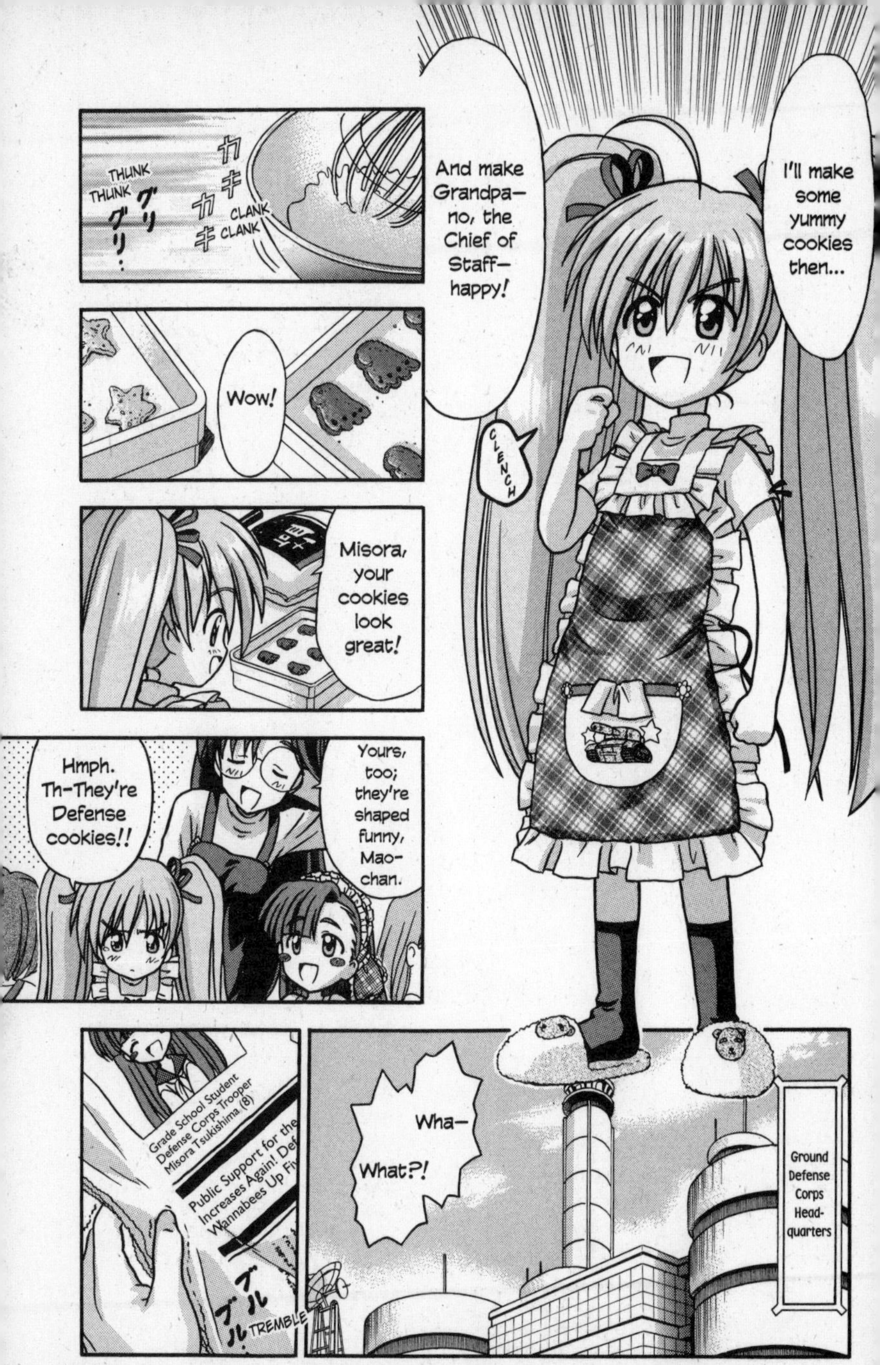
I'll make some yummy cookies then...
And make Grandpa-no, the Chief of Staff-happy!
CLENCH
カキカキ
CLANK CLANK
グリグリ
THUNK THUNK
Wow!
Misora, your cookies look great!
Yours, too; they're shaped funny, Mao-chan.
Hmph. Th-They're Defense cookies!!
Ground Defense Corps Headquarters
Wha-
What?!
Grade School Student Defense Corps Trooper Misora Tsukishima (8)
Public Support for the Increases Again! Def Wannabees Up Fiv
ブルブル
TREMBLE

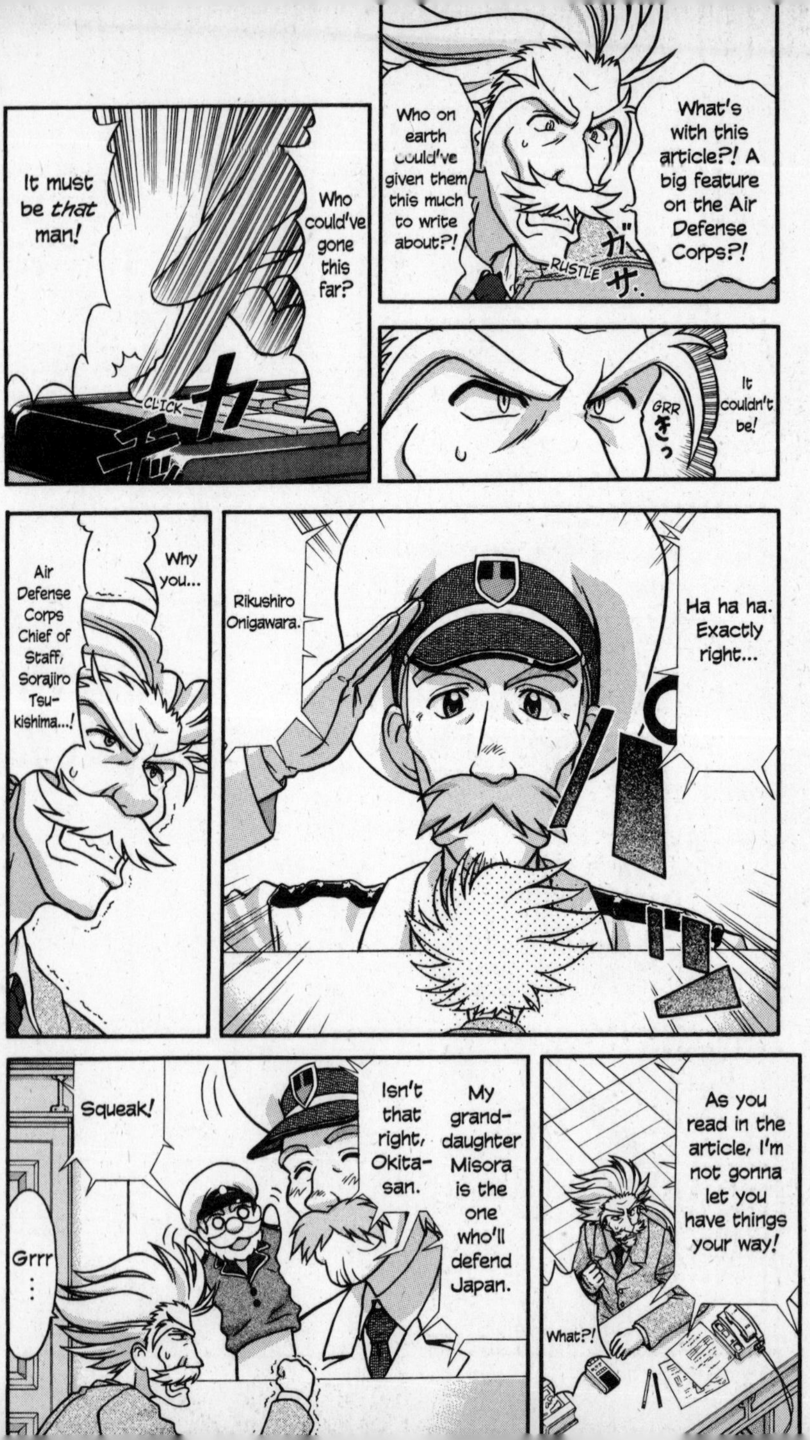
What's with this article?! A big feature on the Air Defense Corps?!
Who on earth could've given them this much to write about?!
RUSTLE
ガサ
It couldn't be!
GRR
Who could've gone this far?
It must be *that* man!
CLICK
Ha ha ha. Exactly right...
Rikushiro Onigawara.
Why you...
Air Defense Corps Chief of Staff, Sorajiro Tsukishima...!
As you read in the article, I'm not gonna let you have things your way!
What?!
My grand-daughter Misora is the one who'll defend Japan.
Isn't that right, Okita-san.
Squeak!
Grrr...

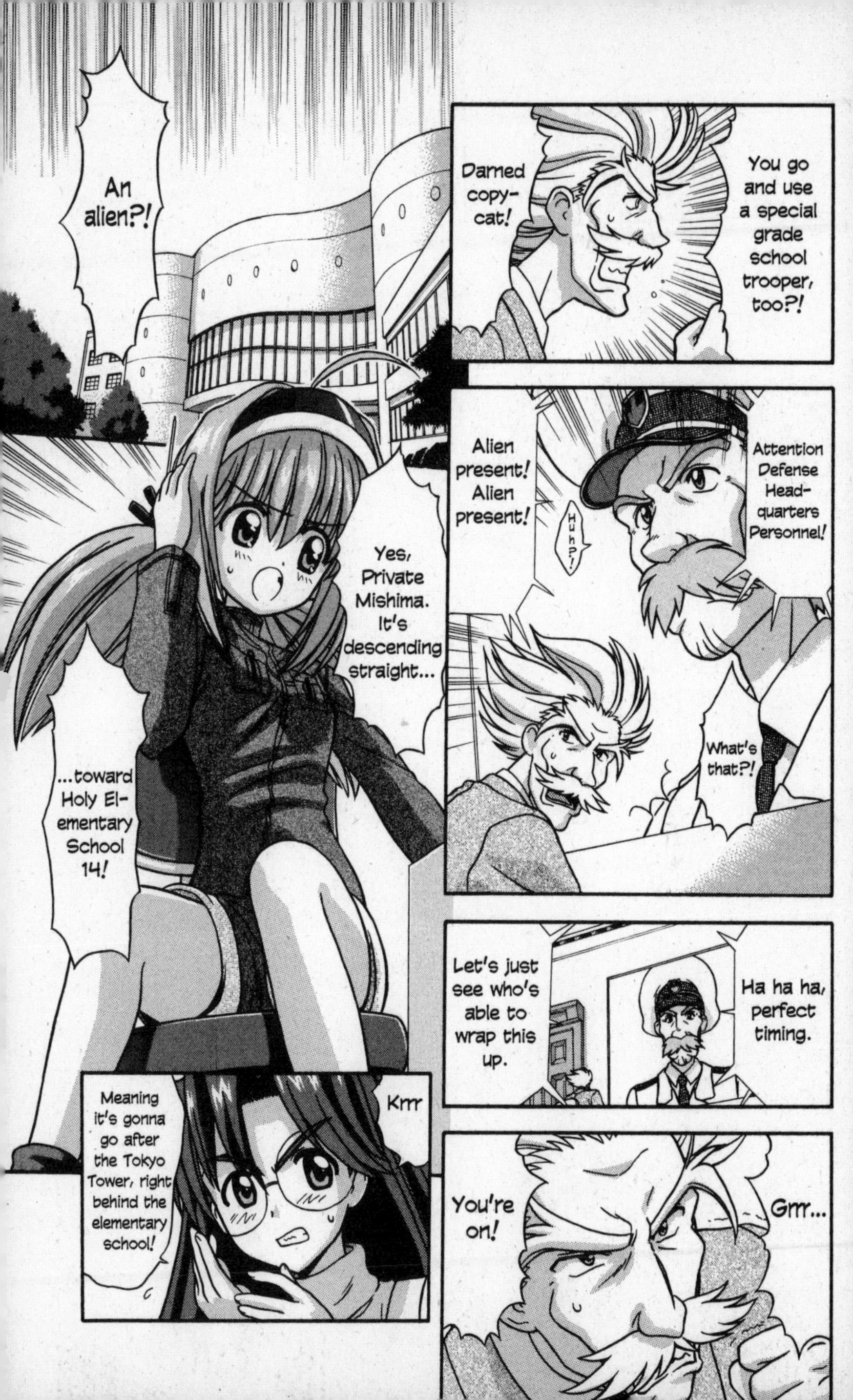

You go and use a special grade school trooper, too?!
Darned copy-cat!
Attention Defense Head-quarters Personnel!
Alien present! Alien present!
Huh?!
What's that?!
Ha ha ha, perfect timing.
Let's just see who's able to wrap this up.
Grrr...
You're on!
An alien?!
Yes, Private Mishima. It's descending straight...
...toward Holy El-ementary School 14!
Krrr
Meaning it's gonna go after the Tokyo Tower, right behind the elementary school!

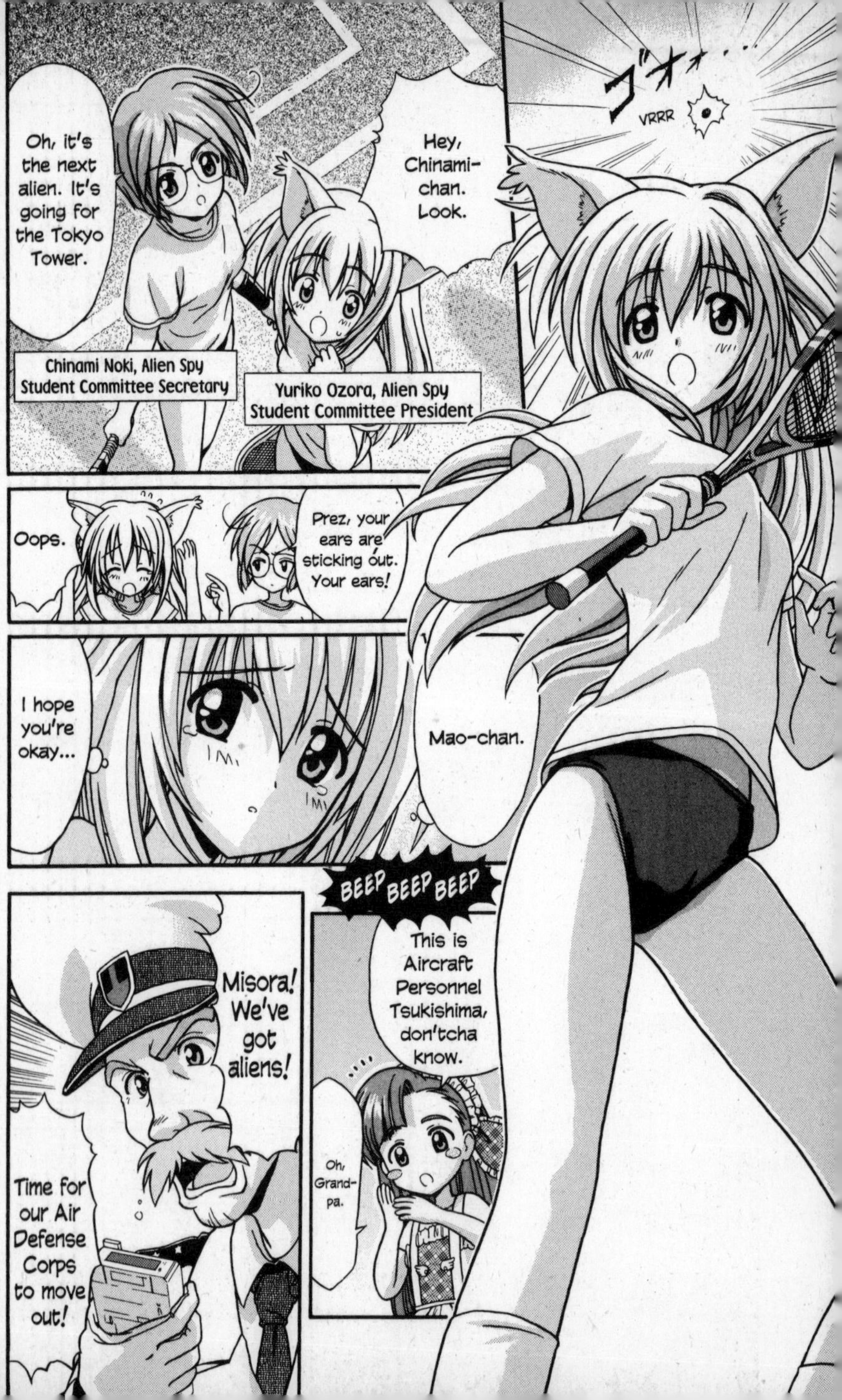
ゴオォ…
VRRR
Hey, Chinami-chan. Look.
Oh, it's the next alien. It's going for the Tokyo Tower.
Yuriko Ozora, Alien Spy Student Committee President
Chinami Noki, Alien Spy Student Committee Secretary
Prez, your ears are sticking out. Your ears!
Oops.
Mao-chan.
I hope you're okay...
BEEP BEEP BEEP
This is Aircraft Personnel Tsukishima, don'tcha know.
Oh, Grandpa.
Misora! We've got aliens!
Time for our Air Defense Corps to move out!

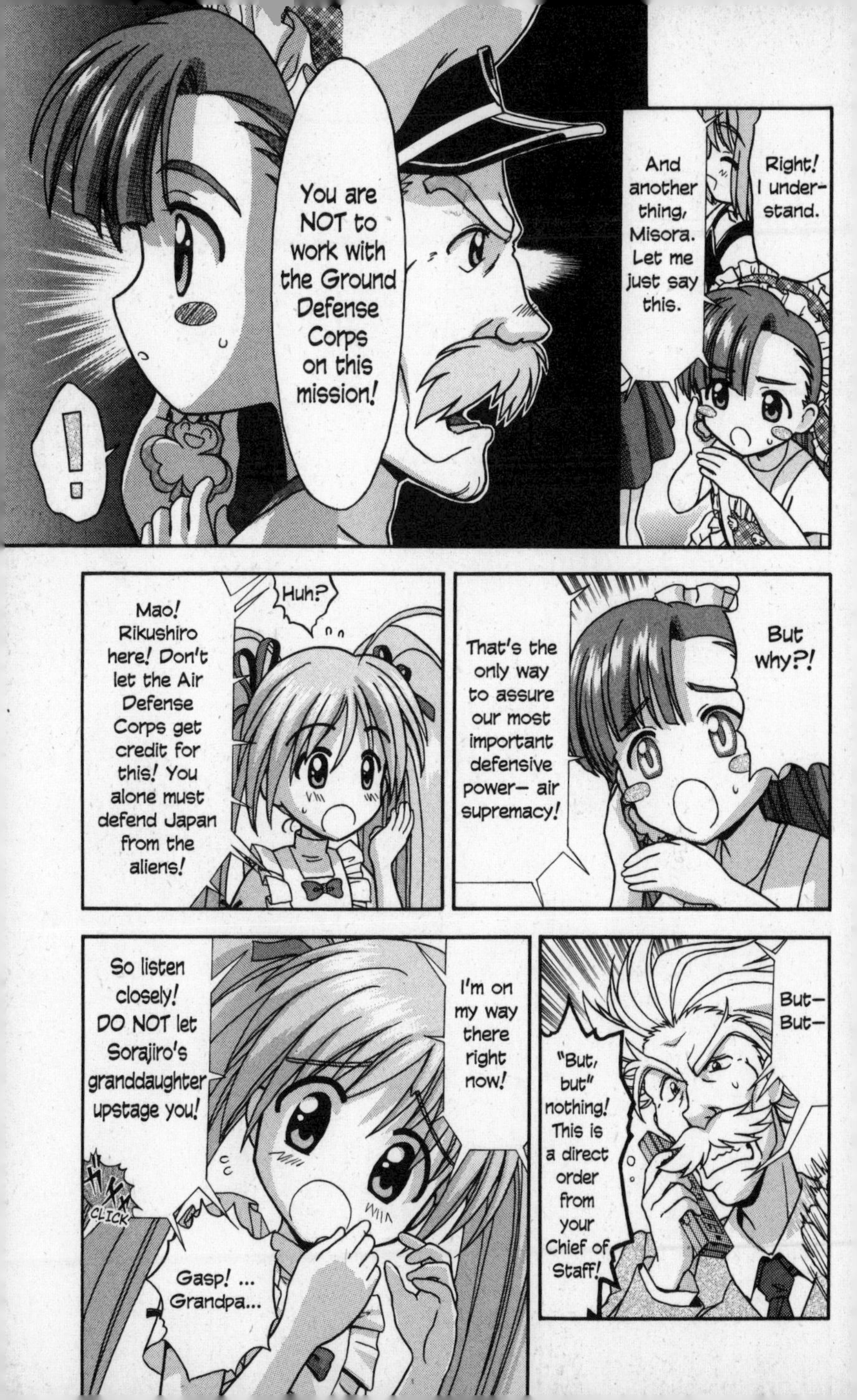
Right! I understand.
And another thing, Misora. Let me just say this.
You are NOT to work with the Ground Defense Corps on this mission!
!
But why?!
That's the only way to assure our most important defensive power— air supremacy!
Huh?
Mao! Rikushiro here! Don't let the Air Defense Corps get credit for this! You alone must defend Japan from the aliens!
But— But—
"But, but" nothing! This is a direct order from your Chief of Staff!
I'm on my way there right now!
So listen closely! DO NOT let Sorajiro's granddaughter upstage you!
CLICK
Gasp! ... Grandpa...

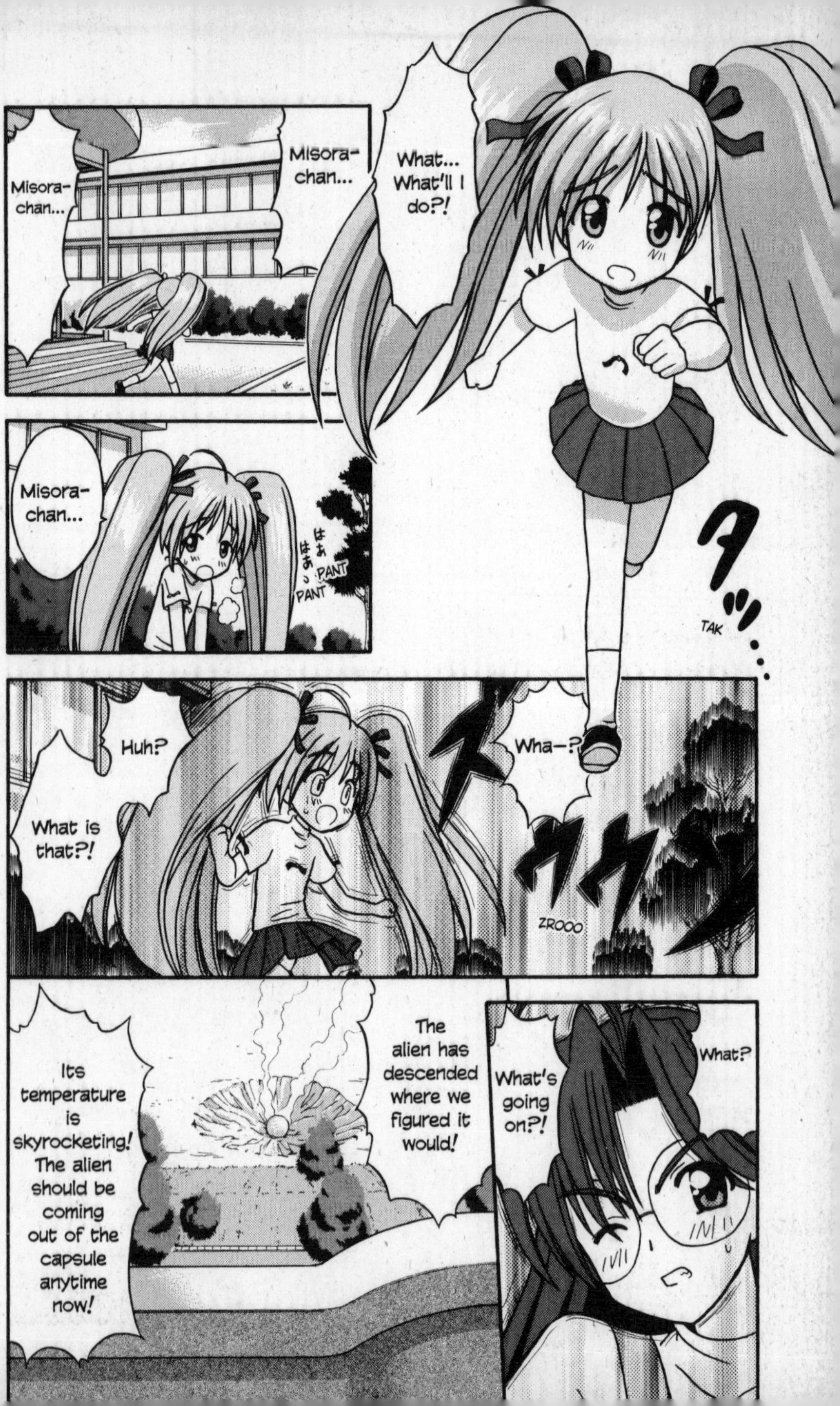

What... What'll I do?!
タッ...
TAK
Misora-chan...
Misora-chan...
Misora-chan...
はあ はあ
PANT PANT
Wha-?
ズウウウ
ZROOO
Huh?
What is that?!
What?
What's going on?!
The alien has descended where we figured it would!
Its temperature is skyrocketing! The alien should be coming out of the capsule anytime now!

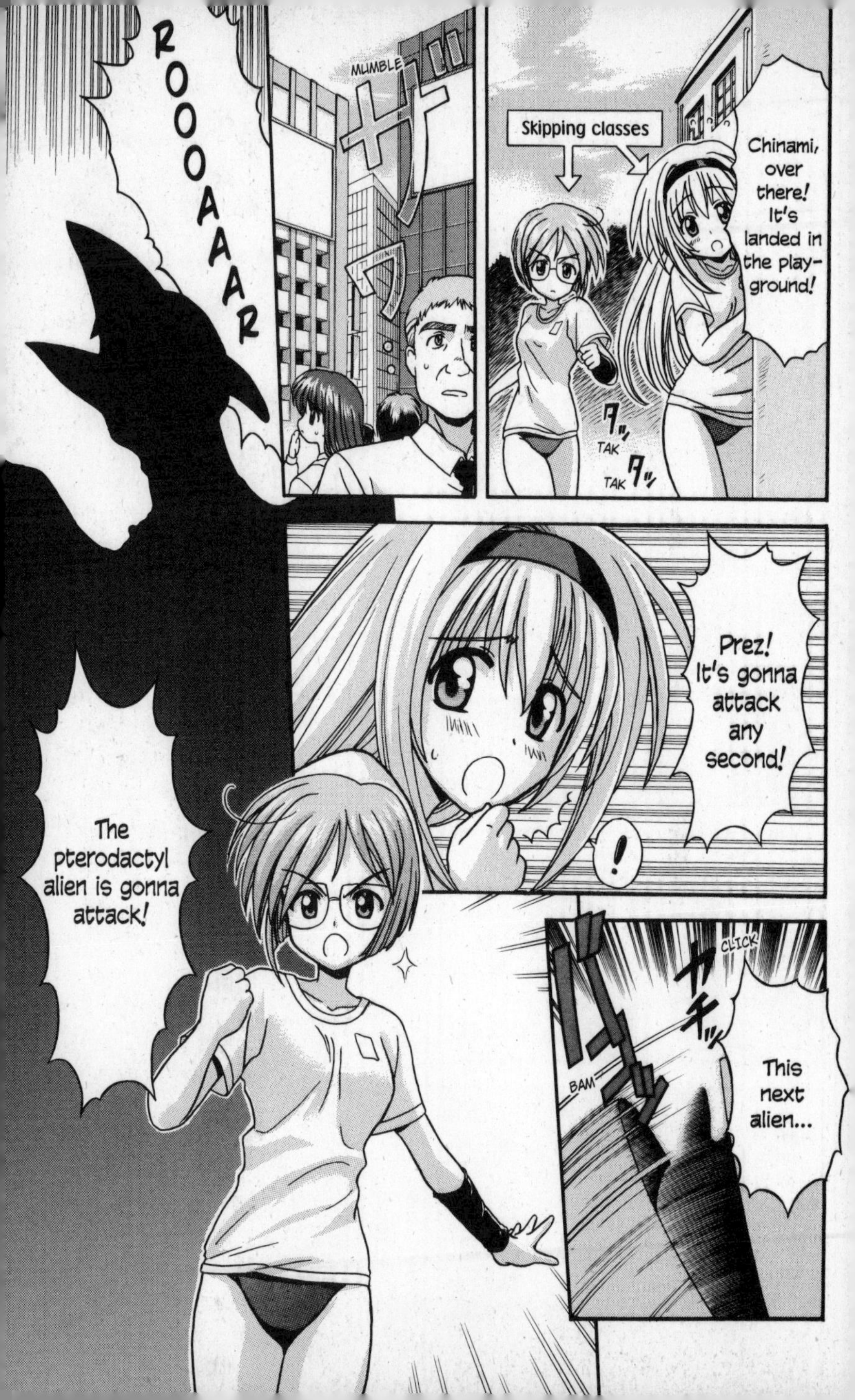

Skipping classes
Chinami, over there! It's landed in the play-ground!
TAK
TAK
MUMBLE
Prez! It's gonna attack any second!
!
CLICK
BAM
This next alien...
ROOOAAAR
The pterodactyl alien is gonna attack!

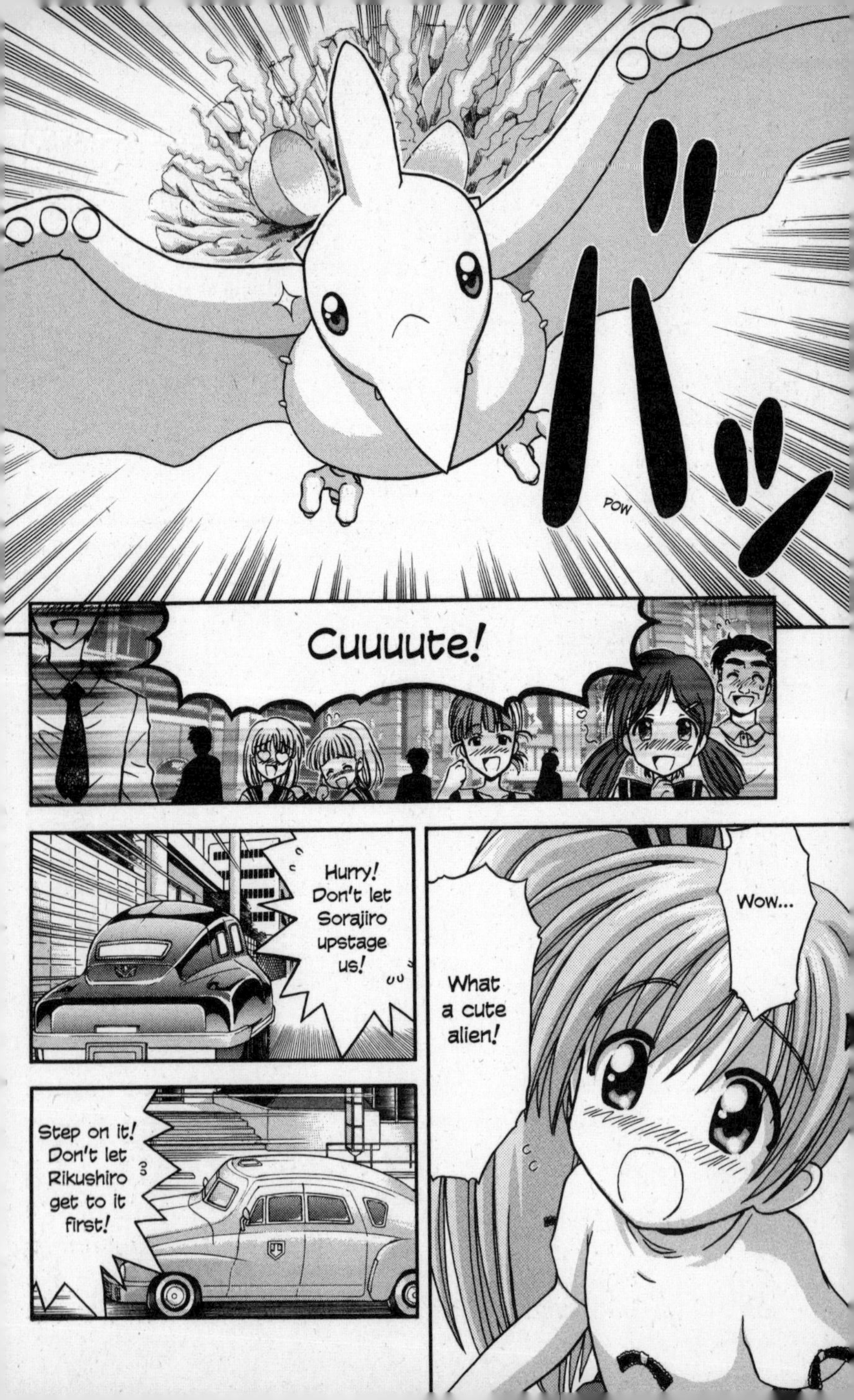
バッ
POW
Cuuuute!
Wow...
What a cute alien!
Hurry! Don't let Sorajiro upstage us!
Step on it! Don't let Rikushiro get to it first!

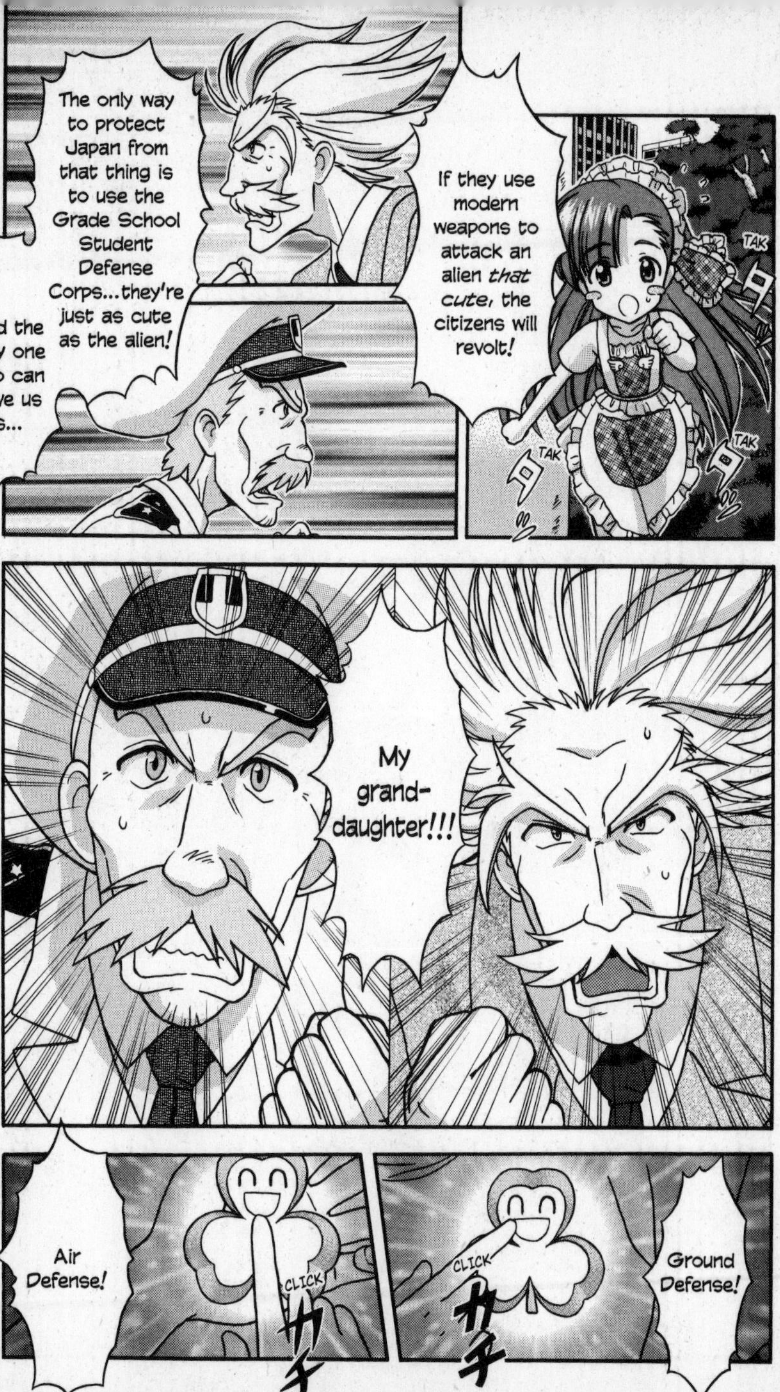
If they use modern weapons to attack an alien *that cute*, the citizens will revolt!
TAK
TAK
TAK
The only way to protect Japan from that thing is to use the Grade School Student Defense Corps...they're just as cute as the alien!
And the only one who can save us is...
My grand-daughter!!!
Ground Defense!
CLICK
Air Defense!
CLICK

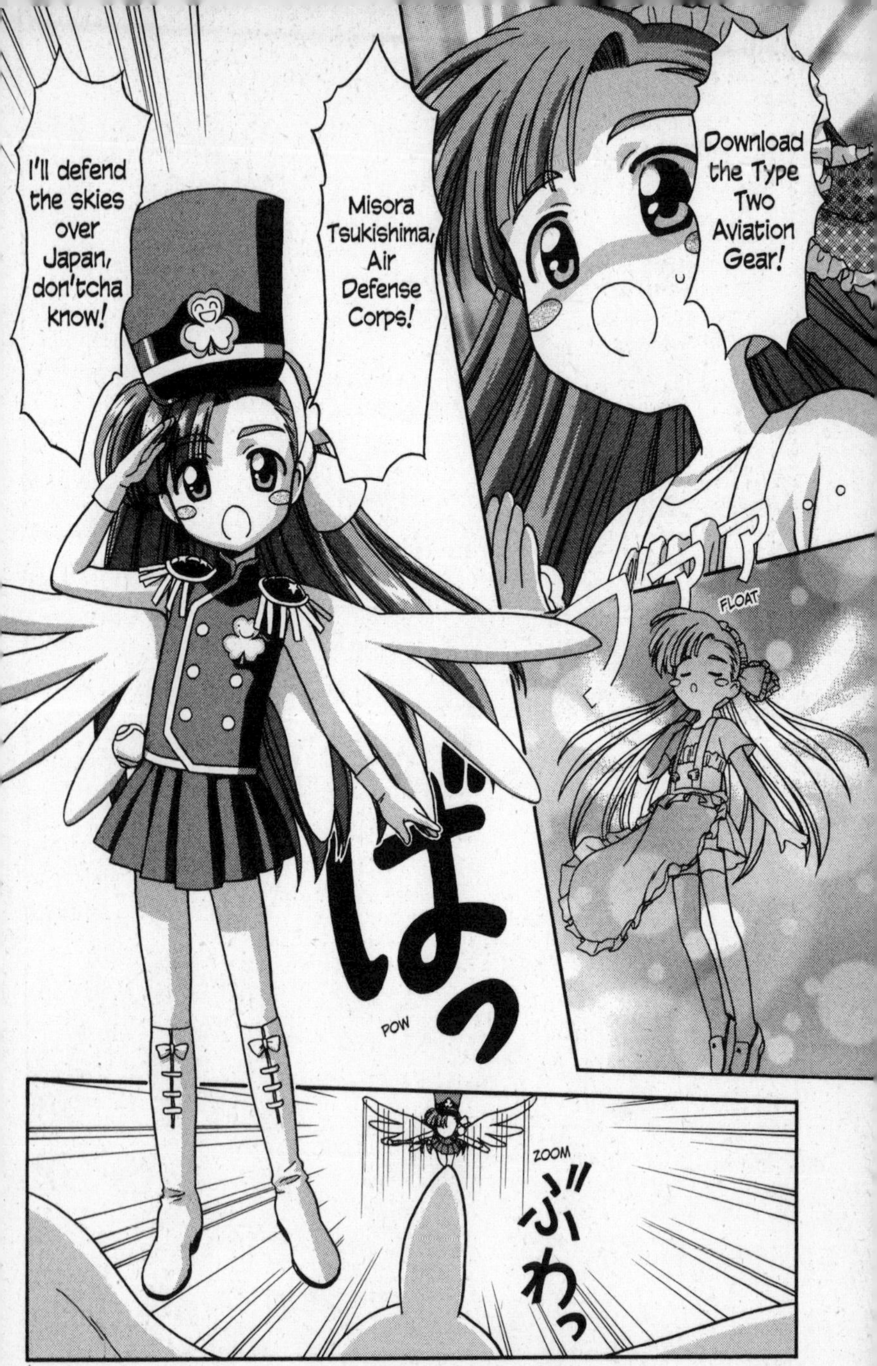
Download the Type Two Aviation Gear!
FLOAT
Misora Tsukishima, Air Defense Corps!
I'll defend the skies over Japan, don'tcha know!
ばっ
POW
ぶわっ
ZOOM

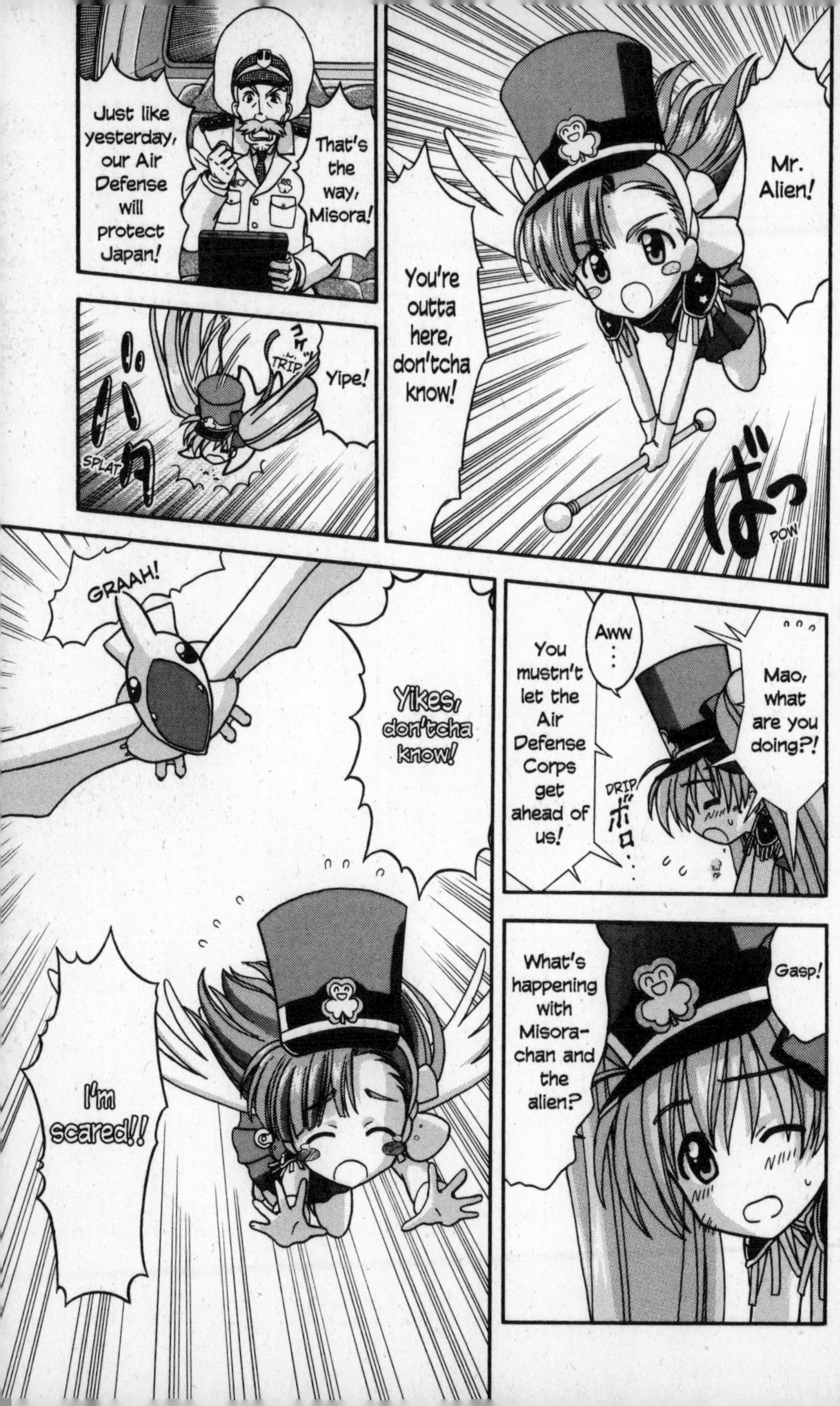
Mr. Alien!
You're outta here, don'tcha know!
POW
That's the way, Misora!
Just like yesterday, our Air Defense will protect Japan!
Yipe!
TRIP
SPLAT
Mao, what are you doing?!
Aww...
You mustn't let the Air Defense Corps get ahead of us!
DRIP
Gasp!
What's happening with Misora-chan and the alien?
GRAAH!
Yikes, don'tcha know!
I'm scared!!

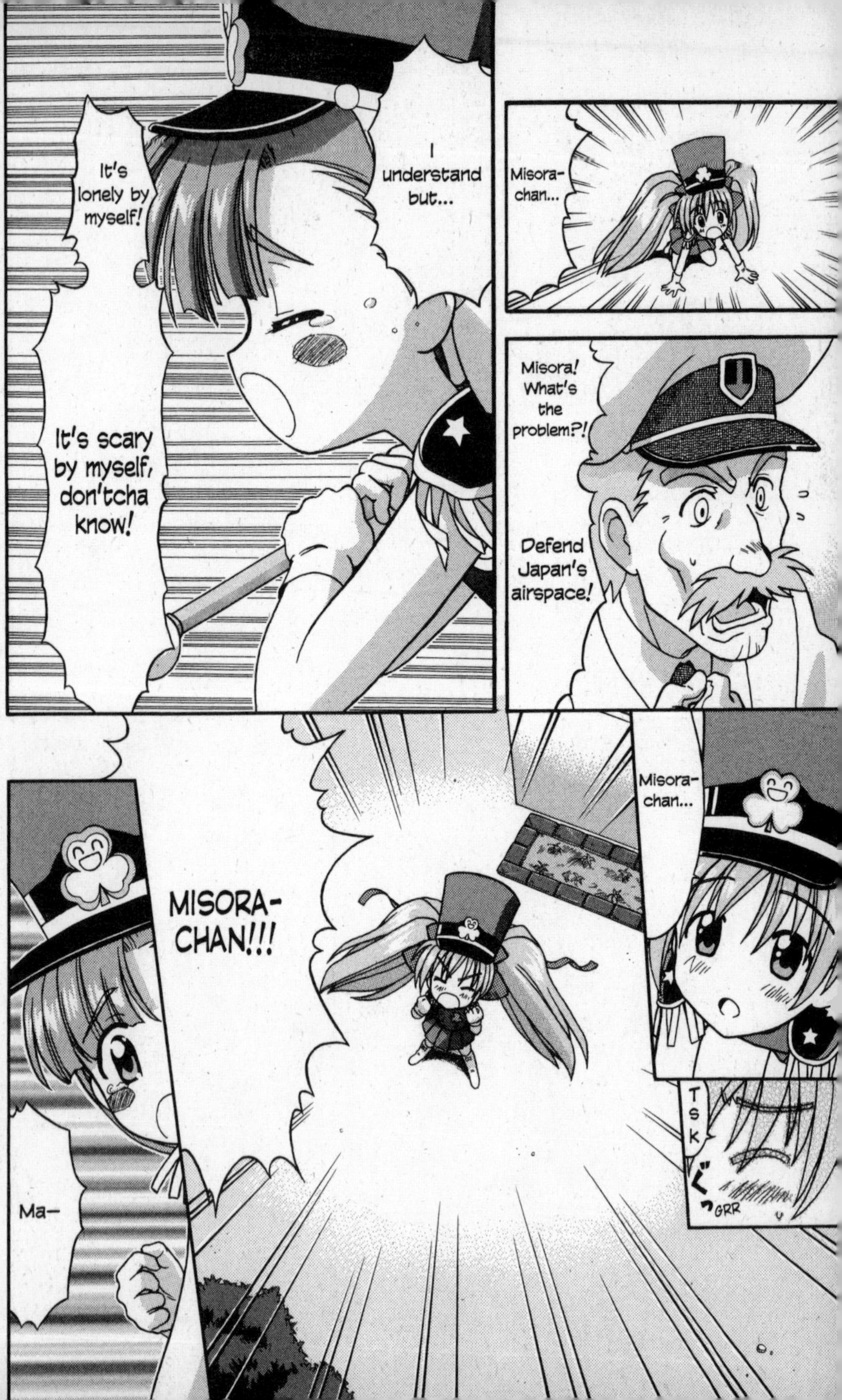
Misora-chan...
Misora! What's the problem?!
Defend Japan's airspace!
I understand but...
It's lonely by myself!
It's scary by myself, don'tcha know!
Misora-chan...
TSK
GRR
MISORA-CHAN!!!
Ma—

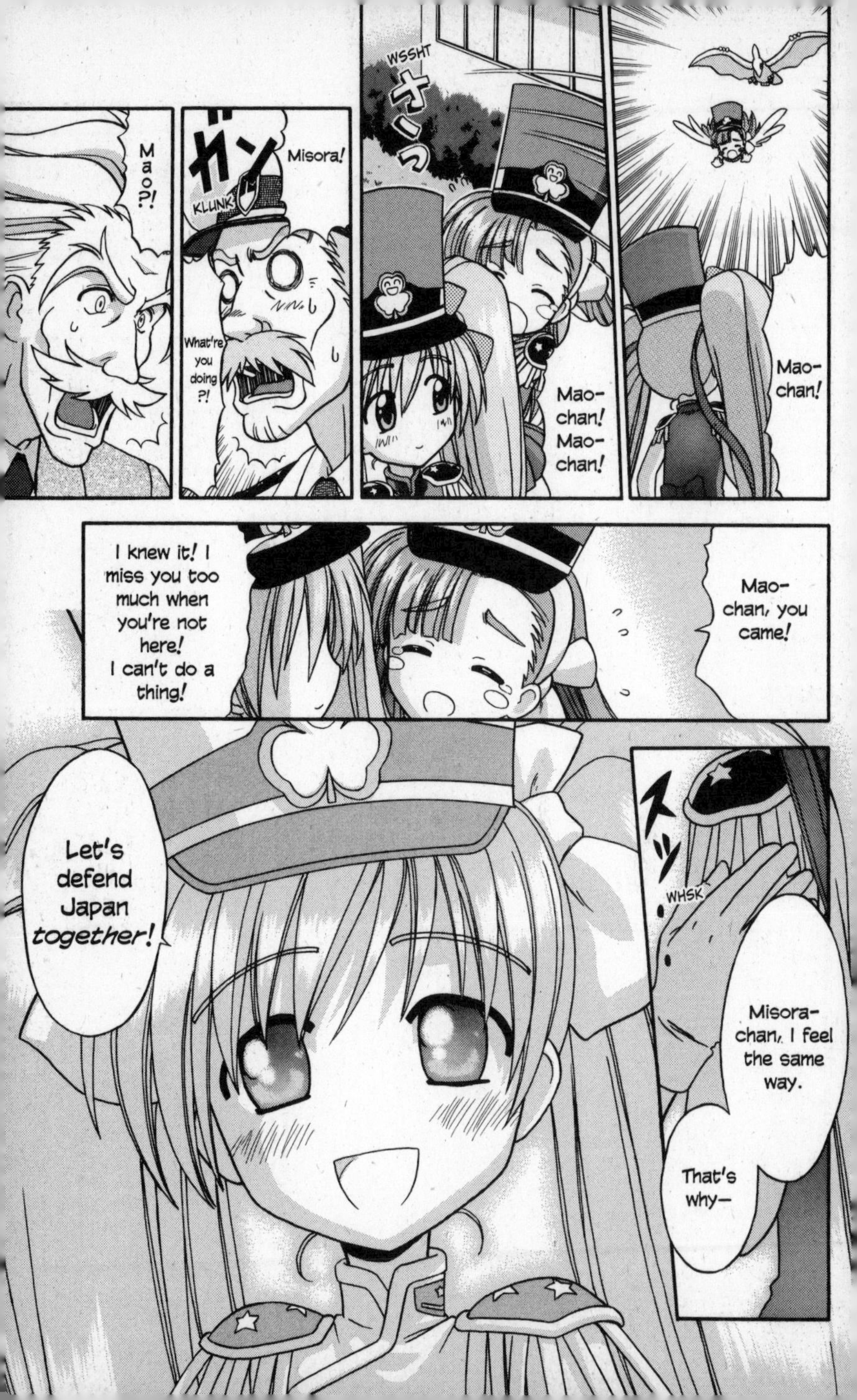
Mao-chan!
WSSHT
さっ
Mao-chan! Mao-chan!
Misora!
ガン
KLUNK
What're you doing?!
Mao?!
Mao-chan, you came!
I knew it! I miss you too much when you're not here! I can't do a thing!
スッ
WHSK
Misora-chan, I feel the same way.
That's why—
Let's defend Japan *together*!

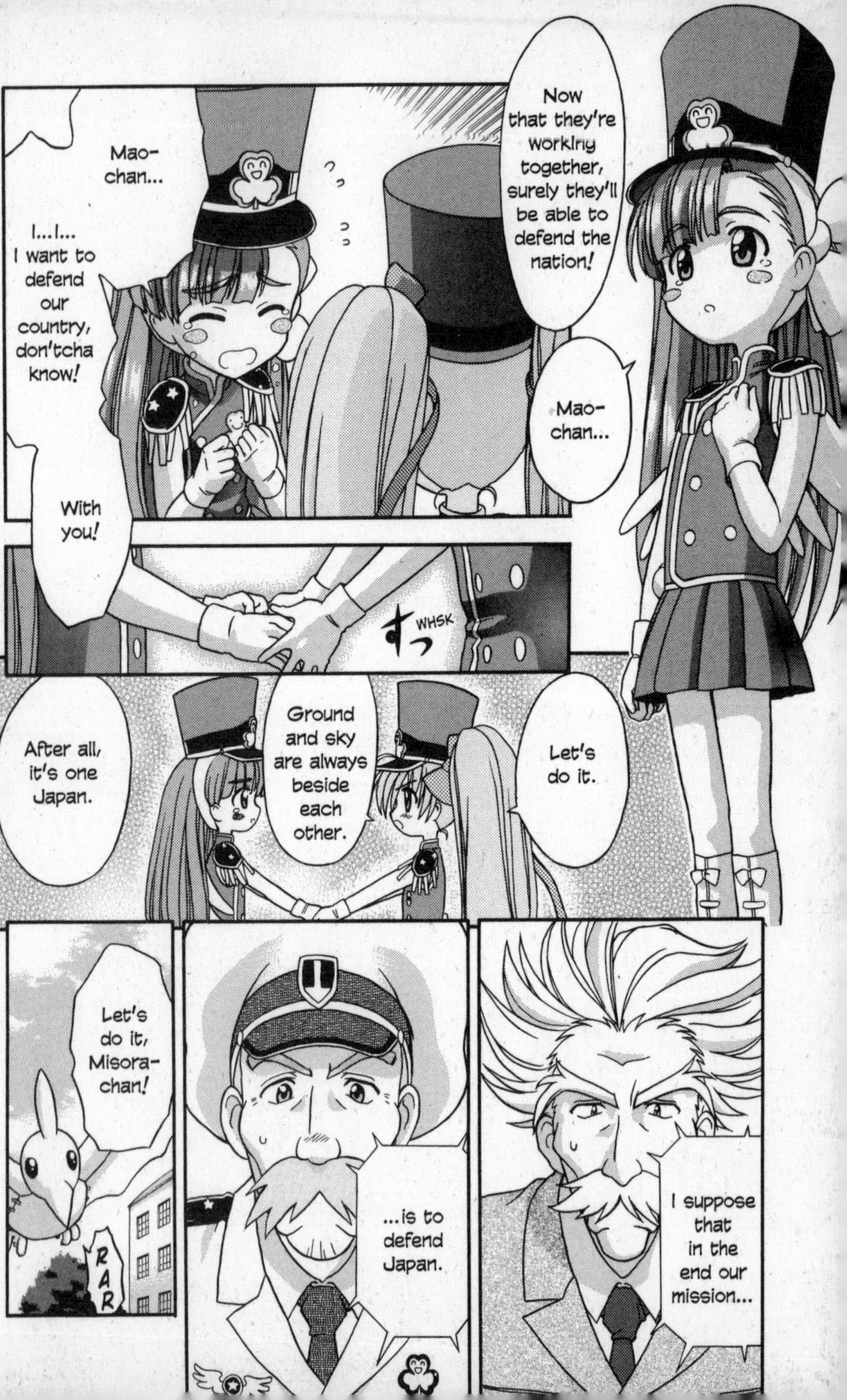

Now that they're working together, surely they'll be able to defend the nation!
Mao-chan...
Mao-chan...
I...I... I want to defend our country, don'tcha know!
With you!
WHSK
Let's do it.
Ground and sky are always beside each other.
After all, it's one Japan.
I suppose that in the end our mission...
...is to defend Japan.
Let's do it, Misora-chan!
RAR

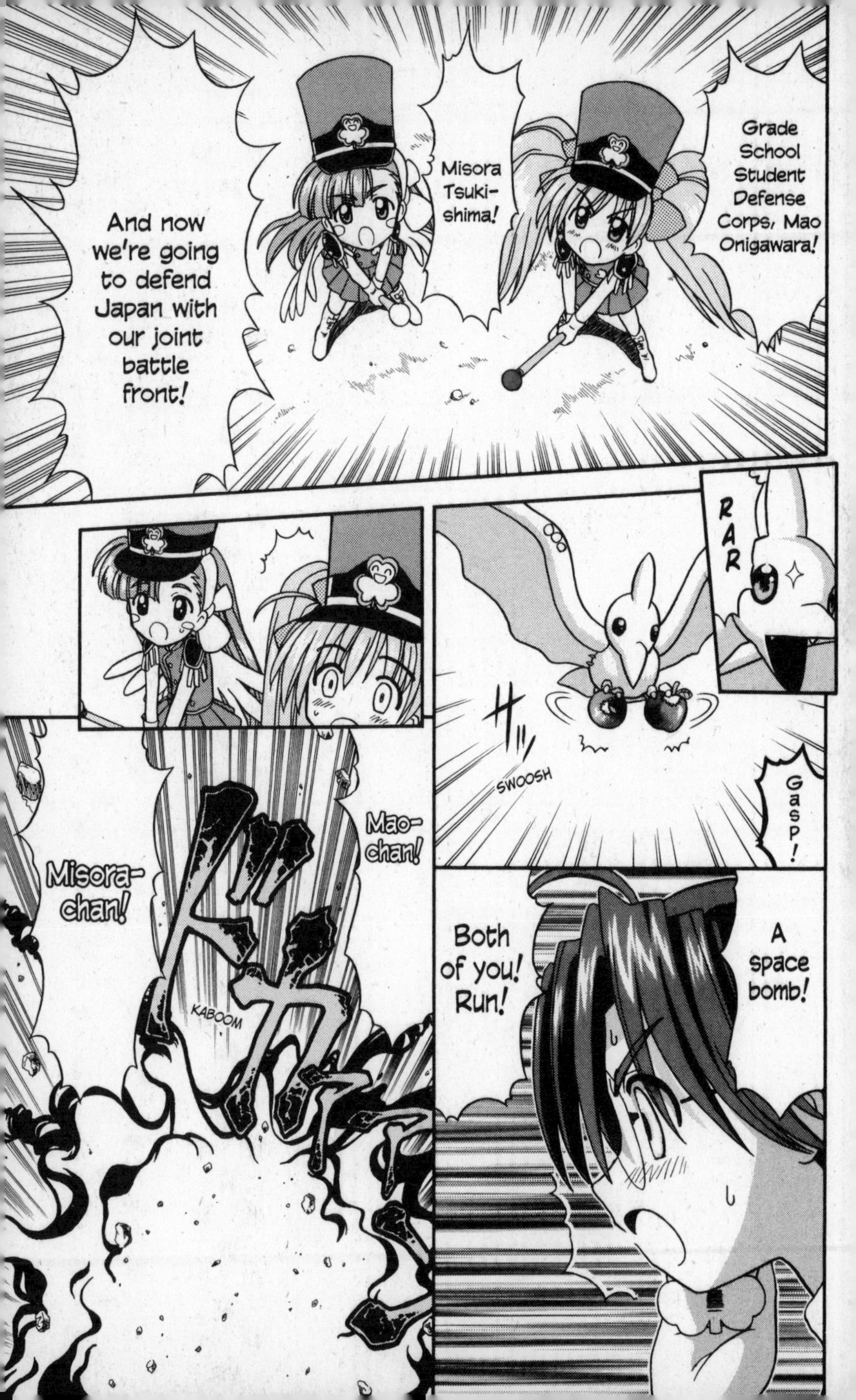
Grade School Student Defense Corps, Mao Onigawara!
Misora Tsukishima!
And now we're going to defend Japan with our joint battle front!
RAR
Gasp!
SWOOSH
A space bomb!
Both of you! Run!
Mao-chan!
Misora-chan!
KABOOM

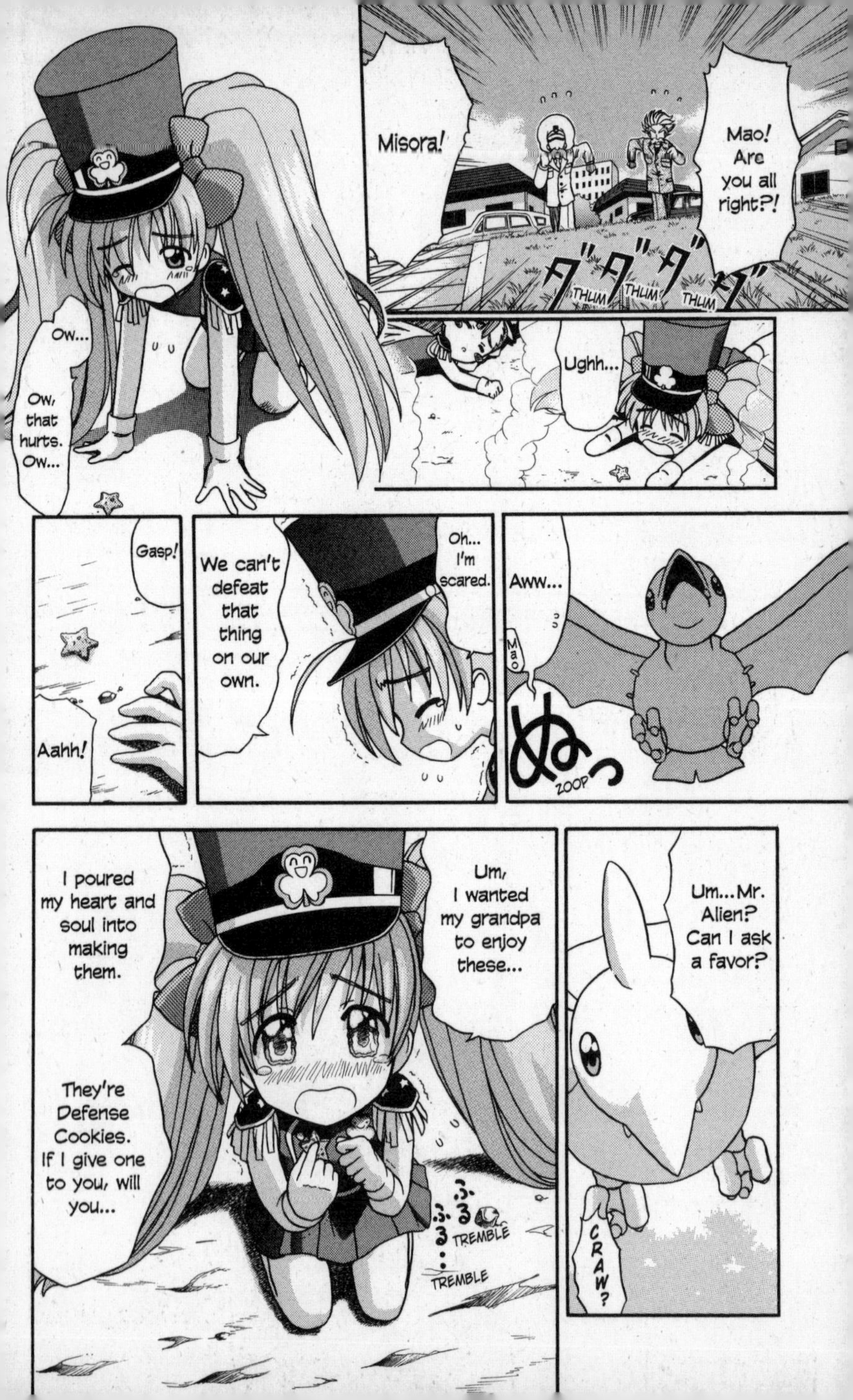
Mao! Are you all right?!
Misora!
ダダダダ
THUM THUM THUM
Ughh...
Ow...
Ow, that hurts. Ow...
Aww...
Mao
ぬっ
ZOOP
Oh... I'm scared.
We can't defeat that thing on our own.
Gasp!
Aahh!
Um...Mr. Alien? Can I ask a favor?
CRAW?
Um, I wanted my grandpa to enjoy these...
I poured my heart and soul into making them.
They're Defense Cookies. If I give one to you, will you...
ふるふる...
TREMBLE
TREMBLE

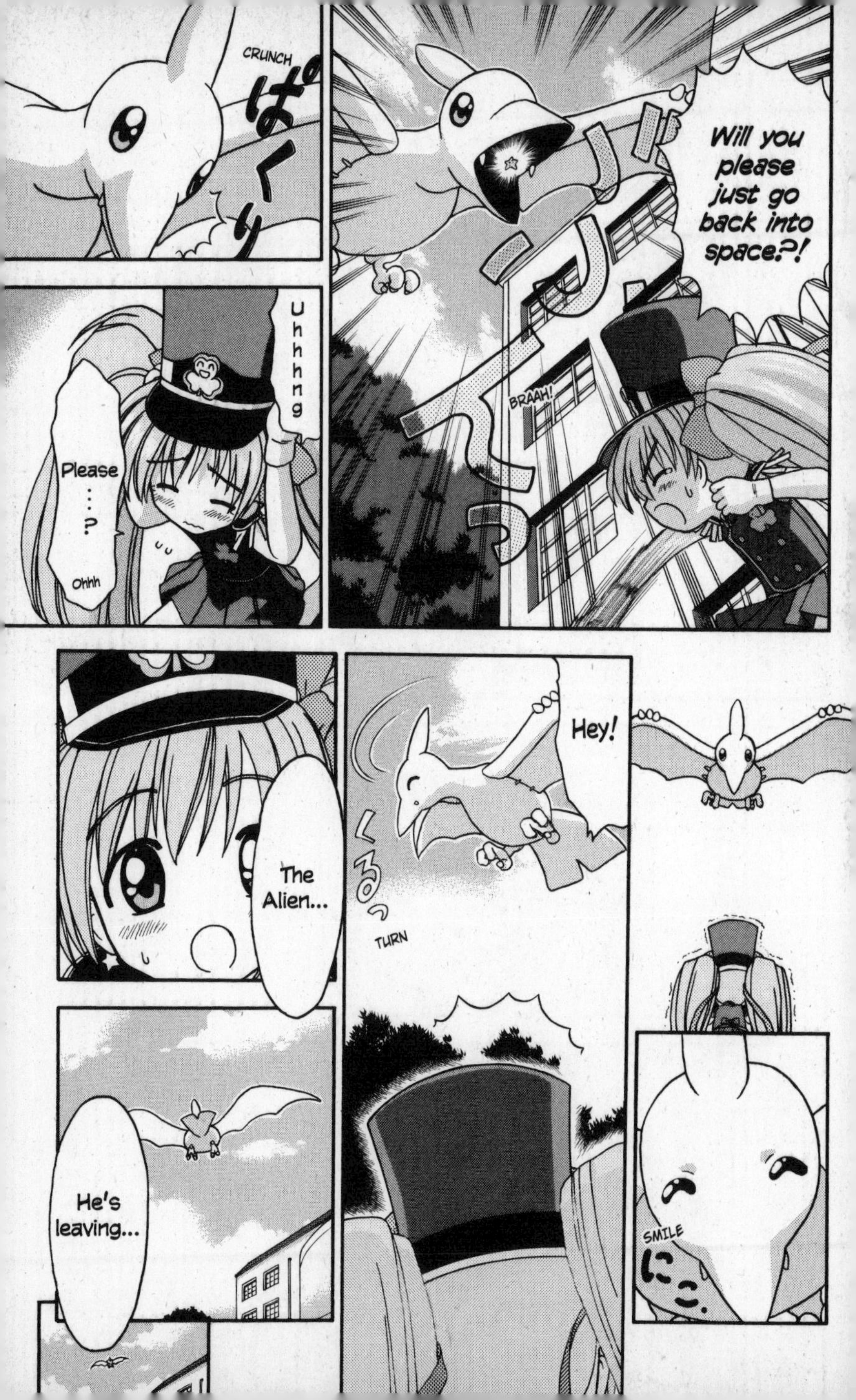
Will you please just go back into space?!
BRAAH!
CRUNCH
ぱくり
Unhhhng
Please...?
Ohhh
Hey!
くるっ
TURN
SMILE
にこっ
The Alien...
He's leaving...

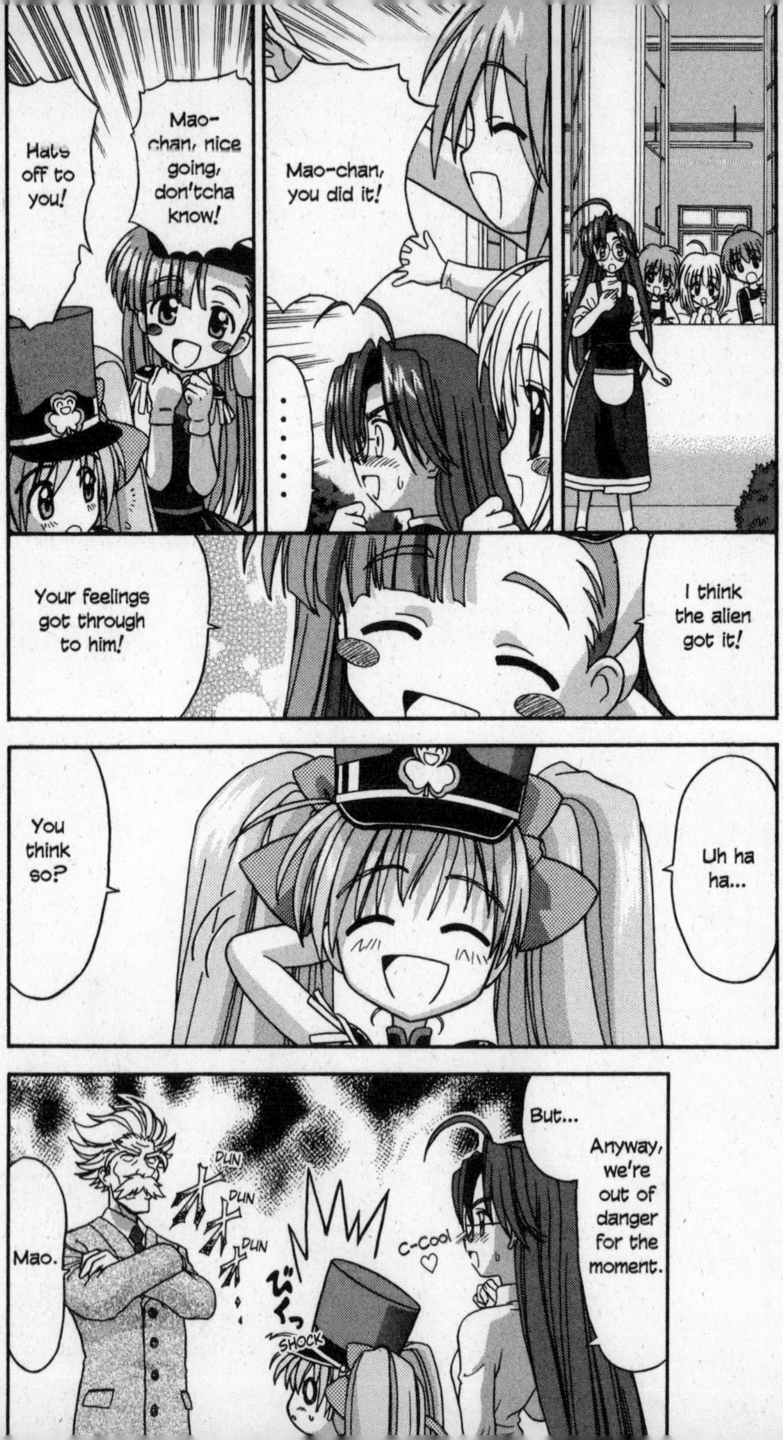
Mao-chan, you did it!
. . . . .
Mao-chan, nice going, don'tcha know!
Hats off to you!
I think the alien got it!
Your feelings got through to him!
Uh ha ha...
You think so?
But...
Anyway, we're out of danger for the moment.
C-Cool ♡
DUN
DUN
DUN
びくっ
SHOCK
Mao.

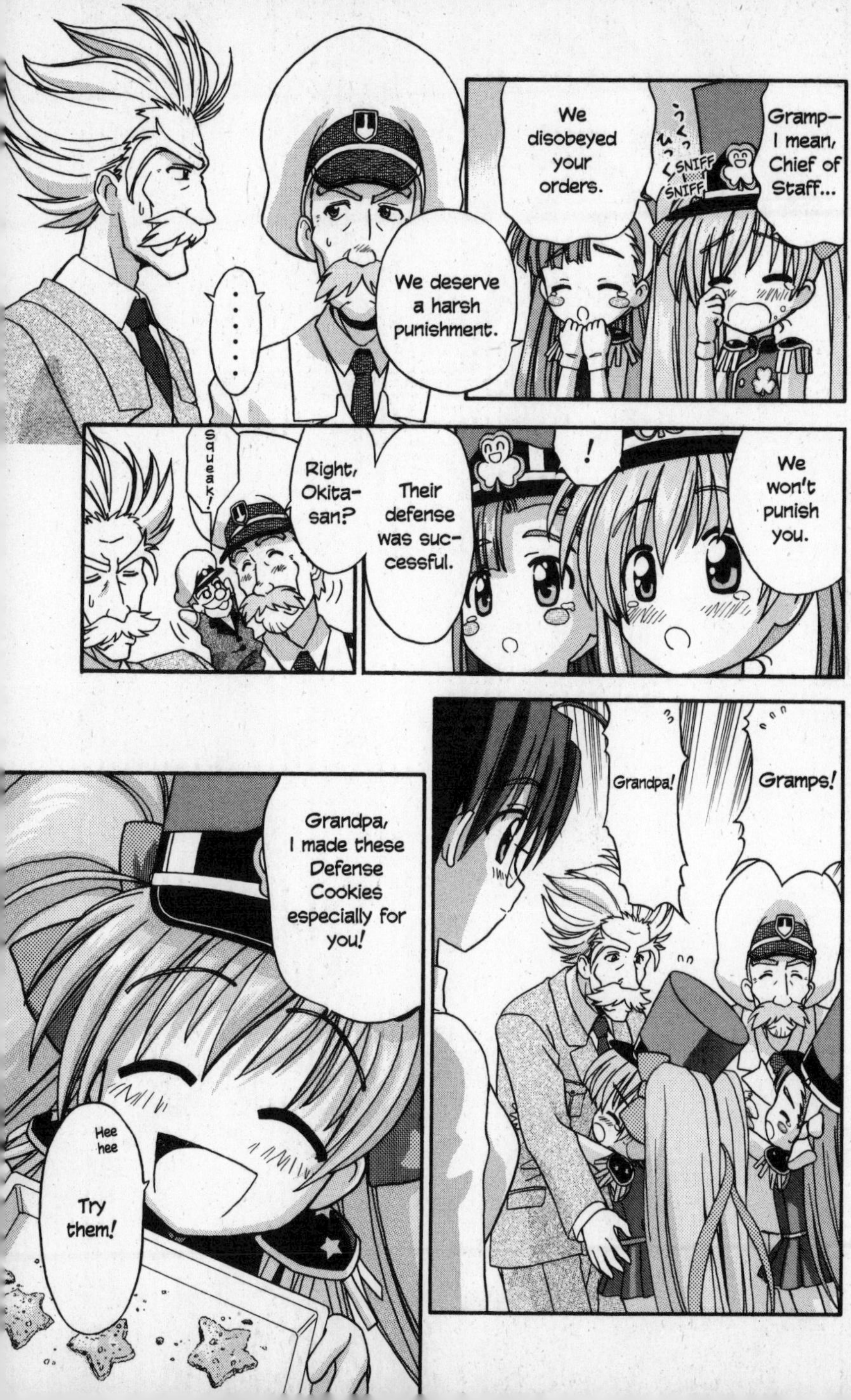

Gramp— I mean, Chief of Staff...
SNIFF SNIFF
We disobeyed your orders.
We deserve a harsh punishment.
......
We won't punish you.
!
Their defense was successful.
Right, Okita-san?
Squeak!
Gramps!
Grandpa!
Grandpa, I made these Defense Cookies especially for you!
Hee hee
Try them!

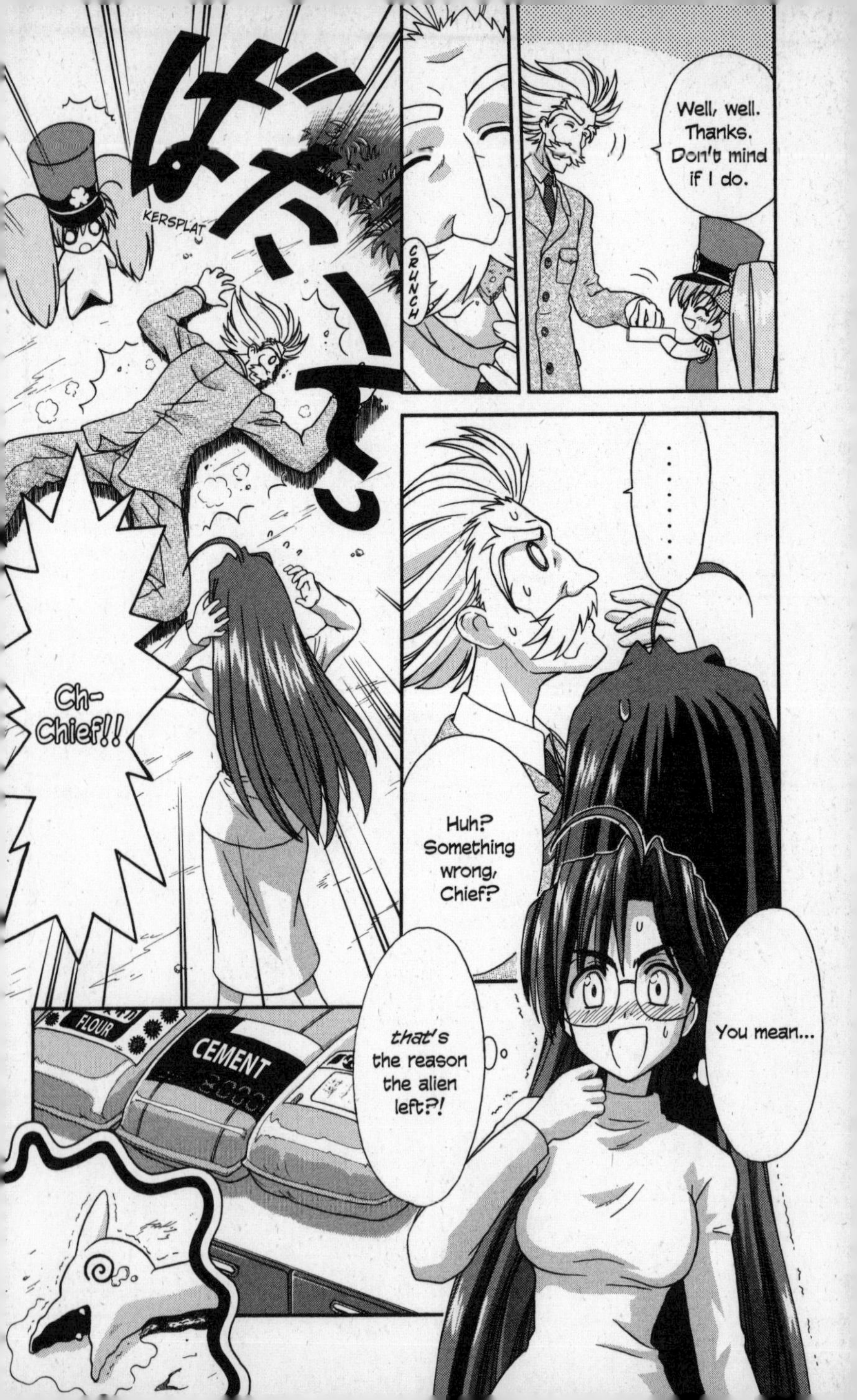
Well, well. Thanks. Don't mind if I do.
CRUNCH
……
Huh? Something wrong, Chief?
KERSPLAT
Ch-Chief!!
You mean...
that's the reason the alien left?!
FLOUR
CEMENT

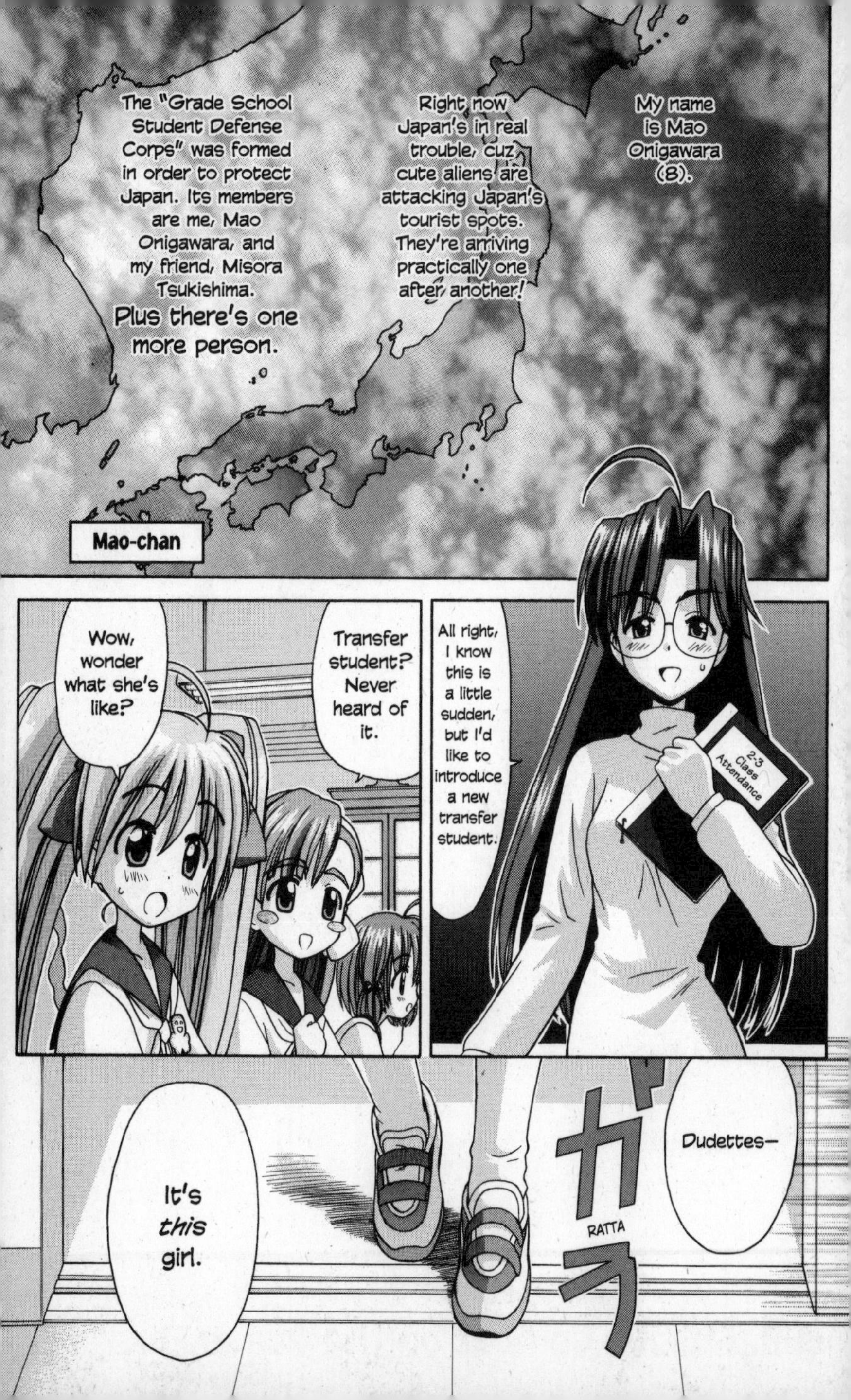
My name is Mao Onigawara (8).
Right now Japan's in real trouble, cuz cute aliens are attacking Japan's tourist spots. They're arriving practically one after another!
The "Grade School Student Defense Corps" was formed in order to protect Japan. Its members are me, Mao Onigawara, and my friend, Misora Tsukishima.
Plus there's one more person.
Mao-chan
All right, I know this is a little sudden, but I'd like to introduce a new transfer student.
2-3 Class Attendance
Transfer student? Never heard of it.
Wow, wonder what she's like?
Dudettes—
RATTA
It's *this* girl.

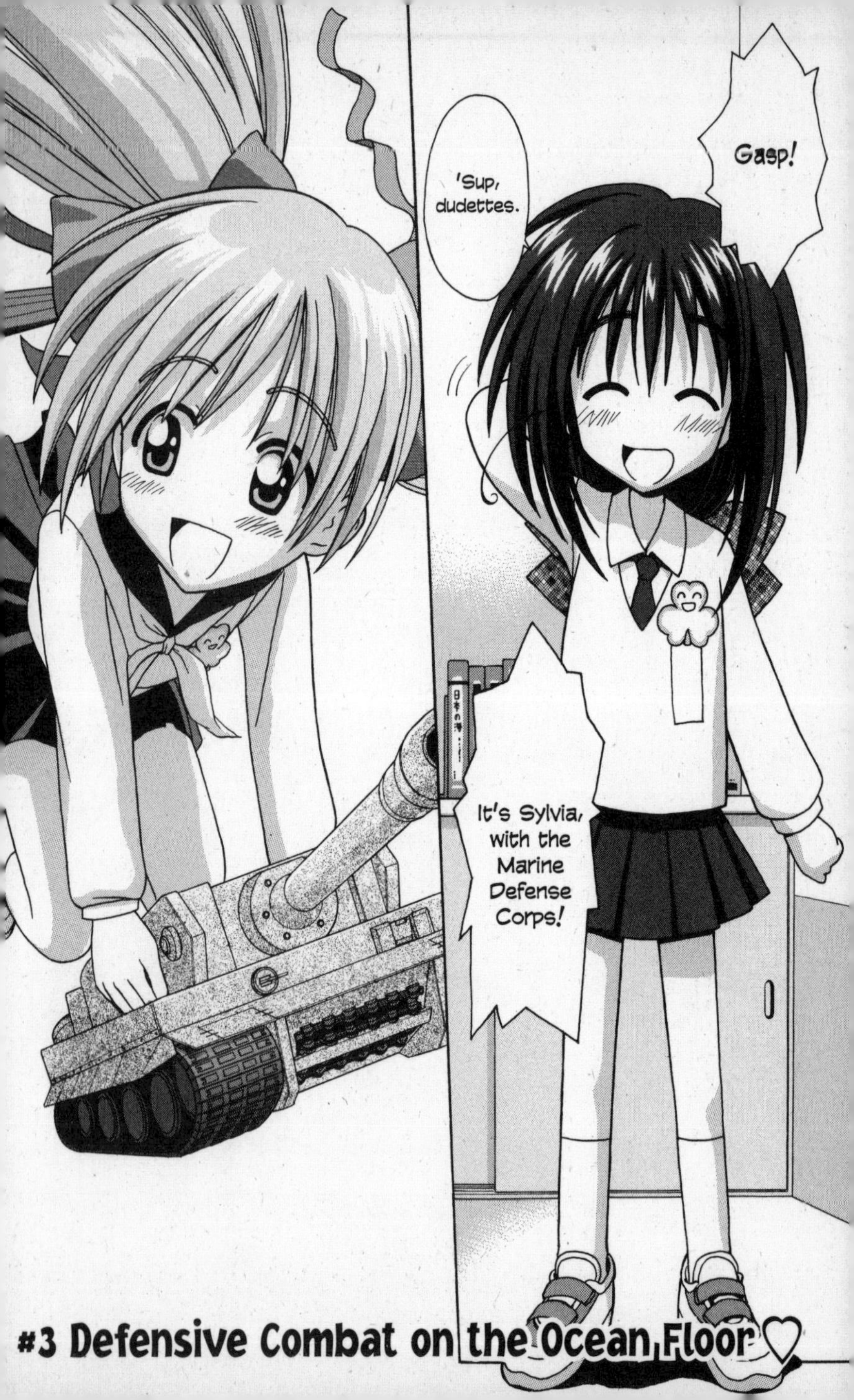
Gasp!
'Sup, dudettes.
It's Sylvia, with the Marine Defense Corps!
#3 Defensive Combat on the Ocean Floor ♡

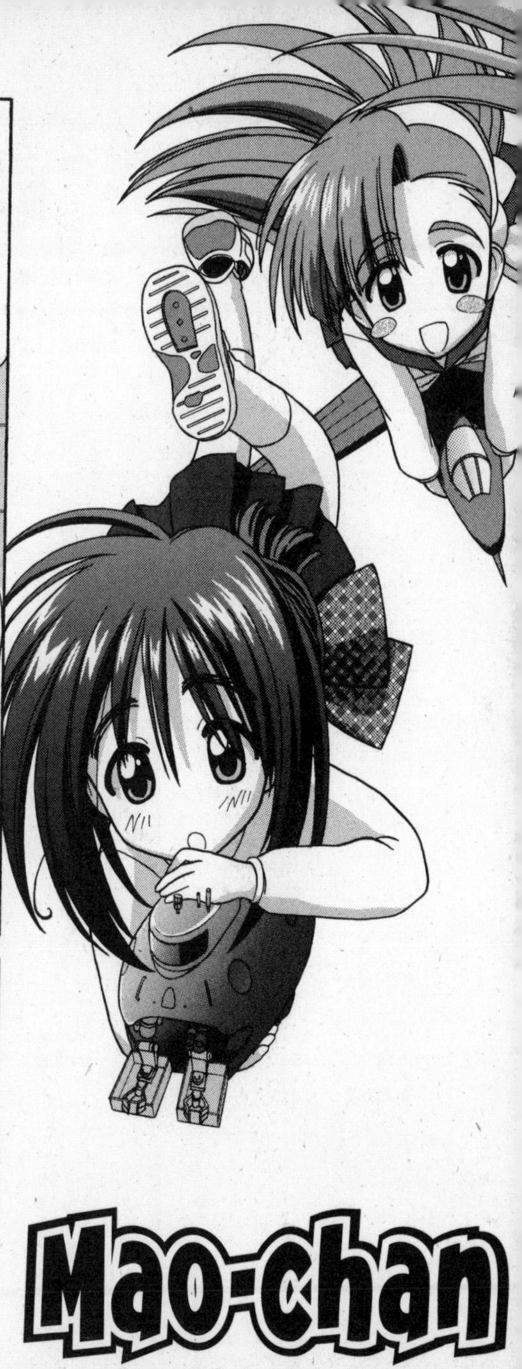
Mao-chan
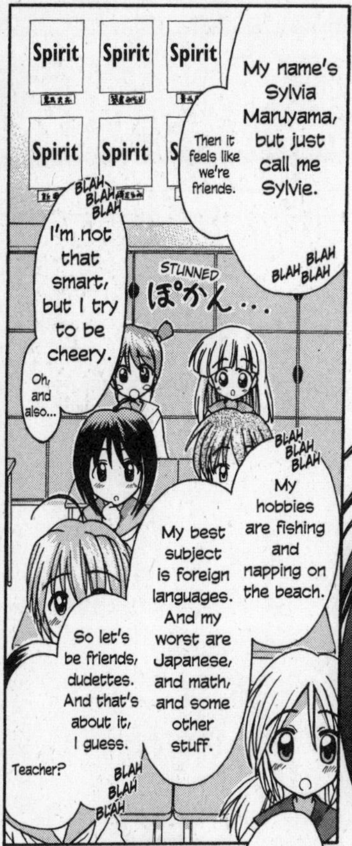
Spirit
Spirit
Spirit
Spirit
Spirit
My name's Sylvia Maruyama, but just call me Sylvie.
Then it feels like we're friends.
BLAH BLAH BLAH
STUNNED
ぽかん…
BLAH BLAH BLAH
I'm not that smart, but I try to be cheery.
Oh, and also...
BLAH BLAH BLAH
My hobbies are fishing and napping on the beach.
My best subject is foreign languages. And my worst are Japanese, and math, and some other stuff.
So let's be friends, dudettes. And that's about it, I guess.
BLAH BLAH BLAH
Teacher?
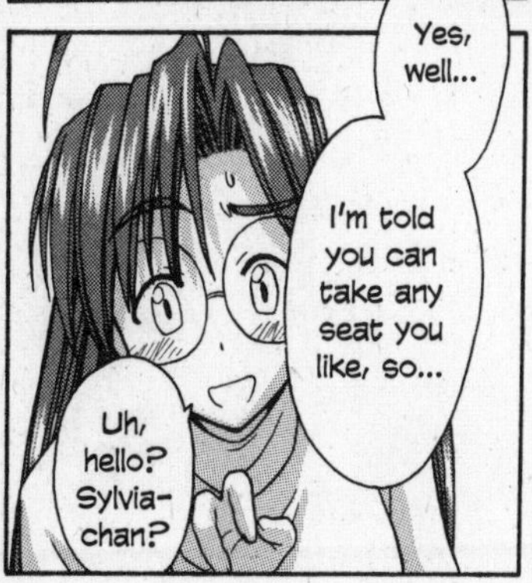
Yes, well...
I'm told you can take any seat you like, so...
Uh, hello? Sylvia-chan?

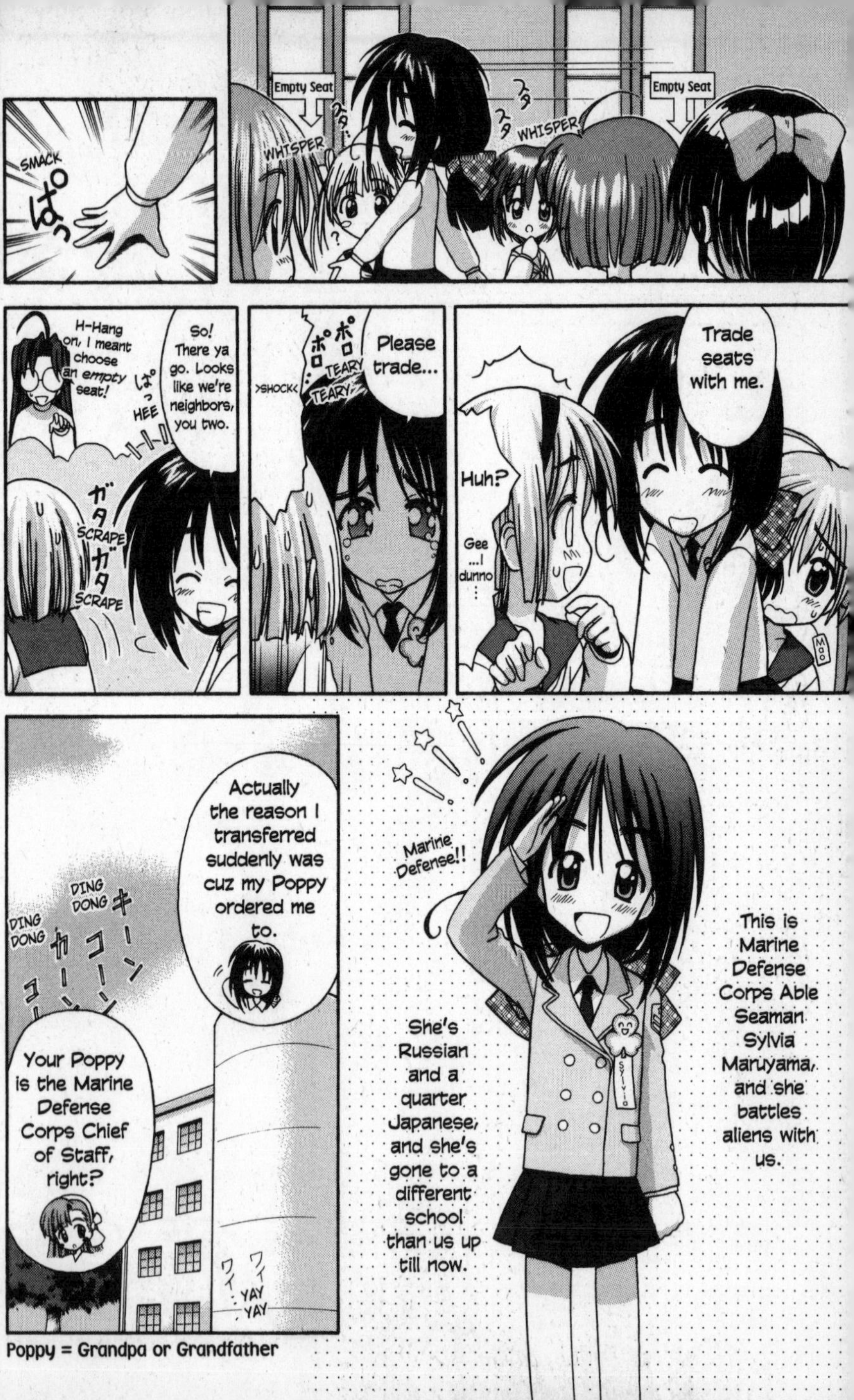
Empty Seat
Empty Seat
スタ
スタ
WHISPER
WHISPER
?
SMACK
ぱっ
Trade seats with me.
Huh?
Gee ...I dunno...
MOO
Please trade...
ポロ
TEARY
ポロ
TEARY
>SHOCK<
So! There ya go. Looks like we're neighbors, you two.
ぱっ
HEE
H-Hang on, I meant choose an *empty* seat!
ガタ
SCRAPE
ガタ
SCRAPE
This is Marine Defense Corps Able Seaman Sylvia Maruyama, and she battles aliens with us.
She's Russian and a quarter Japanese, and she's gone to a different school than us up till now.
Marine Defense!!
SYLVIA
Actually the reason I transferred suddenly was cuz my Poppy ordered me to.
DING DONG
キーンコーン
DING DONG
カーンコーン
Your Poppy is the Marine Defense Corps Chief of Staff, right?
ワイワイ
YAY YAY

Poppy = Grandpa or Grandfather

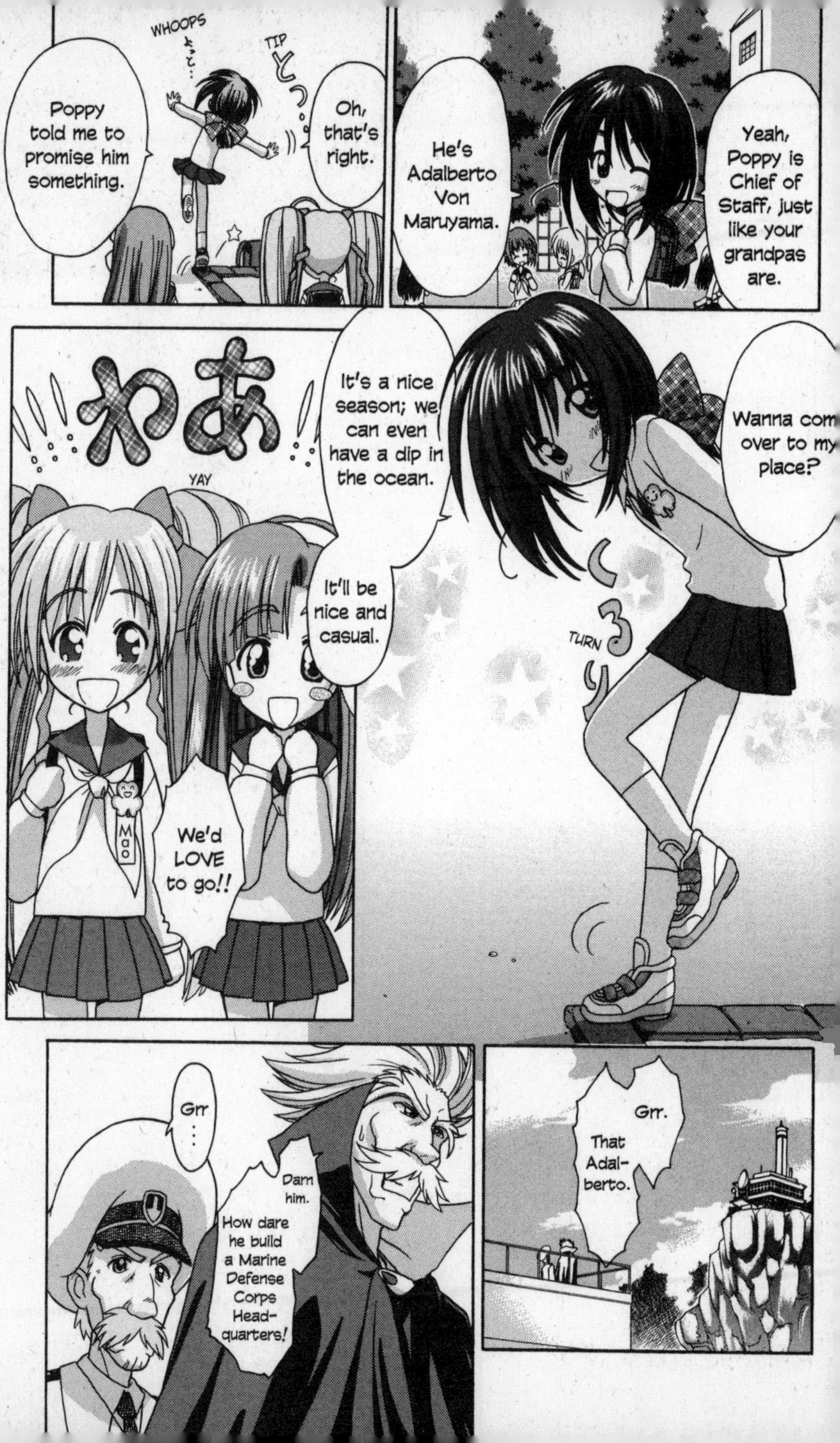
Yeah, Poppy is Chief of Staff, just like your grandpas are.
He's Adalberto Von Maruyama.
Oh, that's right.
TIP
とっ
WHOOPS
Poppy told me to promise him something.
Wanna com over to my place?
TURN
It's a nice season; we can even have a dip in the ocean.
It'll be nice and casual.
わあ
YAY
Mao
We'd LOVE to go!!
Grr.
That Adalberto.
Grr...
Damn him.
How dare he build a Marine Defense Corps Head-quarters!

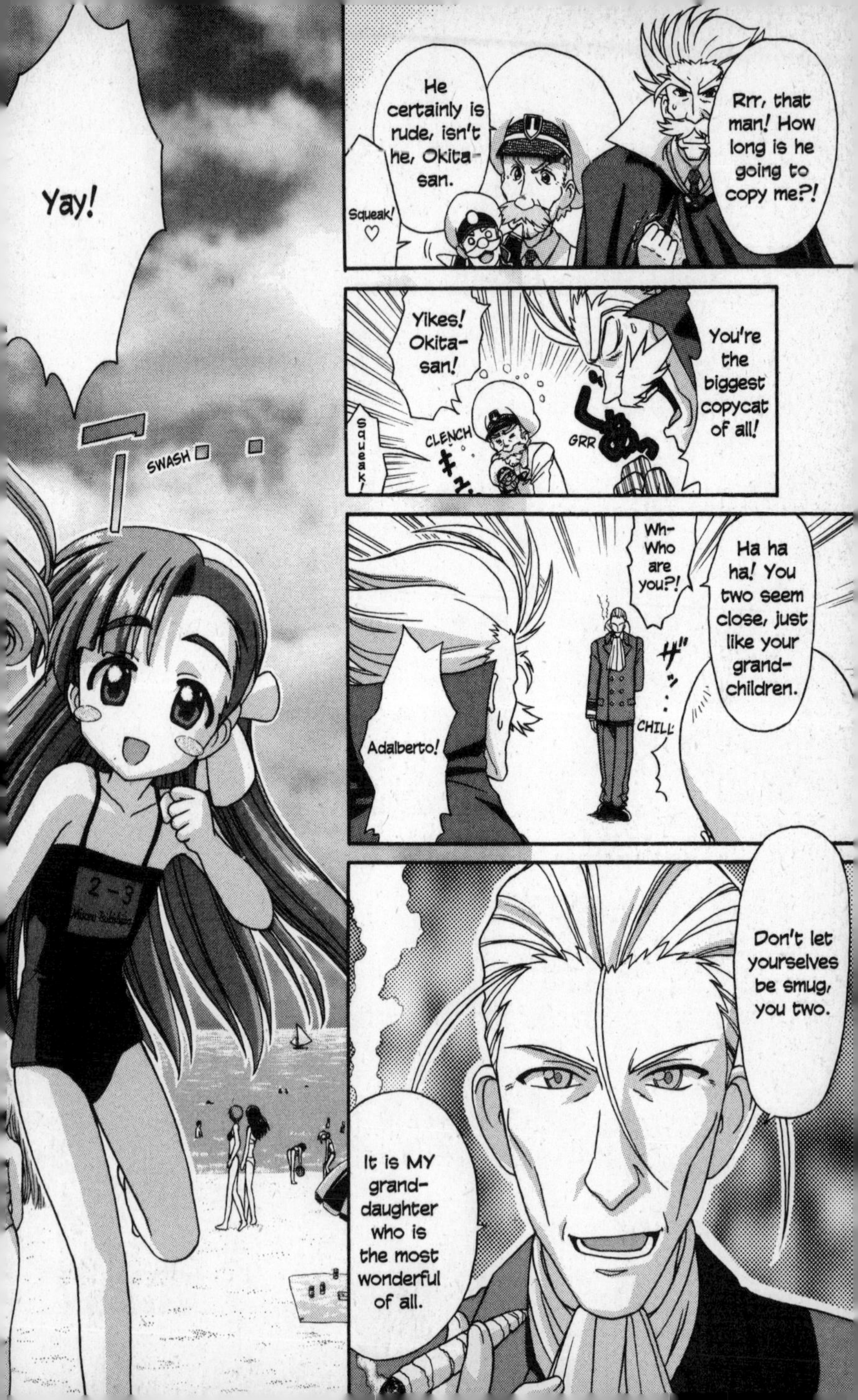
Rrr, that man! How long is he going to copy me?!
He certainly is rude, isn't he, Okita-san.
Squeak! ♡
You're the biggest copycat of all!
GRR
Yikes! Okita-san!
CLENCH
Squeak!
Ha ha ha! You two seem close, just like your grand-children.
Wh-Who are you?!
CHILL
Adalberto!
Don't let yourselves be smug, you two.
It is MY grand-daughter who is the most wonderful of all.
Yay!
SWASH

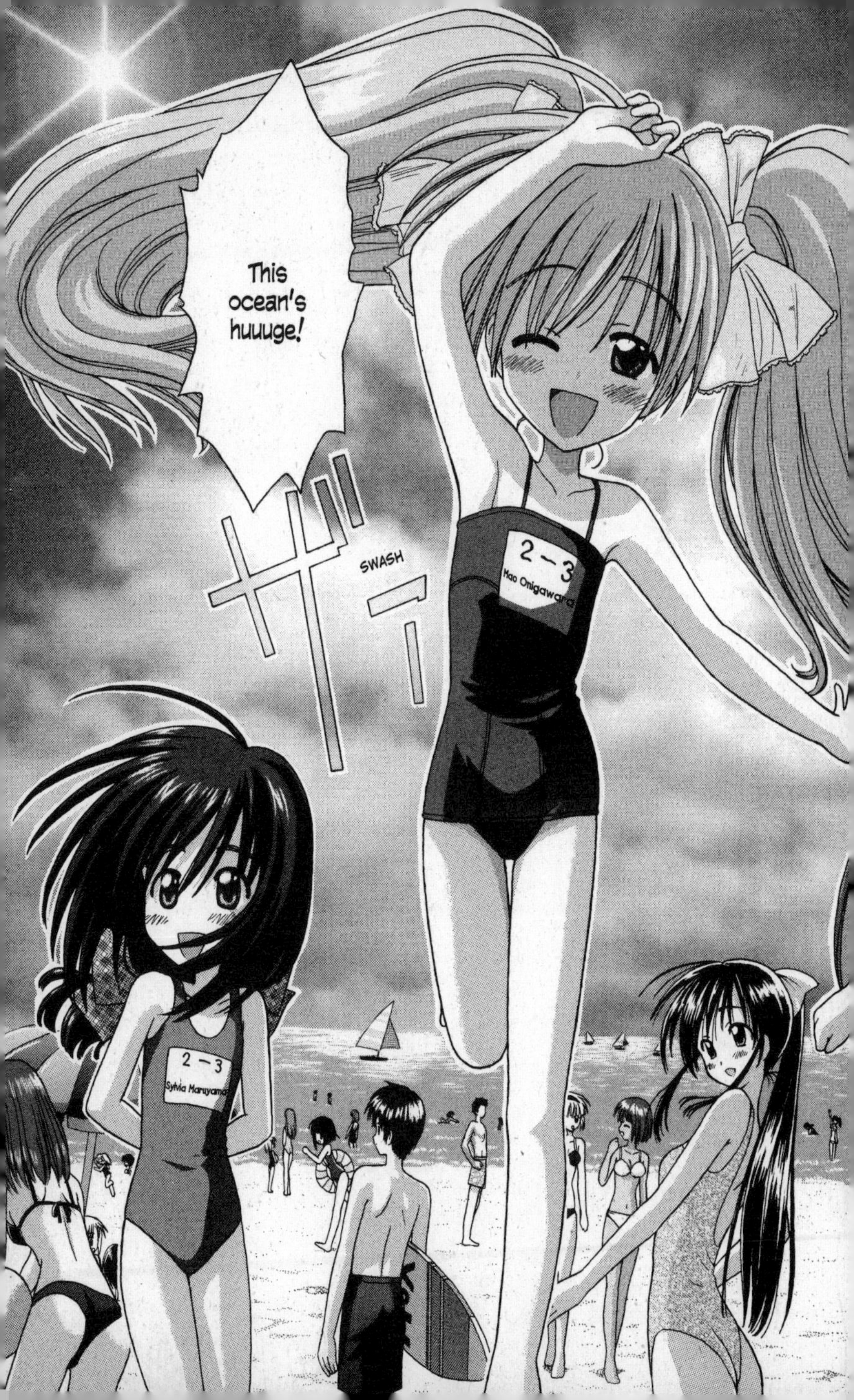
This ocean's huuuge!
SWASH
2—3
Mao Onigawara
2—3
Sylvia Maruyama

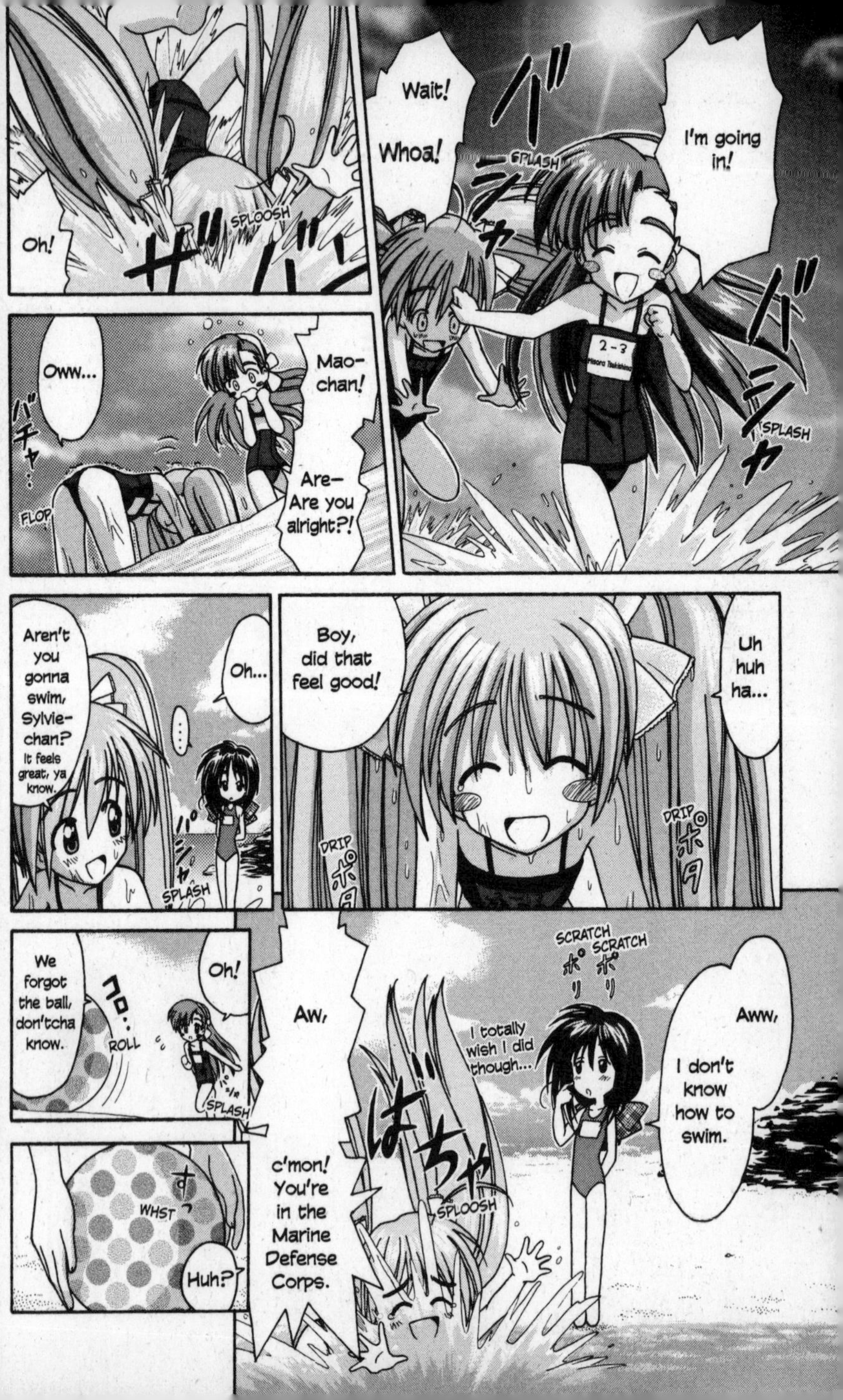
I'm going in!
Wait!
Whoa!
SPLASH
SPLASH
Oh!
SPLOOSH
Mao-chan!
Oww...
Are— Are you alright?!
FLOP
Uh huh ha...
Boy, did that feel good!
DRIP
DRIP
Oh...
Aren't you gonna swim, Sylvie-chan?
It feels great, ya know.
...
SPLASH
Aww,
I don't know how to swim.
SCRATCH SCRATCH
I totally wish I did though...
Aw,
c'mon! You're in the Marine Defense Corps.
SPLOOSH
Oh!
We forgot the ball, don'tcha know.
ROLL
SPLASH
WHST
Huh?

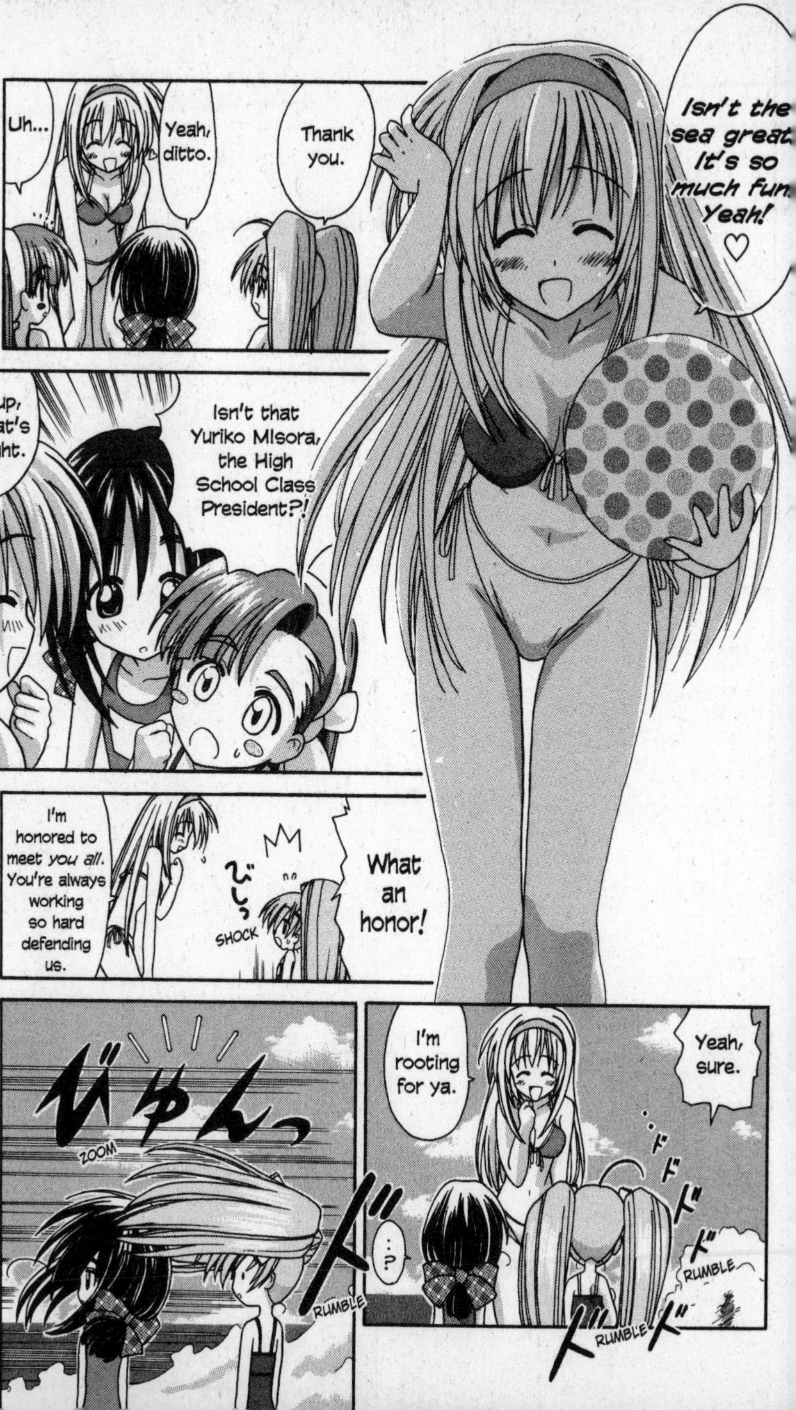
Isn't the sea great. It's so much fun. Yeah! ♡
Thank you.
Yeah, ditto.
Uh...
Isn't that Yuriko Misora, the High School Class President?!
Yup, that's right.
What an honor!
びしっ
SHOCK
I'm honored to meet *you all*. You're always working so hard defending us.
Yeah, sure.
I'm rooting for ya.
...?
RUMBLE
RUMBLE
びゅんっ
ZOOM
RUMBLE

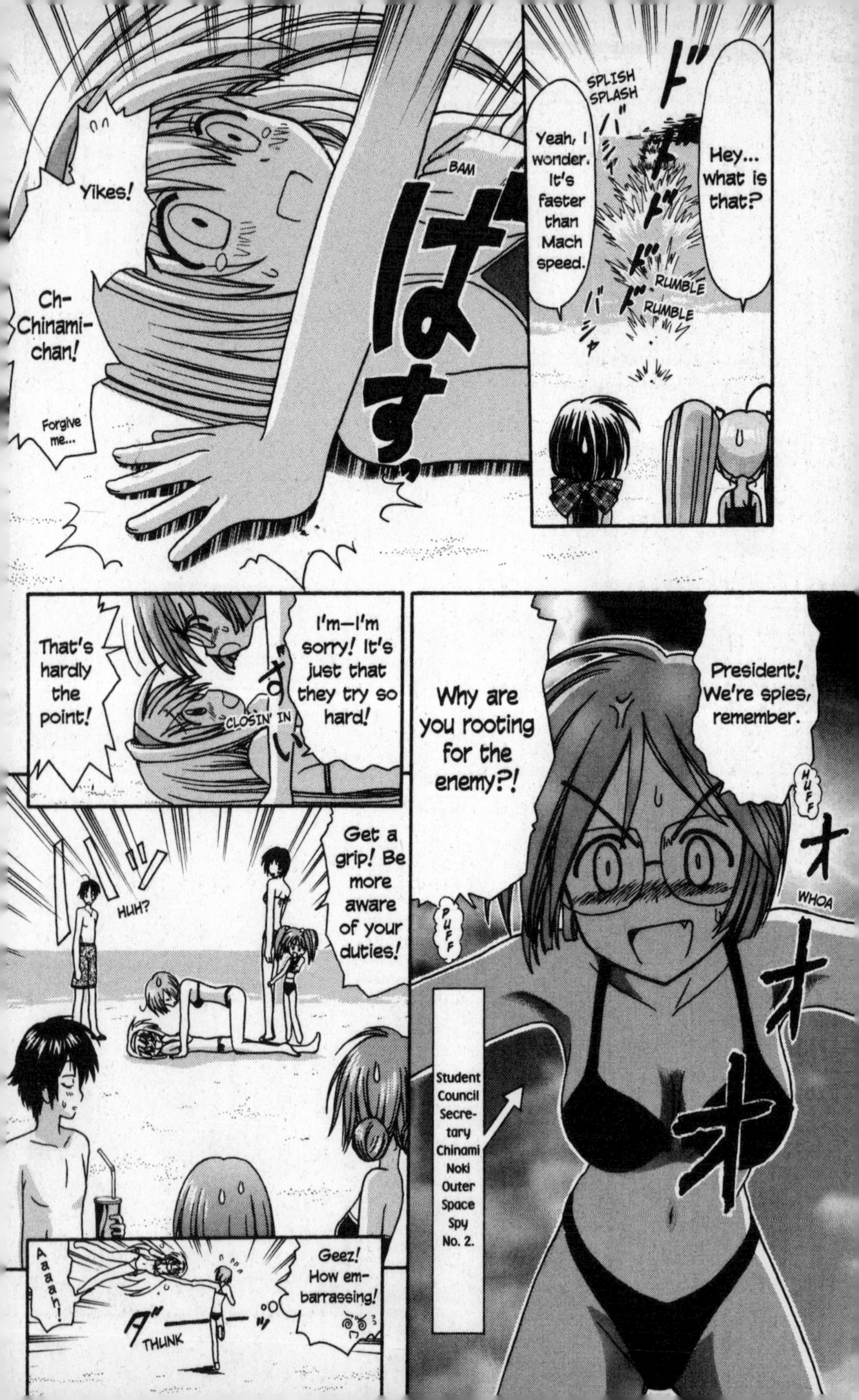
Hey... what is that?
Yeah, I wonder. It's faster than Mach speed.
SPLISH SPLASH
RUMBLE
RUMBLE
BAM
Yikes!
Ch-Chinami-chan!
Forgive me...
President! We're spies, remember.
Why are you rooting for the enemy?!
HUFF
WHOA
PUFF
Student Council Secretary Chinami Noki Outer Space Spy No. 2.
I'm—I'm sorry! It's just that they try so hard!
CLOSIN' IN
That's hardly the point!
Get a grip! Be more aware of your duties!
HUH?
Geez! How embarrassing!
Aaaah!
THUNK

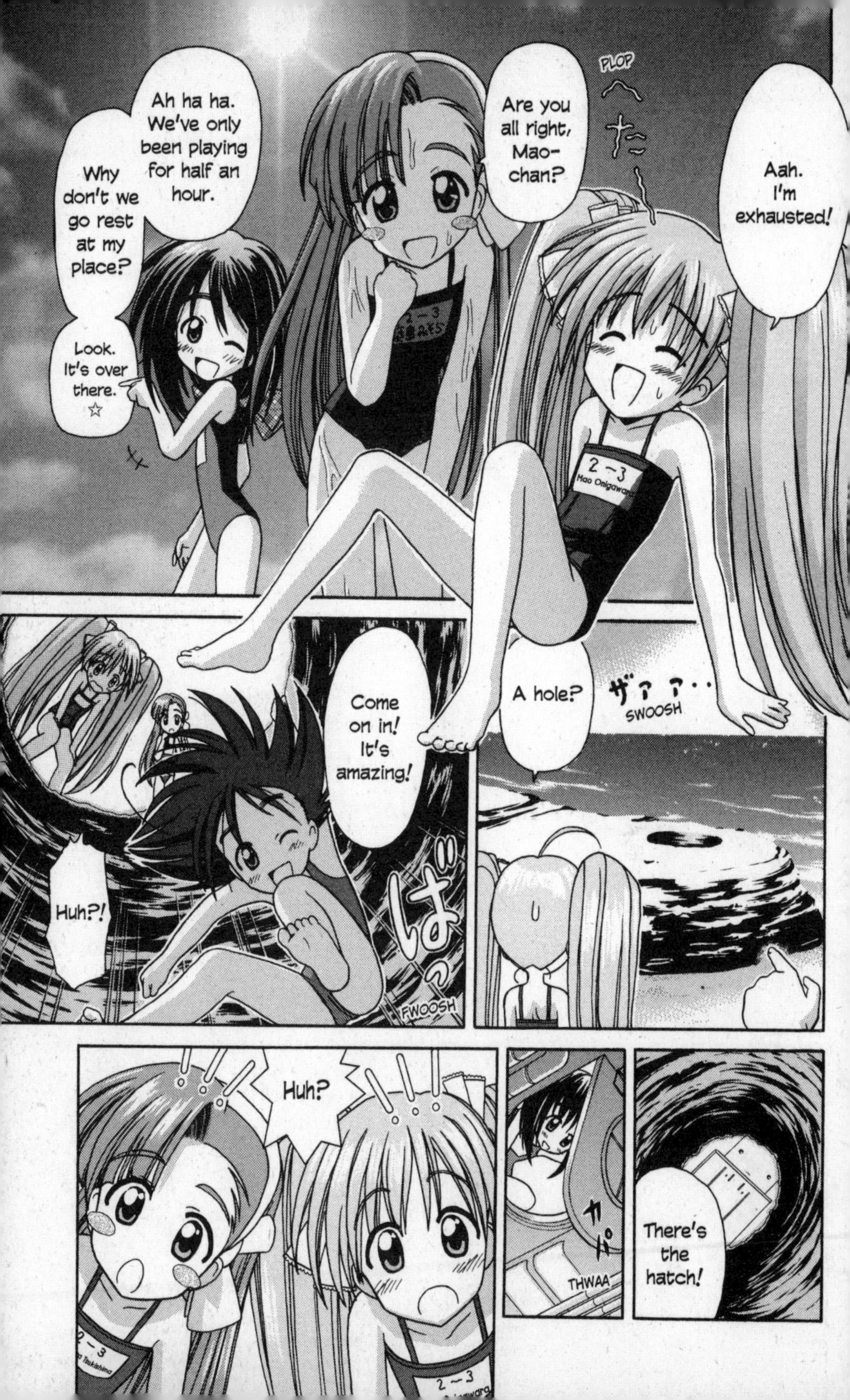
Aah. I'm exhausted!
PLOP
Are you all right, Mao-chan?
Ah ha ha. We've only been playing for half an hour.
Why don't we go rest at my place?
Look. It's over there. ☆
SWOOSH
A hole?
Come on in! It's amazing!
FWOOSH
Huh?!
There's the hatch!
THWAA
Huh?

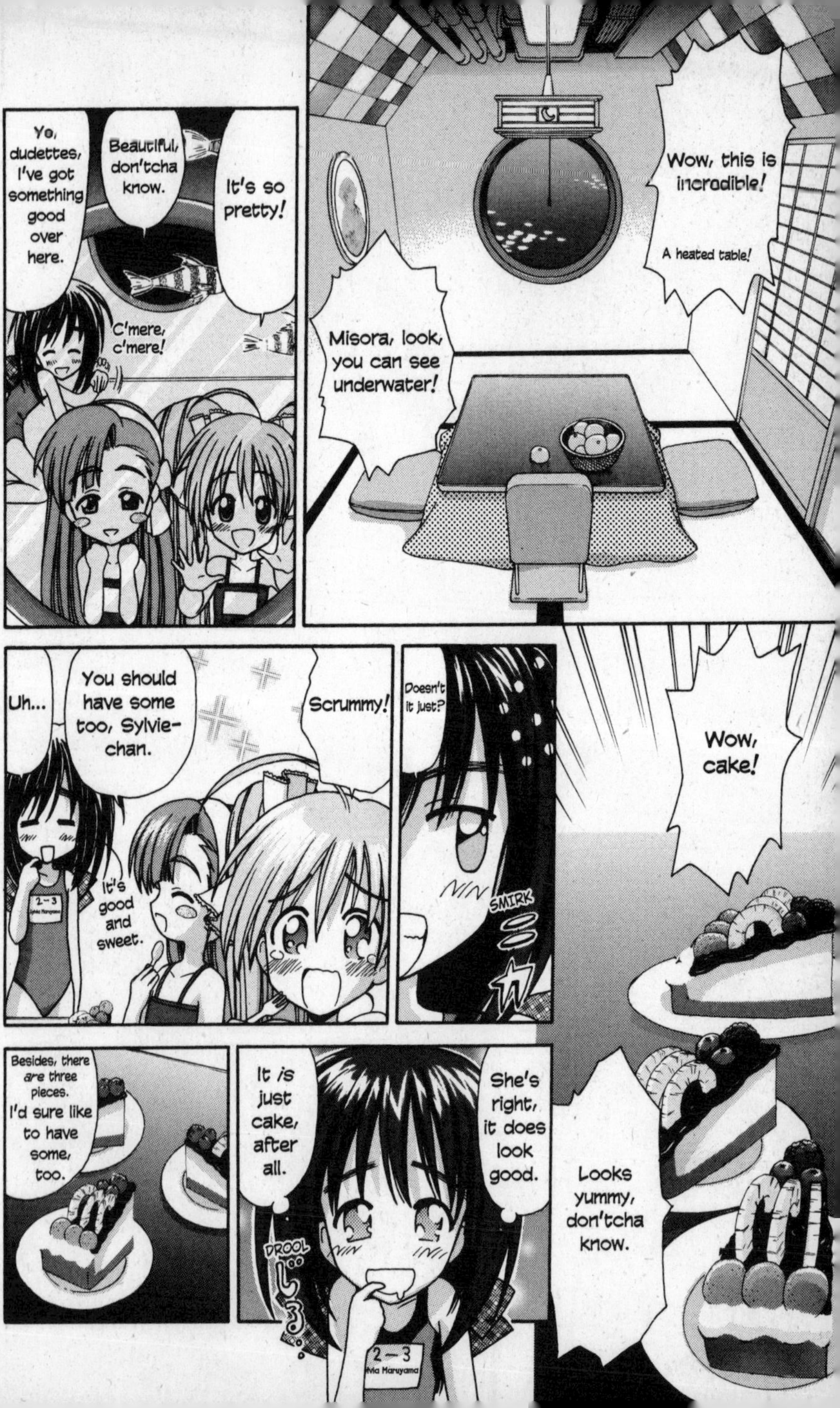

Wow, this is incredible!
A heated table!
Misora, look, you can see underwater!
It's so pretty!
Beautiful, don'tcha know.
Yo, dudettes, I've got something good over here.
C'mere, c'mere!
Wow, cake!
Looks yummy, don'tcha know.
Doesn't it just?
SMIRK
Scrummy!
You should have some too, Sylvie-chan.
Uh...
It's good and sweet.
2-3
She's right, it does look good.
It is just cake, after all.
DROOL
2-3
Besides, there are three pieces.
I'd sure like to have some, too.

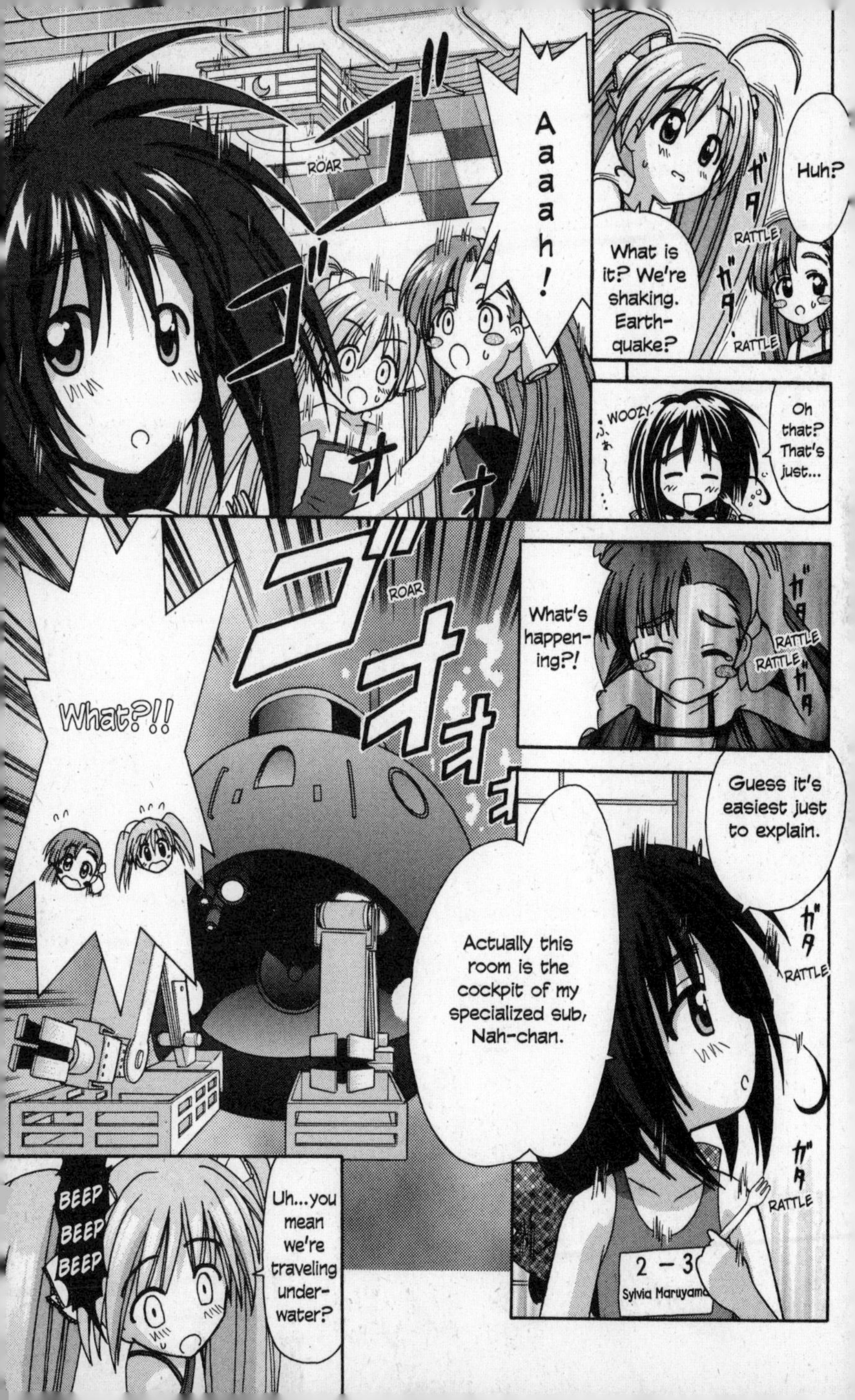
Huh?
What is it? We're shaking. Earthquake?
RATTLE
RATTLE
Oh that? That's just...
WOOZY
ROAR
Aaaah!
What's happening?!
RATTLE
RATTLE
Guess it's easiest just to explain.
Actually this room is the cockpit of my specialized sub, Nah-chan.
RATTLE
RATTLE
2 – 3
Sylvia Maruyama
ROAR
What?!!
BEEP
BEEP
BEEP
Uh...you mean we're traveling underwater?

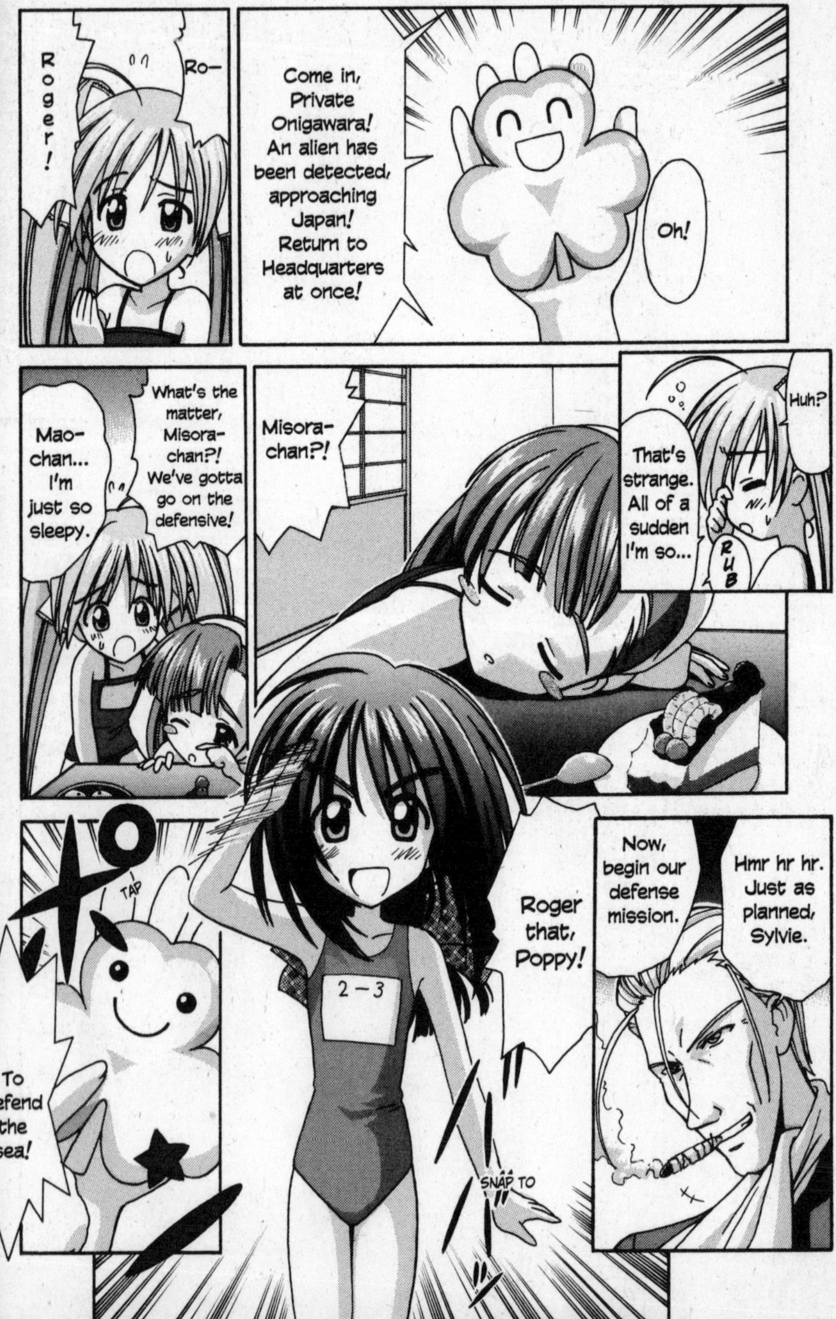
Come in, Private Onigawara! An alien has been detected, approaching Japan! Return to Headquarters at once!
Oh!
Ro—
Roger!
Huh?
That's strange. All of a sudden I'm so...
RUB
Misora-chan?!
What's the matter, Misora-chan?! We've gotta go on the defensive!
Mao-chan... I'm just so sleepy.
Hmr hr hr. Just as planned, Sylvie.
Now, begin our defense mission.
Roger that, Poppy!
2-3
SNAP TO
TAP
To efend the sea!

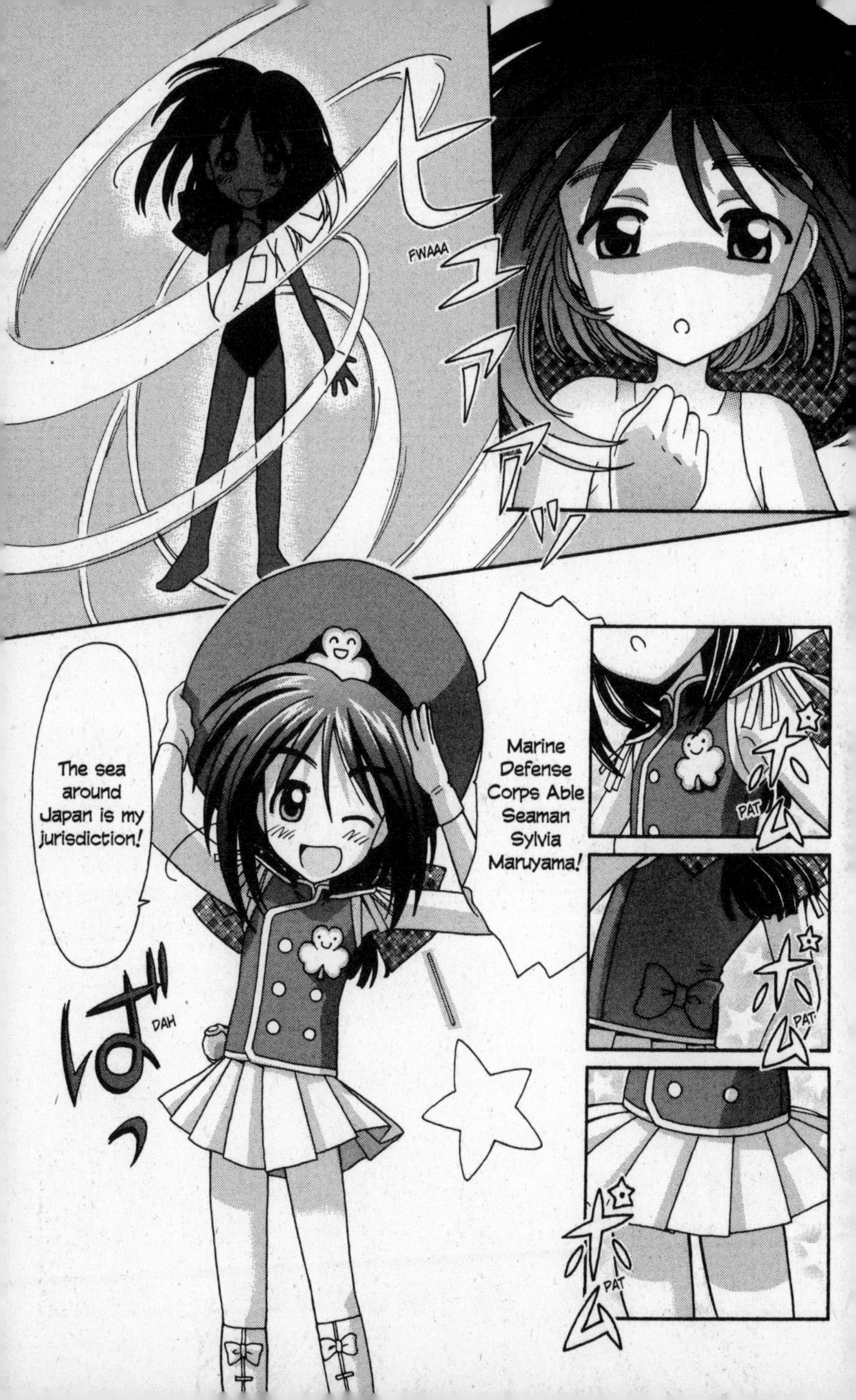
FWAAA
PAT
PAT
PAT
Marine Defense Corps Able Seaman Sylvia Maruyama!
The sea around Japan is my jurisdiction!
DAH

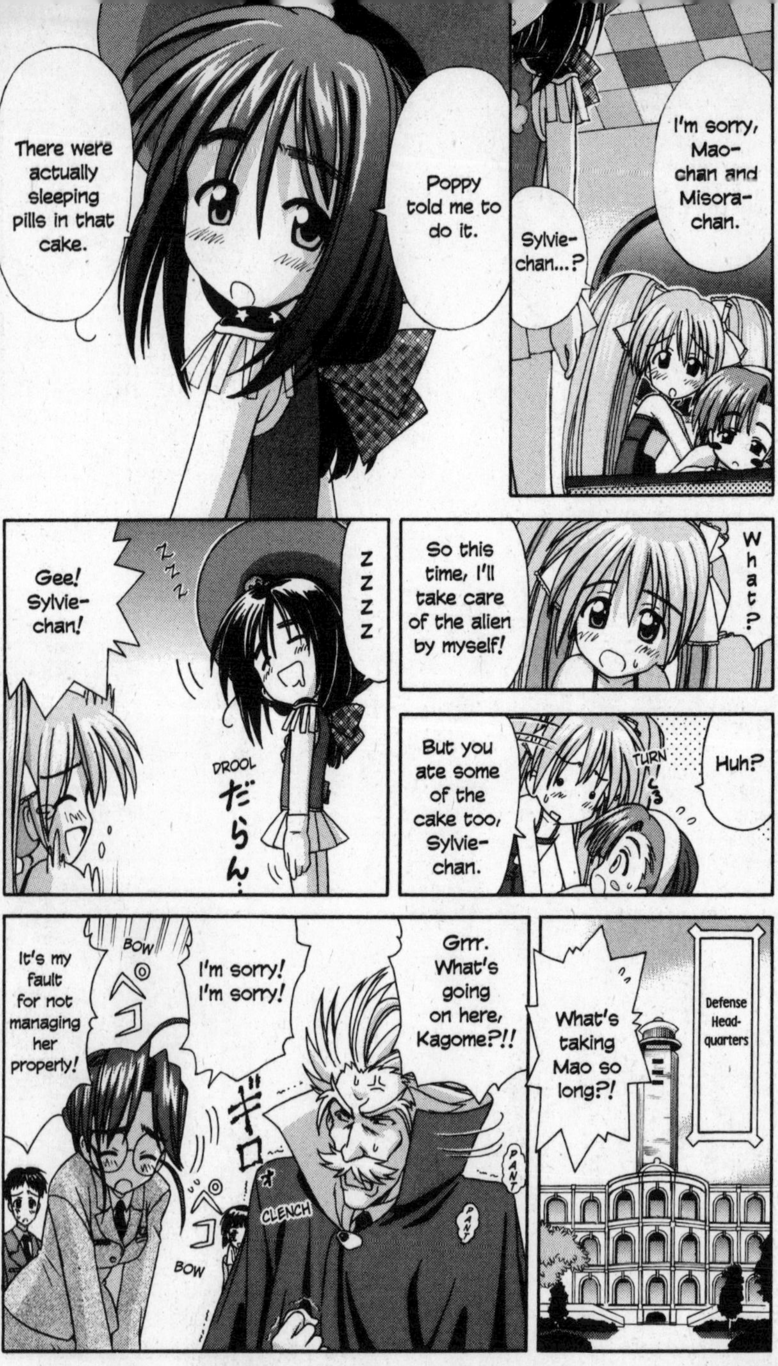
I'm sorry, Mao-chan and Misora-chan.
Sylvie-chan...?
Poppy told me to do it.
There were actually sleeping pills in that cake.
What?
So this time, I'll take care of the alien by myself!
Huh?
TURN
But you ate some of the cake too, Sylvie-chan.
ZZZZ
Gee! Sylvie-chan!
DROOL
だらん…
Defense Headquarters
What's taking Mao so long?!
Grrr. What's going on here, Kagome?!!
PANT
PANT
CLENCH
I'm sorry! I'm sorry!
BOW
It's my fault for not managing her properly!
BOW

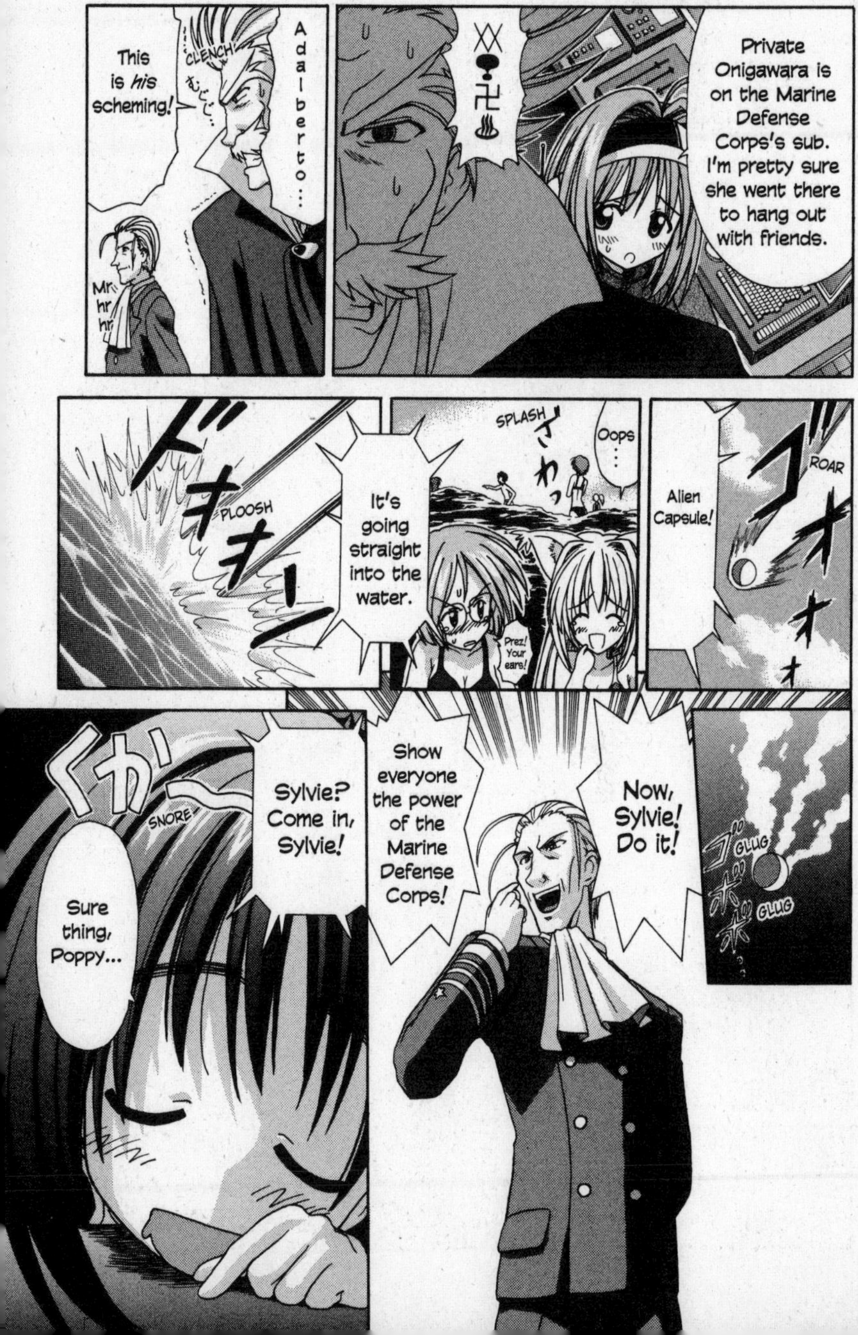
Private Onigawara is on the Marine Defense Corps's sub. I'm pretty sure she went there to hang out with friends.
Adalberto...
CLENCH
This is *his* scheming!
Mr hr hr
ROAR
Alien Capsule!
SPLASH
Oops...
Prez! Your ears!
It's going straight into the water.
PLOOSH
GLUG
GLUG
Now, Sylvie! Do it!
Show everyone the power of the Marine Defense Corps!
Sylvie? Come in, Sylvie!
SNORE
Sure thing, Poppy...

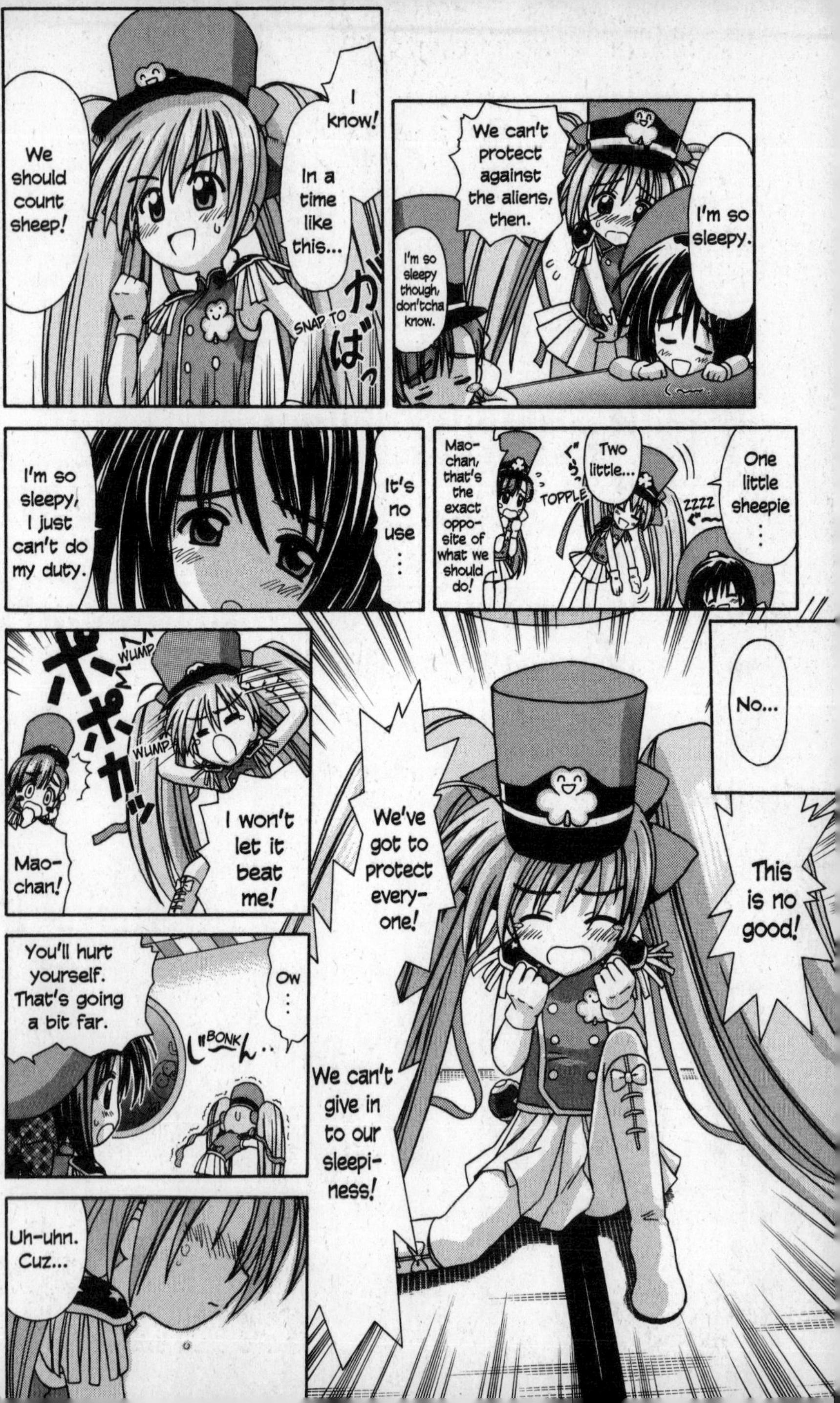
I'm so sleepy.
We can't protect against the aliens, then.
I'm so sleepy though, don'tcha know.
I know!
In a time like this...
SNAP TO
We should count sheep!
One little sheepie ...
ZZZZ
Two little...
TOPPLE
Mao-chan, that's the exact opposite of what we should do!
It's no use ...
I'm so sleepy, I just can't do my duty.
No...
This is no good!
We've got to protect every-one!
We can't give in to our sleepi-ness!
WUMP
WUMP
I won't let it beat me!
Mao-chan!
Ow ...
BONK
You'll hurt yourself. That's going a bit far.
Uh-uhn. Cuz...

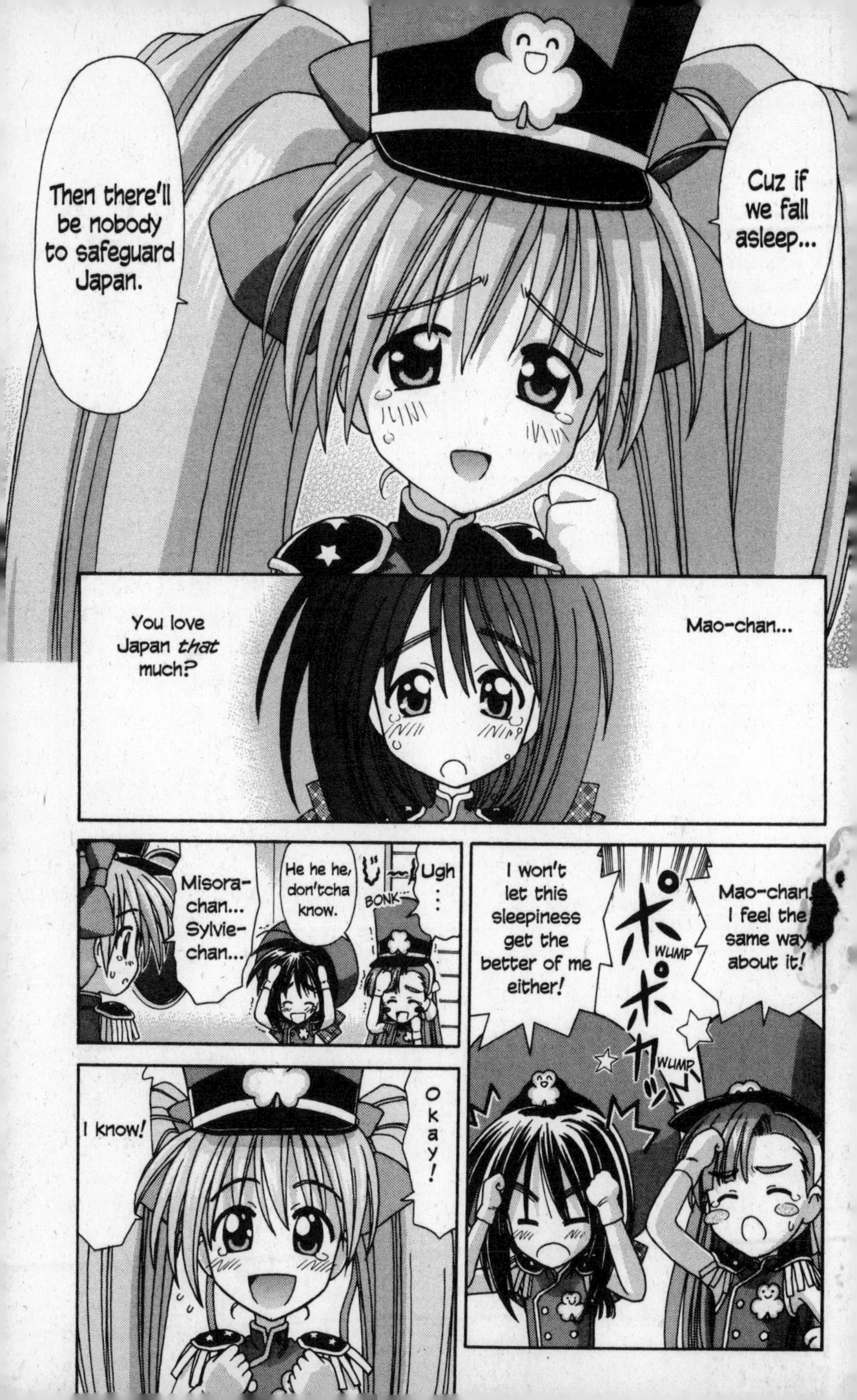
Cuz if we fall asleep...
Then there'll be nobody to safeguard Japan.
Mao-chan...
You love Japan *that* much?
Mao-chan! I feel the same way about it!
ポ
WUMP
ポ
WUMP
I won't let this sleepiness get the better of me either!
Ugh...
BONK
He he he, don'tcha know.
Misora-chan... Sylvie-chan...
Okay!
I know!

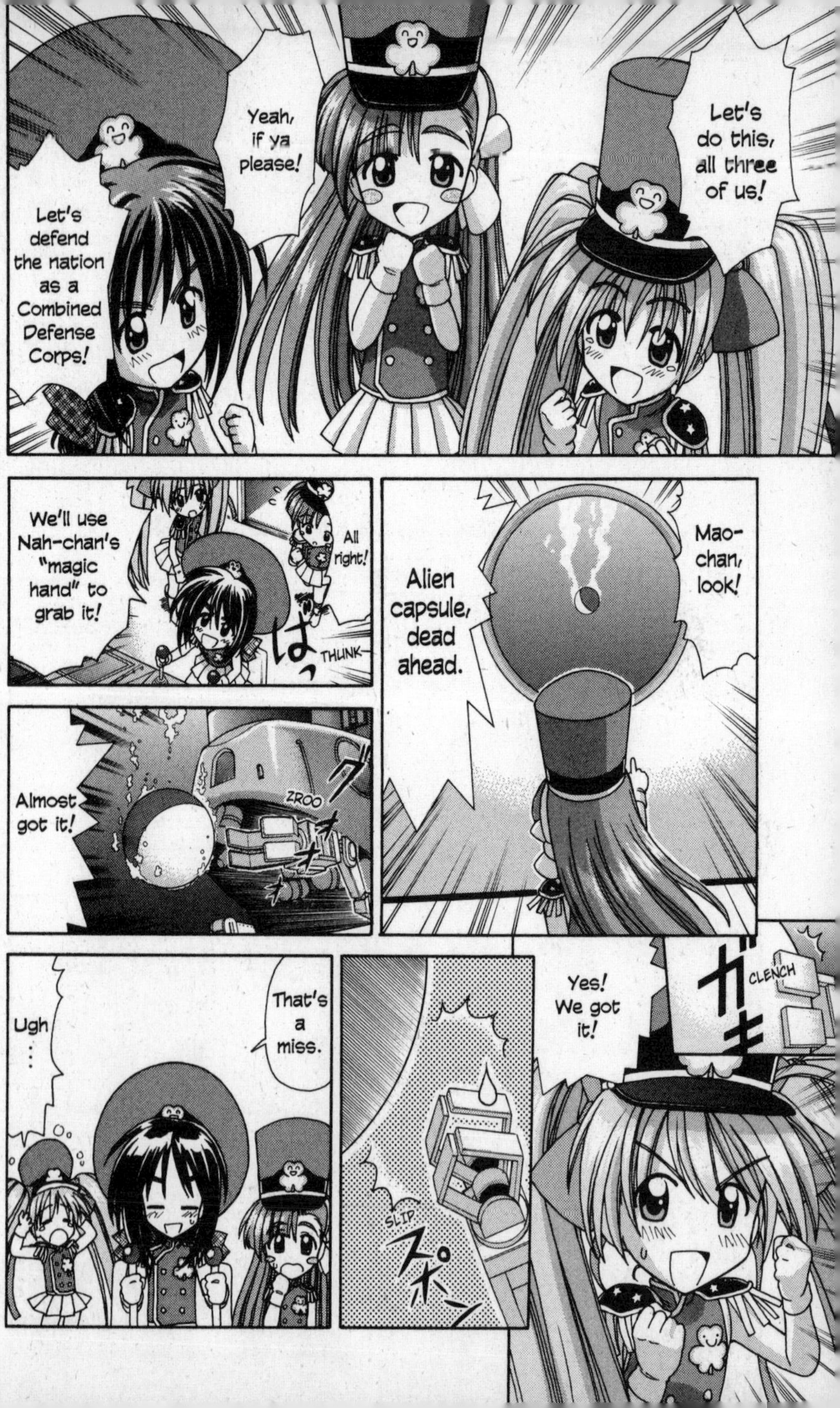
Let's do this, all three of us!
Yeah, if ya please!
Let's defend the nation as a Combined Defense Corps!
Mao-chan, look!
Alien capsule, dead ahead.
We'll use Nah-chan's "magic hand" to grab it!
All right!
THUNK-
ZROO
Almost got it!
CLENCH
Yes! We got it!
SLIP
That's a miss.
Ugh...

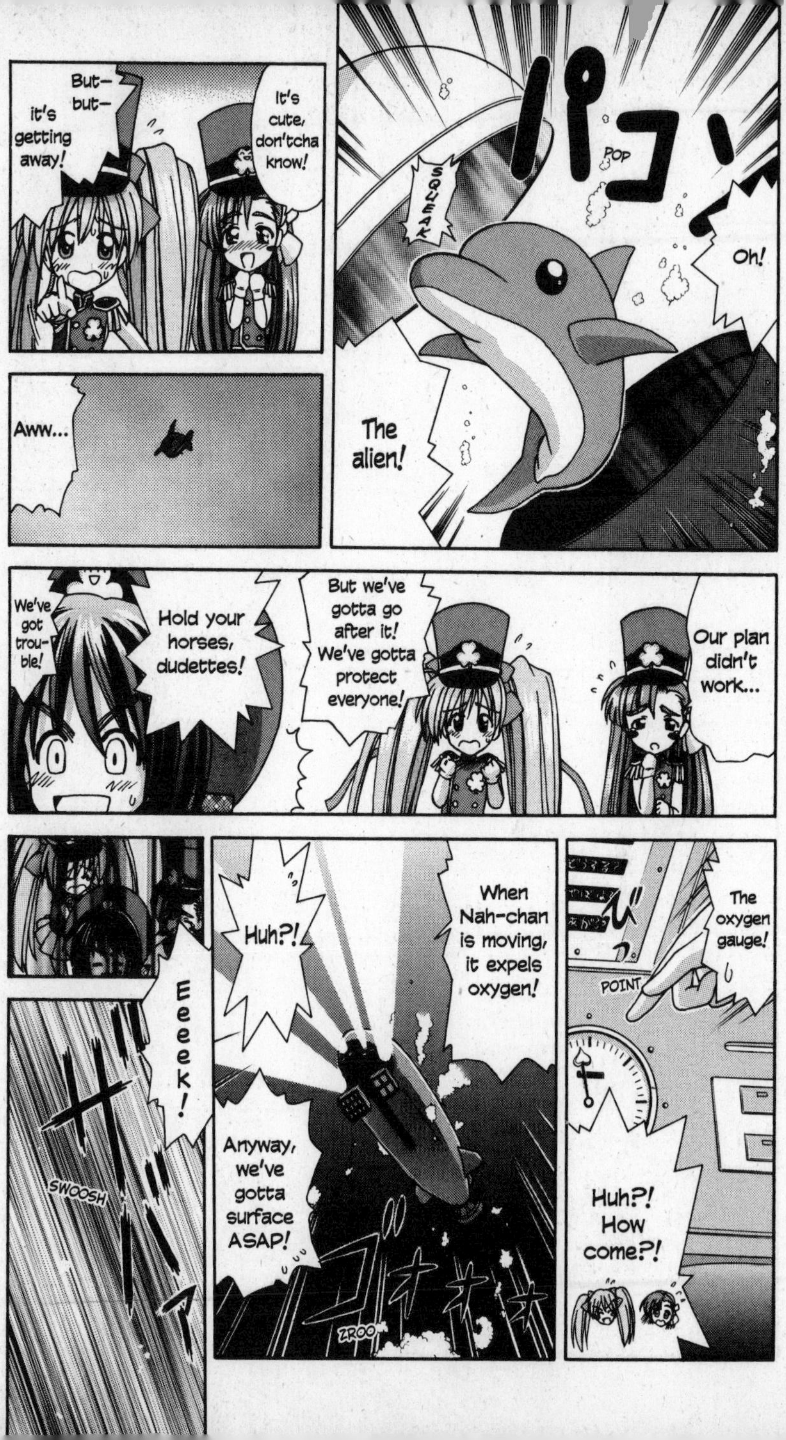
パコン
POP
Oh!
SQUEAK
The alien!
It's cute, don'tcha know!
But— but— it's getting away!
Aww...
Our plan didn't work...
But we've gotta go after it! We've gotta protect everyone!
Hold your horses, dudettes!
We've got trouble!
The oxygen gauge!
POINT
Huh?! How come?!
When Nah-chan is moving, it expels oxygen!
Huh?!
Anyway, we've gotta surface ASAP!
ZROO
Eeeek!
SWOOSH

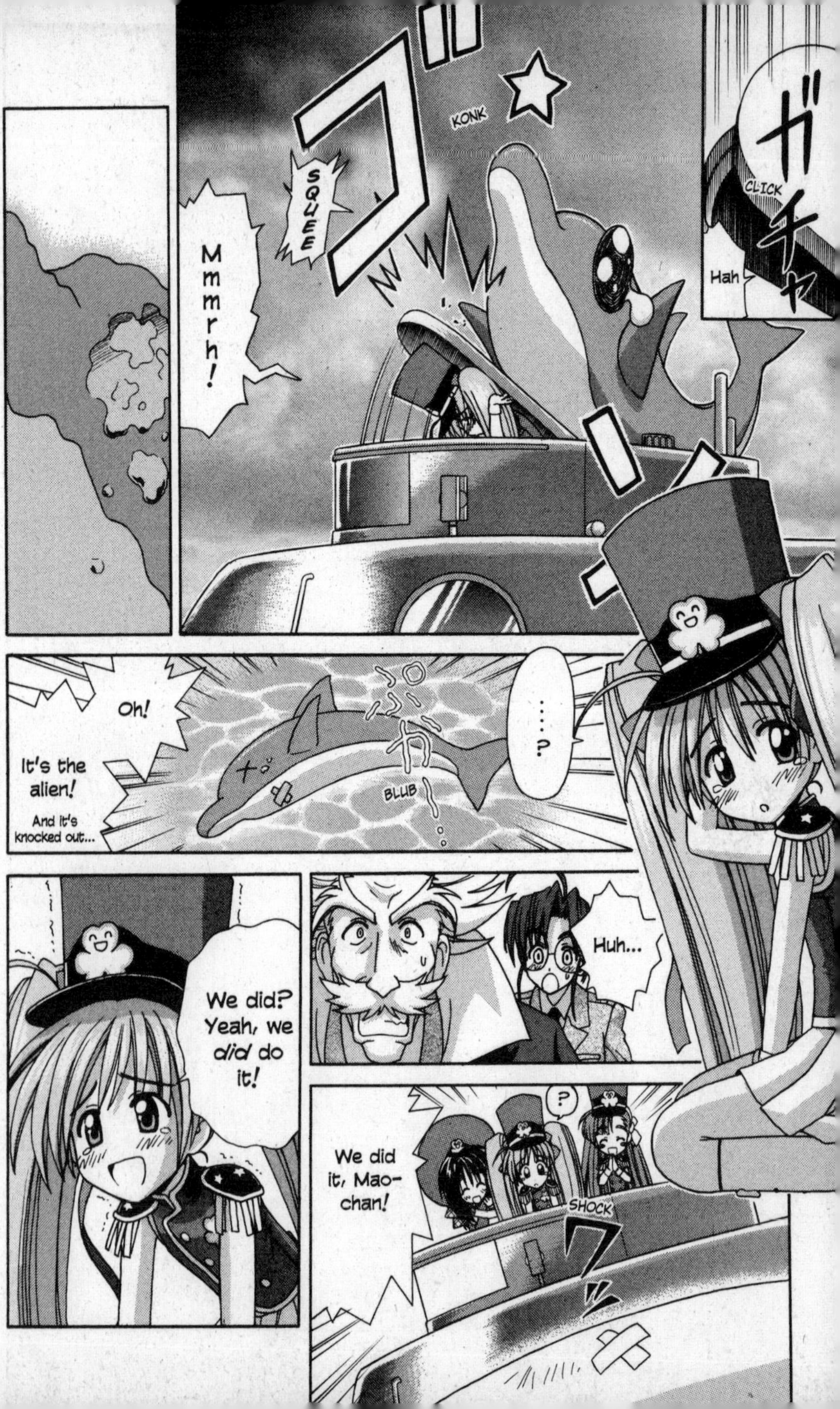
ガチャ
CLICK
Hah
ゴン
KONK
SQUEEE
Mmmrh!
....?
Oh!
It's the alien!
And it's knocked out...
ぷかー
BLUB
Huh...
?
We did it, Mao-chan!
SHOCK
We did? Yeah, we did do it!

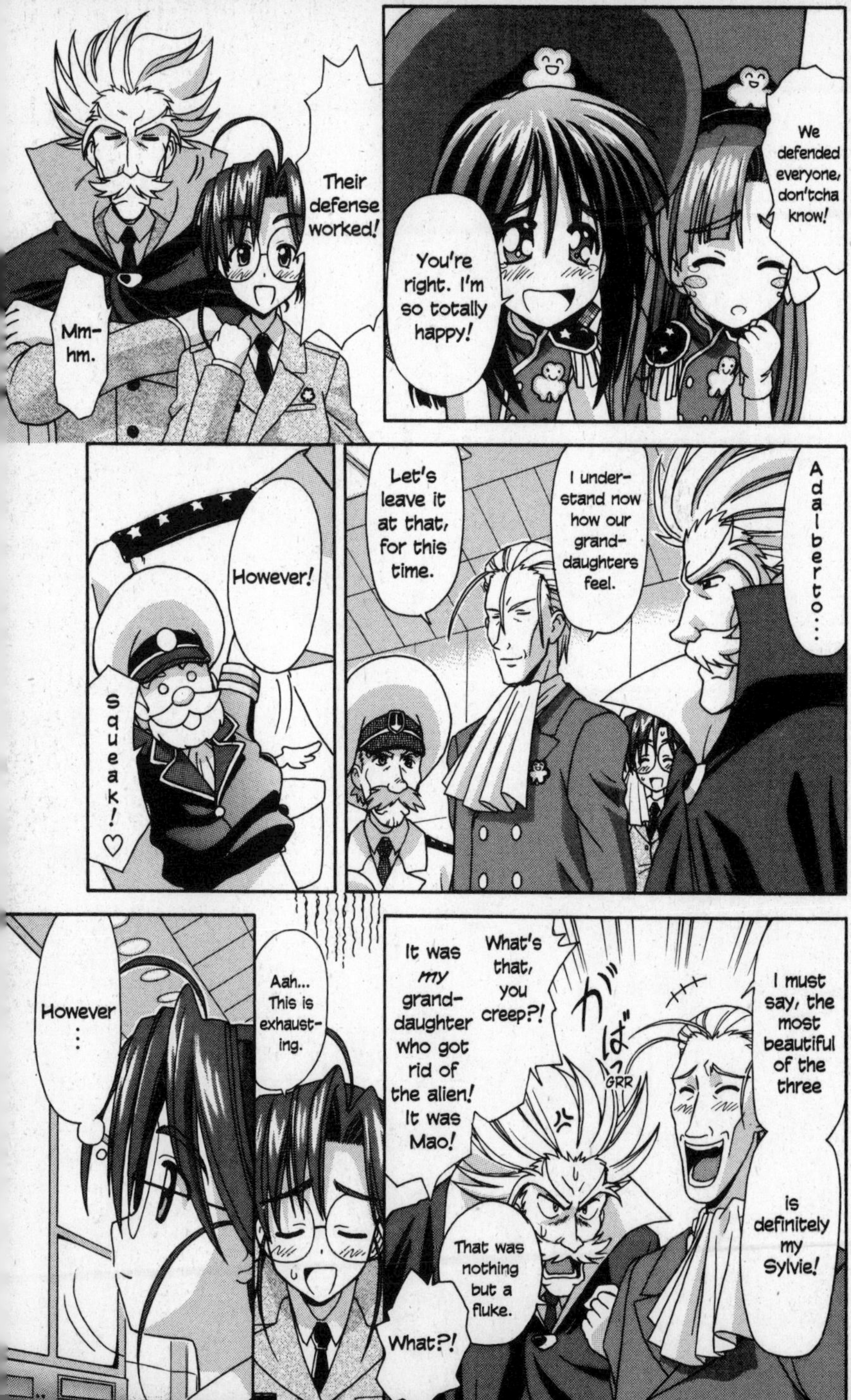
We defended everyone, don'tcha know!
You're right. I'm so totally happy!
Their defense worked!
Mm-hm.
Adalberto...
I under-stand now how our grand-daughters feel.
Let's leave it at that, for this time.
However!
Squeak! ♡
I must say, the most beautiful of the three
is definitely my Sylvie!
がばっ
GRR
What's that, you creep?!
It was *my* grand-daughter who got rid of the alien! It was Mao!
That was nothing but a fluke.
What?!
Aah... This is exhaust-ing.
However...

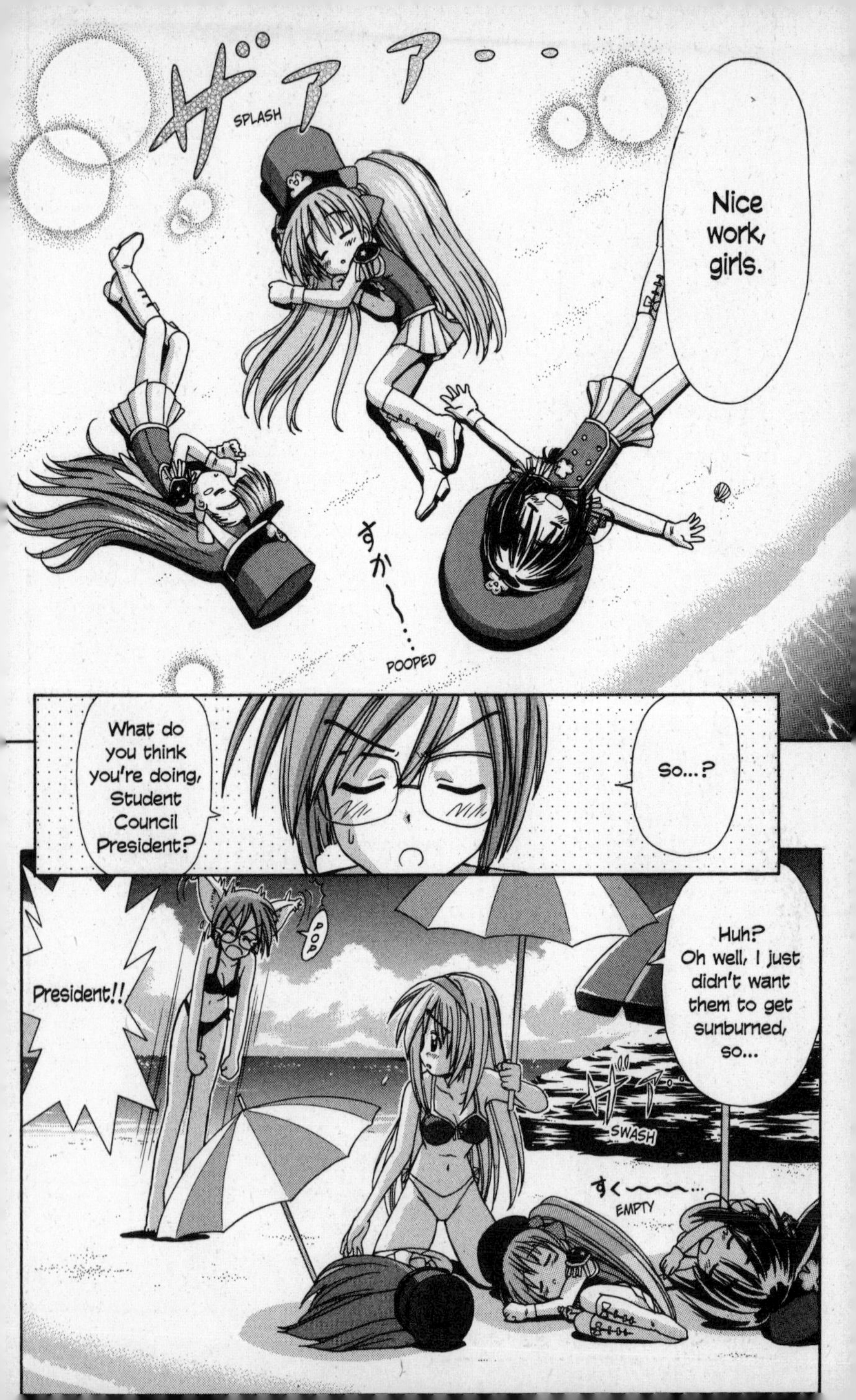

ザアア・・・
SPLASH
Nice work, girls.
すか〜…
POOPED
So...?
What do you think you're doing, Student Council President?
Huh? Oh well, I just didn't want them to get sunburned, so...
SWASH
すく〜〜〜…
EMPTY
POP
President!!

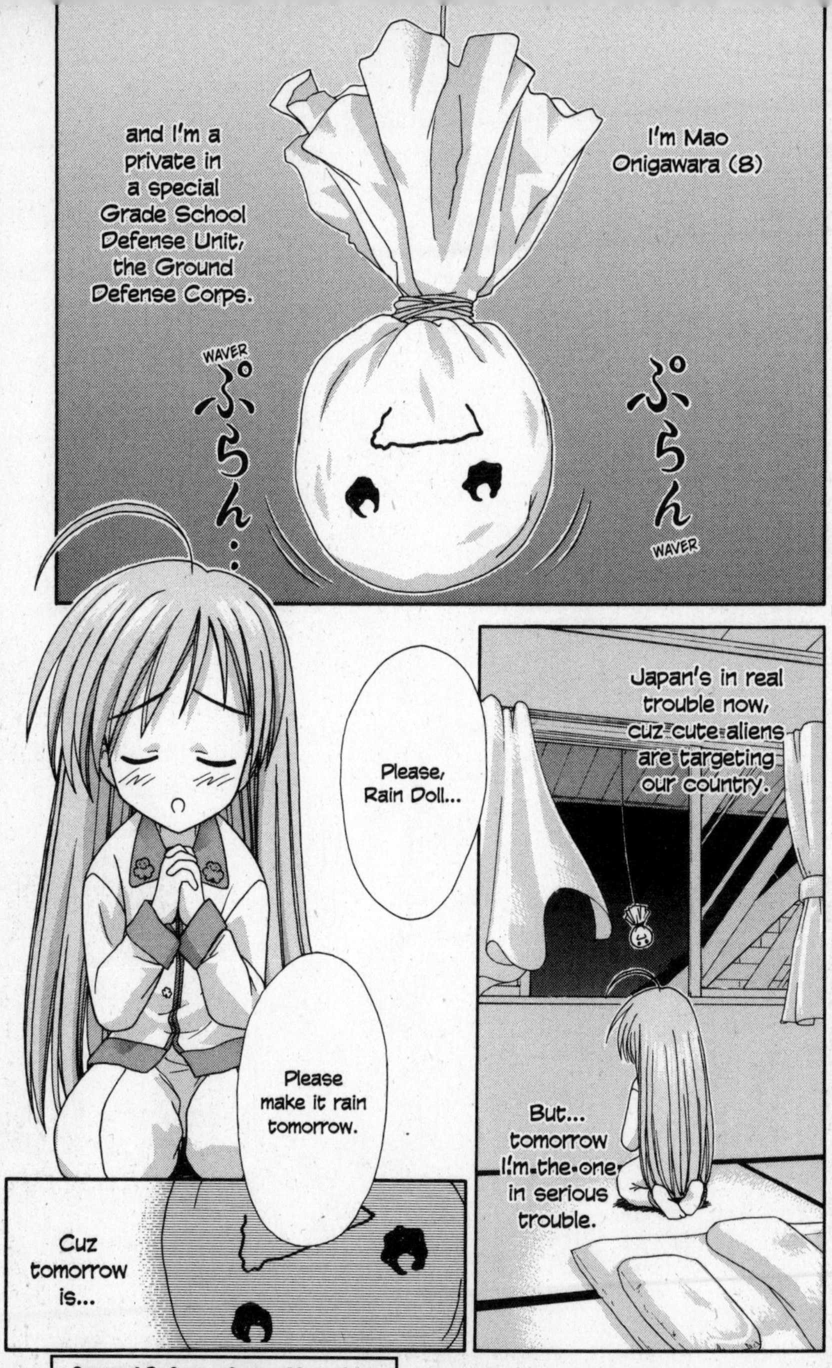
I'm Mao Onigawara (8)
and I'm a private in a special Grade School Defense Unit, the Ground Defense Corps.
ぷらん
WAVER
ぷらん…
WAVER
Japan's in real trouble now, cuz cute aliens are targeting our country.
But... tomorrow I'm the one in serious trouble.
Please, Rain Doll...
Please make it rain tomorrow.
Cuz tomorrow is...

Ground Defense Corps Mao-chan

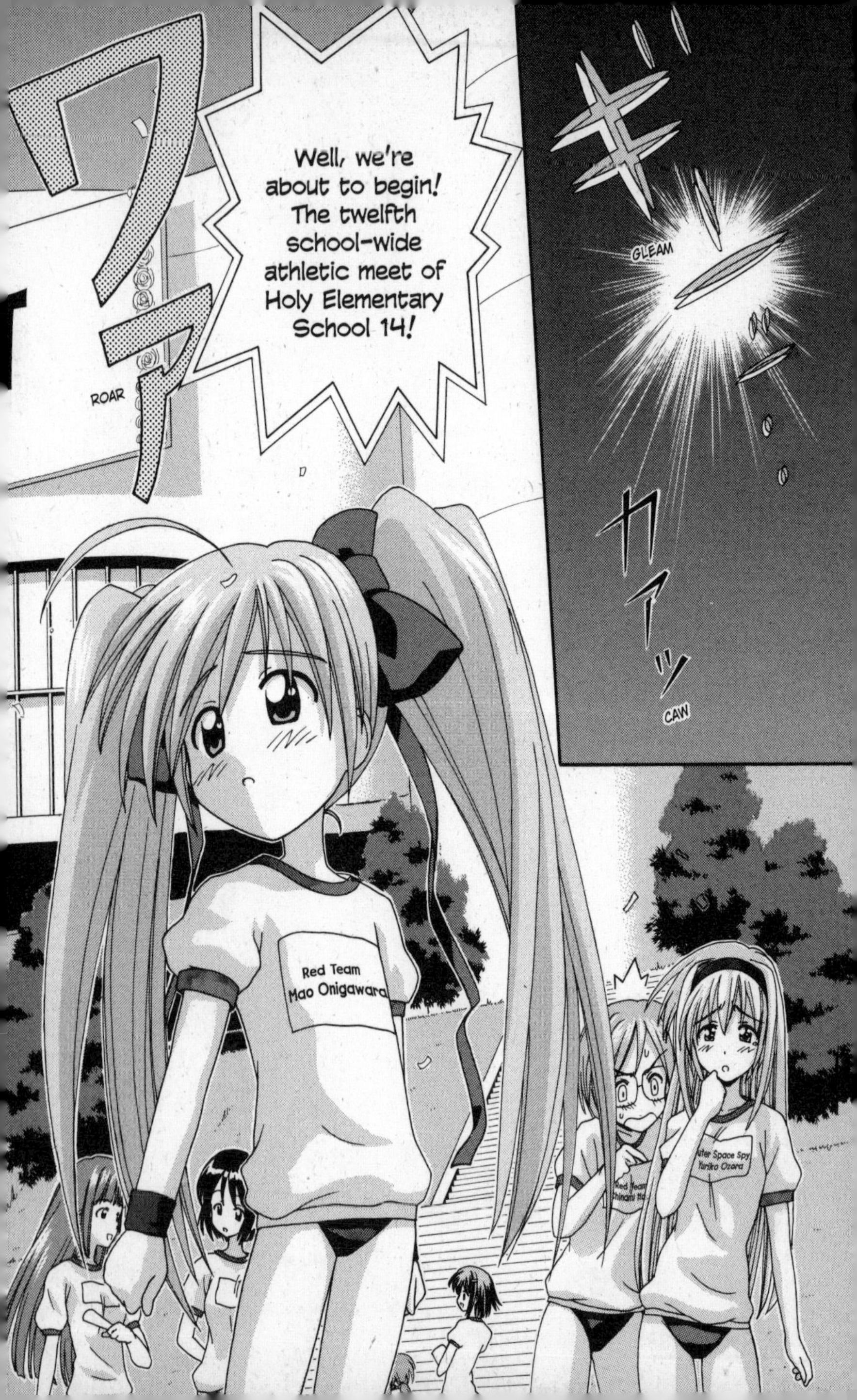
GLEAM
CAW
Well, we're about to begin! The twelfth school-wide athletic meet of Holy Elementary School 14!
ROAR
Red Team Mao Onigawara

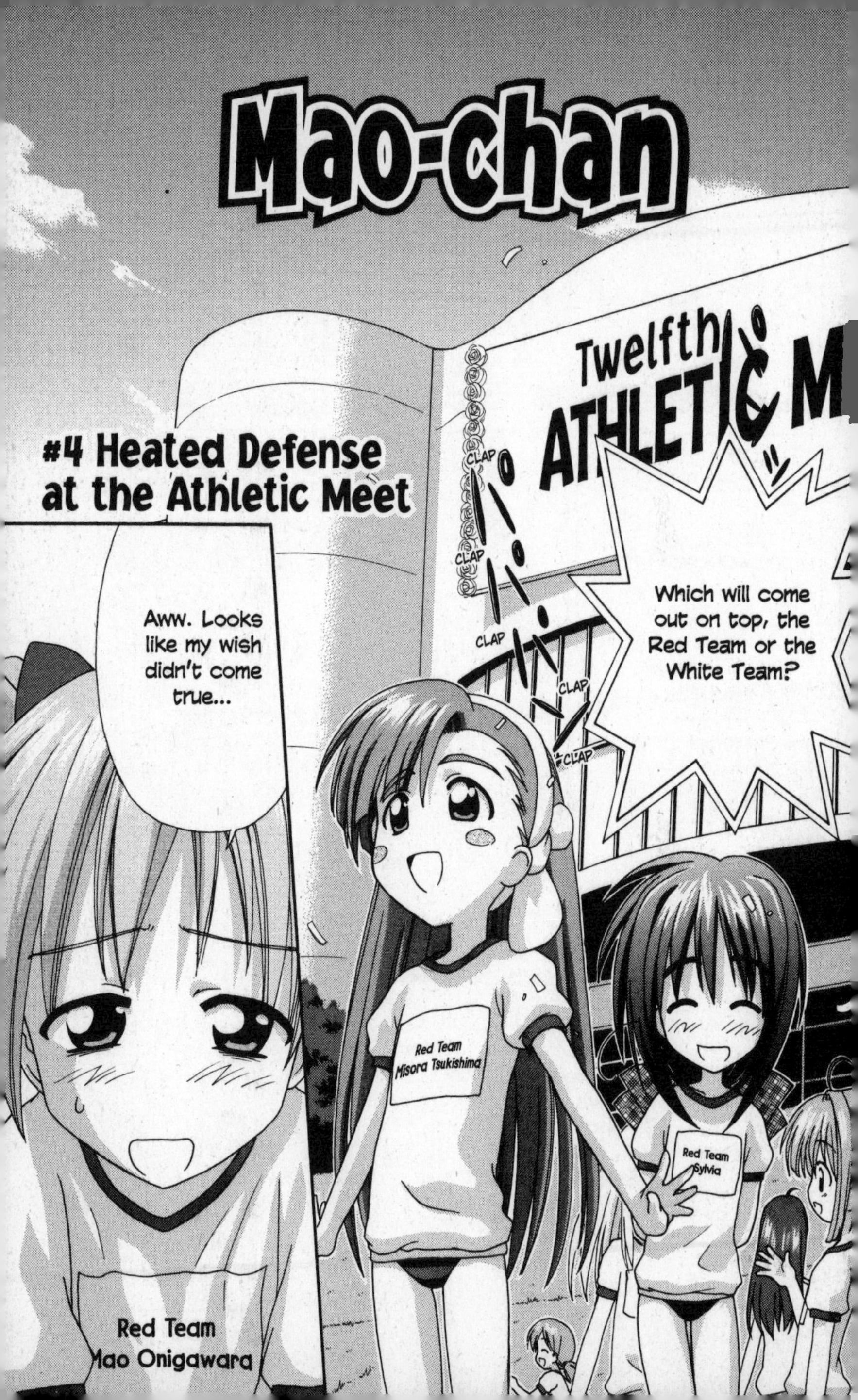
Mao-chan
Twelfth ATHLETIC M
#4 Heated Defense at the Athletic Meet
CLAP CLAP CLAP CLAP CLAP
Which will come out on top, the Red Team or the White Team?
Aww. Looks like my wish didn't come true...
Red Team Sylvia
Red Team Misora Tsukishima
Red Team Mao Onigawara

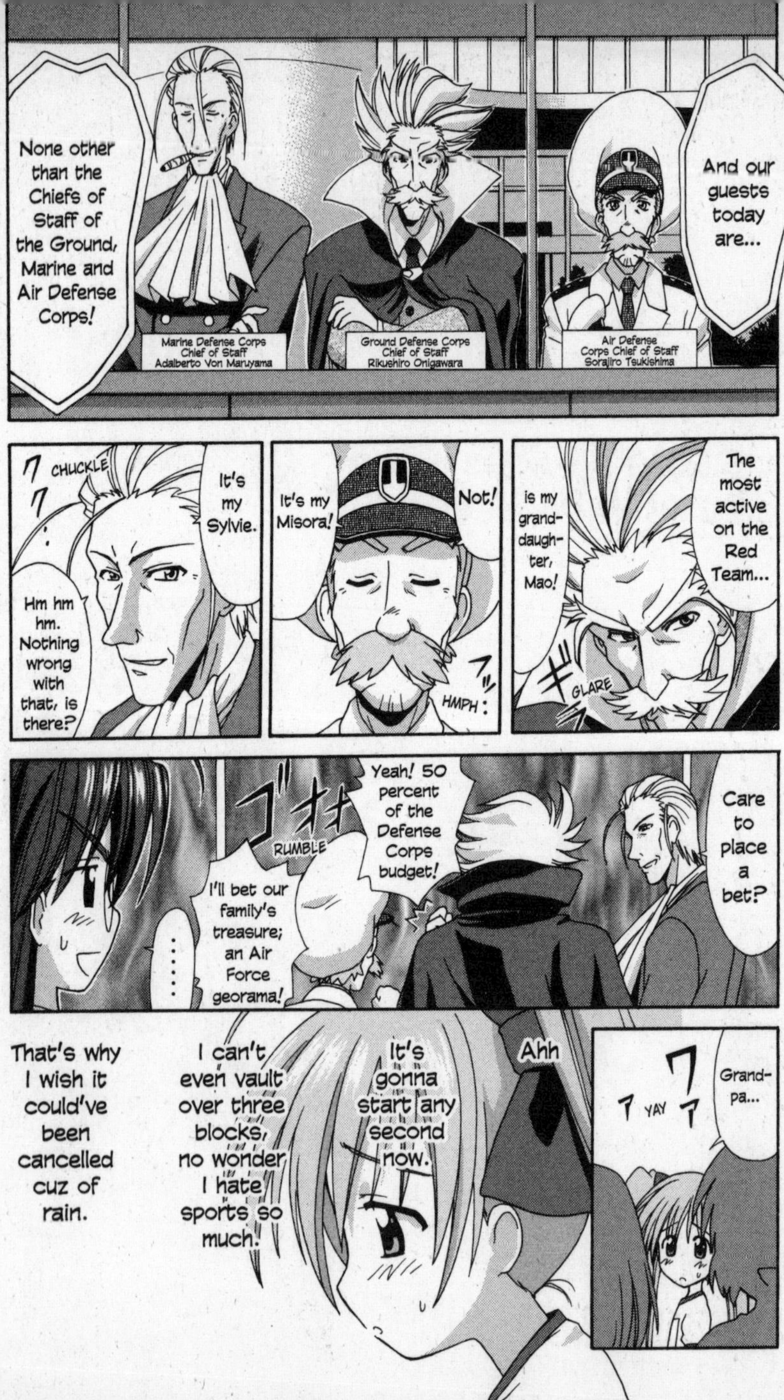
And our guests today are...
None other than the Chiefs of Staff of the Ground, Marine and Air Defense Corps!
Air Defense Corps Chief of Staff Sorajiro Tsukishima
Ground Defense Corps Chief of Staff Rikushiro Onigawara
Marine Defense Corps Chief of Staff Adalberto Von Maruyama
The most active on the Red Team...
is my grand-daugh-ter, Mao!
GLARE
Not!
It's my Misora!
HMPH
It's my Sylvie.
CHUCKLE
Hm hm hm. Nothing wrong with that, is there?
Care to place a bet?
Yeah! 50 percent of the Defense Corps budget!
RUMBLE
I'll bet our family's treasure; an Air Force georama!
......
Grand-pa...
YAY
Ahh
It's gonna start any second now.
I can't even vault over three blocks, no wonder I hate sports so much.
That's why I wish it could've been cancelled cuz of rain.

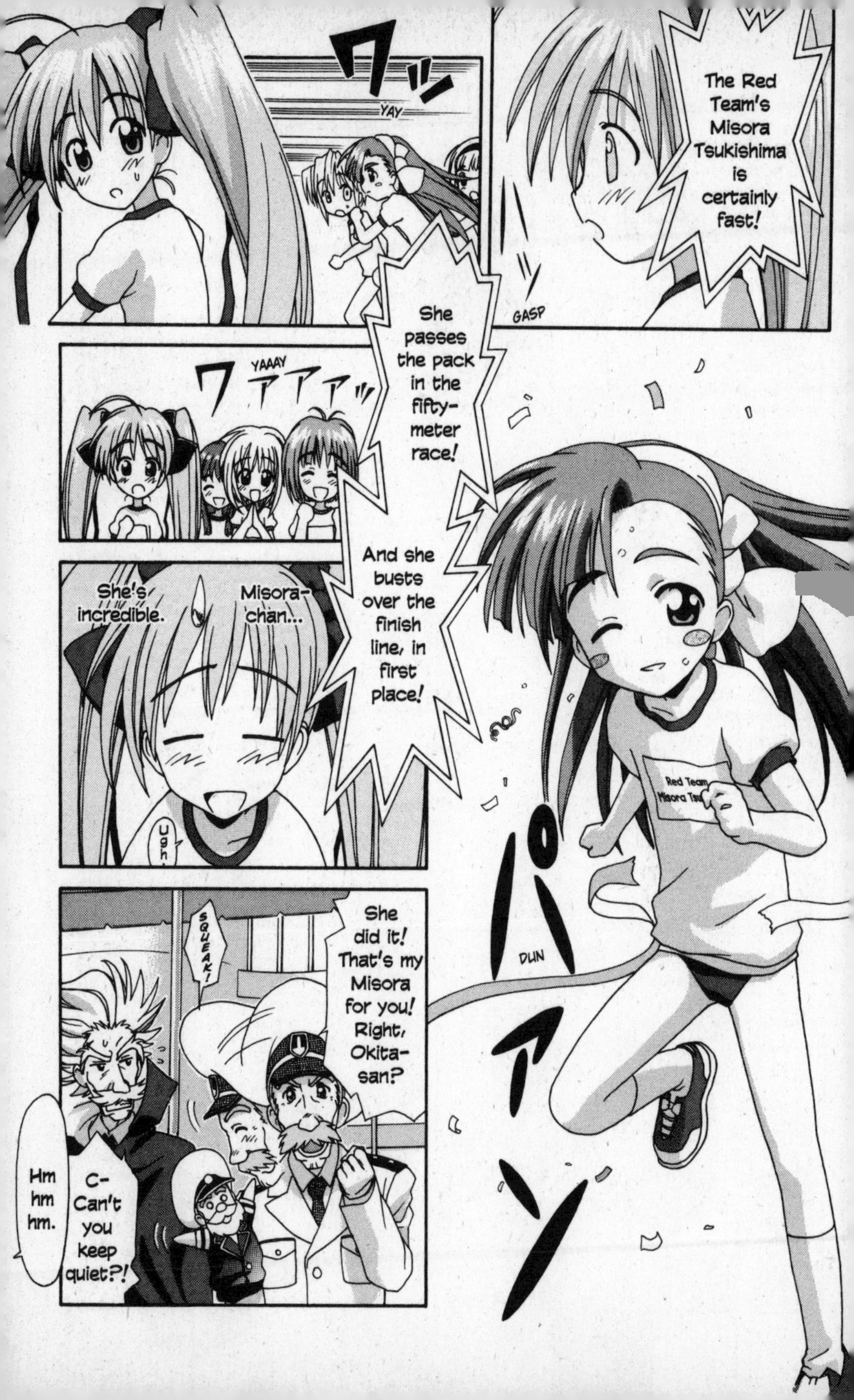
The Red Team's Misora Tsukishima is certainly fast!
GASP
YAY
She passes the pack in the fifty-meter race!
And she busts over the finish line, in first place!
Red Team Misora Tsu
DUN
YAAAY
Misora-chan...
She's incredible.
Ugh
She did it! That's my Misora for you! Right, Okita-san?
SQUEAK!
C-Can't you keep quiet?!
Hm hm hm.

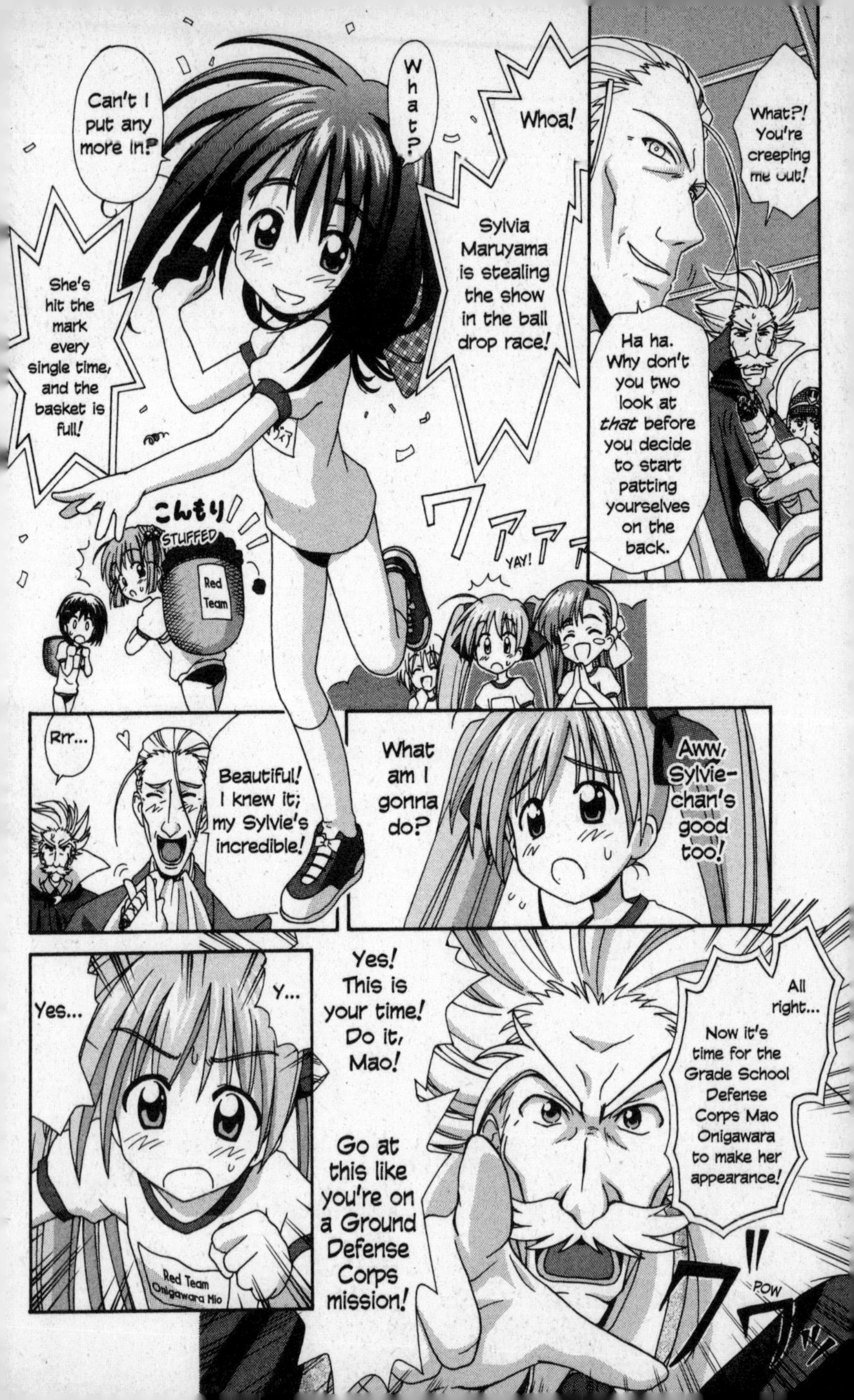

What?! You're creeping me out!
Ha ha. Why don't you two look at *that* before you decide to start patting yourselves on the back.
Whoa!
What?
Sylvia Maruyama is stealing the show in the ball drop race!
Can't I put any more in?
She's hit the mark every single time, and the basket is full!
こんもり
STUFFED
Red Team
ワァァァ
YAY!
Aww, Sylvie-chan's good too!
What am I gonna do?
Beautiful! I knew it; my Sylvie's incredible!
Rrr...
All right... Now it's time for the Grade School Defense Corps Mao Onigawara to make her appearance!
POW
Yes! This is your time! Do it, Mao!
Go at this like you're on a Ground Defense Corps mission!
Y...
Yes...
Red Team Onigawara Mio

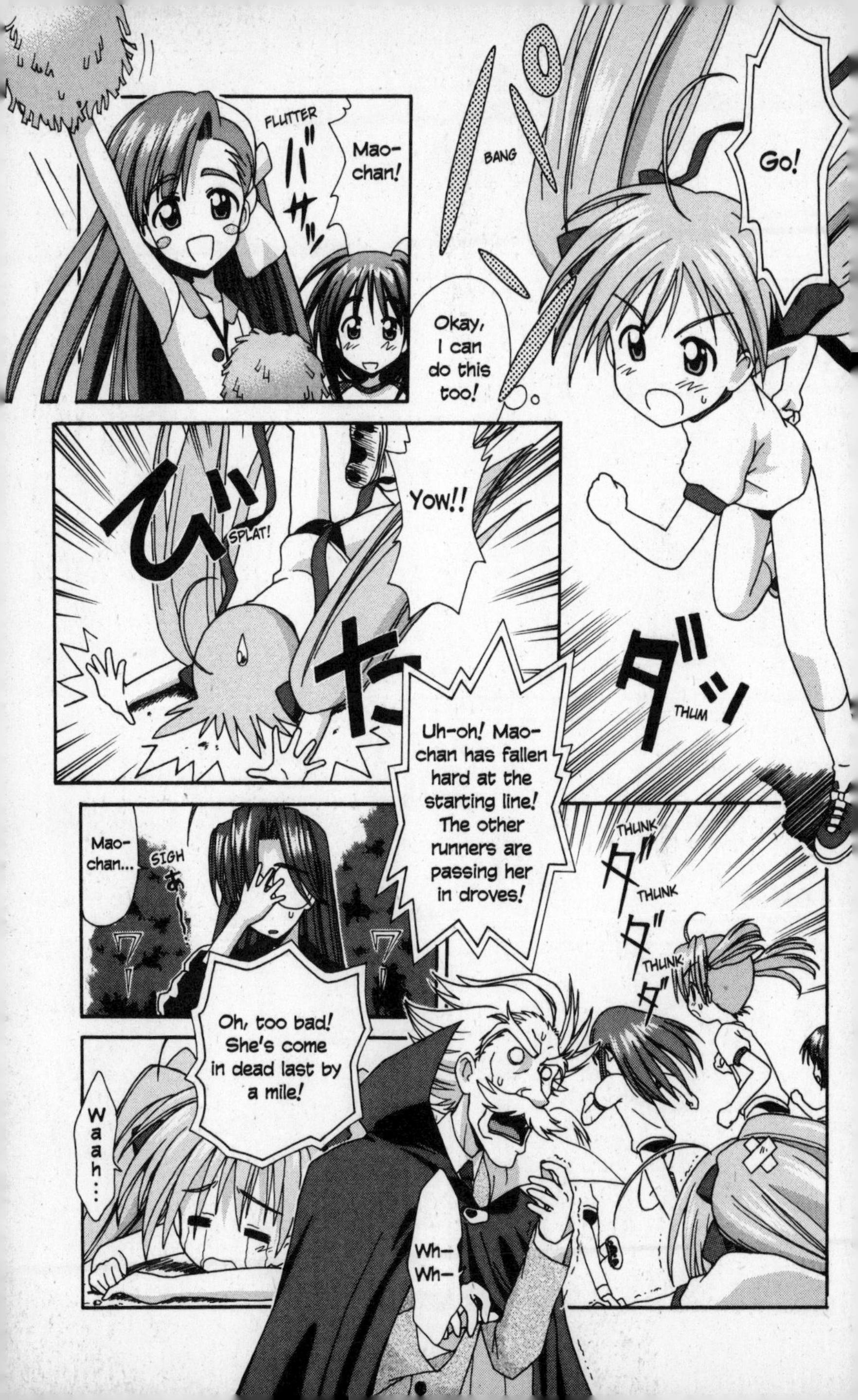
Go!
BANG
THUM
FLUTTER
Mao-chan!
Okay, I can do this too!
YOW!!
SPLAT!
THUNK
THUNK
THUNK
Uh-oh! Mao-chan has fallen hard at the starting line! The other runners are passing her in droves!
Mao-chan...
SIGH
Oh, too bad! She's come in dead last by a mile!
Wh- Wh-
Waah...

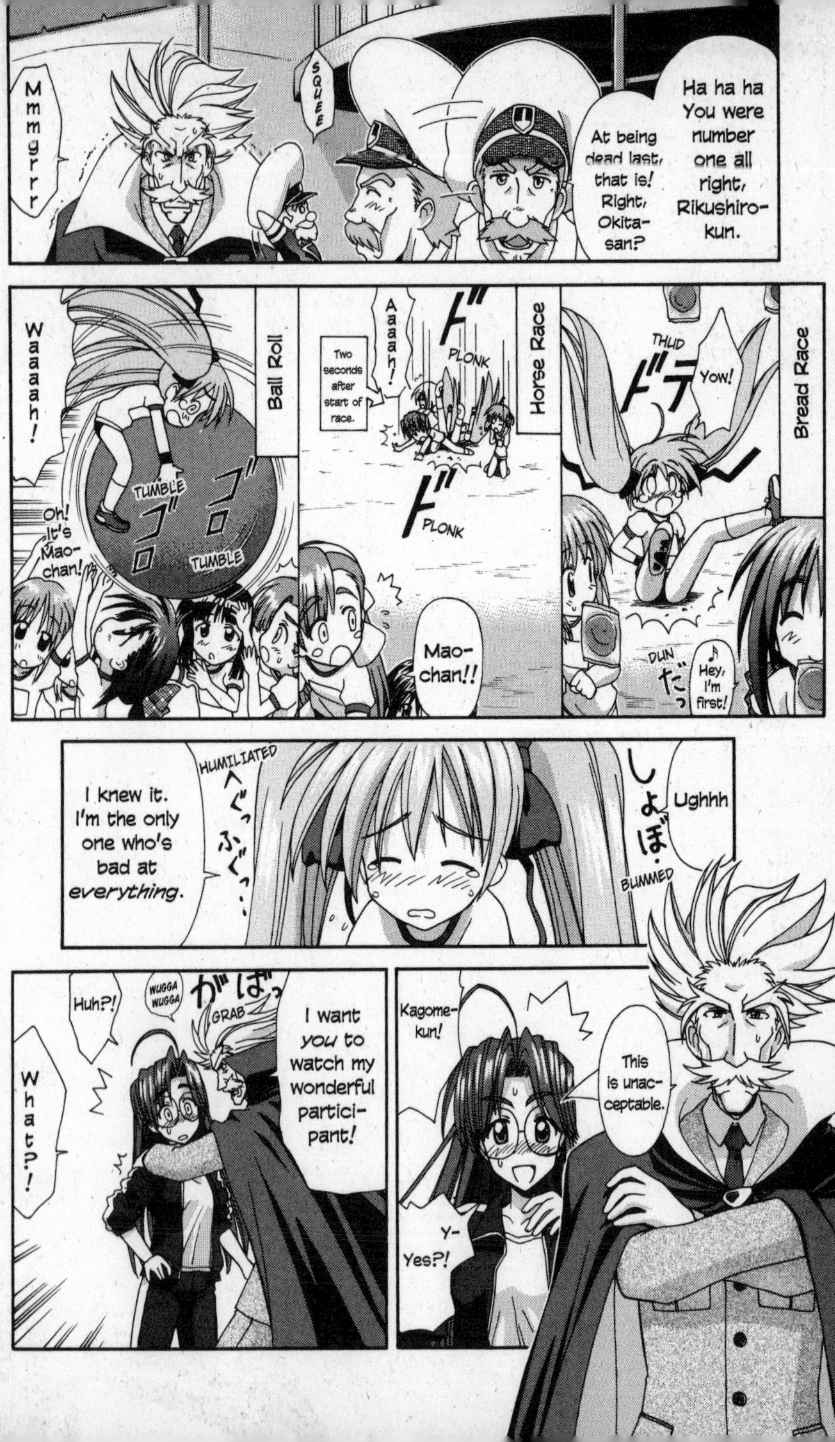
Ha ha ha You were number one all right, Rikushiro-kun.
At being dead last, that is! Right, Okita-san?
SQUEE
Mmmgrrr
Bread Race
THUD
ドテ
Yow!
♪ Hey, I'm first!
DUN
だっ
Horse Race
ド
PLONK
Aaaah!
Two seconds after start of race.
ド
PLONK
Mao-chan!!
Ball Roll
Waaaaah!
TUMBLE
ゴロゴロ
TUMBLE
Oh! It's Mao-chan!
Ughhh
しょぼ・
BUMMED
へぐっふぐっ
HUMILIATED
I knew it. I'm the only one who's bad at *everything*.
Kagome-kun!
This is unacceptable.
Y- Yes?!
I want *you* to watch my wonderful partici-pant!
がばっ
GRAB
WUGGA WUGGA
Huh?!
What?!

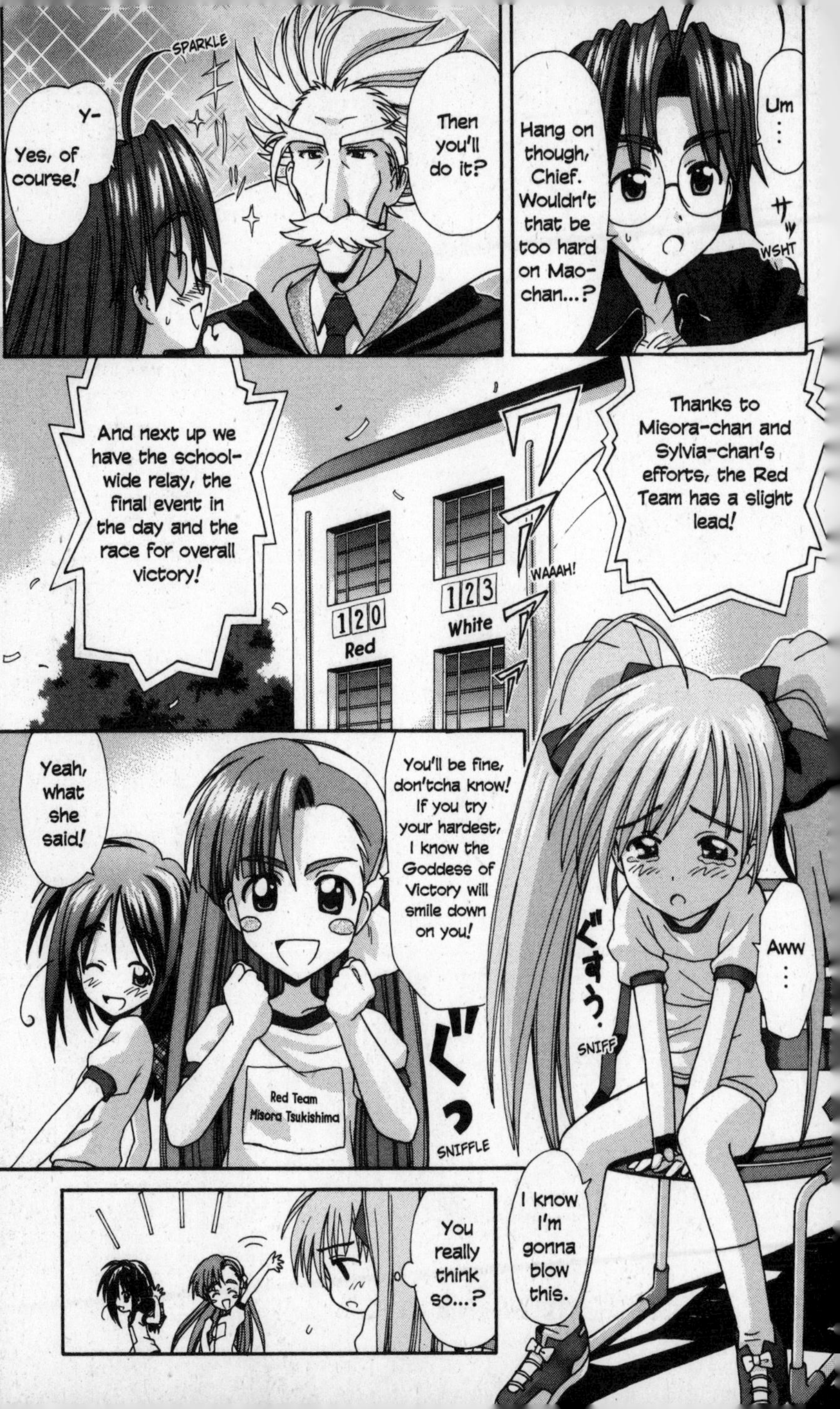
Um...
Hang on though, Chief. Wouldn't that be too hard on Mao-chan...?
WSHT
Then you'll do it?
SPARKLE
Y- Yes, of course!
Thanks to Misora-chan and Sylvia-chan's efforts, the Red Team has a slight lead!
WAAAH!
123
White
120
Red
And next up we have the school-wide relay, the final event in the day and the race for overall victory!
Aww...
SNIFF
I know I'm gonna blow this.
You'll be fine, don'tcha know! If you try your hardest, I know the Goddess of Victory will smile down on you!
SNIFFLE
Red Team Misora Tsukishima
Yeah, what she said!
You really think so...?

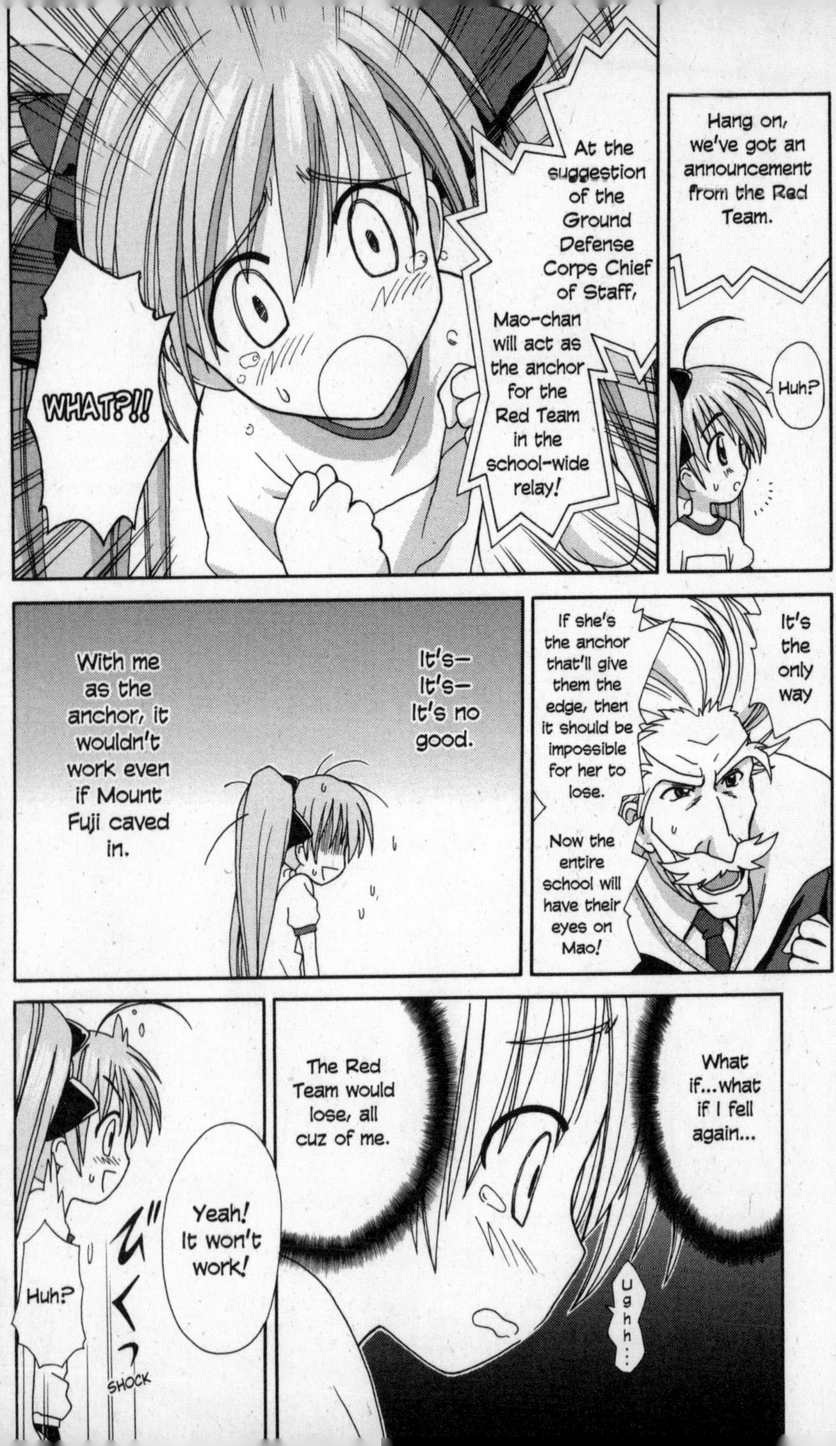
Hang on, we've got an announcement from the Red Team.
Huh?
At the suggestion of the Ground Defense Corps Chief of Staff, Mao-chan will act as the anchor for the Red Team in the school-wide relay!
WHAT?!!
It's the only way
If she's the anchor that'll give them the edge, then it should be impossible for her to lose.
Now the entire school will have their eyes on Mao!
It's— It's— It's no good.
With me as the anchor, it wouldn't work even if Mount Fuji caved in.
What if...what if I fell again...
The Red Team would lose, all cuz of me.
Ughh...
Yeah! It won't work!
SHOCK
Huh?

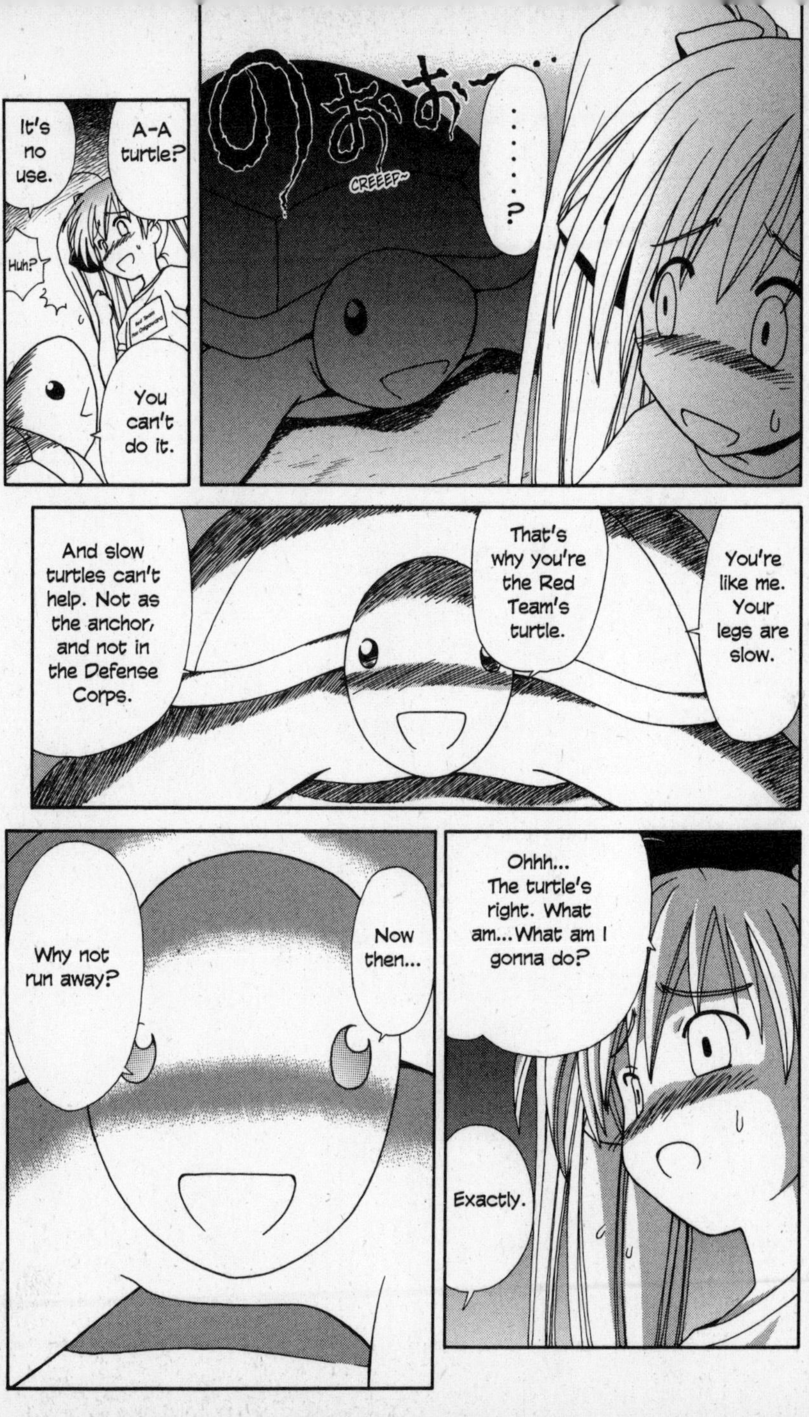
のおお～
CREEEP~
......?
A-A turtle?
It's no use.
Huh?
You can't do it.
You're like me. Your legs are slow.
That's why you're the Red Team's turtle.
And slow turtles can't help. Not as the anchor, and not in the Defense Corps.
Ohhh... The turtle's right. What am...What am I gonna do?
Exactly.
Now then...
Why not run away?

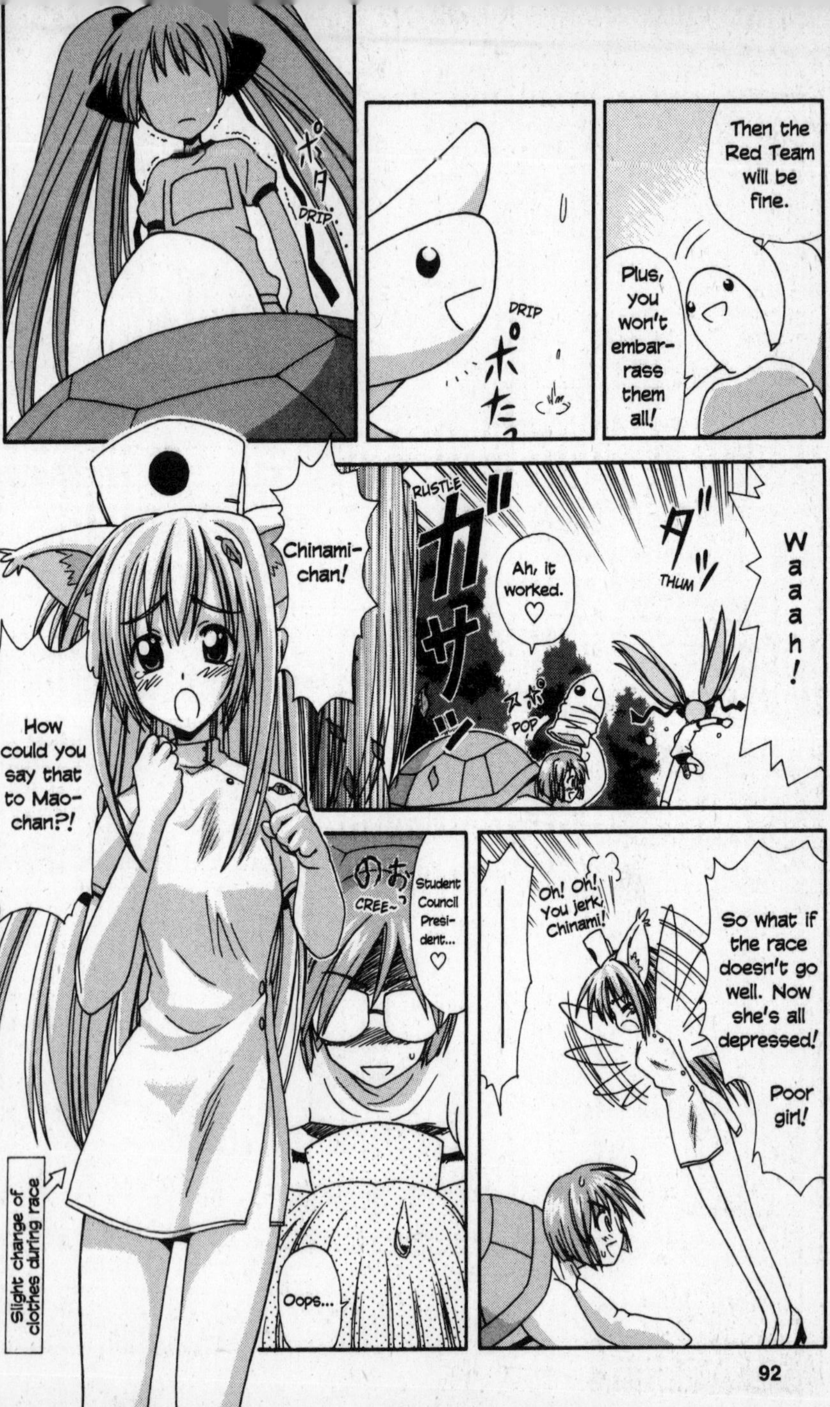
Then the Red Team will be fine.
Plus, you won't embarrass them all!
DRIP
DRIP
Waaah!
THUM
Ah, it worked. ♡
RUSTLE
POP
Oh! Oh! You jerk, Chinami!
So what if the race doesn't go well. Now she's all depressed!
Poor girl!
Student Council President... ♡
CREE~
Oops...
Chinami-chan!
How could you say that to Mao-chan?!
Slight change of clothes during race

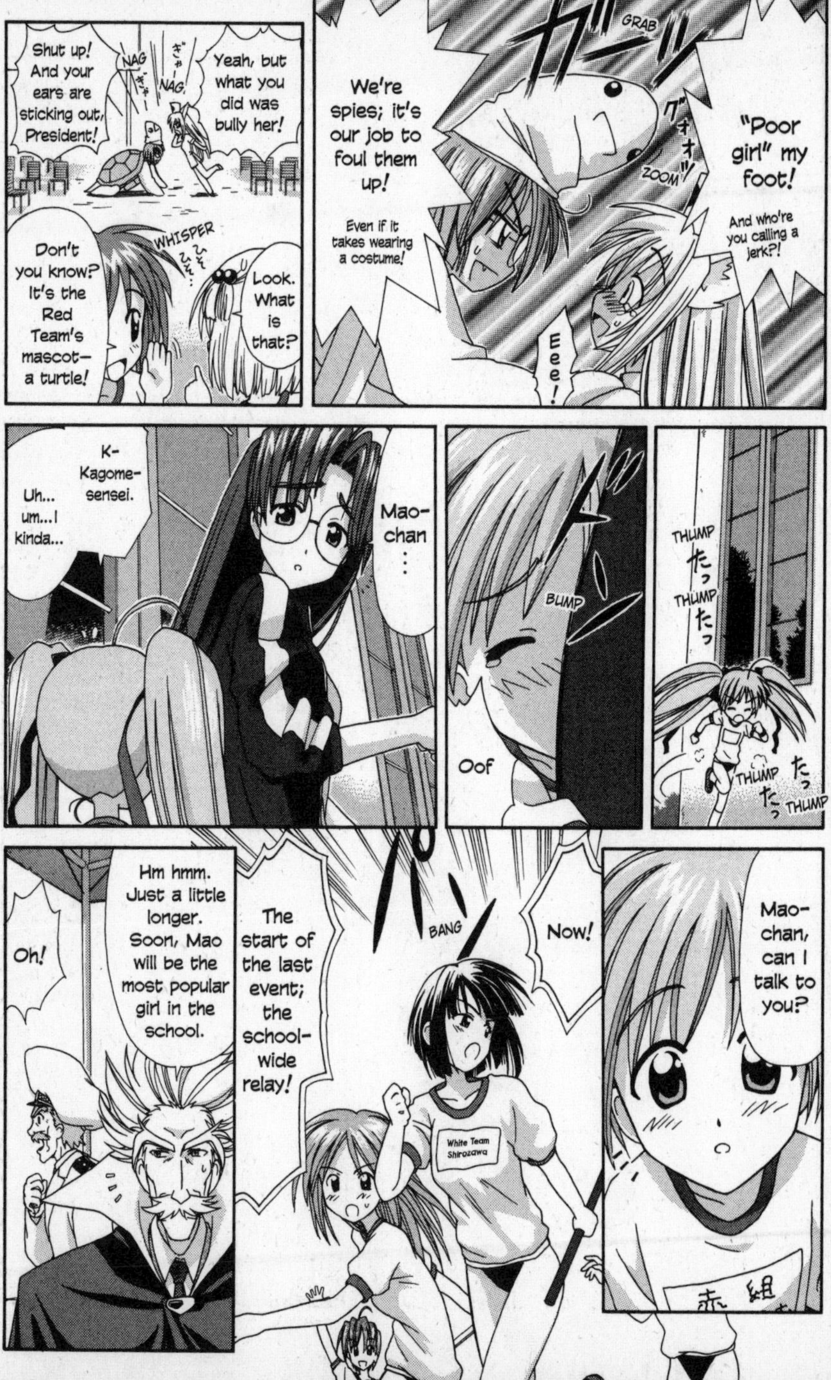
GRAB
"Poor girl" my foot!
And who're you calling a jerk?!
ZOOM
We're spies; it's our job to foul them up!
Even if it takes wearing a costume!
Eee!
Yeah, but what you did was bully her!
NAG
NAG
Shut up! And your ears are sticking out, President!
Look. What is that?
WHISPER
Don't you know? It's the Red Team's mascot—a turtle!
THUMP
THUMP
THUMP
THUMP
BUMP
Oof
Mao-chan...
K-Kagome-sensei.
Uh... um...I kinda...
Mao-chan, can I talk to you?
赤組
Now!
BANG
The start of the last event; the school-wide relay!
White Team Shirozawa
Hm hmm. Just a little longer. Soon, Mao will be the most popular girl in the school.
Oh!

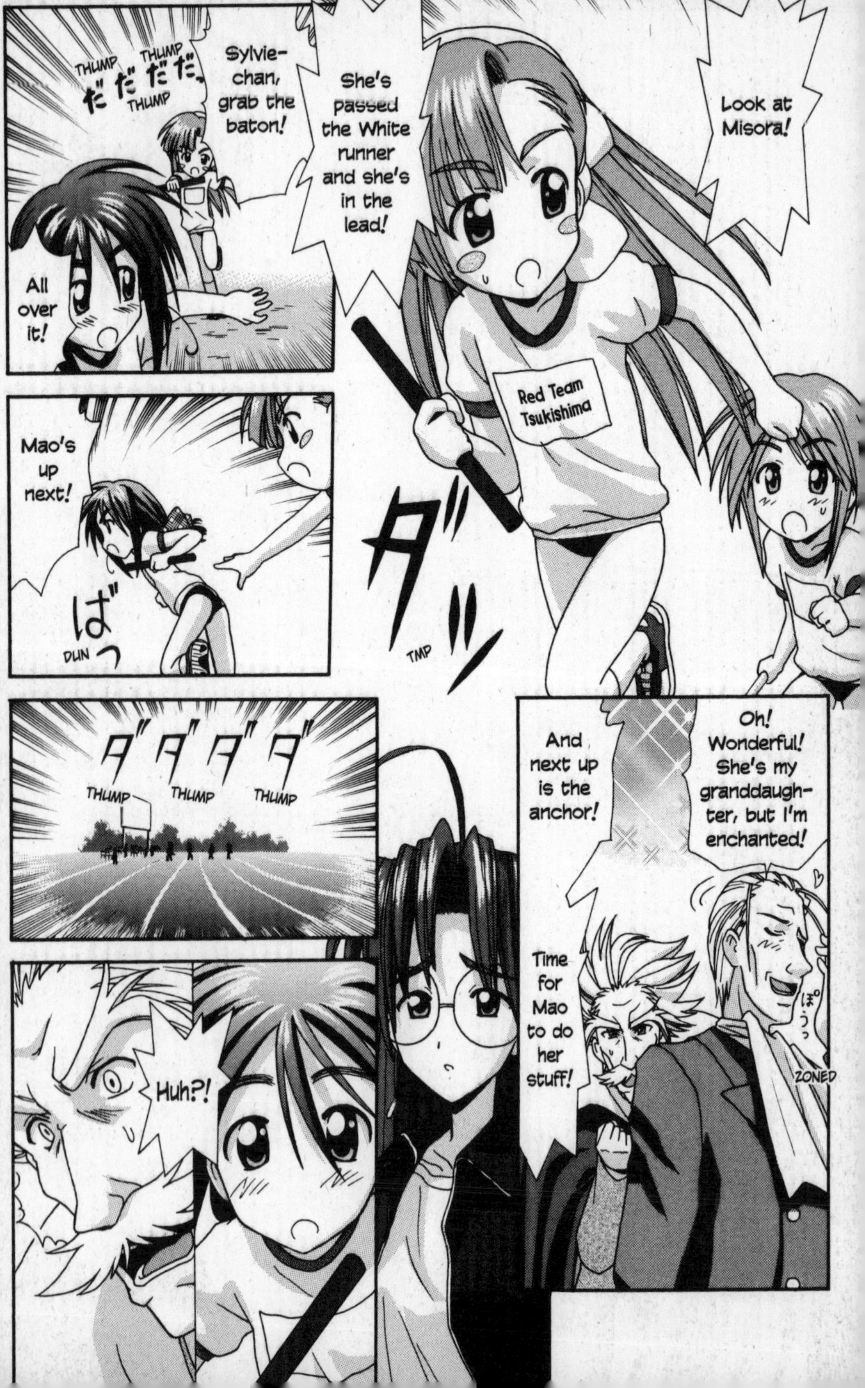
Look at Misora!
She's passed the White runner and she's in the lead!
Red Team Tsukishima
ダッ
TMP
Sylvie-chan, grab the baton!
だだだだ
THUMP THUMP THUMP
All over it!
Mao's up next!
ばっ
DUN
Oh! Wonderful! She's my granddaughter, but I'm enchanted!
And next up is the anchor!
Time for Mao to do her stuff!
ぽうっ
ZONED
ダダダダ
THUMP THUMP THUMP
Huh?!

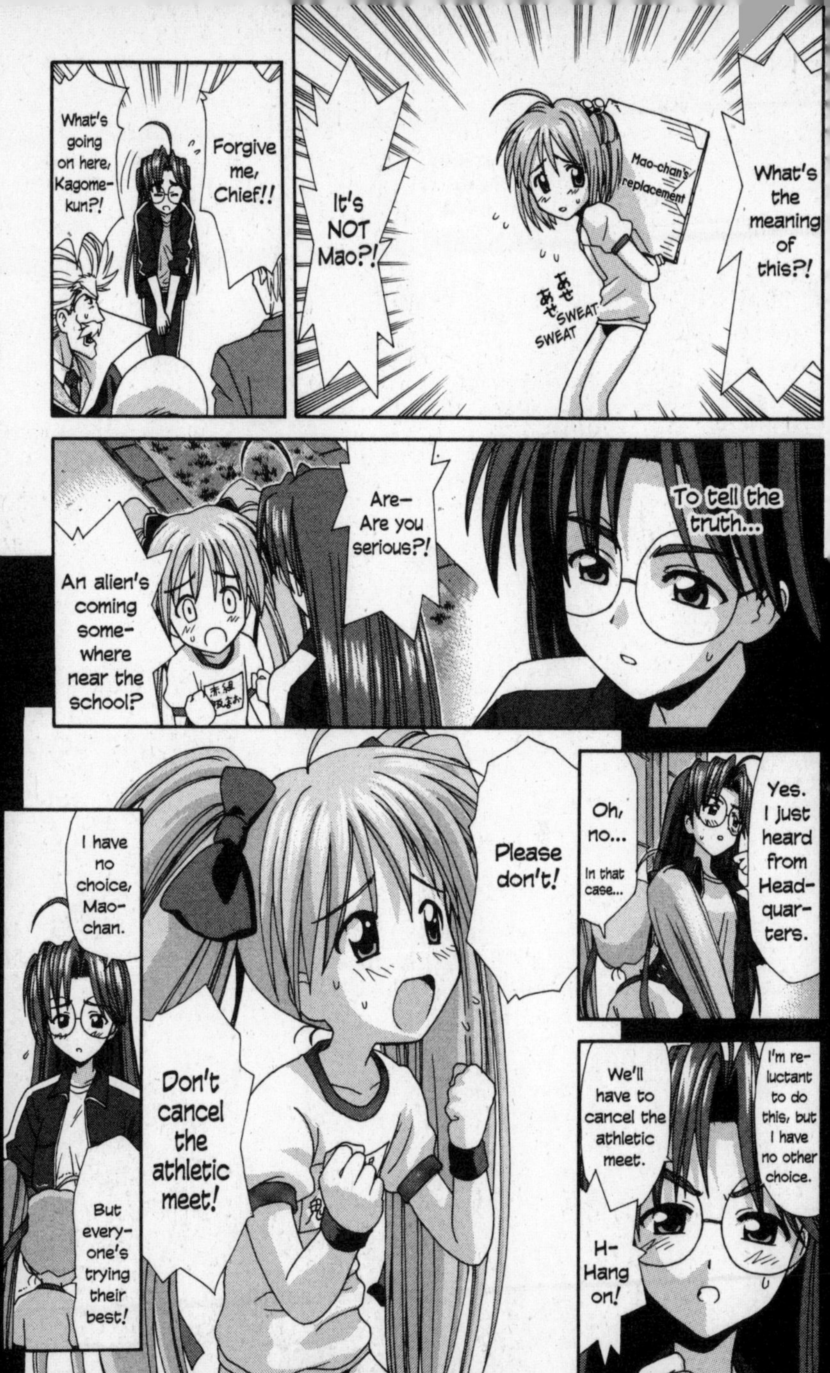
What's the meaning of this?!
It's NOT Mao?!
Mao-chan's replacement
あせ あせ
SWEAT SWEAT
Forgive me, Chief!!
What's going on here, Kagome-kun?!
To tell the truth...
Are— Are you serious?!
An alien's coming some-where near the school?
Yes. I just heard from Head-quar-ters.
Oh, no...
In that case...
I'm re-luctant to do this, but I have no other choice.
We'll have to cancel the athletic meet.
H-Hang on!
Please don't!
Don't cancel the athletic meet!
I have no choice, Mao-chan.
But every-one's trying their best!

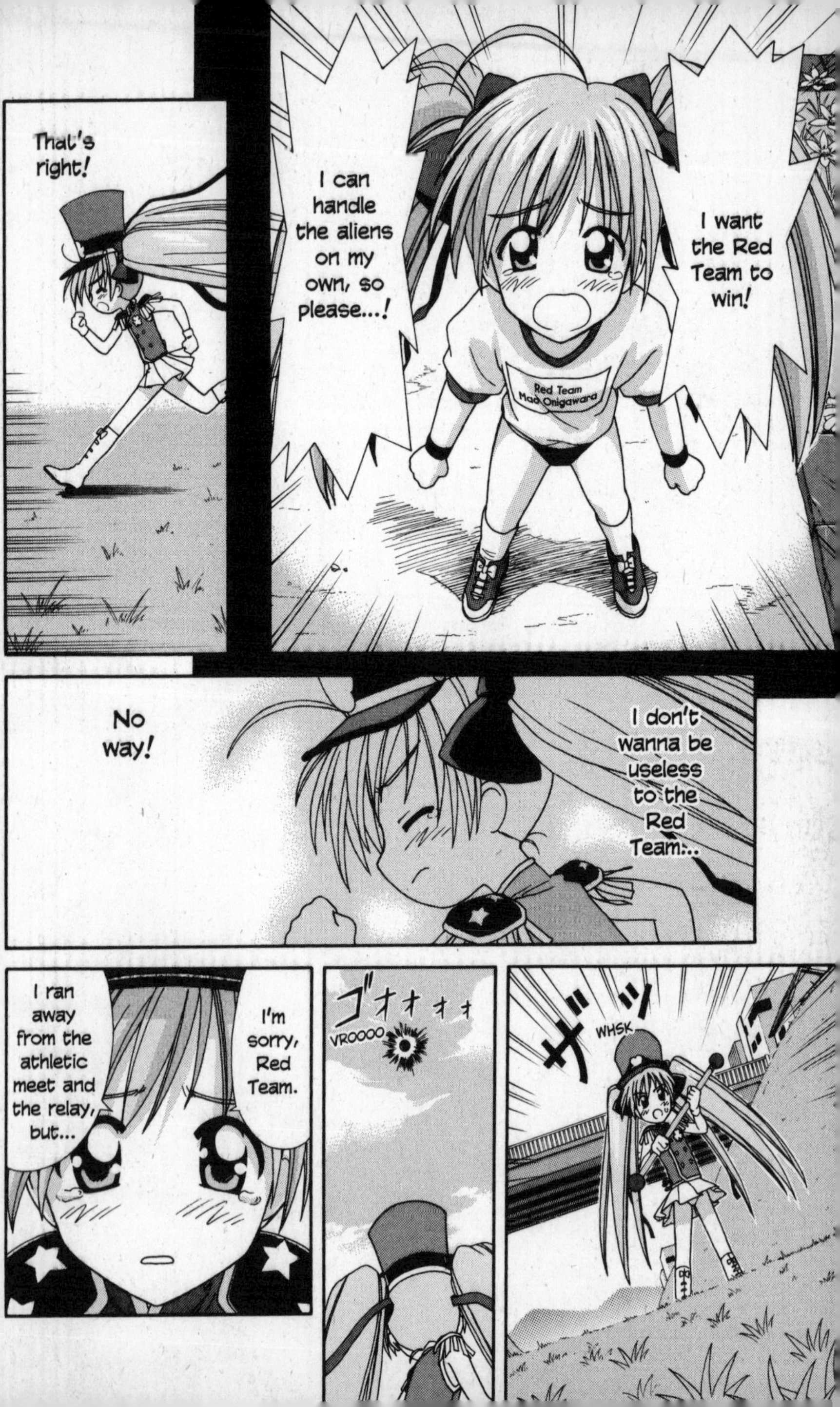
I want the Red Team to win!
I can handle the aliens on my own, so please...!
Red Team Mao Onigawara
That's right!
I don't wanna be useless to the Red Team...
No way!
ガッ
WHSK
ゴオオオオ
VROOOO
I'm sorry, Red Team.
I ran away from the athletic meet and the relay, but...

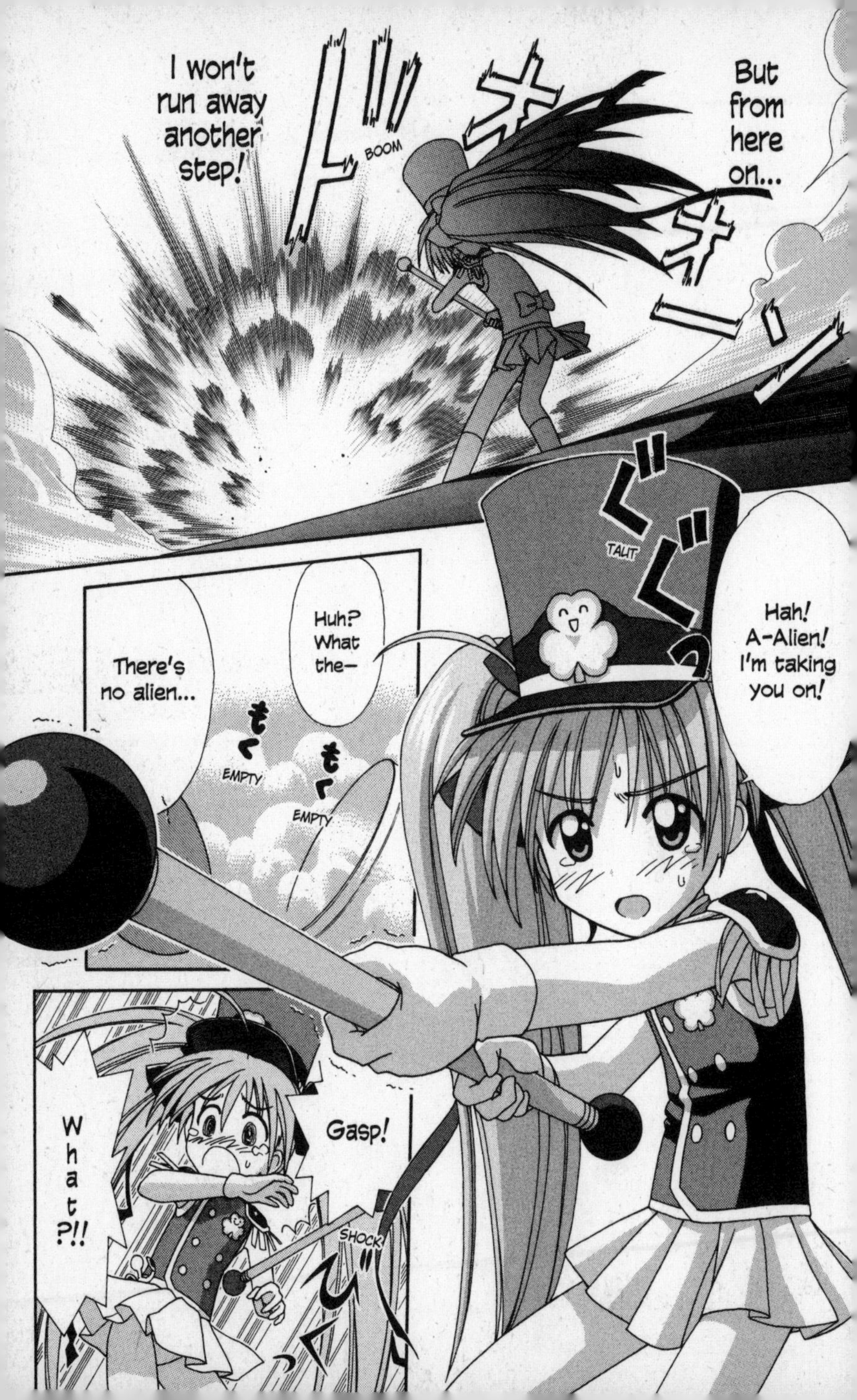
But from here on...
BOOM
I won't run away another step!
TAUT
Hah! A-Alien! I'm taking you on!
Huh? What the—
EMPTY
EMPTY
There's no alien...
Gasp!
What?!!
SHOCK

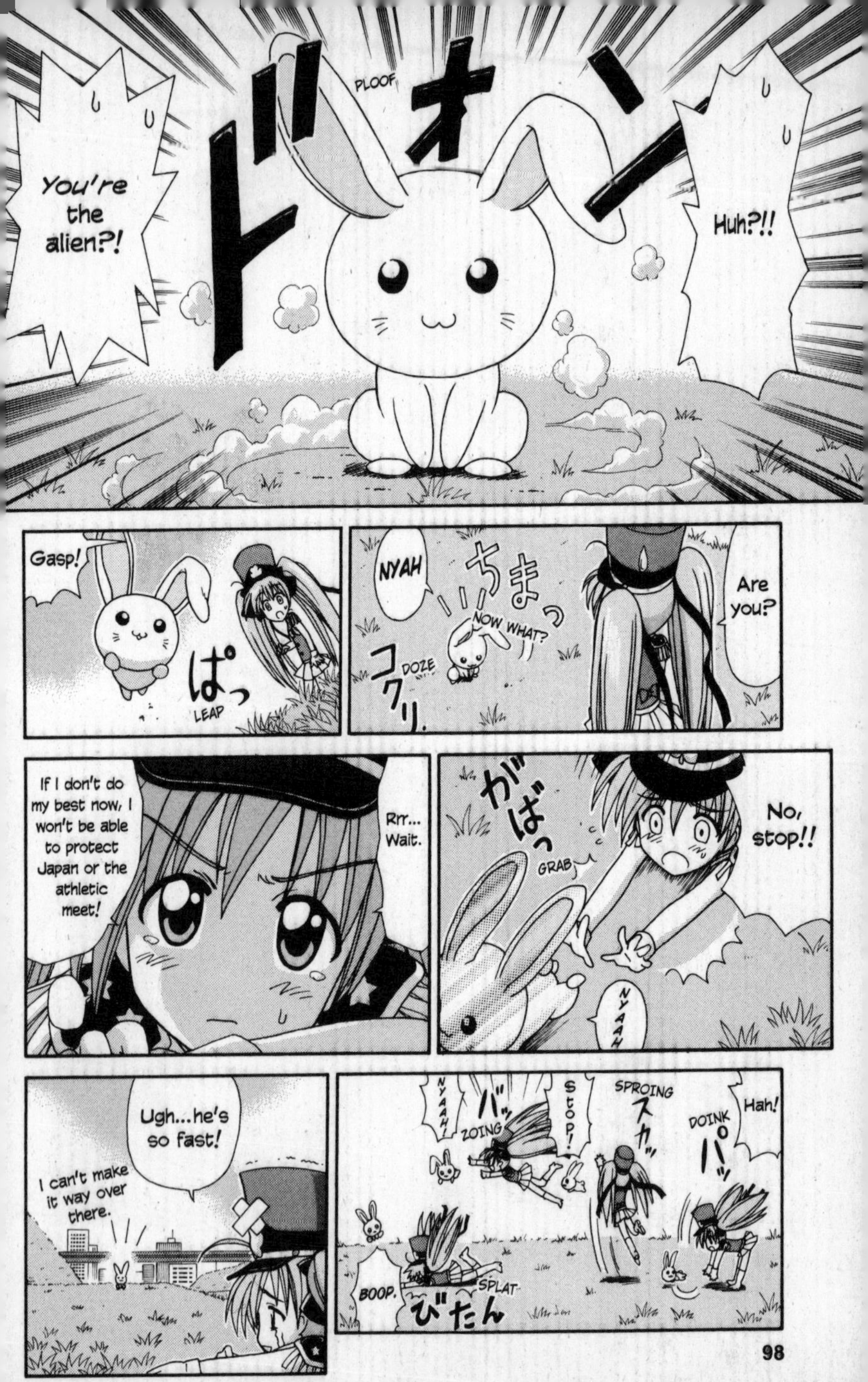
Huh?!!
ドオン
PLOOF
You're the alien?!
Are you?
NYAH
ちまっ
NOW WHAT?
コクリ
DOZE
ぱっ
LEAP
Gasp!
No, stop!!
がばっ
GRAB
NYAAH
Rrr... Wait.
If I don't do my best now, I won't be able to protect Japan or the athletic meet!
Hah!
パッ
DOINK
スカッ
SPROING
STOP!
バッ
ZOING
NYAAH!
びたん
SPLAT
BOOP.
Ugh...he's so fast!
I can't make it way over there.

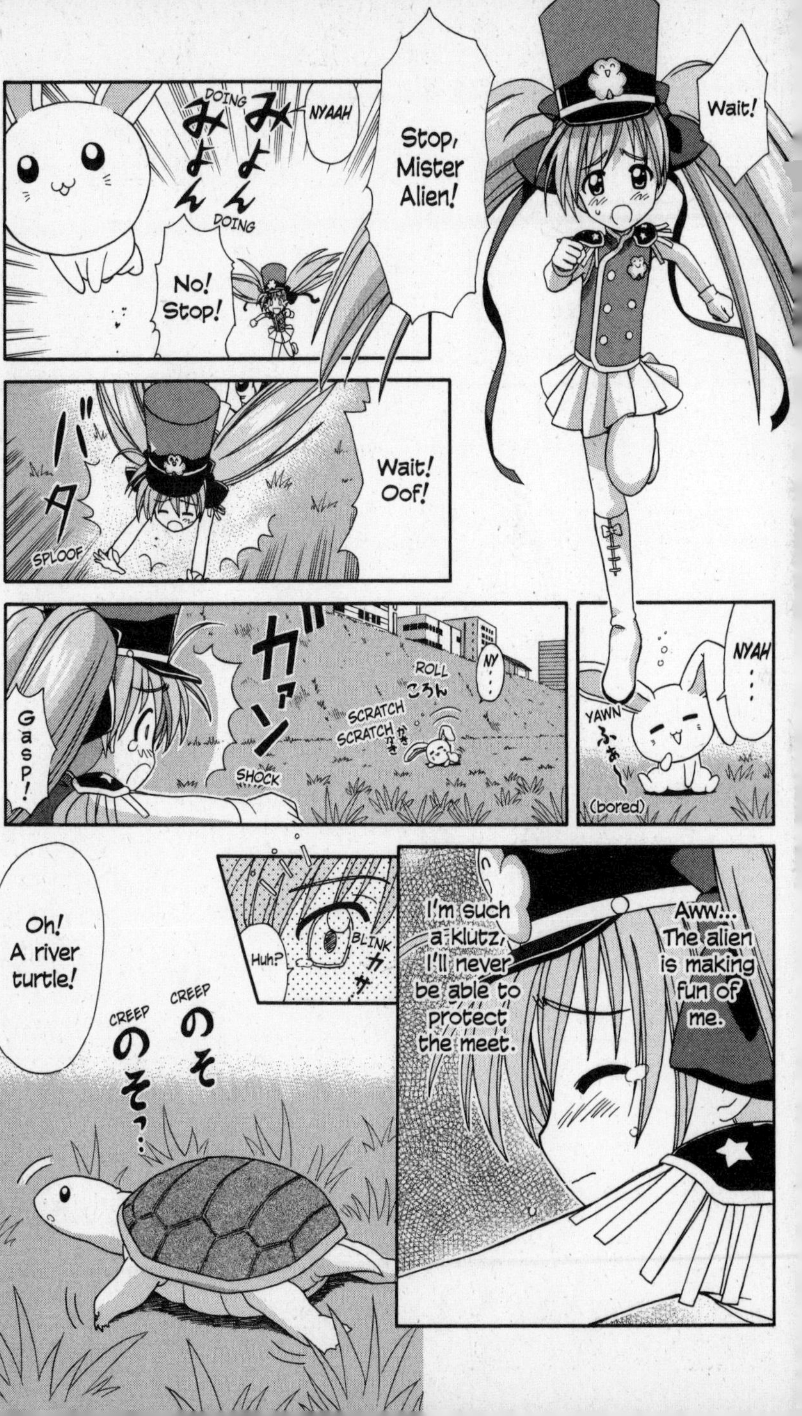
Wait!
Stop, Mister Alien!
NYAAH
DOING
みょん
みょん
DOING
No! Stop!
Wait! Oof!
バタ
SPLOOF
NYAH...
YAWN
ふぁ~
(bored)
NY...
ROLL
ころん
SCRATCH SCRATCH
かきかき
ガァン
SHOCK
Gasp!
Aww... The alien is making fun of me.
I'm such a klutz, I'll never be able to protect the meet.
BLINK
Huh?
Oh! A river turtle!
CREEP
のそ
CREEP
のそっ...

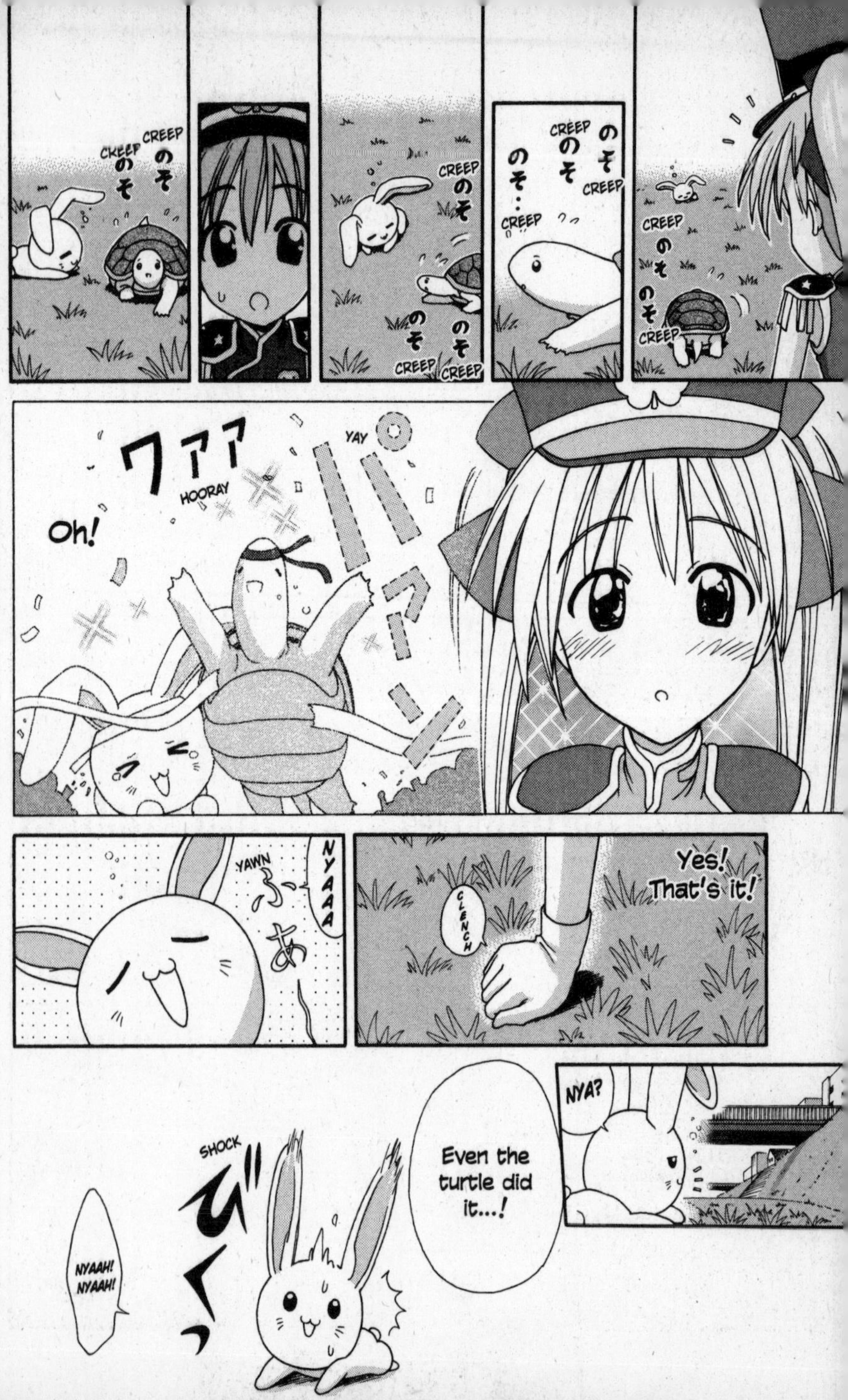
CREEP
のそ
のそ
CREEP
CREEP
のそ
CREEP
のそ
CREEP
のそ…
CREEP
CREEP
のそ
のそ
CREEP
のそ
CREEP
CREEP
のそ
CKEEP
のそ
YAY
パアーン
ワアア
HOORAY
Oh!
Yes! That's it!
CLENCH
NYAAA
YAWN
ふぁ
NYA?
Even the turtle did it...!
SHOCK
NYAAH! NYAAH!

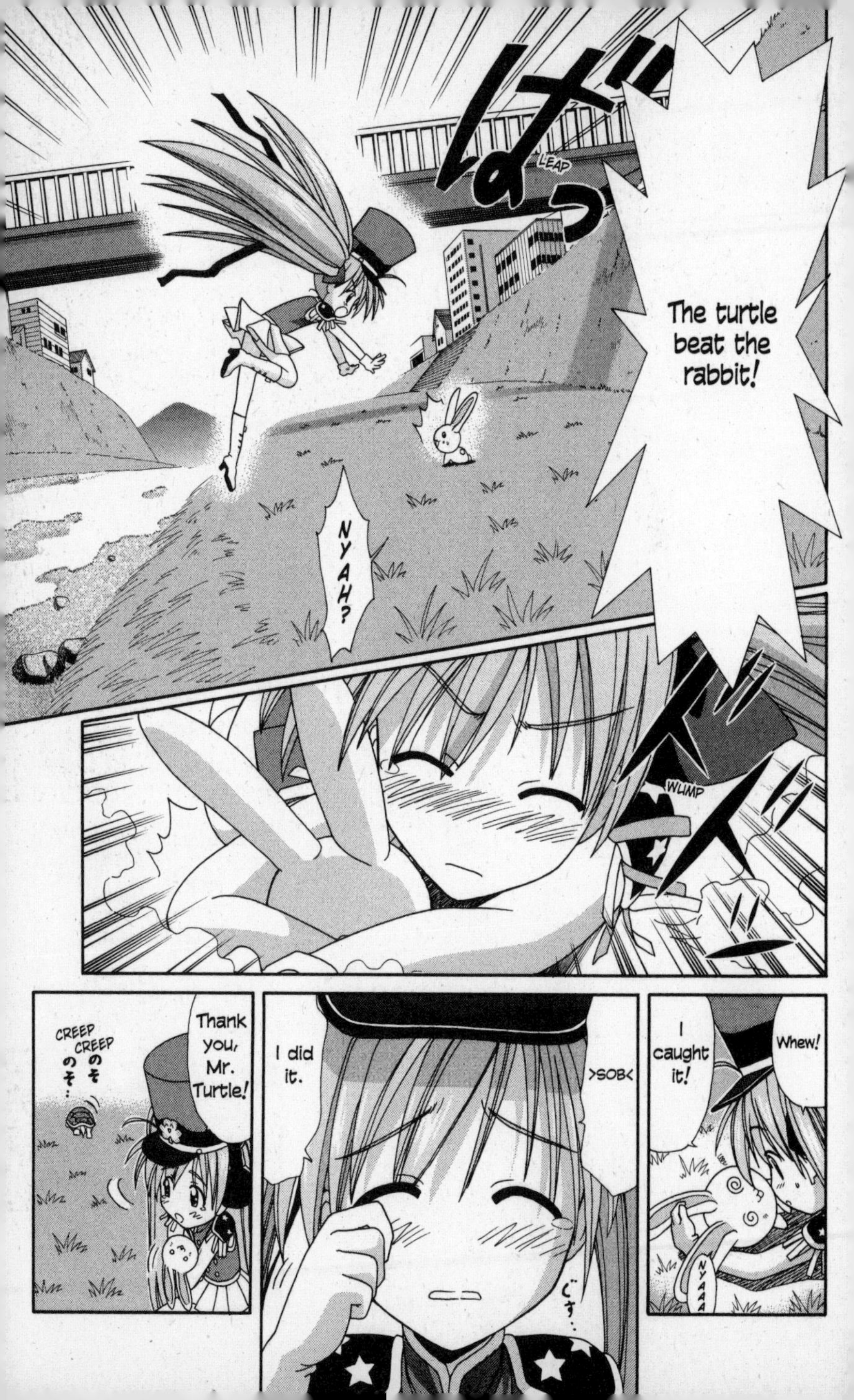
The turtle beat the rabbit!
LEAP
NYAH?
WUMP
Whew!
I caught it!
NYAAA
>SOB<
I did it.
Thank you, Mr. Turtle!
CREEP CREEP

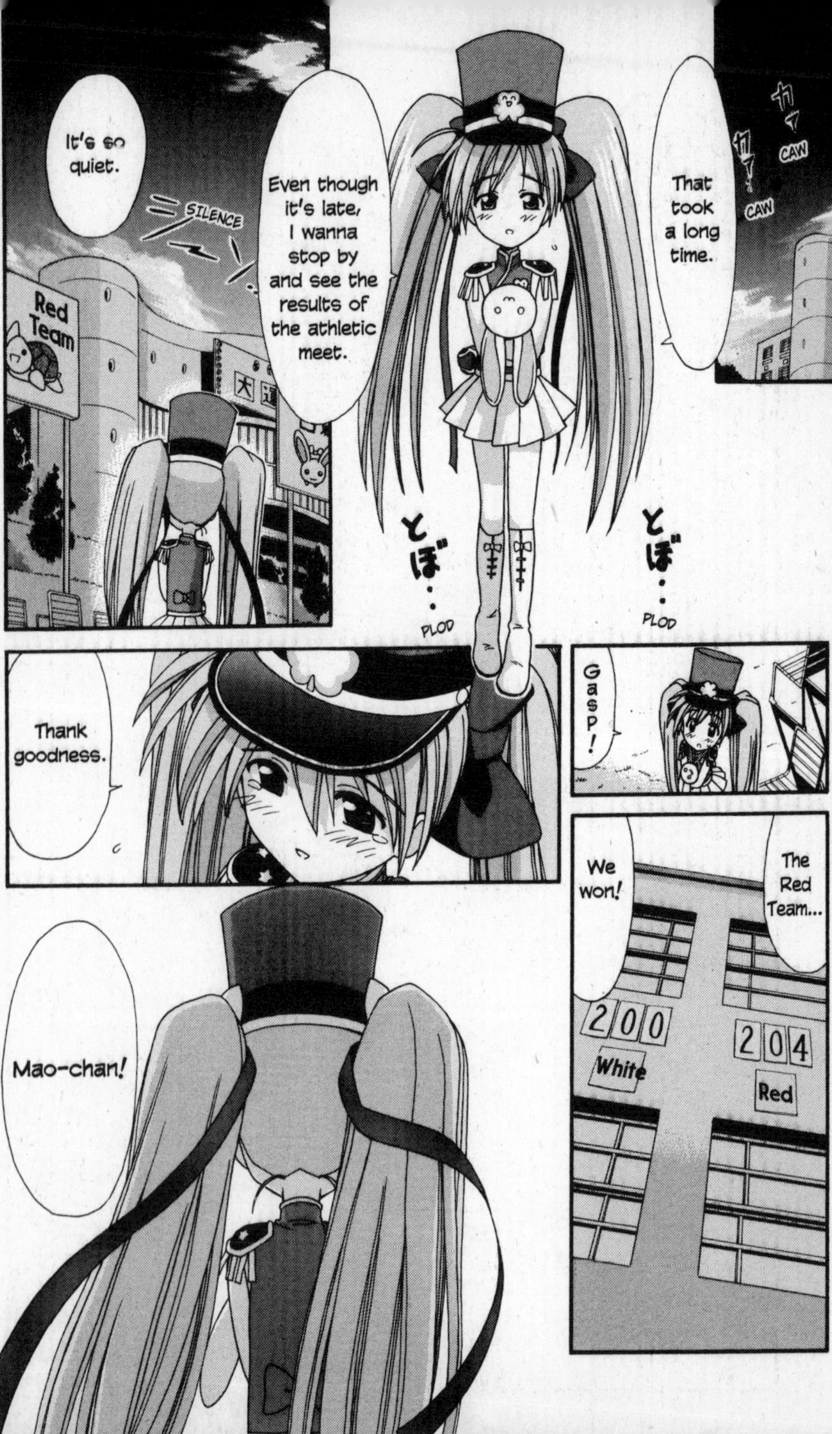
カァ
CAW
カァ
CAW
That took a long time.
Even though it's late, I wanna stop by and see the results of the athletic meet.
とぼ・・
PLOD
とぼ・・
PLOD
It's so quiet.
SILENCE
Red Team
Gasp!
The Red Team...
We won!
200
White
204
Red
Thank goodness.
Mao-chan!

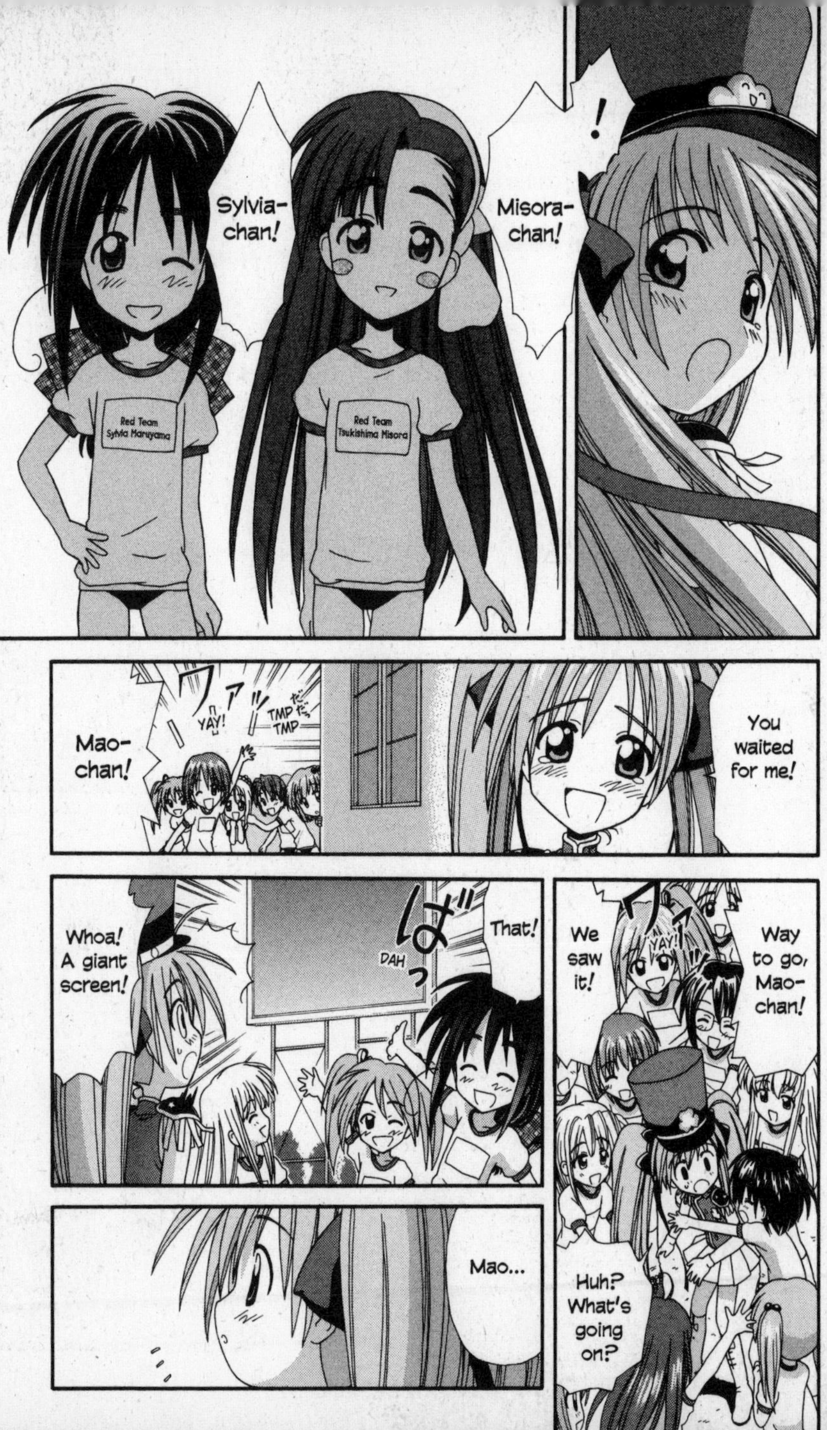
!
Misora-chan!
Red Team Tsukishima Misora
Sylvia-chan!
Red Team Sylvia Maruyama
You waited for me!
TMP TMP
YAY!
Mao-chan!
Way to go, Mao-chan!
YAY!
We saw it!
Huh? What's going on?
That!
DAH
Whoa! A giant screen!
Mao...

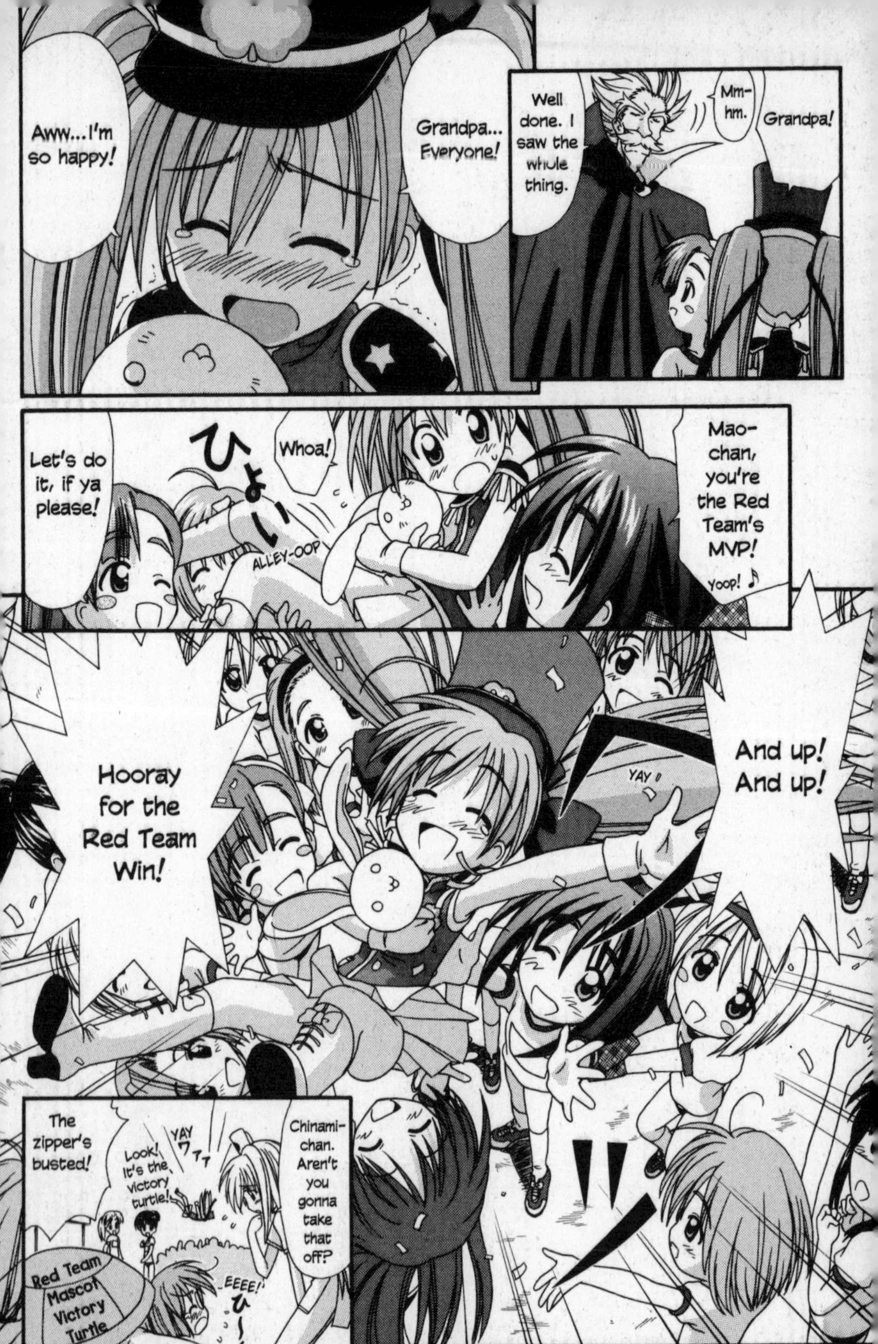
Grandpa!
Mm-hm.
Well done. I saw the whole thing.
Grandpa... Everyone!
Aww...I'm so happy!
Mao-chan, you're the Red Team's MVP!
Yoop! ♪
Whoa!
ひょい
ALLEY-OOP
Let's do it, if ya please!
And up! And up!
YAY
Hooray for the Red Team Win!
!!
Chinami-chan. Aren't you gonna take that off?
YAY ワァァ
Look! It's the victory turtle!
The zipper's busted!
EEEE! ひ〜ん
Red Team Mascot Victory Turtle

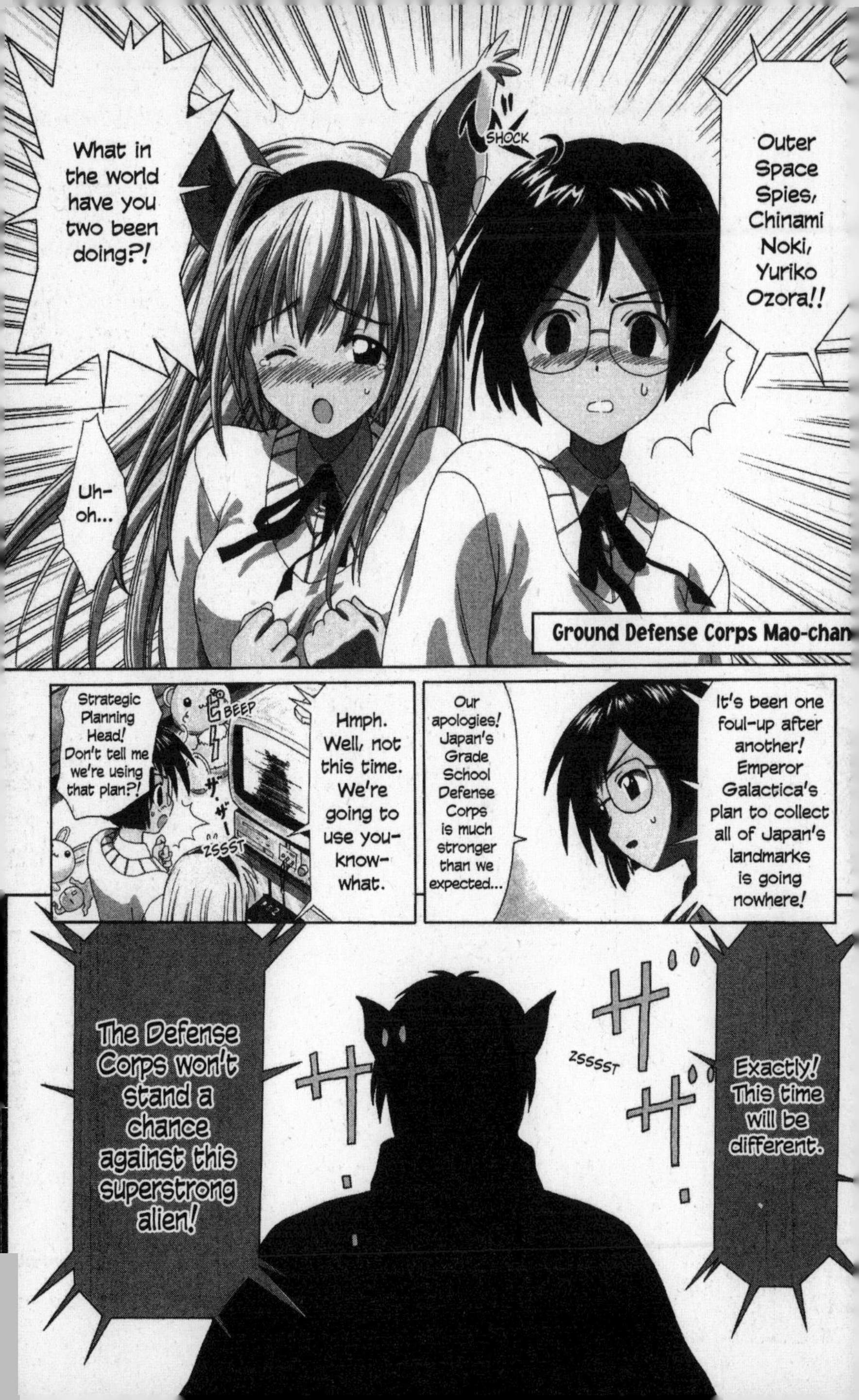
Outer Space Spies, Chinami Noki, Yuriko Ozora!!
SHOCK
What in the world have you two been doing?!
Uh-oh...
Ground Defense Corps Mao-chan
It's been one foul-up after another! Emperor Galactica's plan to collect all of Japan's landmarks is going nowhere!
Our apologies! Japan's Grade School Defense Corps is much stronger than we expected...
Hmph. Well, not this time. We're going to use you-know-what.
Strategic Planning Head! Don't tell me we're using that plan?!
BEEP
ZSSST
Exactly! This time will be different.
ZSSSST
The Defense Corps won't stand a chance against this superstrong alien!

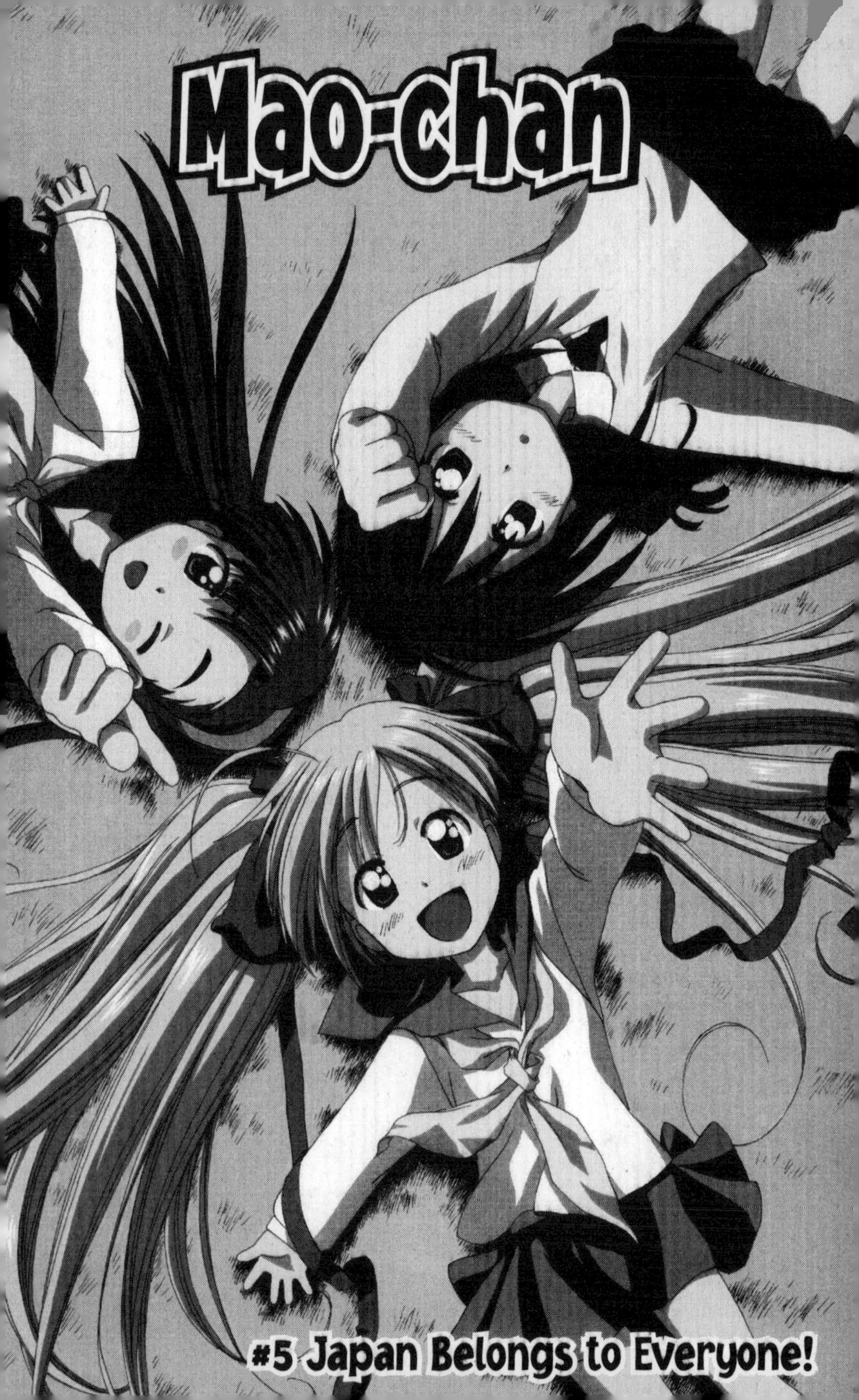
Mao-chan
#5 Japan Belongs to Everyone!

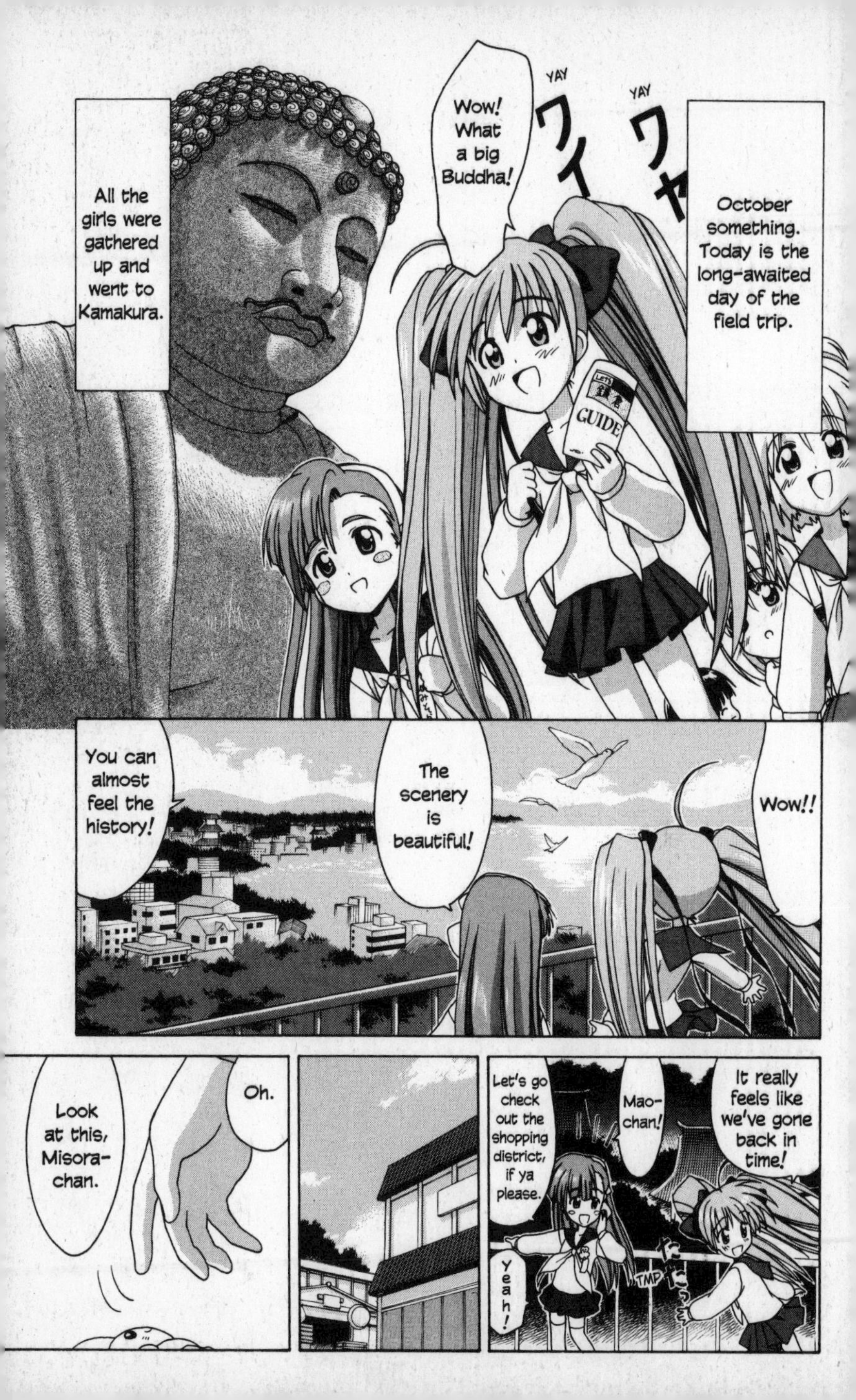
October something. Today is the long-awaited day of the field trip.
YAY
YAY
Wow! What a big Buddha!
All the girls were gathered up and went to Kamakura.
GUIDE
Wow!!
The scenery is beautiful!
You can almost feel the history!
It really feels like we've gone back in time!
Mao-chan!
Let's go check out the shopping district, if ya please.
Yeah!
TMP
Oh.
Look at this, Misora-chan.

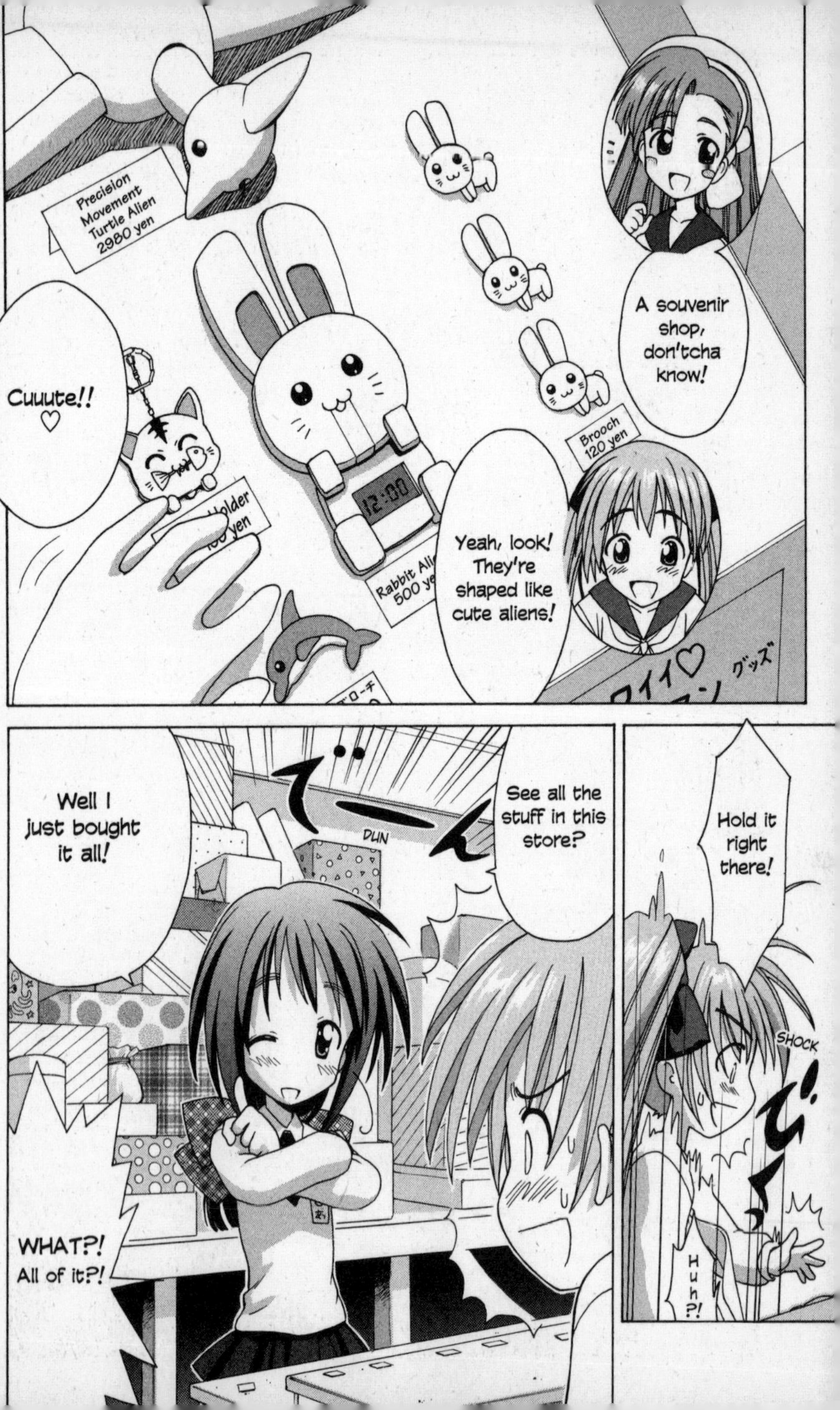
A souvenir shop, don'tcha know!
Brooch 120 yen
グッズ
Yeah, look! They're shaped like cute aliens!
Precision Movement Turtle Alien 2980 yen
Cuuute!! ♡
Hold it right there!
SHOCK
Huh?!
See all the stuff in this store?
DUN
Well I just bought it all!
WHAT?! All of it?!

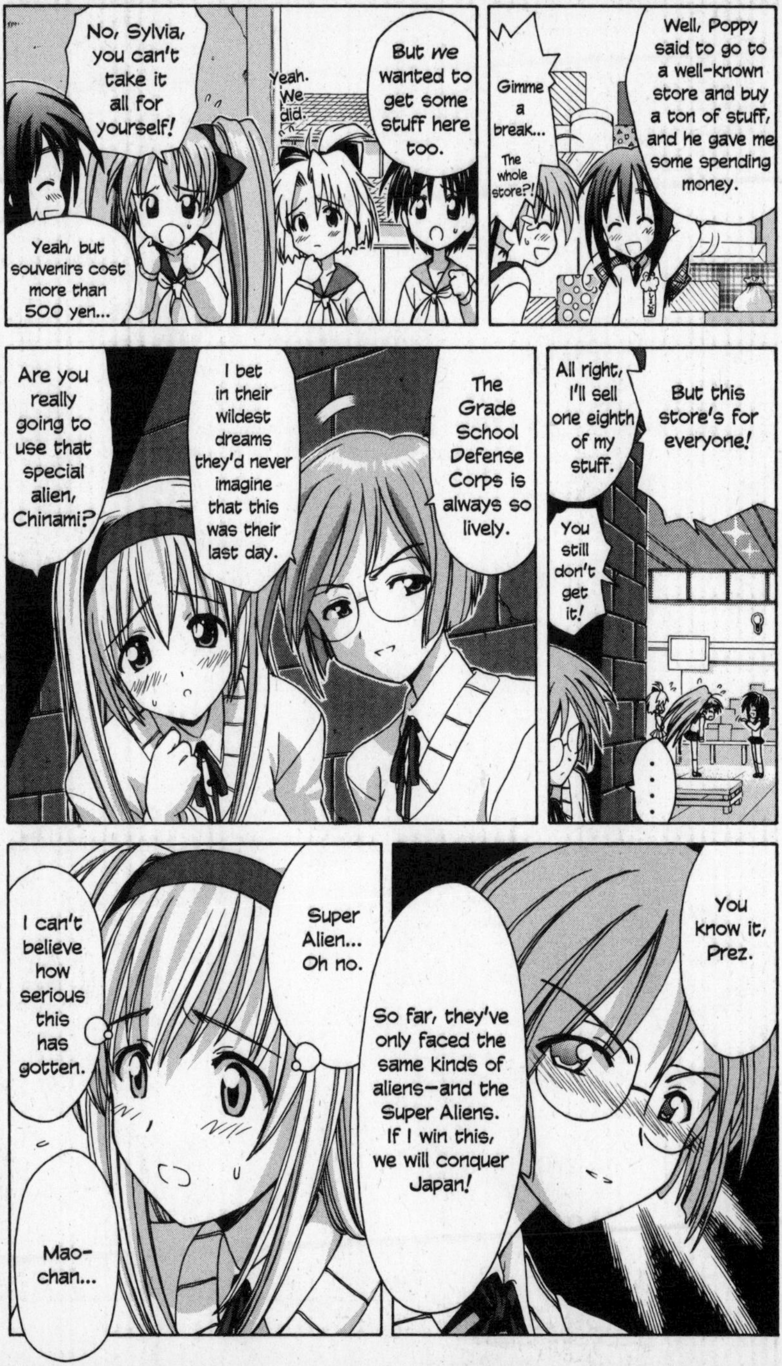

Well, Poppy said to go to a well-known store and buy a ton of stuff, and he gave me some spending money.
Gimme a break...
The whole store?!
But we wanted to get some stuff here too.
Yeah. We did.
No, Sylvia, you can't take it all for yourself!
Yeah, but souvenirs cost more than 500 yen...
But this store's for everyone!
All right, I'll sell one eighth of my stuff.
You still don't get it!
...
The Grade School Defense Corps is always so lively.
I bet in their wildest dreams they'd never imagine that this was their last day.
Are you really going to use that special alien, Chinami?
You know it, Prez.
So far, they've only faced the same kinds of aliens—and the Super Aliens. If I win this, we will conquer Japan!
Super Alien... Oh no.
I can't believe how serious this has gotten.
Mao-chan...

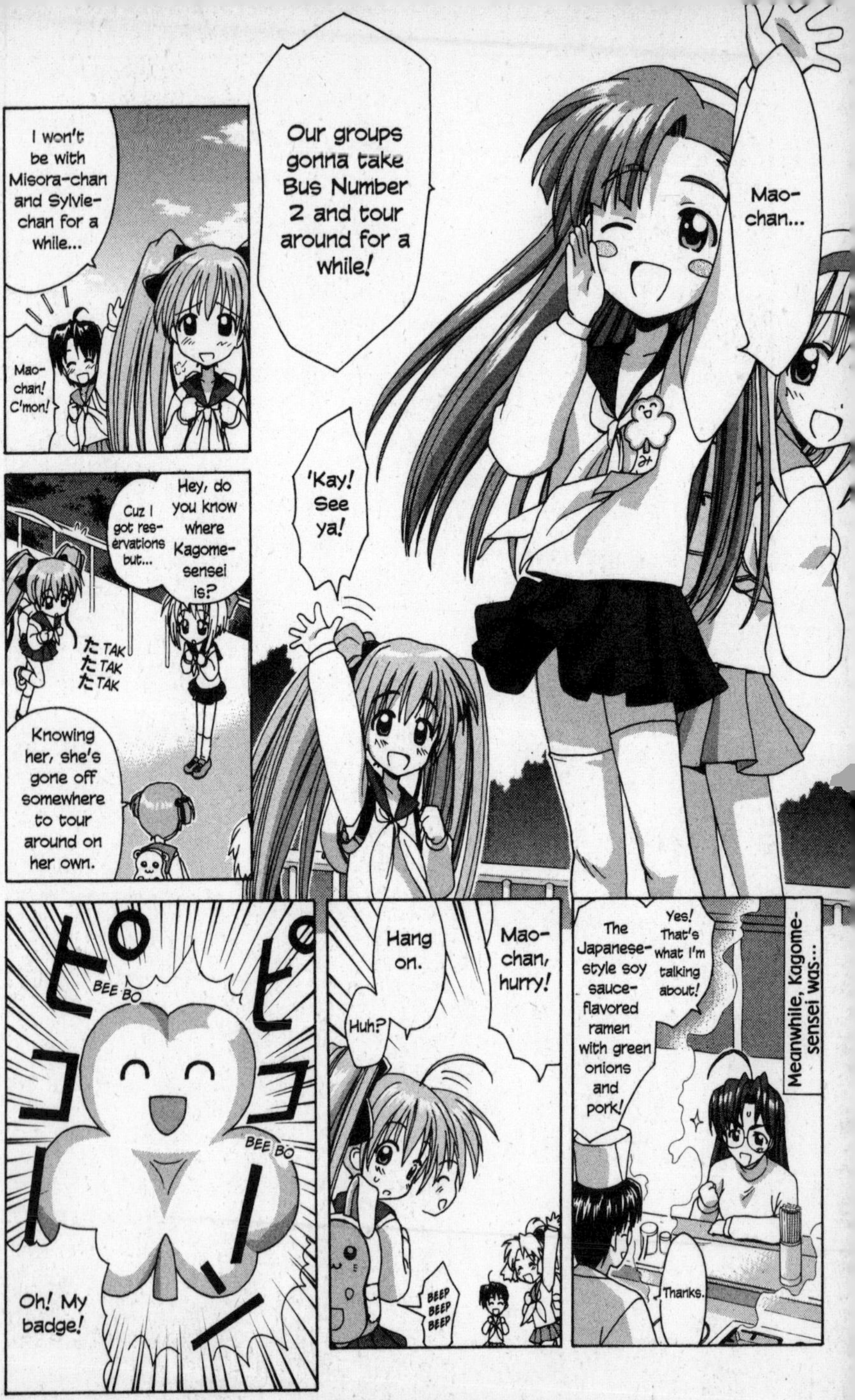
Mao-chan...
Our groups gonna take Bus Number 2 and tour around for a while!
'Kay! See ya!
I won't be with Misora-chan and Sylvie-chan for a while...
Mao-chan! C'mon!
Hey, do you know where Kagome-sensei is?
Cuz I got reservations but...
たTAK たTAK たTAK
Knowing her, she's gone off somewhere to tour around on her own.
Meanwhile, Kagome-sensei was...
Yes! That's what I'm talking about!
The Japanese-style soy sauce-flavored ramen with green onions and pork!
Thanks.
Mao-chan, hurry!
Hang on.
Huh?
BEEP BEEP BEEP
BEE BO
BEE BO
Oh! My badge!

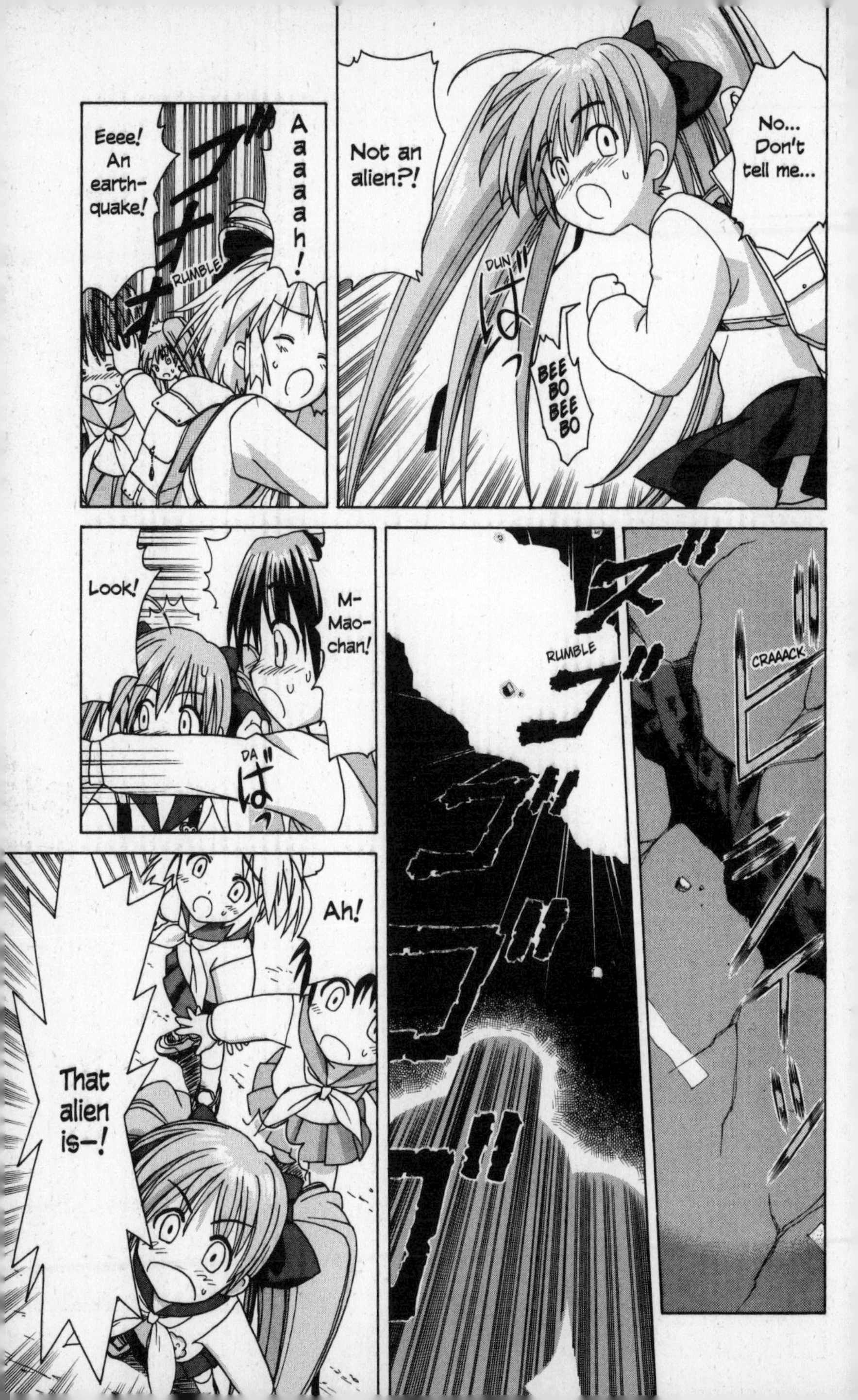
No... Don't tell me...
Not an alien?!
DUN
BEE BO BEE BO
Aaaaah!
Eeee! An earthquake!
RUMBLE
CRAAACK
RUMBLE
M-Mao-chan!
Look!
DA
Ah!
That alien is—!

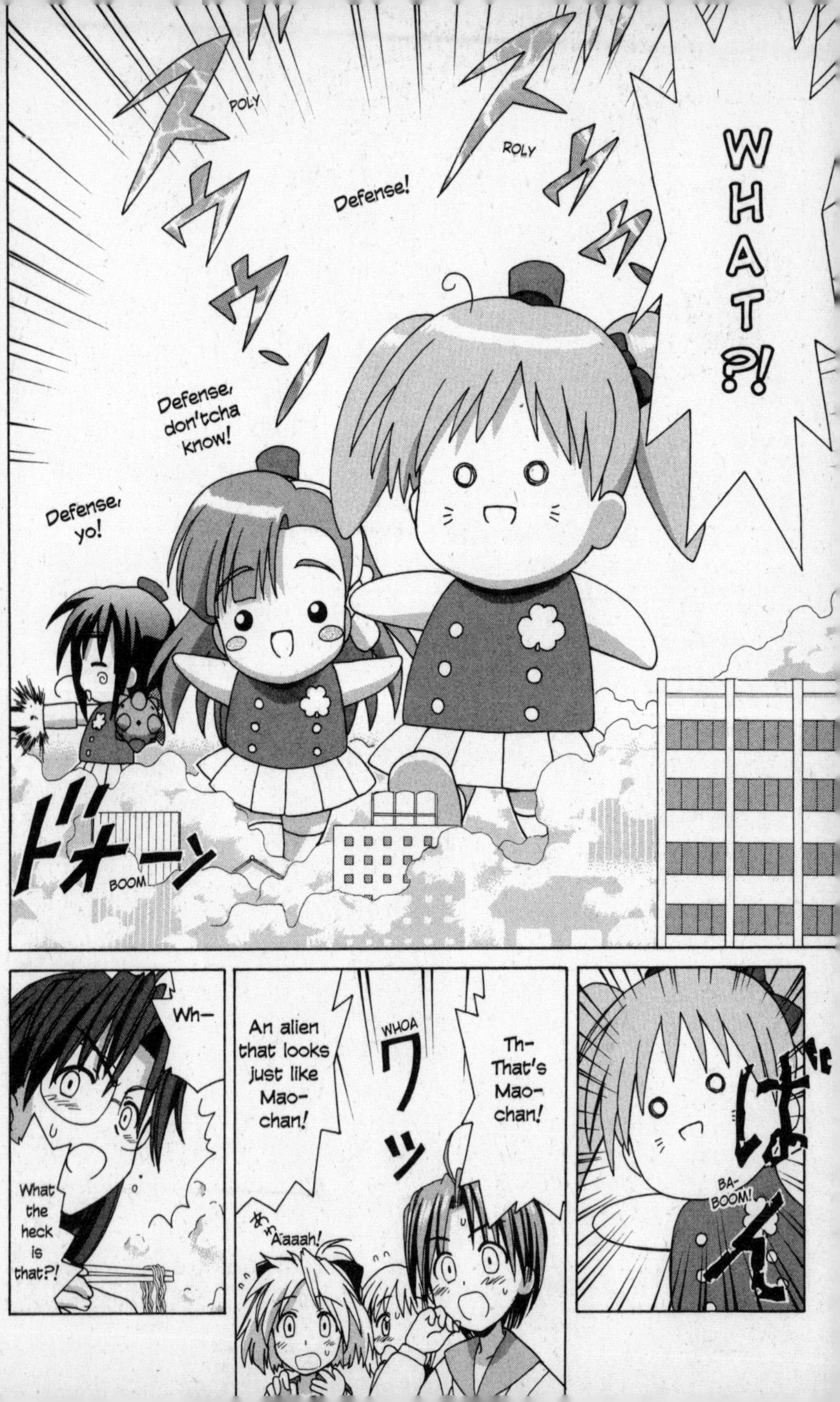
WHAT?!
ROLY
Defense!
POLY
Defense, don'tcha know!
Defense, yo!
BOOM
BA-BOOM!
Th- That's Mao-chan!
WHOA
An alien that looks just like Mao-chan!
Aaaah!
Wh-
What the heck is that?!

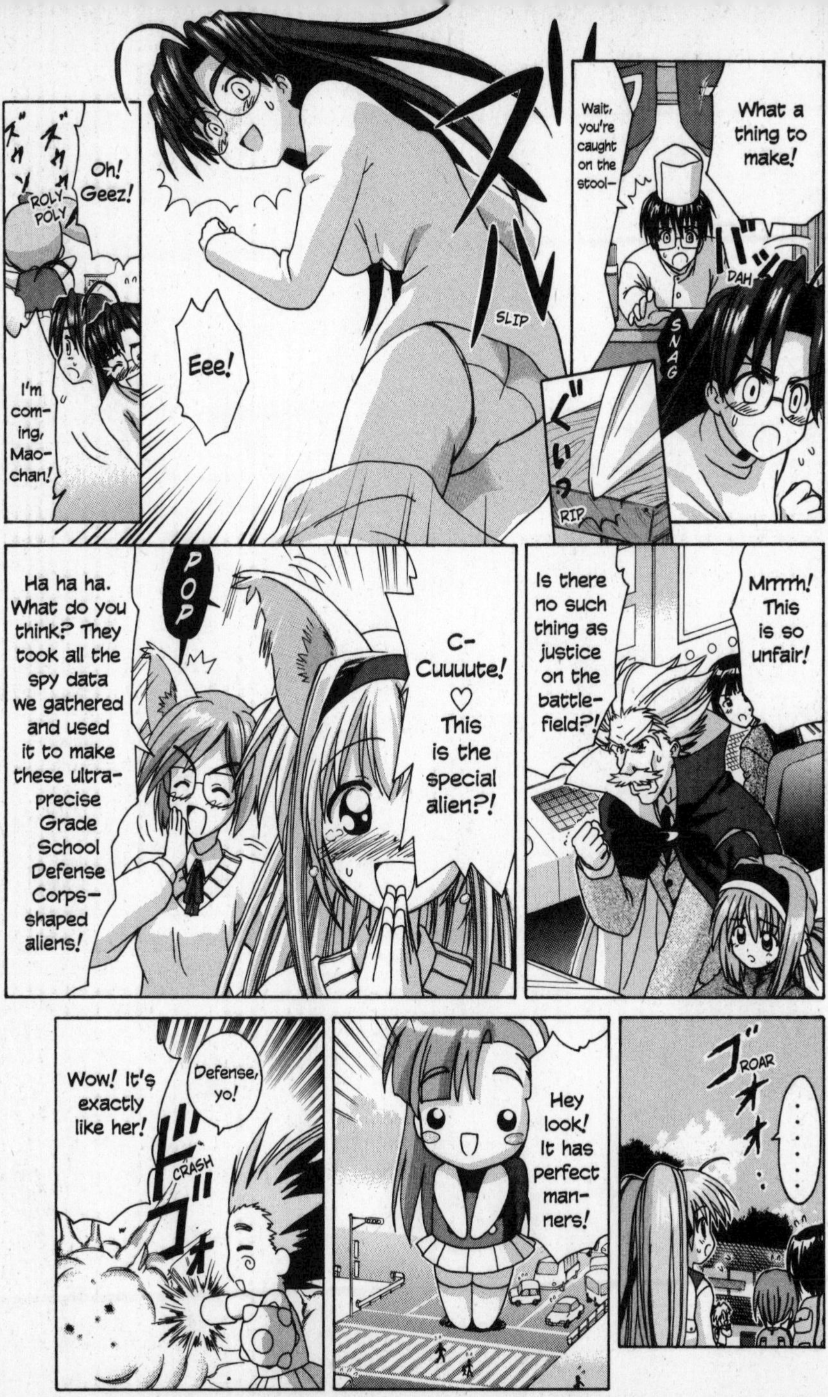
What a thing to make!
Wait, you're caught on the stool—
DAH
SNAG
RIP
SLIP
Eee!
Oh! Geez!
ROLY POLY
I'm com-ing, Mao-chan!
Mrrrh! This is so unfair!
Is there no such thing as justice on the battle-field?!
C-Cuuuute! ♡ This is the special alien?!
POP
Ha ha ha. What do you think? They took all the spy data we gathered and used it to make these ultra-precise Grade School Defense Corps-shaped aliens!
ROAR
......
Hey look! It has perfect man-ners!
Defense, yo!
Wow! It's exactly like her!
CRASH

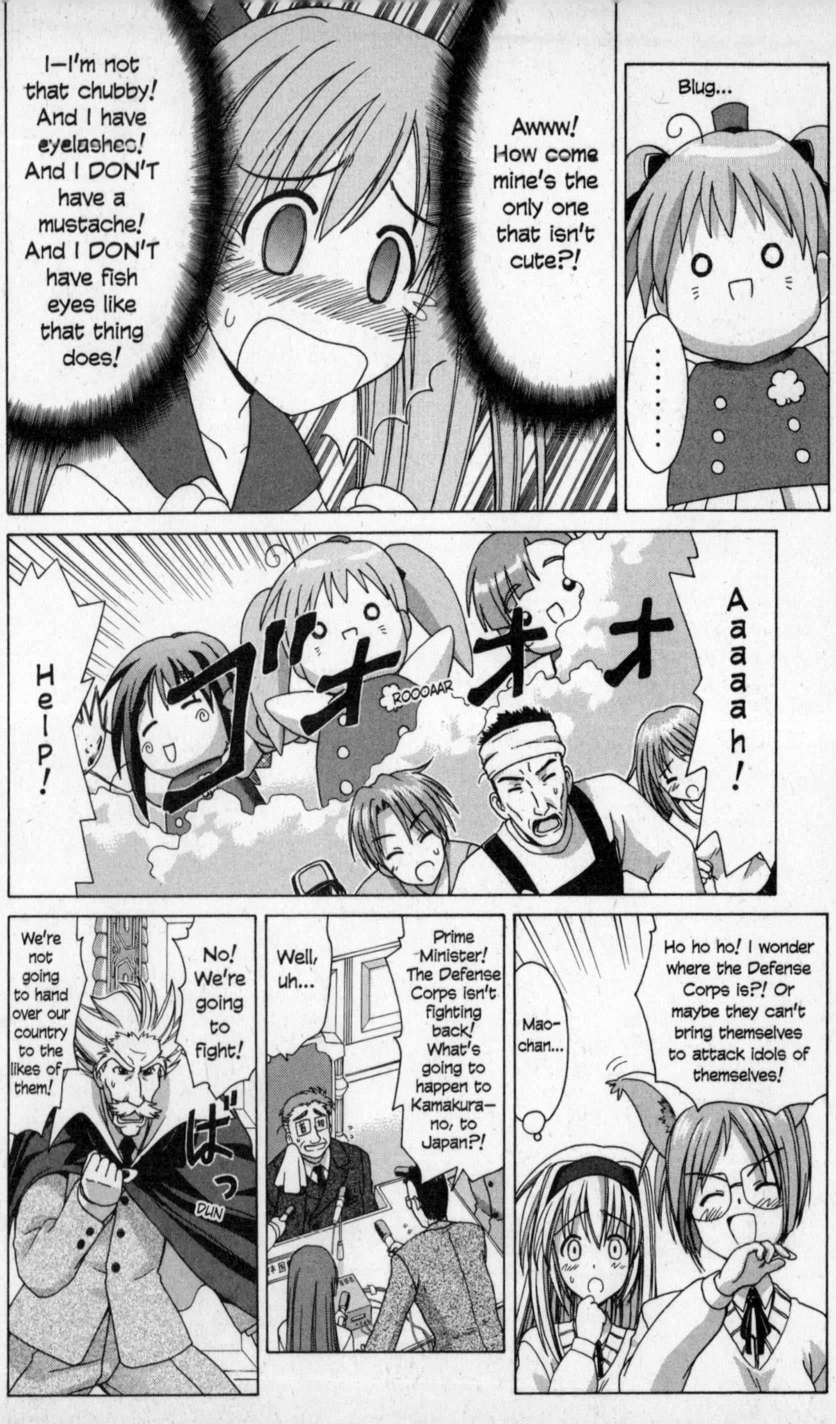

Blug...
......
Awww! How come mine's the only one that isn't cute?!
I—I'm not that chubby! And I have eyelashes! And I DON'T have a mustache! And I DON'T have fish eyes like that thing does!
Aaaaah!
ゴオオ
ROOOAAR
Help!
Ho ho ho! I wonder where the Defense Corps is?! Or maybe they can't bring themselves to attack idols of themselves!
Mao-chan...
Prime Minister! The Defense Corps isn't fighting back! What's going to happen to Kamakura-no, to Japan?!
Well, uh...
No! We're going to fight!
We're not going to hand over our country to the likes of them!
ばっ
DUN

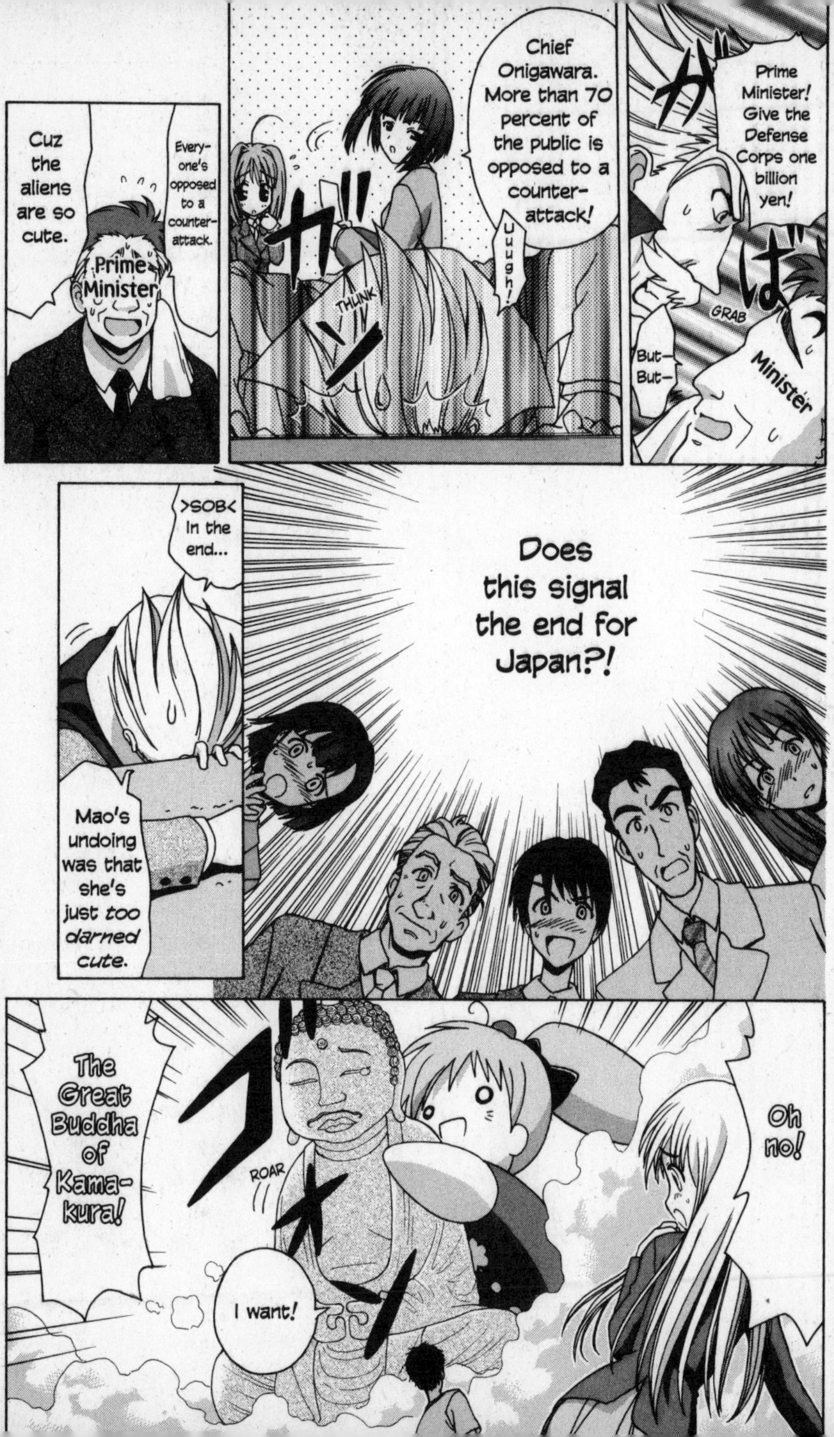

Prime Minister! Give the Defense Corps one billion yen!
GRAB
Minister
But— But—
Chief Onigawara. More than 70 percent of the public is opposed to a counter-attack!
Uuugh!
THUNK
Every-one's opposed to a counter-attack.
Cuz the aliens are so cute.
Prime Minister
Does this signal the end for Japan?!
>SOB< In the end...
Mao's undoing was that she's just *too darned* cute.
Oh no!
I want!
ROAR
The Great Buddha of Kama-kura!

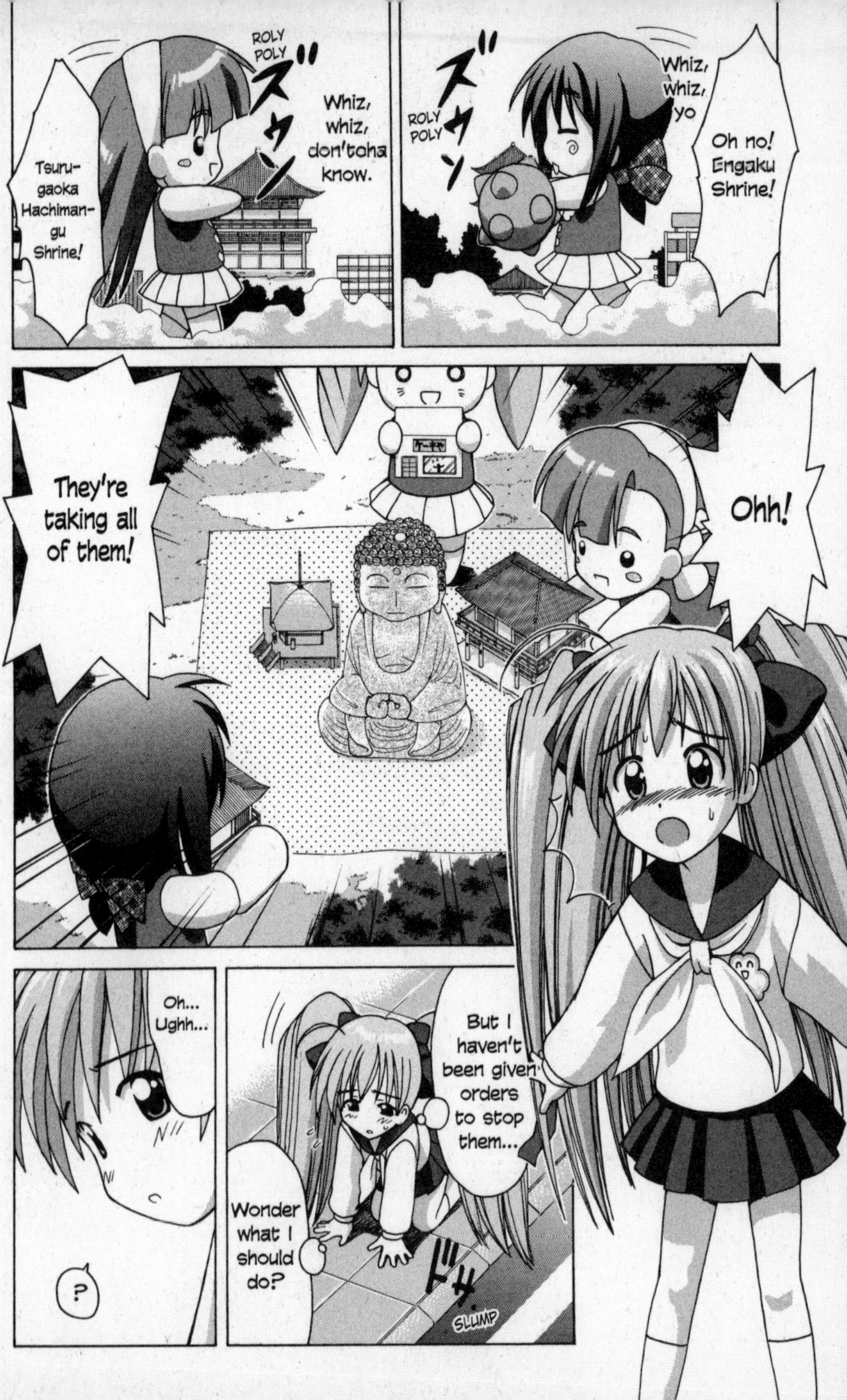

Whiz, whiz, yo
Oh no! Engaku Shrine!
ROLY POLY
ROLY POLY
Whiz, whiz, don'toha know.
Tsuru-gaoka Hachiman-gu Shrine!
Ohh!
They're taking all of them!
But I haven't been given orders to stop them...
Wonder what I should do?
SLUMP
Oh... Ughh...
?

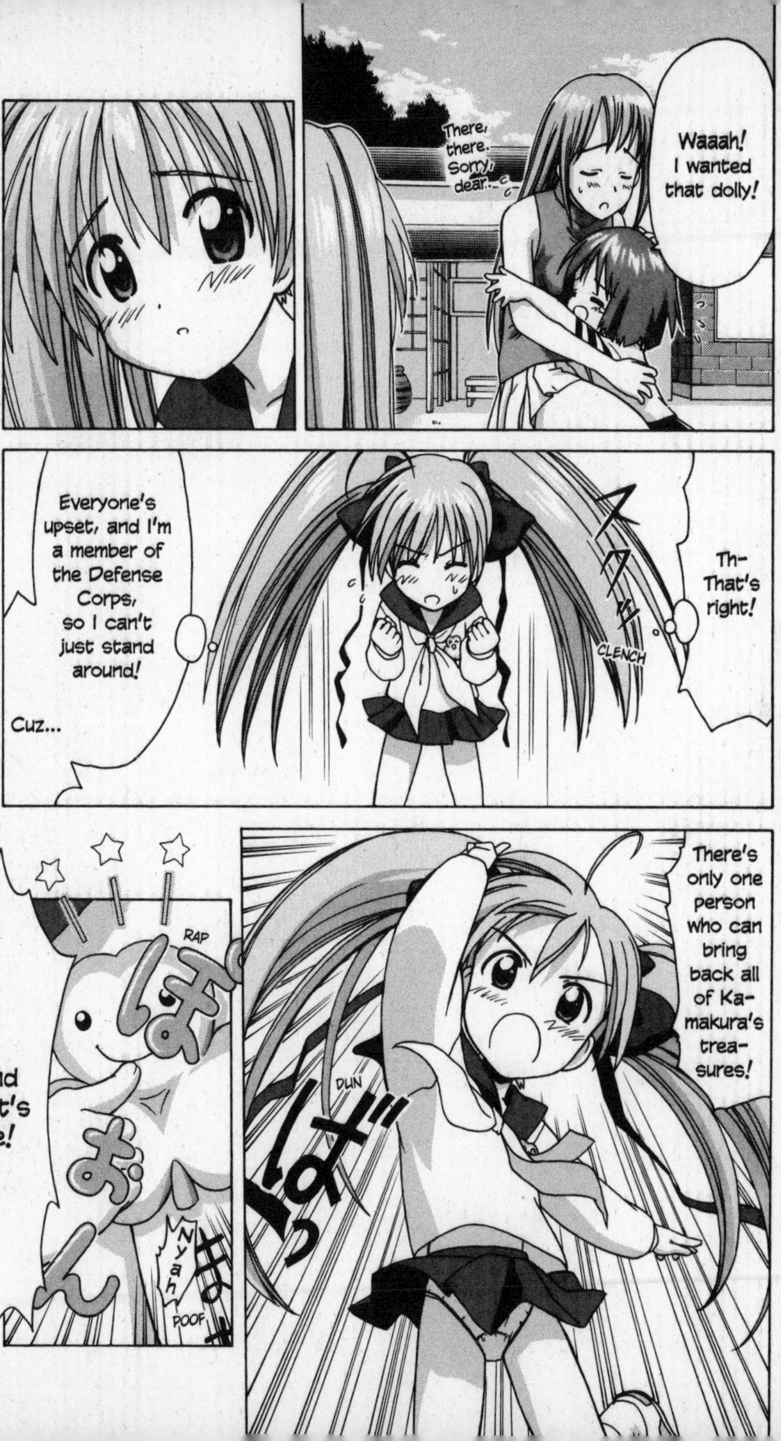
Waaah! I wanted that dolly!
There, there. Sorry, dear.
Th- That's right!
CLENCH
Everyone's upset, and I'm a member of the Defense Corps, so I can't just stand around!
Cuz...
There's only one person who can bring back all of Kamakura's treasures!
DUN
And that's me!
RAP
Nyah
POOF

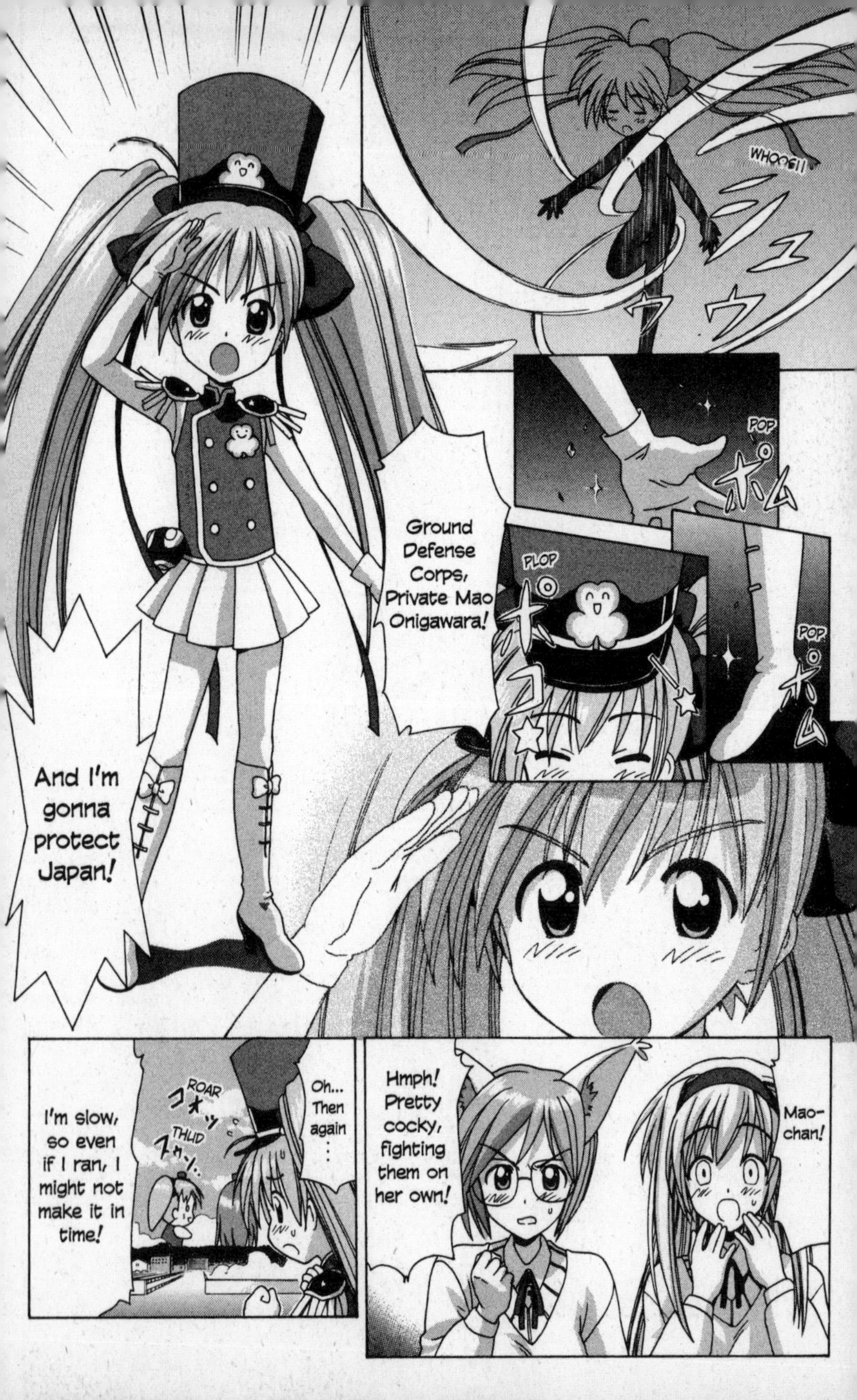
WHOOSH!!
POP
PLOP
POP
Ground Defense Corps, Private Mao Onigawara!
And I'm gonna protect Japan!
Mao-chan!
Hmph! Pretty cocky, fighting them on her own!
Oh... Then again...
ROAR
THUD
I'm slow, so even if I ran, I might not make it in time!

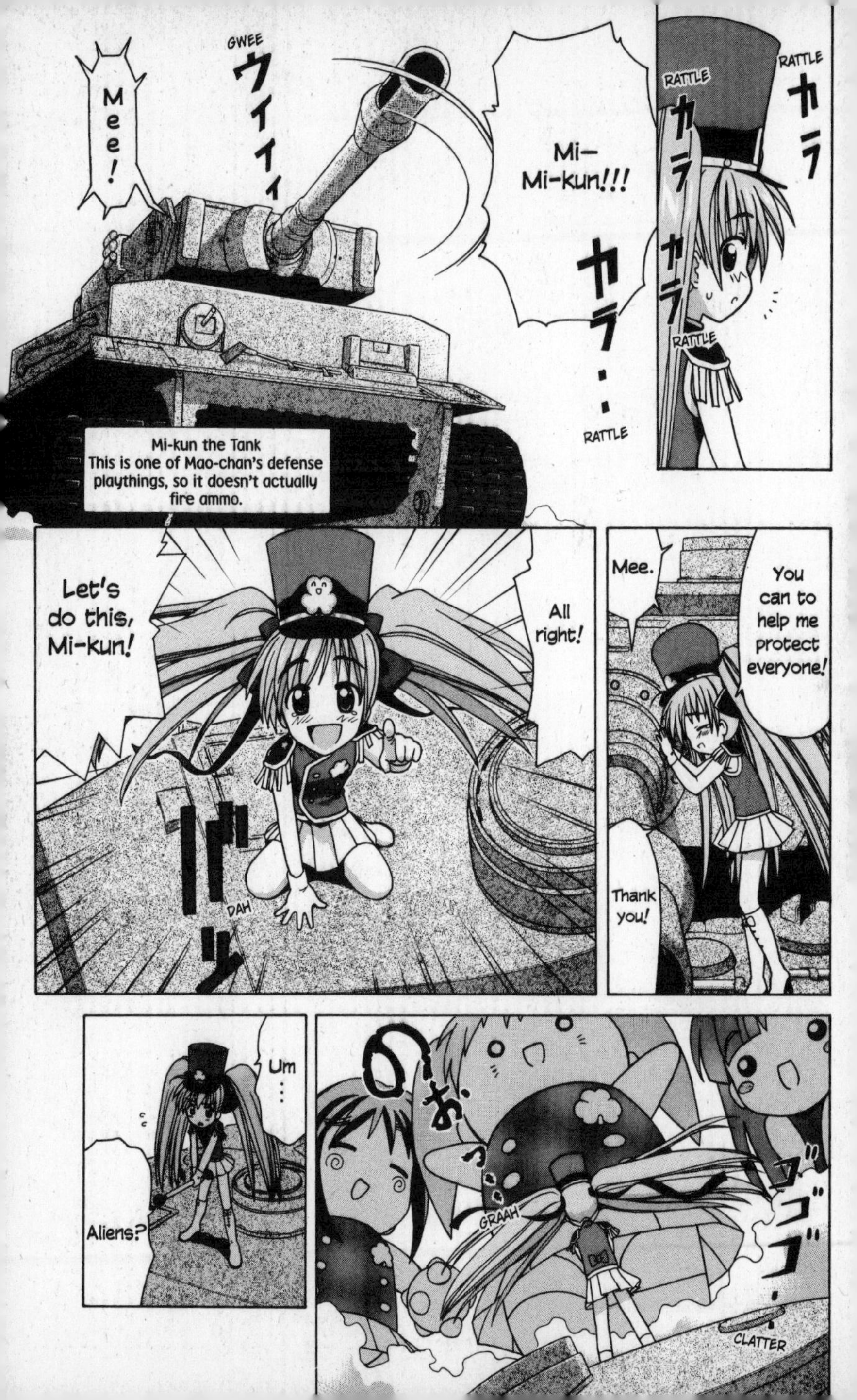

RATTLE
カラ
RATTLE
カラ
カラ
RATTLE
Mi–
Mi-kun!!!
カラ…
RATTLE
GWEE
ウィィィ
Mee!
Mi-kun the Tank
This is one of Mao-chan's defense playthings, so it doesn't actually fire ammo.
You can to help me protect everyone!
Mee.
Thank you!
All right!
Let's do this, Mi-kun!
ダッ
DAH
ゴゴゴ…
CLATTER
GRAAH
Um…
Aliens?

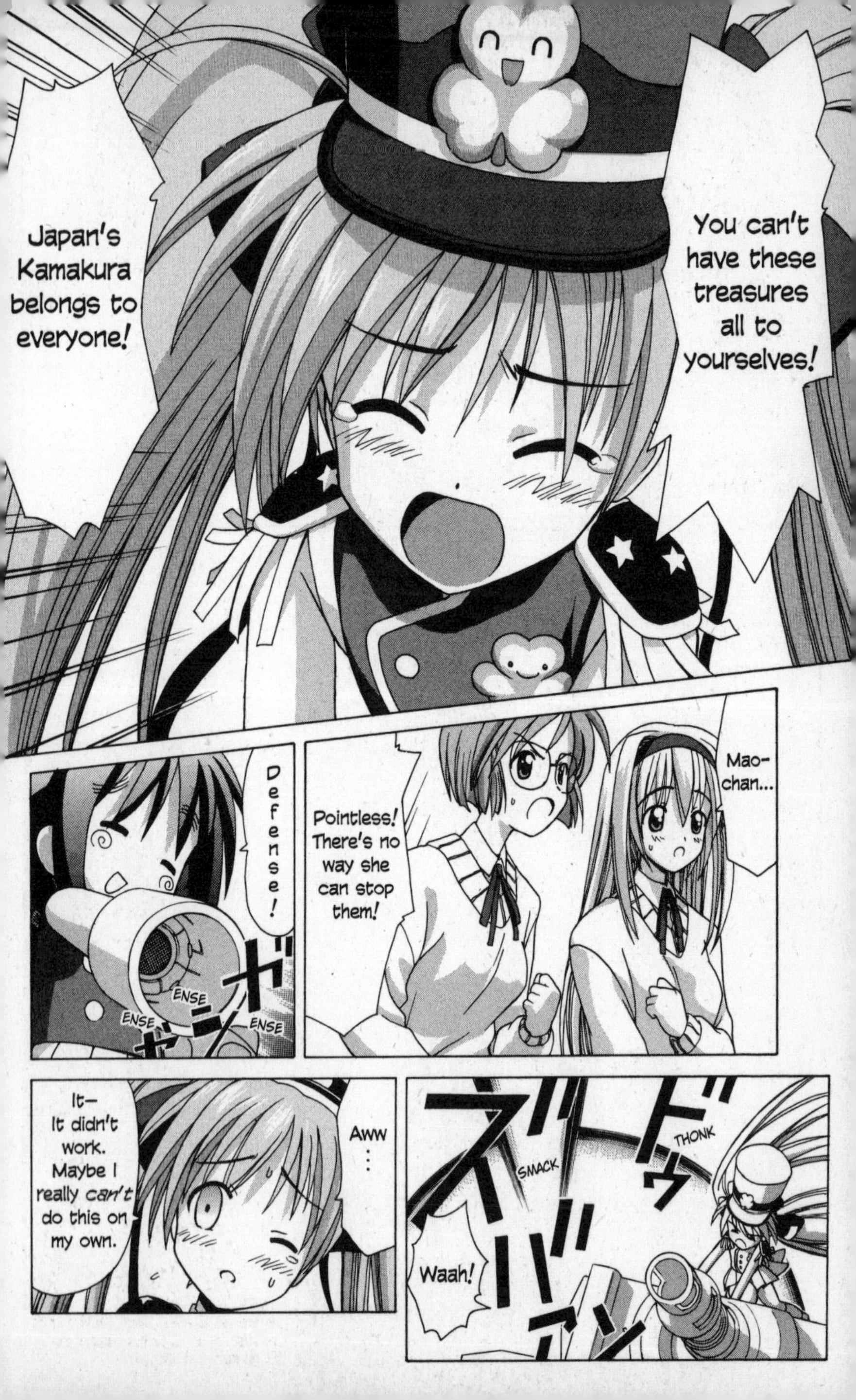
You can't have these treasures all to yourselves!
Japan's Kamakura belongs to everyone!
Mao-chan...
Pointless! There's no way she can stop them!
Defense!
ENSE
ENSE
ENSE
THONK
SMACK
Waah!
Aww...
It— It didn't work. Maybe I really *can't* do this on my own.

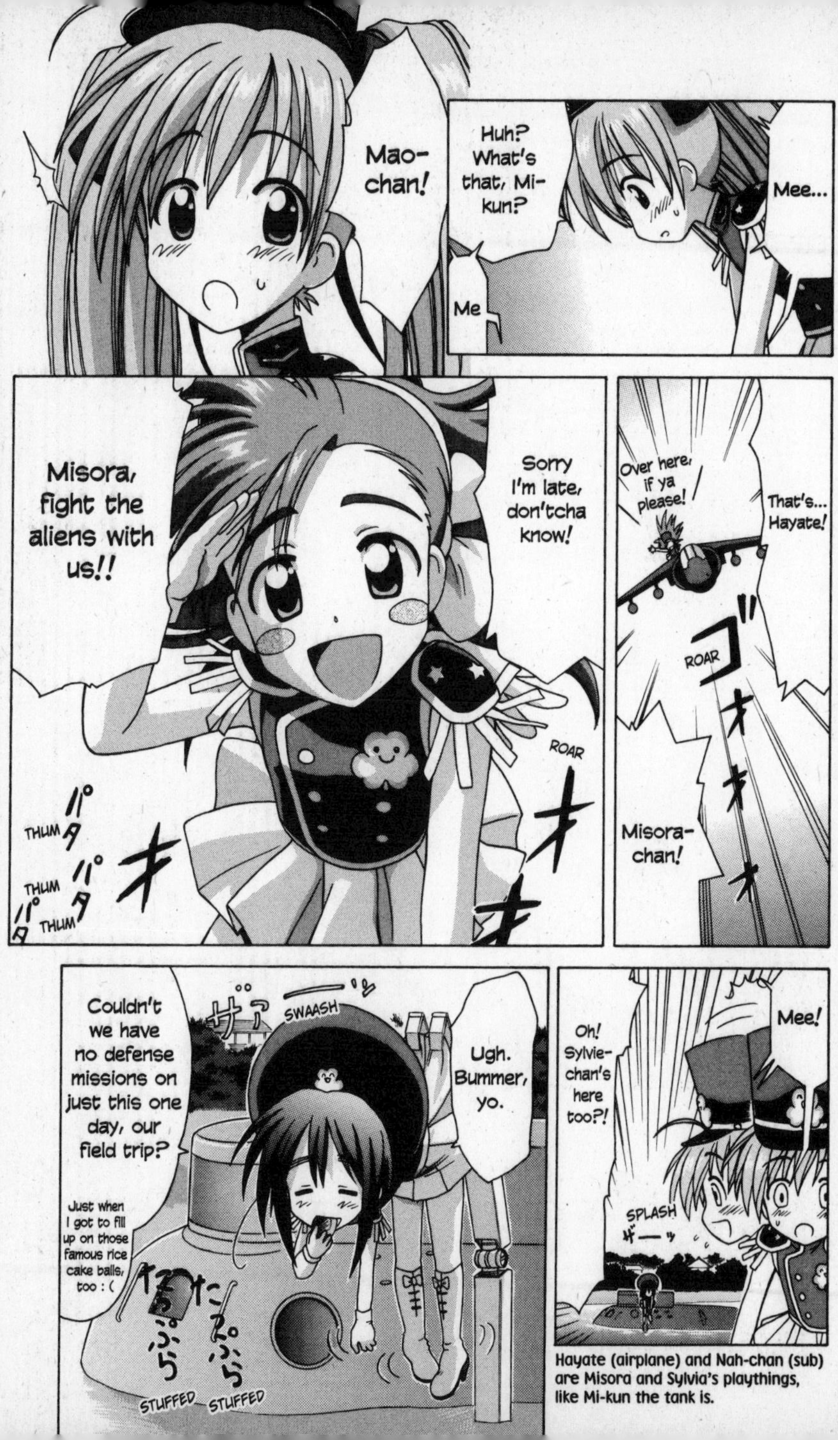
Mee...
Huh? What's that, Mi-kun?
Me
Mao-chan!
That's... Hayate!
Over here, if ya please!
ROAR
Misora-chan!
Sorry I'm late, don'tcha know!
Misora, fight the aliens with us!!
ROAR
THUM
THUM
THUM
Mee!
Oh! Sylvie-chan's here too?!
SPLASH
SWAASH
Ugh. Bummer, yo.
Couldn't we have no defense missions on just this one day, our field trip?
Just when I got to fill up on those famous rice cake balls, too : (
STUFFED
STUFFED

Hayate (airplane) and Nah-chan (sub) are Misora and Sylvia's playthings, like Mi-kun the tank is.

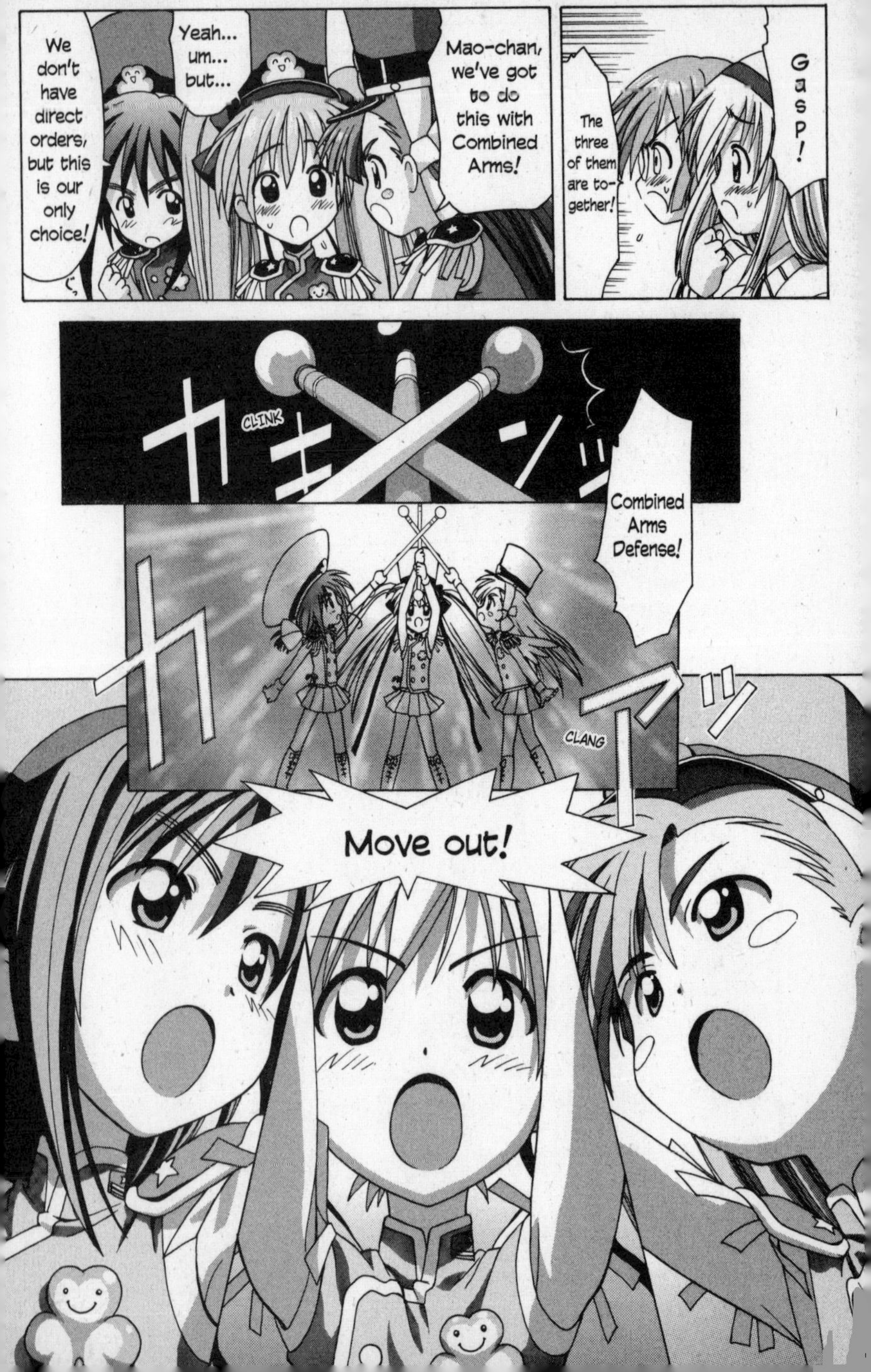
Gasp!
The three of them are together!
Mao-chan, we've got to do this with Combined Arms!
Yeah... um... but...
We don't have direct orders, but this is our only choice!
CLINK
Combined Arms Defense!
CLANG
Move out!

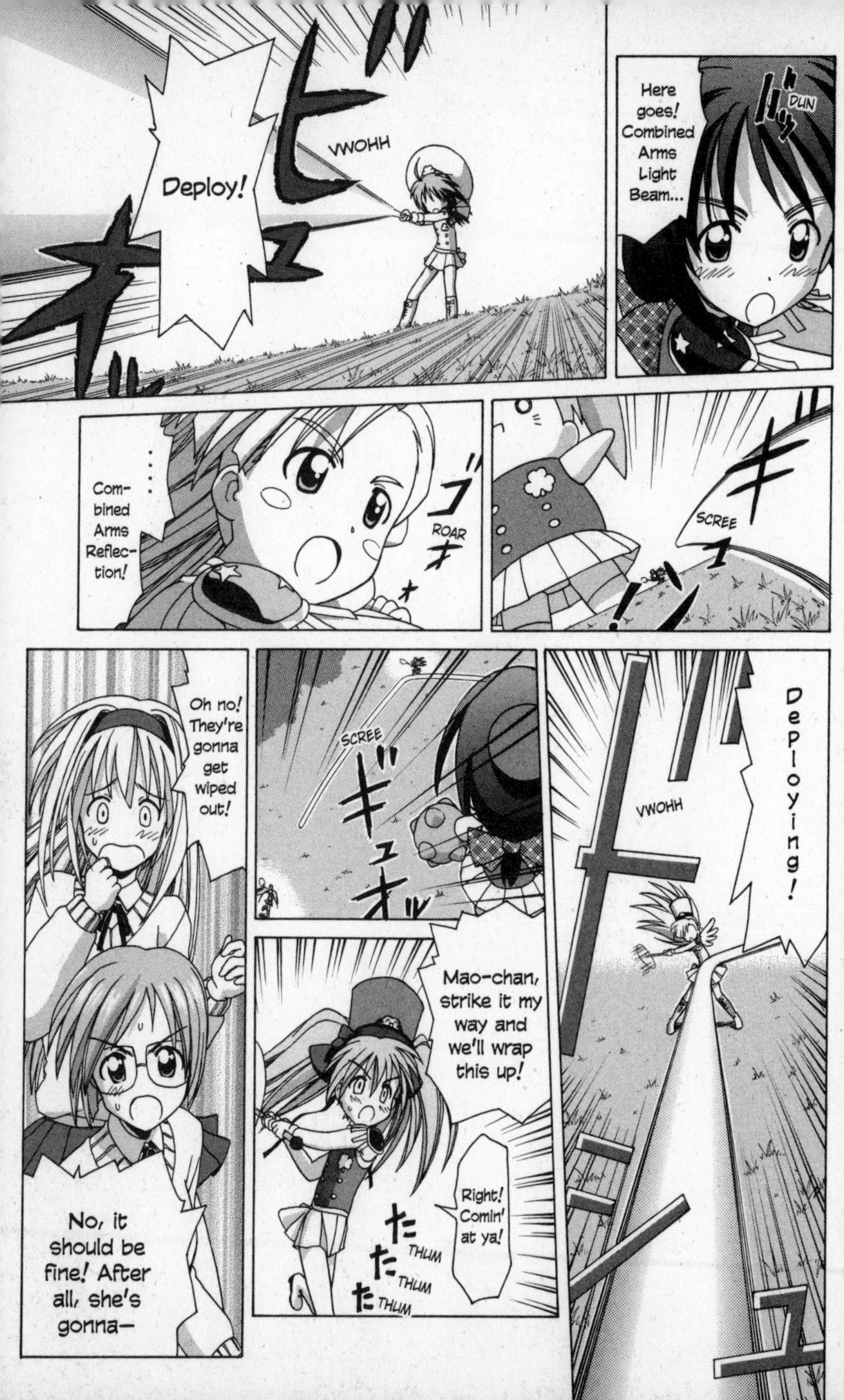

Here goes! Combined Arms Light Beam...
DUN
VWOHH
Deploy!
SCREE
!
...
Combined Arms Reflection!
ROAR
Deploying!
VWOHH
SCREE
Mao-chan, strike it my way and we'll wrap this up!
Right! Comin' at ya!
THUM
THUM
THUM
Oh no! They're gonna get wiped out!
No, it should be fine! After all, she's gonna–

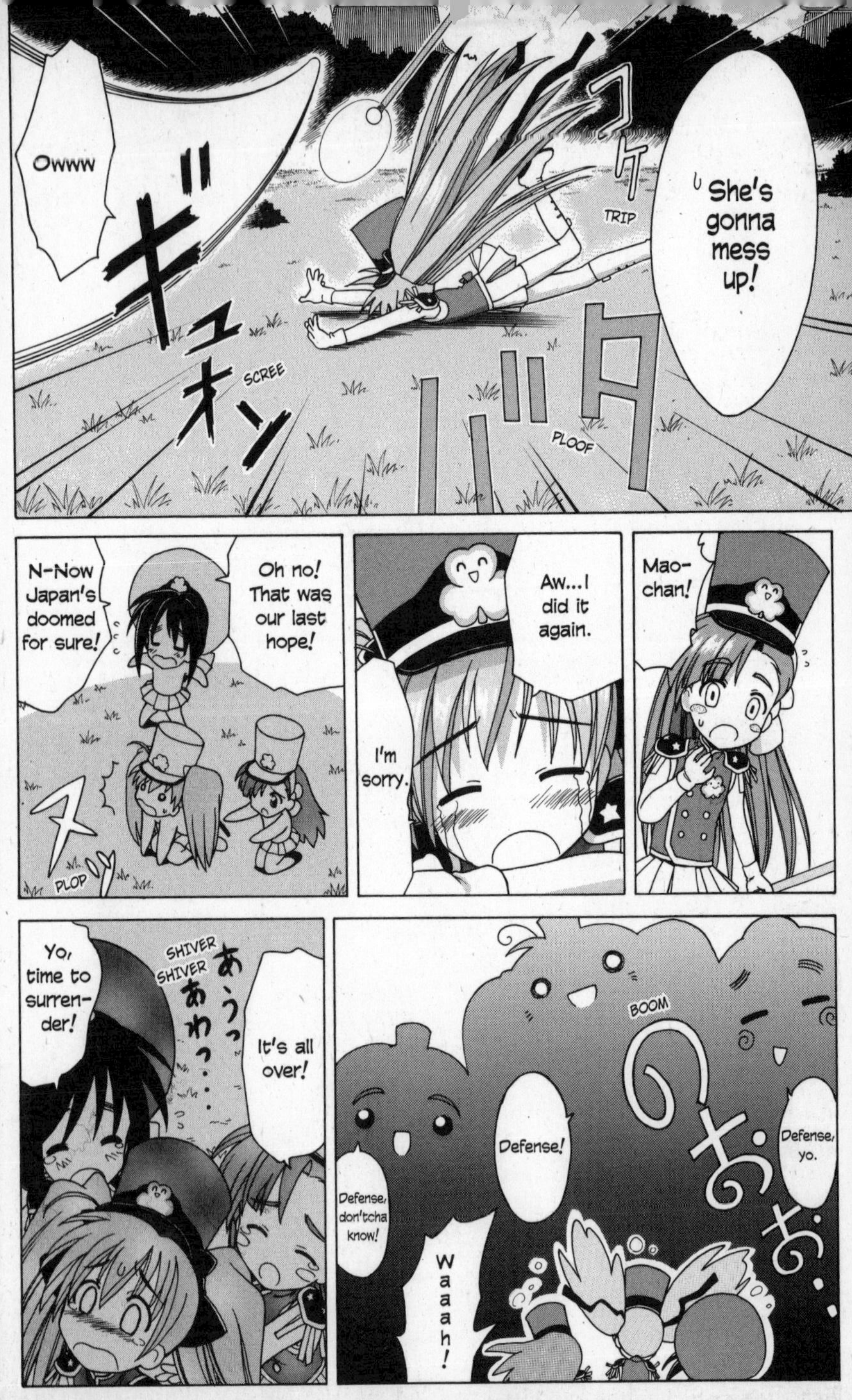
She's gonna mess up!
コケ
TRIP
バタ
PLOOF
ギュオン
SCREE
Owww
Mao-chan!
Aw...I did it again.
I'm sorry.
Oh no! That was our last hope!
N-Now Japan's doomed for sure!
PLOP
BOOM
Defense, yo.
Defense!
Defense, don'tcha know!
Waaah!
It's all over!
SHIVER SHIVER
あうっ あわっ...
Yo, time to surrender!

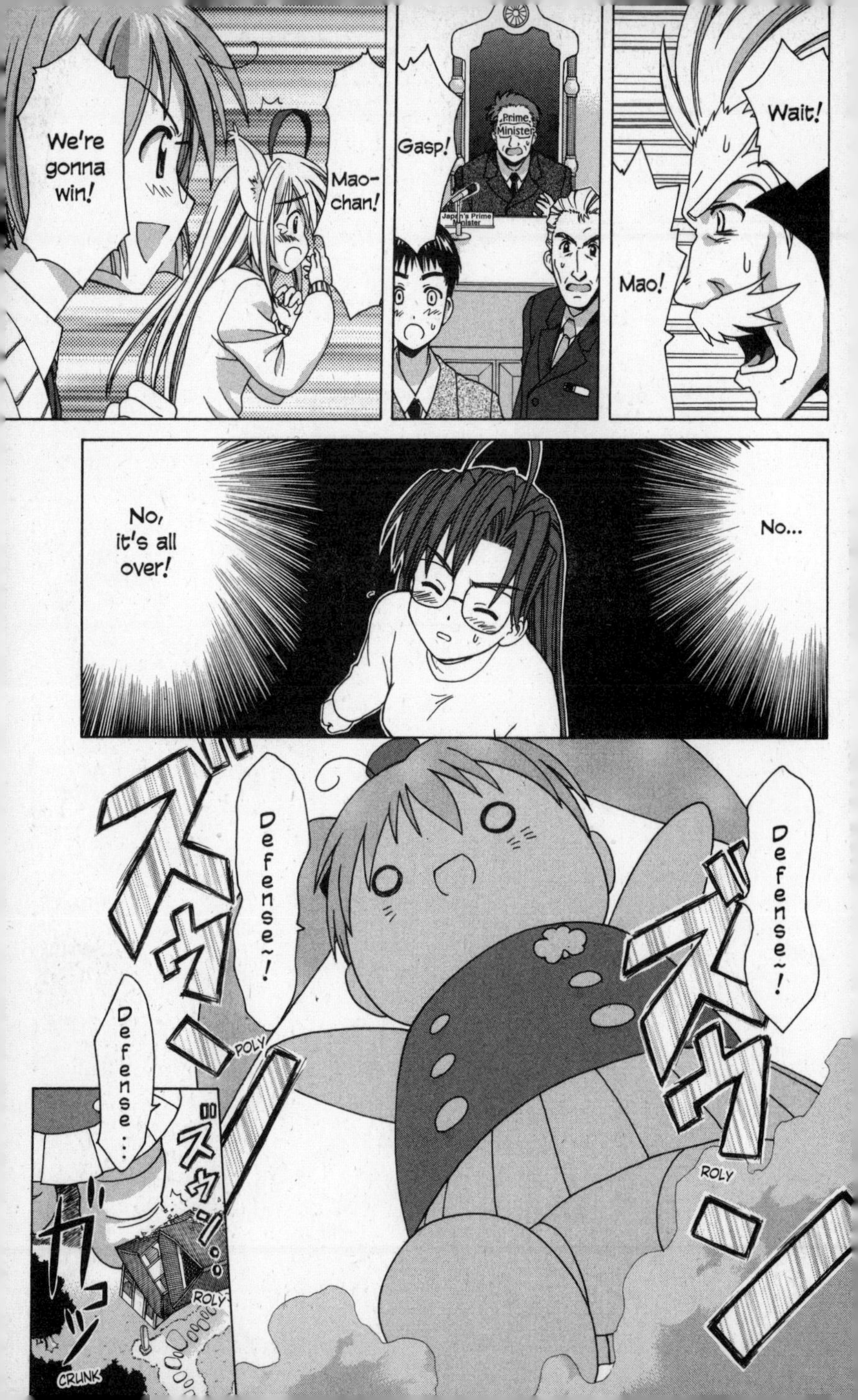
Wait!
Mao!
Gasp!
Prime Minister
Japan's Prime Minister
Mao-chan!
We're gonna win!
No...
No, it's all over!
Defense~!
ROLY
Defense~!
POLY
Defense...
ROLY
CRUNK

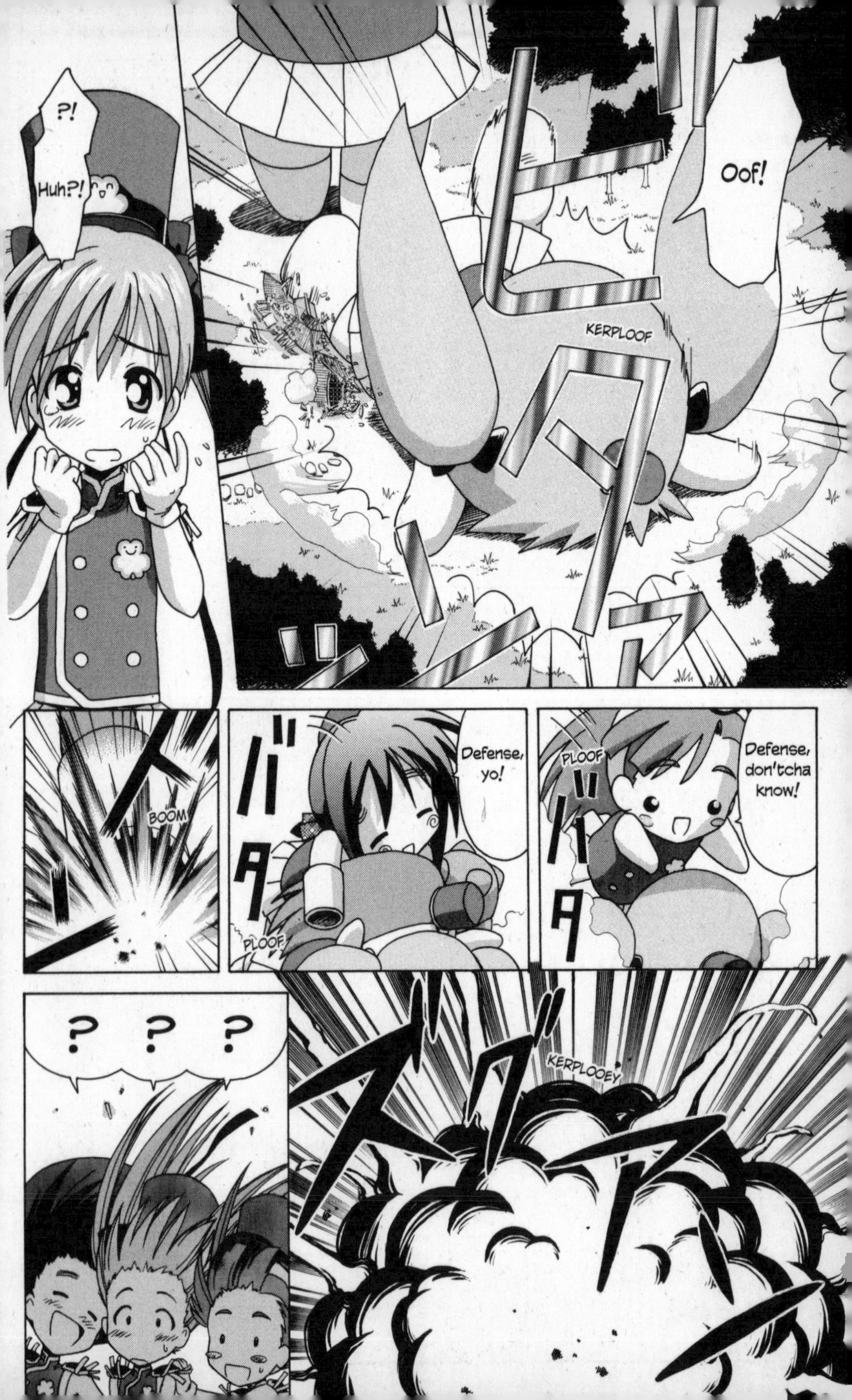
Oof!
KERPLOOF
?!
Huh?!
PLOOF
Defense, don'tcha know!
Defense, yo!
PLOOF
BOOM
KERPLOOEY
? ? ?

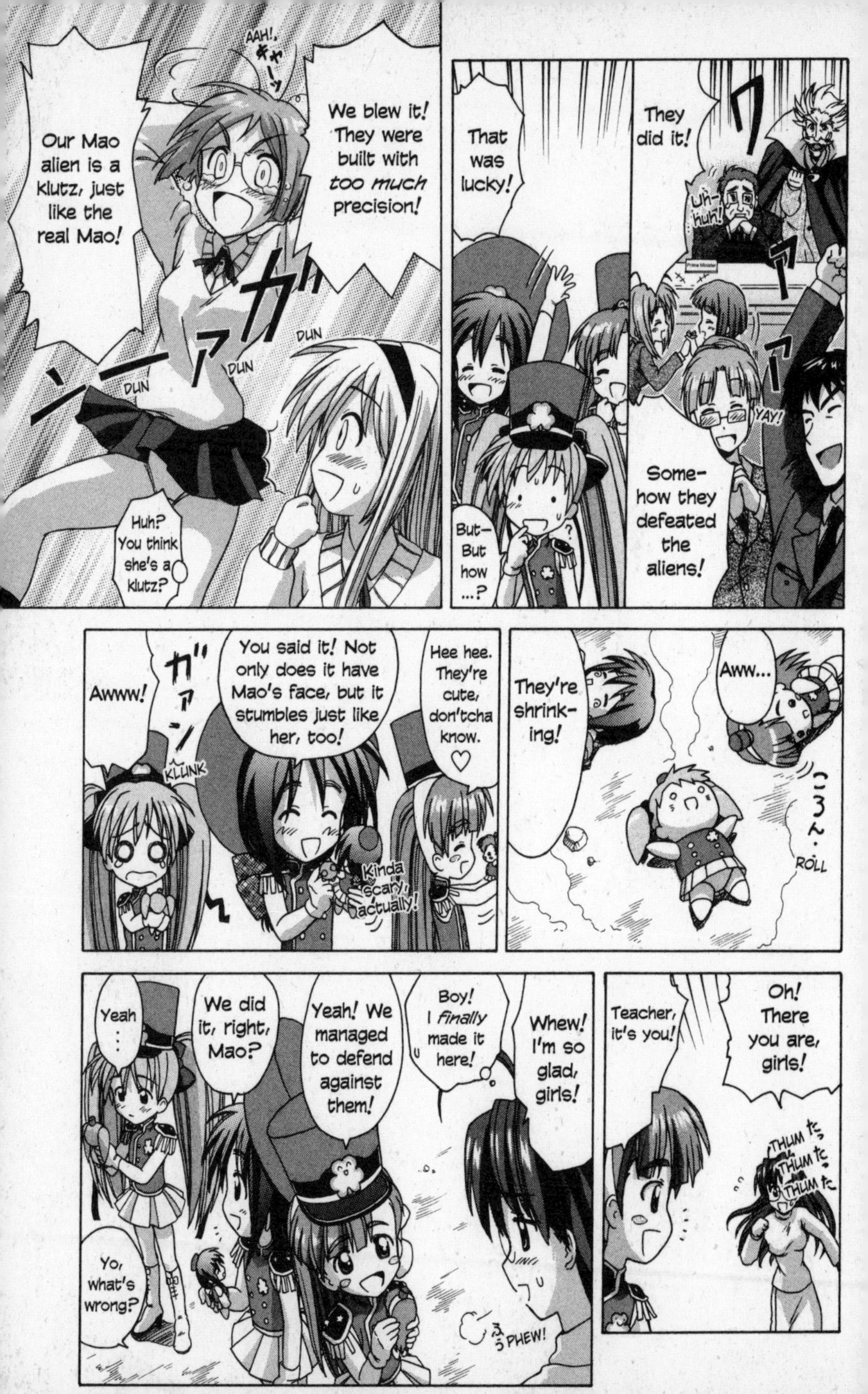

They did it!
Uh-huh!
YAY!
Some-how they defeated the aliens!
That was lucky!
But— But how ...?
AAH!
We blew it! They were built with *too much* precision!
Our Mao alien is a klutz, just like the real Mao!
DUN
DUN
DUN
Huh? You think she's a klutz?
Aww...
ROLL
They're shrink-ing!
Hee hee. They're cute, don'tcha know. ♡
You said it! Not only does it have Mao's face, but it stumbles just like her, too!
Awww!
KLUNK
Kinda scary, actually!
Oh! There you are, girls!
Teacher, it's you!
THUM
THUM
THUM
Whew! I'm so glad, girls!
Boy! I *finally* made it here!
Yeah! We managed to defend against them!
We did it, right, Mao?
Yeah ...
Yo, what's wrong?
PHEW!

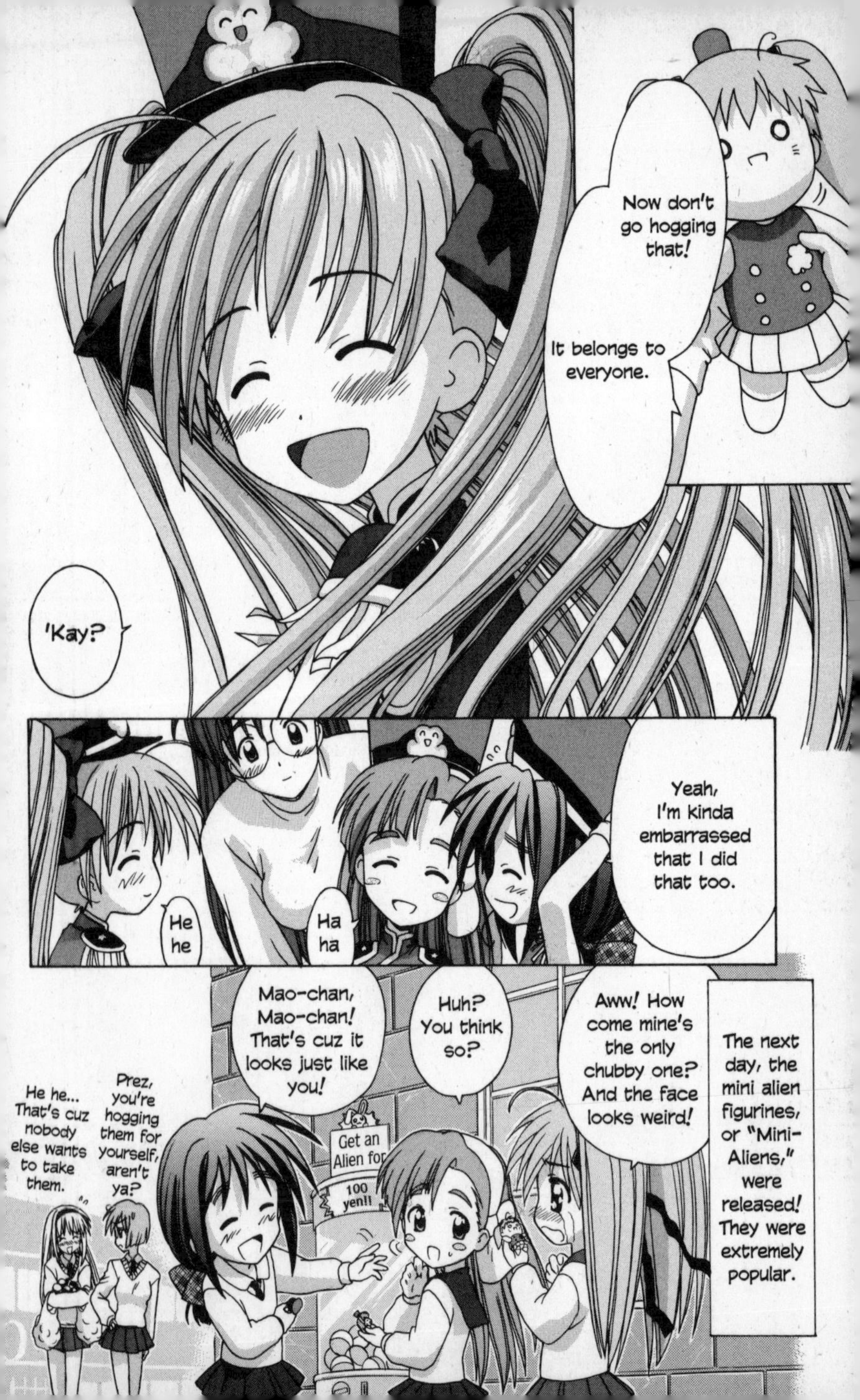
Now don't go hogging that!
It belongs to everyone.
'Kay?
Yeah, I'm kinda embarrassed that I did that too.
Ha ha
He he
The next day, the mini alien figurines, or "Mini-Aliens," were released! They were extremely popular.
Aww! How come mine's the only chubby one? And the face looks weird!
Huh? You think so?
Mao-chan, Mao-chan! That's cuz it looks just like you!
Get an Alien for 100 yen!!
Prez, you're hogging them for yourself, aren't ya?
He he... That's cuz nobody else wants to take them.

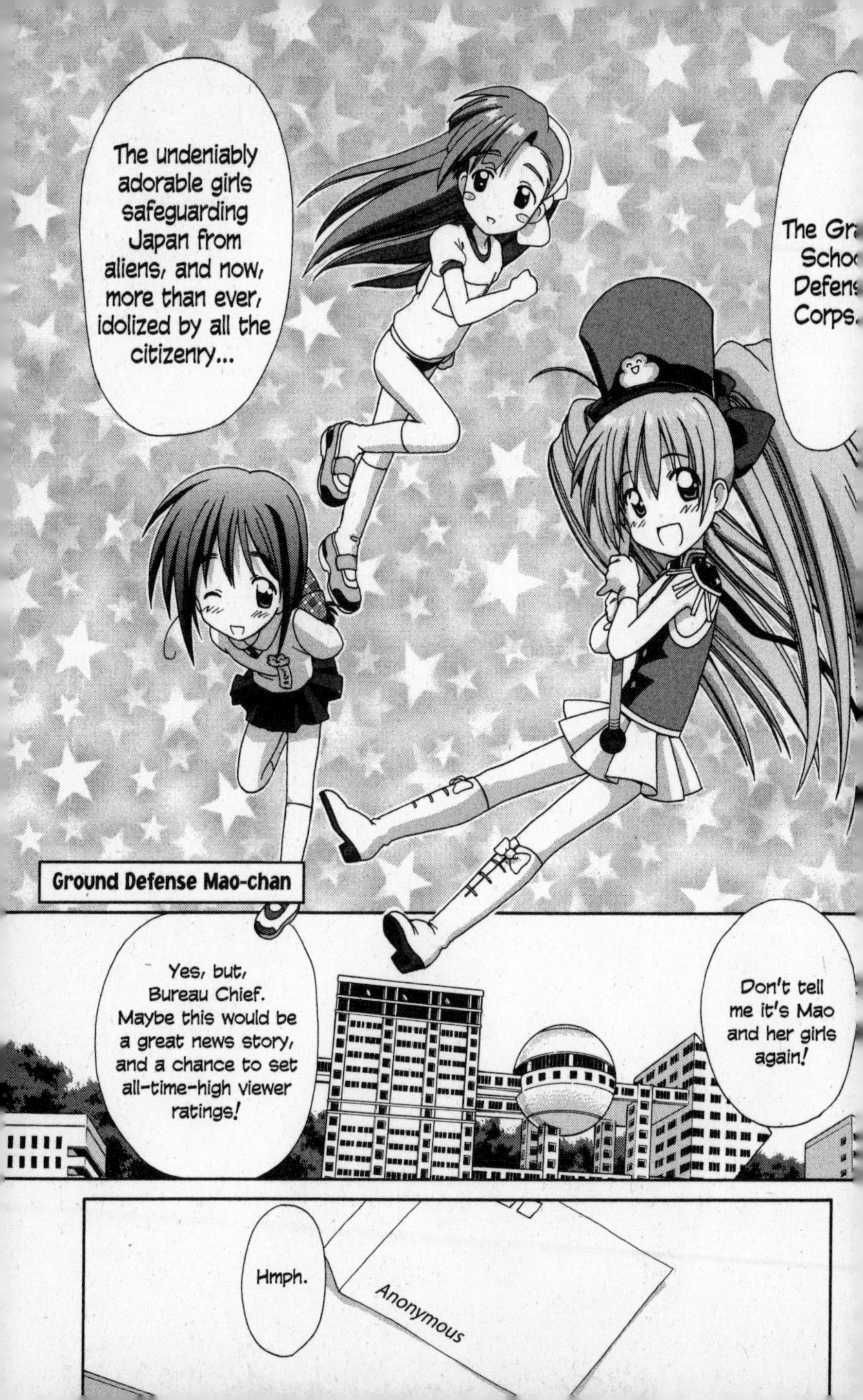
The Gr Scho Defens Corps.
The undeniably adorable girls safeguarding Japan from aliens, and now, more than ever, idolized by all the citizenry...
Ground Defense Mao-chan
Don't tell me it's Mao and her girls again!
Yes, but, Bureau Chief. Maybe this would be a great news story, and a chance to set all-time-high viewer ratings!
Hmph.
Anonymous

Mao-chan

#6 Secret Defensive Combat

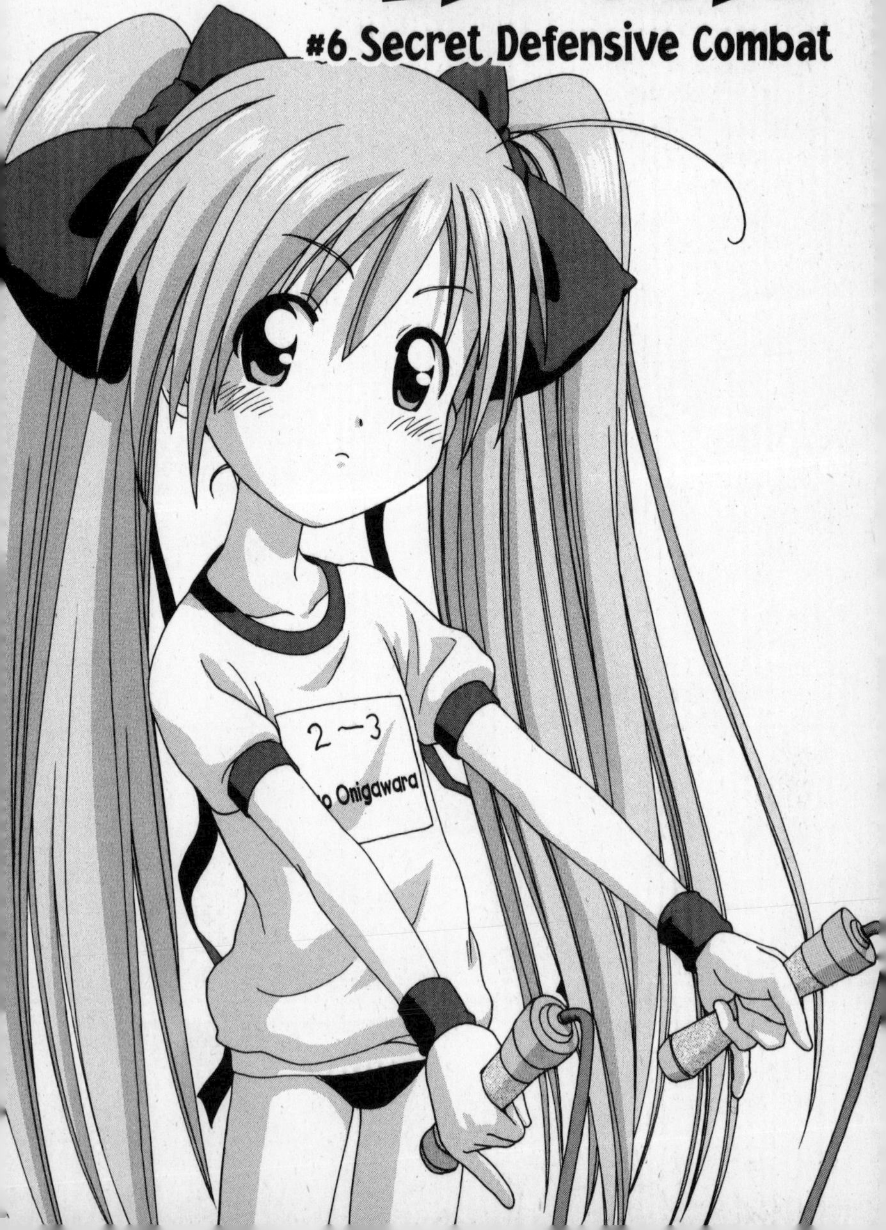
2—3
Onigawara

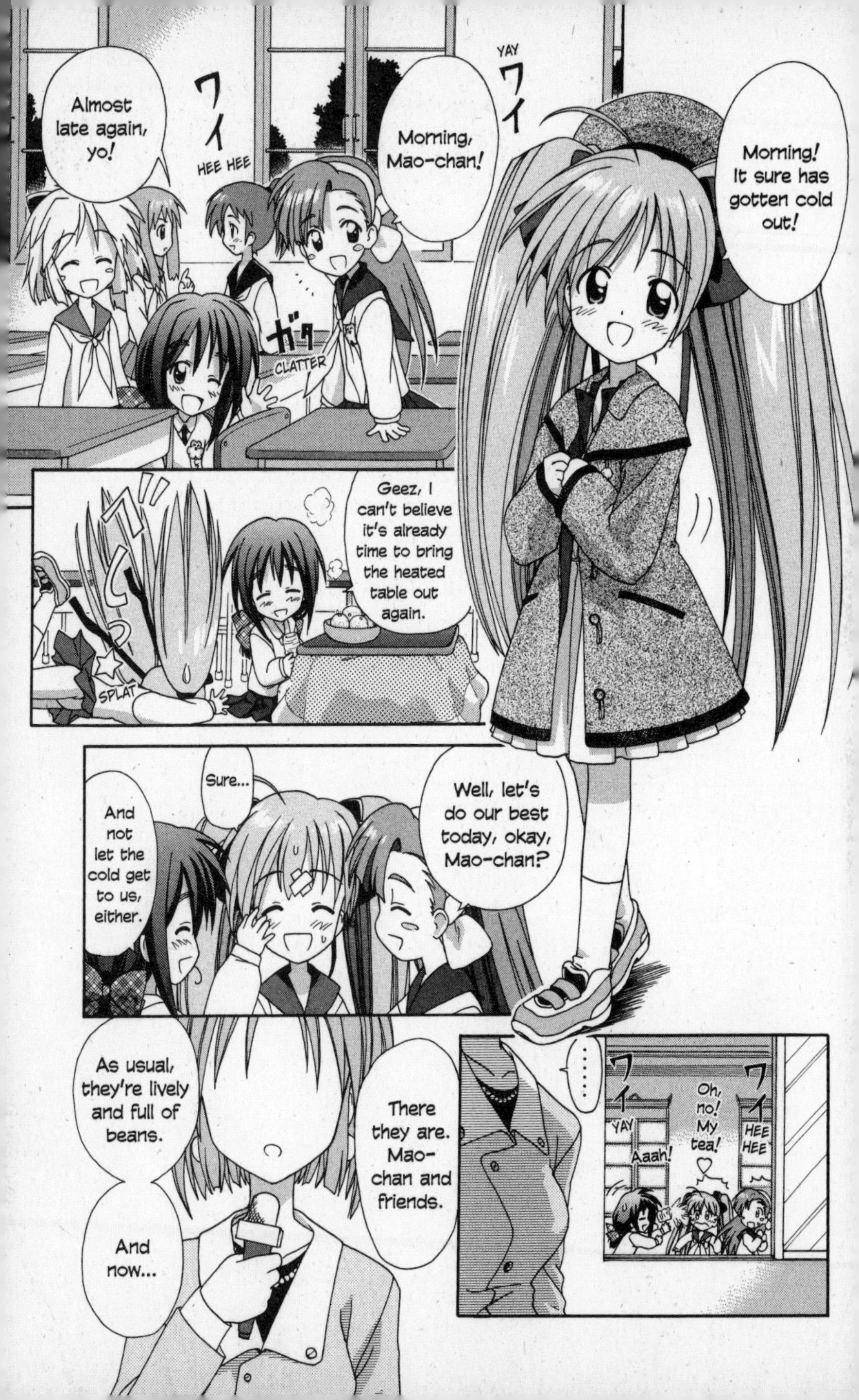
Morning! It sure has gotten cold out!
YAY
ワイ
Morning, Mao-chan!
ワイ
HEE HEE
Almost late again, yo!
ガタ
CLATTER
Geez, I can't believe it's already time to bring the heated table out again.
SPLAT
Well, let's do our best today, okay, Mao-chan?
Sure...
And not let the cold get to us, either.
ワイ
HEE HEE
Oh, no! My tea!
ワイ
YAY
Aaah!
......
There they are. Mao-chan and friends.
As usual, they're lively and full of beans.
And now...

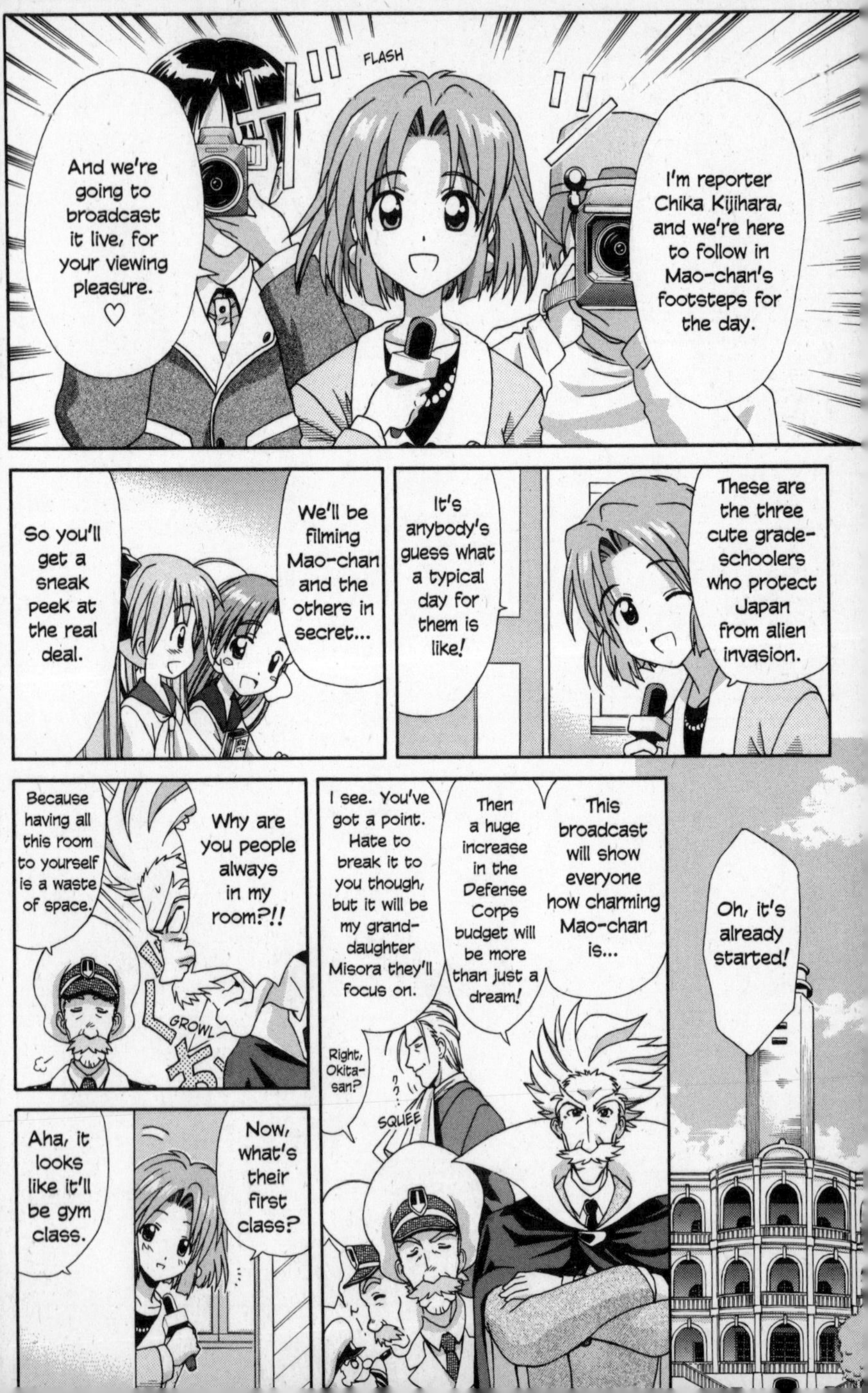
FLASH
I'm reporter Chika Kijihara, and we're here to follow in Mao-chan's footsteps for the day.
And we're going to broadcast it live, for your viewing pleasure. ♡
These are the three cute grade-schoolers who protect Japan from alien invasion.
It's anybody's guess what a typical day for them is like!
We'll be filming Mao-chan and the others in secret...
So you'll get a sneak peek at the real deal.
Oh, it's already started!
This broadcast will show everyone how charming Mao-chan is...
Then a huge increase in the Defense Corps budget will be more than just a dream!
I see. You've got a point. Hate to break it to you though, but it will be my grand-daughter Misora they'll focus on.
Right, Okita-san?
SQUEE
Why are you people always in my room?!!
Because having all this room to yourself is a waste of space.
GROWL
Now, what's their first class?
Aha, it looks like it'll be gym class.

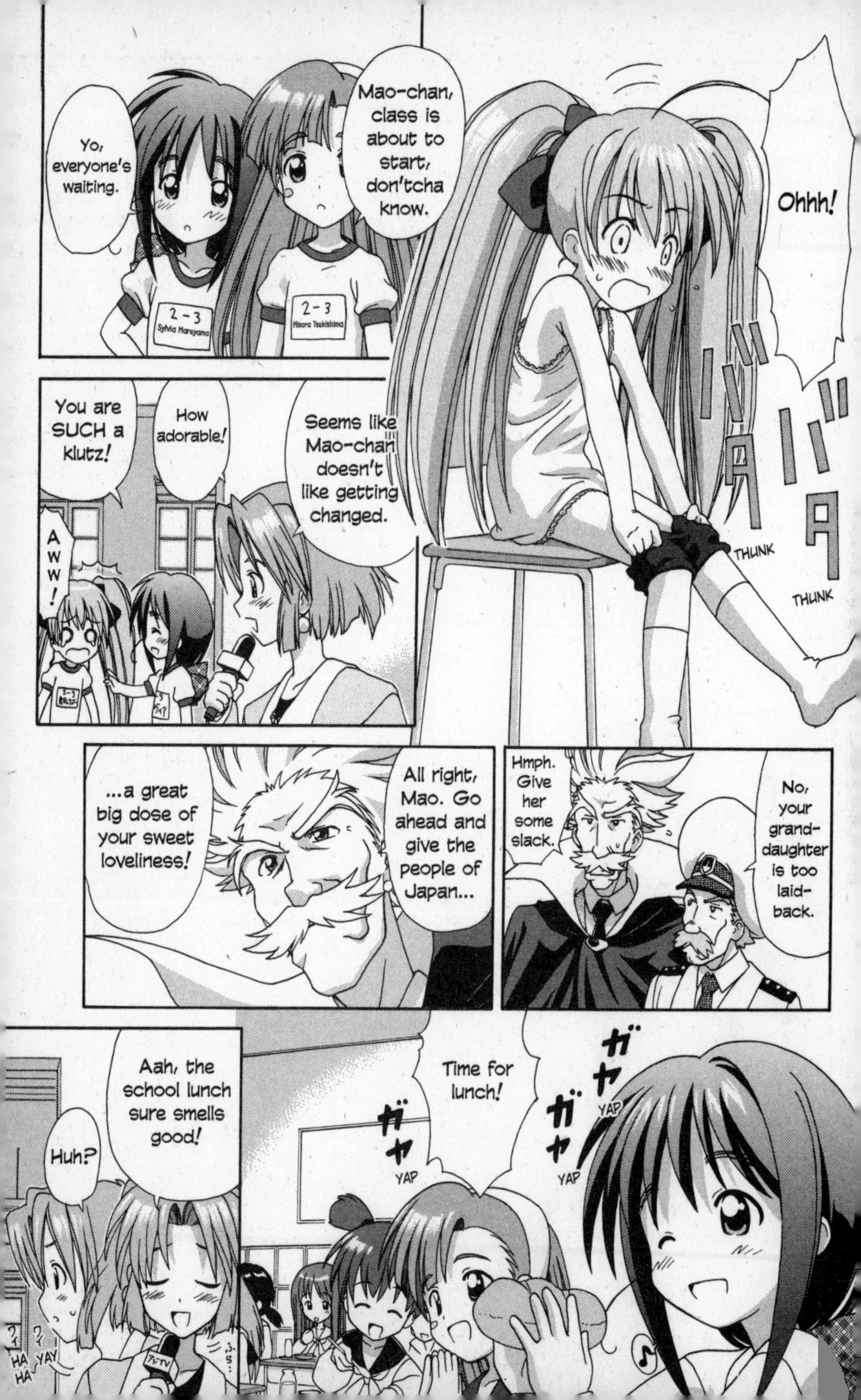
Ohhh!
THUNK
THUNK
Mao-chan, class is about to start, don'tcha know.
Yo, everyone's waiting.
2-3 Misora Tsukishima
2-3 Sylvia Maruyama
Seems like Mao-chan doesn't like getting changed.
How adorable!
You are SUCH a klutz!
AWW!
No, your grand-daughter is too laid-back.
Hmph. Give her some slack.
All right, Mao. Go ahead and give the people of Japan...
...a great big dose of your sweet loveliness!
Time for lunch!
ガヤ ガヤ
YAP
YAP
ガヤ
YAP
Aah, the school lunch sure smells good!
Huh?
HA HA YAY

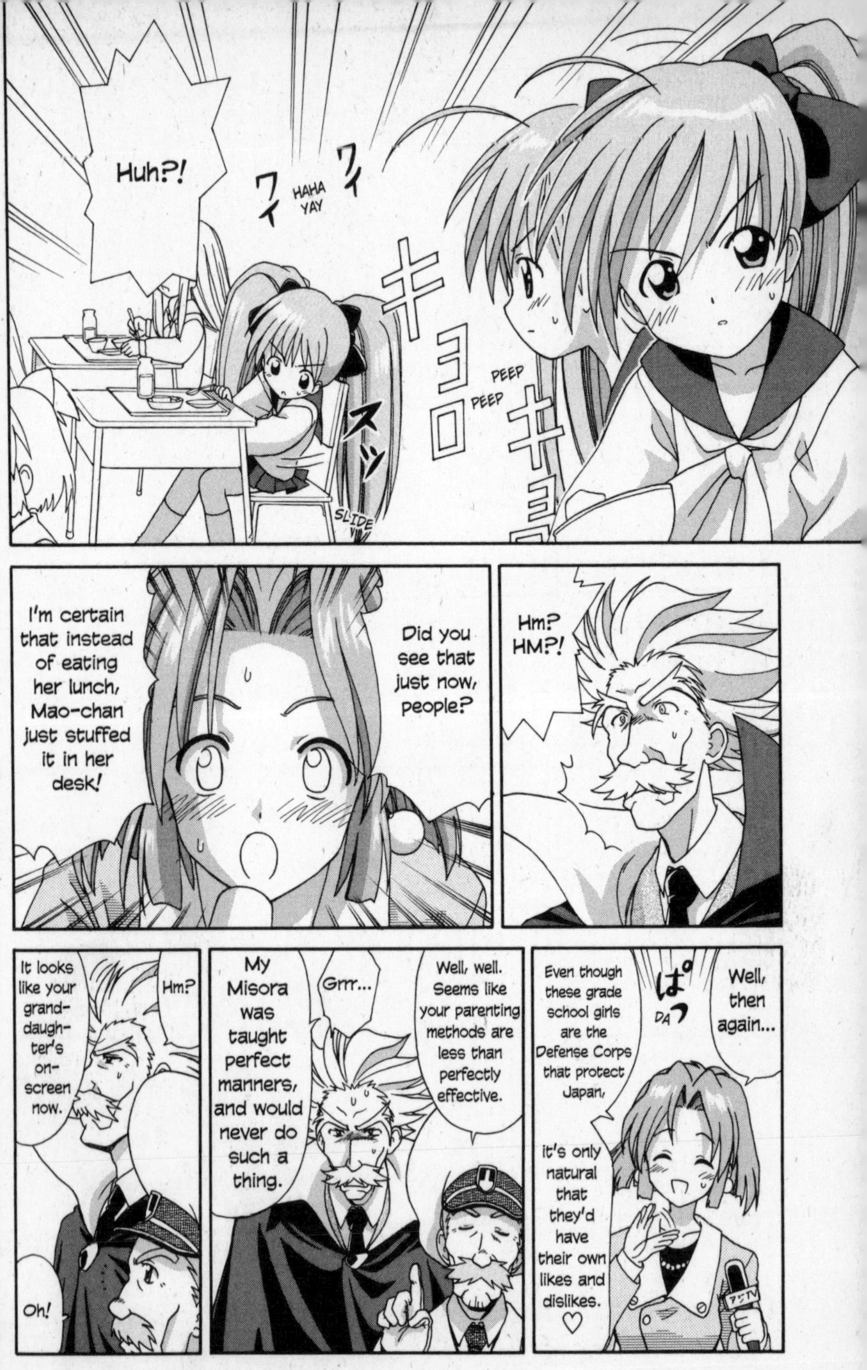
キョロ
PEEP
キョロ
PEEP
ワイ
ワイ
HAHA YAY
Huh?!
スッ
SLIDE
Hm? HM?!
Did you see that just now, people?
I'm certain that instead of eating her lunch, Mao-chan just stuffed it in her desk!
Well, then again...
ぱっ
DA
Even though these grade school girls are the Defense Corps that protect Japan,
it's only natural that they'd have their own likes and dislikes. ♡
Well, well. Seems like your parenting methods are less than perfectly effective.
Grrr...
My Misora was taught perfect manners, and would never do such a thing.
Hm?
It looks like your grand-daugh-ter's on-screen now.
Oh!

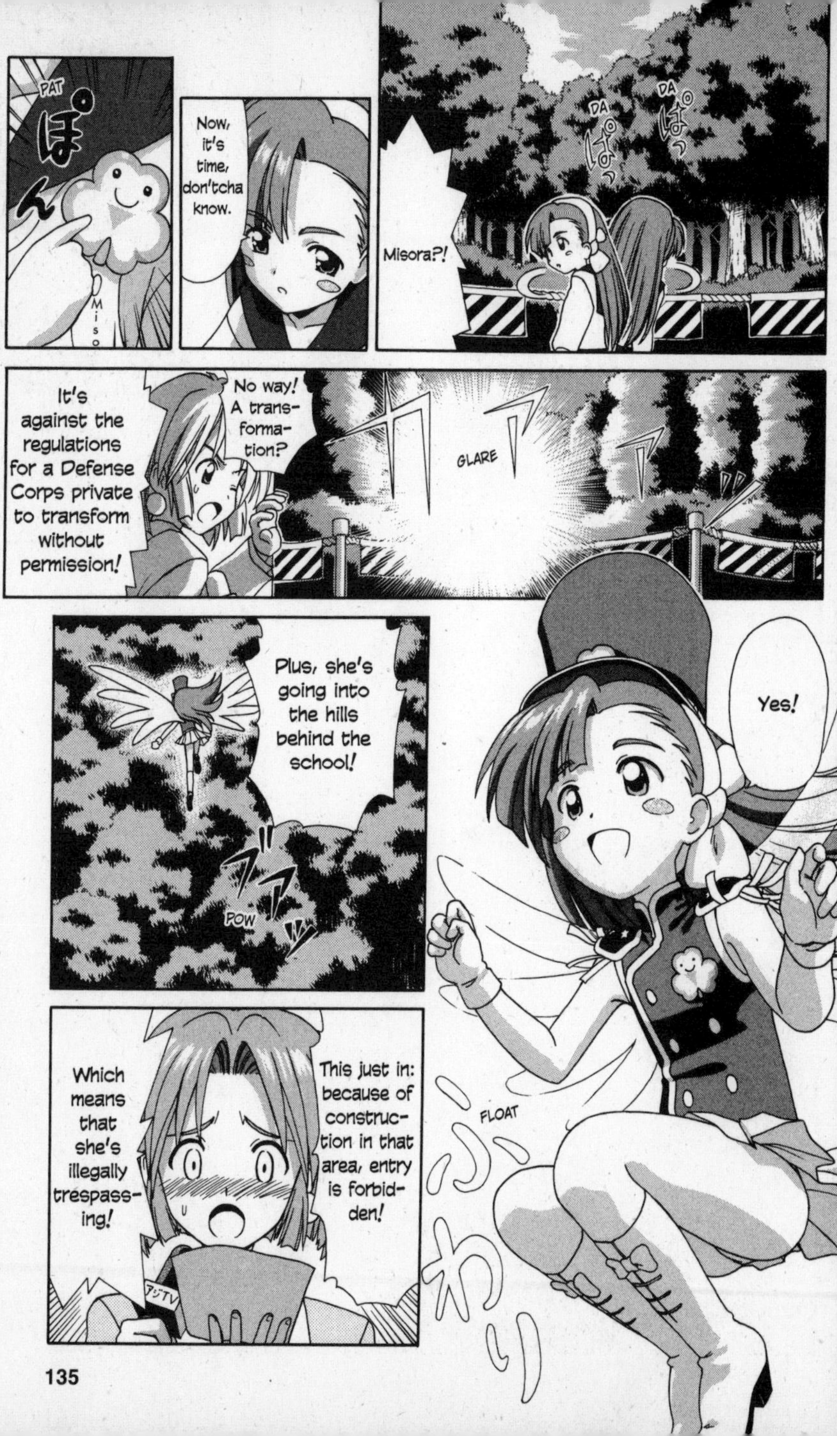
DA
DA
Misora?!
Now, it's time, don'tcha know.
PAT
Miso
GLARE
No way! A transformation?
It's against the regulations for a Defense Corps private to transform without permission!
Yes!
FLOAT
Plus, she's going into the hills behind the school!
POW
This just in: because of construction in that area, entry is forbidden!
Which means that she's illegally trespassing!

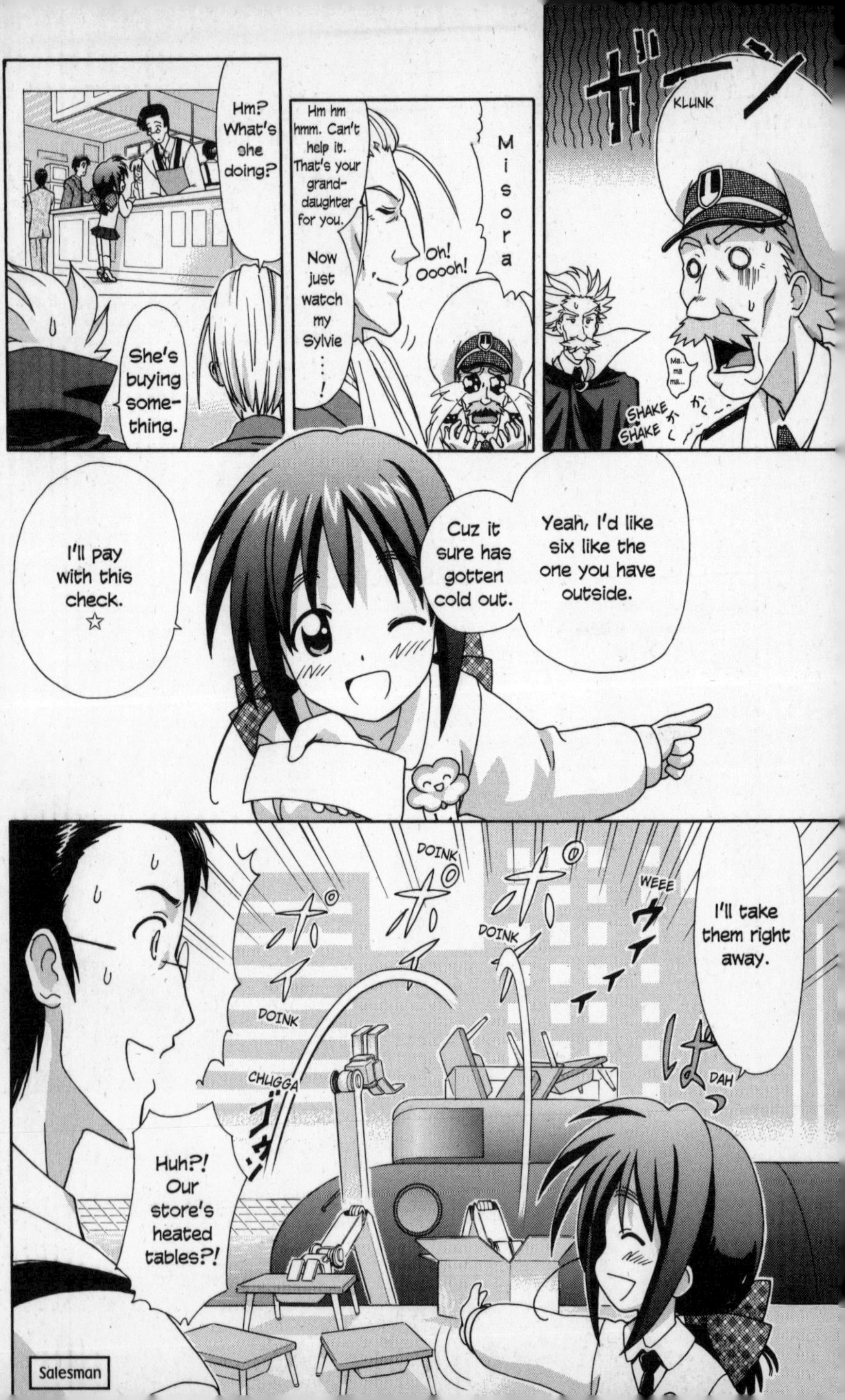
KLUNK
Ma... ma... ma...
SHAKE SHAKE
Misora
Oh! Ooooh!
Hm hm hmm. Can't help it. That's your granddaughter for you.
Now just watch my Sylvie...!
Hm? What's she doing?
She's buying something.
Yeah, I'd like six like the one you have outside.
Cuz it sure has gotten cold out.
I'll pay with this check. ☆
I'll take them right away.
DAH
WEEE
DOINK
DOINK
DOINK
CHUGGA
Huh?! Our store's heated tables?!
Salesman

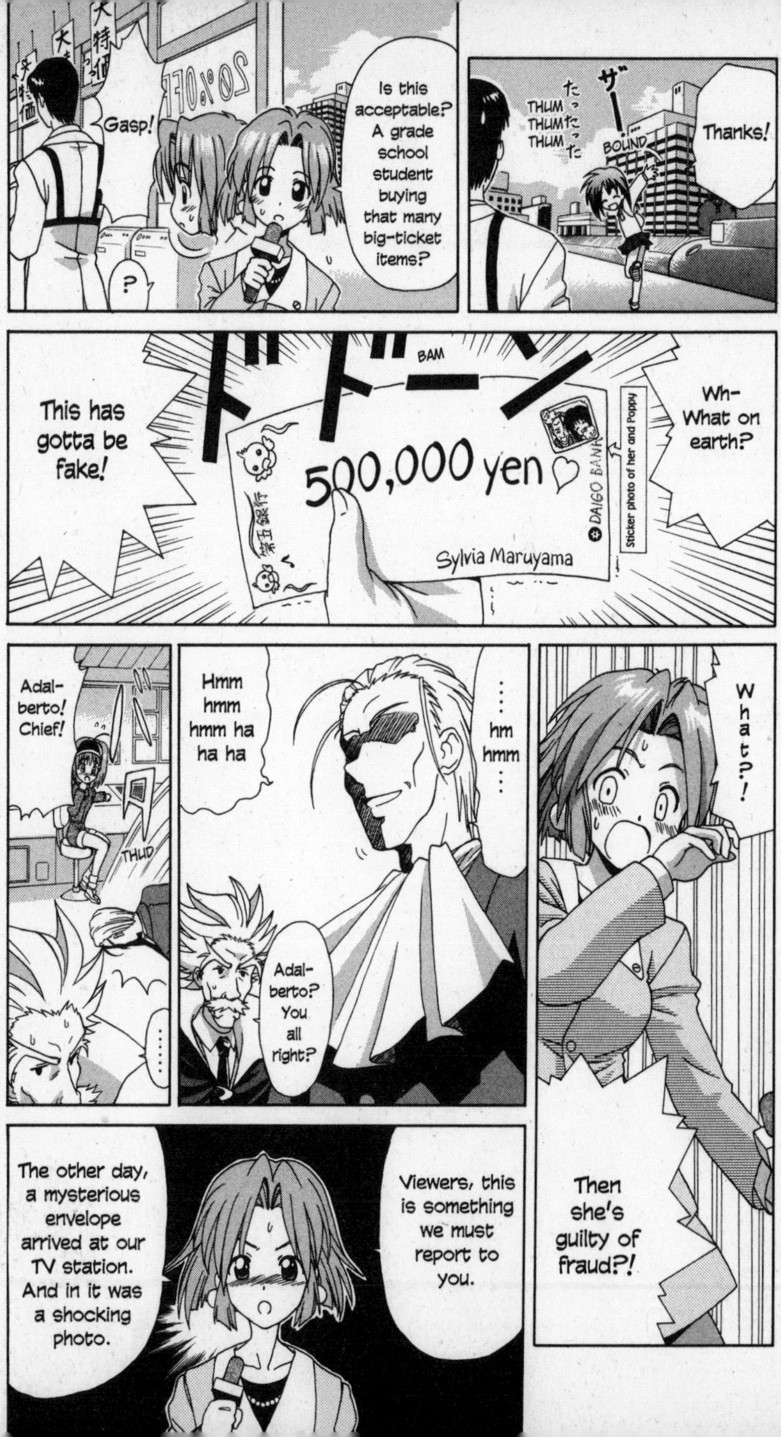
Thanks!
THUM THUM THUM
たったった
ザー
BOUND
Is this acceptable? A grade school student buying that many big-ticket items?
Gasp!
?
Wh- What on earth?
BAM
ドドーン
500,000 yen
DAIGO BANK
Sticker photo of her and Poppy
Sylvia Maruyama
This has gotta be fake!
What?!
Then she's guilty of fraud?!
...hm hmm...
Hmm hmm hmm ha ha ha
Adalberto? You all right?
Adalberto! Chief!
THUD
......
Viewers, this is something we must report to you.
The other day, a mysterious envelope arrived at our TV station. And in it was a shocking photo.

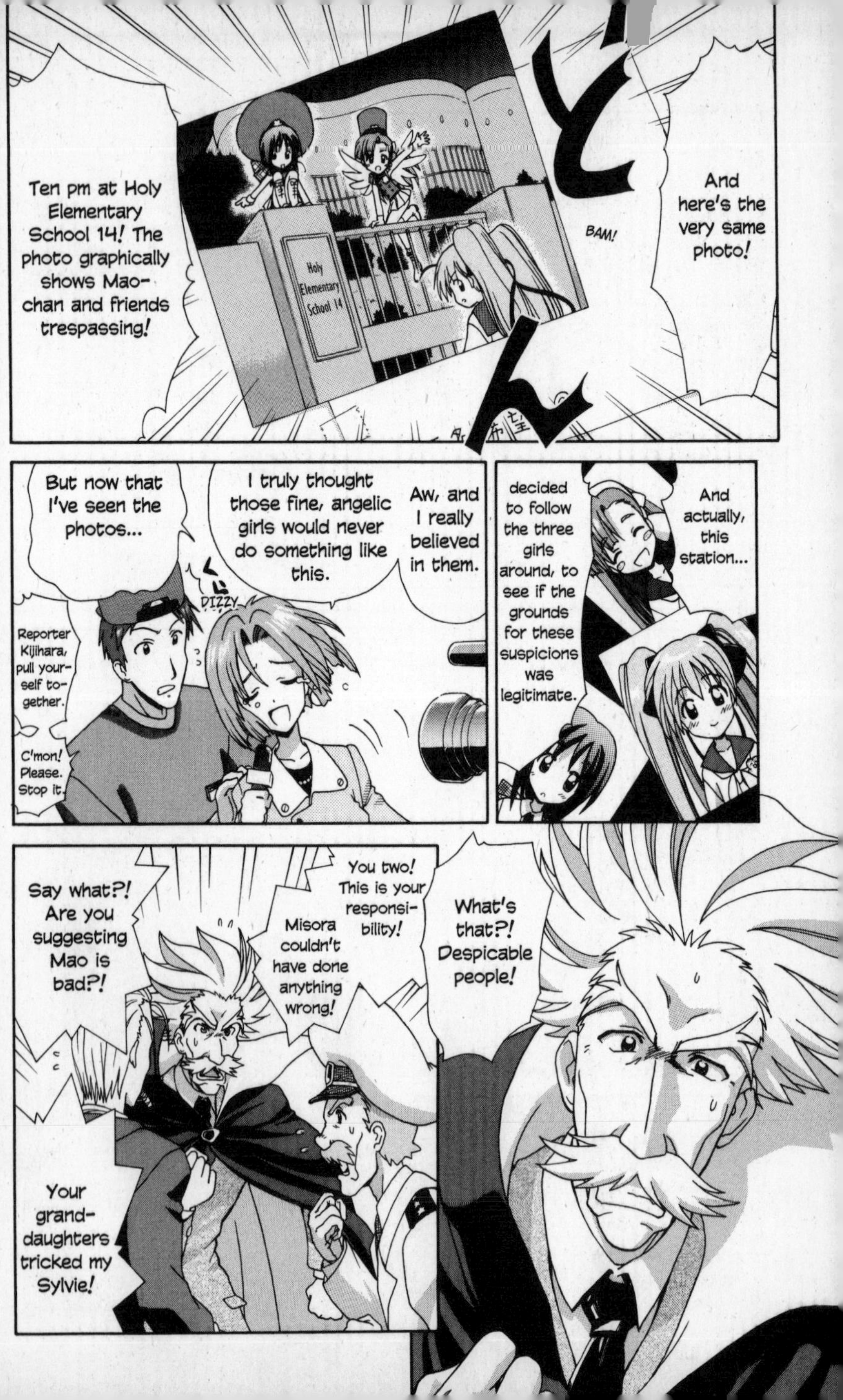
And here's the very same photo!
BAM!
Holy Elementary School 14
Ten pm at Holy Elementary School 14! The photo graphically shows Mao-chan and friends trespassing!
And actually, this station...
decided to follow the three girls around, to see if the grounds for these suspicions was legitimate.
Aw, and I really believed in them.
I truly thought those fine, angelic girls would never do something like this.
DIZZY
But now that I've seen the photos...
Reporter Kijihara, pull yourself together.
C'mon! Please. Stop it.
What's that?! Despicable people!
You two! This is your responsibility!
Misora couldn't have done anything wrong!
Say what?! Are you suggesting Mao is bad?!
Your granddaughters tricked my Sylvie!

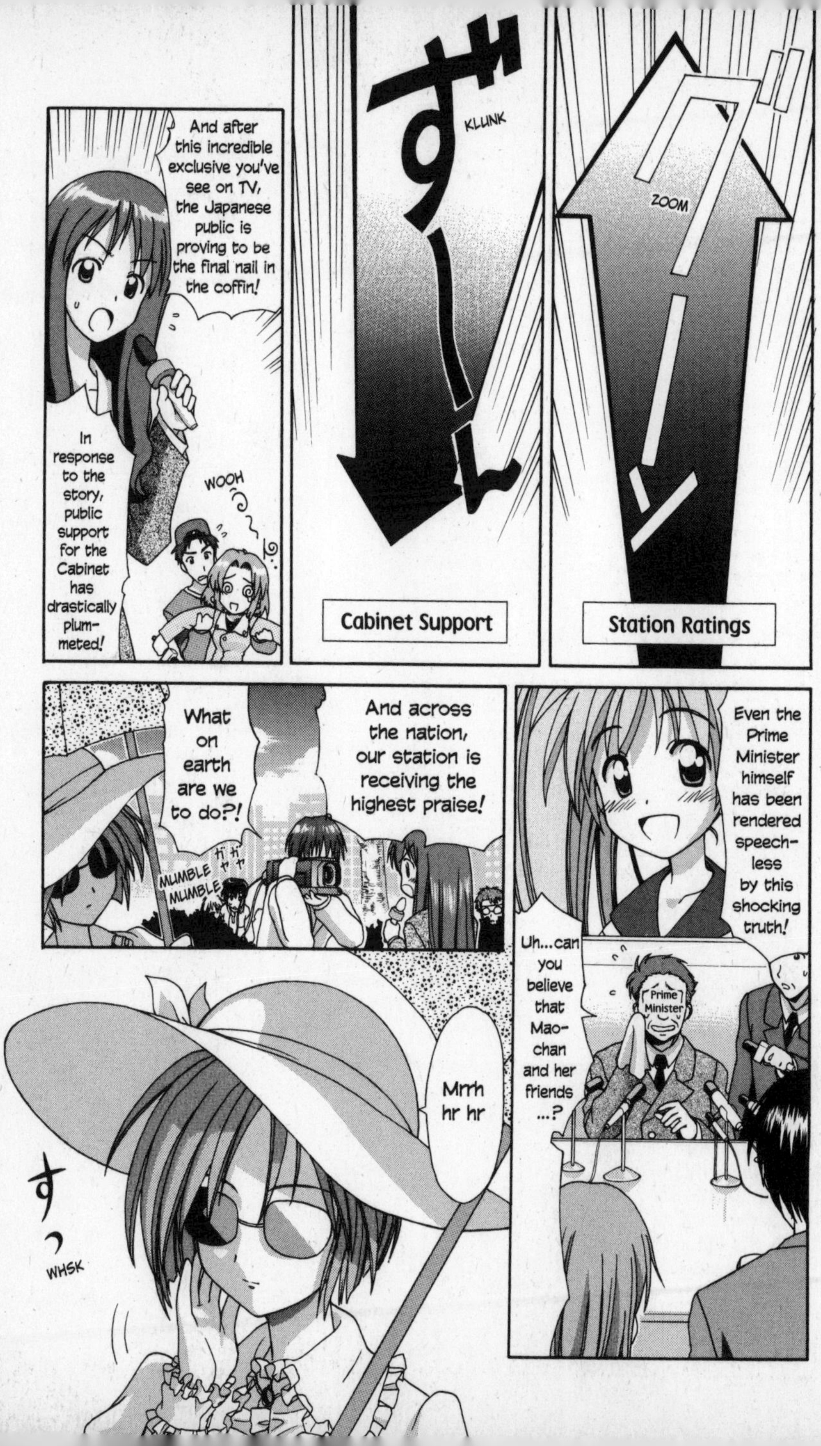

ZOOM
Station Ratings
ずーん
KLUNK
Cabinet Support
And after this incredible exclusive you've see on TV, the Japanese public is proving to be the final nail in the coffin!
In response to the story, public support for the Cabinet has drastically plum-meted!
WOOH
Even the Prime Minister himself has been rendered speech-less by this shocking truth!
And across the nation, our station is receiving the highest praise!
What on earth are we to do?!
MUMBLE MUMBLE
Uh...can you believe that Mao-chan and her friends ...?
Prime Minister
Mrrh hr hr
WHSK

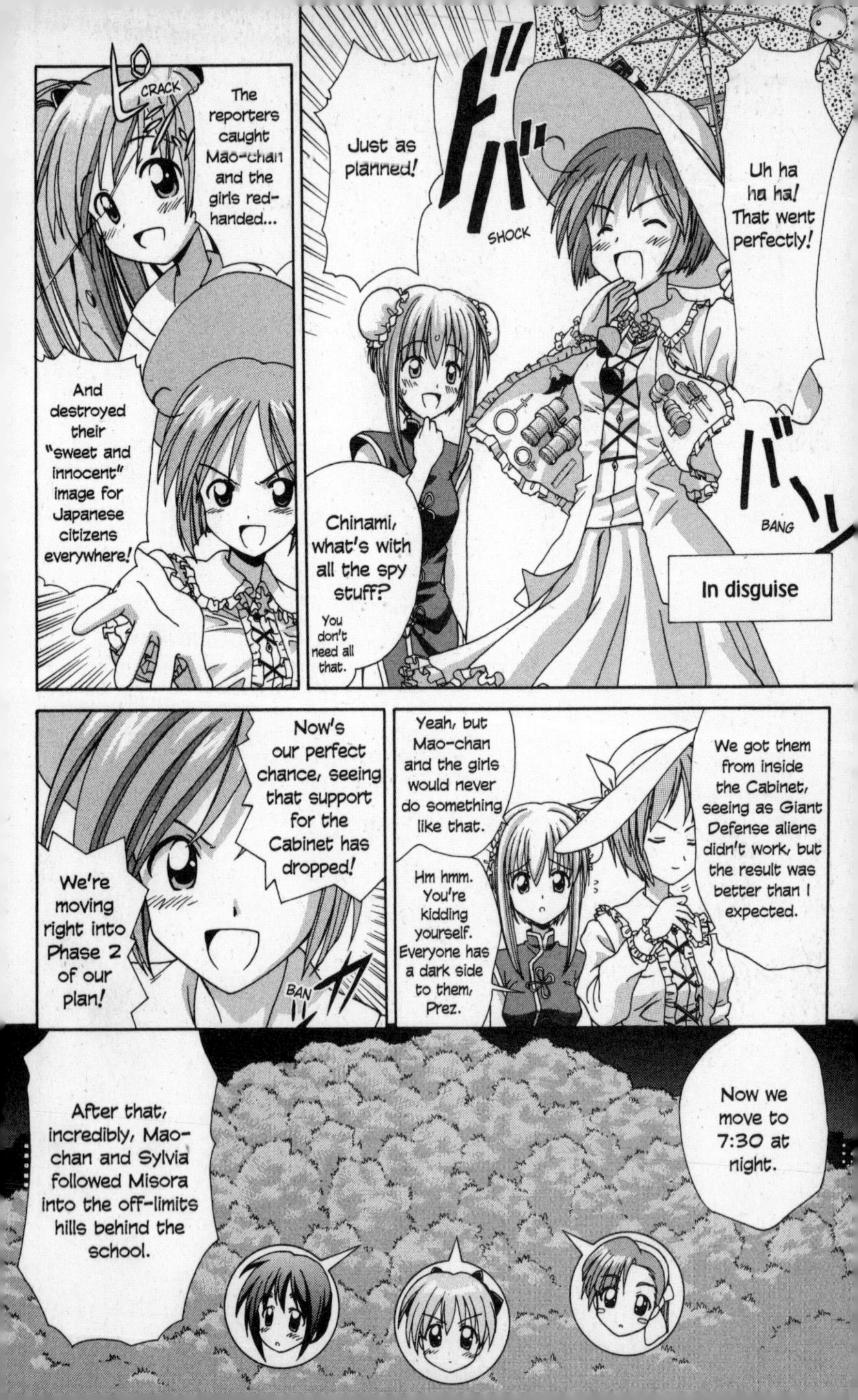
Uh ha ha ha! That went perfectly!
Just as planned!
SHOCK
BANG
In disguise
Chinami, what's with all the spy stuff?
You don't need all that.
CRACK
The reporters caught Mao-chan and the girls red-handed...
And destroyed their "sweet and innocent" image for Japanese citizens everywhere!
We got them from inside the Cabinet, seeing as Giant Defense aliens didn't work, but the result was better than I expected.
Yeah, but Mao-chan and the girls would never do something like that.
Hm hmm. You're kidding yourself. Everyone has a dark side to them, Prez.
Now's our perfect chance, seeing that support for the Cabinet has dropped!
We're moving right into Phase 2 of our plan!
BAN
Now we move to 7:30 at night.
After that, incredibly, Mao-chan and Sylvia followed Misora into the off-limits hills behind the school.

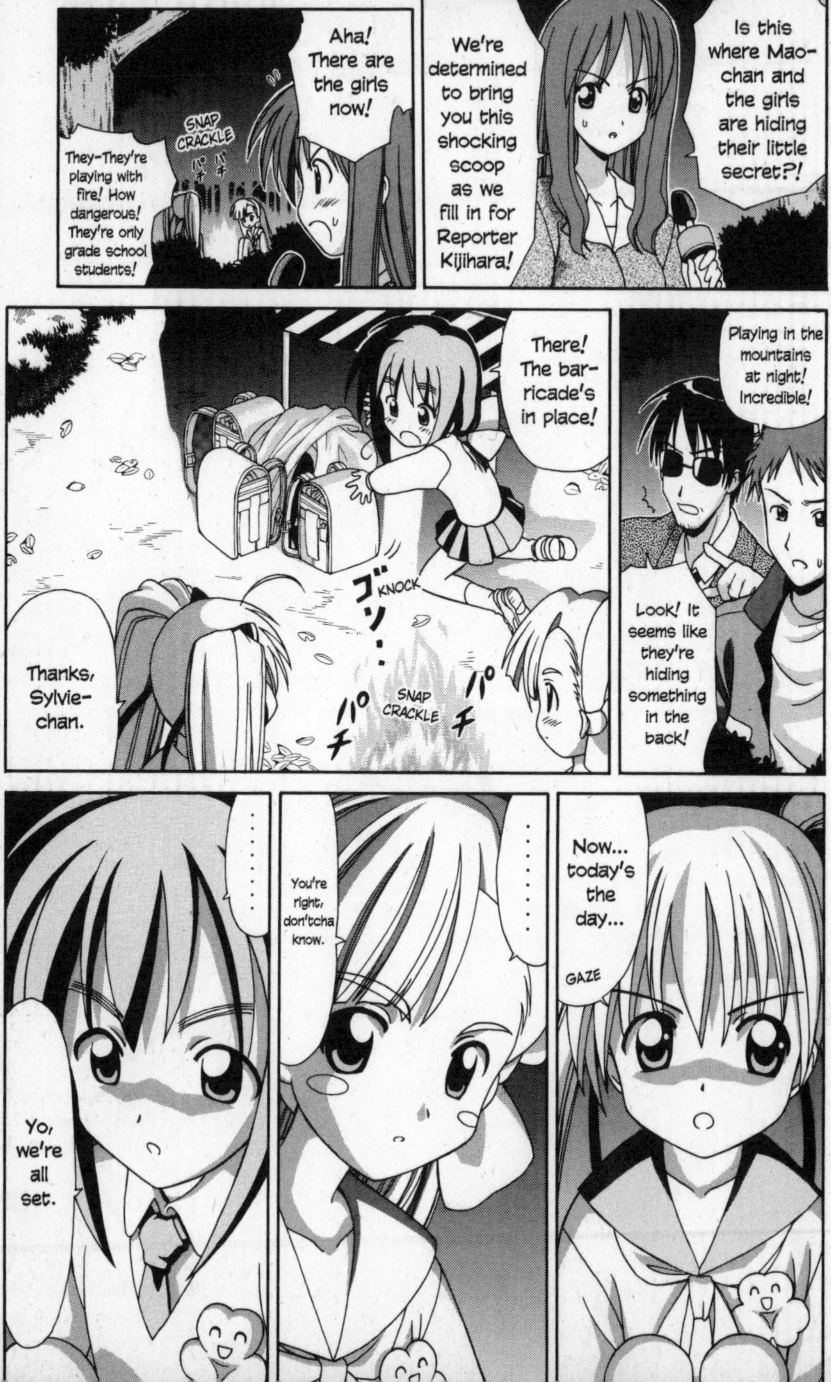

Is this where Mao-chan and the girls are hiding their little secret?!
We're determined to bring you this shocking scoop as we fill in for Reporter Kijihara!
Aha! There are the girls now!
SNAP CRACKLE
パチ パチ
They-They're playing with fire! How dangerous! They're only grade school students!
Playing in the mountains at night! Incredible!
Look! It seems like they're hiding something in the back!
There! The barricade's in place!
ゴツ・・
KNOCK
パチ パチ
SNAP CRACKLE
Thanks, Sylvie-chan.
Now... today's the day...
......
GAZE
......
You're right, don'tcha know.
......
Yo, we're all set.

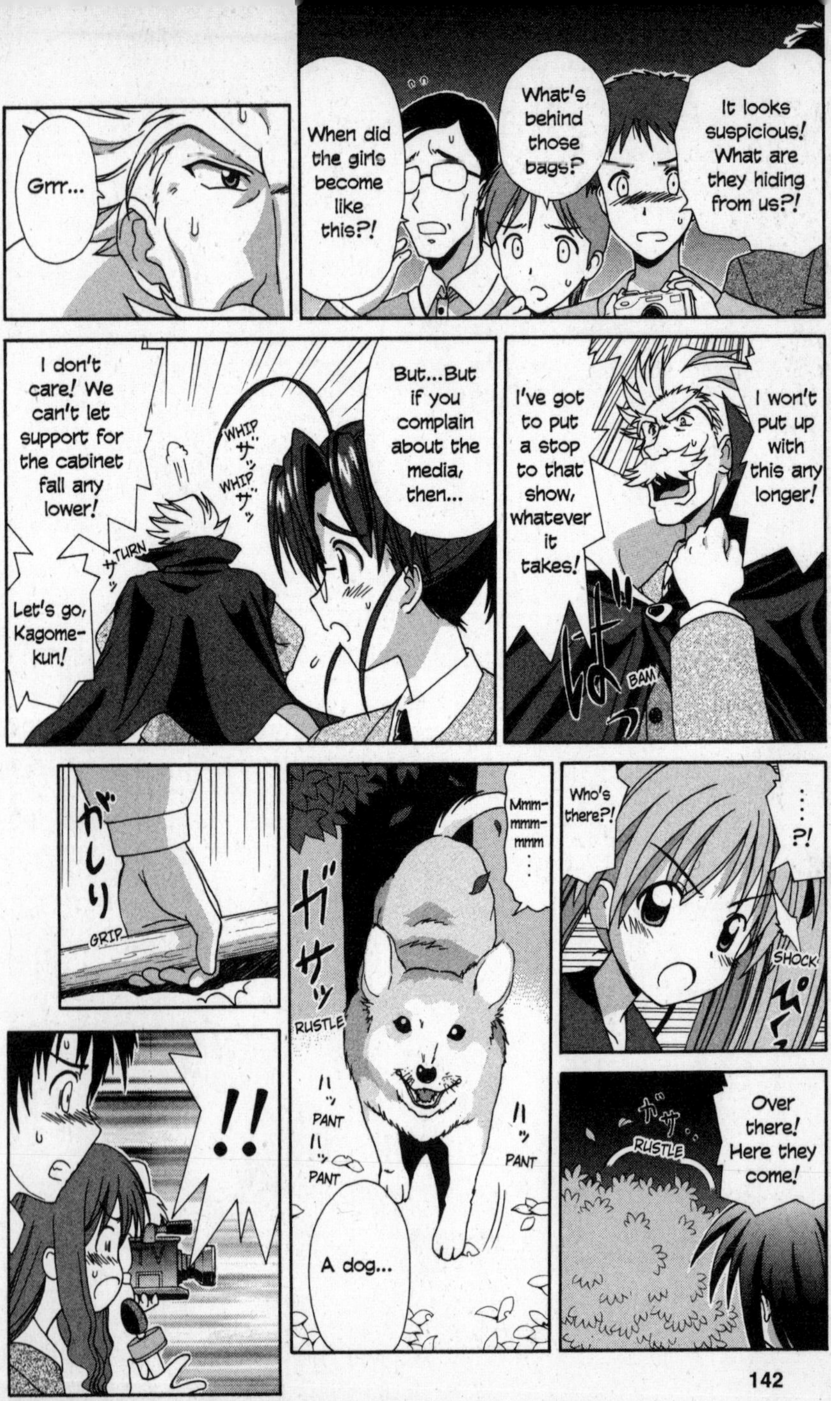
It looks suspicious! What are they hiding from us?!
What's behind those bags?
When did the girls become like this?!
Grrr...
I won't put up with this any longer!
I've got to put a stop to that show, whatever it takes!
BAM
But...But if you complain about the media, then...
WHIP
WHIP
I don't care! We can't let support for the cabinet fall any lower!
TURN
Let's go, Kagome-kun!
...?!
Who's there?!
SHOCK
Over there! Here they come!
RUSTLE
Mmm-mmm-mmm...
RUSTLE
PANT
PANT
PANT
A dog...
GRIP
!!

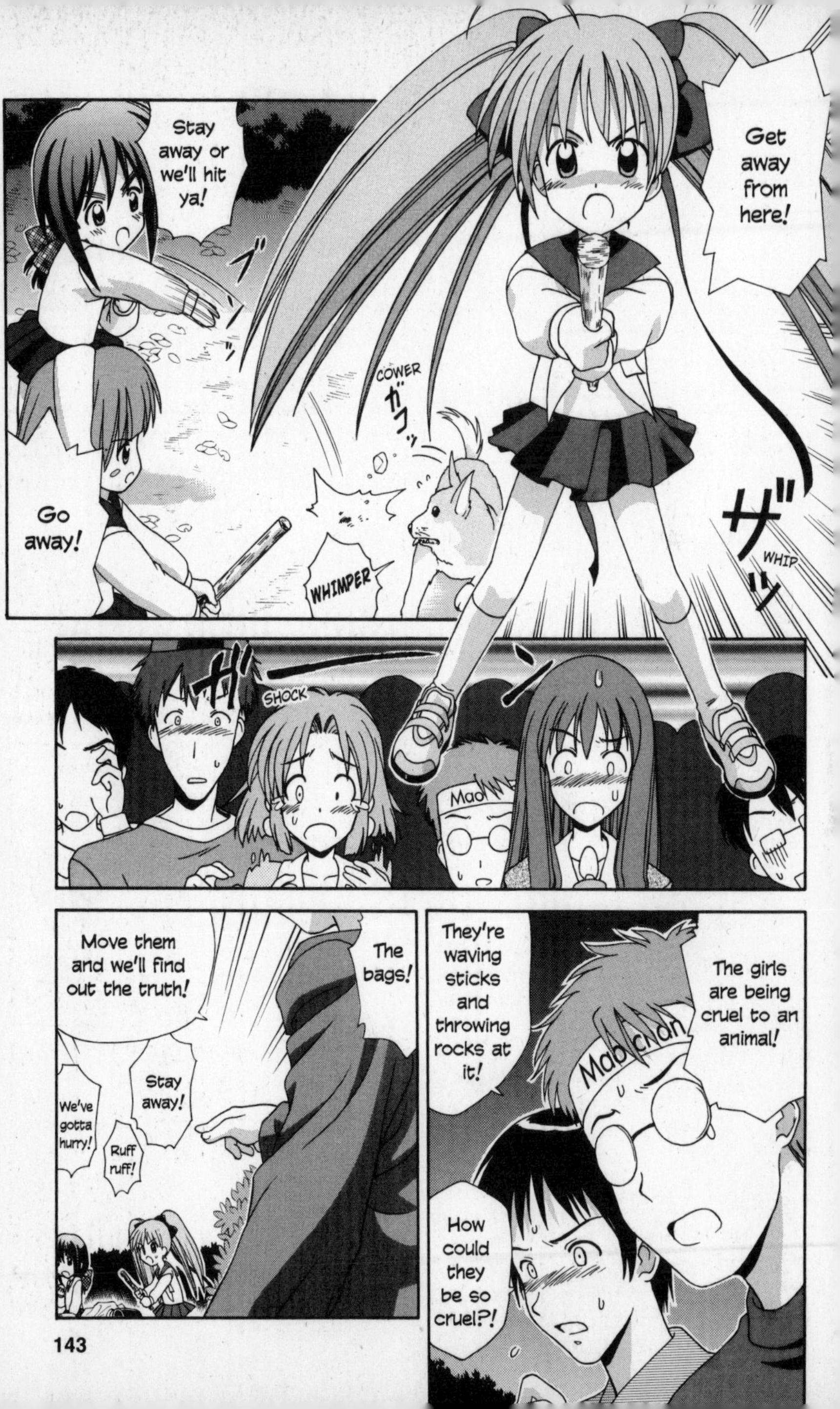
Get away from here!
WHIP
COWER
Stay away or we'll hit ya!
WHIMPER
Go away!
SHOCK
Mao
The girls are being cruel to an animal!
Mao chan
They're waving sticks and throwing rocks at it!
How could they be so cruel?!
The bags!
Move them and we'll find out the truth!
Stay away!
Ruff ruff!
We've gotta hurry!

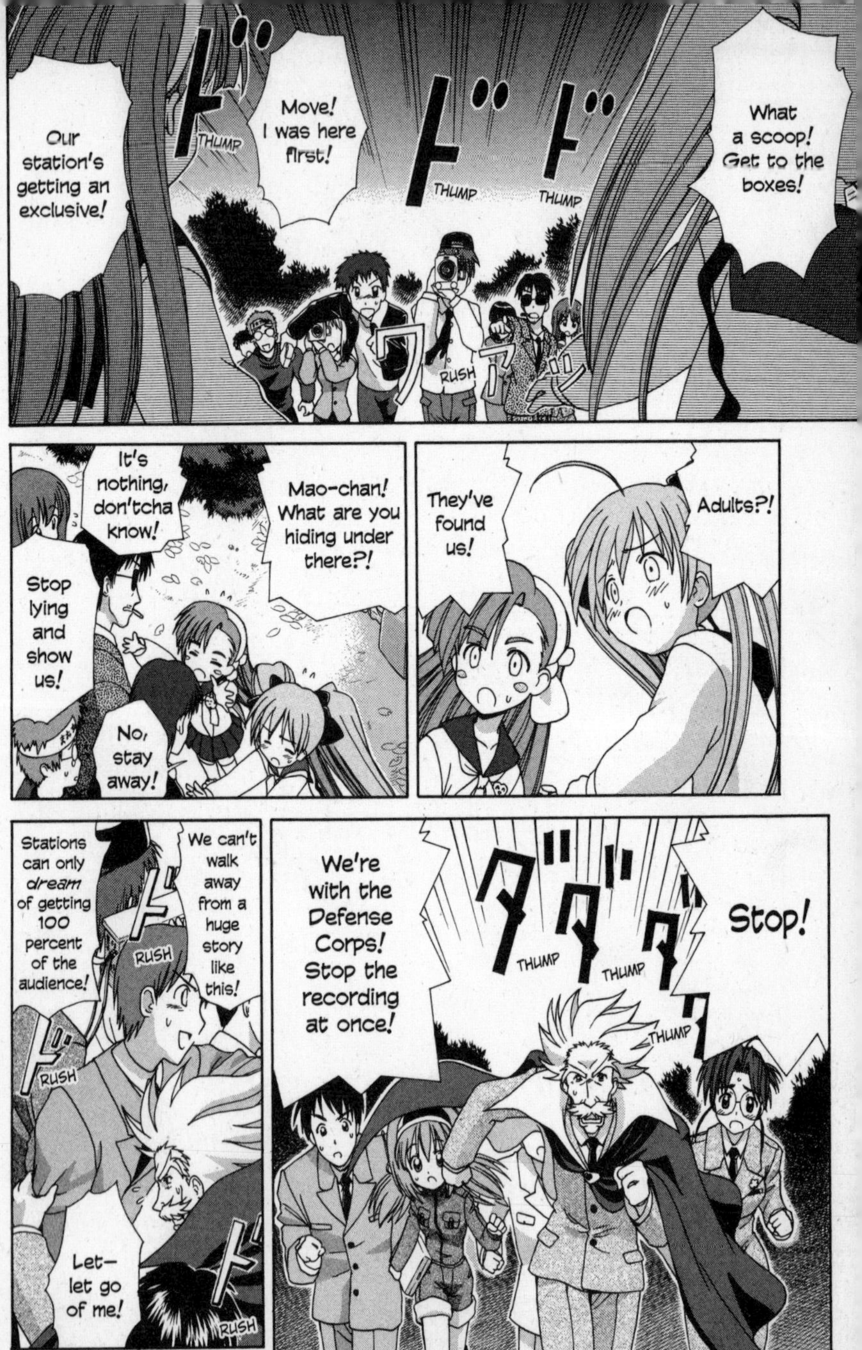
What a scoop! Get to the boxes!
THUMP
THUMP
Move! I was here first!
THUMP
Our station's getting an exclusive!
RUSH
Adults?!
They've found us!
Mao-chan! What are you hiding under there?!
It's nothing, don'tcha know!
Stop lying and show us!
No, stay away!
Stop!
We're with the Defense Corps! Stop the recording at once!
THUMP
THUMP
THUMP
We can't walk away from a huge story like this!
Stations can only *dream* of getting 100 percent of the audience!
RUSH
RUSH
Let—let go of me!
RUSH

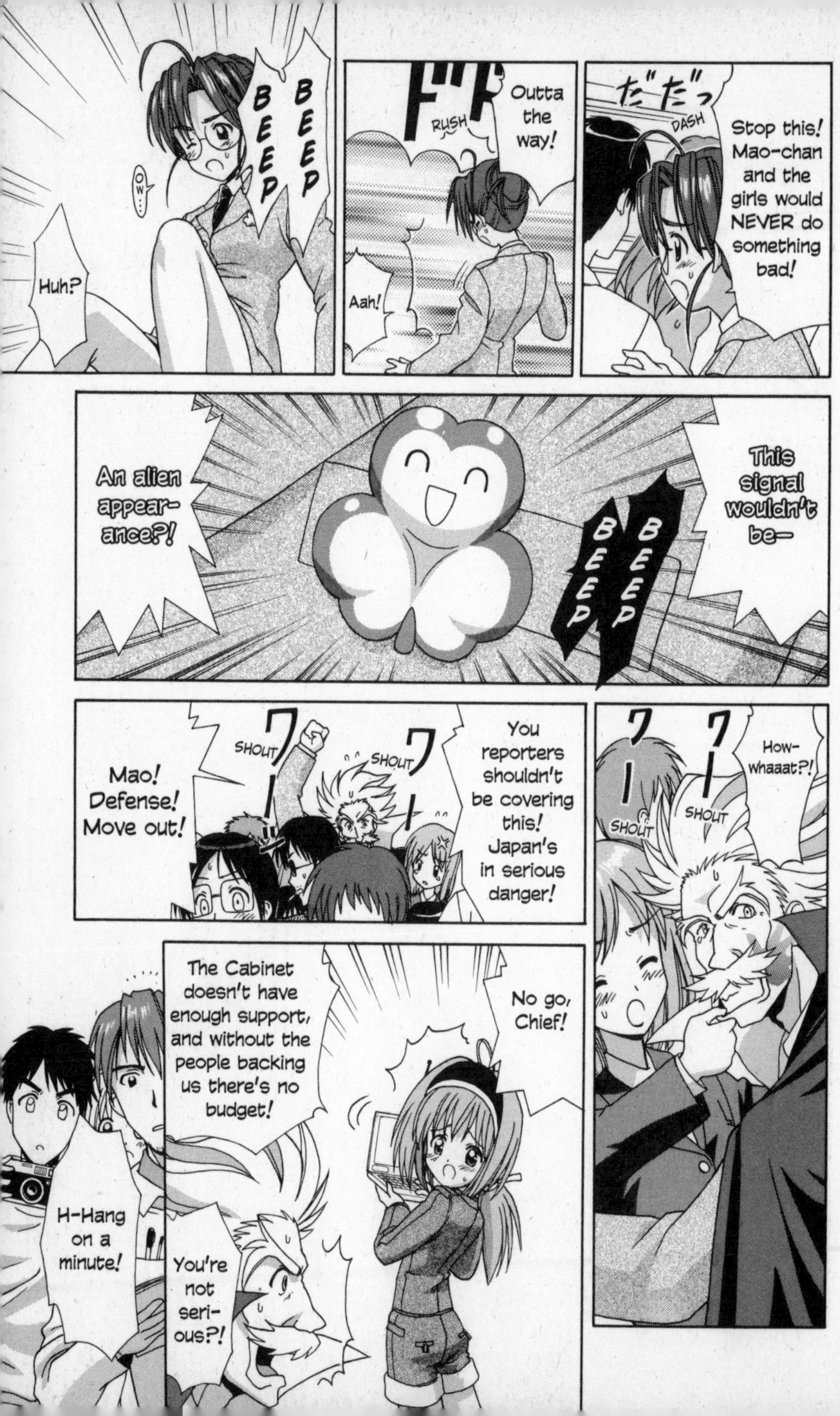
だだっ
DASH
Stop this! Mao-chan and the girls would NEVER do something bad!
ドド
RUSH
Outta the way!
Aah!
BEEP BEEP
OW...
Huh?
This signal wouldn't be-
BEEP BEEP
An alien appearance?!
ワー ワー
How-whaaat?!
SHOUT
SHOUT
ワー ワー
You reporters shouldn't be covering this! Japan's in serious danger!
SHOUT
SHOUT
Mao! Defense! Move out!
No go, Chief!
The Cabinet doesn't have enough support, and without the people backing us there's no budget!
You're not seri-ous?!
H-Hang on a minute!

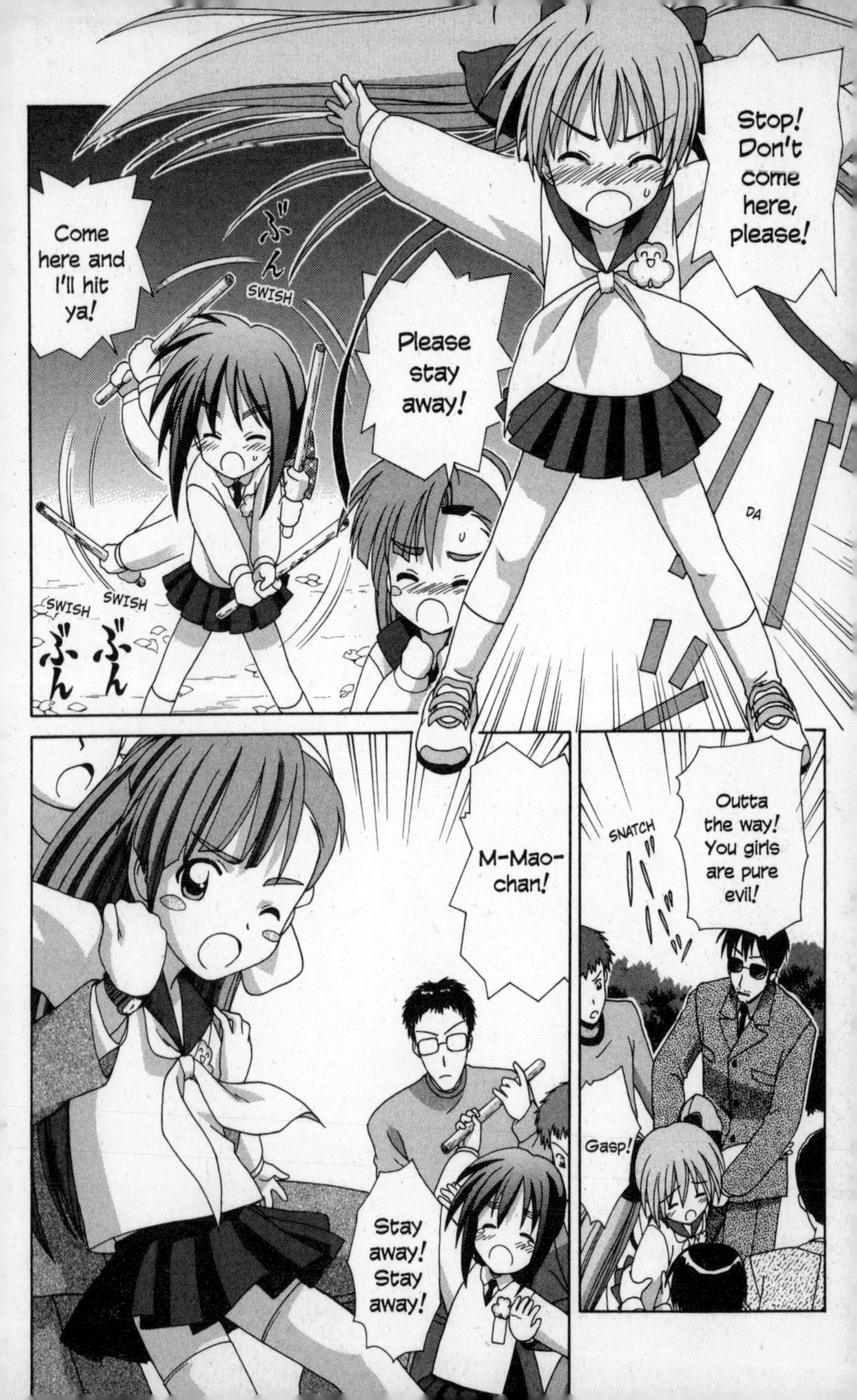
Stop! Don't come here, please!
DA
Please stay away!
ぶん
SWISH
Come here and I'll hit ya!
SWISH
ぶん
SWISH
ぶん
Outta the way! You girls are pure evil!
SNATCH
Gasp!
M-Mao-chan!
Stay away! Stay away!

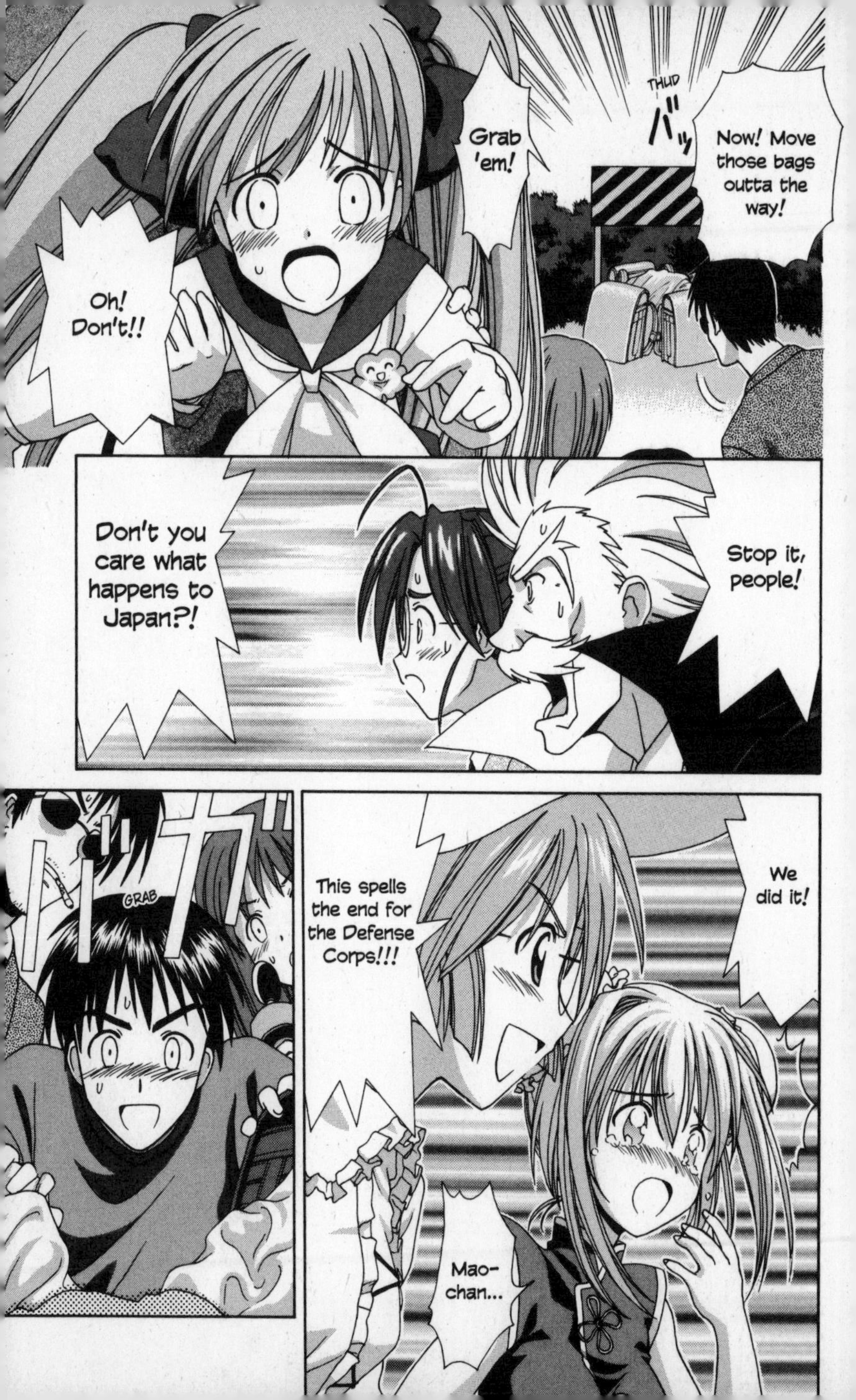
THUD
Now! Move those bags outta the way!
Grab 'em!
Oh! Don't!!
Stop it, people!
Don't you care what happens to Japan?!
We did it!
This spells the end for the Defense Corps!!!
Mao-chan...
GRAB

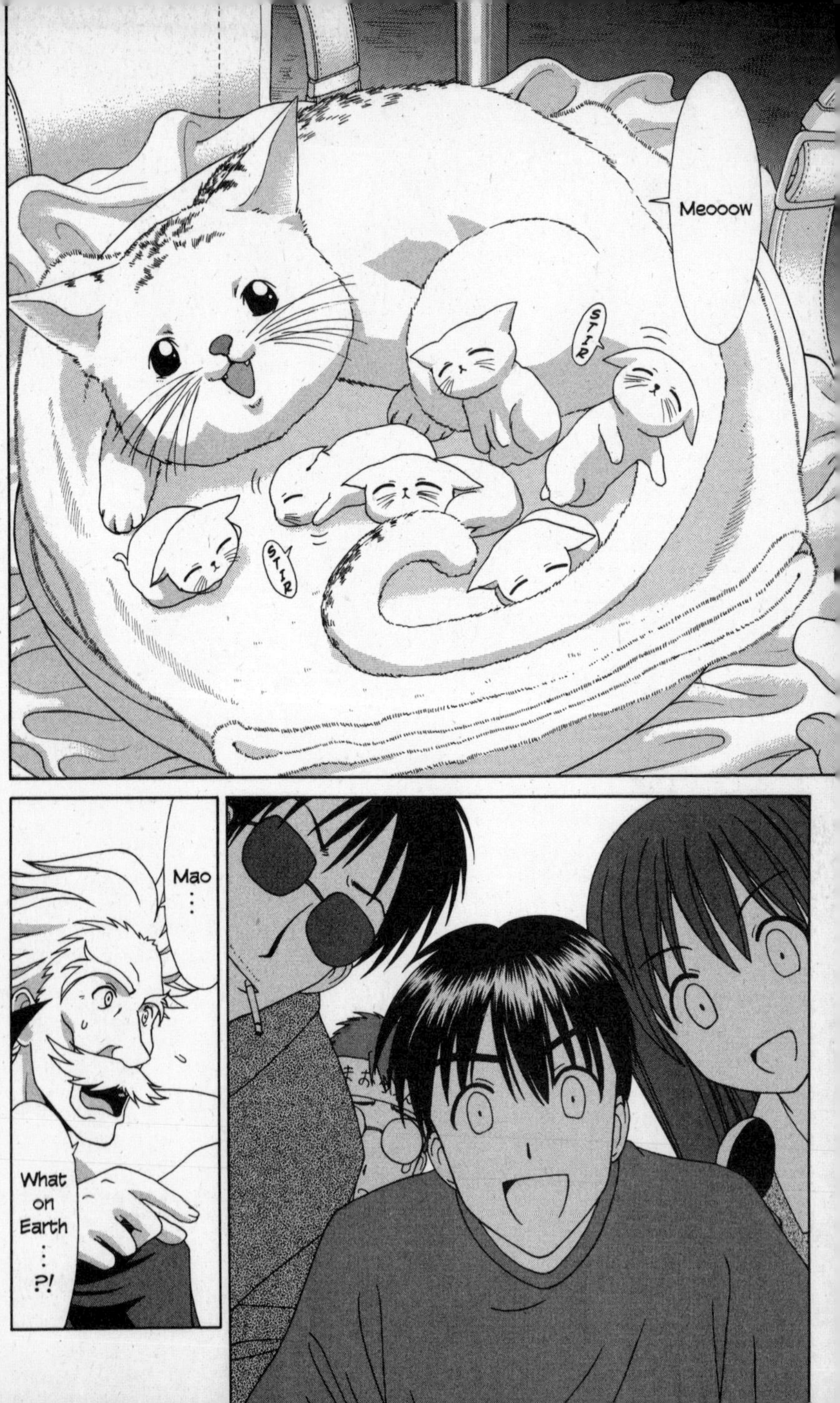
Meooow
STIR
STIR
Mao . . .
What on Earth . . . ?!

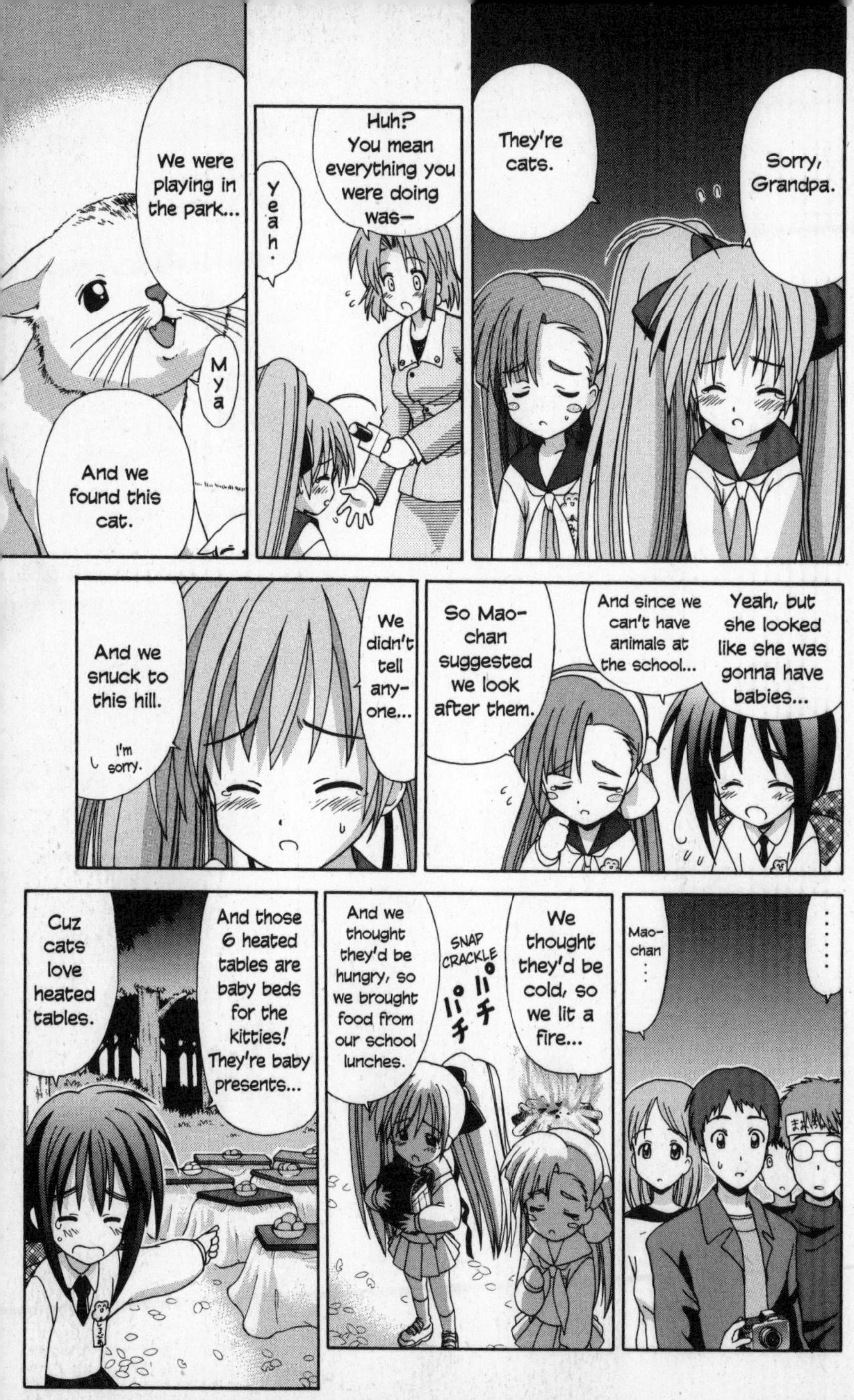
Sorry, Grandpa.
They're cats.
Huh? You mean everything you were doing was—
Yeah.
We were playing in the park...
Mya
And we found this cat.
Yeah, but she looked like she was gonna have babies...
And since we can't have animals at the school...
So Mao-chan suggested we look after them.
We didn't tell anyone...
And we snuck to this hill.
I'm sorry.
......
Mao-chan...
We thought they'd be cold, so we lit a fire...
SNAP CRACKLE
パチパチ
And we thought they'd be hungry, so we brought food from our school lunches.
And those 6 heated tables are baby beds for the kitties! They're baby presents...
Cuz cats love heated tables.

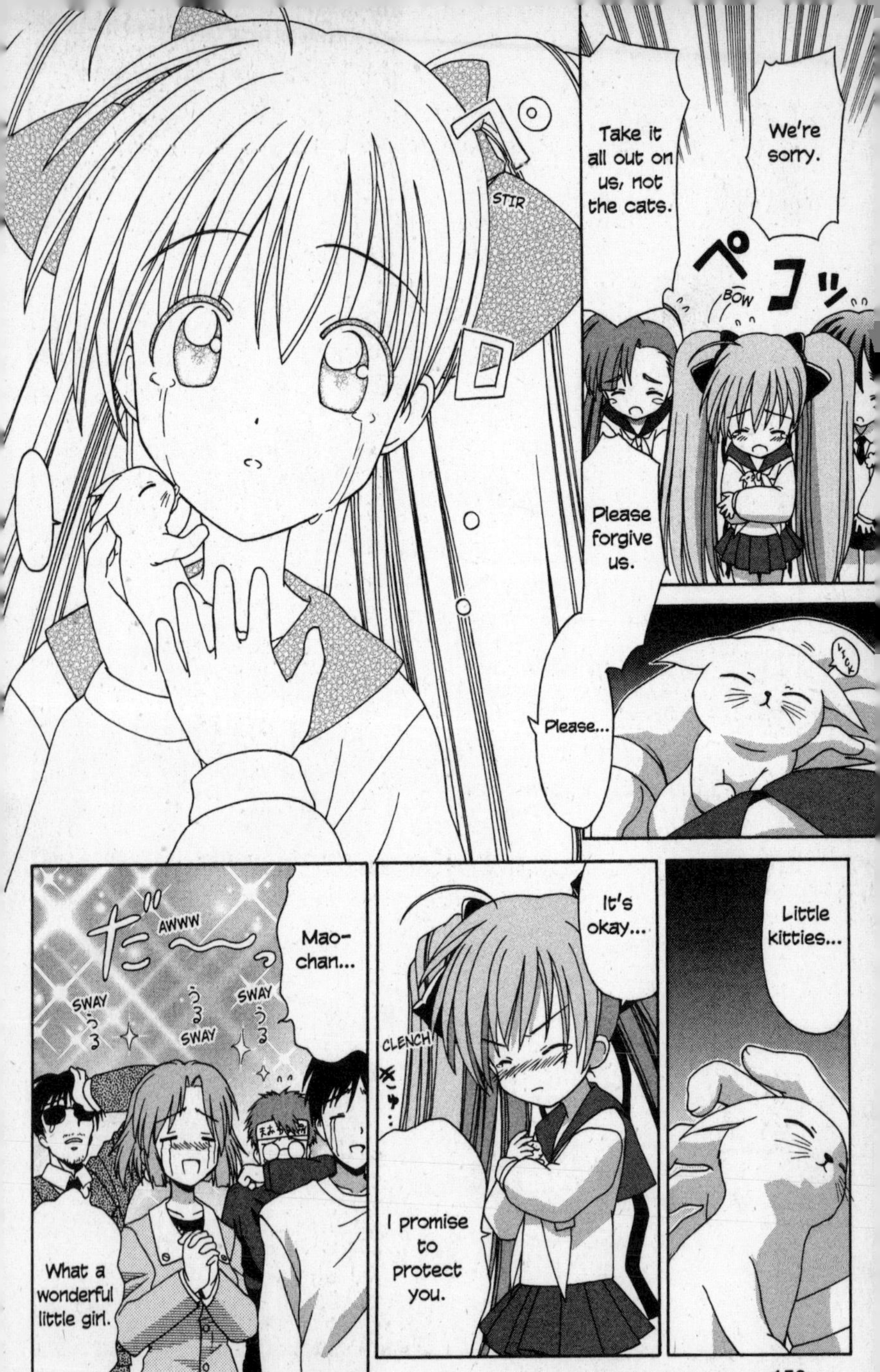
We're sorry.
Take it all out on us, not the cats.
BOW
Please forgive us.
Please...
STIR
Little kitties...
It's okay...
CLENCH
I promise to protect you.
AWWW
Mao-chan...
SWAY
SWAY
SWAY
What a wonderful little girl.

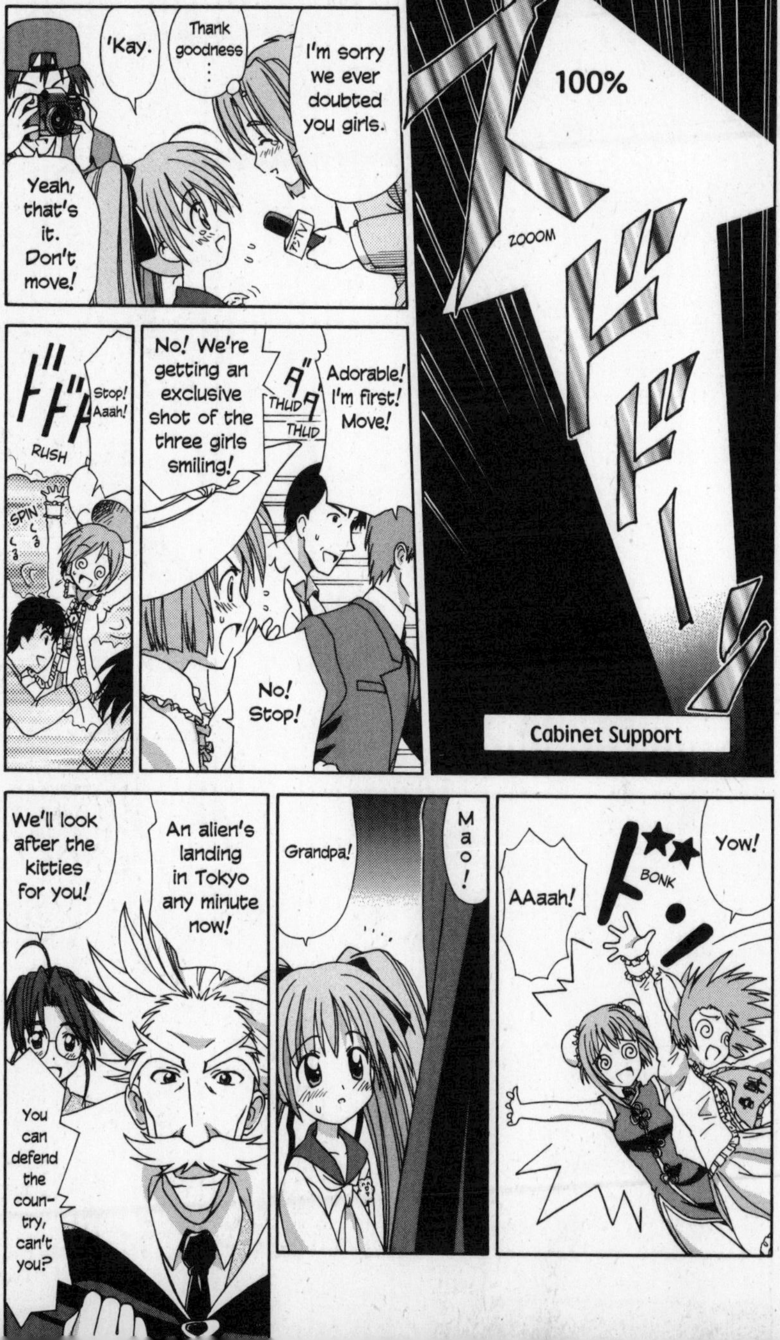
100%
ZOOOM
Cabinet Support
I'm sorry we ever doubted you girls.
Thank goodness...
'Kay.
Yeah, that's it. Don't move!
Adorable! I'm first! Move!
THUD
THUD
No! We're getting an exclusive shot of the three girls smiling!
No! Stop!
Stop! Aaah!
RUSH
SPIN
Yow!
BONK
AAaah!
Mao!
Grandpa!
...
An alien's landing in Tokyo any minute now!
We'll look after the kitties for you!
You can defend the country, can't you?

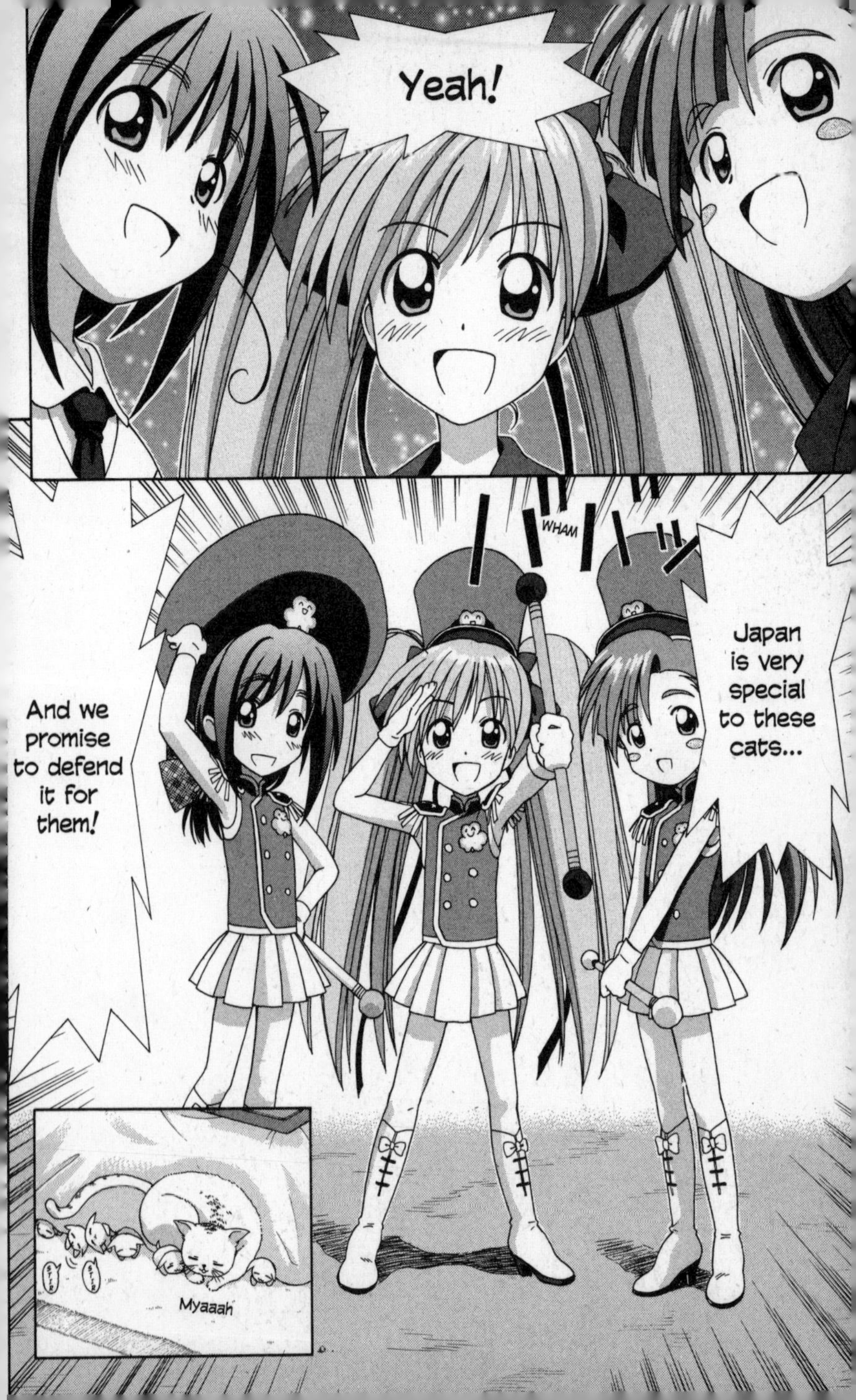
Yeah!
Japan is very special to these cats...
WHAM
And we promise to defend it for them!
STIR
STIR
Myaaah

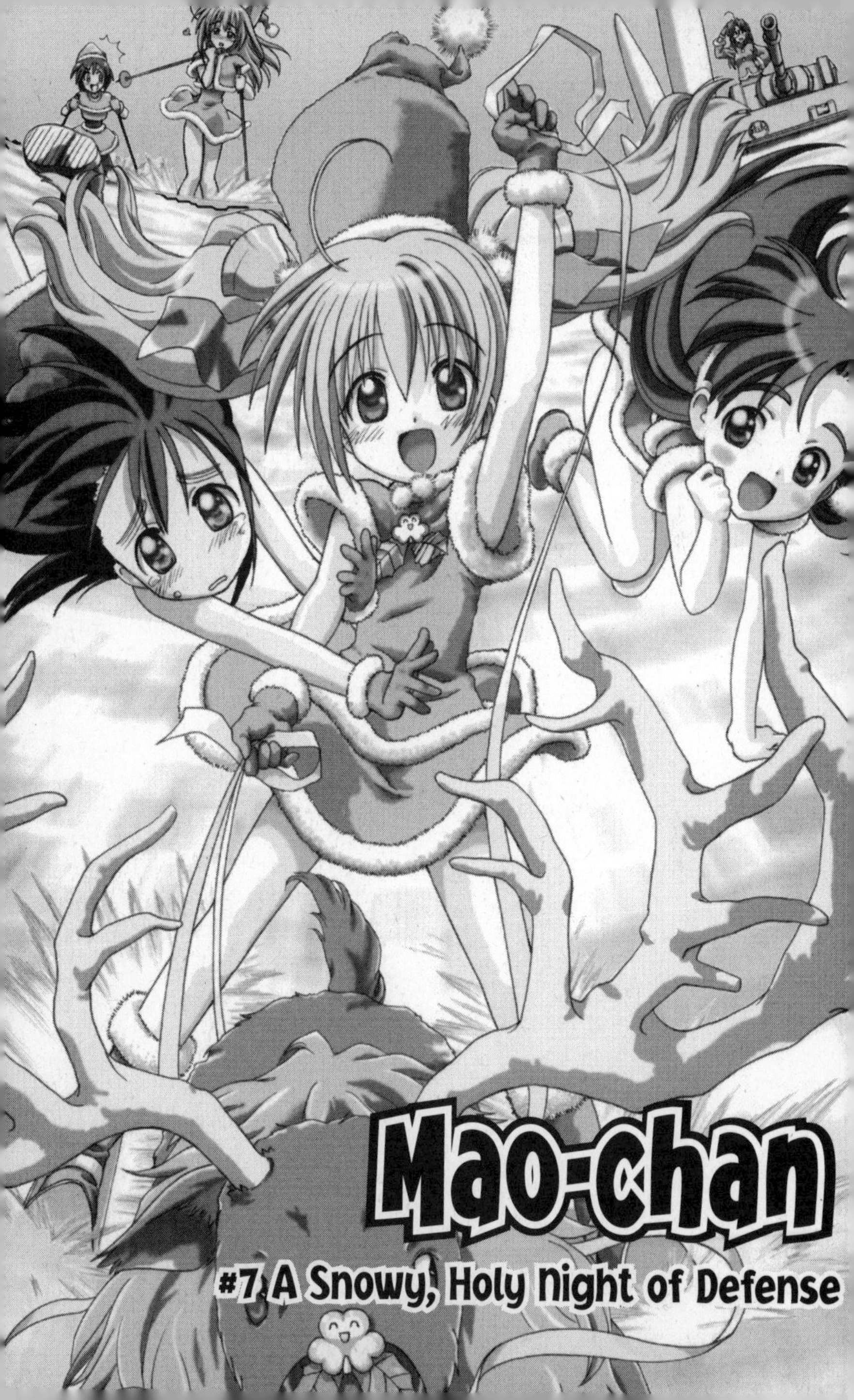
Mao-chan
#7 A Snowy, Holy Night of Defense

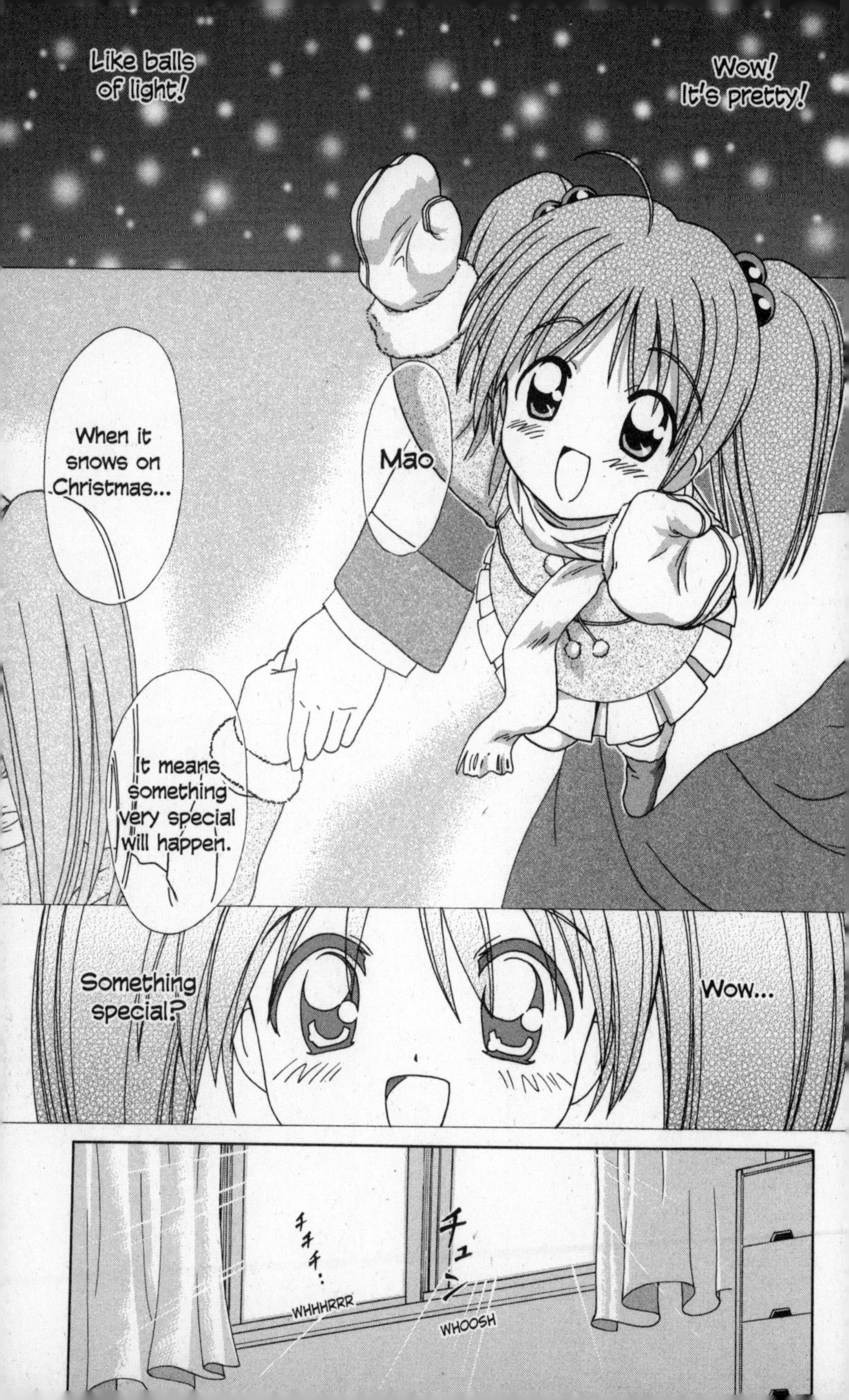
Wow! It's pretty!
Like balls of light!
Mao
When it snows on Christmas...
It means something very special will happen.
Wow...
Something special?
チュン
WHOOSH
チチチ‥
WHHHRRR

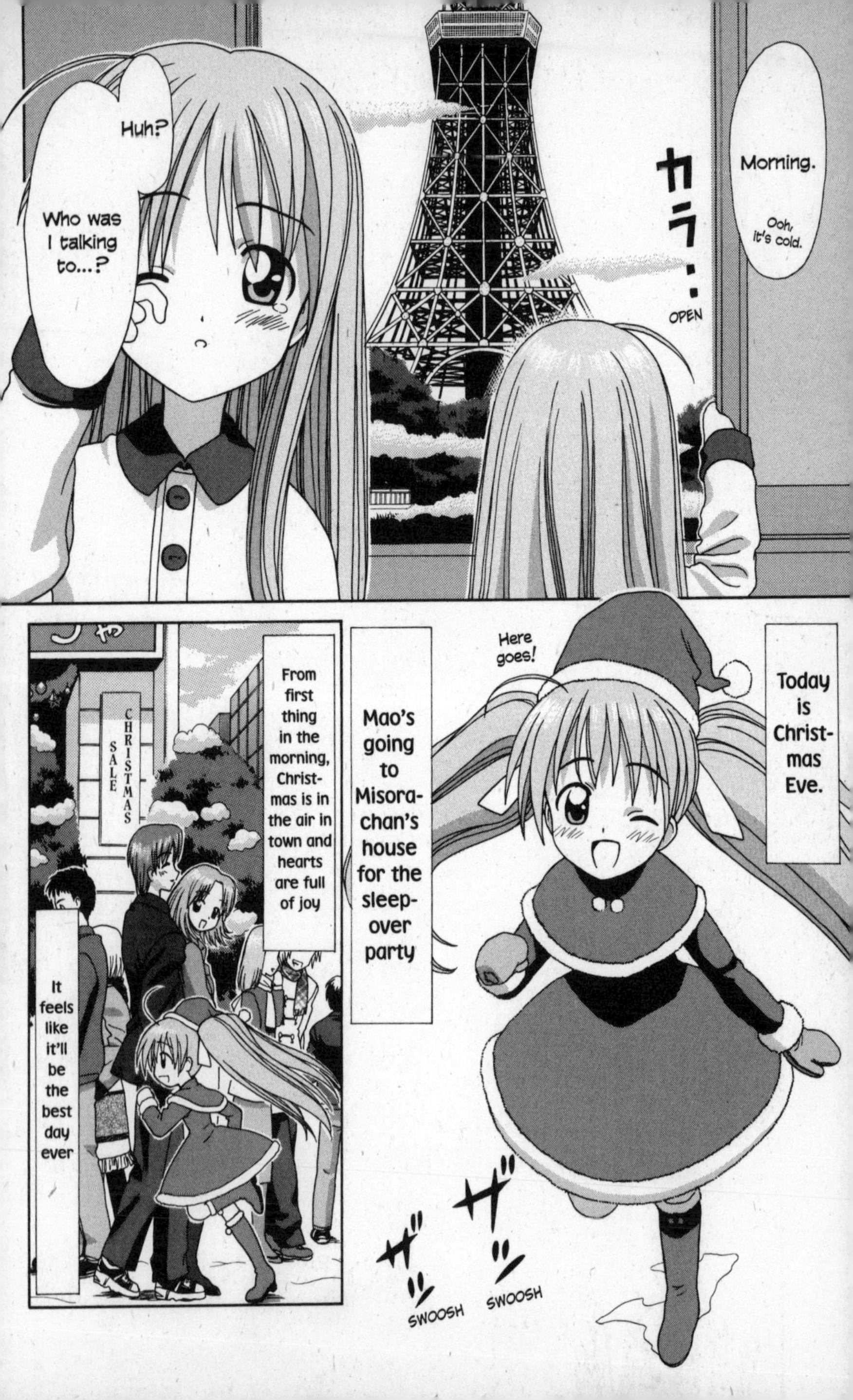
Morning.
Ooh, it's cold.
カラ・・
OPEN
Huh?
Who was I talking to...?
Today is Christmas Eve.
Here goes!
Mao's going to Misora-chan's house for the sleep-over party
ザッ
SWOOSH
ザッ
SWOOSH
From first thing in the morning, Christmas is in the air in town and hearts are full of joy
CHRISTMAS SALE
It feels like it'll be the best day ever

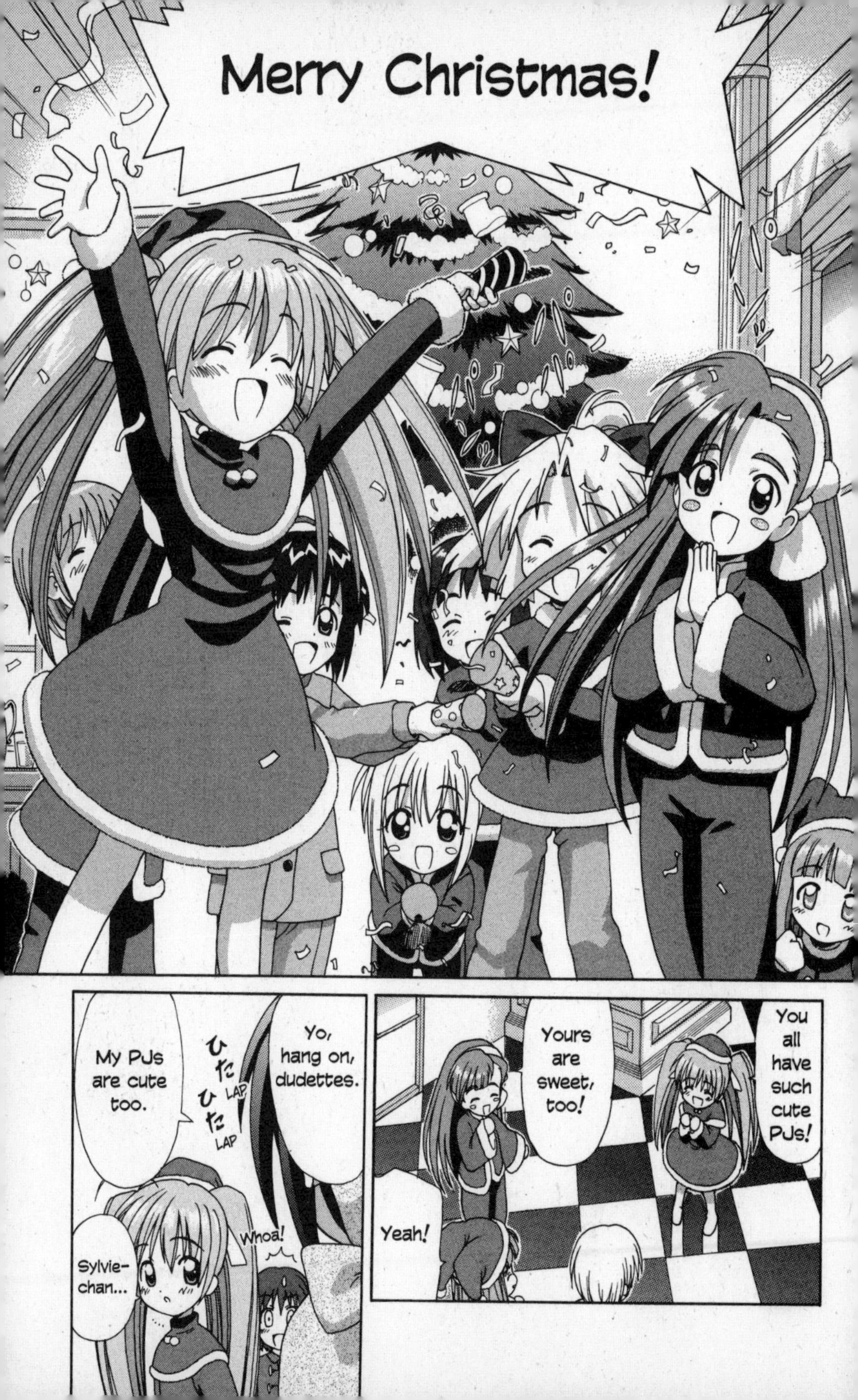
Merry Christmas!
You all have such cute PJs!
Yours are sweet, too!
Yeah!
Yo, hang on, dudettes.
ひた ひた LAP LAP
My PJs are cute too.
Whoa!
Sylvie-chan...

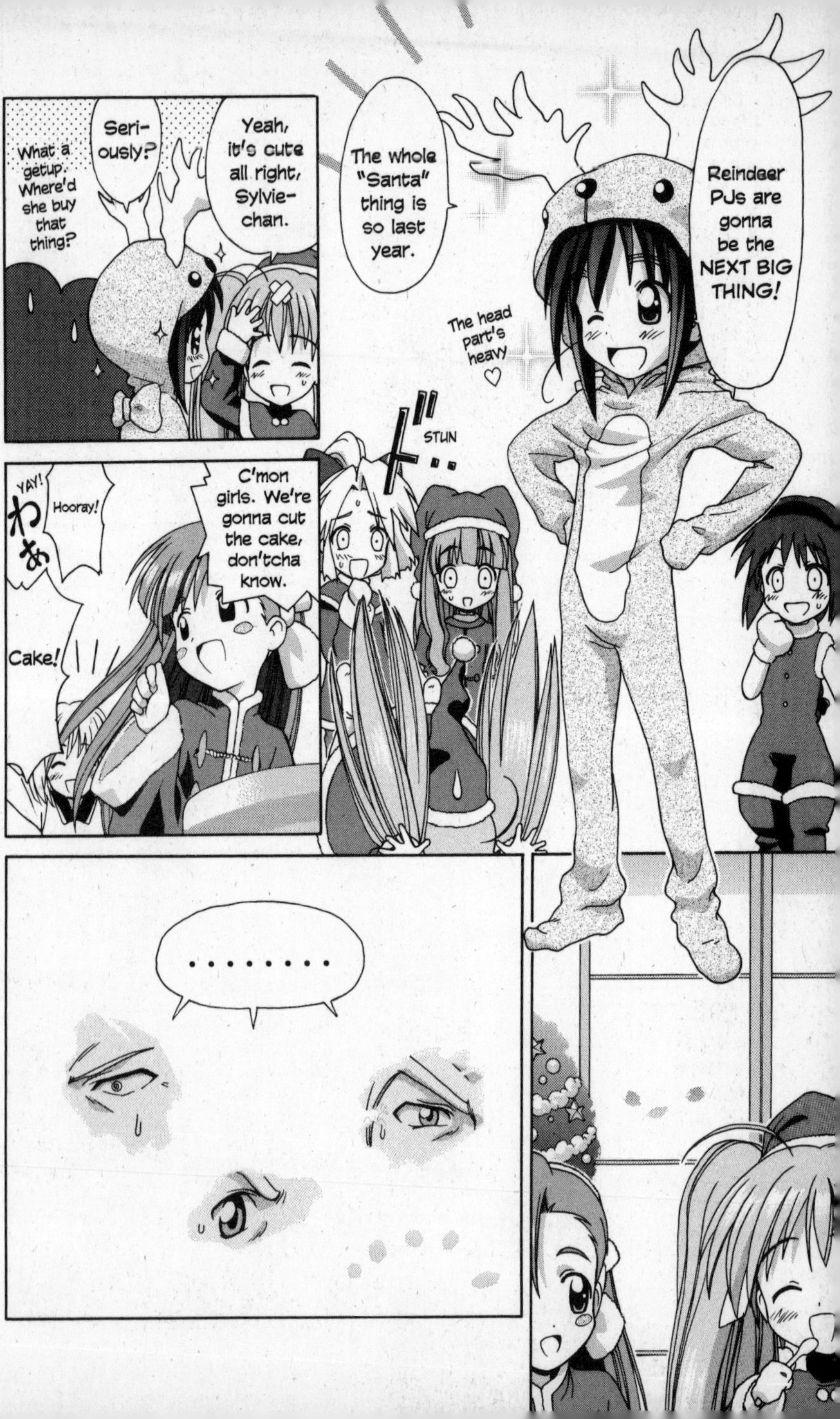
Reindeer PJs are gonna be the NEXT BIG THING!
The whole "Santa" thing is so last year.
The head part's heavy ♡
STUN
Yeah, it's cute all right, Sylvie-chan.
Seri-ously?
What a getup. Where'd she buy that thing?
C'mon girls. We're gonna cut the cake, don'tcha know.
Hooray!
YAY!
わあ
Cake!
....

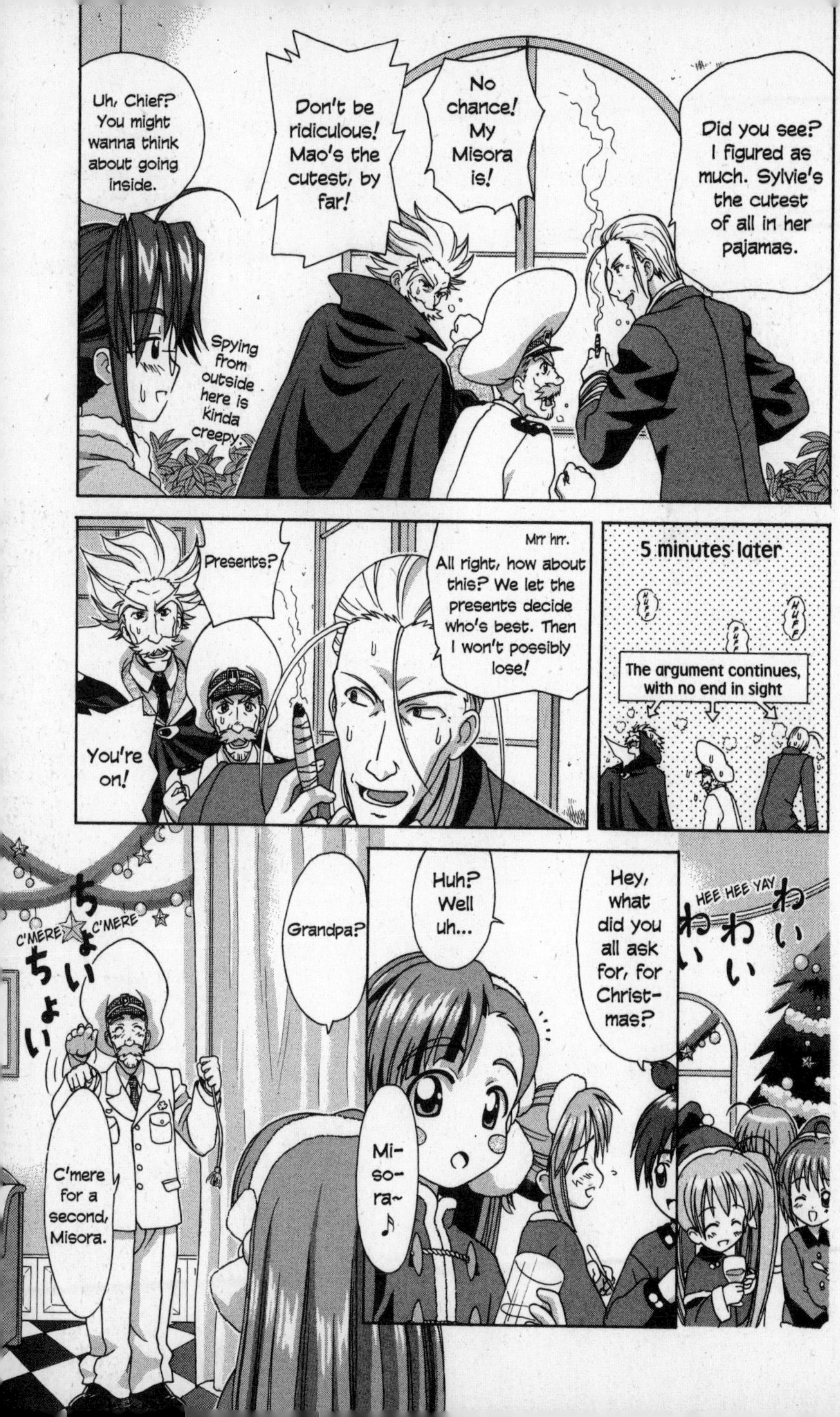
Did you see? I figured as much. Sylvie's the cutest of all in her pajamas.
No chance! My Misora is!
Don't be ridiculous! Mao's the cutest, by far!
Uh, Chief? You might wanna think about going inside.
Spying from outside here is kinda creepy.
5 minutes later
HUFF
PUFF
HUFF
The argument continues, with no end in sight
Mrr hrr.
All right, how about this? We let the presents decide who's best. Then I won't possibly lose!
Presents?
You're on!
わいわい
HEE HEE YAY
Hey, what did you all ask for, for Christmas?
Huh? Well uh...
Grandpa?
Mi-so-ra~♪
ちょいちょい
C'MERE C'MERE
C'mere for a second, Misora.

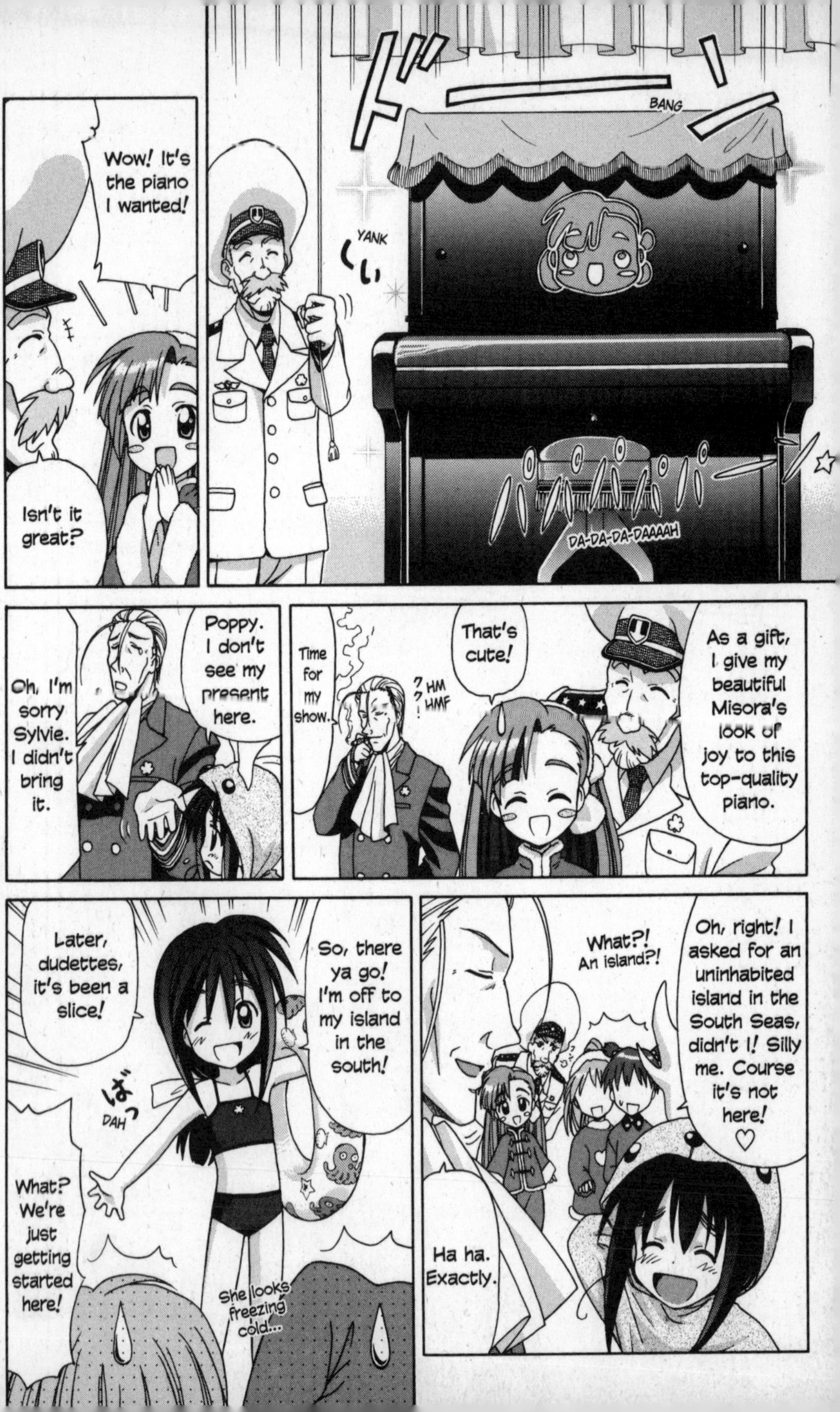
BANG
YANK
DA-DA-DA-DAAAAH
Wow! It's the piano I wanted!
Isn't it great?
As a gift, I give my beautiful Misora's look of joy to this top-quality piano.
That's cute!
HM HMF
Time for my show.
Poppy. I don't see my present here.
Oh, I'm sorry Sylvie. I didn't bring it.
Oh, right! I asked for an uninhabited island in the South Seas, didn't I! Silly me. Course it's not here! ♡
What?! An island?!
Ha ha. Exactly.
So, there ya go! I'm off to my island in the south!
Later, dudettes, it's been a slice!
DAH
What? We're just getting started here!
She looks freezing cold...

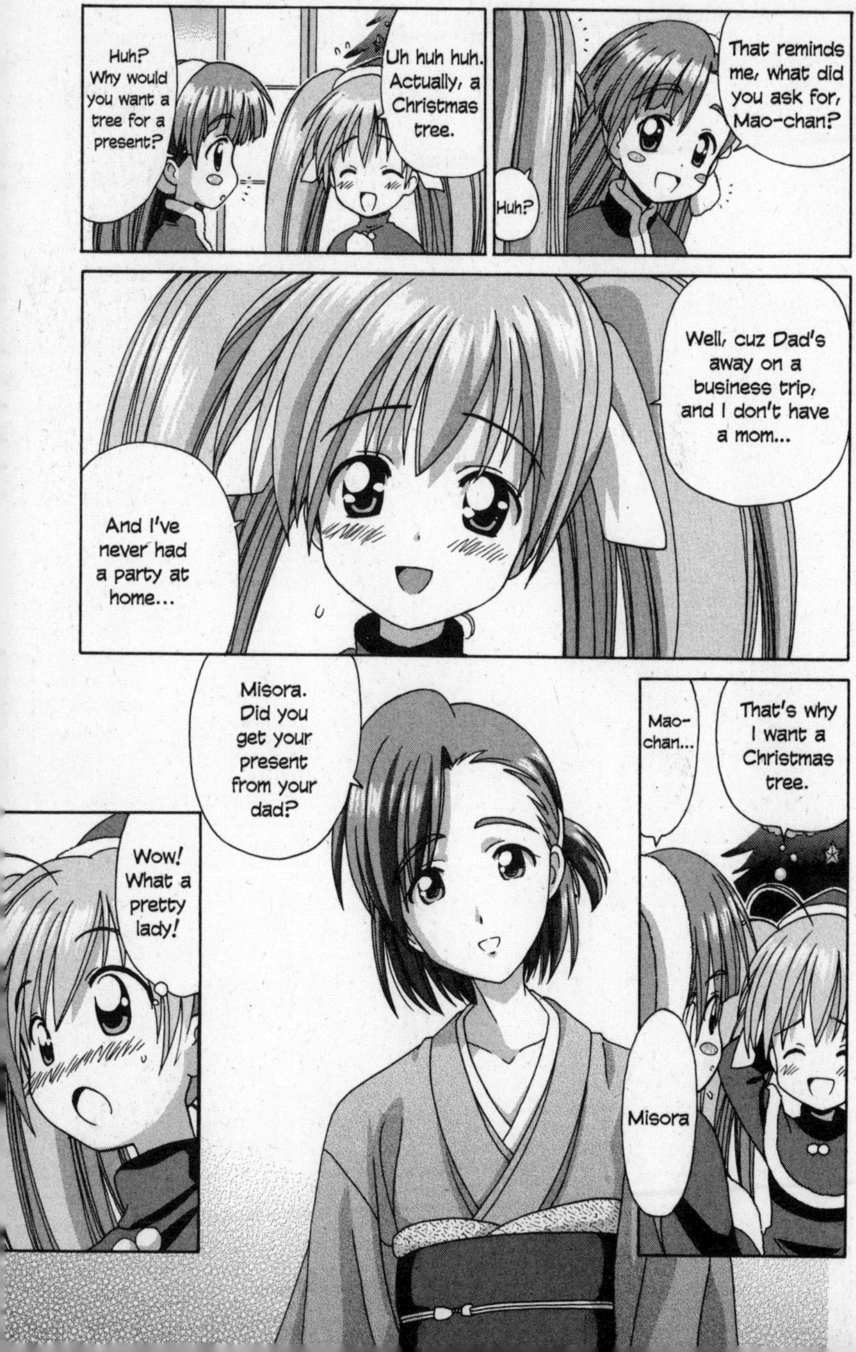
That reminds me, what did you ask for, Mao-chan?
Huh?
Uh huh huh. Actually, a Christmas tree.
Huh? Why would you want a tree for a present?
Well, cuz Dad's away on a business trip, and I don't have a mom...
And I've never had a party at home...
That's why I want a Christmas tree.
Mao-chan...
Misora
Misora. Did you get your present from your dad?
Wow! What a pretty lady!

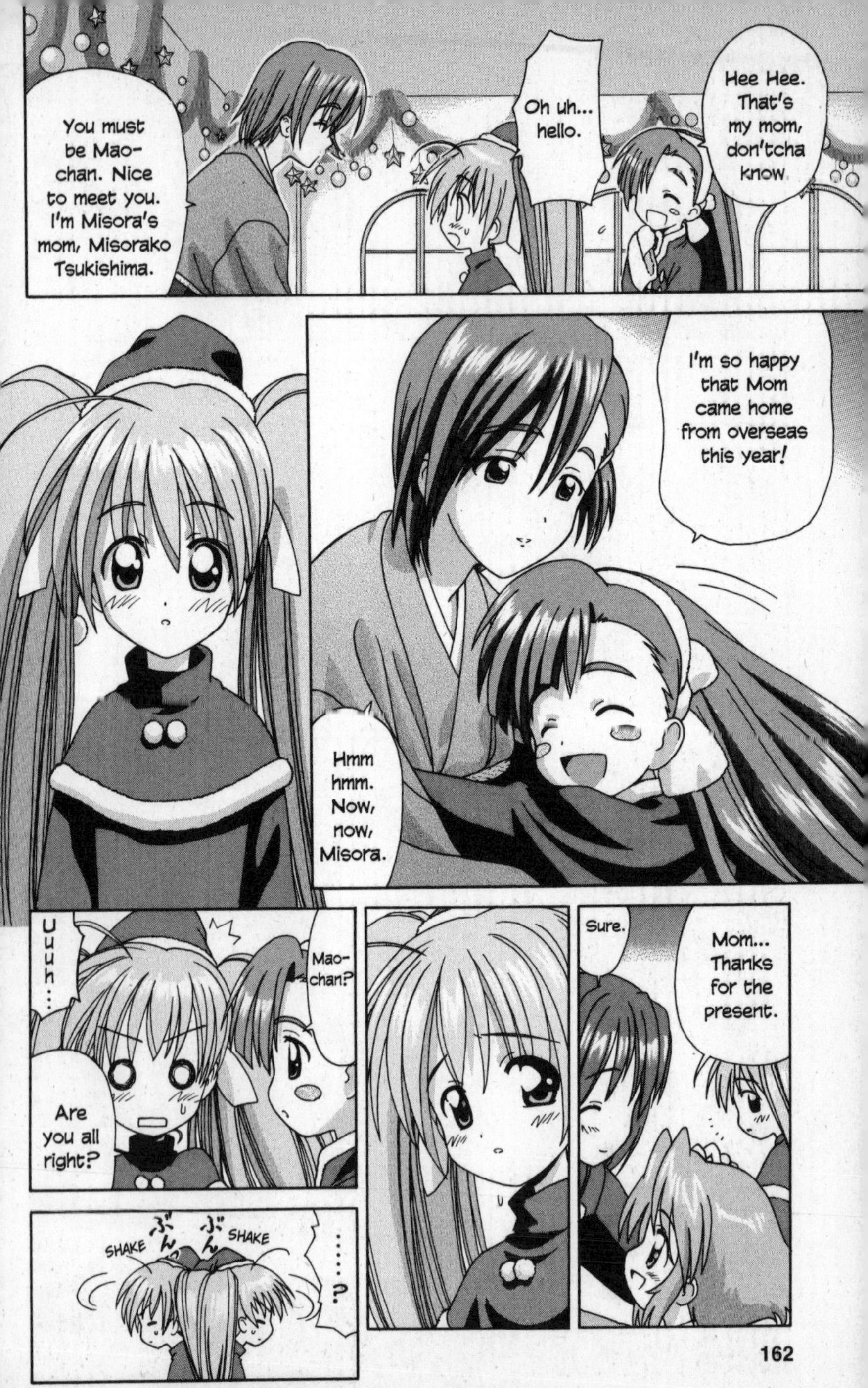
Hee Hee. That's my mom, don'tcha know.
Oh uh... hello.
You must be Mao-chan. Nice to meet you. I'm Misora's mom, Misorako Tsukishima.
I'm so happy that Mom came home from overseas this year!
Hmm hmm. Now, now, Misora.
Mom... Thanks for the present.
Sure.
Mao-chan?
Uuuh...
Are you all right?
......?
ぶん SHAKE
ぶん SHAKE

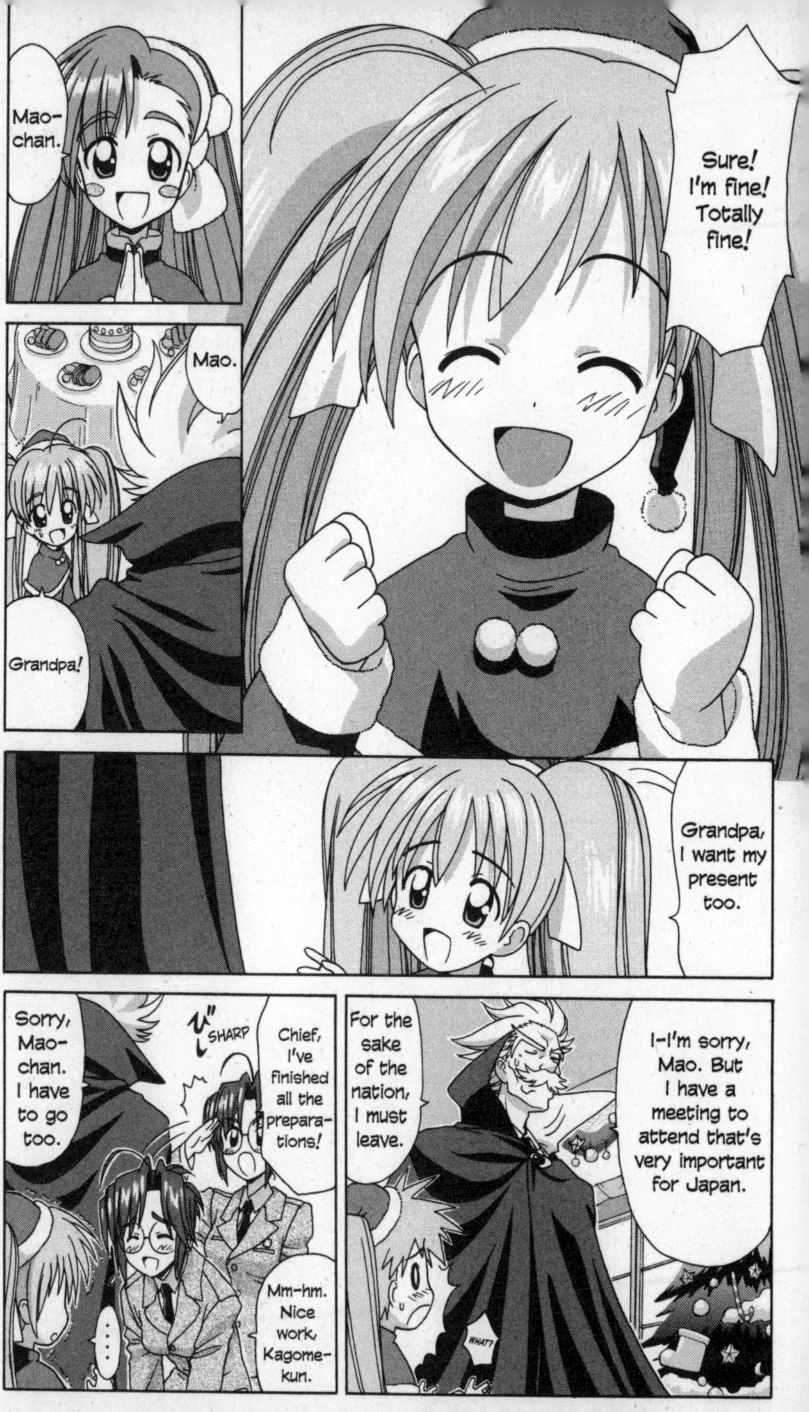
Sure! I'm fine! Totally fine!
Mao-chan.
Mao.
Grandpa!
Grandpa, I want my present too.
I-I'm sorry, Mao. But I have a meeting to attend that's very important for Japan.
For the sake of the nation, I must leave.
WHAT?
Chief, I've finished all the preparations!
SHARP
Sorry, Mao-chan. I have to go too.
Mm-hm. Nice work, Kagome-kun.
....

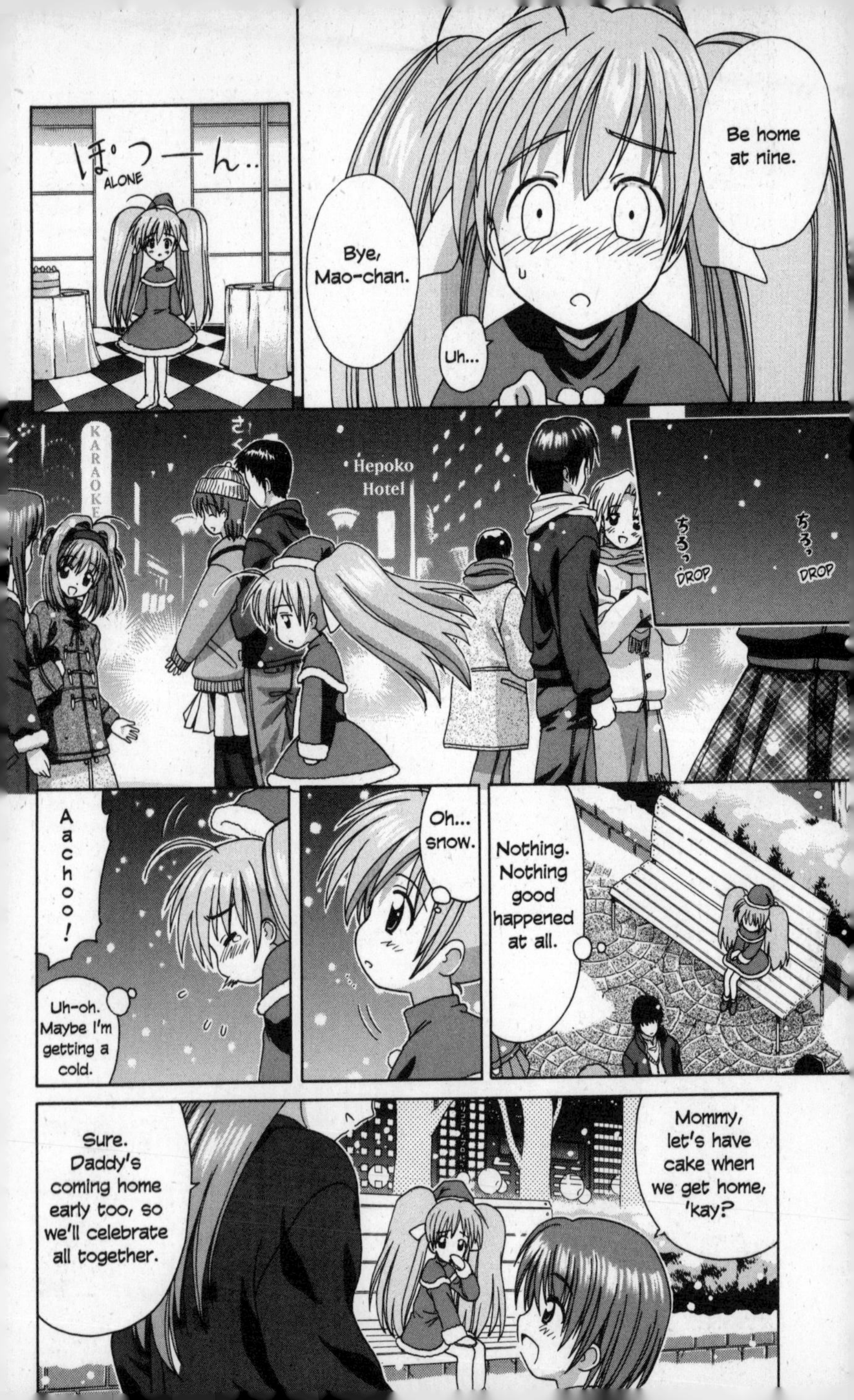
Be home at nine.
Bye, Mao-chan.
Uh...
ぽつーん..
ALONE
ちろっ
DROP
ちろっ
DROP
Hepoko Hotel
KARAOKE
さく
Nothing. Nothing good happened at all.
Oh... snow.
Aachoo!
Uh-oh. Maybe I'm getting a cold.
Mommy, let's have cake when we get home, 'kay?
Sure. Daddy's coming home early too, so we'll celebrate all together.

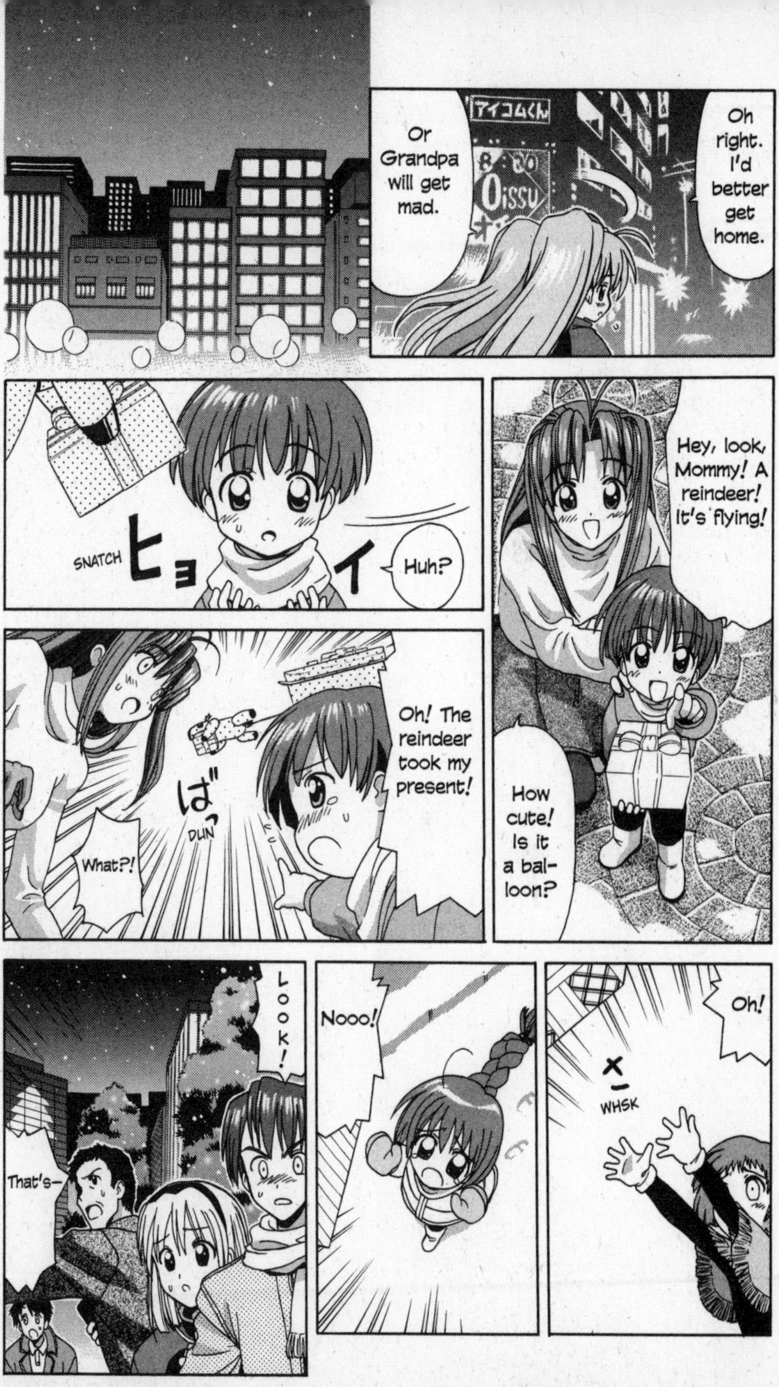

Oh right. I'd better get home.
Or Grandpa will get mad.
Hey, look, Mommy! A reindeer! It's flying!
How cute! Is it a balloon?
Huh?
ヒョイ
SNATCH
Oh! The reindeer took my present!
ばっ
DUN
What?!
Oh!
WHSK
Nooo!
LOOK!
That's—

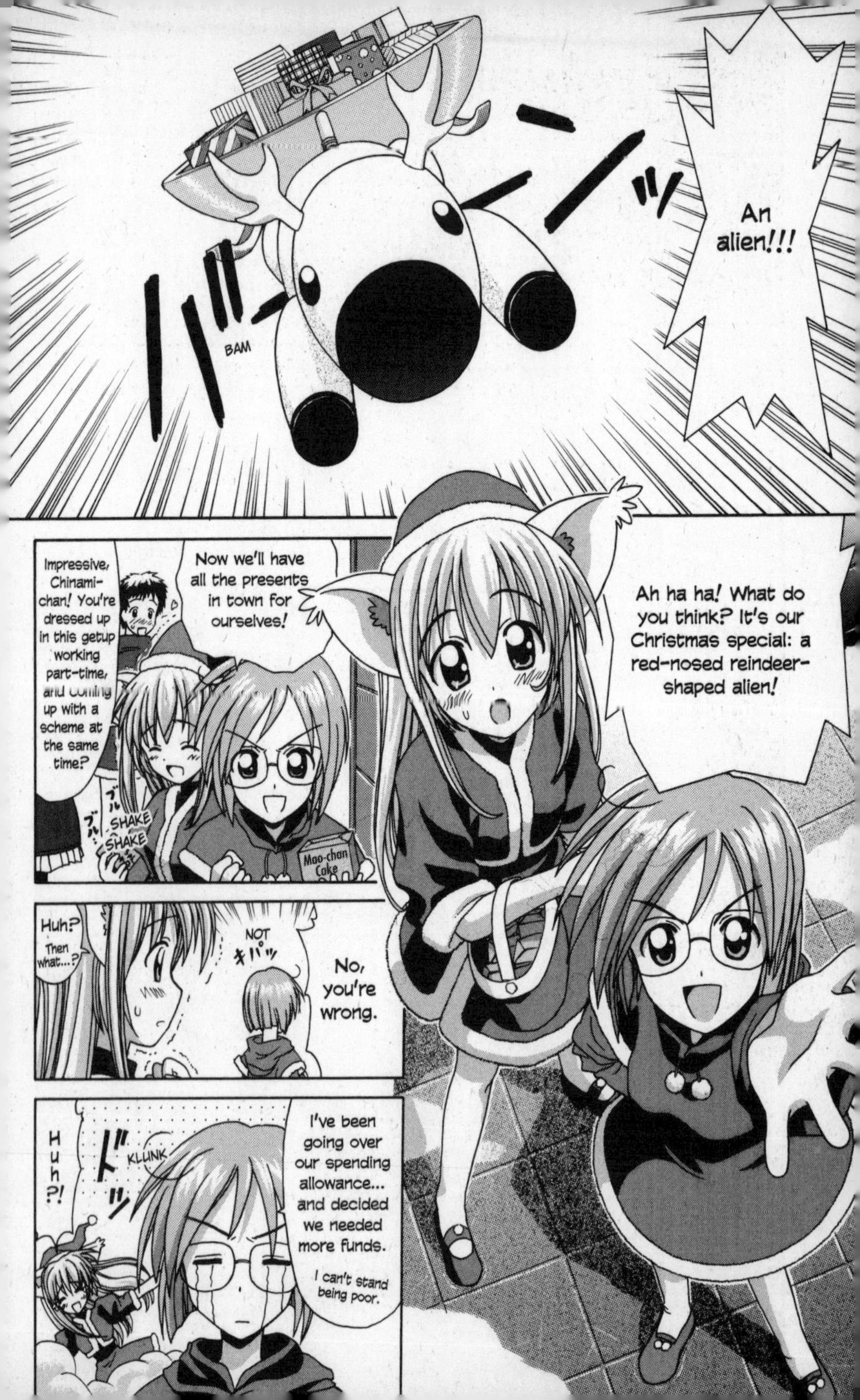
An alien!!!
BAM
Ah ha ha! What do you think? It's our Christmas special: a red-nosed reindeer-shaped alien!
Now we'll have all the presents in town for ourselves!
Impressive, Chinami-chan! You're dressed up in this getup working part-time, and coming up with a scheme at the same time?
SHAKE SHAKE
Mao-chan Cake
NOT
No, you're wrong.
Huh? Then what...?
I've been going over our spending allowance... and decided we needed more funds.
I can't stand being poor.
KLUNK
Huh?!

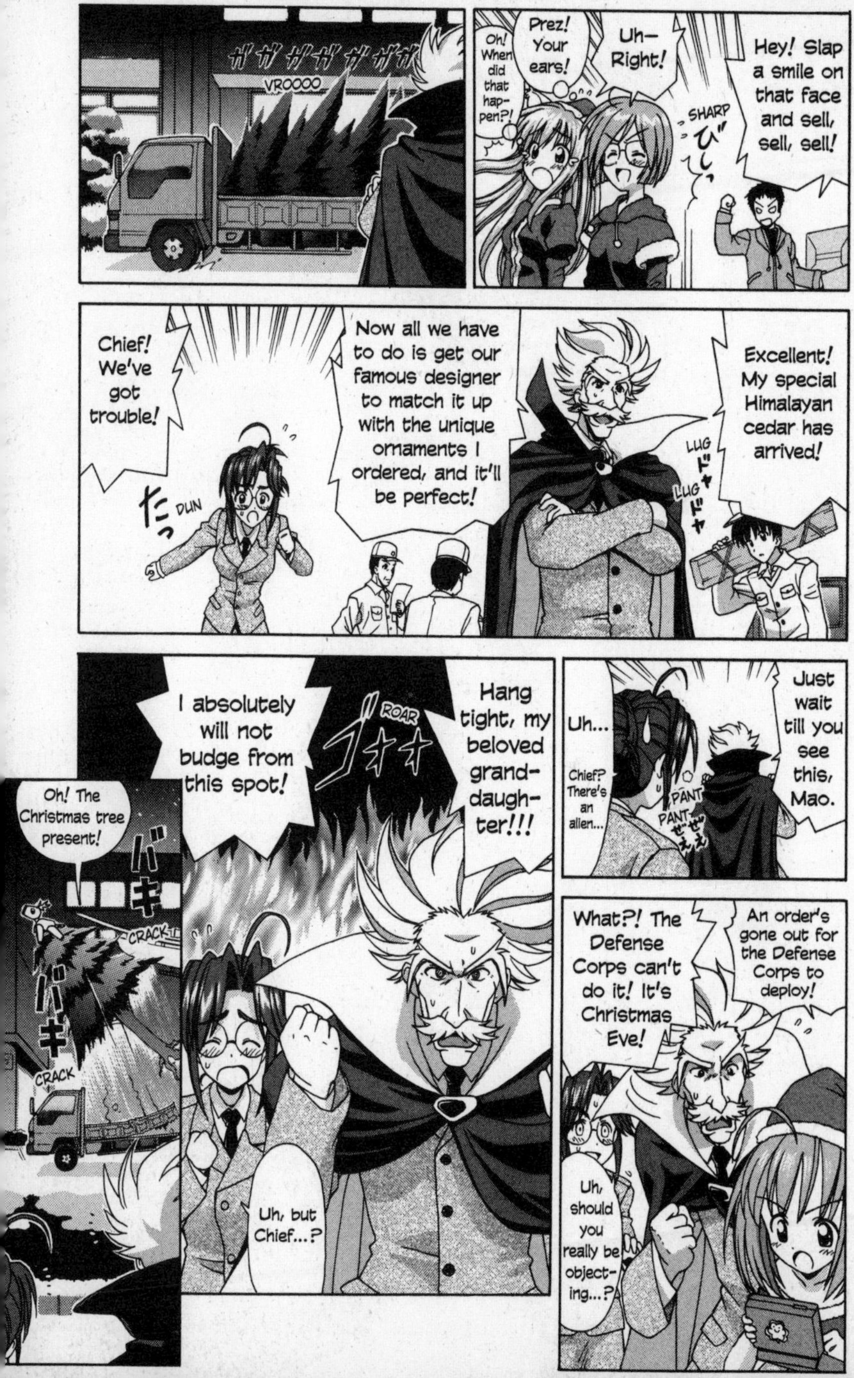
Hey! Slap a smile on that face and sell, sell, sell!
Uh— Right!
SHARP
Prez! Your ears!
Oh! When did that hap-pen?!
VROOOO
Excellent! My special Himalayan cedar has arrived!
LUG
LUG
Now all we have to do is get our famous designer to match it up with the unique ornaments I ordered, and it'll be perfect!
Chief! We've got trouble!
DUN
Just wait till you see this, Mao.
PANT PANT
Uh...
Chief? There's an alien...
An order's gone out for the Defense Corps to deploy!
What?! The Defense Corps can't do it! It's Christmas Eve!
Uh, should you really be objecting...?
Hang tight, my beloved grand-daugh-ter!!!
ROAR
I absolutely will not budge from this spot!
Uh, but Chief...?
Oh! The Christmas tree present!
CRACK
CRACK

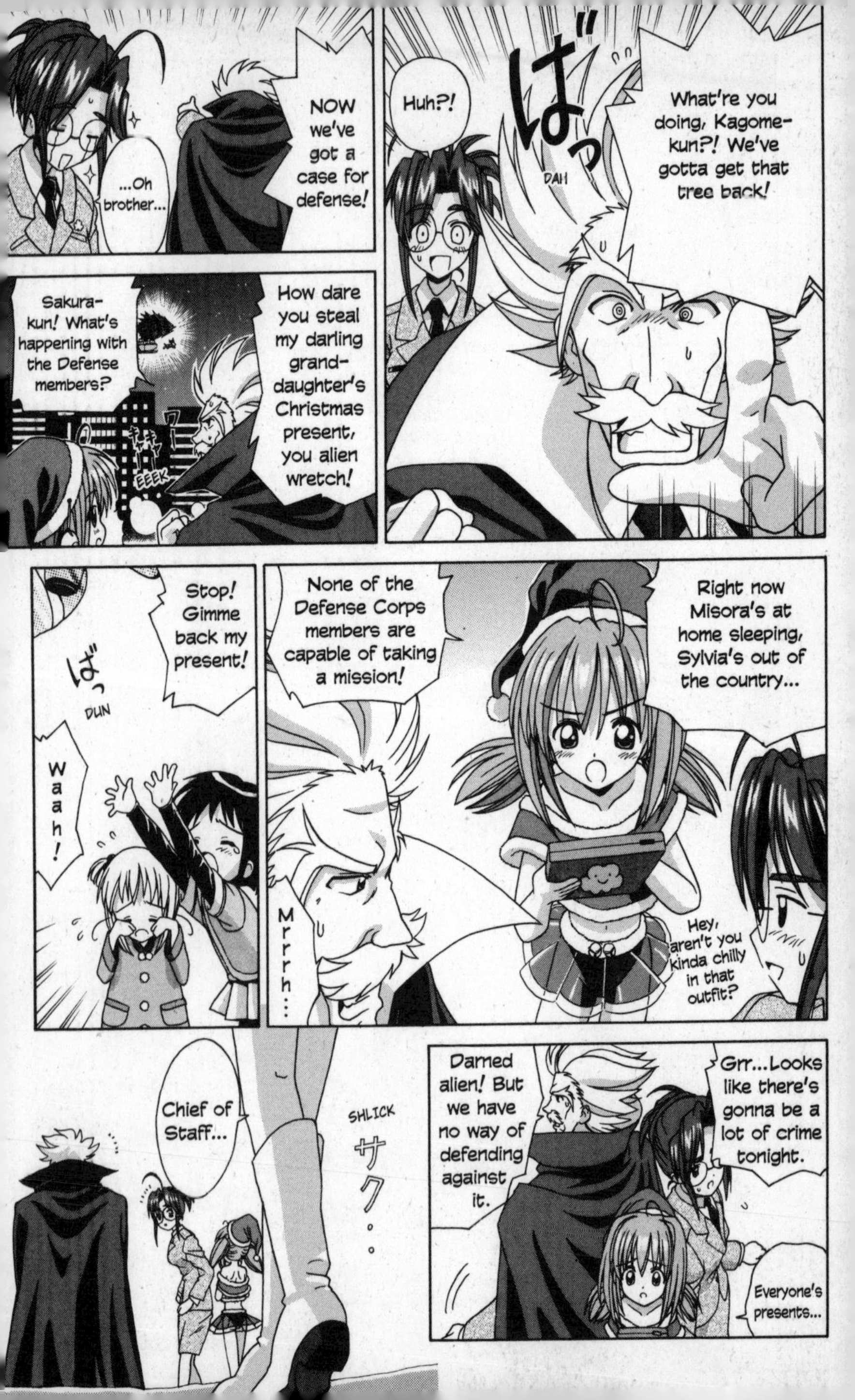
ばっ
DAH
What're you doing, Kagome-kun?! We've gotta get that tree back!
Huh?!
NOW we've got a case for defense!
...Oh brother...
How dare you steal my darling grand-daughter's Christmas present, you alien wretch!
Sakura-kun! What's happening with the Defense members?
EEEK
Right now Misora's at home sleeping, Sylvia's out of the country...
None of the Defense Corps members are capable of taking a mission!
Hey, aren't you kinda chilly in that outfit?
Mrrrh...
Stop! Gimme back my present!
ばっ
DUN
Waah!
Grr...Looks like there's gonna be a lot of crime tonight.
Darned alien! But we have no way of defending against it.
Everyone's presents...
SHLICK
サク。。
Chief of Staff...

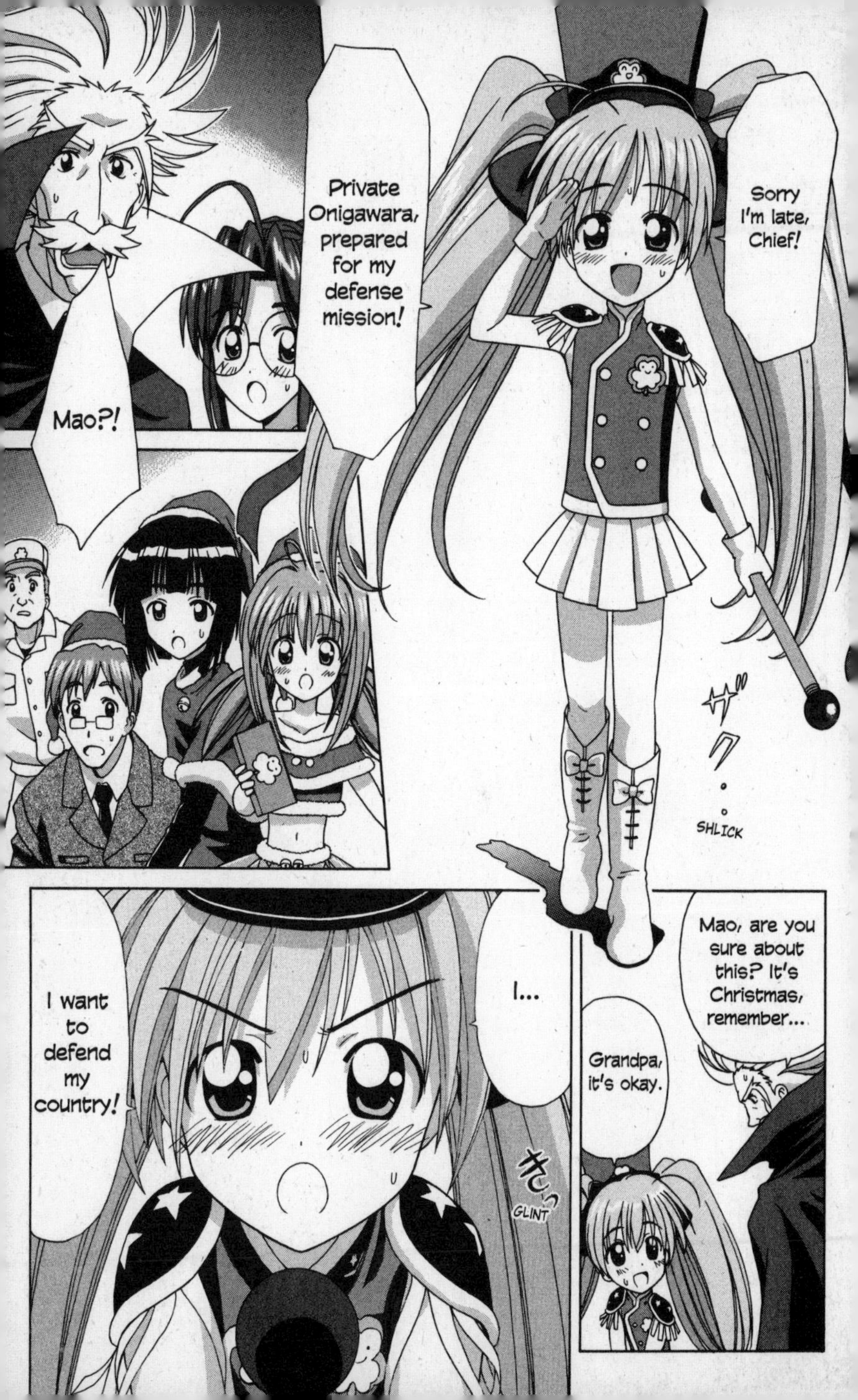
Sorry I'm late, Chief!
Private Onigawara, prepared for my defense mission!
SHLICK
Mao?!
Mao, are you sure about this? It's Christmas, remember...
Grandpa, it's okay.
I...
I want to defend my country!
GLINT

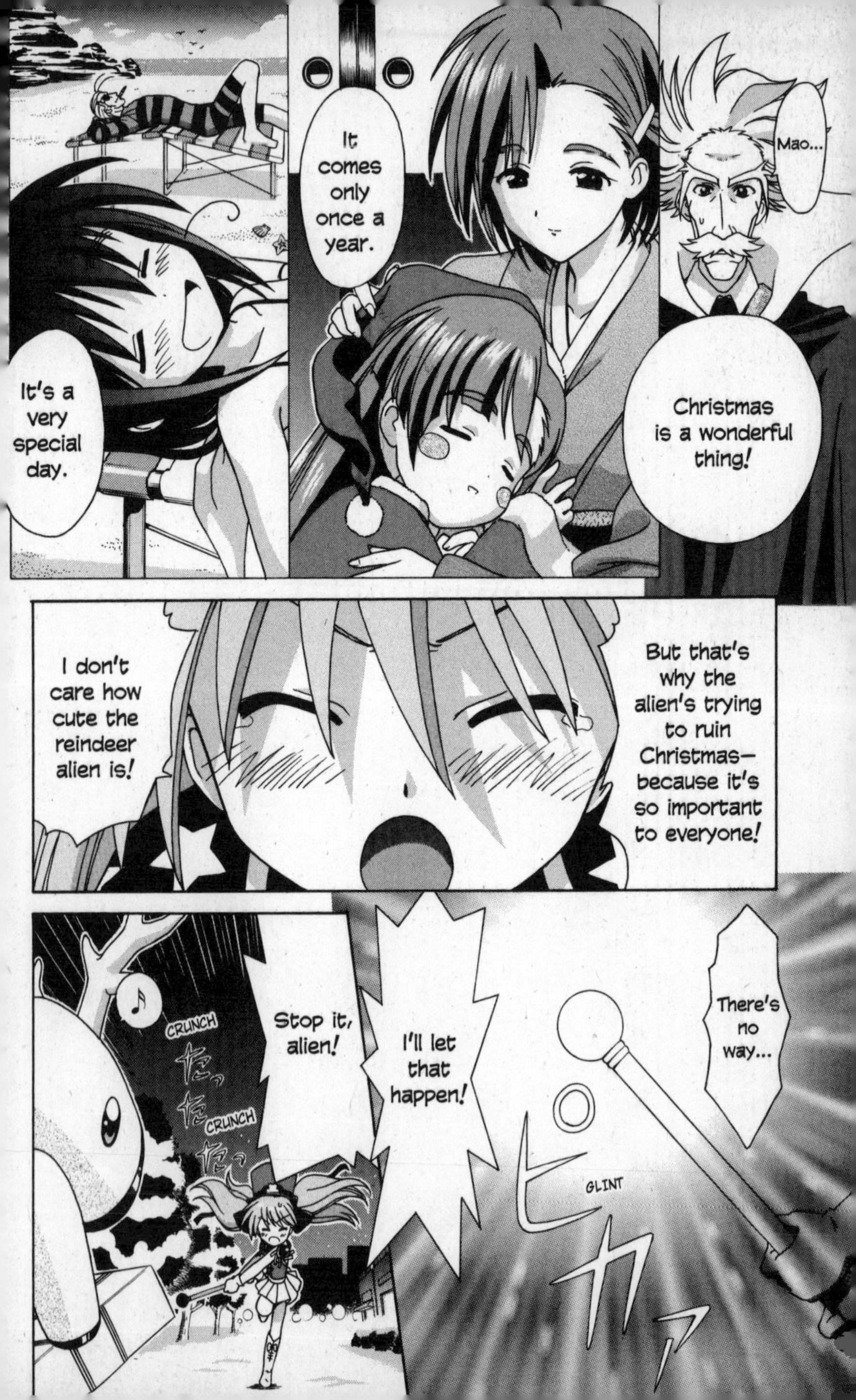
Mao...
Christmas is a wonderful thing!
It comes only once a year.
It's a very special day.
But that's why the alien's trying to ruin Christmas—because it's so important to everyone!
I don't care how cute the reindeer alien is!
There's no way...
I'll let that happen!
GLINT
Stop it, alien!
CRUNCH
CRUNCH

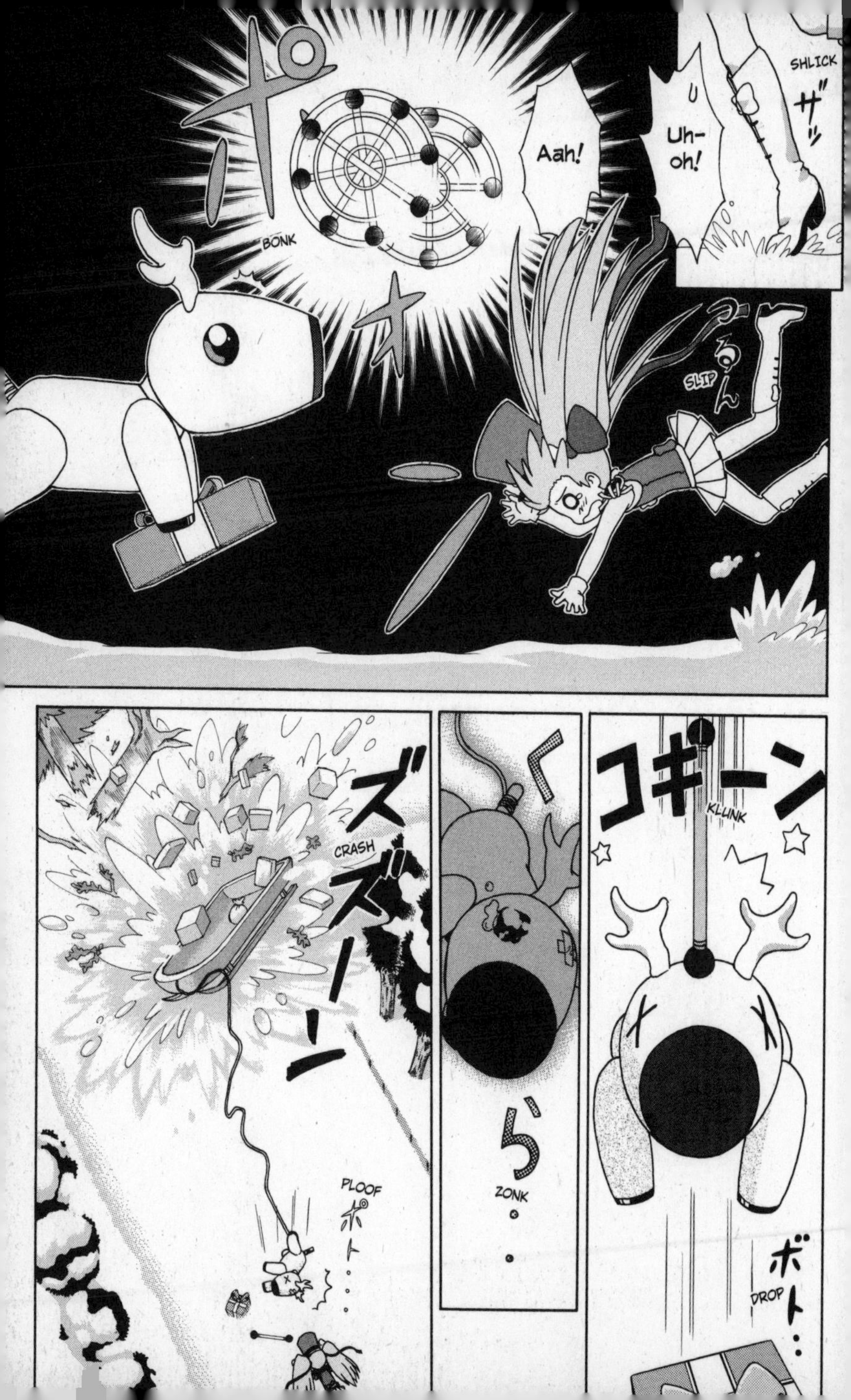
SHLICK
ザッ
Uh-oh!
Aah!
BONK
SLIP
つるん
コキーン
KLUNK
ボト…
DROP
くら
ZONK
ズズーン
CRASH
ポト…
PLOOF

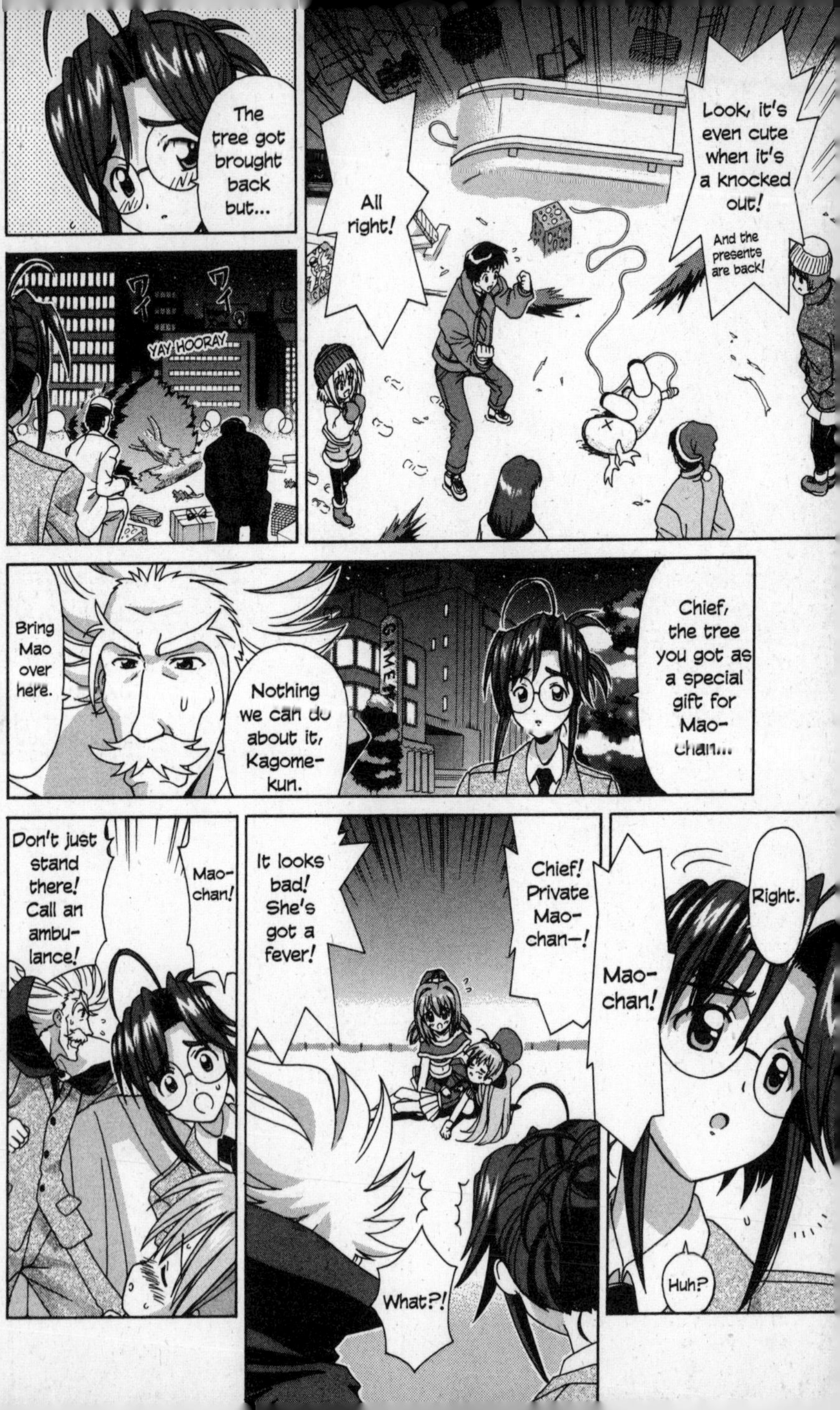
Look, it's even cute when it's a knocked out!
And the presents are back!
All right!
The tree got brought back but...
YAY HOORAY
Chief, the tree you got as a special gift for Mao-chan...
Nothing we can do about it, Kagome-kun.
Bring Mao over here.
Right.
Mao-chan!
Huh?
Chief! Private Mao-chan—!
It looks bad! She's got a fever!
What?!
Mao-chan!
Don't just stand there! Call an ambulance!

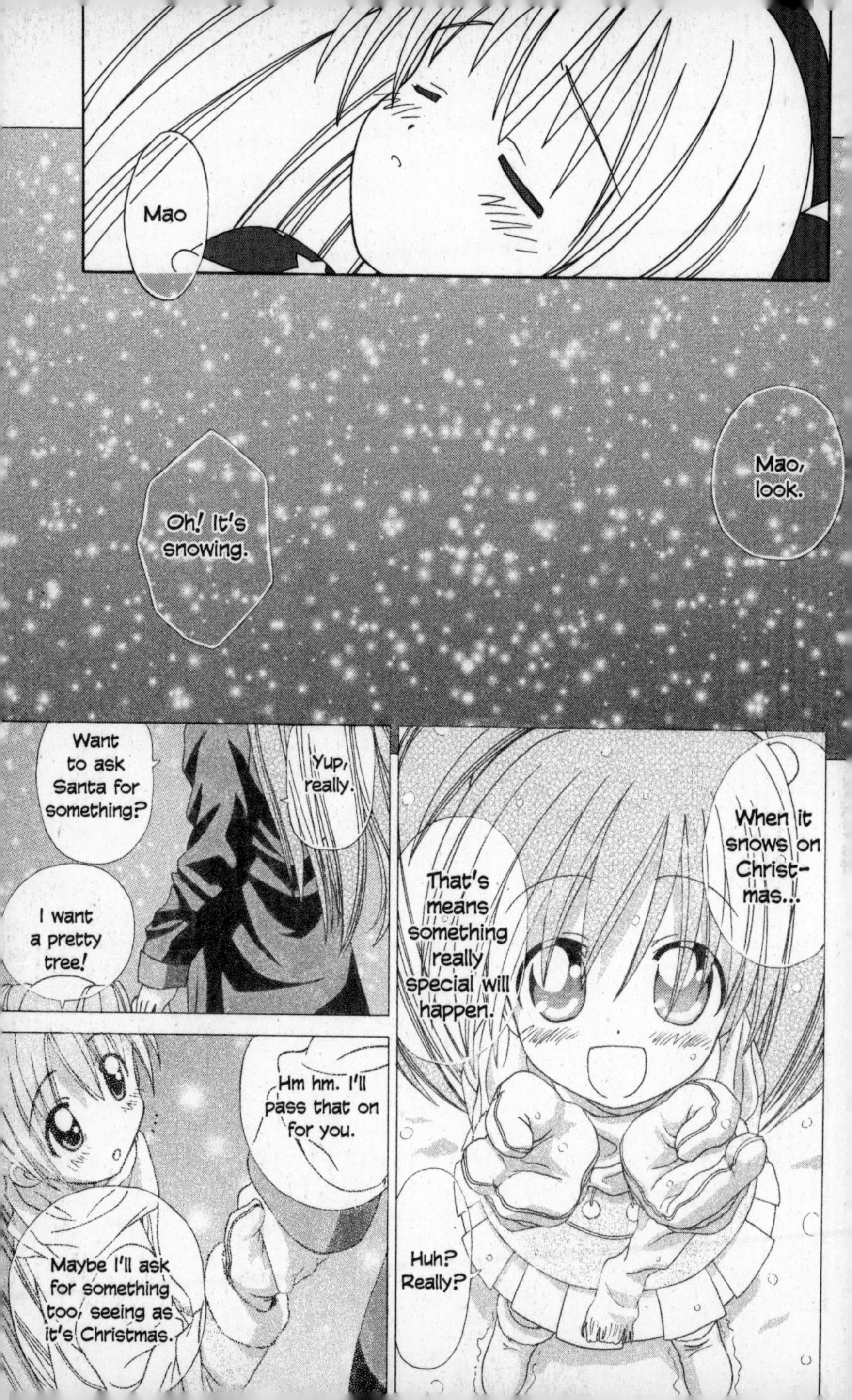
Mao
Mao, look.
Oh! It's snowing.
When it snows on Christmas...
That's means something really special will happen.
Huh? Really?
Yup, really.
Want to ask Santa for something?
I want a pretty tree!
Hm hm. I'll pass that on for you.
Maybe I'll ask for something too, seeing as it's Christmas.

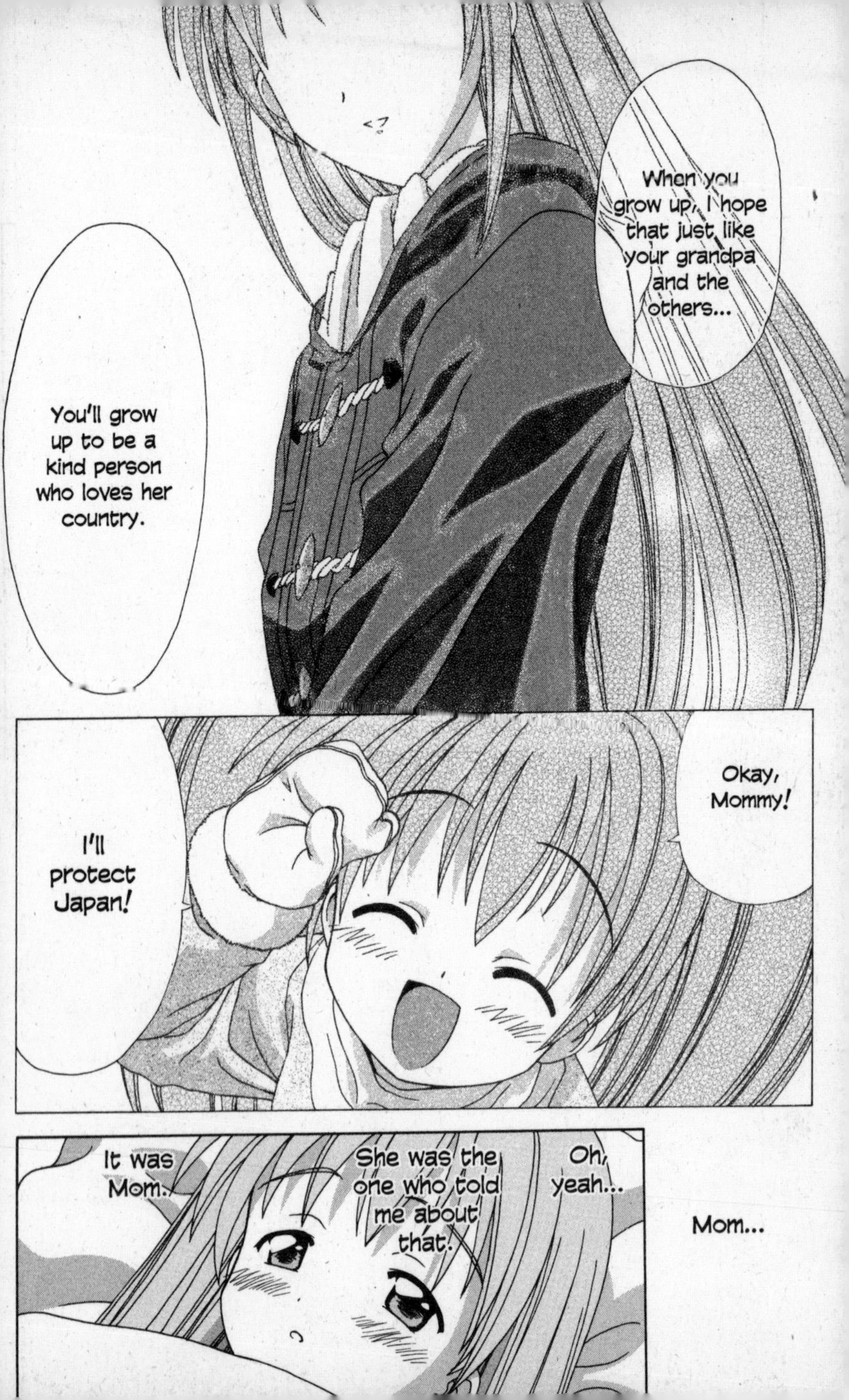
When you grow up, I hope that just like your grandpa and the others...
You'll grow up to be a kind person who loves her country.
Okay, Mommy!
I'll protect Japan!
Mom...
Oh, yeah...
She was the one who told me about that.
It was Mom.

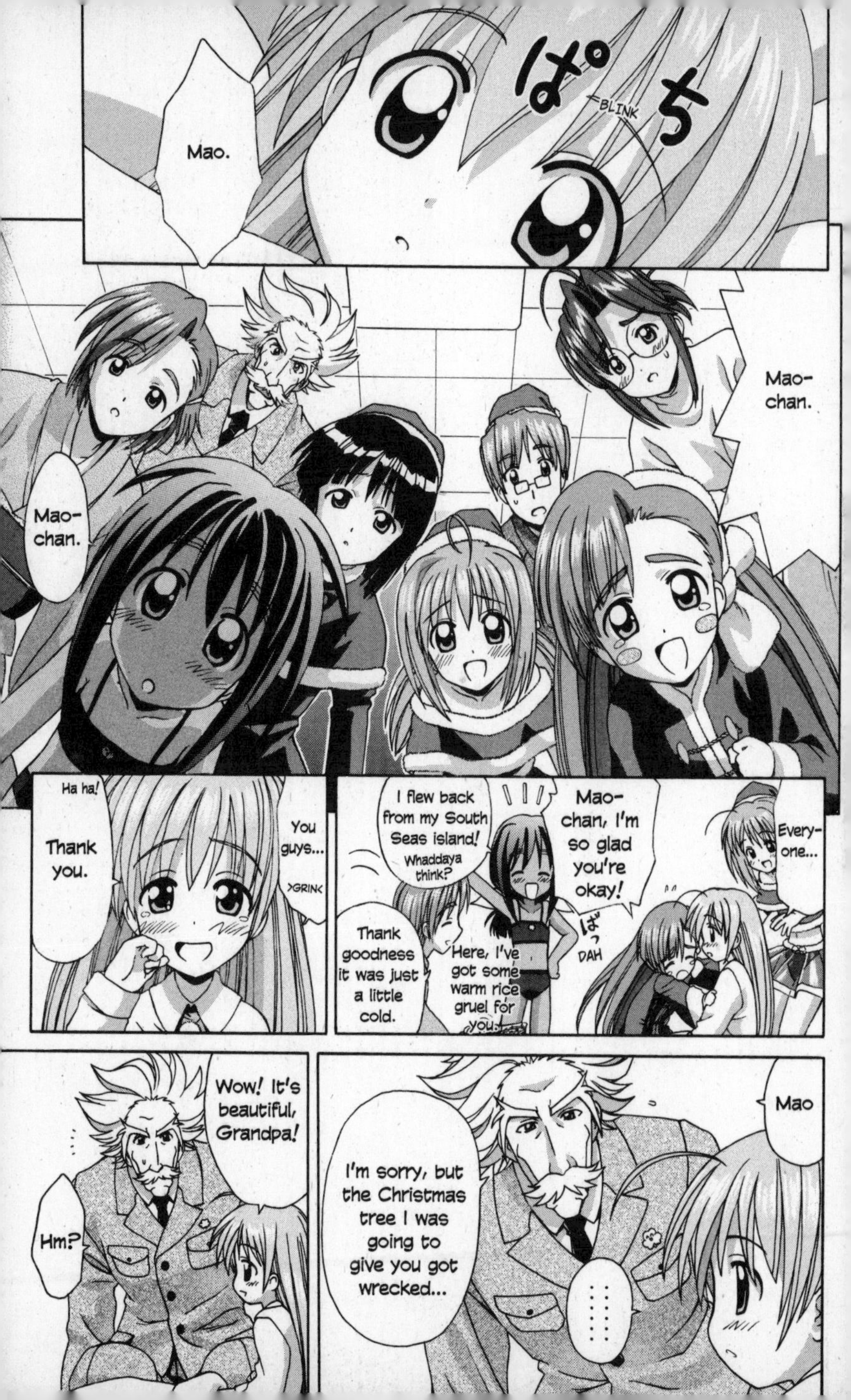
ぱち
BLINK
Mao.
Mao-chan.
Mao-chan.
Every-one...
Mao-chan, I'm so glad you're okay!
ばっ
DAH
I flew back from my South Seas island!
Whaddaya think?
Here, I've got some warm rice gruel for you.
Thank goodness it was just a little cold.
You guys...
>GRIN<
Ha ha!
Thank you.
Mao
I'm sorry, but the Christmas tree I was going to give you got wrecked...
......
Wow! It's beautiful, Grandpa!
Hm?

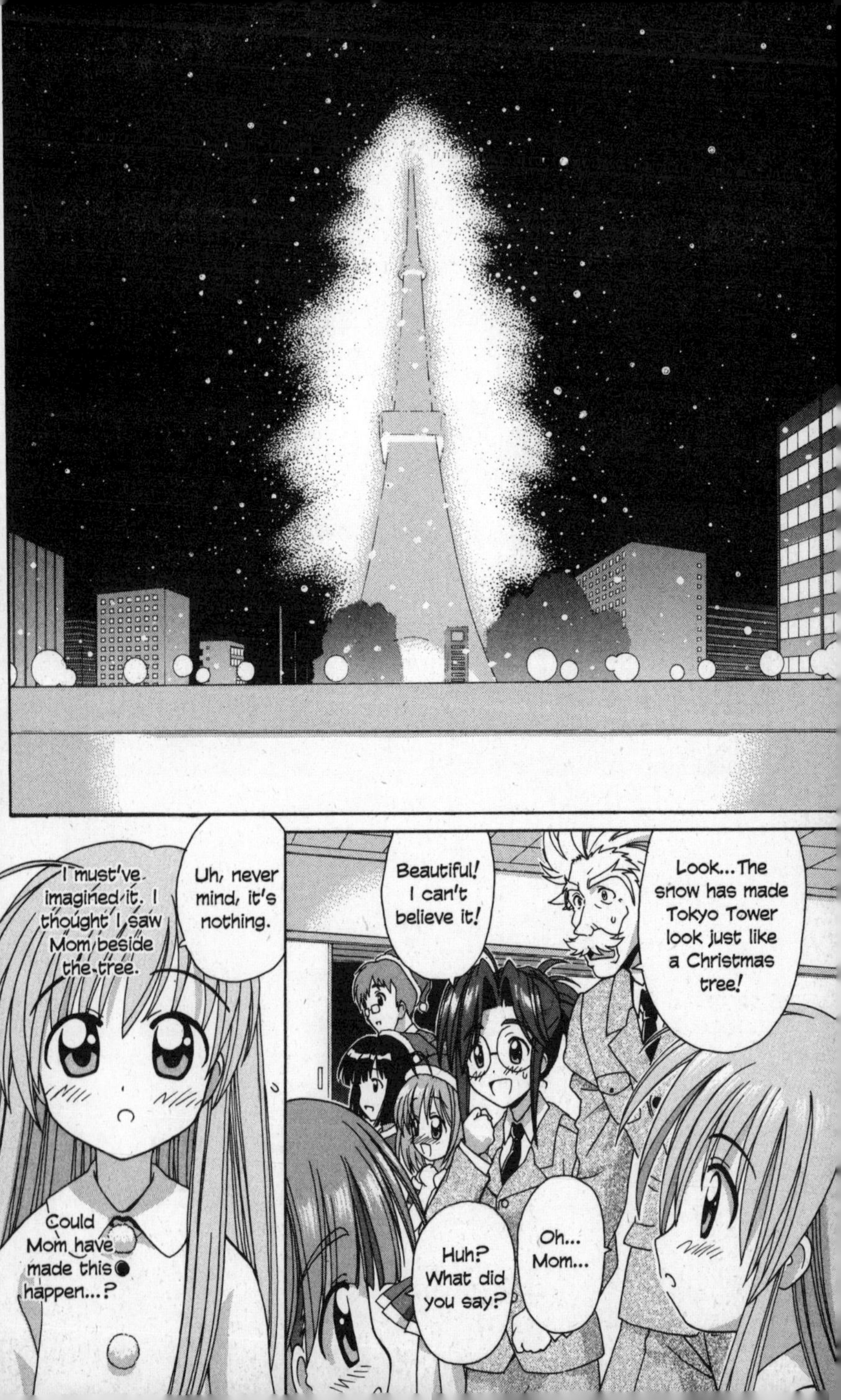
Look... The snow has made Tokyo Tower look just like a Christmas tree!
Beautiful! I can't believe it!
Oh... Mom...
Huh? What did you say?
Uh, never mind, it's nothing.
I must've imagined it. I thought I saw Mom beside the tree.
Could Mom have made this happen...?

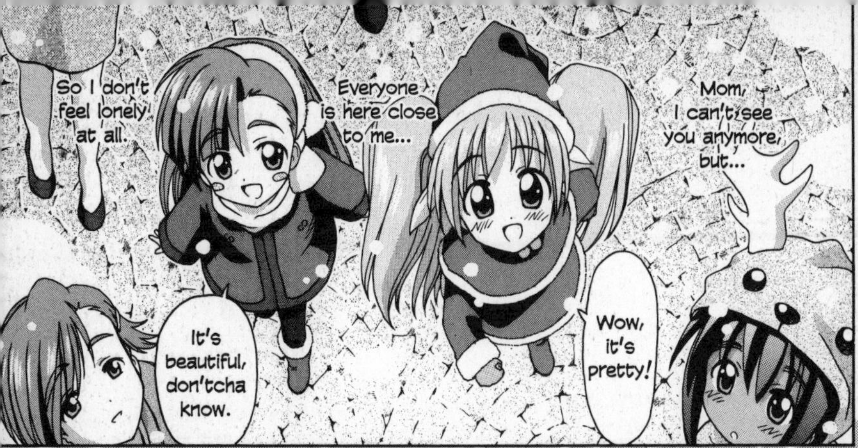
Mom, I can't see you anymore, but...
Everyone is here close to me...
So I don't feel lonely at all.
Wow, it's pretty!
It's beautiful, don'tcha know.
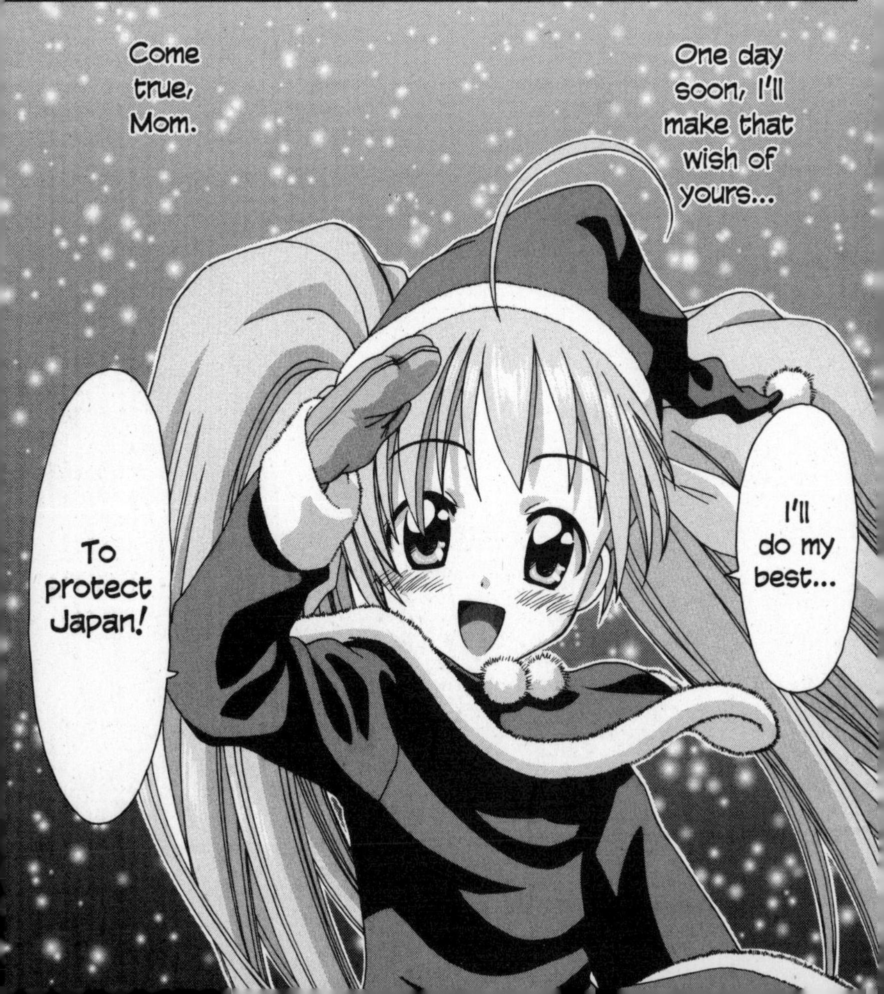
One day soon, I'll make that wish of yours...
Come true, Mom.
I'll do my best...
To protect Japan!

Mao-chan

2

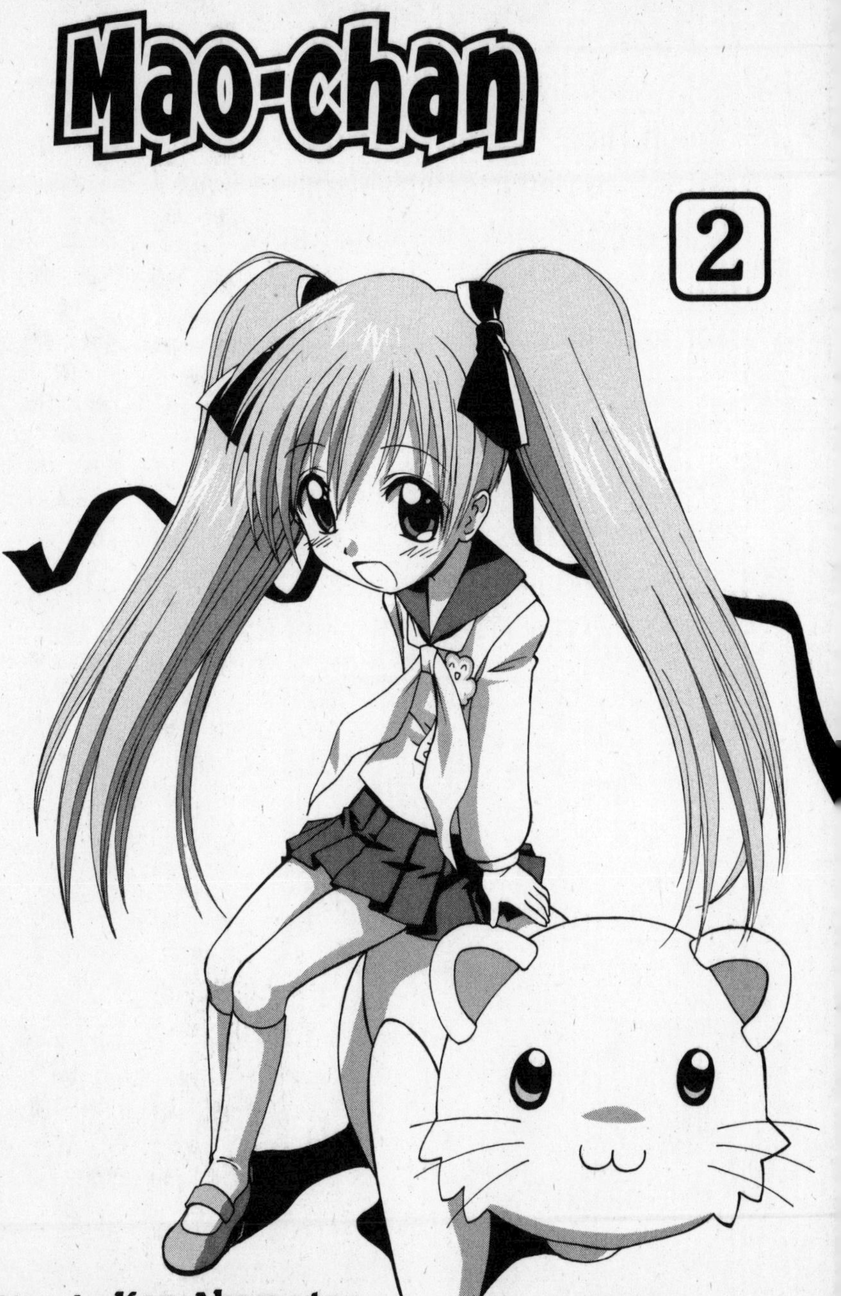

Story by **Ken Akamatsu**

Art by **RAN**

CONTENTS

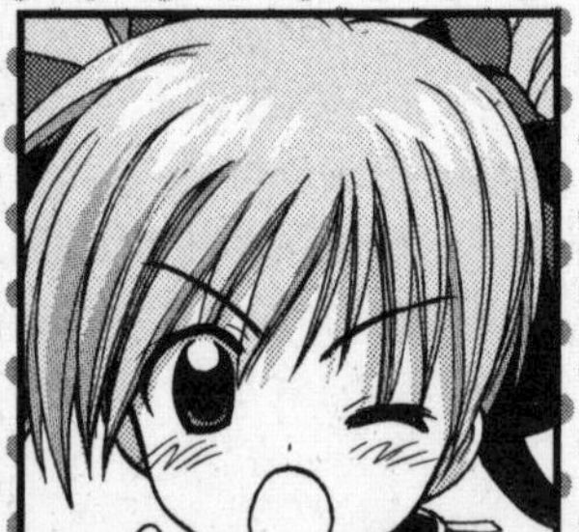

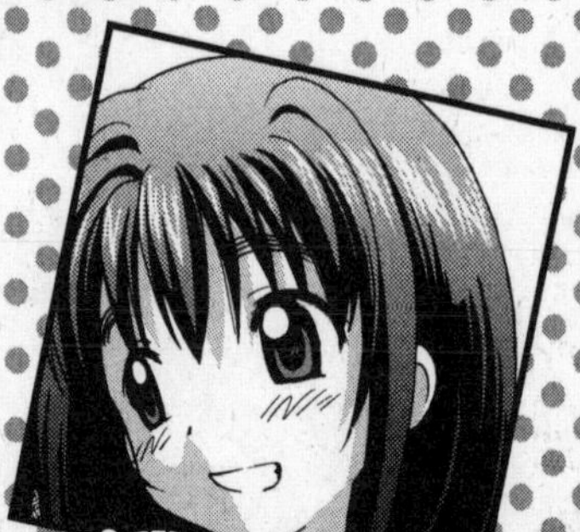

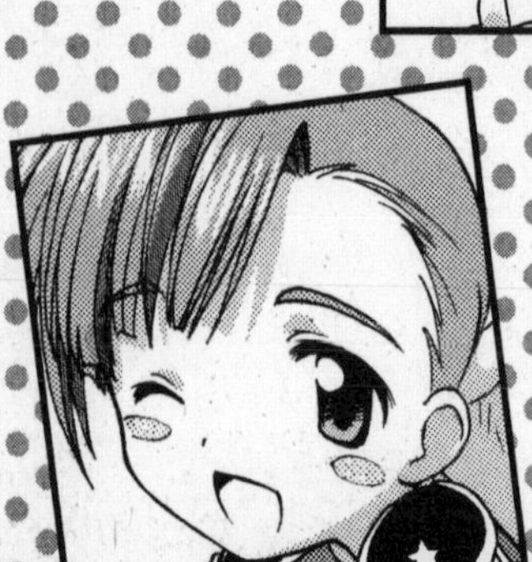

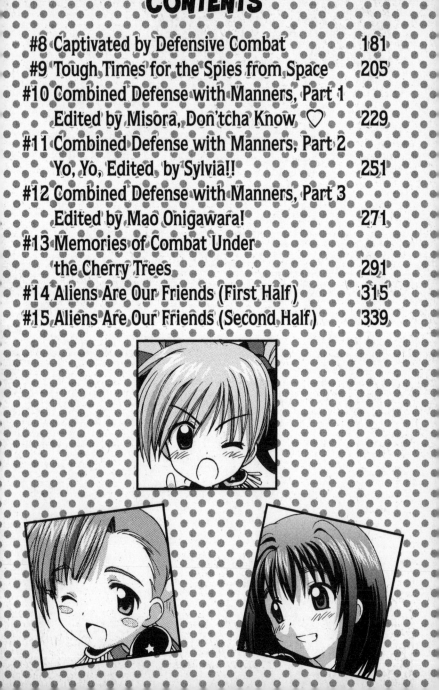

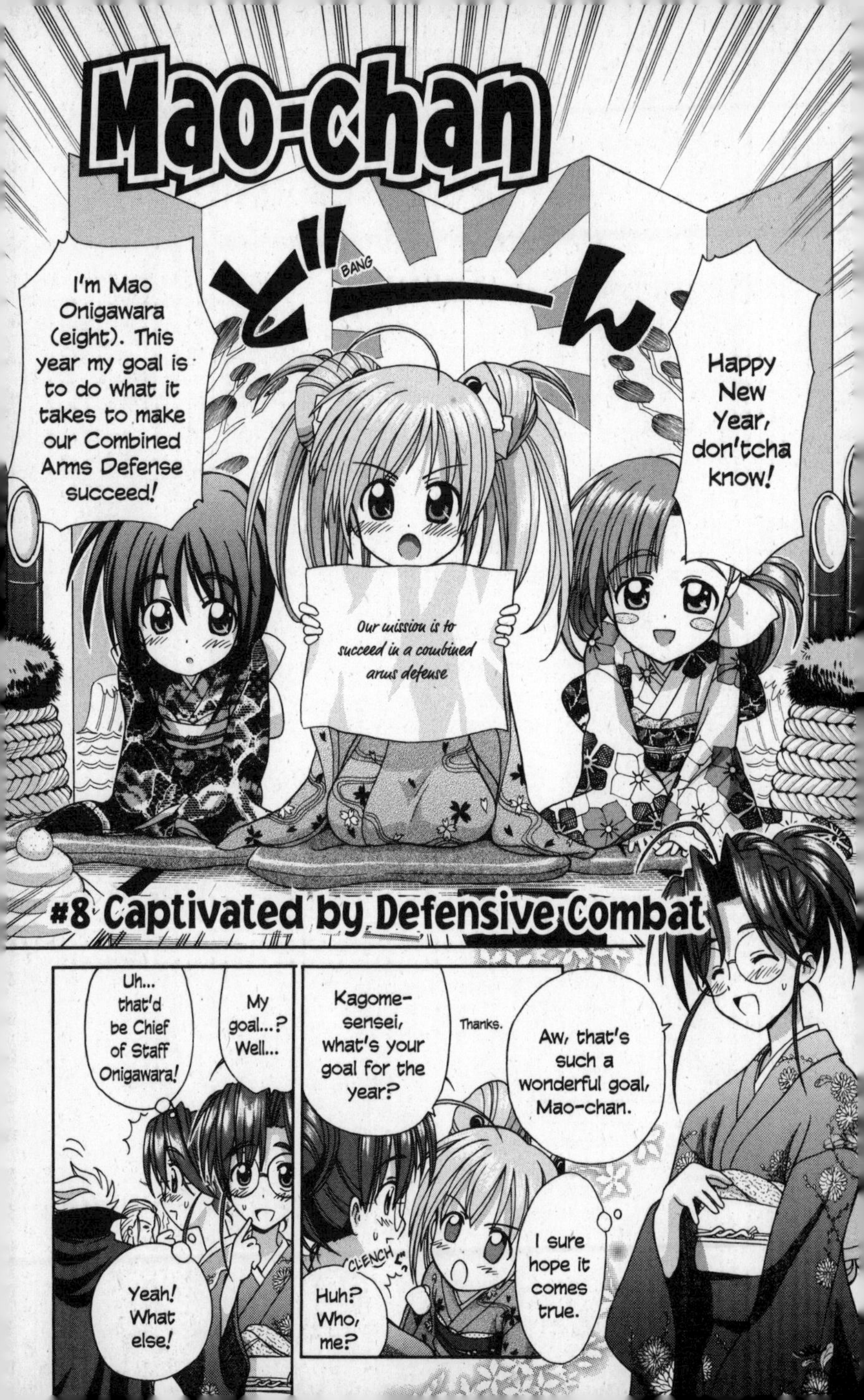
Mao-chan
Happy New Year, don'tcha know!
BANG
I'm Mao Onigawara (eight). This year my goal is to do what it takes to make our Combined Arms Defense succeed!
Our mission is to succeed in a combined arms defense
#8 Captivated by Defensive Combat
Aw, that's such a wonderful goal, Mao-chan.
Thanks.
Kagome-sensei, what's your goal for the year?
I sure hope it comes true.
CLENCH
Huh? Who, me?
My goal...? Well...
Uh... that'd be Chief of Staff Onigawara!
Yeah! What else!

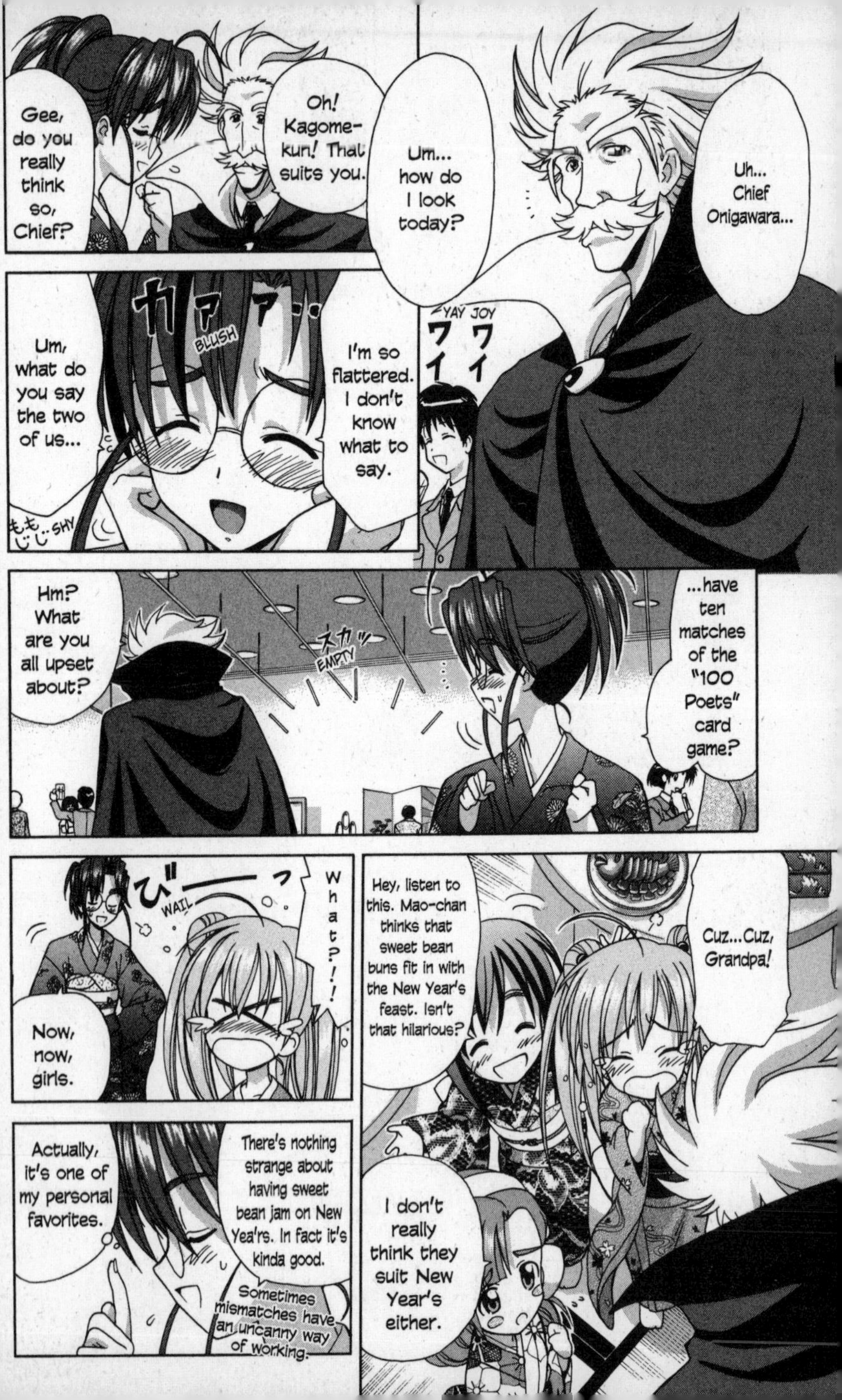
Uh... Chief Onigawara...
Um... how do I look today?
ワイ ワイ YAY JOY
Oh! Kagome-kun! That suits you.
Gee, do you really think so, Chief?
カァ BLUSH
I'm so flattered. I don't know what to say.
Um, what do you say the two of us...
もじもじ.. SHY
...have ten matches of the "100 Poets" card game?
スカッ EMPTY
Hm? What are you all upset about?
Cuz...Cuz, Grandpa!
Hey, listen to this. Mao-chan thinks that sweet bean buns fit in with the New Year's feast. Isn't that hilarious?
What?!!
び——っ WAIL
Now, now, girls.
I don't really think they suit New Year's either.
There's nothing strange about having sweet bean jam on New Year's. In fact it's kinda good.
Actually, it's one of my personal favorites.
Sometimes mismatches have an uncanny way of working.

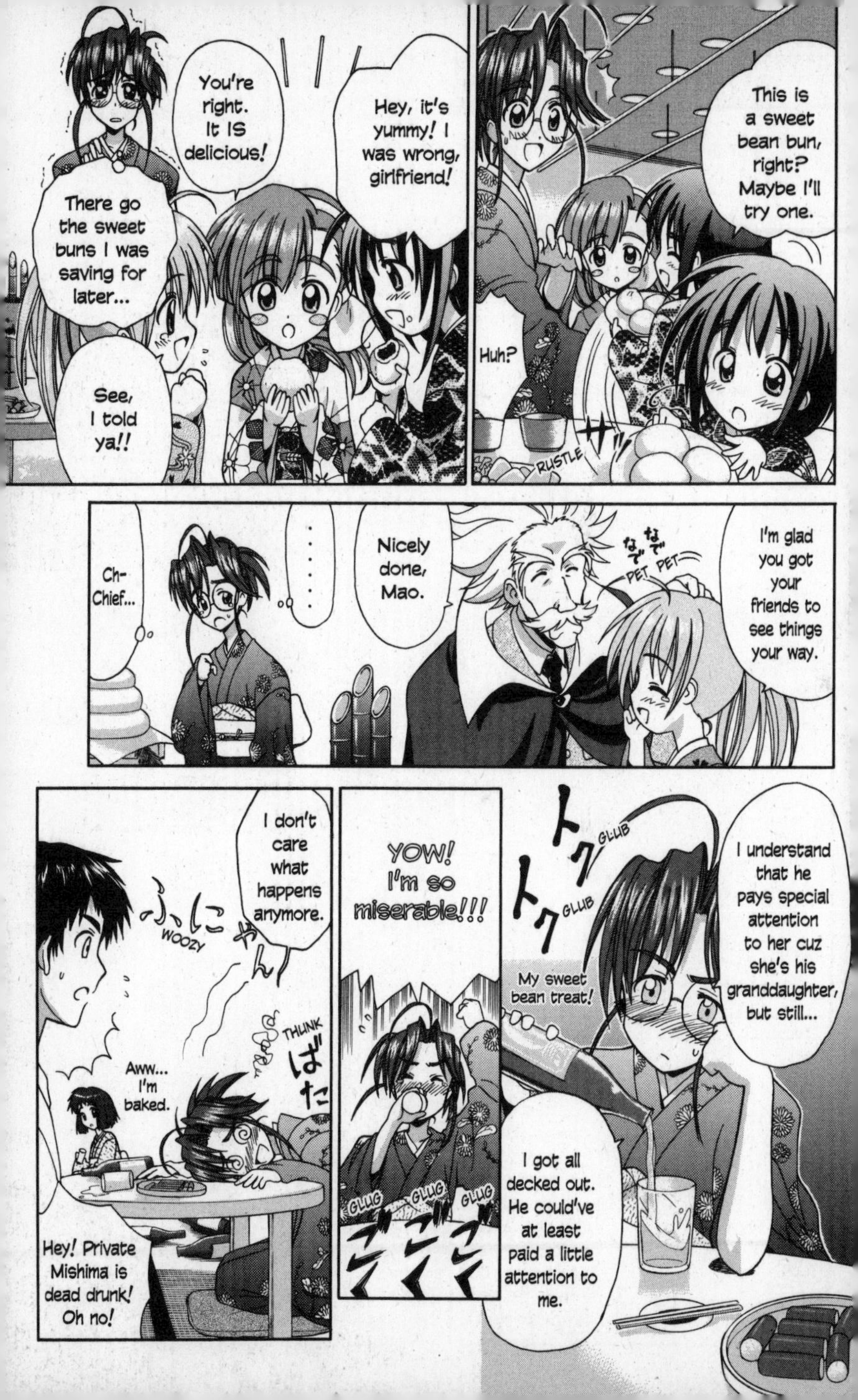
This is a sweet bean bun, right? Maybe I'll try one.
Huh?
RUSTLE
Hey, it's yummy! I was wrong, girlfriend!
You're right. It IS delicious!
There go the sweet buns I was saving for later...
See, I told ya!!
I'm glad you got your friends to see things your way.
なでなで
PET PET
Nicely done, Mao.
......
Ch-Chief...
トク
GLUB
トク
GLUB
I understand that he pays special attention to her cuz she's his granddaughter, but still...
My sweet bean treat!
I got all decked out. He could've at least paid a little attention to me.
YOW! I'm so miserable!!!
GLUG GLUG GLUG
I don't care what happens anymore.
WOOZY
THUNK
ばた
Aww... I'm baked.
Hey! Private Mishima is dead drunk! Oh no!

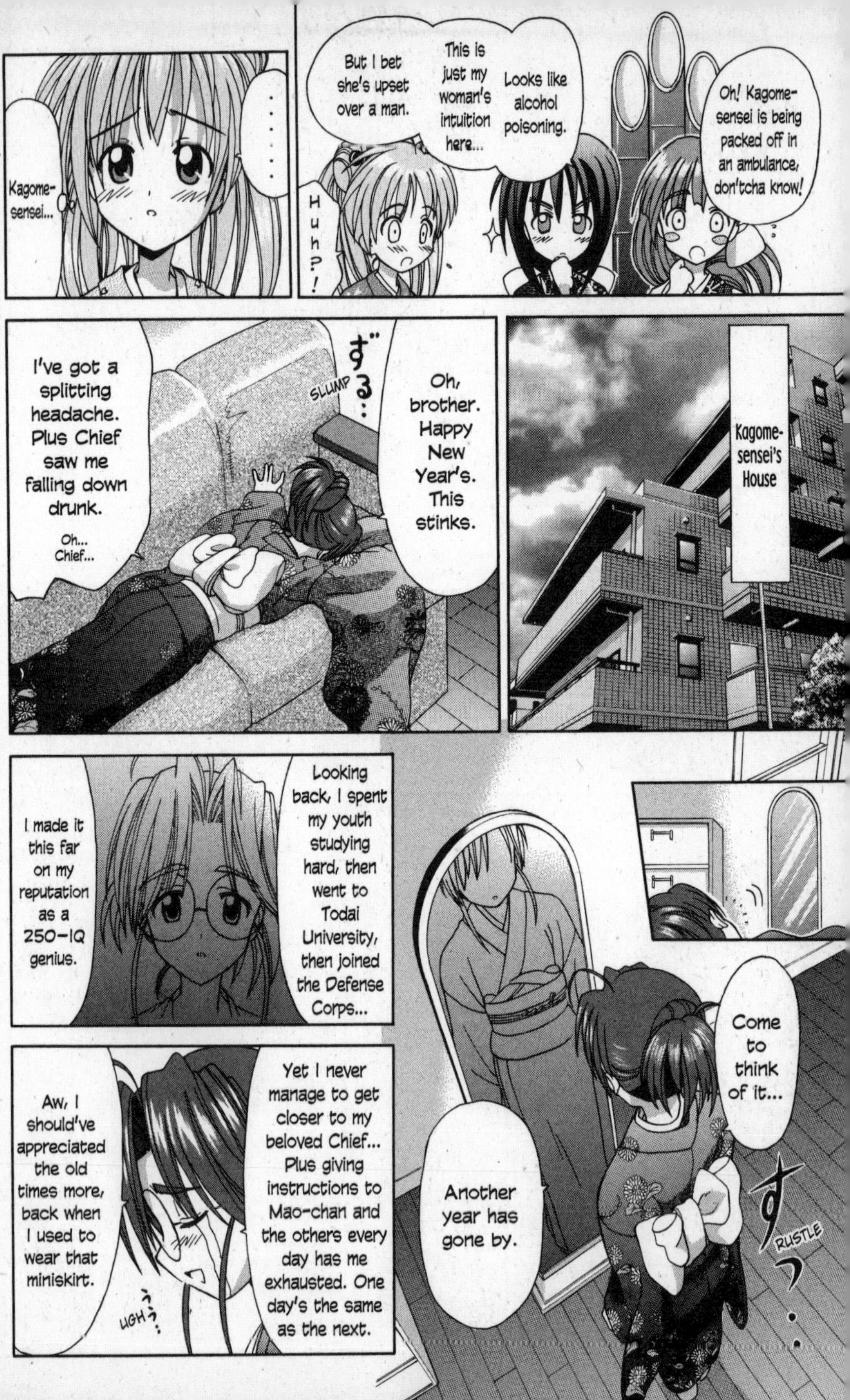
Oh! Kagome-sensei is being packed off in an ambulance, don'tcha know!
Looks like alcohol poisoning.
This is just my woman's intuition here...
But I bet she's upset over a man.
Huh?!
......
Kagome-sensei...
Kagome-sensei's House
Oh, brother. Happy New Year's. This stinks.
ずる
SLUMP
I've got a splitting headache. Plus Chief saw me falling down drunk.
Oh... Chief...
Come to think of it...
す
RUSTLE
Another year has gone by.
Looking back, I spent my youth studying hard, then went to Todai University, then joined the Defense Corps...
I made it this far on my reputation as a 250-IQ genius.
Yet I never manage to get closer to my beloved Chief... Plus giving instructions to Mao-chan and the others every day has me exhausted. One day's the same as the next.
Aw, I should've appreciated the old times more, back when I used to wear that miniskirt.
UGH

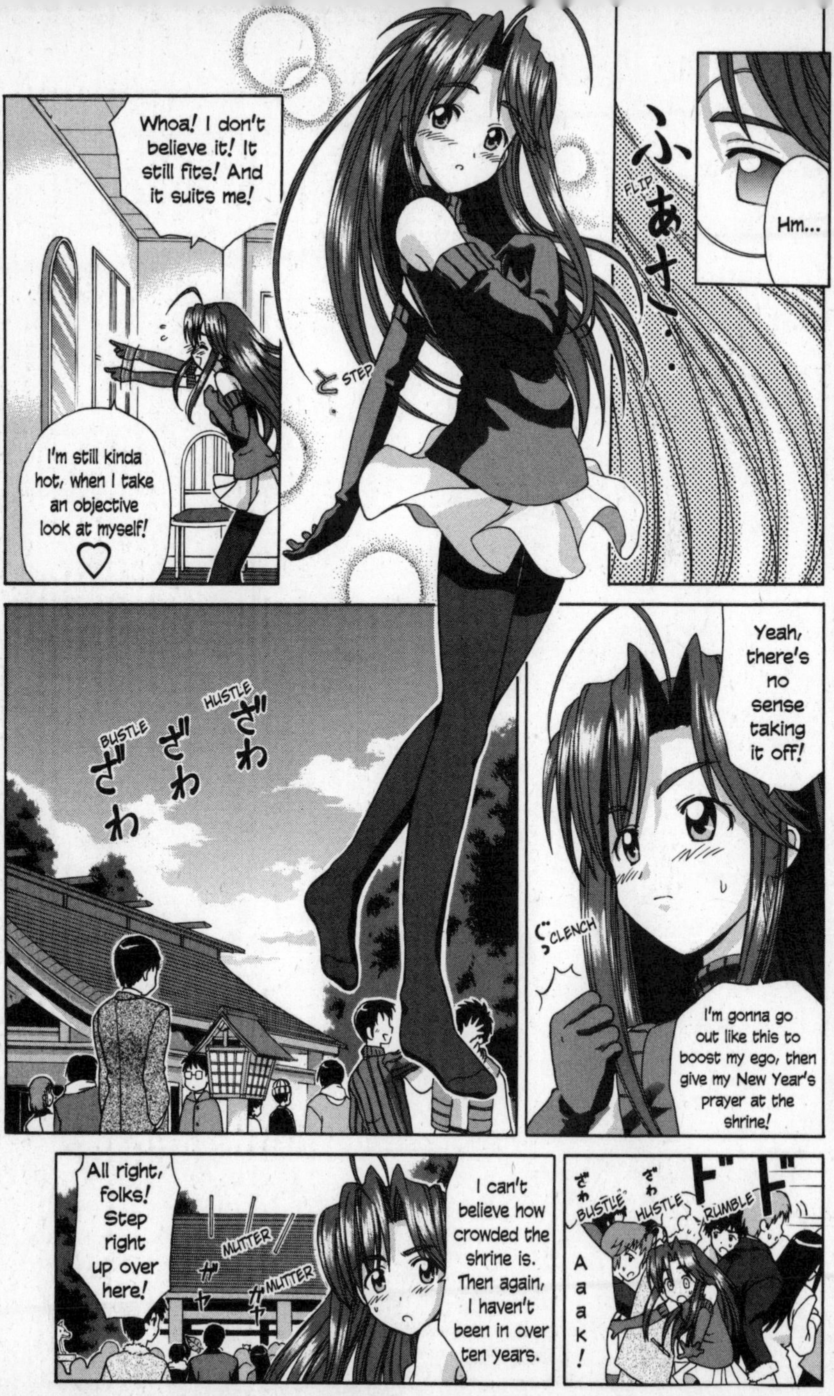
Hm...
ふぁさ…
FLIP
と STEP
Whoa! I don't believe it! It still fits! And it suits me!
I'm still kinda hot, when I take an objective look at myself! ♡
Yeah, there's no sense taking it off!
ぐっ CLENCH
I'm gonna go out like this to boost my ego, then give my New Year's prayer at the shrine!
ざわ HUSTLE
ざわ
ざわ BUSTLE
ドド RUMBLE
ざわ HUSTLE
ざわ BUSTLE
Aaak!
I can't believe how crowded the shrine is. Then again, I haven't been in over ten years.
ガヤ MUTTER
ガヤ MUTTER
All right, folks! Step right up over here!

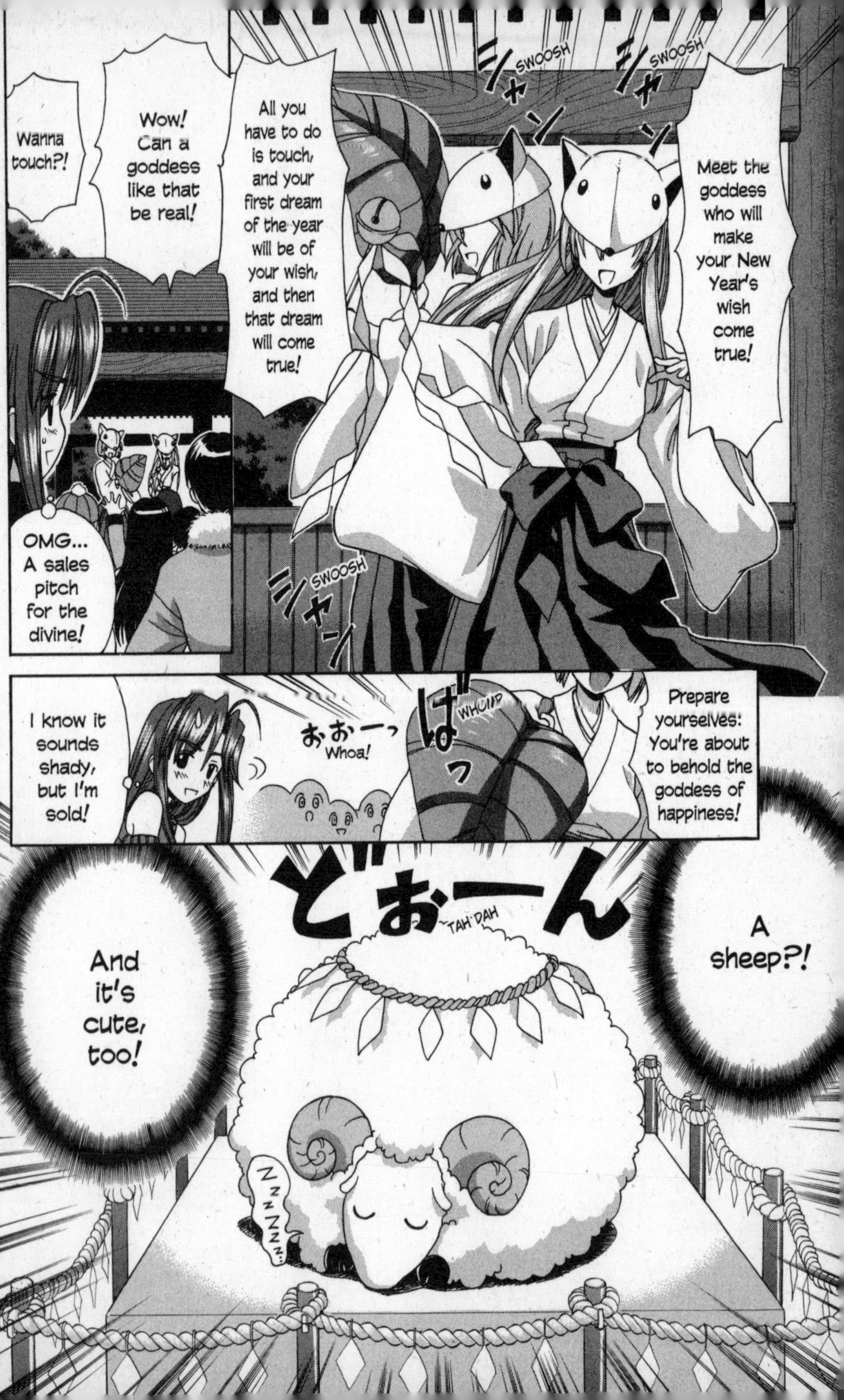

Meet the goddess who will make your New Year's wish come true!
シャン SWOOSH
シャン SWOOSH
All you have to do is touch, and your first dream of the year will be of your wish, and then that dream will come true!
Wow! Can a goddess like that be real!
Wanna touch?!
シャーン SWOOSH
OMG... A sales pitch for the divine!
Prepare yourselves: You're about to behold the goddess of happiness!
ばっ WHUP
おおーっ Whoa!
I know it sounds shady, but I'm sold!
どおーん TAH DAH
A sheep?!
And it's cute, too!
ZzzZzz...

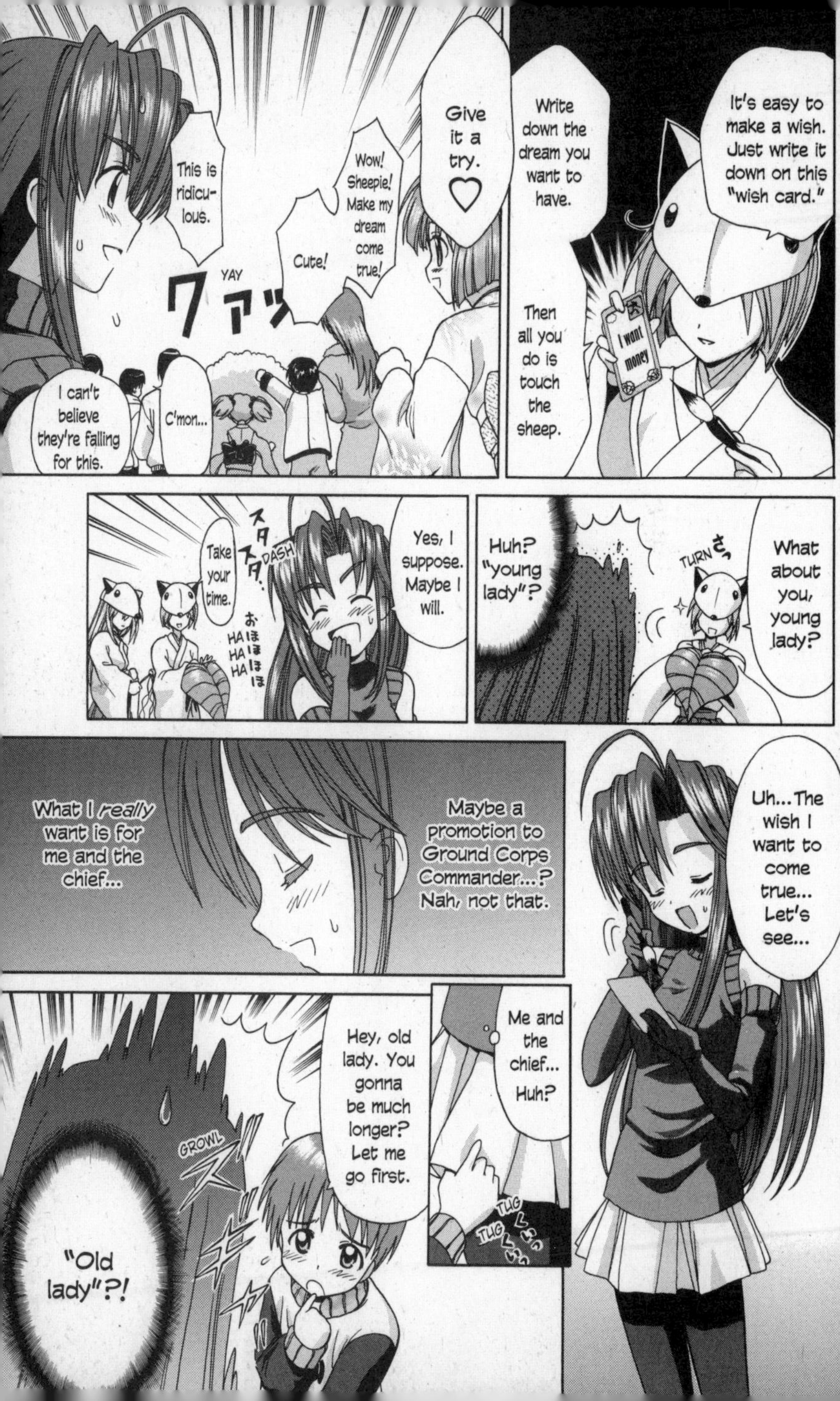
It's easy to make a wish. Just write it down on this "wish card."
Write down the dream you want to have.
I want money
Then all you do is touch the sheep.
Give it a try. ♡
Wow! Sheepie! Make my dream come true!
Cute!
YAY
This is ridiculous.
C'mon...
I can't believe they're falling for this.
What about you, young lady?
TURN
Huh? "young lady"?
Yes, I suppose. Maybe I will.
DASH
Take your time.
HA HA HA HA
Uh...The wish I want to come true... Let's see...
Maybe a promotion to Ground Corps Commander...? Nah, not that.
What I *really* want is for me and the chief...
Me and the chief... Huh?
TUG TUG
Hey, old lady. You gonna be much longer? Let me go first.
GROWL
"Old lady"?!

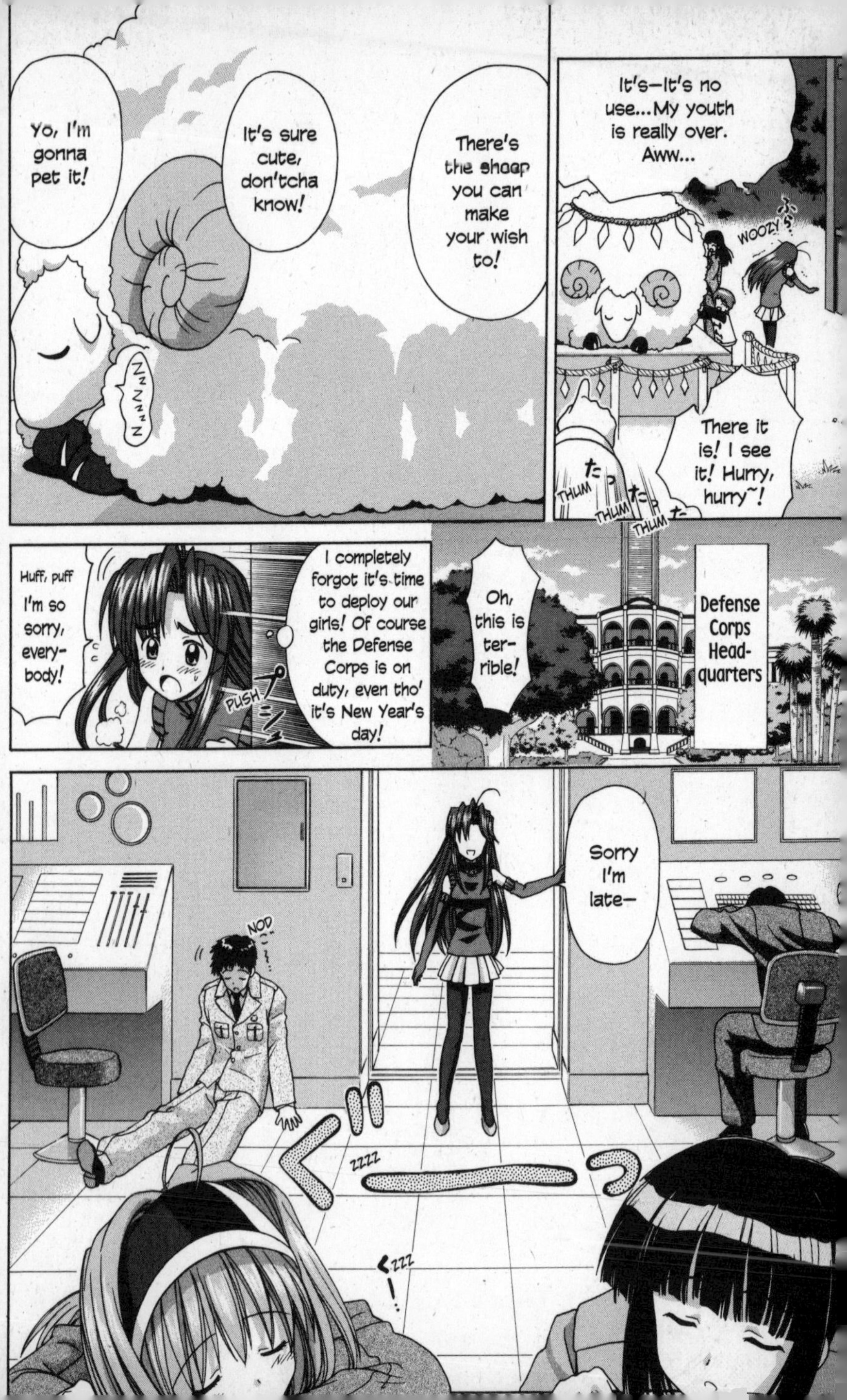
It's—It's no use...My youth is really over. Aww...
ふら
WOOZY
There it is! I see it! Hurry, hurry~!
THUM
THUM
THUM
There's the sheep you can make your wish to!
It's sure cute, don'tcha know!
Yo, I'm gonna pet it!
Defense Corps Headquarters
Oh, this is terrible!
I completely forgot it's time to deploy our girls! Of course the Defense Corps is on duty, even tho' it's New Year's day!
PUSH
Huff, puff
I'm so sorry, everybody!
Sorry I'm late–
NOD
zzzz
zzz

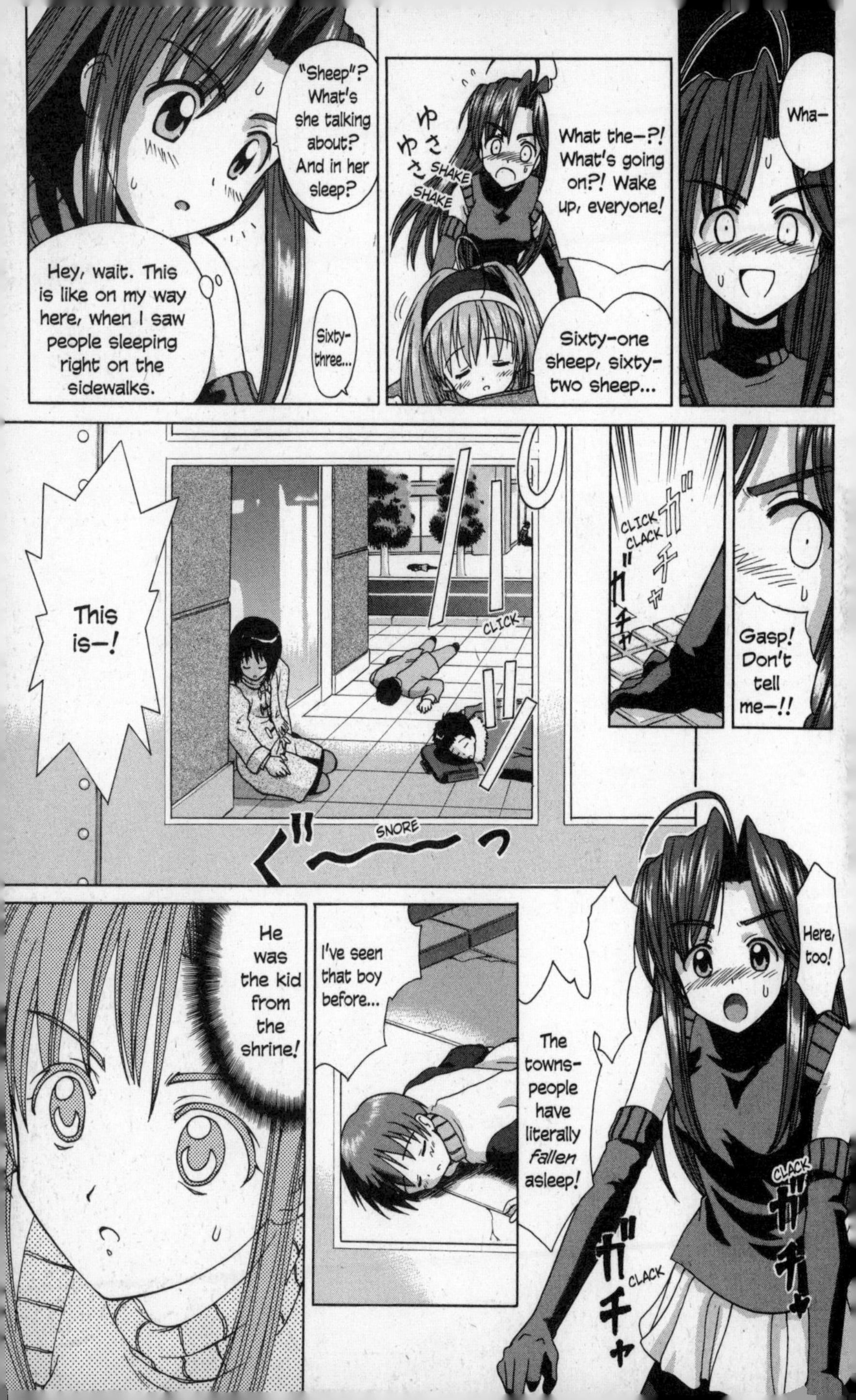
Wha-
What the-?! What's going on?! Wake up, everyone!
ゆさ ゆさ
SHAKE SHAKE
Sixty-one sheep, sixty-two sheep...
Sixty-three...
"Sheep"? What's she talking about? And in her sleep?
Hey, wait. This is like on my way here, when I saw people sleeping right on the sidewalks.
Gasp! Don't tell me-!!
ガチャ ガチャ
CLICK CLACK
CLICK
This is-!
ぐ~~っ
SNORE
Here, too!
The towns-people have literally *fallen* asleep!
ガチャ ガチャ
CLACK CLACK
I've seen that boy before...
He was the kid from the shrine!

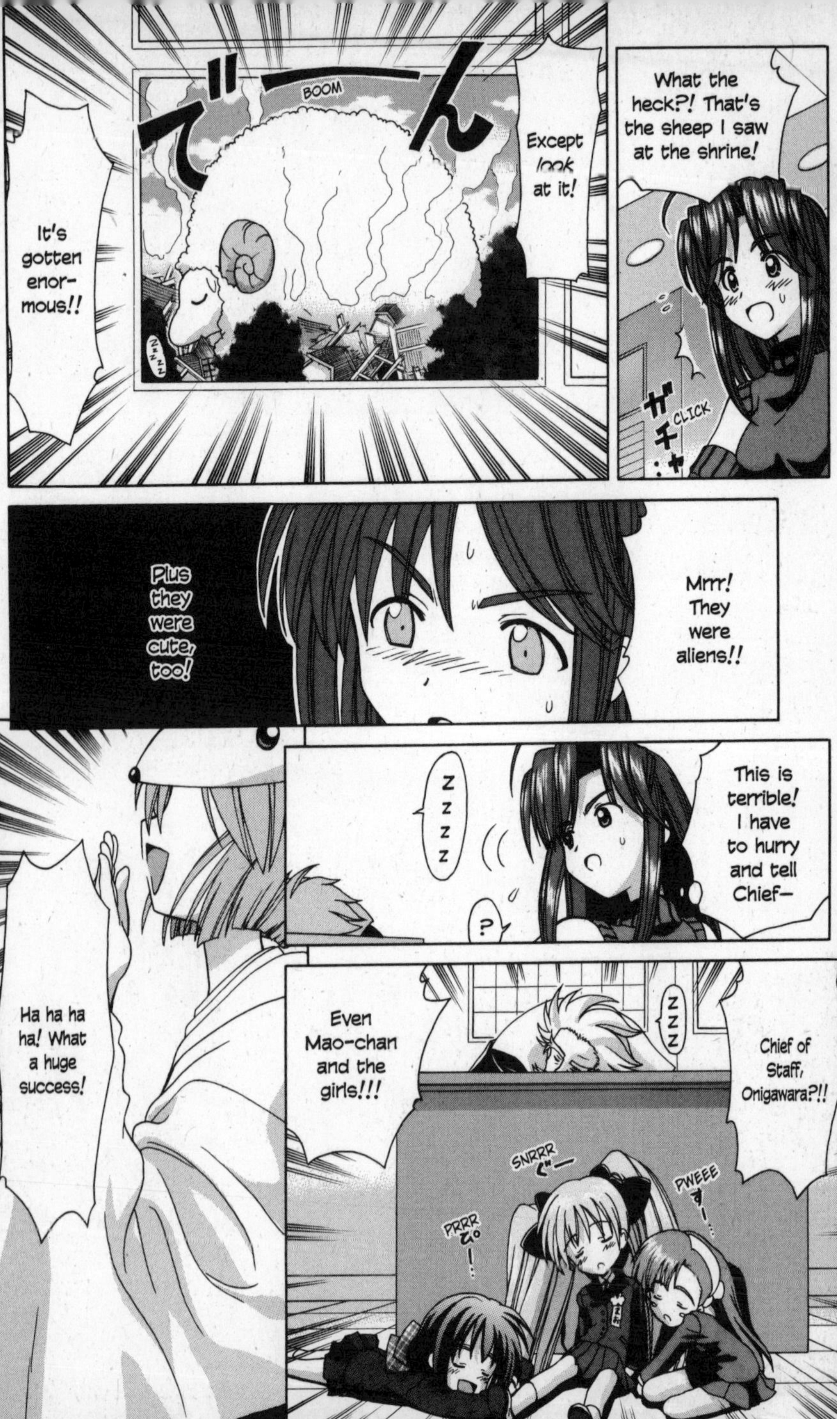
What the heck?! That's the sheep I saw at the shrine!
ガチャ
CLICK
でーん
BOOM
Except *look* at it!
It's gotten enor-mous!!
Z z z z
Mrrr! They were aliens!!
Plus they were cute, too!
This is terrible! I have to hurry and tell Chief–
Z z z z
?
Chief of Staff, Onigawara?!!
Z Z Z
Even Mao-chan and the girls!!!
SNRRR
ぐー
PWEEE
すー…
PRRR
ぴー…
Ha ha ha ha! What a huge success!

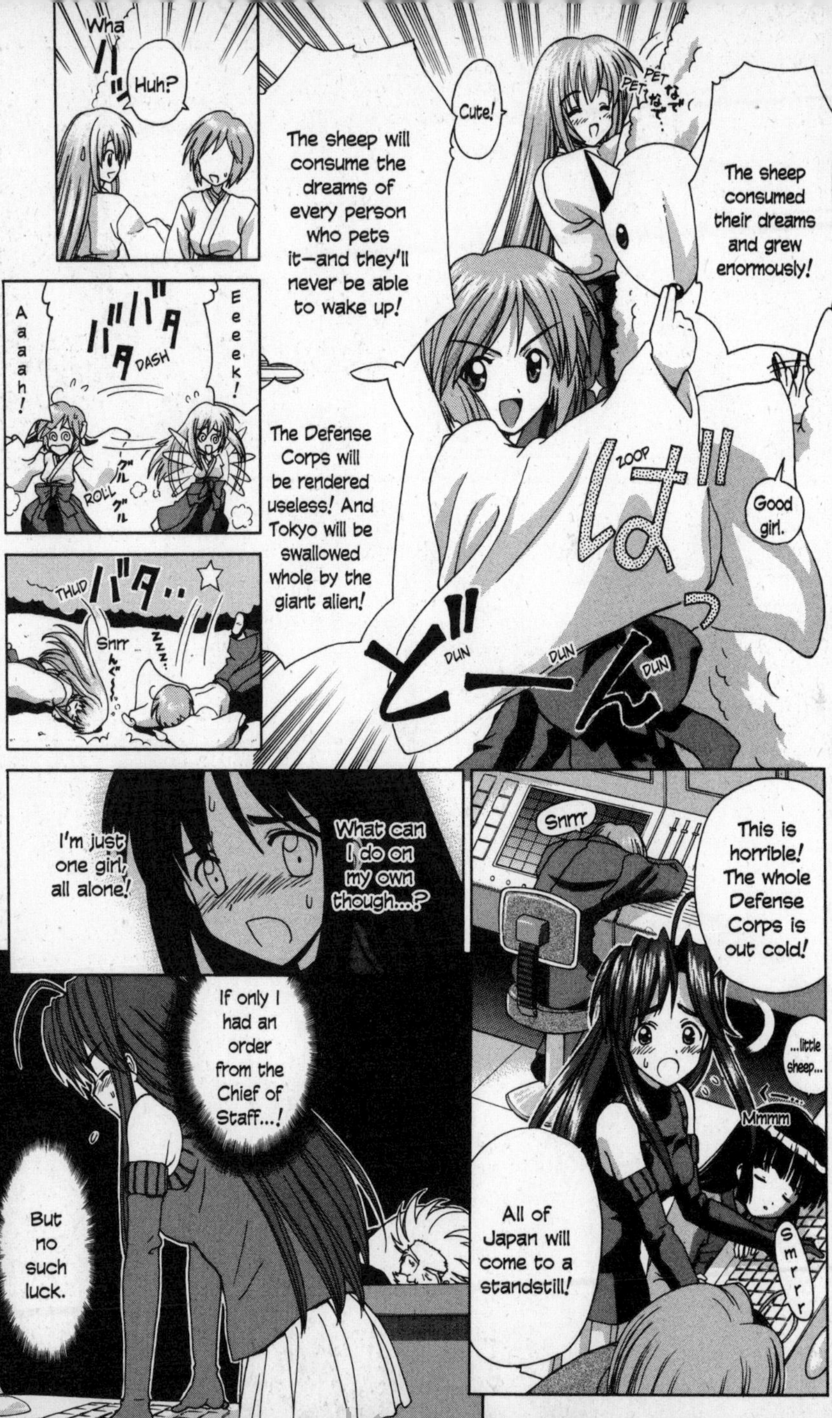
Cute!
PET PET
The sheep consumed their dreams and grew enormously!
ZOOP
Good girl.
DUN
DUN
DUN
The sheep will consume the dreams of every person who pets it—and they'll never be able to wake up!
Huh?
Wha
The Defense Corps will be rendered useless! And Tokyo will be swallowed whole by the giant alien!
Eeeek!
DASH
Aaaah!
ROLL
THUD
Snrr
ZZZ
This is horrible! The whole Defense Corps is out cold!
Snrr
...little sheep...
Mmmm
All of Japan will come to a standstill!
Smrrr
What can I do on my own though...?
I'm just one girl, all alone!
If only I had an order from the Chief of Staff...!
But no such luck.

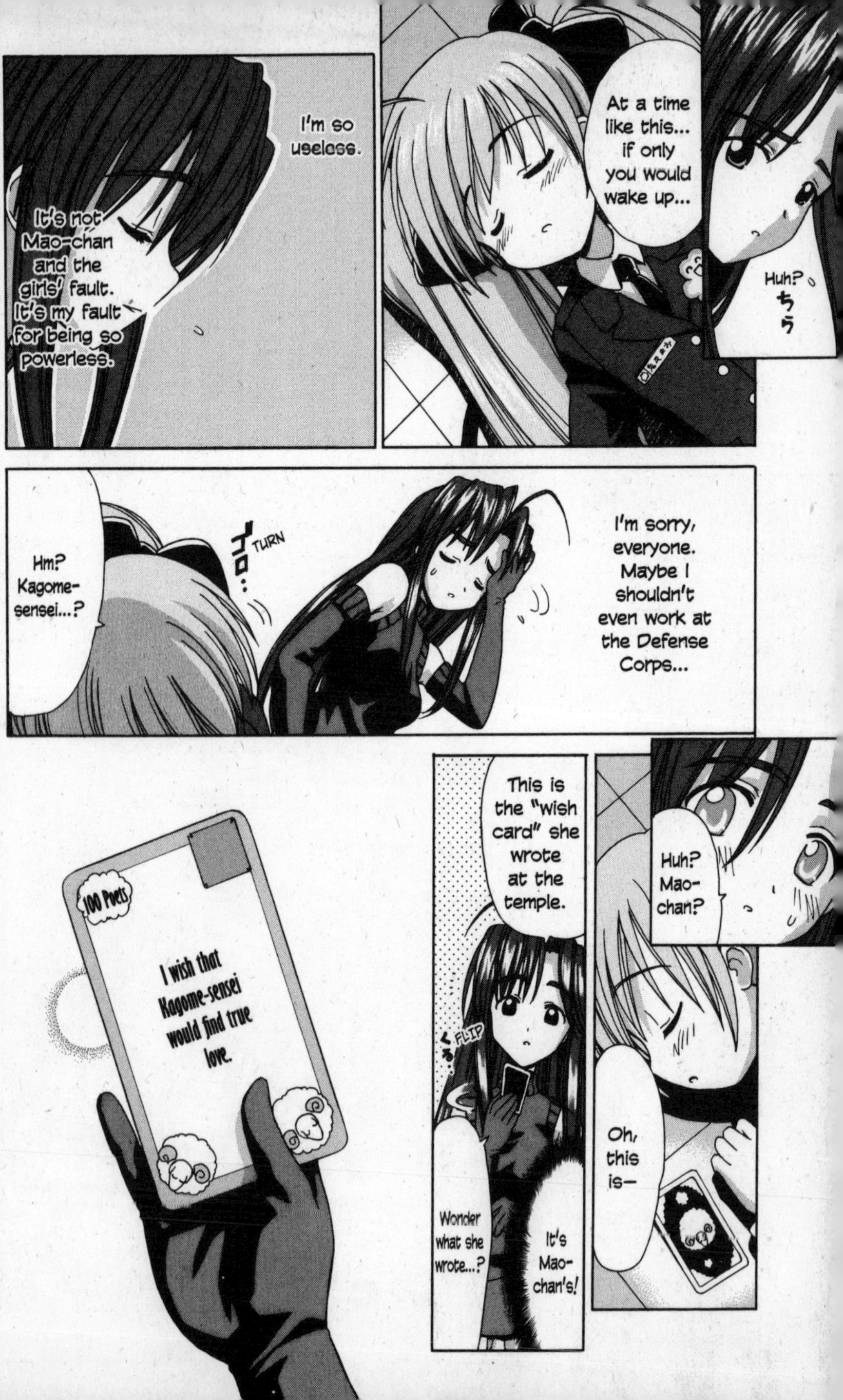
At a time like this... if only you would wake up...
Huh?
ちら
I'm so useless.
It's not Mao-chan and the girls' fault. It's my fault for being so powerless.
I'm sorry, everyone. Maybe I shouldn't even work at the Defense Corps...
TURN
Hm? Kagome-sensei...?
Huh? Mao-chan?
Oh, this is—
It's Mao-chan's!
This is the "wish card" she wrote at the temple.
FLIP
Wonder what she wrote...?
100 Poets
I wish that Kagome-sensei would find true love.

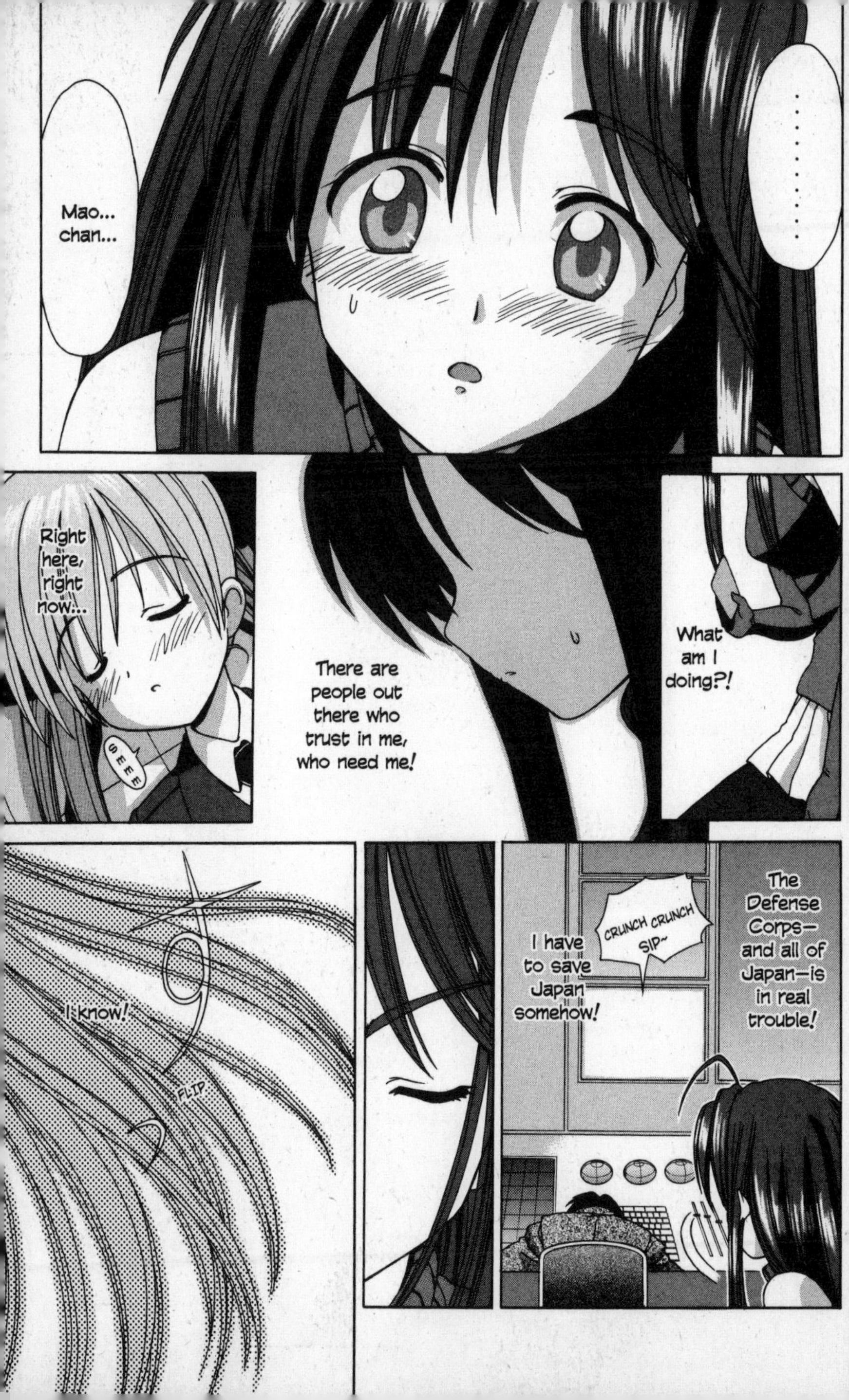

......
Mao... chan...
What am I doing?!
There are people out there who trust in me, who need me!
Right here, right now...
SEEE
The Defense Corps—and all of Japan—is in real trouble!
CRUNCH CRUNCH SIP~
I have to save Japan somehow!
I know!
FLIP

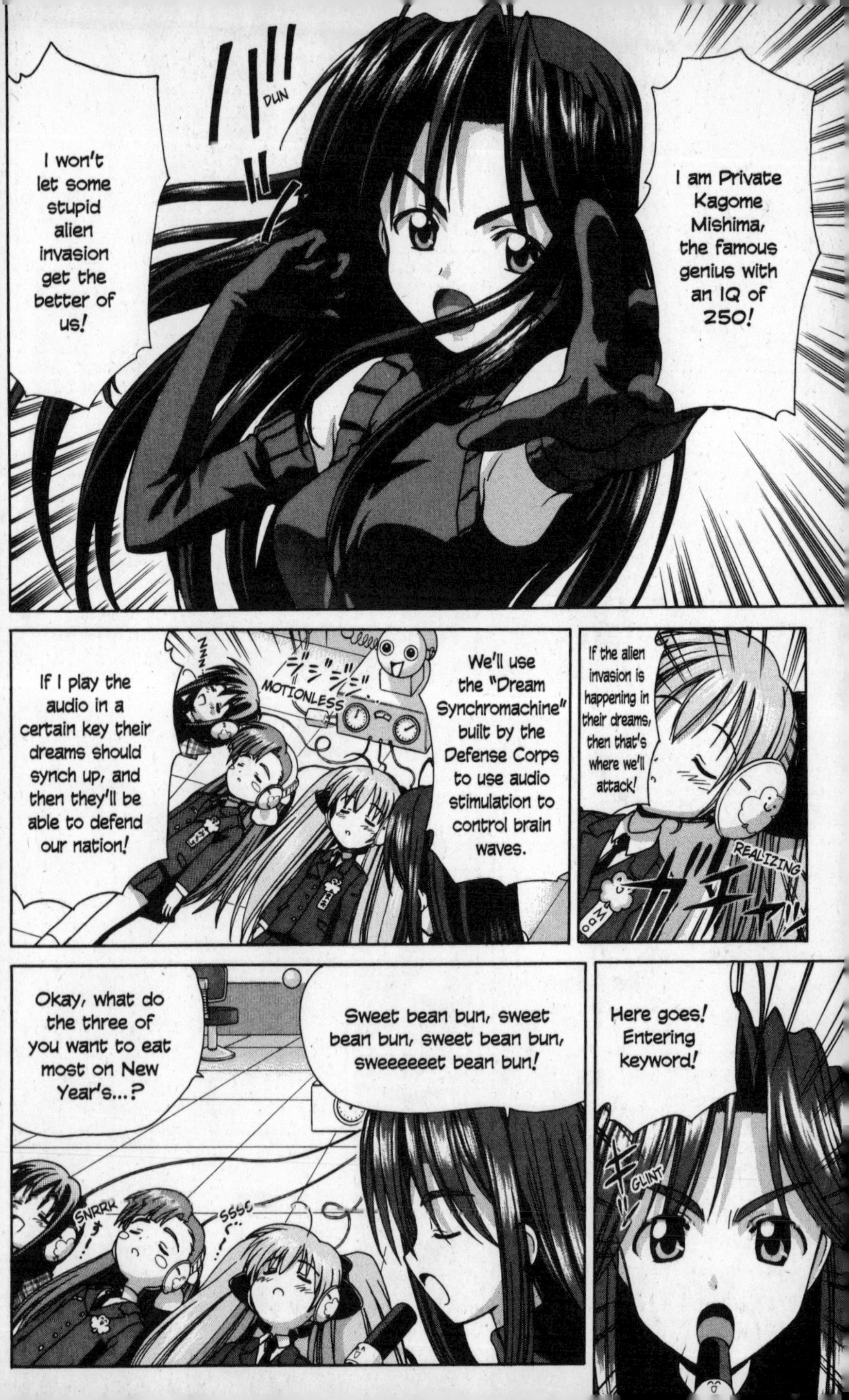
DUN
I am Private Kagome Mishima, the famous genius with an IQ of 250!
I won't let some stupid alien invasion get the better of us!
If the alien invasion is happening in their dreams, then that's where we'll attack!
REALIZING
We'll use the "Dream Synchromachine" built by the Defense Corps to use audio stimulation to control brain waves.
MOTIONLESS
ZZZ
If I play the audio in a certain key their dreams should synch up, and then they'll be able to defend our nation!
Here goes! Entering keyword!
GLINT
Sweet bean bun, sweet bean bun, sweet bean bun, sweeeeeet bean bun!
Okay, what do the three of you want to eat most on New Year's...?
SNRRK
SSSC

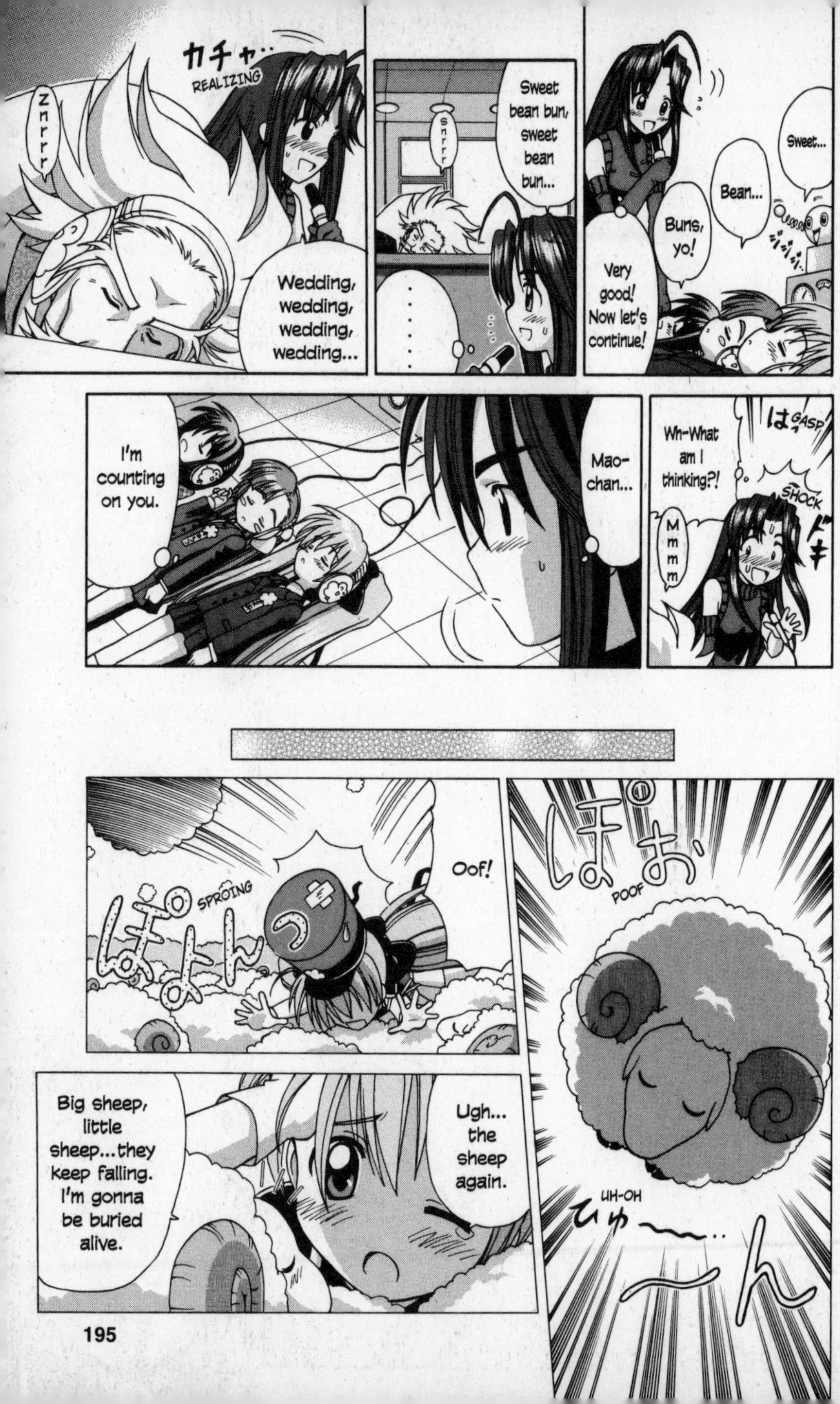

Sweet...
Bean...
Buns, yo!
Very good! Now let's continue!
Sweet bean bun, sweet bean bun...
snrrr
......
カチャ.. REALIZING
Znrrr
Wedding, wedding, wedding, wedding...
は GASP
Wh-What am I thinking?!
SHOCK ドキ
Mmmm
Mao-chan...
I'm counting on you.
ぽぉ POOF
ひゅ~~ん UH-OH
Oof!
ぽよんっ SPROING
Ugh... the sheep again.
Big sheep, little sheep...they keep falling. I'm gonna be buried alive.

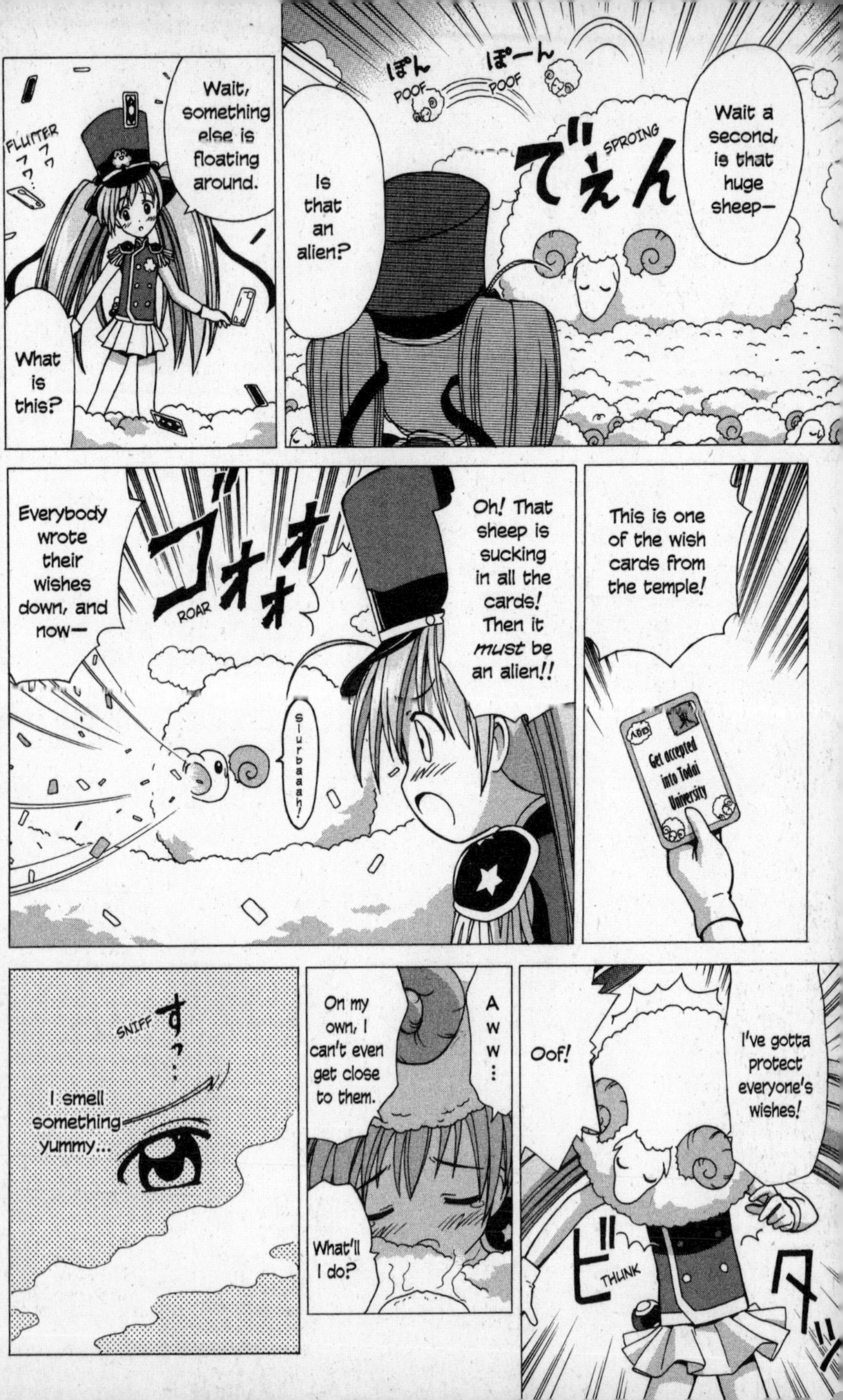
ぽん
POOF
ぽーん
POOF
Wait a second, is that huge sheep—
でぇん
SPROING
Is that an alien?
Wait, something else is floating around.
FLUTTER
What is this?
This is one of the wish cards from the temple!
Get accepted into Todai University
Oh! That sheep is sucking in all the cards! Then it *must* be an alien!!
ゴォォォ
ROAR
Slurbaaah!
Everybody wrote their wishes down, and now—
I've gotta protect everyone's wishes!
Oof!
ビ
THUNK
タッ
Aww...
On my own, I can't even get close to them.
What'll I do?
SNIFF
I smell something yummy...

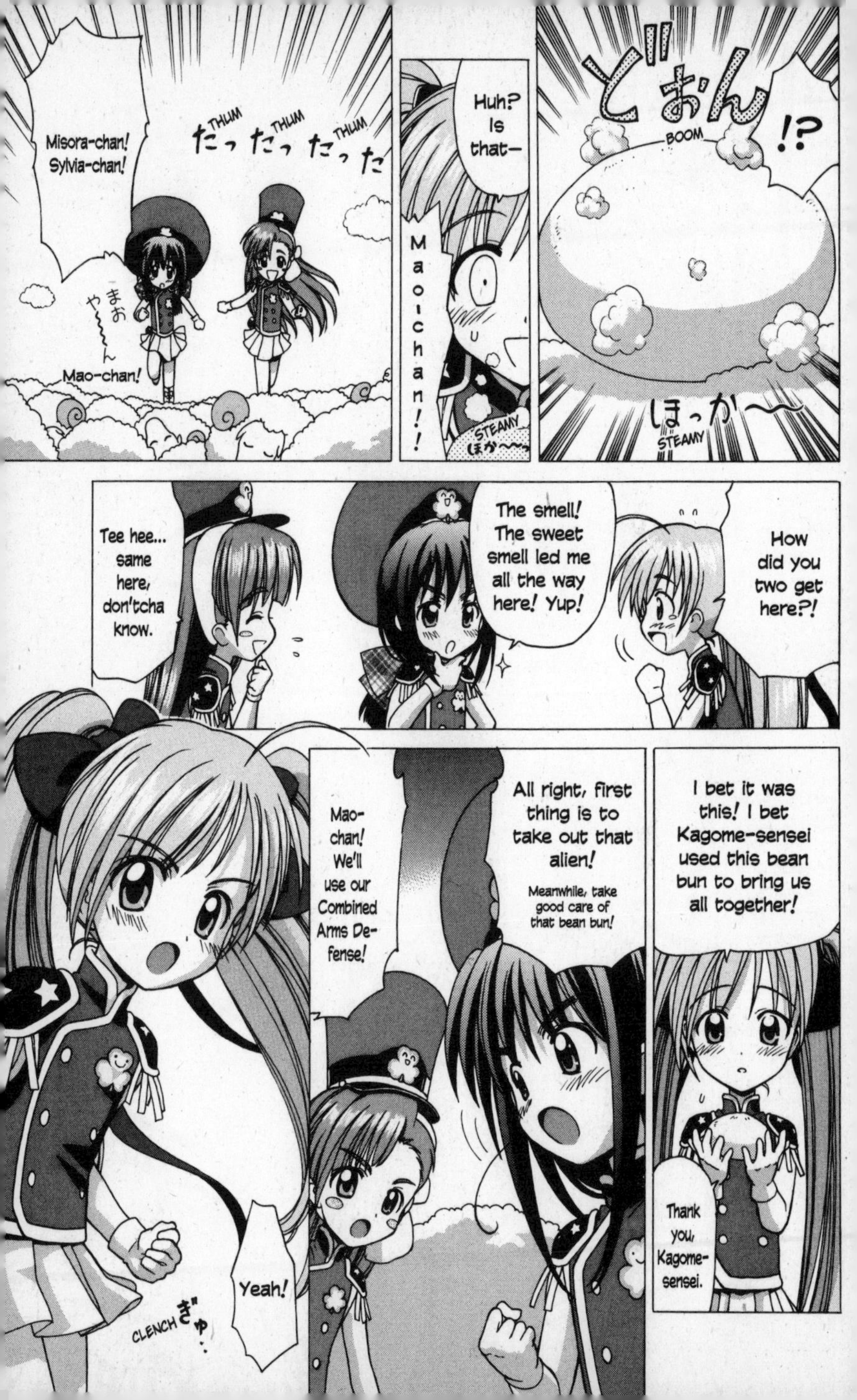
どおん
BOOM
!?
ほっか〜〜
STEAMY
Huh? Is that—
Mao-chan!!
STEAMY
ほか〜〜
Misora-chan! Sylvia-chan!
THUM たっ THUM たっ THUM たった
まおや〜〜ん
Mao-chan!
How did you two get here?!
The smell! The sweet smell led me all the way here! Yup!
Tee hee... same here, don'tcha know.
I bet it was this! I bet Kagome-sensei used this bean bun to bring us all together!
Thank you, Kagome-sensei.
All right, first thing is to take out that alien!
Meanwhile, take good care of that bean bun!
Mao-chan! We'll use our Combined Arms Defense!
Yeah!
CLENCH ぎゅ..

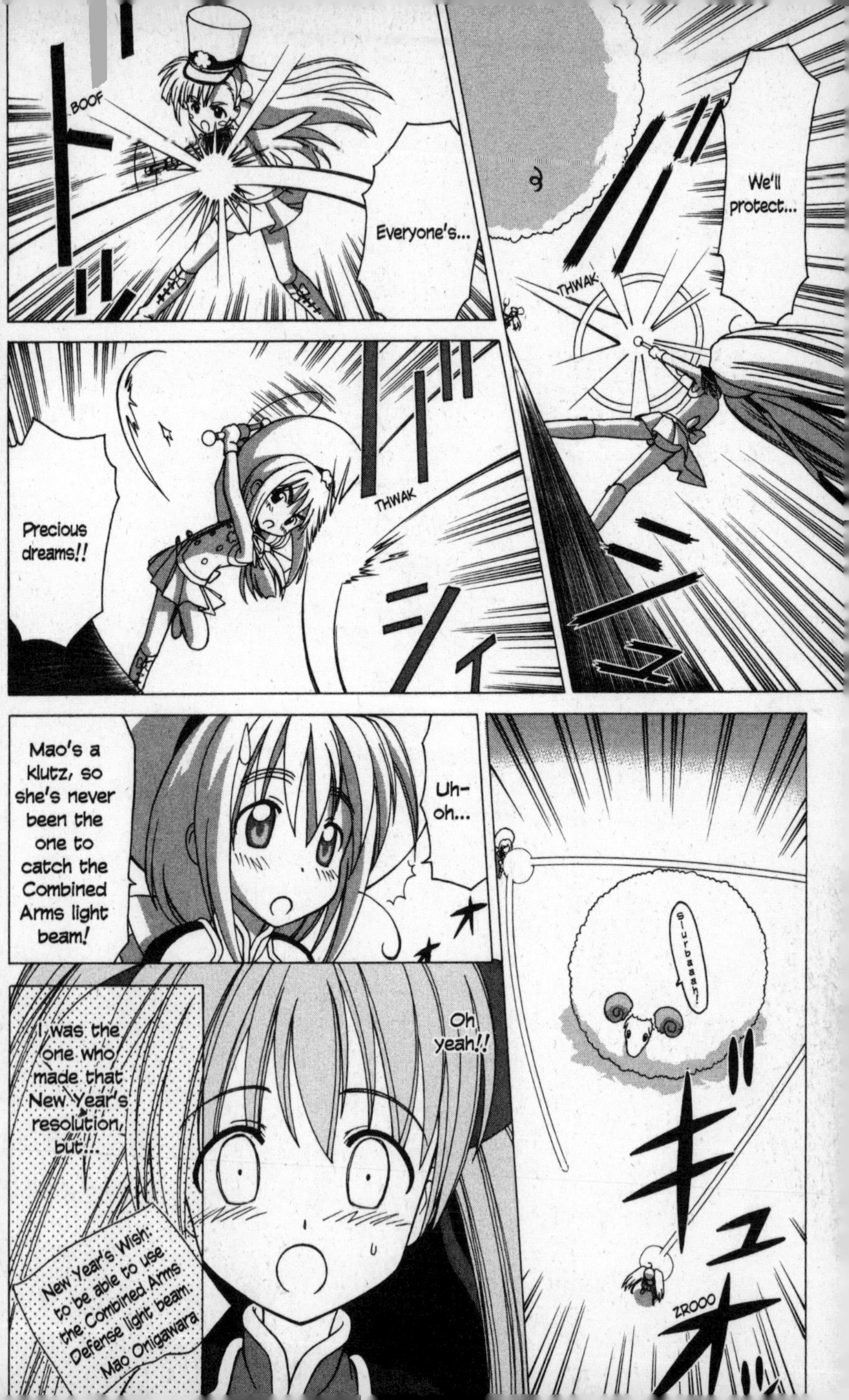

We'll protect...
THWAK
BOOF
Everyone's...
THWAK
Precious dreams!!
Slurbaaah!
ZROOO
Uh-oh...
Mao's a klutz, so she's never been the one to catch the Combined Arms light beam!
Oh yeah!!
I was the one who made that New Year's resolution, but!...
New Year's Wish: to be able to use the Combined Arms Defense light beam. Mao Onigawara

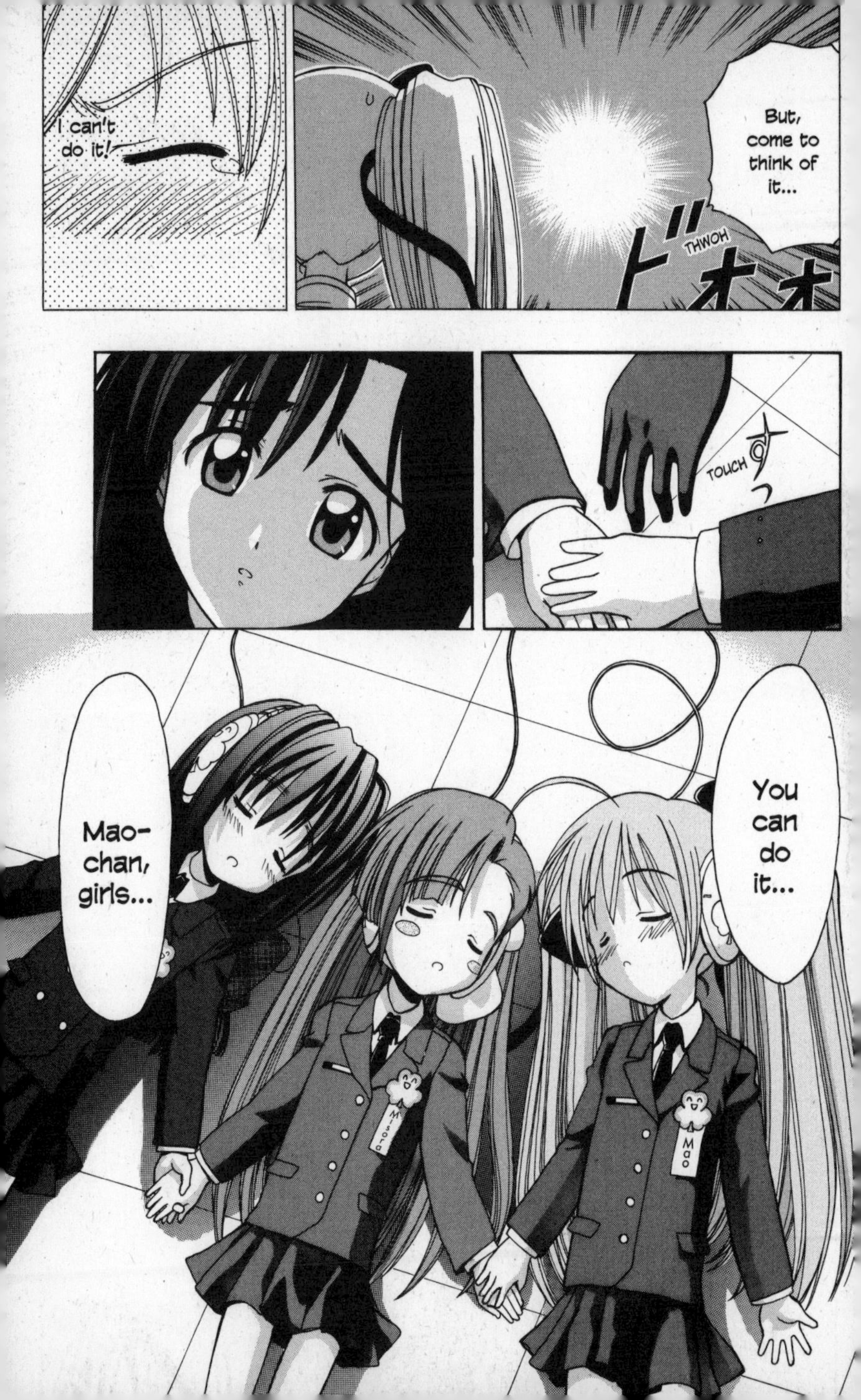
But, come to think of it...
THWOH
I can't do it!
TOUCH
You can do it...
Mao-chan, girls...
Misora
Mao

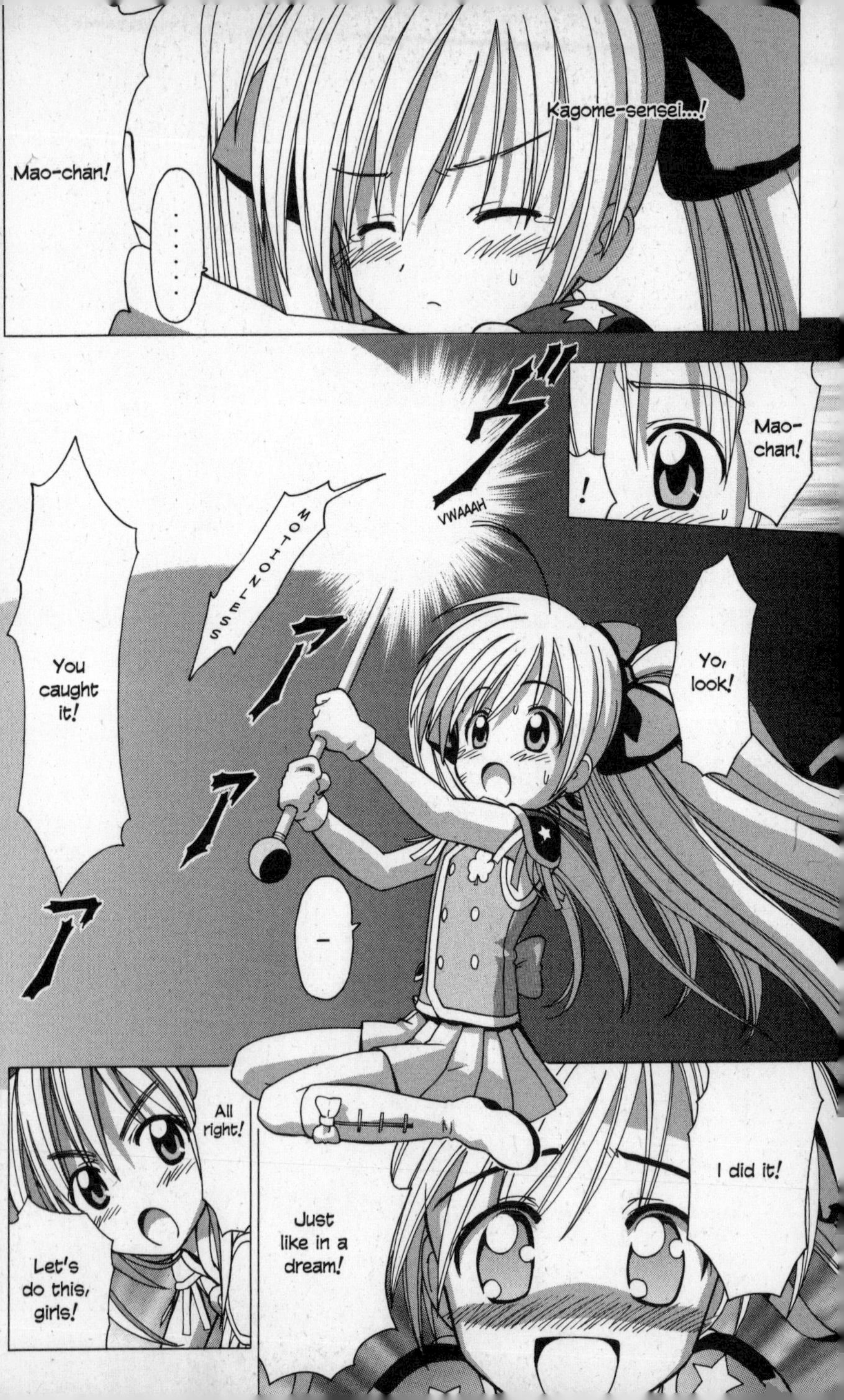
Kagome-sensei...!
......
Mao-chan!
Mao-chan!
!
Yo, look!
VWAAAH
MOTIONLESS
You caught it!
I did it!
Just like in a dream!
All right!
Let's do this, girls!

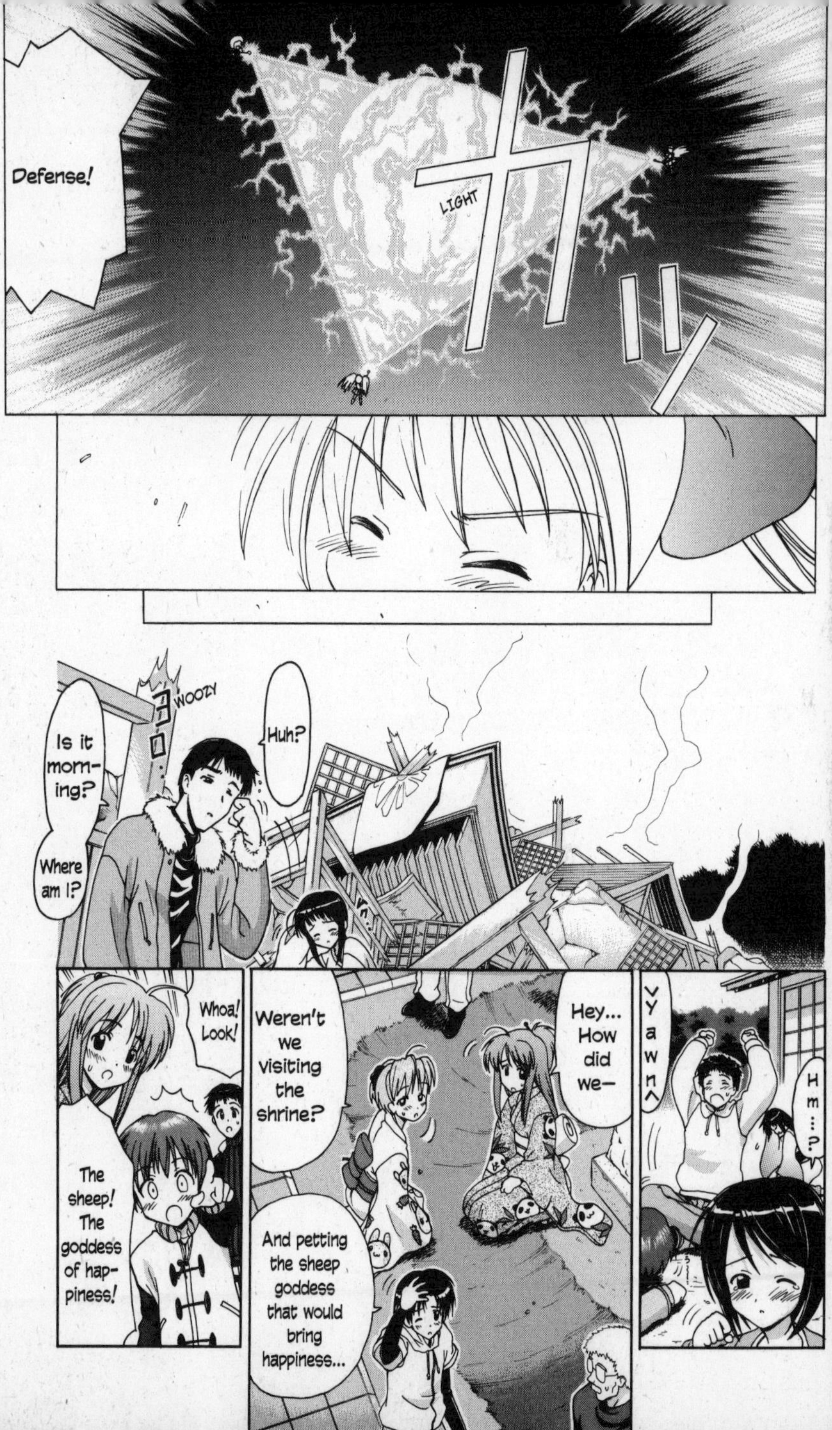
Defense!
LIGHT
Huh?
WOOZY
Is it morning?
Where am I?
Yawn
Hm...?
Hey... How did we—
Weren't we visiting the shrine?
And petting the sheep goddess that would bring happiness...
Whoa! Look!
The sheep! The goddess of happiness!

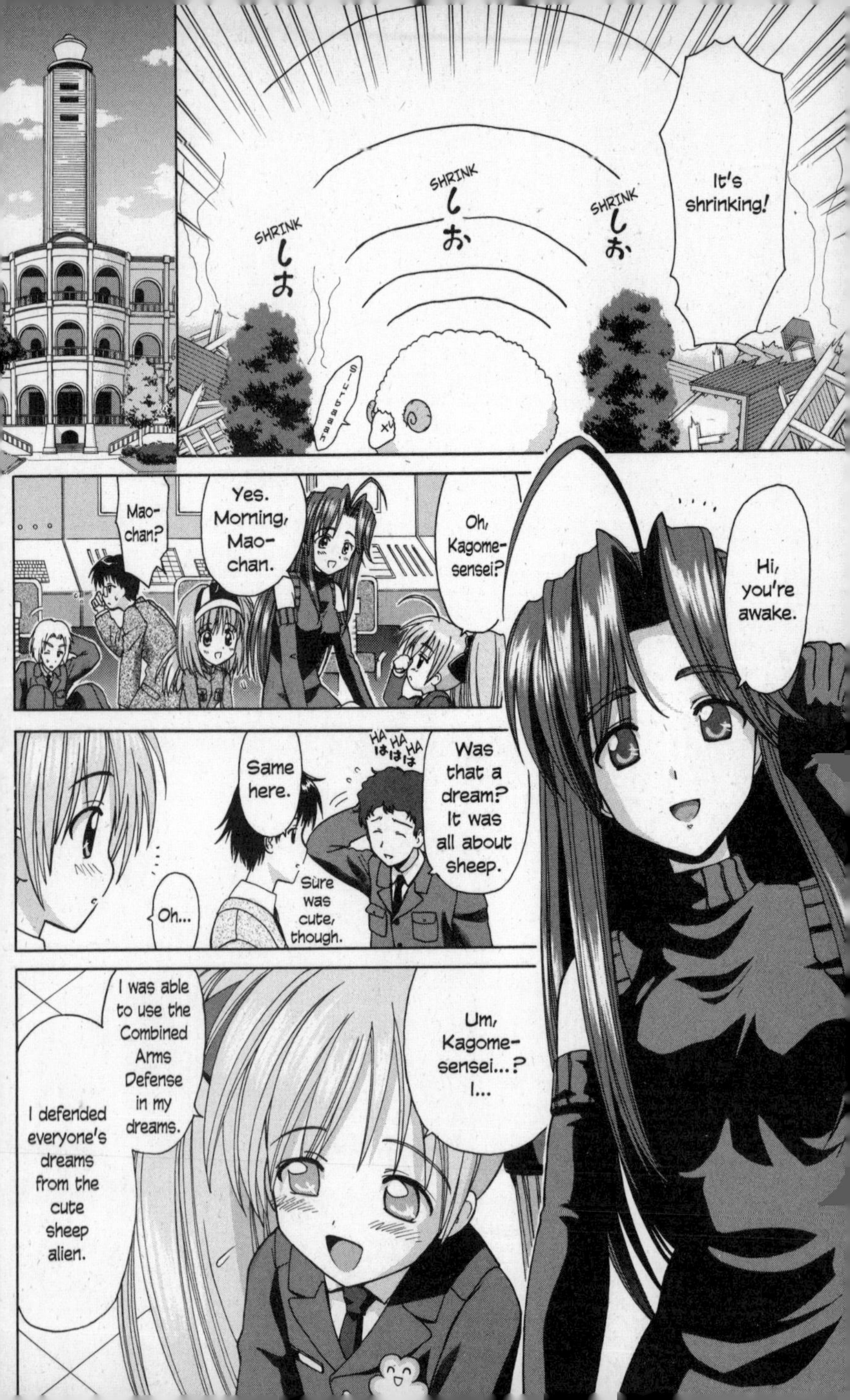
It's shrinking!
SHRINK しお
SHRINK しお
SHRINK しお
Hi, you're awake.
Oh, Kagome-sensei?
Yes. Morning, Mao-chan.
Mao-chan?
Was that a dream? It was all about sheep.
HA HA HA はははは
Same here.
Sure was cute, though.
Oh...
Um, Kagome-sensei...? I...
I was able to use the Combined Arms Defense in my dreams.
I defended everyone's dreams from the cute sheep alien.

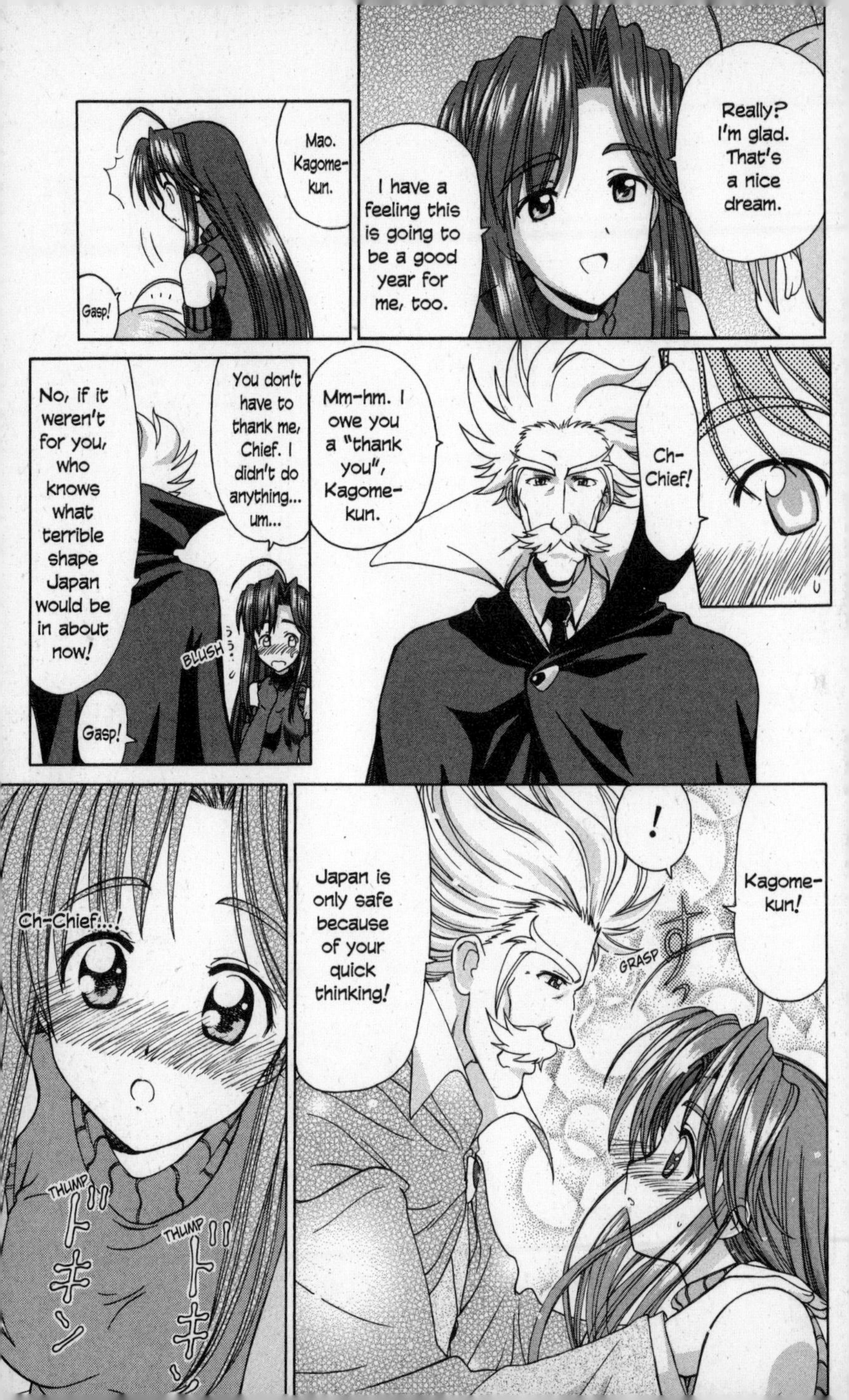
Really? I'm glad. That's a nice dream.
I have a feeling this is going to be a good year for me, too.
Mao. Kagome-kun.
Gasp!
Ch-Chief!
Mm-hm. I owe you a "thank you", Kagome-kun.
You don't have to thank me, Chief. I didn't do anything... um...
No, if it weren't for you, who knows what terrible shape Japan would be in about now!
BLUSH
Gasp!
!
Kagome-kun!
GRASP
Japan is only safe because of your quick thinking!
Ch-Chief...!
THUMP
ドキン
THUMP
ドキン

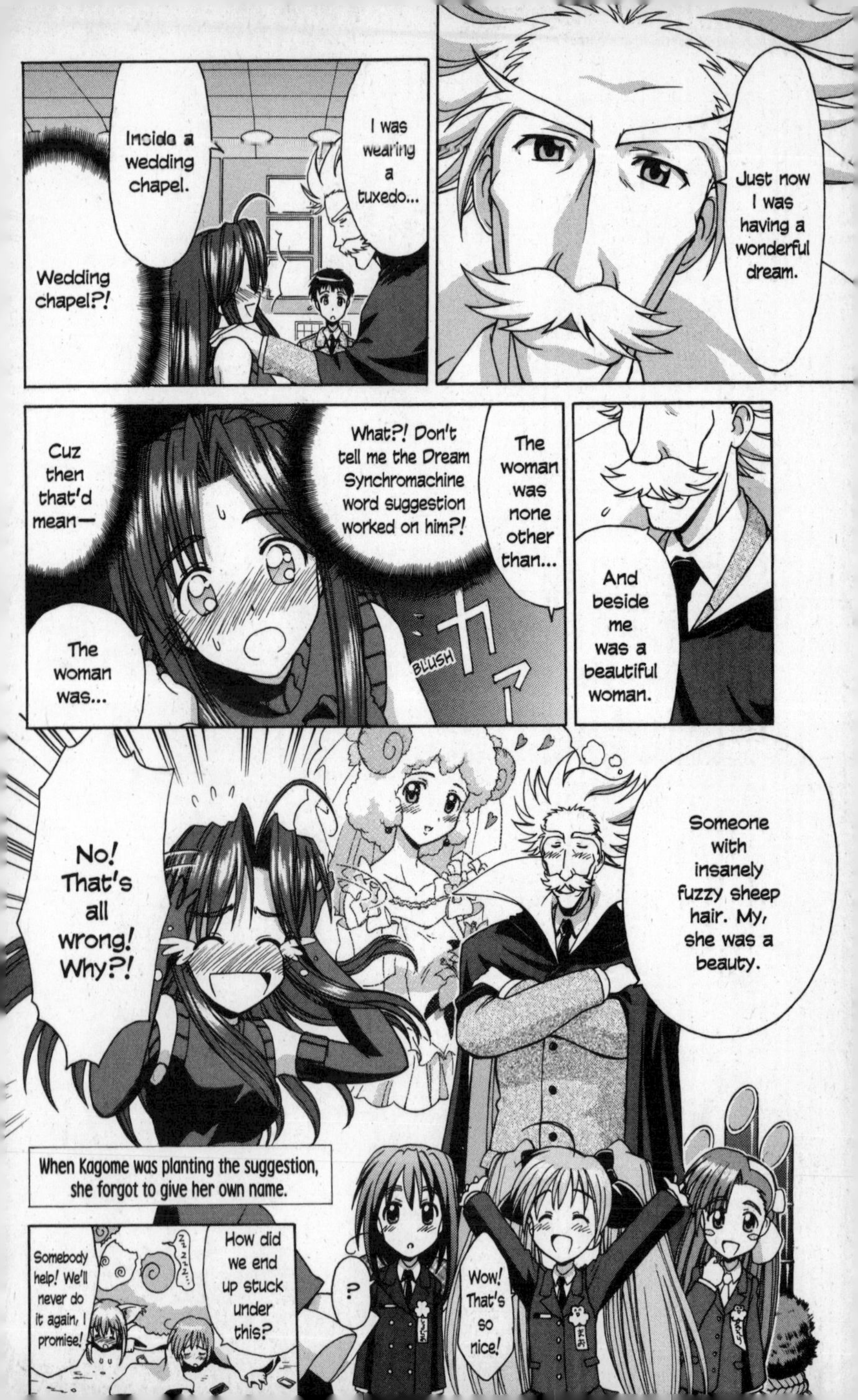

Just now I was having a wonderful dream.
I was wearing a tuxedo...
Inside a wedding chapel.
Wedding chapel?!
And beside me was a beautiful woman.
The woman was none other than...
What?! Don't tell me the Dream Synchromachine word suggestion worked on him?!
BLUSH
Cuz then that'd mean—
The woman was...
Someone with insanely fuzzy sheep hair. My, she was a beauty.
No! That's all wrong! Why?!
When Kagome was planting the suggestion, she forgot to give her own name.
Wow! That's so nice!
?
How did we end up stuck under this?
Somebody help! We'll never do it again, I promise!

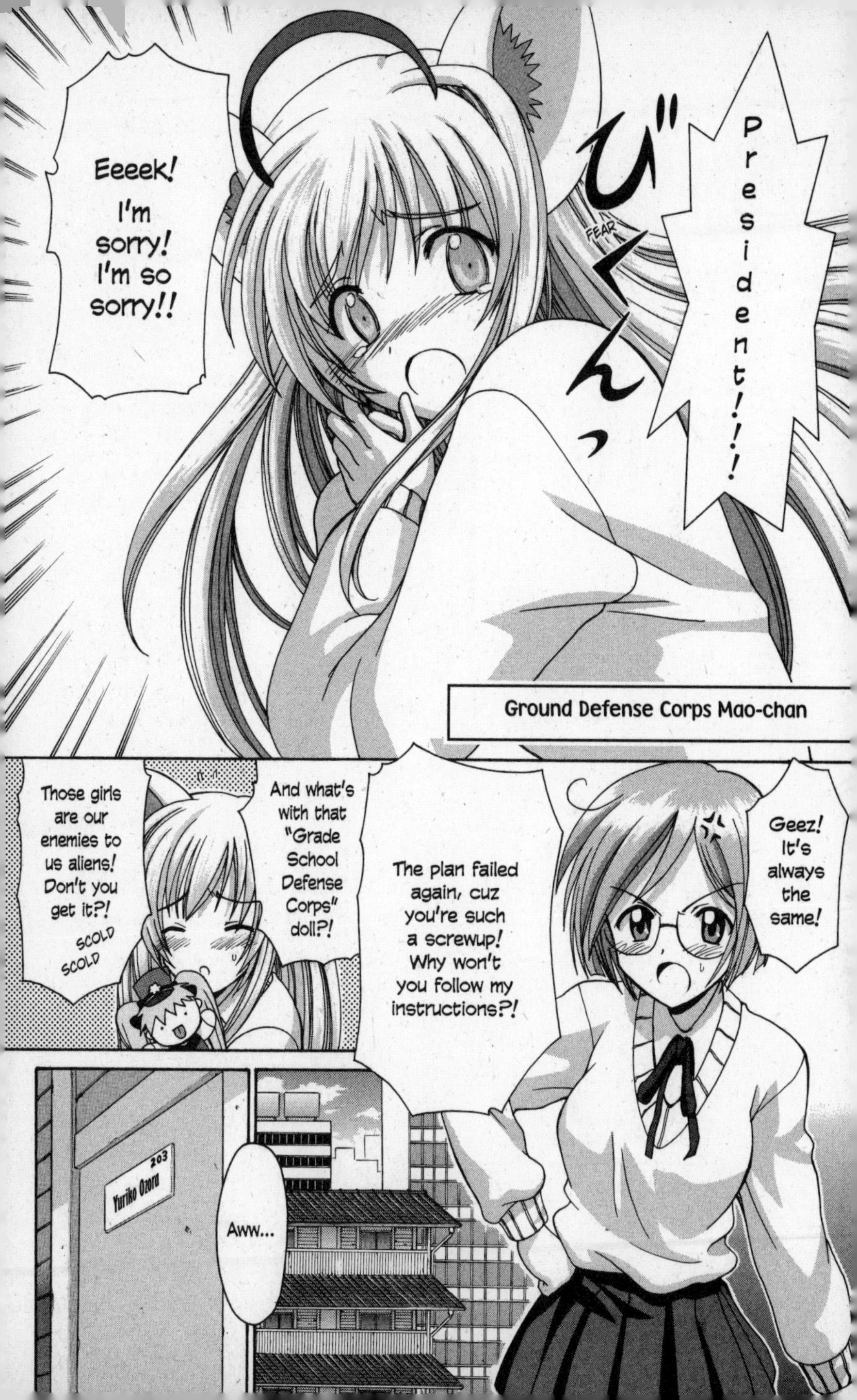
President!!!
FEAR
Eeeek! I'm sorry! I'm so sorry!!
Ground Defense Corps Mao-chan
Geez! It's always the same!
The plan failed again, cuz you're such a screwup! Why won't you follow my instructions?!
And what's with that "Grade School Defense Corps" doll?!
Those girls are our enemies to us aliens! Don't you get it?!
SCOLD SCOLD
203 Yuriko Ozora
Aww...

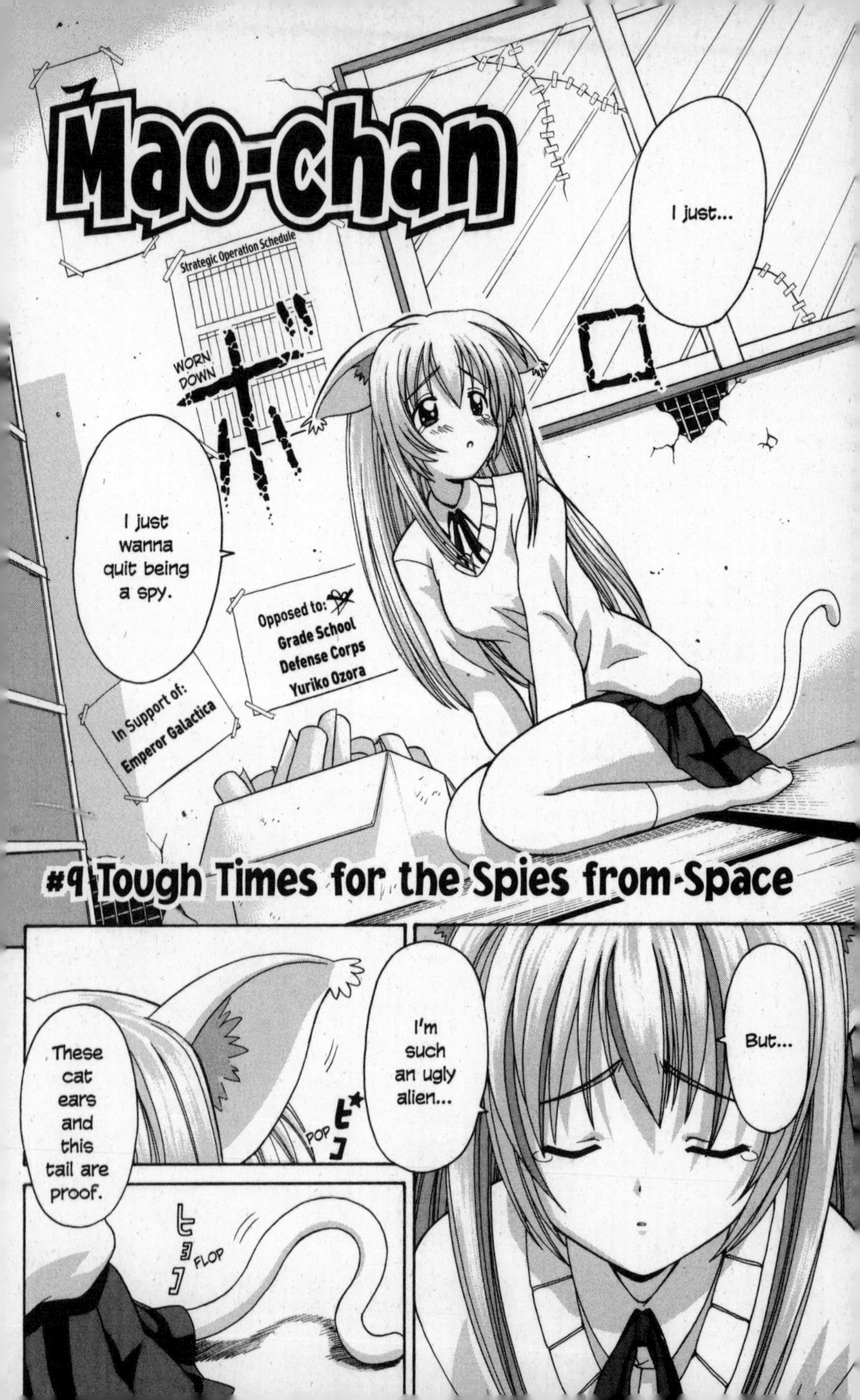
Mao-chan
Strategic Operation Schedule
WORN DOWN
I just...
I just wanna quit being a spy.
Opposed to: Grade School Defense Corps Yuriko Ozora
In Support of: Emperor Galactica
#9 Tough Times for the Spies from Space
But...
I'm such an ugly alien...
POP
These cat ears and this tail are proof.
FLOP

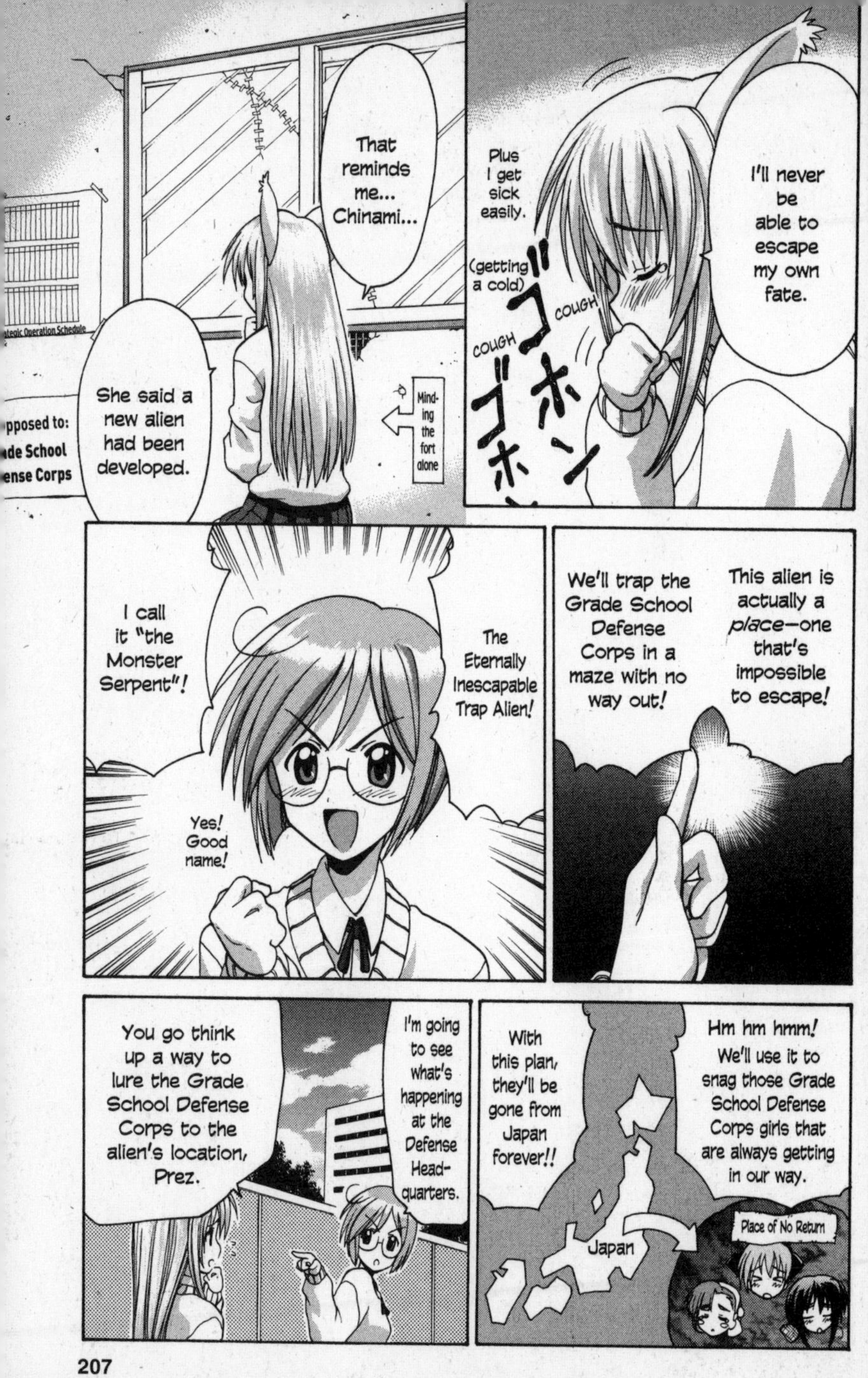
I'll never be able to escape my own fate.
Plus I get sick easily.
(getting a cold)
COUGH
COUGH
ゴホンゴホン
That reminds me... Chinami...
She said a new alien had been developed.
Minding the fort alone
ategic Operation Schedule
pposed to:
de School
ense Corps
This alien is actually a *place*—one that's impossible to escape!
We'll trap the Grade School Defense Corps in a maze with no way out!
The Eternally Inescapable Trap Alien!
I call it "the Monster Serpent"!
Yes! Good name!
Hm hm hmm! We'll use it to snag those Grade School Defense Corps girls that are always getting in our way.
With this plan, they'll be gone from Japan forever!!
Japan
Place of No Return
I'm going to see what's happening at the Defense Headquarters.
You go think up a way to lure the Grade School Defense Corps to the alien's location, Prez.

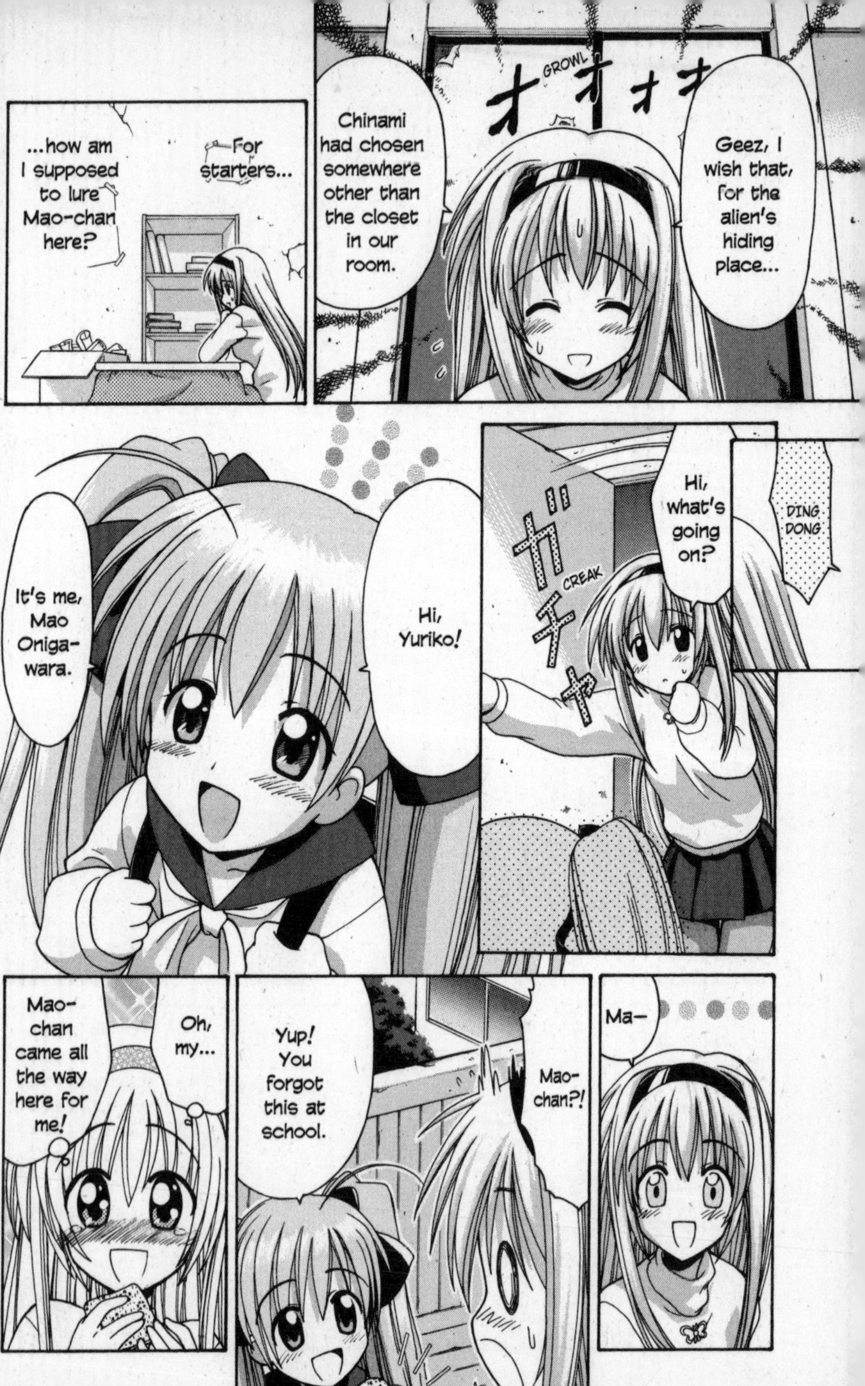
GROWL
Geez, I wish that, for the alien's hiding place...
Chinami had chosen somewhere other than the closet in our room.
For starters...
...how am I supposed to lure Mao-chan here?
DING DONG
Hi, what's going on?
CREAK
Hi, Yuriko!
It's me, Mao Oniga-wara.
Ma—
Mao-chan?!
Yup! You forgot this at school.
Oh, my...
Mao-chan came all the way here for me!

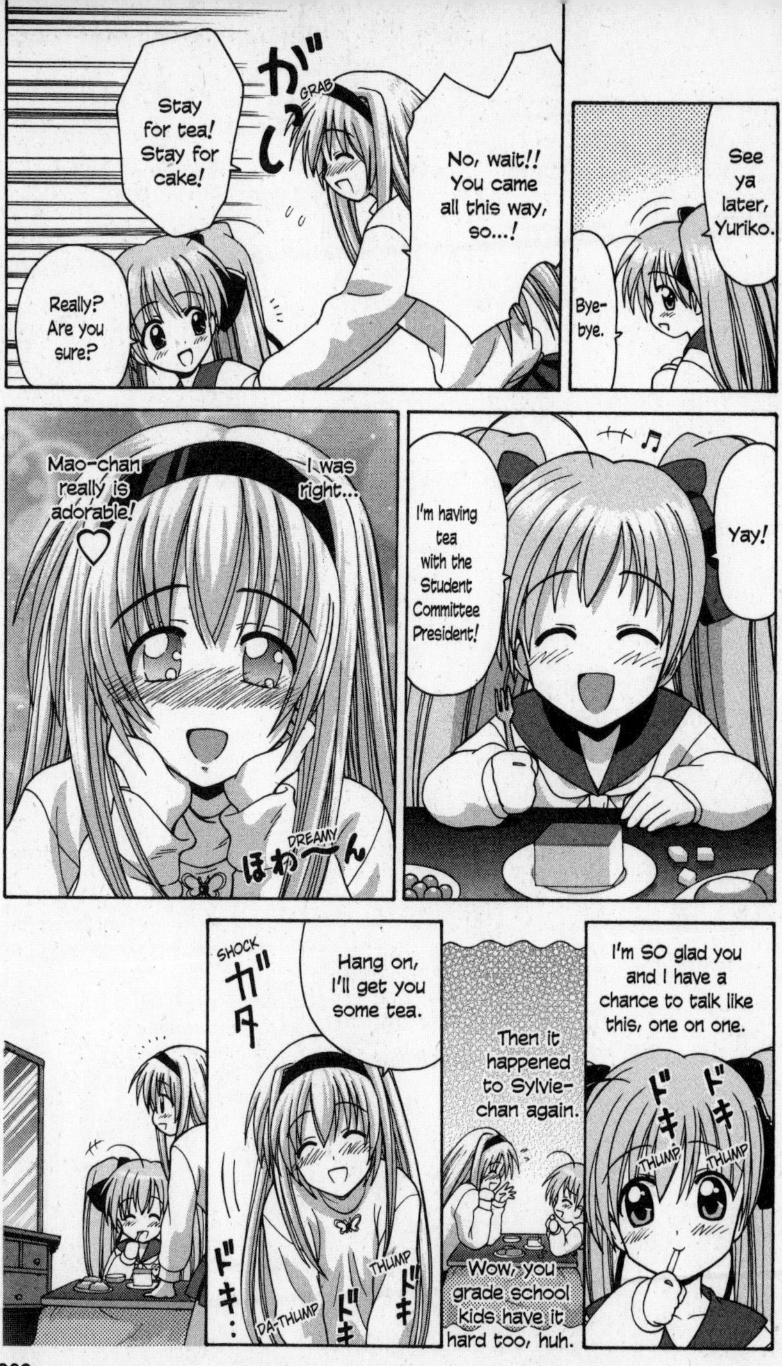
See ya later, Yuriko.
Bye-bye.
No, wait!! You came all this way, so...!
GRAB
がしっ
Stay for tea! Stay for cake!
Really? Are you sure?
Yay!
I'm having tea with the Student Committee President!
I was right...
Mao-chan really is adorable! ♡
DREAMY
ほわ～ん
I'm SO glad you and I have a chance to talk like this, one on one.
ドキ ドキ
THUMP THUMP
Then it happened to Sylvie-chan again.
Wow, you grade school kids have it hard too, huh.
Hang on, I'll get you some tea.
SHOCK
ガタ
THUMP
ドキ
ドキ
DA-THUMP
ドキ…

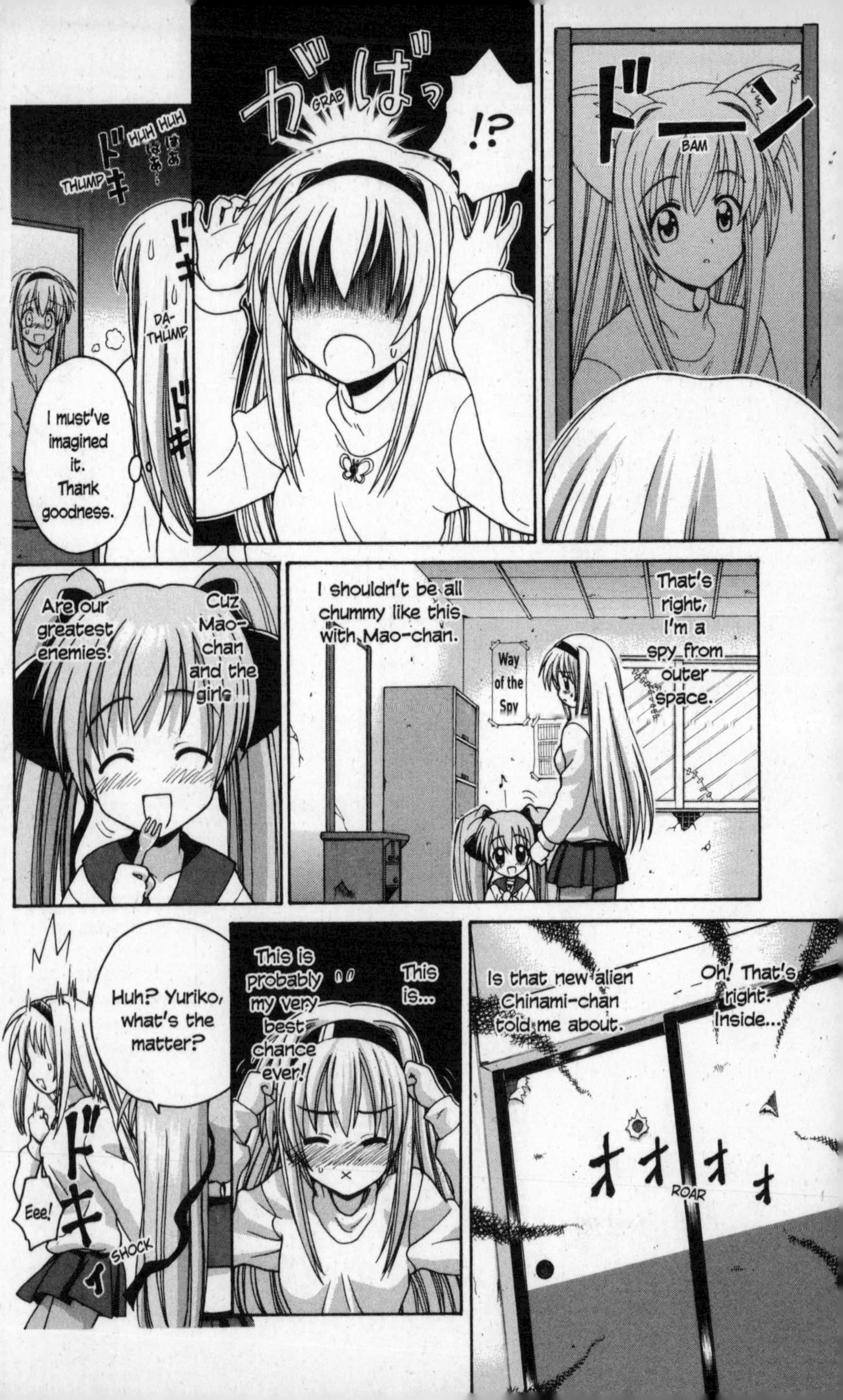
ドーン
BAM
ガばっ
GRAB
!?
ドキ
THUMP
HUH HUH
はぁはぁ…
DA-THUMP
I must've imagined it. Thank goodness.
That's right, I'm a spy from outer space.
I shouldn't be all chummy like this with Mao-chan.
Way of the Spy
Cuz Mao-chan and the girls
Are our greatest enemies.
Oh! That's right. Inside...
Is that new alien Chinami-chan told me about.
オオオオ
ROAR
This is...
This is probably my very best chance ever!
Huh? Yuriko, what's the matter?
Eee!
SHOCK

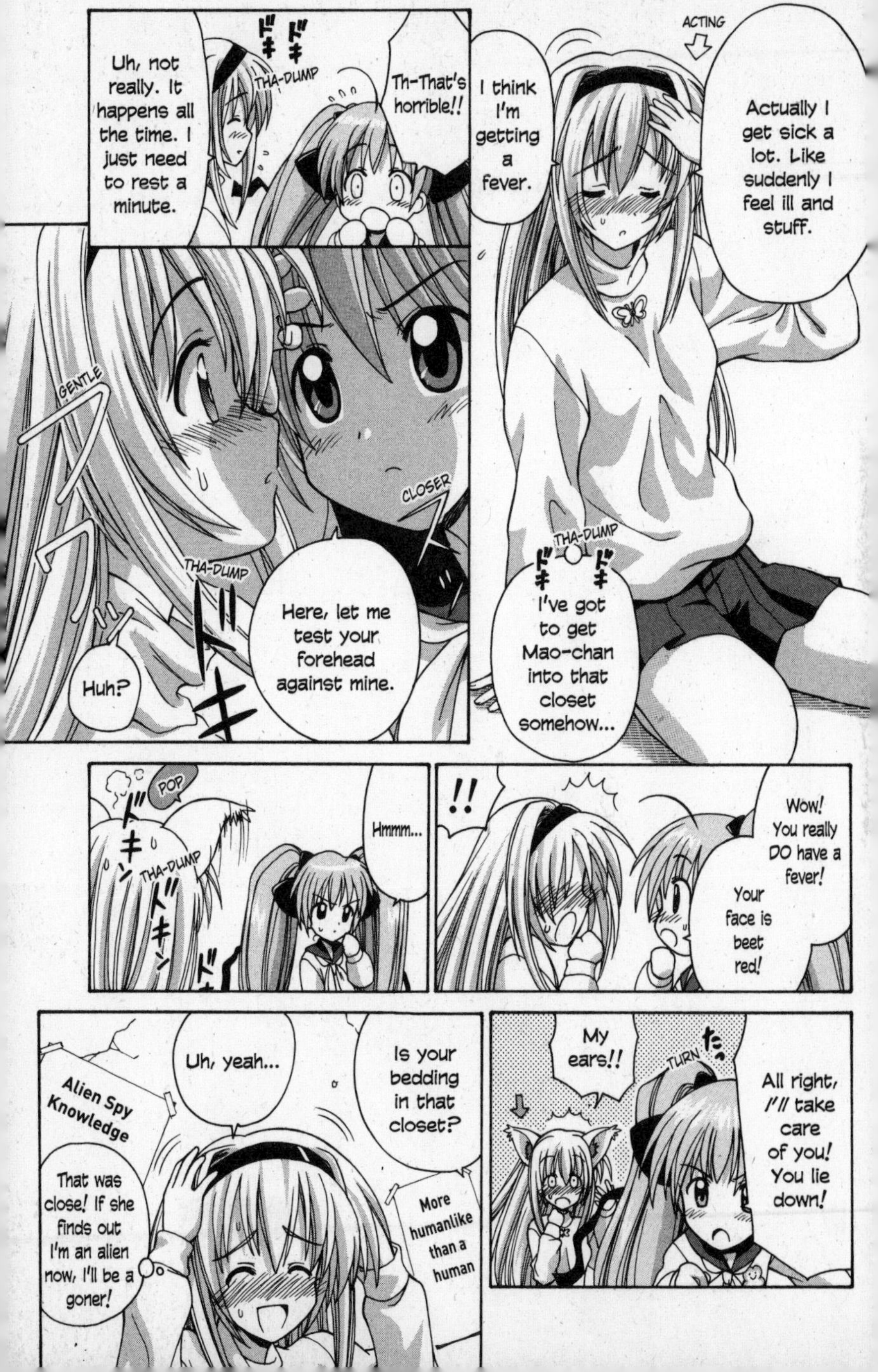
ACTING
Actually I get sick a lot. Like suddenly I feel ill and stuff.
I think I'm getting a fever.
THA-DUMP
ドキ ドキ
I've got to get Mao-chan into that closet somehow...
Th-That's horrible!!
ドキ ドキ
THA-DUMP
Uh, not really. It happens all the time. I just need to rest a minute.
CLOSER
Here, let me test your forehead against mine.
THA-DUMP
ドキ
GENTLE
Huh?
Wow! You really DO have a fever!
Your face is beet red!
!!
Hmmm...
POP
THA-DUMP
ドキン
All right, I'll take care of you! You lie down!
TURN
My ears!!
Is your bedding in that closet?
Uh, yeah...
More humanlike than a human
Alien Spy Knowledge
That was close! If she finds out I'm an alien now, I'll be a goner!

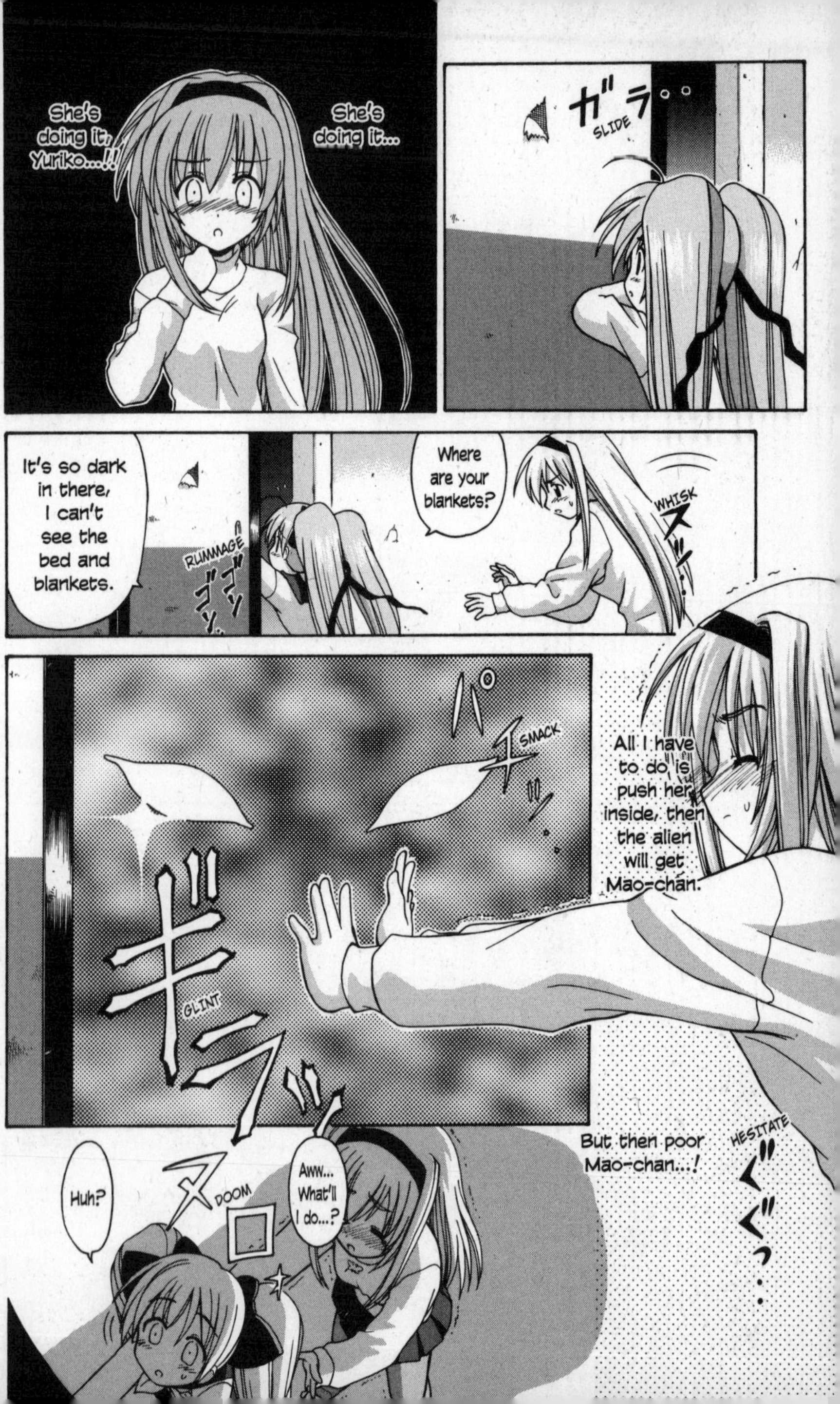
ガラ
SLIDE
She's doing it...
She's doing it, Yuriko...!!
WHISK
Where are your blankets?
RUMMAGE
It's so dark in there, I can't see the bed and blankets.
All I have to do is push her inside, then the alien will get Mao-chan.
SMACK
GLINT
HESITATE
But then poor Mao-chan...!
Aww... What'll I do...?
DOOM
Huh?

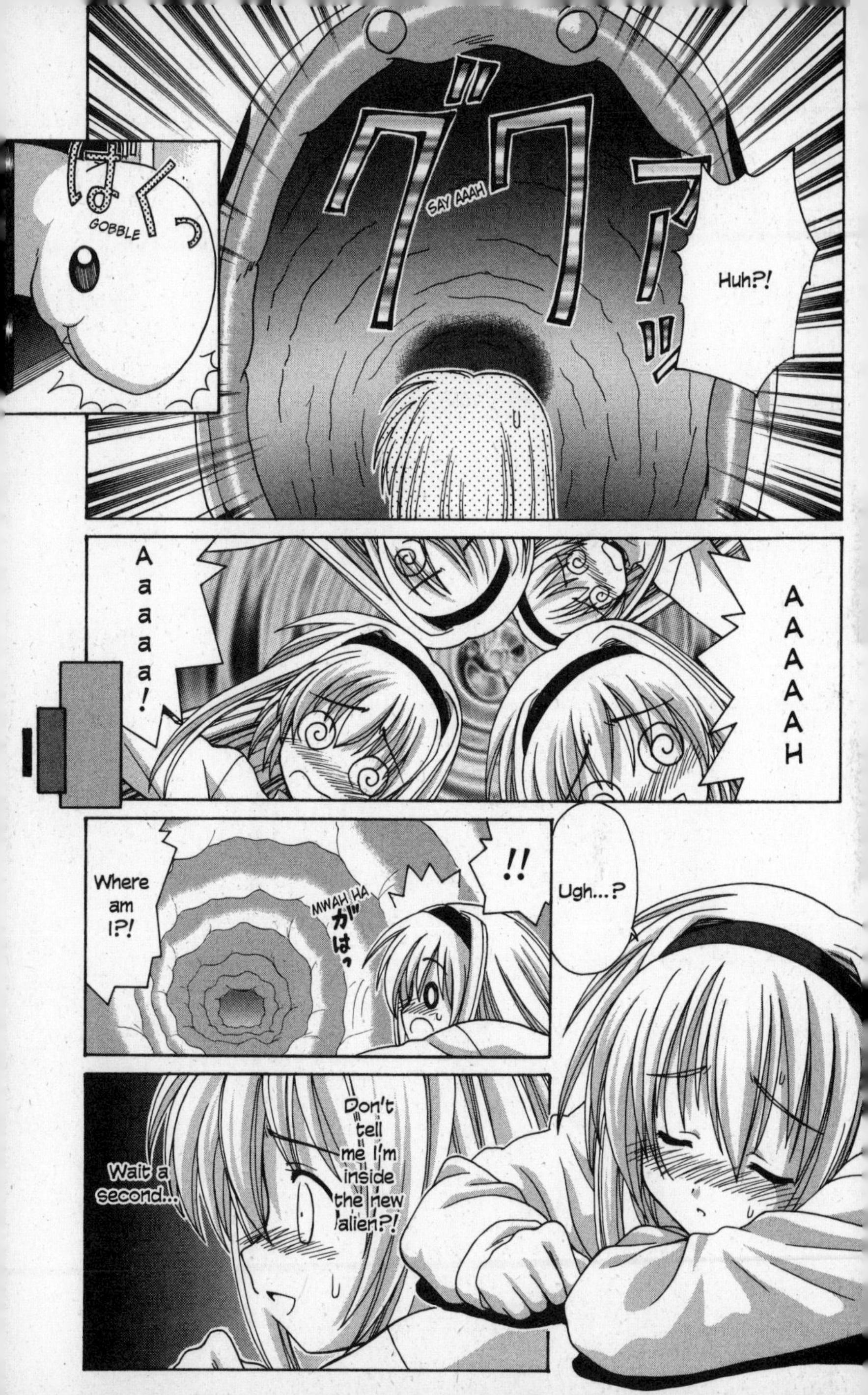
Huh?!
SAY AAAH
GOBBLE
AAAAAH
Aaaaa!
Ugh...?
!!
MWAH HA
Where am I?!
Don't tell me I'm inside the new alien?!
Wait a second...

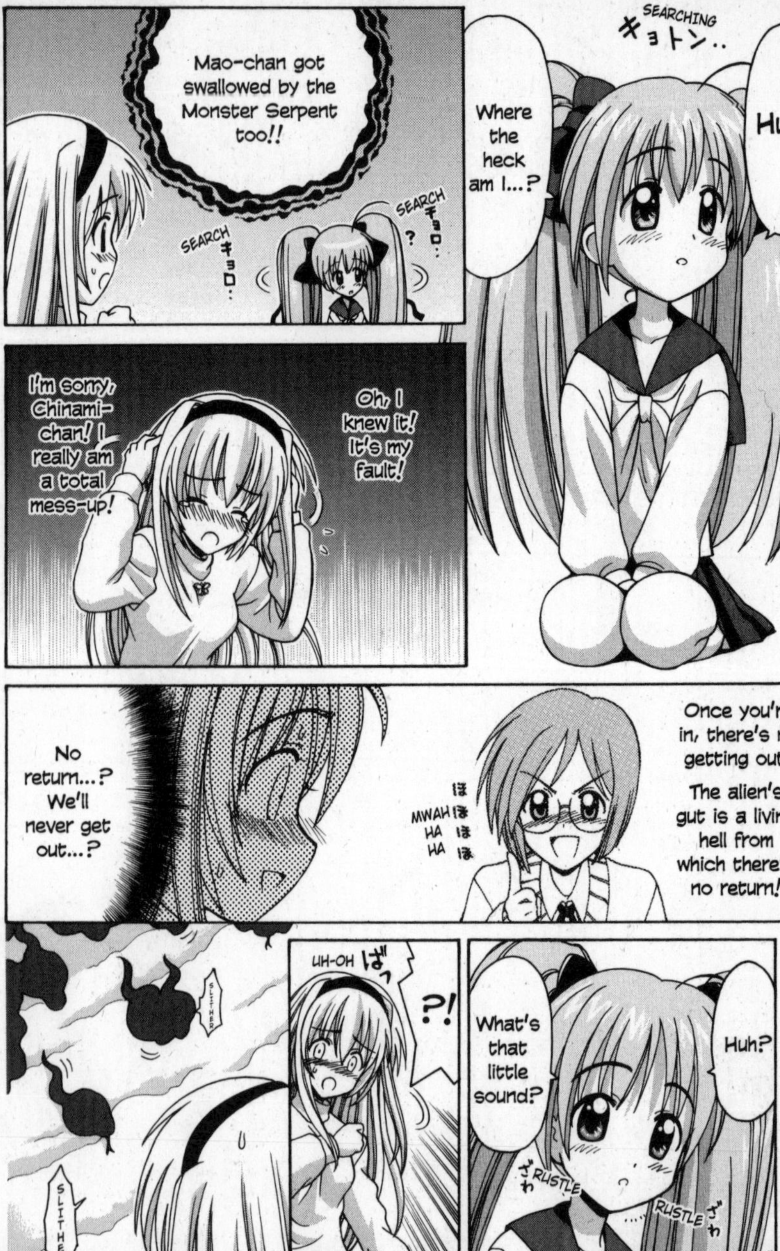
SEARCHING キョトン..
Huh?
Where the heck am I...?
Mao-chan got swallowed by the Monster Serpent too!!
SEARCH キョロ..
?
SEARCH キョロ..
Oh, I knew it! It's my fault!
I'm sorry, Chinami-chan! I really am a total mess-up!
Once you're in, there's no getting out!
The alien's gut is a living hell from which there's no return!
MWAH HA HA HA ほほほほ
No return...? We'll never get out...?
Huh?
What's that little sound?
RUSTLE ざわ
RUSTLE ざわ
RUSTLE ざわ
UH-OH ばっ
?!
SLITHER
SLITHER

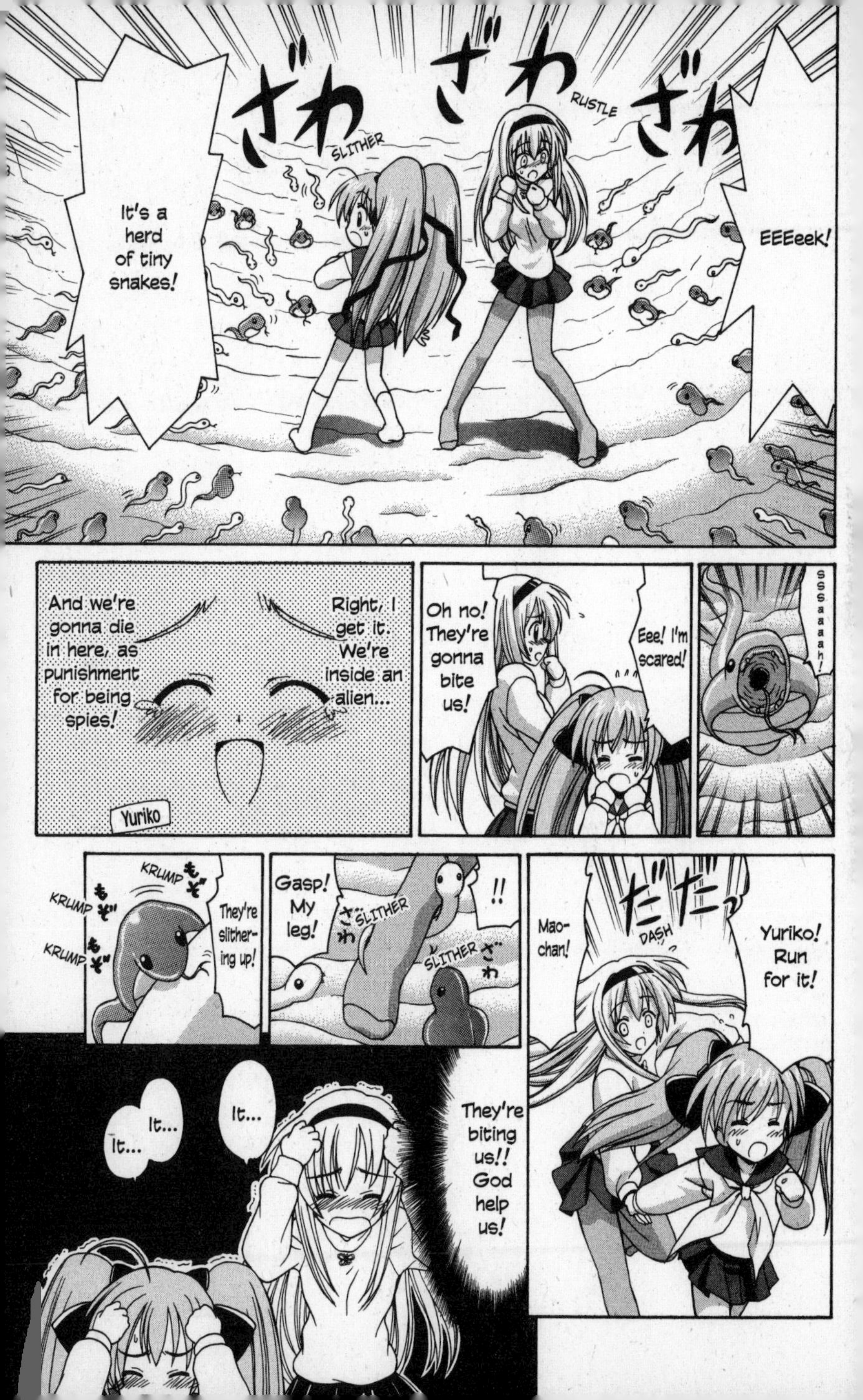
EEEeek!
ざわ
RUSTLE
ざわ
ざわ
SLITHER
It's a herd of tiny snakes!
SSaaaah!
Eee! I'm scared!
Oh no! They're gonna bite us!
Right, I get it. We're inside an alien...
And we're gonna die in here, as punishment for being spies!
Yuriko
Yuriko! Run for it!
だだっ
DASH
Mao-chan!
They're biting us!! God help us!
!!
Gasp! My leg!
ざわ
SLITHER
SLITHER
ざわ
They're slither-ing up!
もぞ
KRUMP
もぞ
KRUMP
もぞ
KRUMP
It...
It...
It...

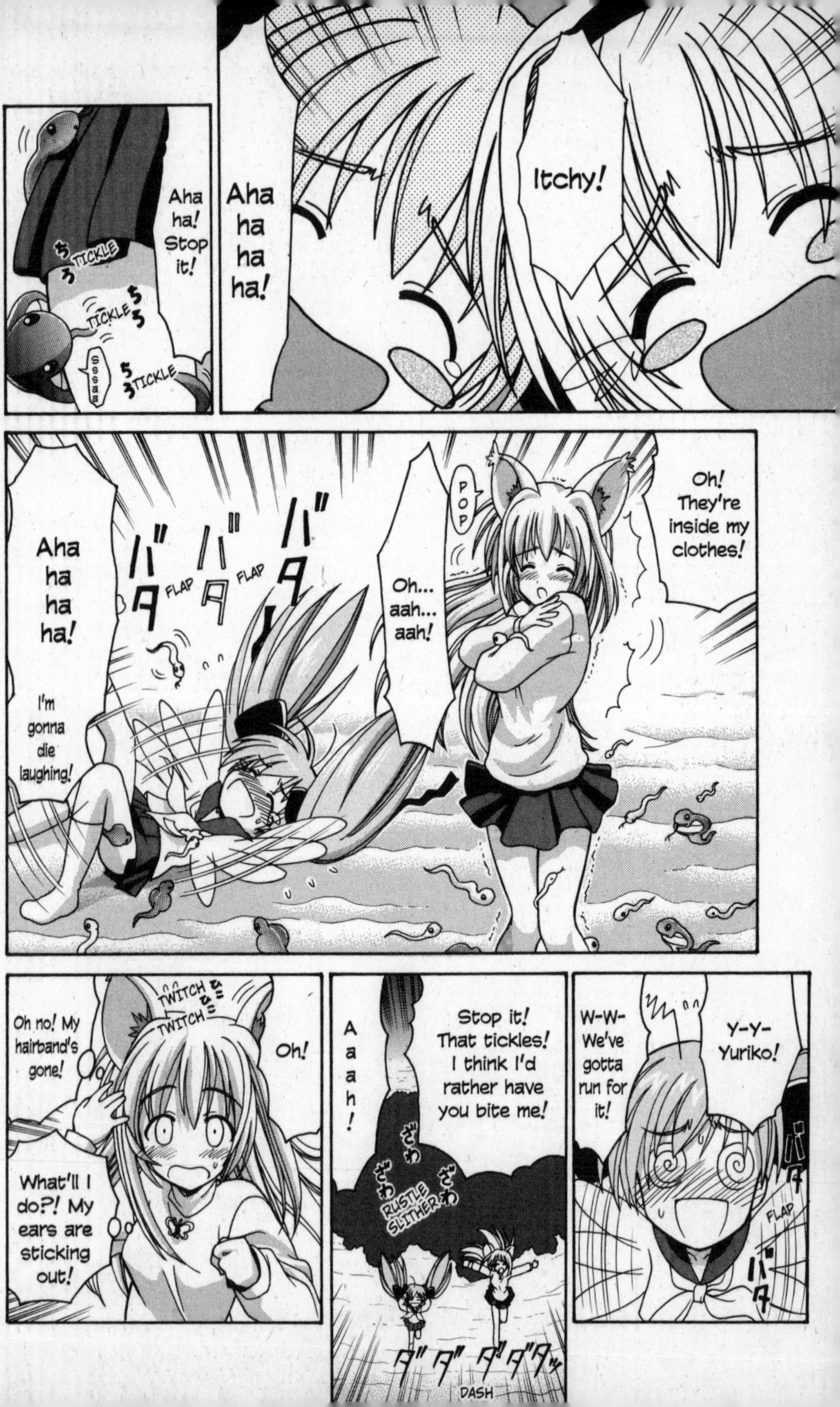
Itchy!
Aha ha ha ha!
Aha ha! Stop it!
TICKLE
TICKLE
Sssaa
TICKLE
Oh! They're inside my clothes!
POP
Oh... aah... aah!
FLAP
FLAP
Aha ha ha ha!
I'm gonna die laughing!
Y-Y-Yuriko!
W-W-We've gotta run for it!
FLAP
Stop it! That tickles! I think I'd rather have you bite me!
Aaah!
RUSTLE SLITHER
DASH
Oh!
TWITCH
TWITCH
Oh no! My hairband's gone!
What'll I do?! My ears are sticking out!

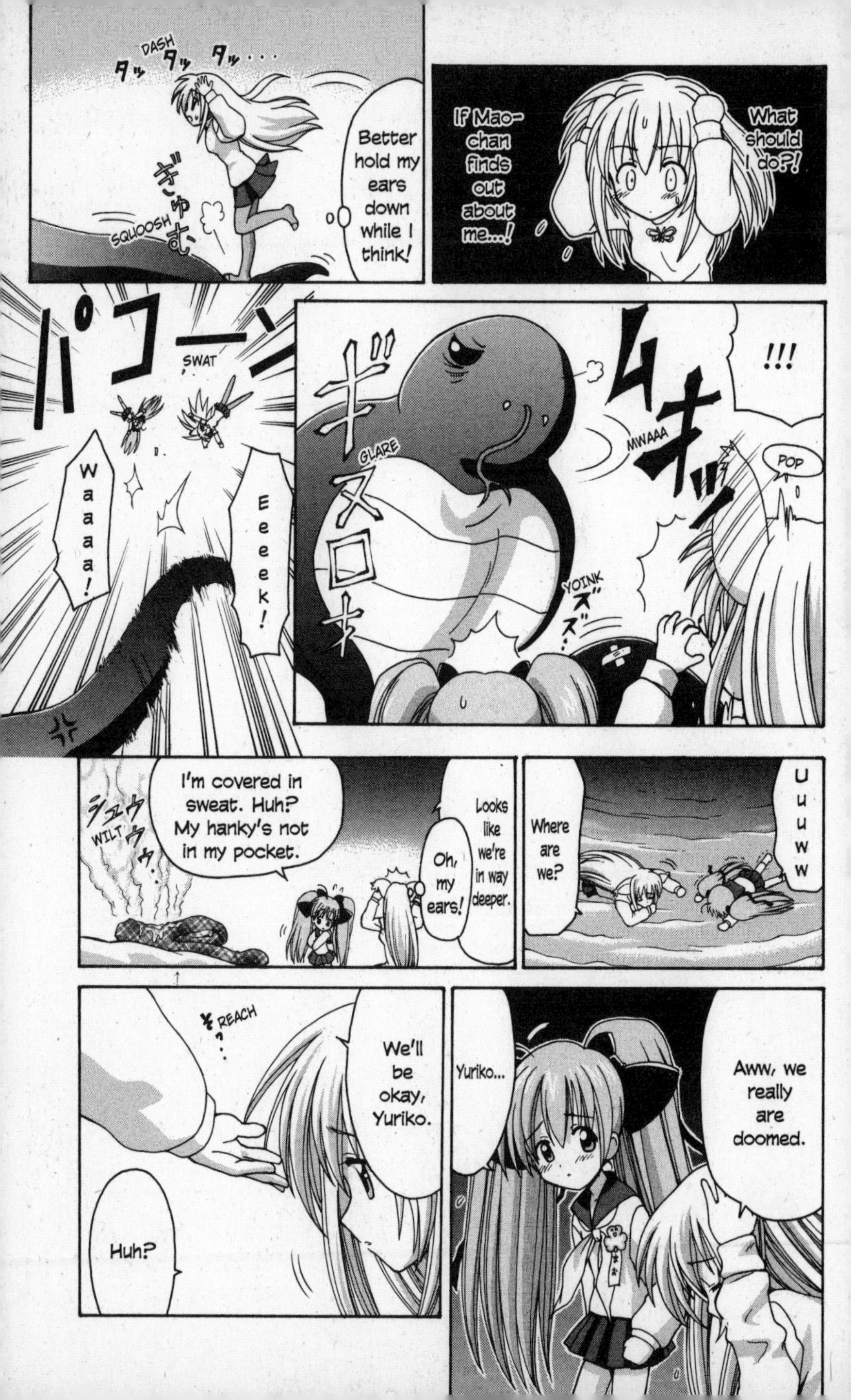
What should I do?!
If Mao-chan finds out about me...!
DASH
Better hold my ears down while I think!
SQUOOSH
!!!
POP
MWAAA
GLARE
YOINK
SWAT
Eeeek!
Waaaa!
Uuuww
Where are we?
Looks like we're in way deeper.
Oh, my ears!
I'm covered in sweat. Huh? My hanky's not in my pocket.
WILT
Aww, we really are doomed.
Yuriko...
We'll be okay, Yuriko.
REACH
Huh?

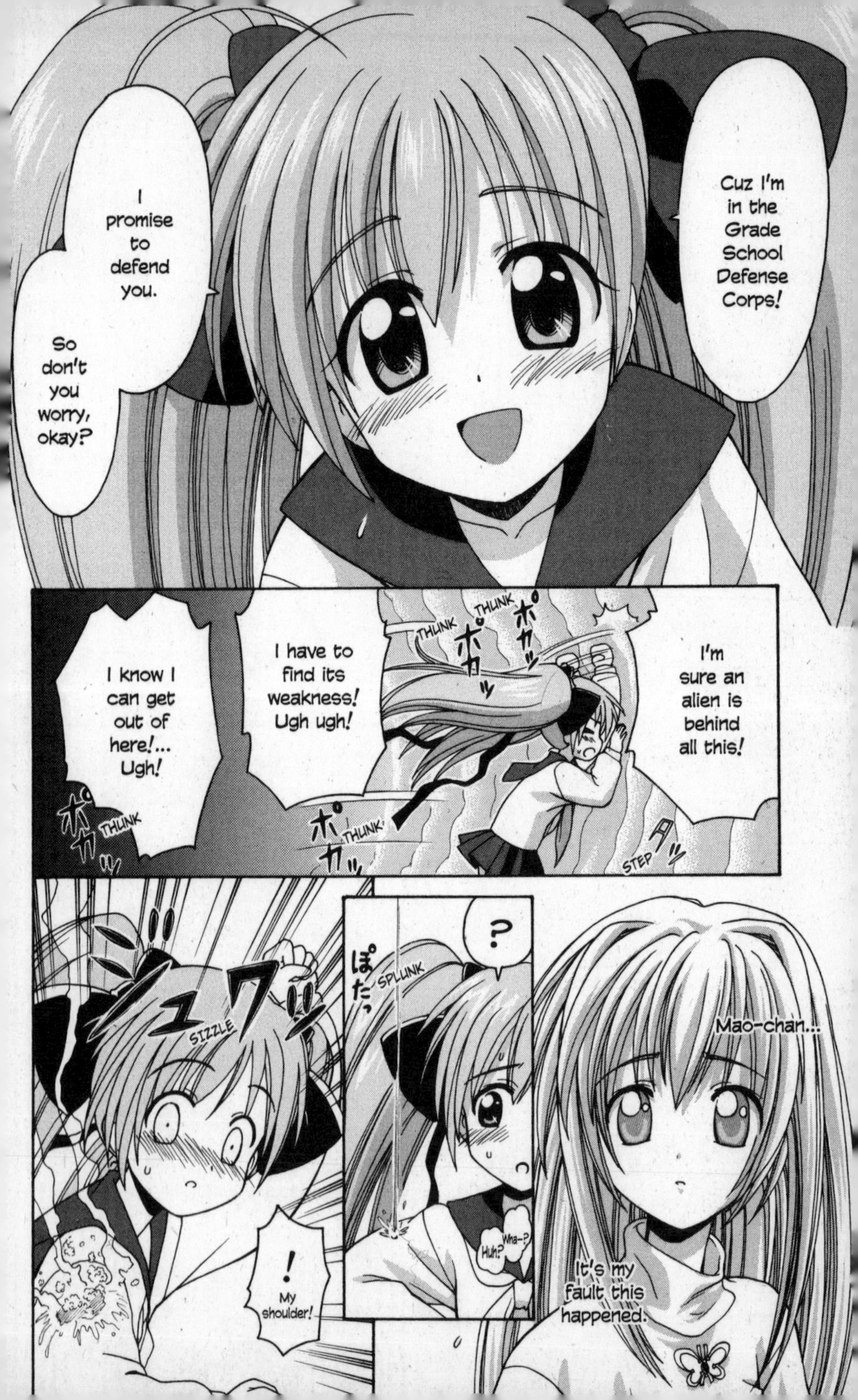

Cuz I'm in the Grade School Defense Corps!
I promise to defend you.
So don't you worry, okay?
I'm sure an alien is behind all this!
STEP
THUNK
THUNK
THUNK
I have to find its weakness! Ugh ugh!
THUNK
I know I can get out of here!... Ugh!
THUNK
Mao-chan...
It's my fault this happened.
?
ぽたっ
SPLUNK
Wha-?
Huh?
SIZZLE
!
My shoulder!

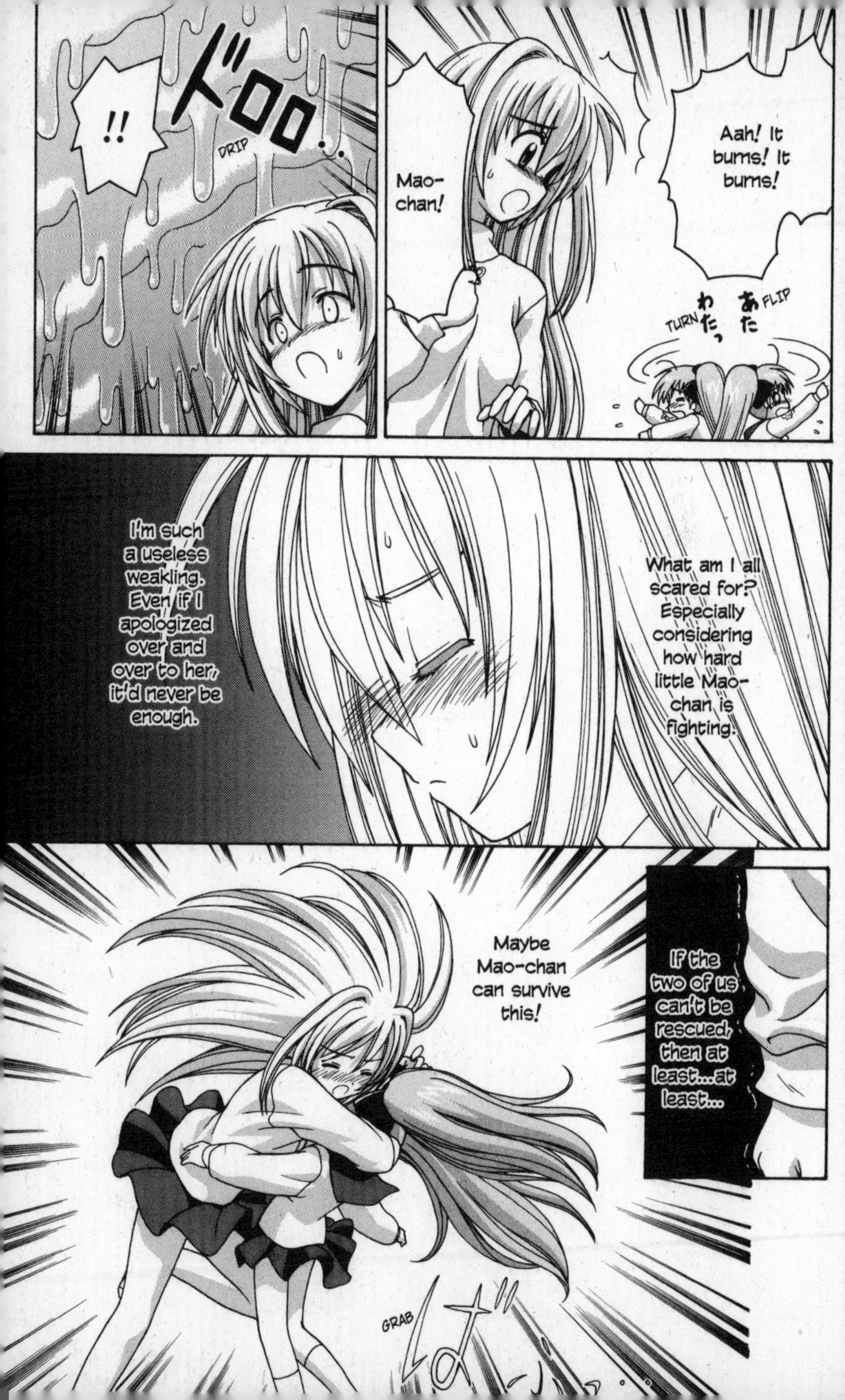
Aah! It burns! It burns!
Mao-chan!
あた FLIP
わたっ TURN
ドOO...
DRIP
!!
What am I all scared for? Especially considering how hard little Mao-chan is fighting.
I'm such a useless weakling. Even if I apologized over and over to her, it'd never be enough.
If the two of us can't be rescued, then at least...at least...
Maybe Mao-chan can survive this!
GRAB

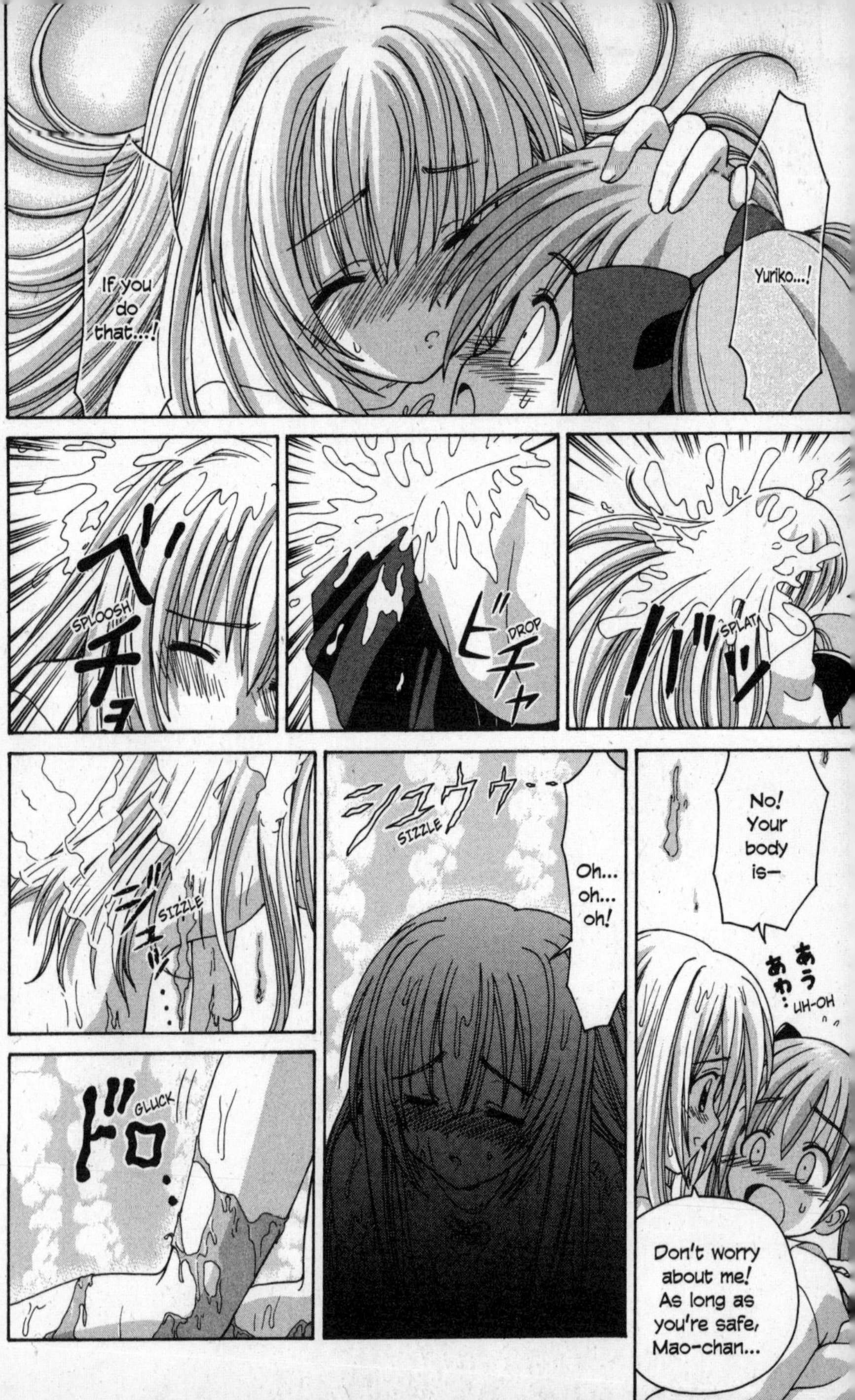

Yuriko...!
If you do that...!
SPLAT
DROP
SPLOOSH
No! Your body is—
UH-OH
Don't worry about me! As long as you're safe, Mao-chan...
SIZZLE
Oh... oh... oh!
SIZZLE
GLUCK

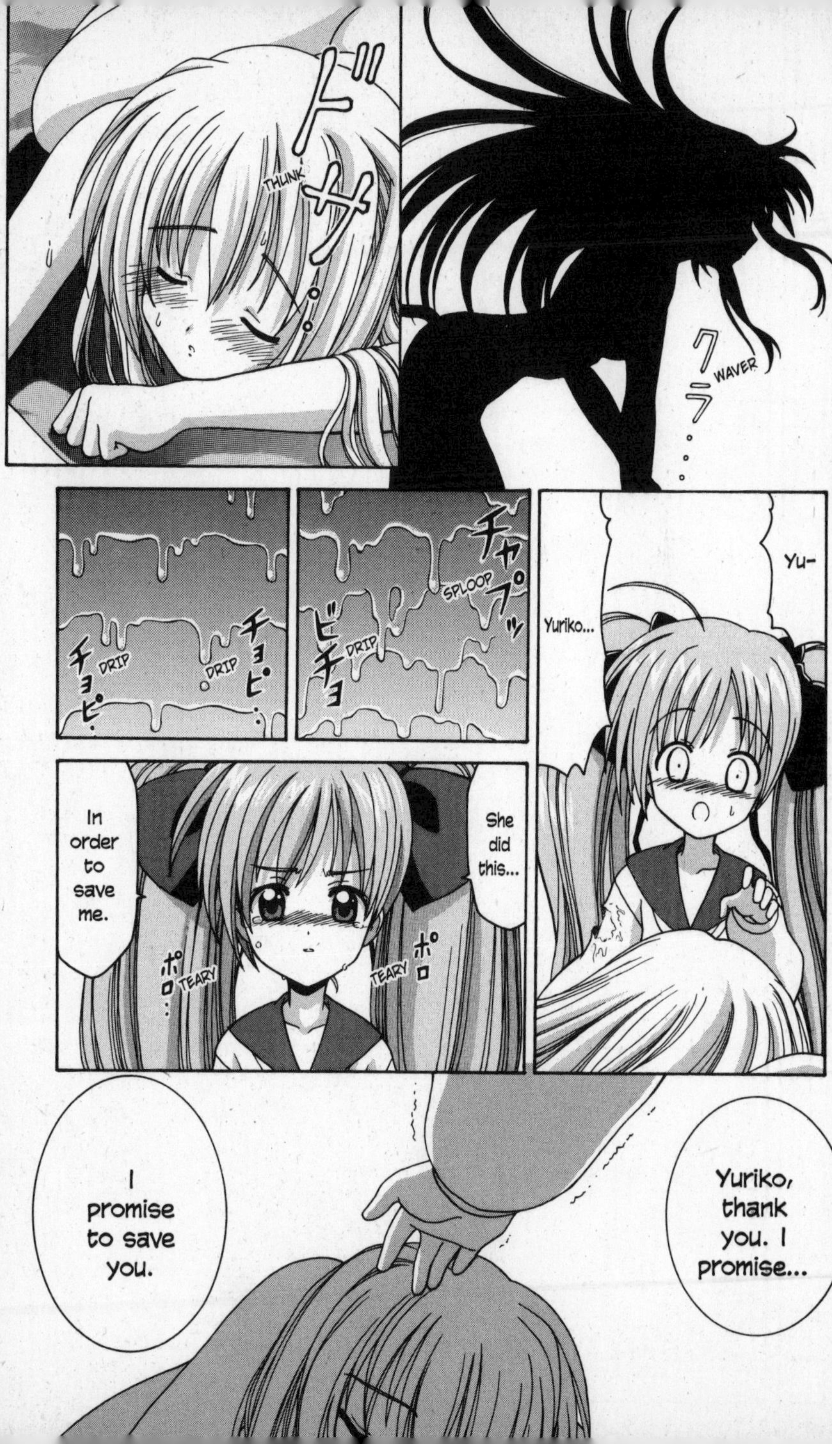
クラ…
WAVER
ドサ
THUNK
Yu-
Yuriko...
チャプッ
SPLOOP
ビチョ
DRIP
チョピ
DRIP
チョピ
DRIP
She did this...
In order to save me.
ポロ
TEARY
ポロ
TEARY
Yuriko, thank you. I promise...
I promise to save you.

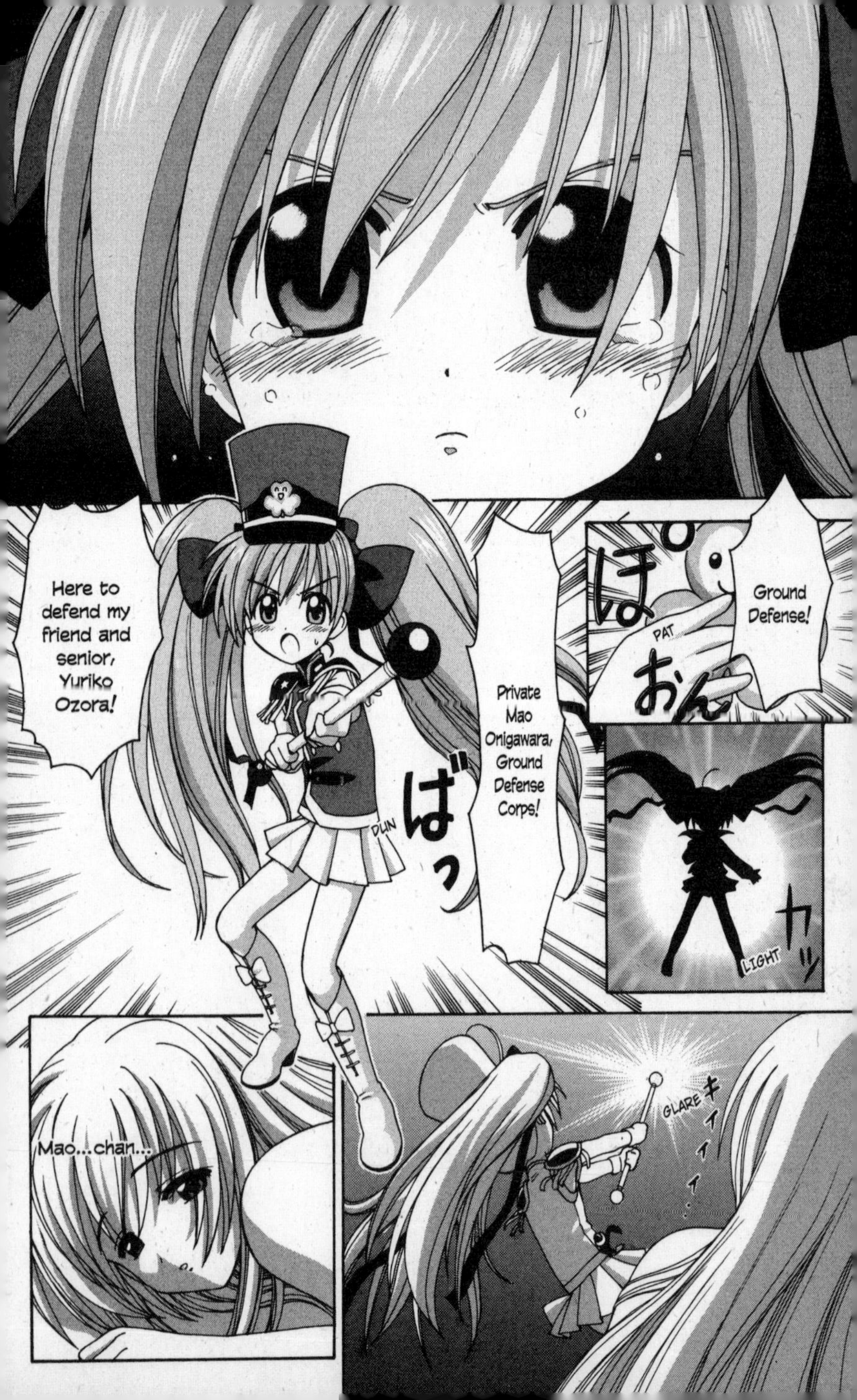
Ground Defense!
ぽおん
PAT
カッ
LIGHT
Private Mao Onigawara, Ground Defense Corps!
Here to defend my friend and senior, Yuriko Ozora!
ばっ
DUN
キイイイ…
GLARE
Mao...chan...

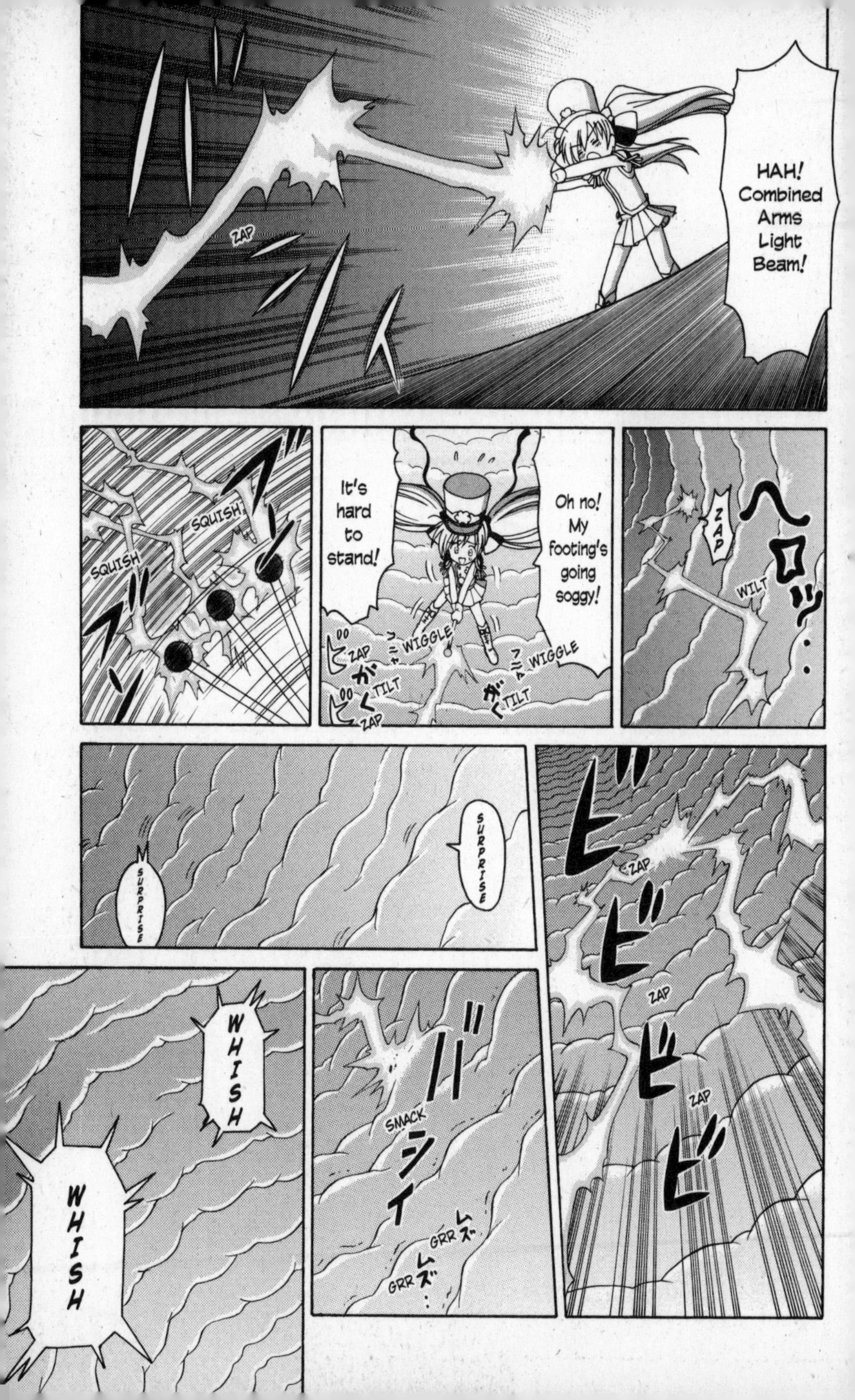
HAH! Combined Arms Light Beam!
ZAP
ZAP
WILT
Oh no! My footing's going soggy!
It's hard to stand!
WIGGLE
WIGGLE
TILT
TILT
ZAP
ZAP
SQUISH
SQUISH
ZAP
ZAP
ZAP
SURPRISE
SURPRISE
SMACK
GRR
GRR
WHISH
WHISH

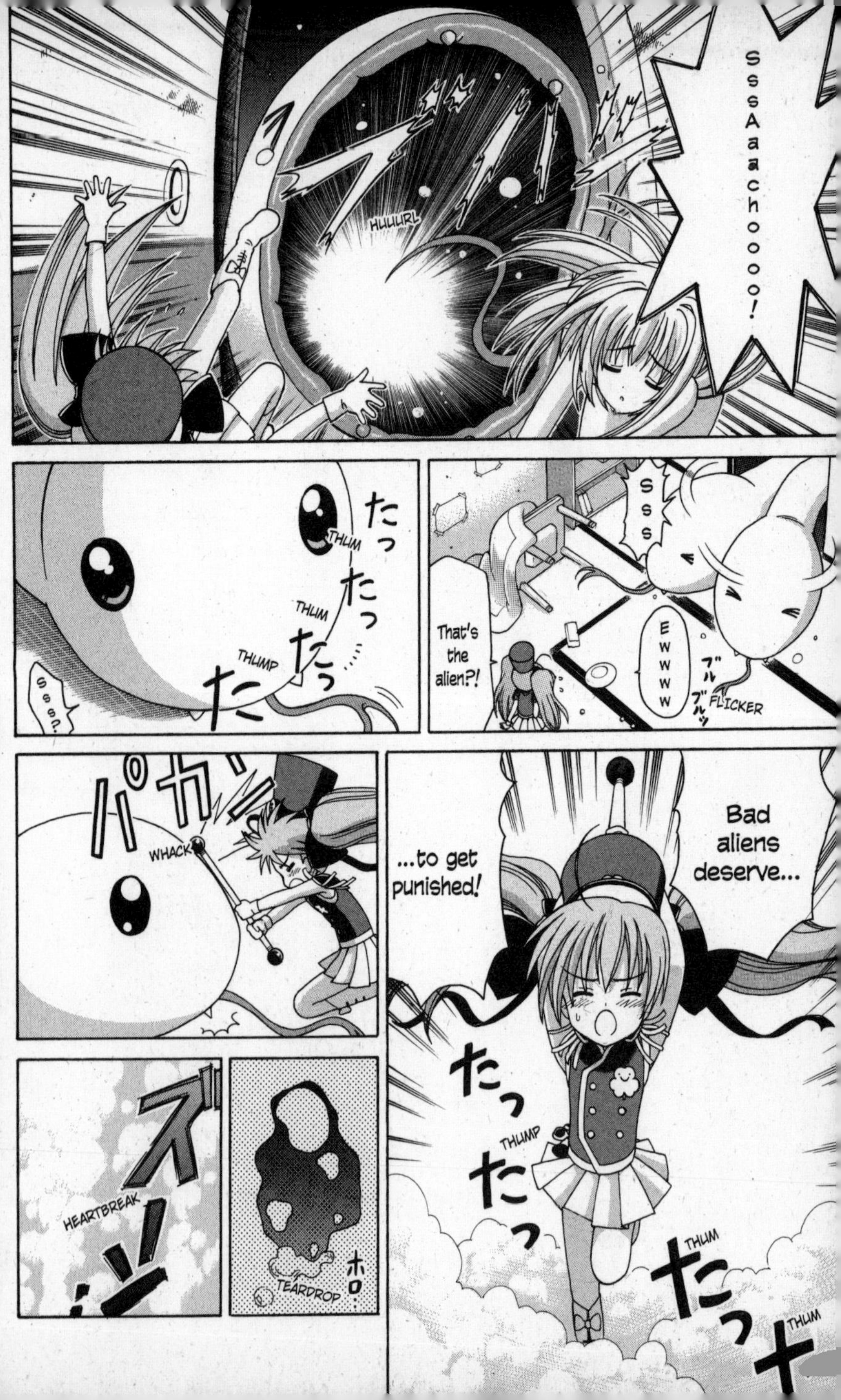
SssAaachoooooo!
HUUURL
Sss
EWWWW
ブルブルッ
FLICKER
That's the alien?!
たっ
THUM
たっ
THUM
たっ……
THUMP
た
Sss?
Bad aliens deserve...
...to get punished!
たっ
THUMP
たっ
THUM
たっ
THUM
パカ
WHACK
ホロ
TEARDROP
ズーン!
HEARTBREAK

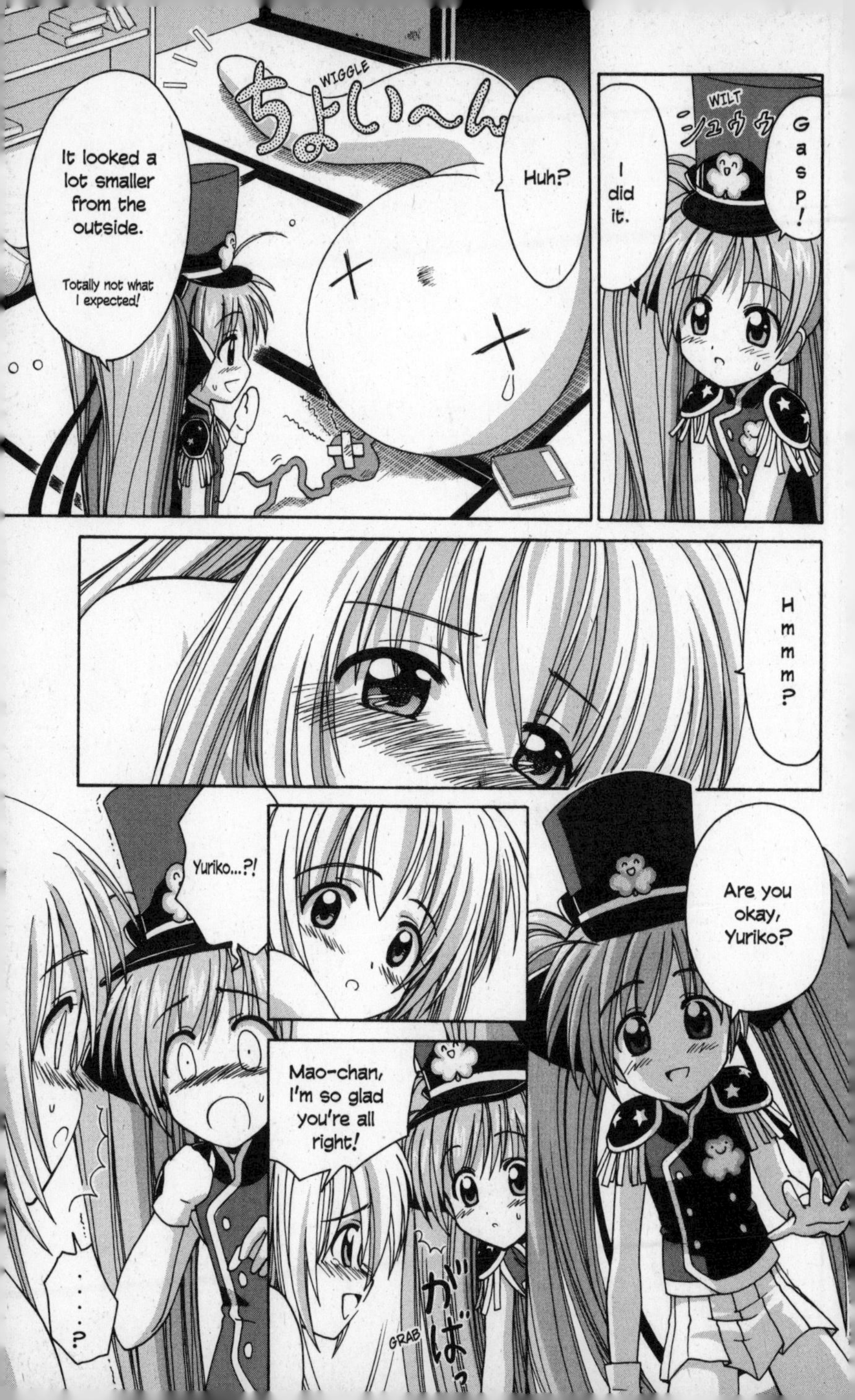
Gasp!
WILT
シュウウ
I did it.
WIGGLE
ちょい～ん
Huh?
It looked a lot smaller from the outside.
Totally not what I expected!
Hmmm?
Are you okay, Yuriko?
Mao-chan, I'm so glad you're all right!
GRAB
がばっ
Yuriko...?!
....?

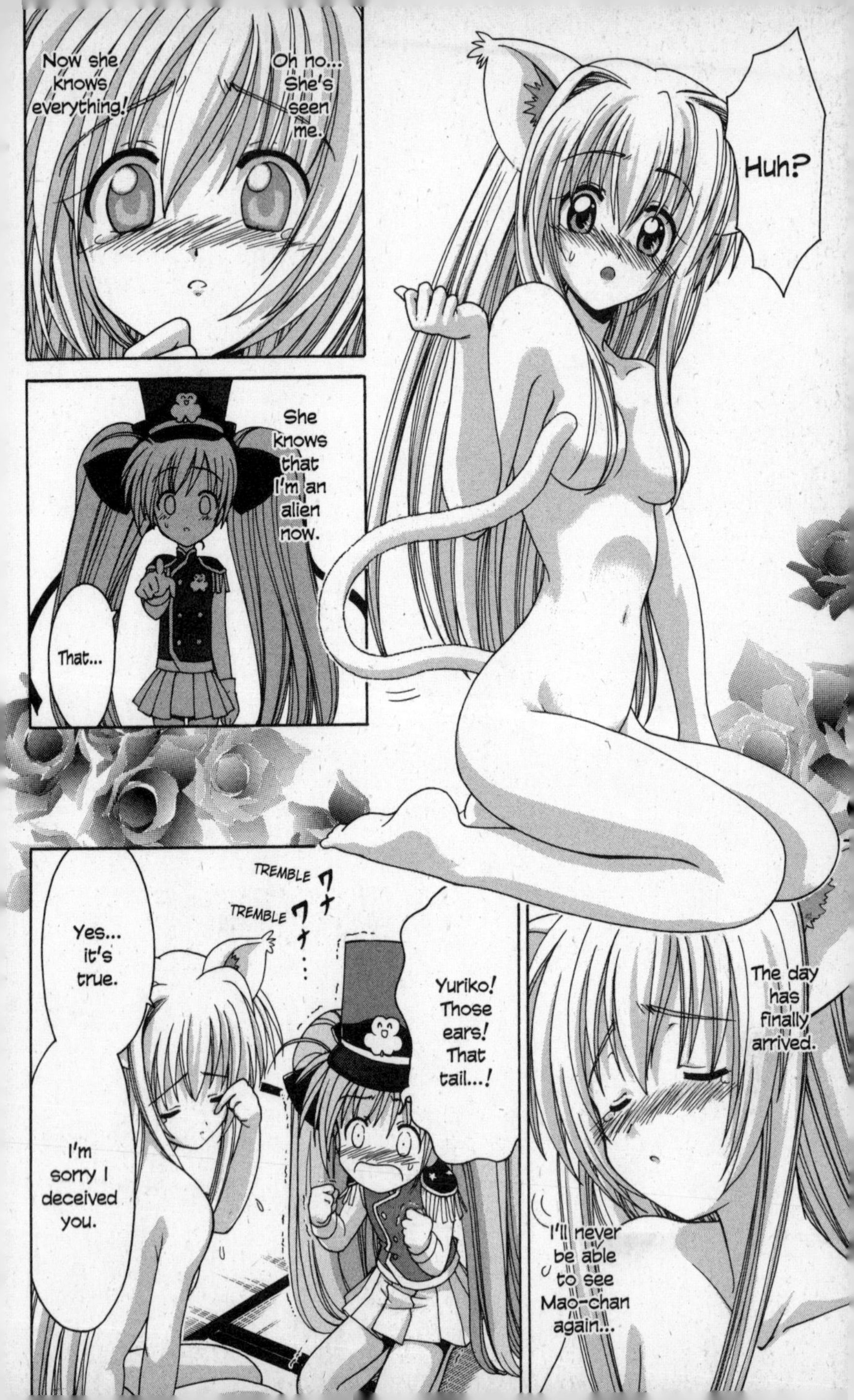
Huh?
Oh no... She's seen me.
Now she knows everything!
She knows that I'm an alien now.
That...
The day has finally arrived.
I'll never be able to see Mao-chan again...
TREMBLE
TREMBLE
Yuriko! Those ears! That tail...!
Yes... it's true.
I'm sorry I deceived you.

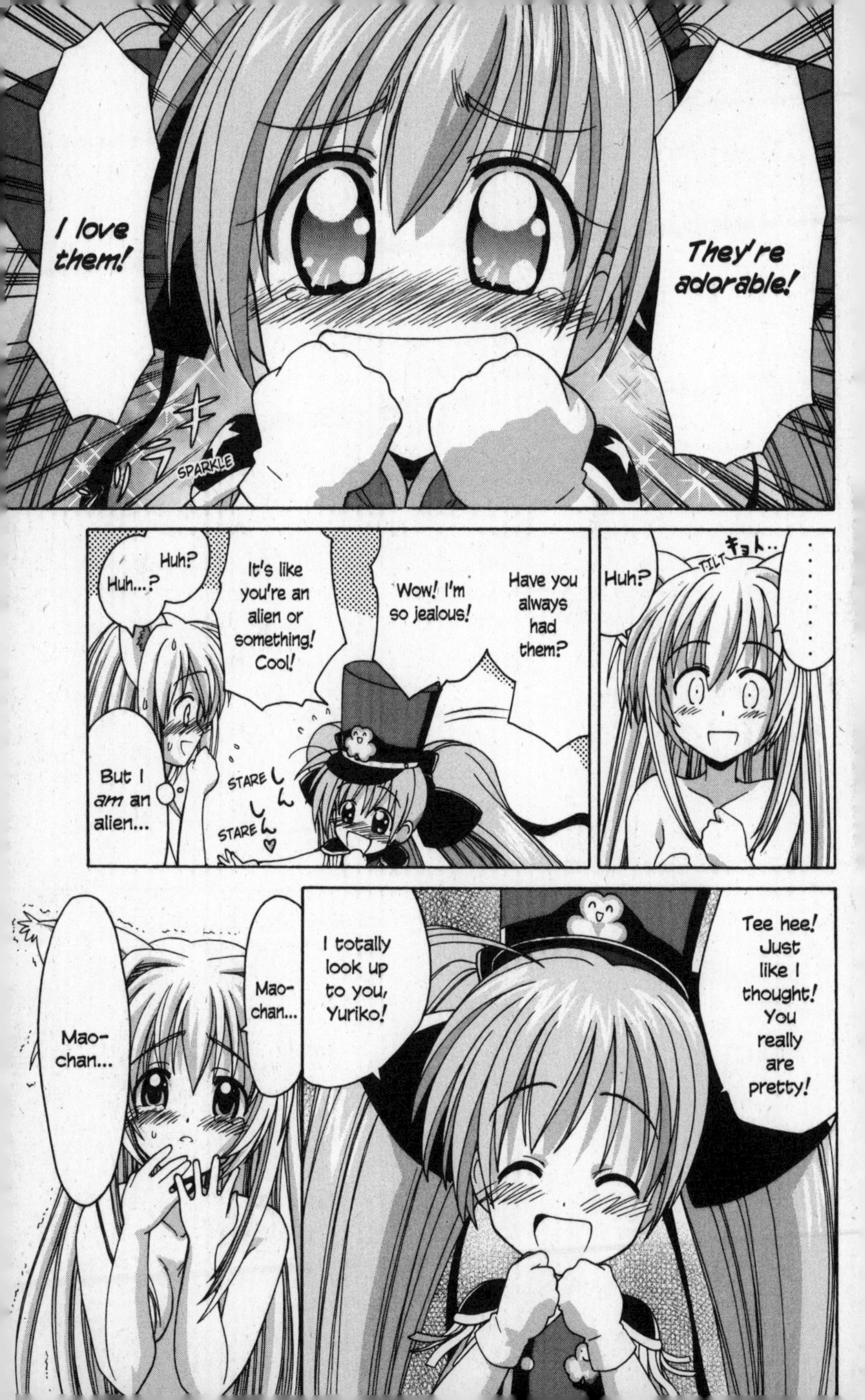
They're adorable!
I love them!
SPARKLE
TILT キョト...
. . . .
Huh?
Have you always had them?
Wow! I'm so jealous!
It's like you're an alien or something! Cool!
Huh? Huh...?
STARE しん
STARE しん
But I *am* an alien...
Tee hee! Just like I thought! You really are pretty!
I totally look up to you, Yuriko!
Mao-chan...
Mao-chan...

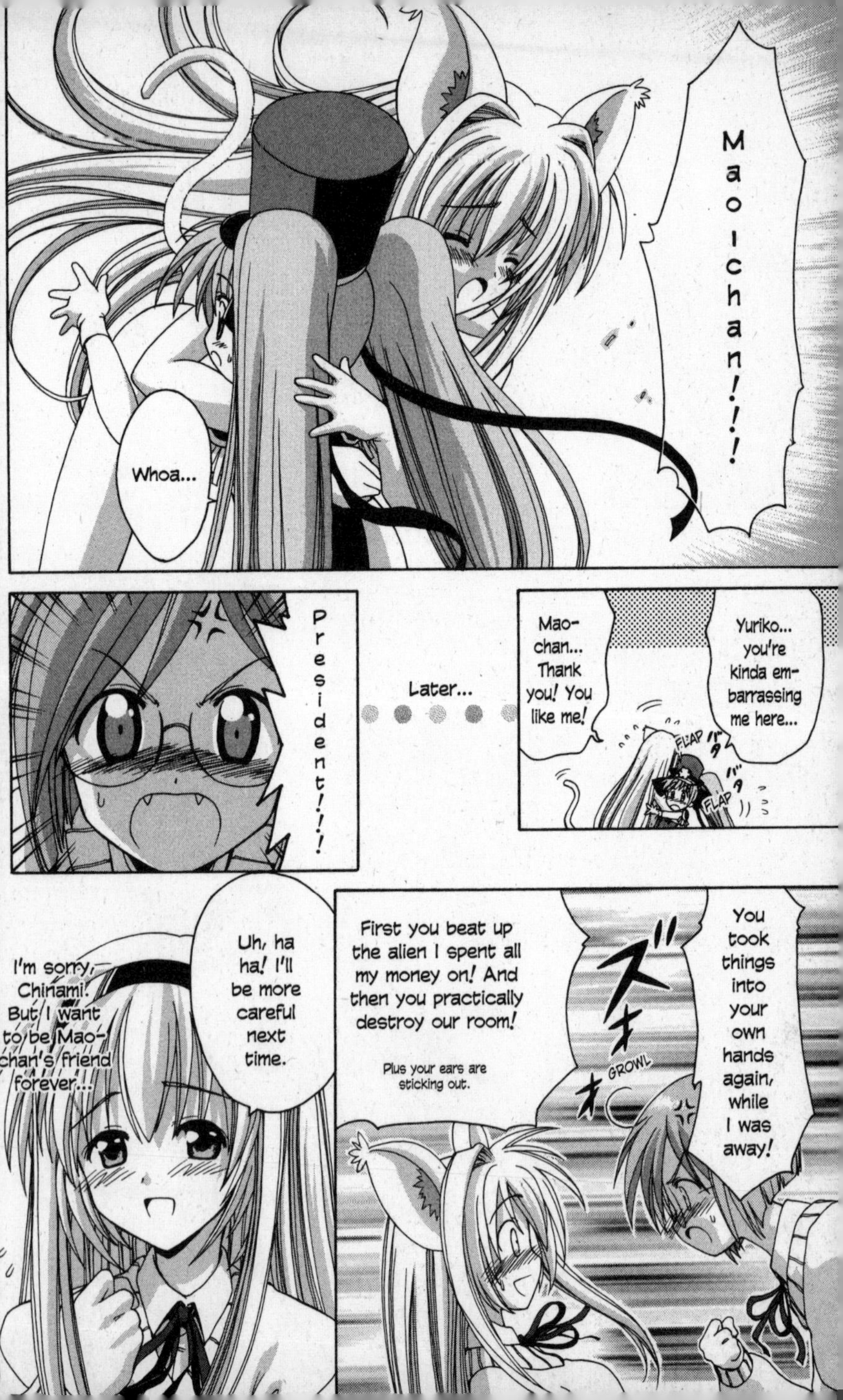

Mao-chan!!!
Whoa...
Yuriko... you're kinda embarrassing me here...
Mao-chan... Thank you! You like me!
FLAP
FLAP
Later...
President!!!
You took things into your own hands again, while I was away!
First you beat up the alien I spent all my money on! And then you practically destroy our room!
Plus your ears are sticking out.
GROWL
Uh, ha ha! I'll be more careful next time.
I'm sorry, Chinami! But I want to be Mao-chan's friend forever...

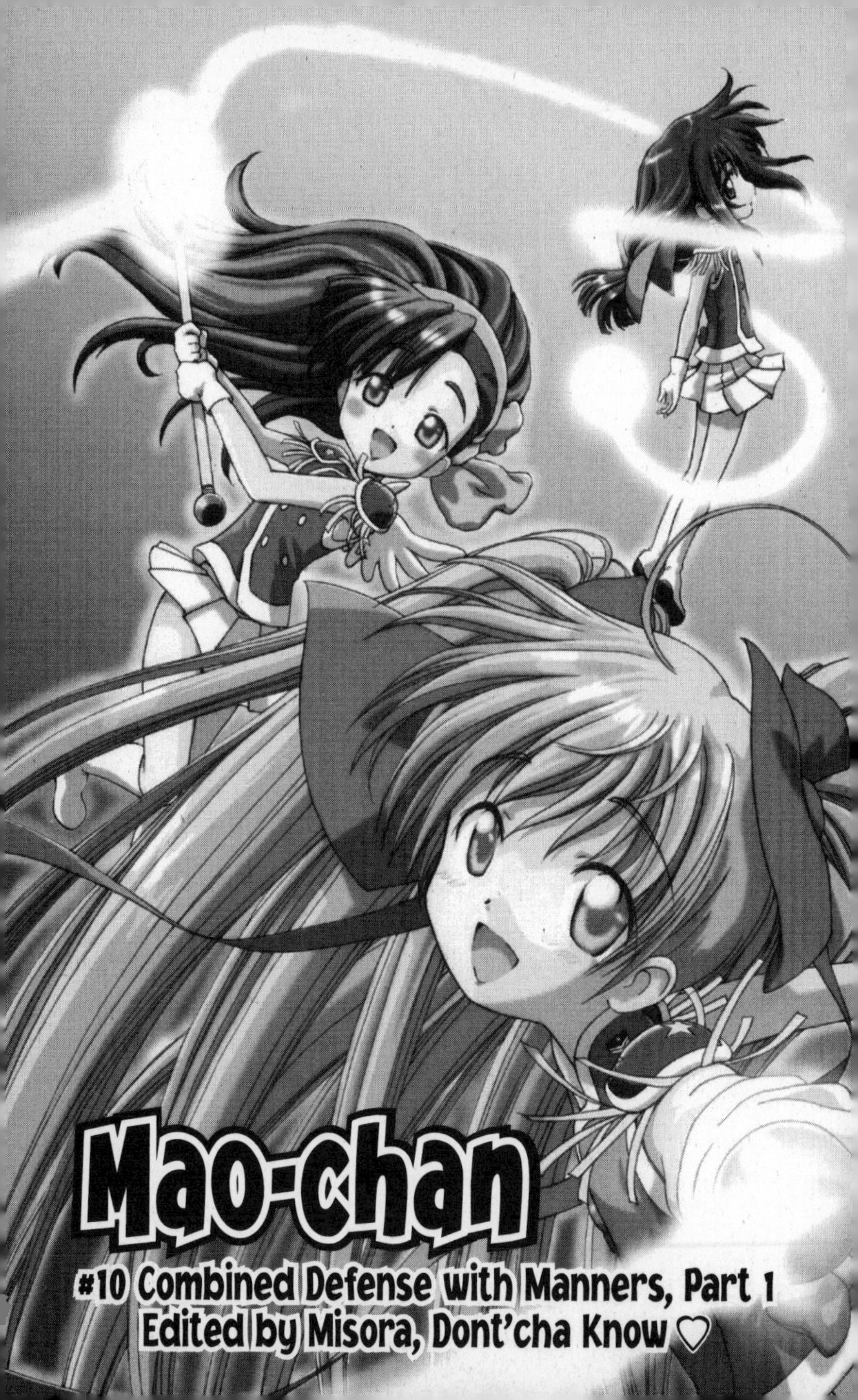
Mao-chan
#10 Combined Defense with Manners, Part 1
Edited by Misora, Dont'cha Know ♡

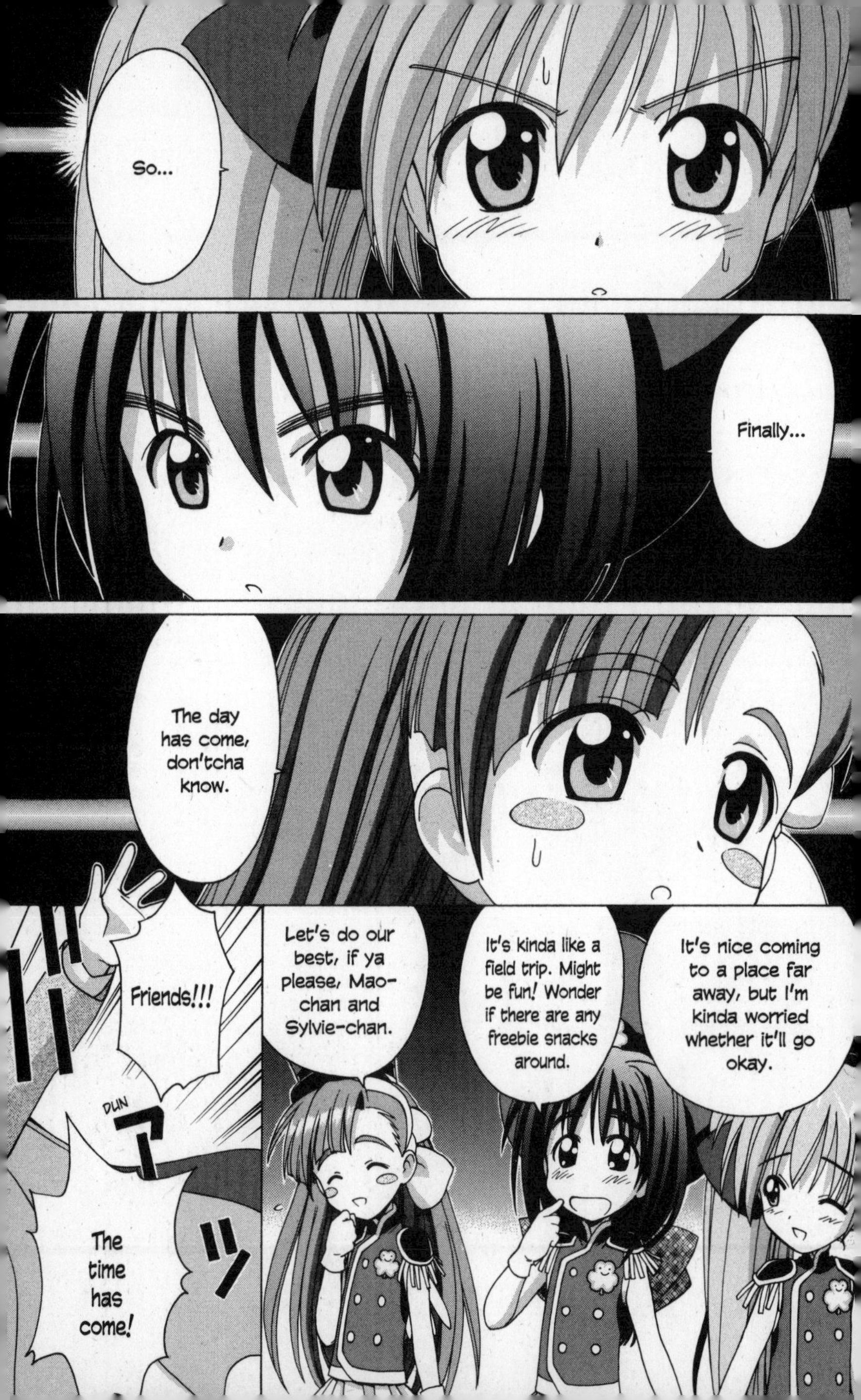
So...
Finally...
The day has come, don'tcha know.
It's nice coming to a place far away, but I'm kinda worried whether it'll go okay.
It's kinda like a field trip. Might be fun! Wonder if there are any freebie snacks around.
Let's do our best, if ya please, Mao-chan and Sylvie-chan.
Friends!!!
DUN
The time has come!

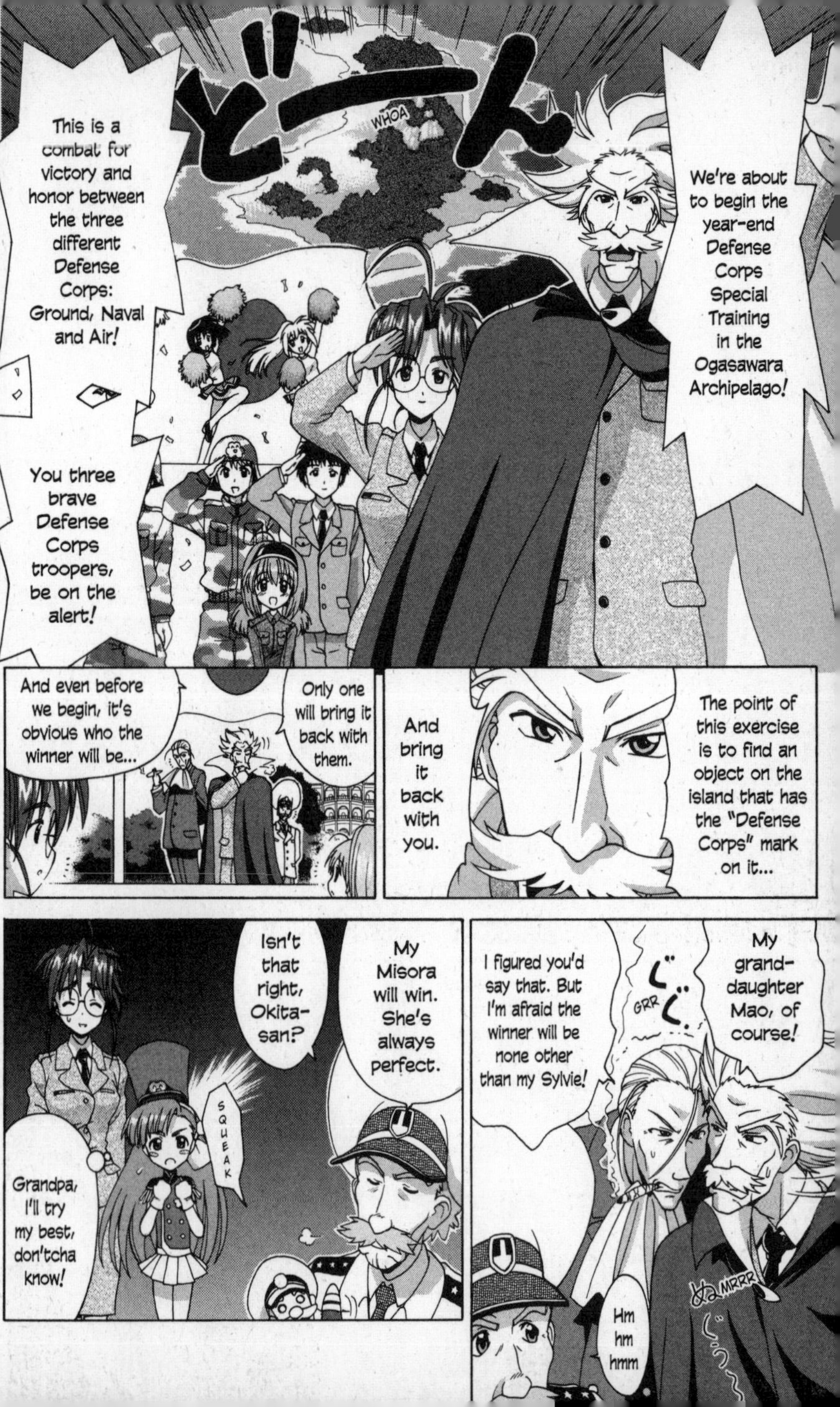
We're about to begin the year-end Defense Corps Special Training in the Ogasawara Archipelago!
どーん
WHOA
This is a combat for victory and honor between the three different Defense Corps: Ground, Naval and Air!
You three brave Defense Corps troopers, be on the alert!
The point of this exercise is to find an object on the island that has the "Defense Corps" mark on it...
And bring it back with you.
Only one will bring it back with them.
And even before we begin, it's obvious who the winner will be...
My grand-daughter Mao, of course!
じじ
GRR
I figured you'd say that. But I'm afraid the winner will be none other than my Sylvie!
Hm hm hmm
ぬ MRRR
My Misora will win. She's always perfect.
Isn't that right, Okita-san?
SQUEAK
Grandpa, I'll try my best, don'tcha know!

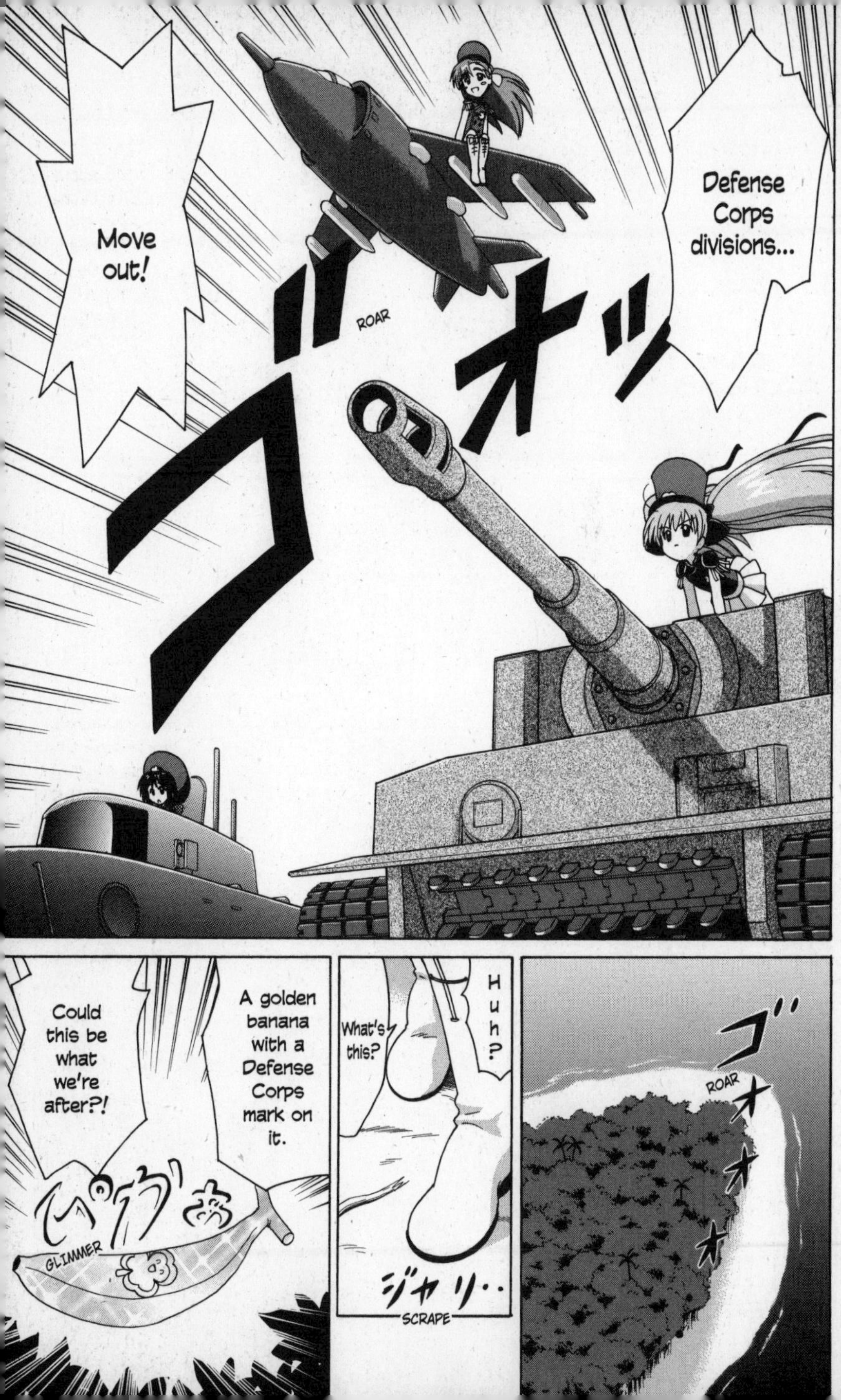
Defense Corps divisions...
Move out!
ゴオッ
ROAR
ゴオオオ
ROAR
Huh?
What's this?
ジャリ‥
SCRAPE
A golden banana with a Defense Corps mark on it.
Could this be what we're after?!
GLIMMER

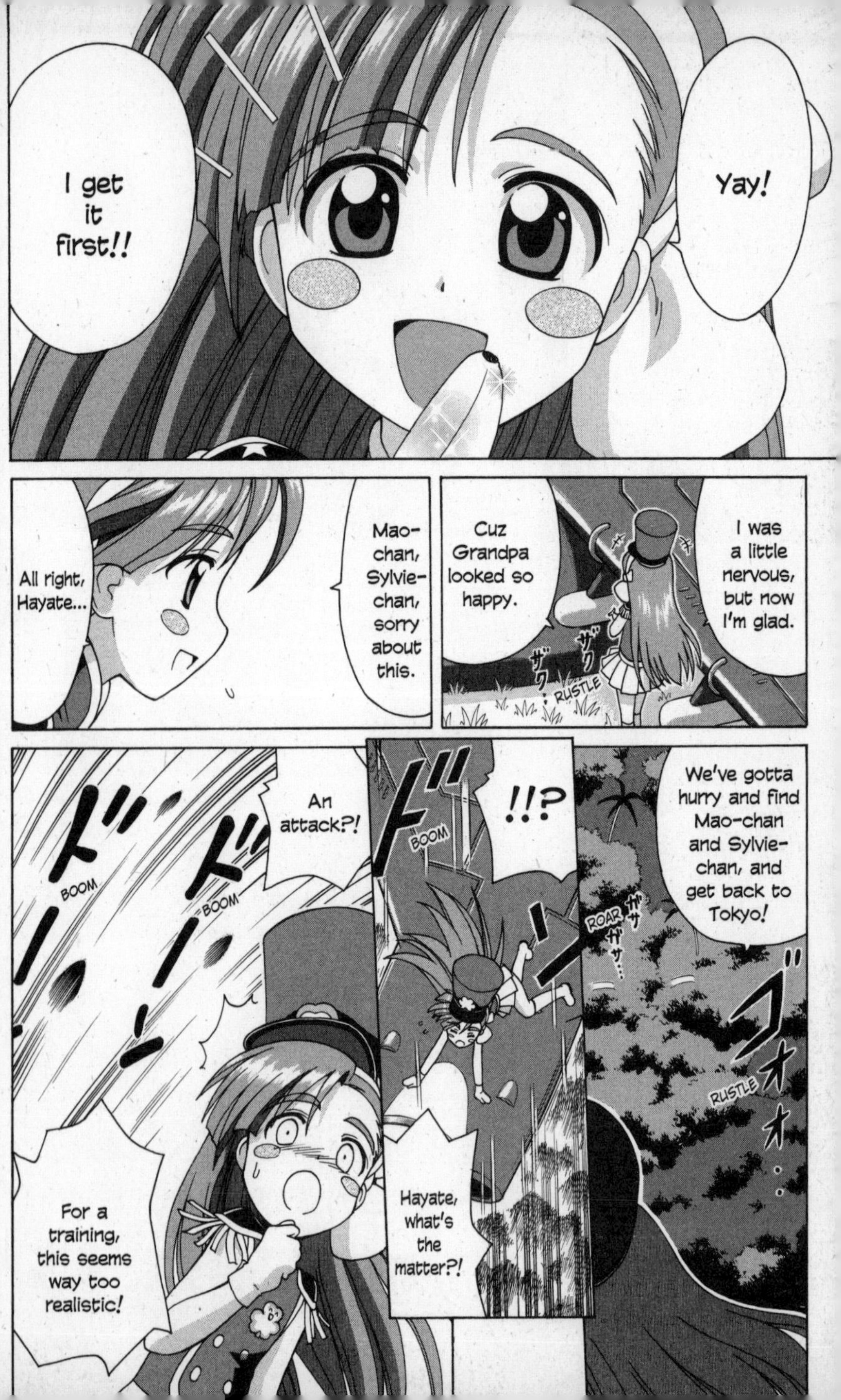
Yay!
I get it first!!
I was a little nervous, but now I'm glad.
Cuz Grandpa looked so happy.
ザク
ザク
RUSTLE
Mao-chan, Sylvie-chan, sorry about this.
All right, Hayate...
We've gotta hurry and find Mao-chan and Sylvie-chan, and get back to Tokyo!
ガサ
ガサ…
ROAR
ゴォォ…
RUSTLE
!!?
ド
BOOM
Hayate, what's the matter?!
An attack?!
ドー
BOOM
ドーン
BOOM
For a training, this seems way too realistic!

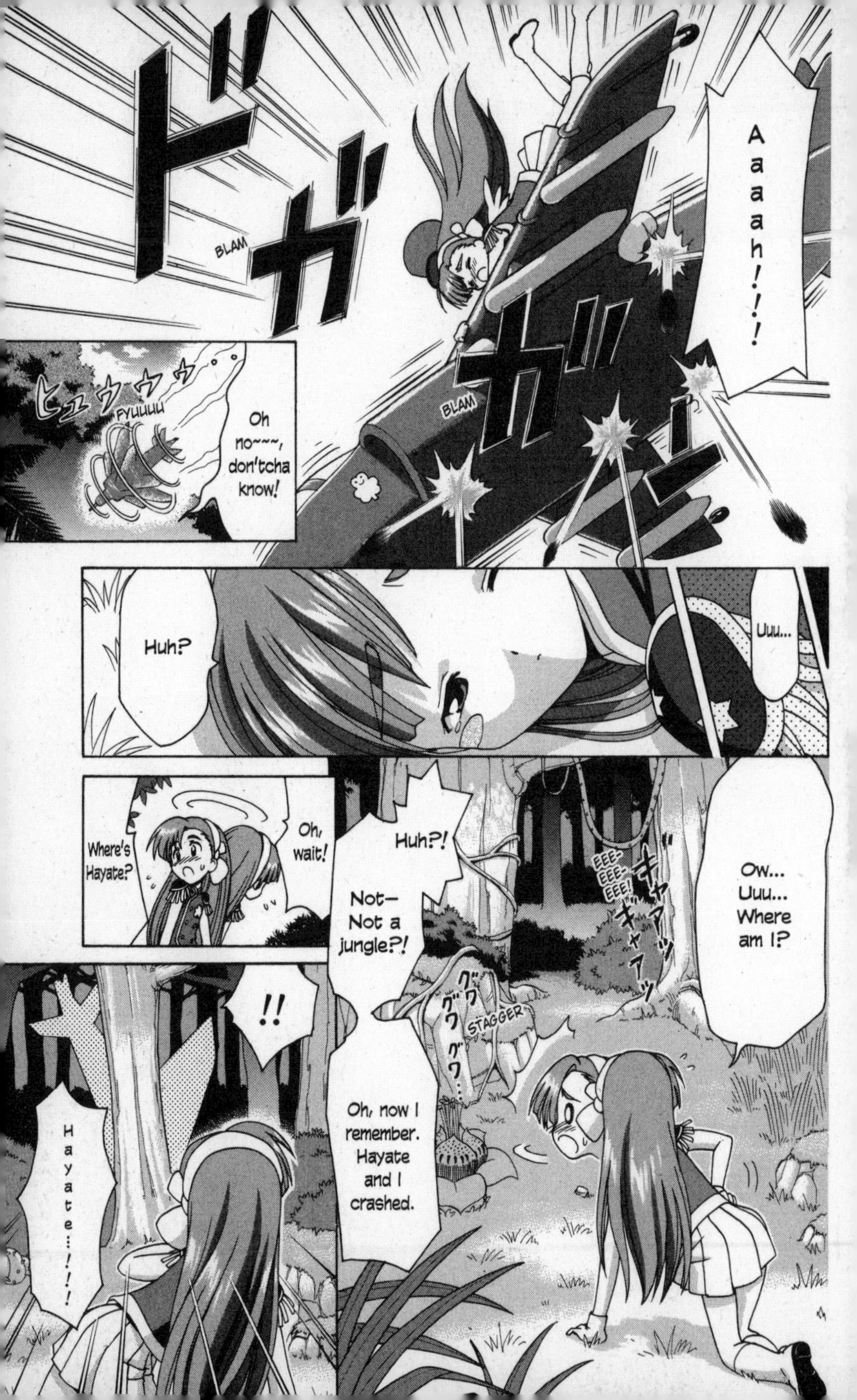
Aaaah!!!!
ドガ
BLAM
ガガ
BLAM
ヒュウウウ
FYUUUU
Oh no~~~, don'tcha know!
Uuu...
Huh?
Ow... Uuu... Where am I?
ギャアッギャアッ
EEE-EEE-EEE!
Huh?!
Not— Not a jungle?!
STAGGER
Oh, now I remember. Hayate and I crashed.
Oh, wait!
Where's Hayate?
!!
Hayate...!!!

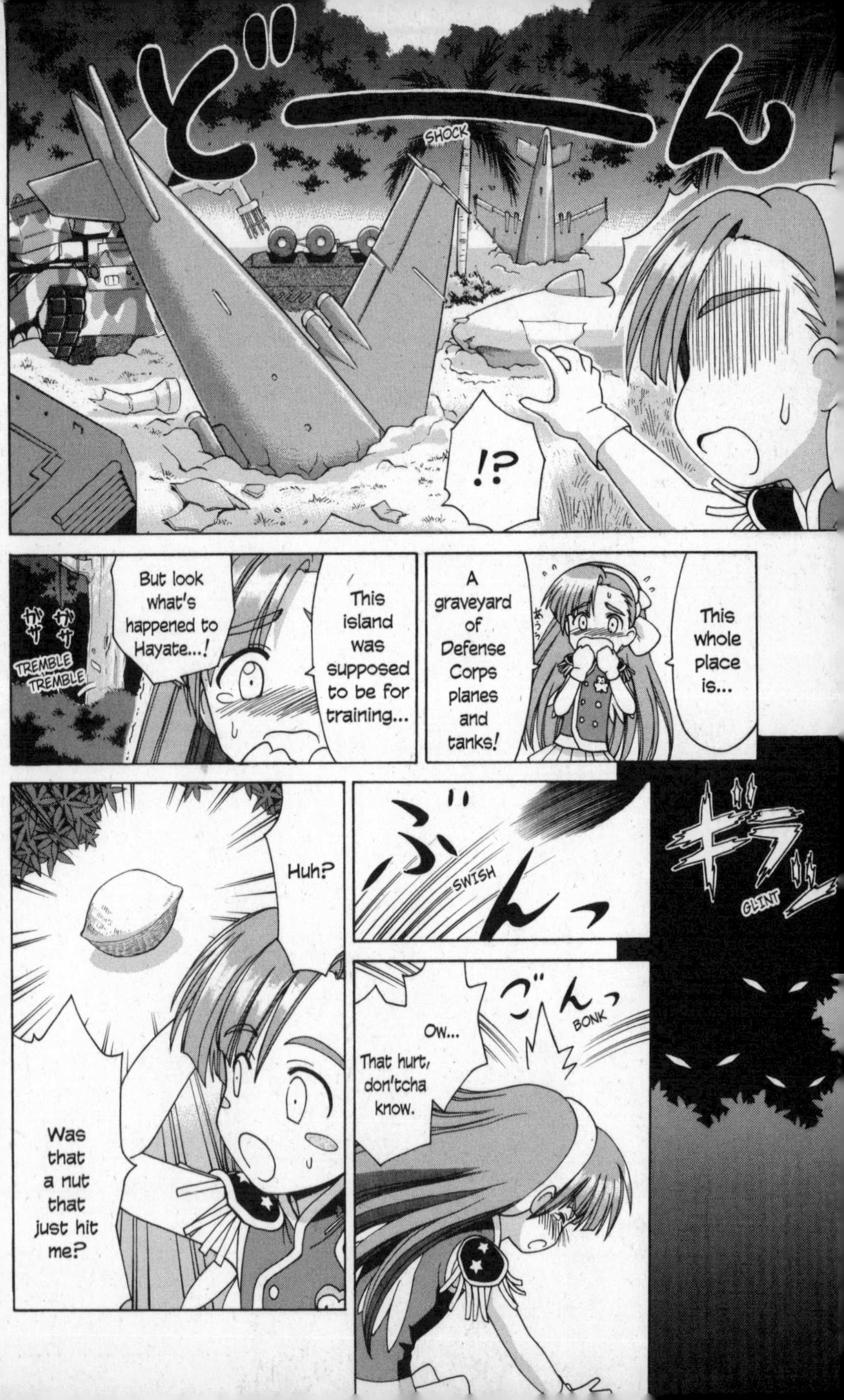
どーーん
SHOCK
!?
This whole place is...
あうう
A graveyard of Defense Corps planes and tanks!
This island was supposed to be for training...
But look what's happened to Hayate...!
ガサ ガサ
TREMBLE TREMBLE
ギラッ
GLINT
ぶんっ
SWISH
ごんっ
BONK
Ow...
That hurt, don'tcha know.
Huh?
Was that a nut that just hit me?

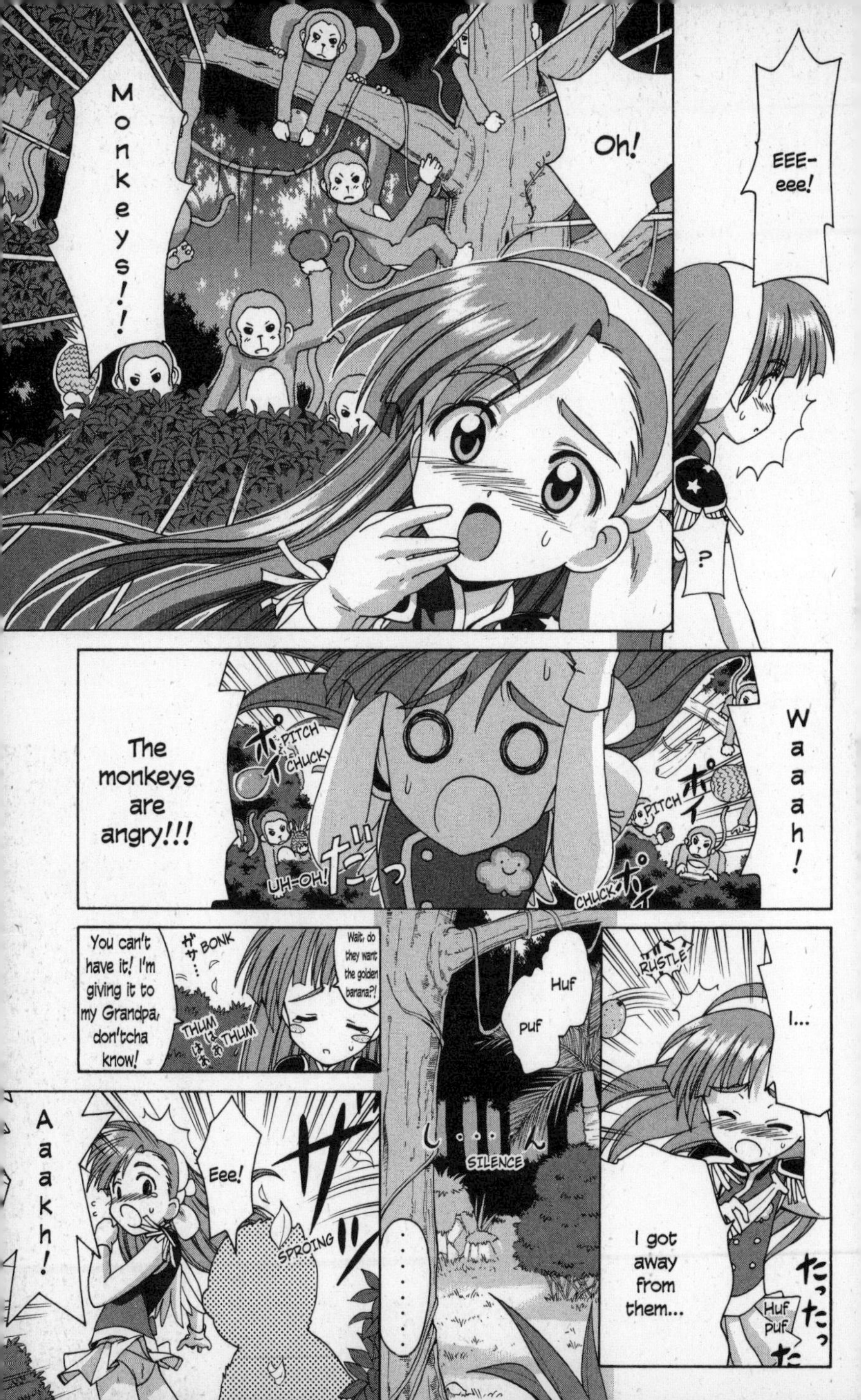
EEE-eee!
Oh!
Monkeys!!
?
Waaah!
PITCH
CHUCK
The monkeys are angry!!!
PITCH
CHUCK
UH-OH!
RUSTLE
I...
I got away from them...
Huf puf
Huf
puf
SILENCE
......
Wait, do they want the golden banana?!
BONK
THUM THUM
You can't have it! I'm giving it to my Grandpa, don'tcha know!
Eee!
SPROING
Aaakh!

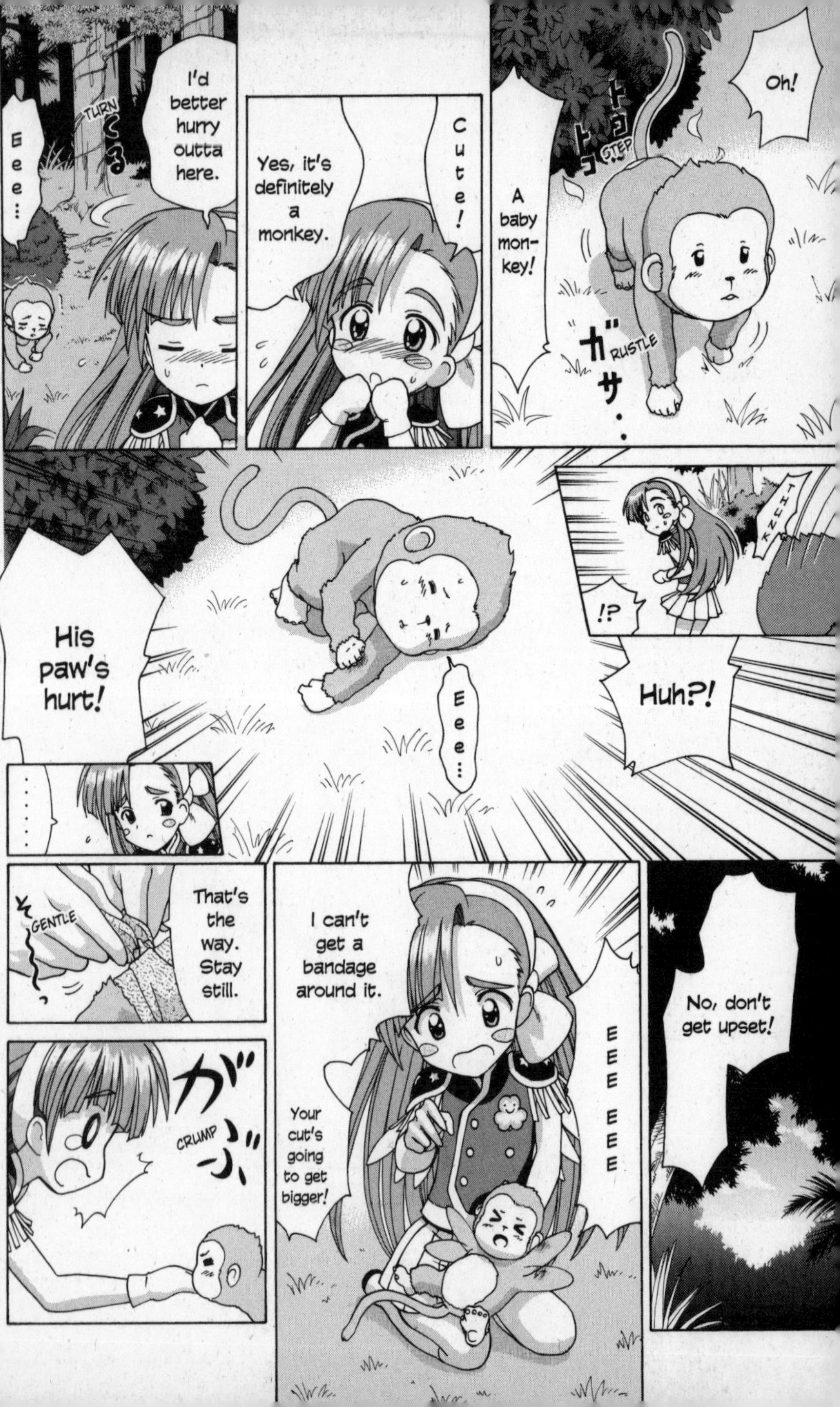
Oh!
STEP
A baby mon-key!
RUSTLE
Cute!
Yes, it's definitely a monkey.
I'd better hurry outta here.
TURN
Eee...
THUNK
!?
Huh?!
Eee...
His paw's hurt!
......
No, don't get upset!
I can't get a bandage around it.
EEE EEE
Your cut's going to get bigger!
That's the way. Stay still.
GENTLE
CRUMP

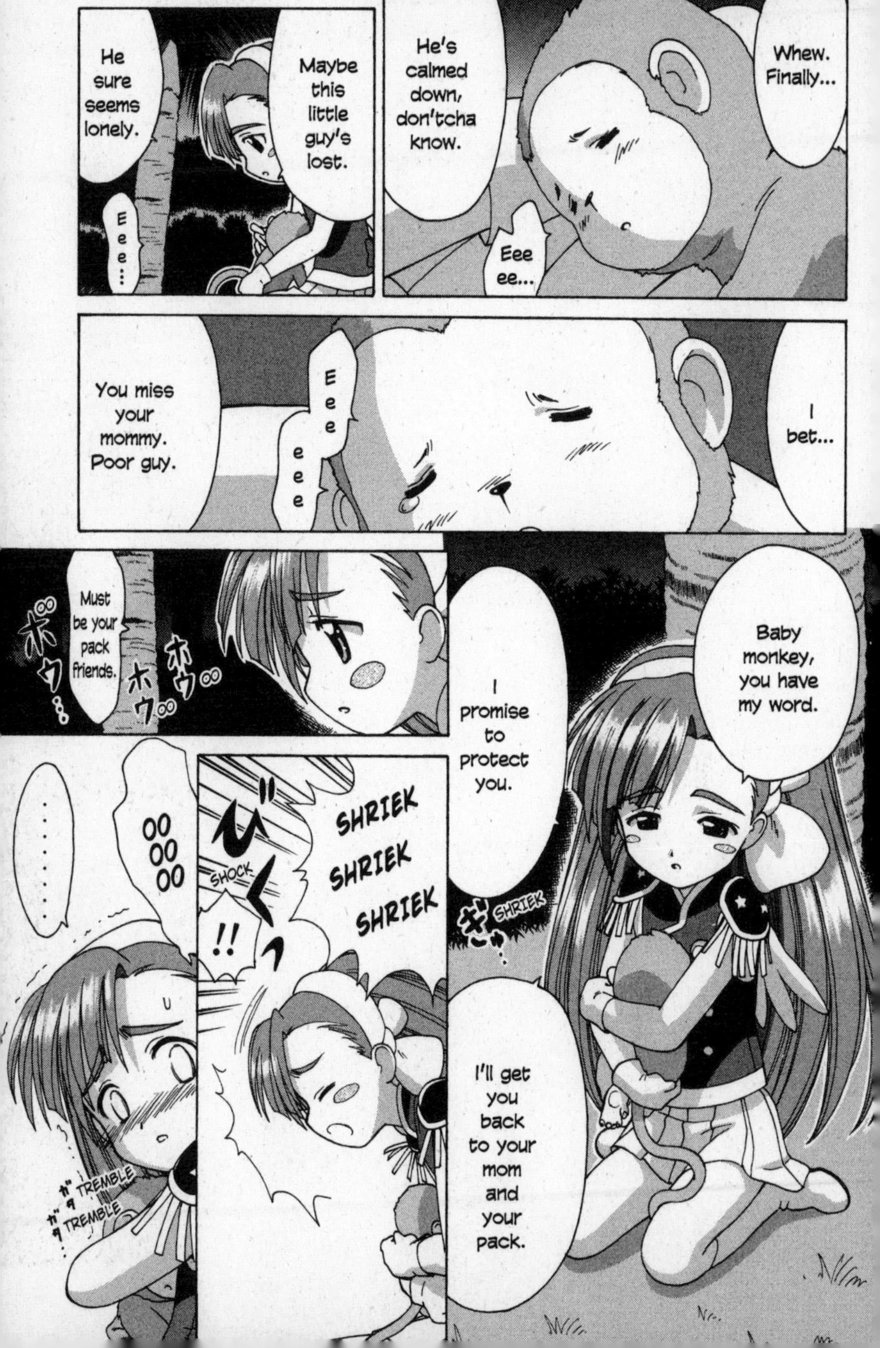
Whew. Finally...
He's calmed down, don'tcha know.
Eee ee...
Maybe this little guy's lost.
He sure seems lonely.
Eee...
I bet...
Eee eee
You miss your mommy. Poor guy.
Baby monkey, you have my word.
I promise to protect you.
SHRIEK
I'll get you back to your mom and your pack.
Must be your pack friends.
SHRIEK
SHRIEK
SHRIEK
SHOCK
!!
OO OO OO
......
TREMBLE
TREMBLE

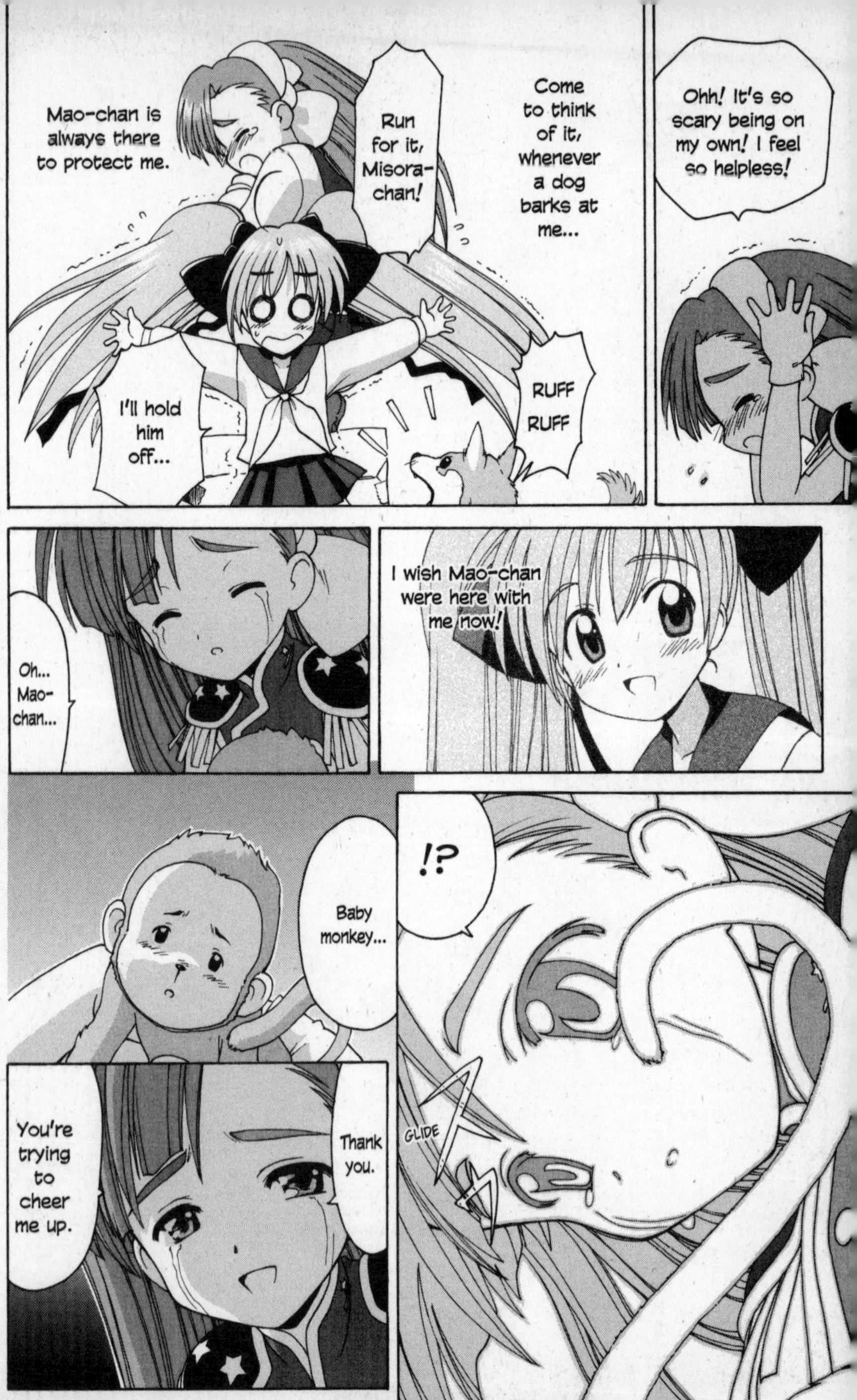
Ohh! It's so scary being on my own! I feel so helpless!
Come to think of it, whenever a dog barks at me...
Run for it, Misora-chan!
Mao-chan is always there to protect me.
RUFF RUFF
I'll hold him off...
I wish Mao-chan were here with me now!
Oh... Mao-chan...
!?
GLIDE
Baby monkey...
Thank you.
You're trying to cheer me up.

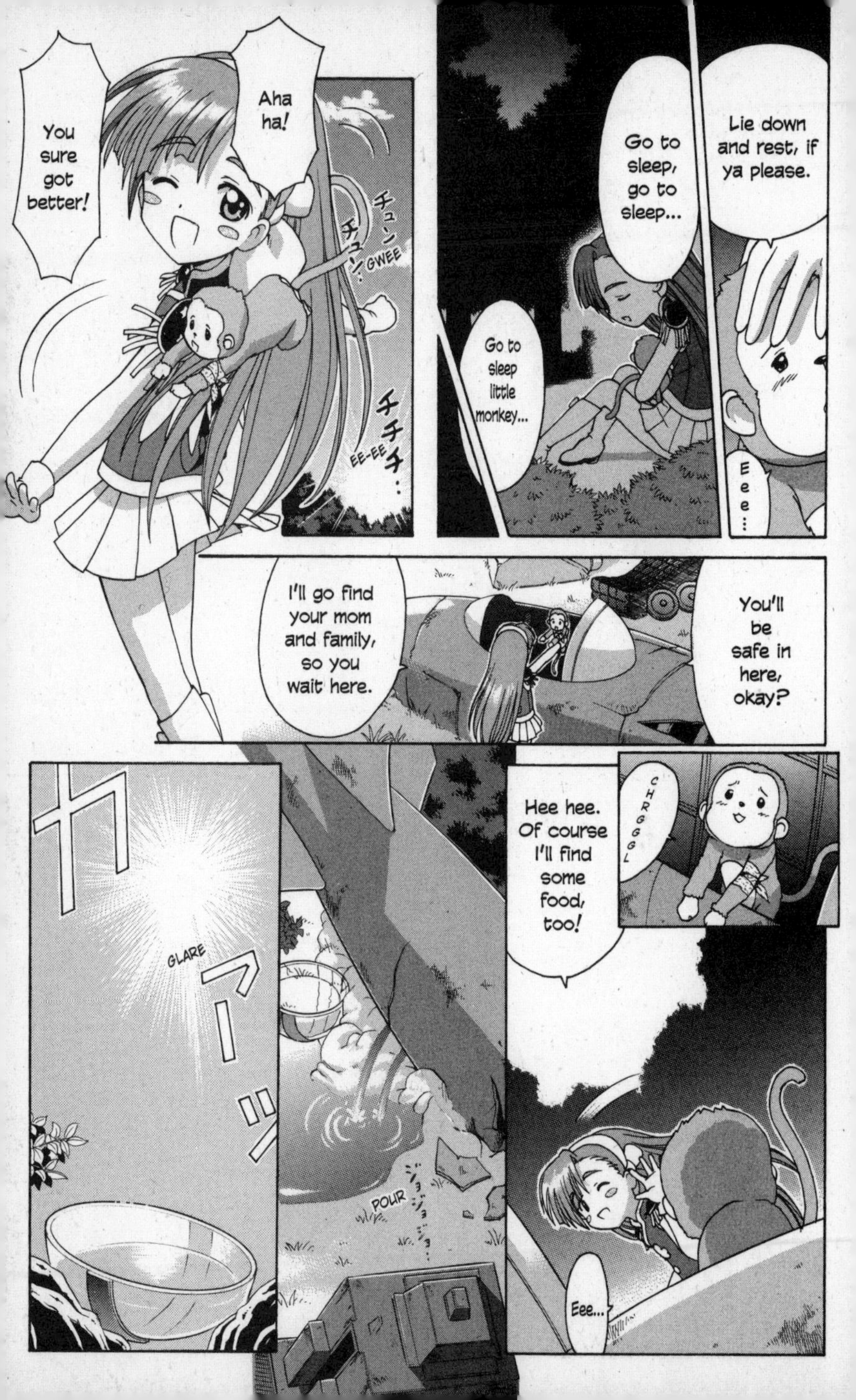

Lie down and rest, if ya please.
Eee...
Go to sleep, go to sleep...
Go to sleep little monkey...
You'll be safe in here, okay?
I'll go find your mom and family, so you wait here.
Aha ha!
You sure got better!
チュンチュン!
GWEE
チチチ...
EE-EE
CHRGGGL
Hee hee. Of course I'll find some food, too!
Eee...
POUR
GLARE

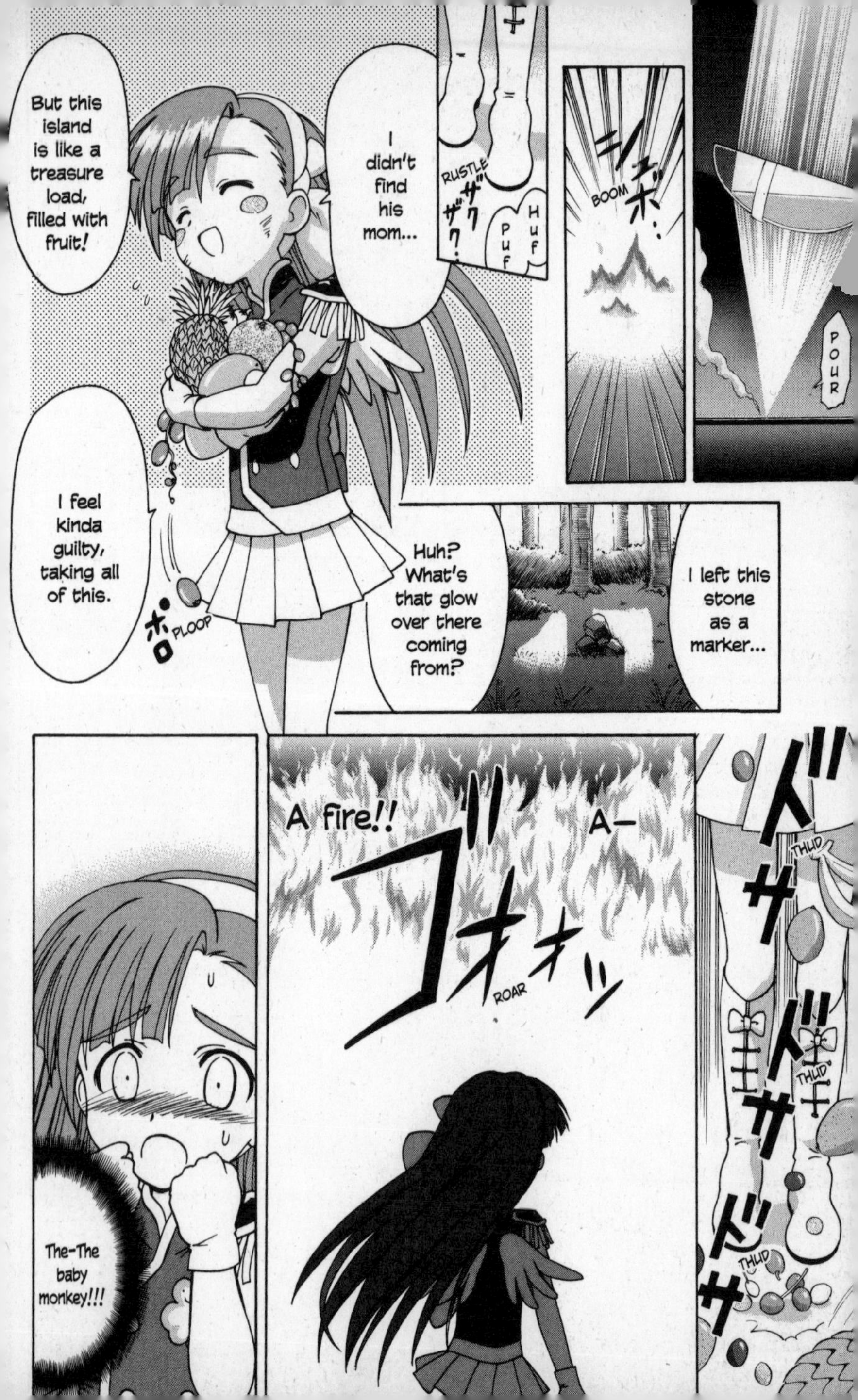
POUR
BOOM
RUSTLE
ザク ザク
Huf
Puf
I didn't find his mom...
But this island is like a treasure load, filled with fruit!
I feel kinda guilty, taking all of this.
ポロ
PLOOP
I left this stone as a marker...
Huh? What's that glow over there coming from?
THUD
THUD
THUD
A—
A fire!!
ゴオオッ
ROAR
The-The baby monkey!!!

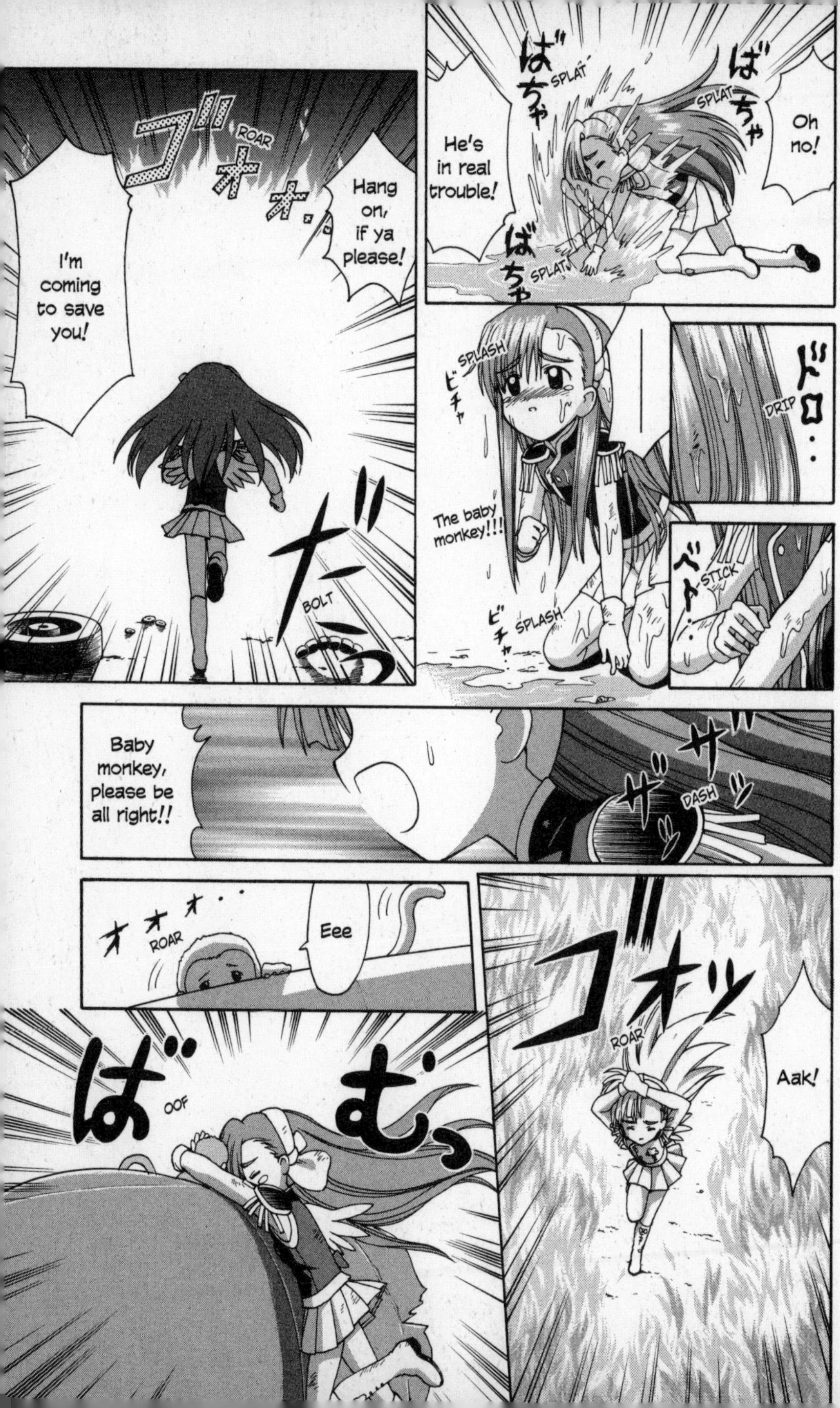

ばちゃ
SPLAT
ばちゃ
SPLAT
Oh no!
He's in real trouble!
ばちゃ
SPLAT
ドロ・・
DRIP
ベト・・
STICK
ビチャ
SPLASH
The baby monkey!!!
ビチャ・・
SPLASH
ゴオオ。
ROAR
Hang on, if ya please!
I'm coming to save you!
ダーっ
BOLT
ザザザッ
DASH
Baby monkey, please be all right!!
ゴオッ
ROAR
Aak!
Eee
オオオ・・
ROAR
ばむっ
OOF

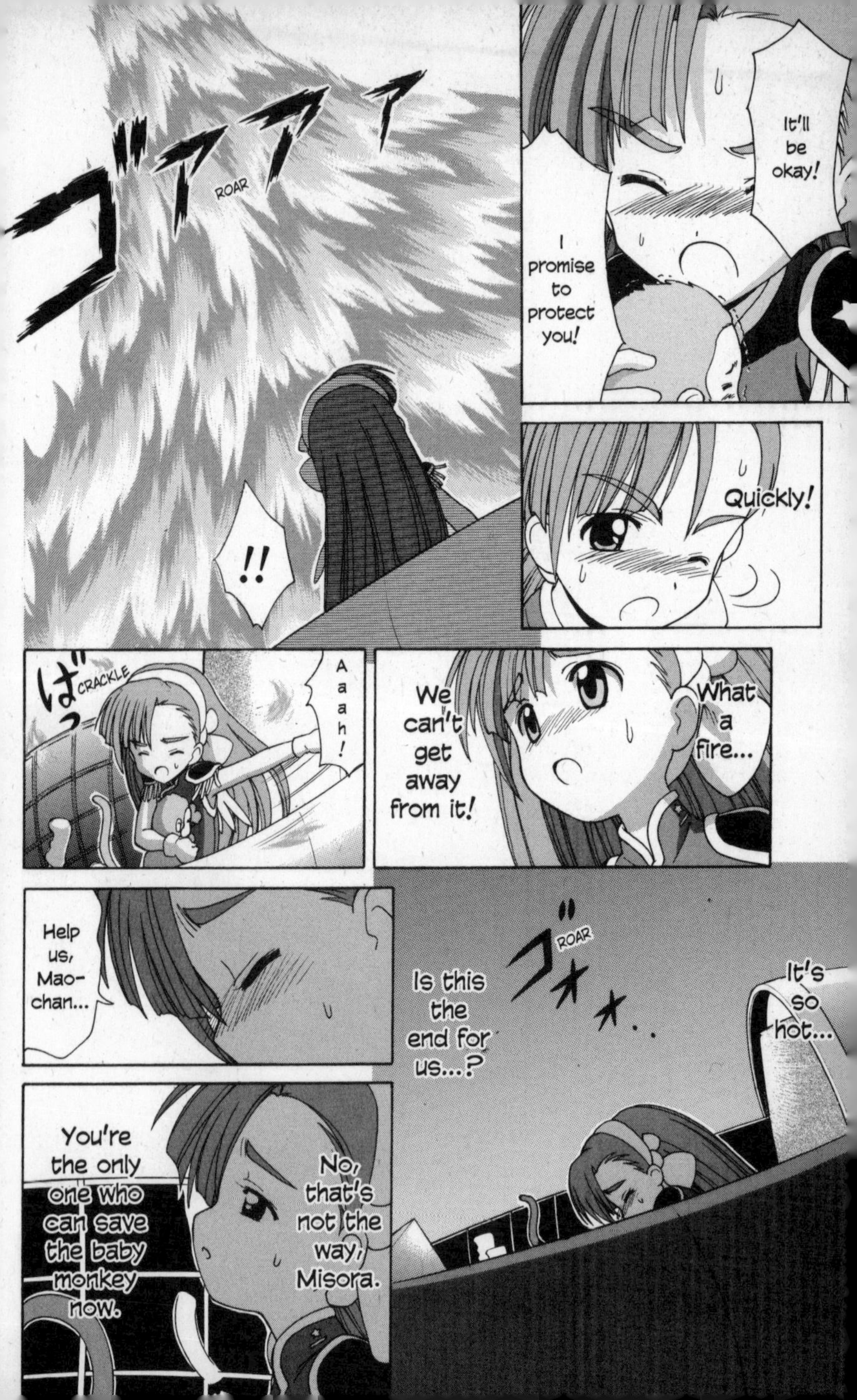
It'll be okay!
I promise to protect you!
Quickly!
ゴアアア
ROAR
!!
What a fire...
We can't get away from it!
Aaah!
ばっ
CRACKLE
It's so hot...
ゴォ
ROAR
Is this the end for us...?
Help us, Mao-chan...
No, that's not the way, Misora.
You're the only one who can save the baby monkey now.

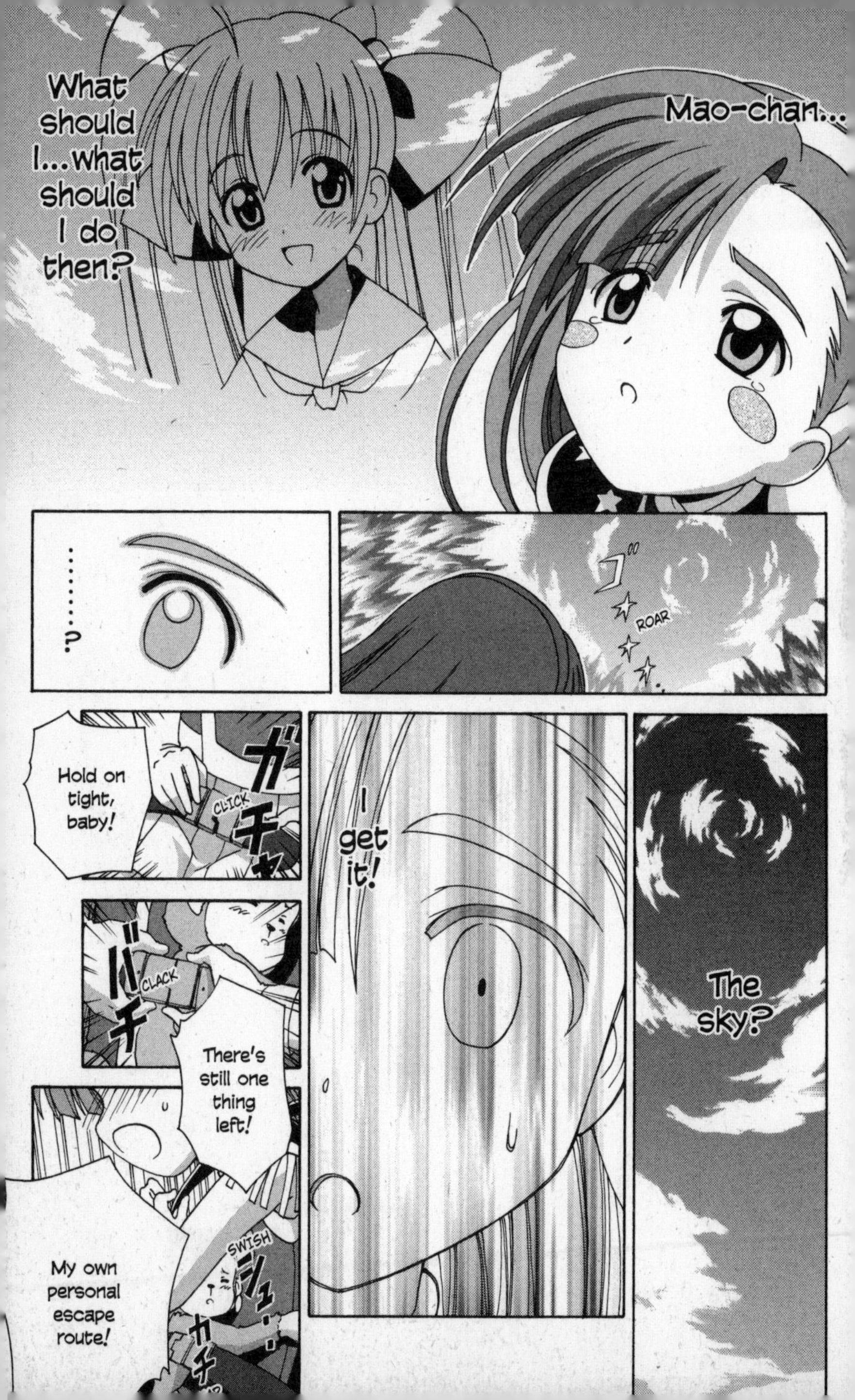
Mao-chan...
What should I...what should I do then?
ゴ
ROAR
......?
The sky?
I get it!
Hold on tight, baby!
ガチャ
CLICK
バチ
CLACK
There's still one thing left!
My own personal escape route!
SWISH
カチ

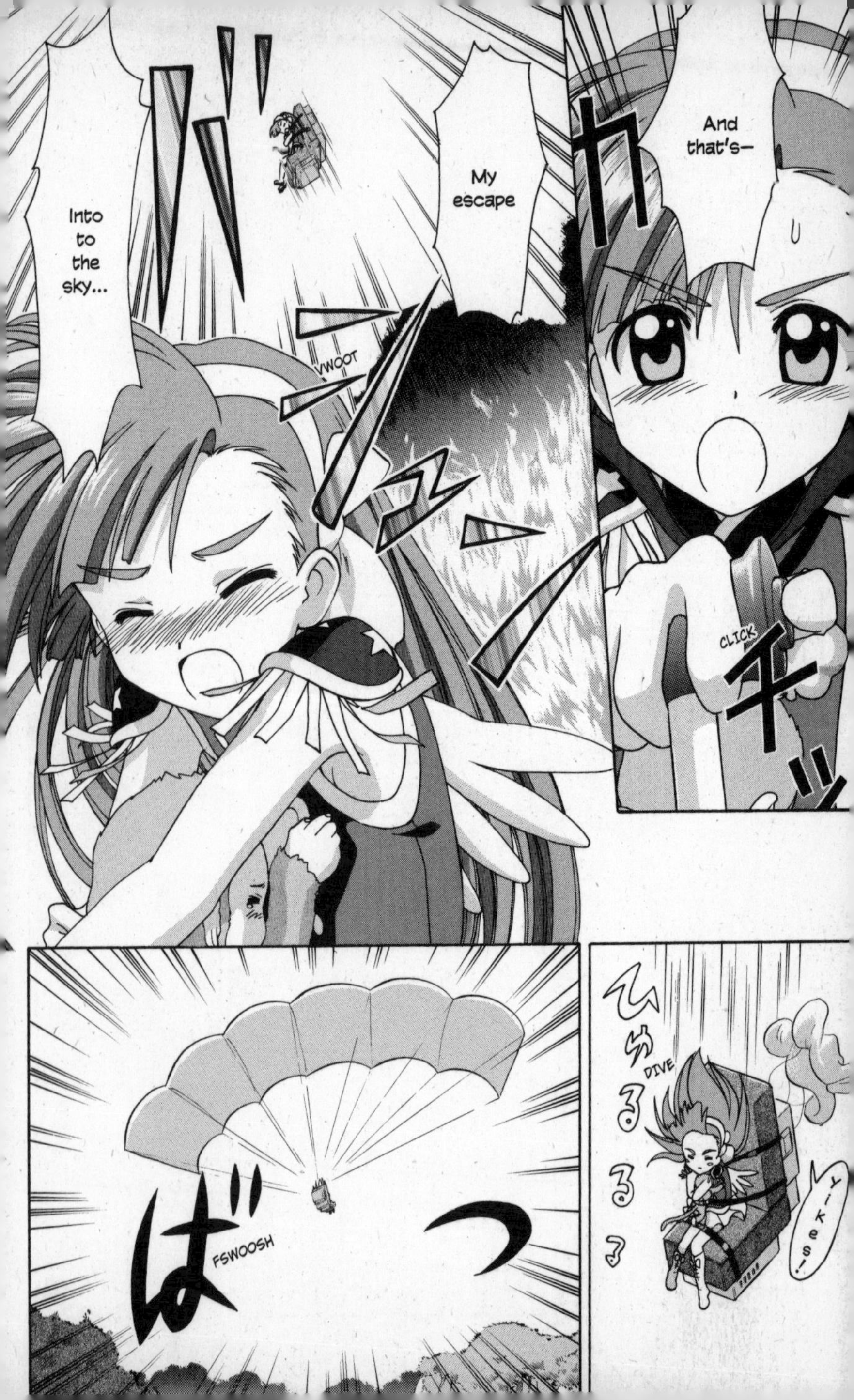
And that's—
CLICK
My escape
Into to the sky...
VWOOT
DIVE
Yikes!
FSWOOSH

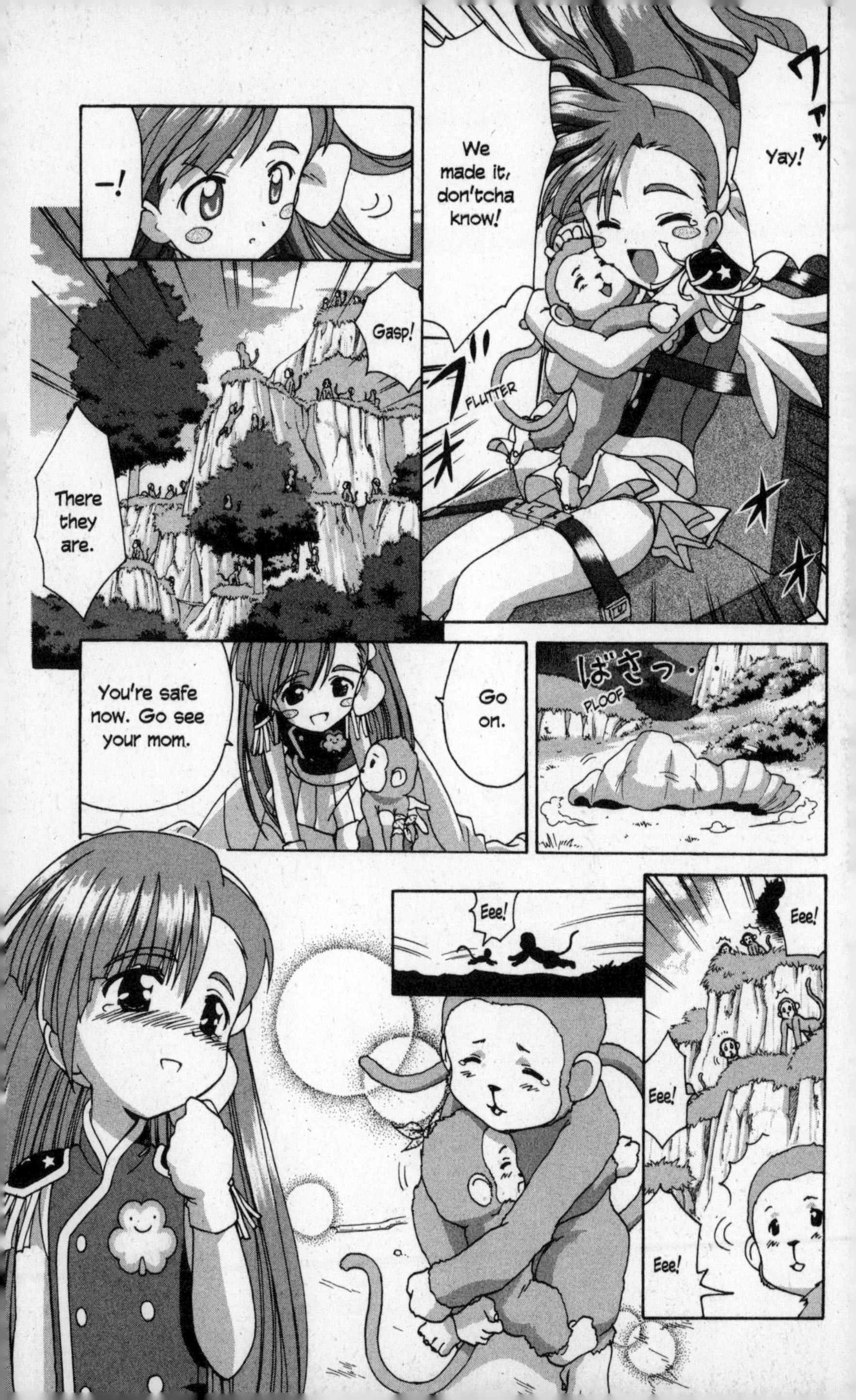
ワァッ
Yay!
We made it, don'tcha know!
FLUTTER
—!
Gasp!
There they are.
ばさっ
PLOOF
Go on.
You're safe now. Go see your mom.
Eee!
Eee!
Eee!
Eee!

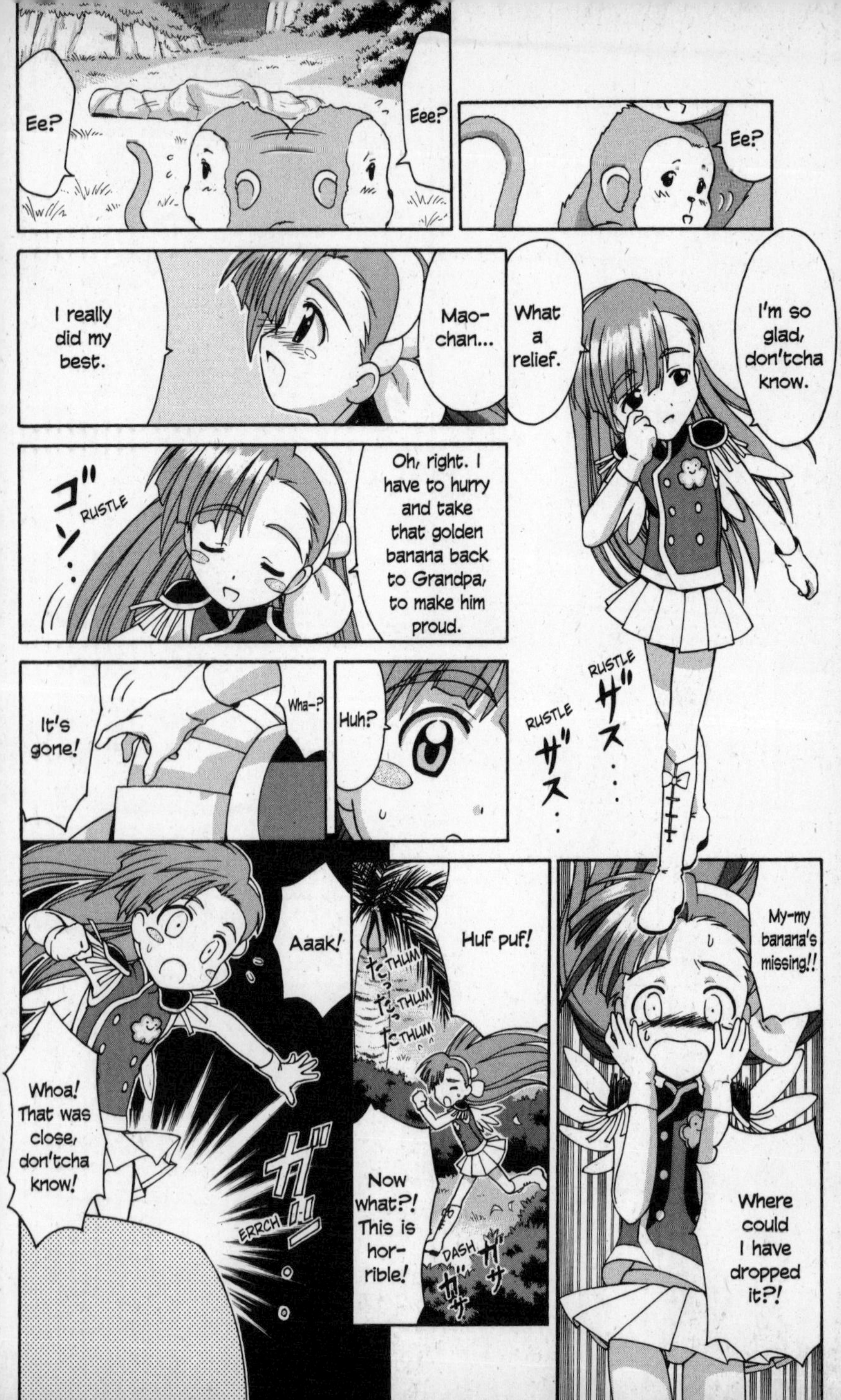
Ee?
Eee?
Ee?
I'm so glad, don'tcha know.
What a relief.
RUSTLE ザス...
RUSTLE ザス...
Mao-chan...
I really did my best.
Oh, right. I have to hurry and take that golden banana back to Grandpa, to make him proud.
RUSTLE ゴソ...
Huh?
Wha-?
It's gone!
My-my banana's missing!!
Where could I have dropped it?!
Huf puf!
THUM たっ
THUM たっ
THUM たっ
Now what?! This is horrible!
DASH ガサ ガサ
Aaak!
ERRCH
Whoa! That was close, don'tcha know!

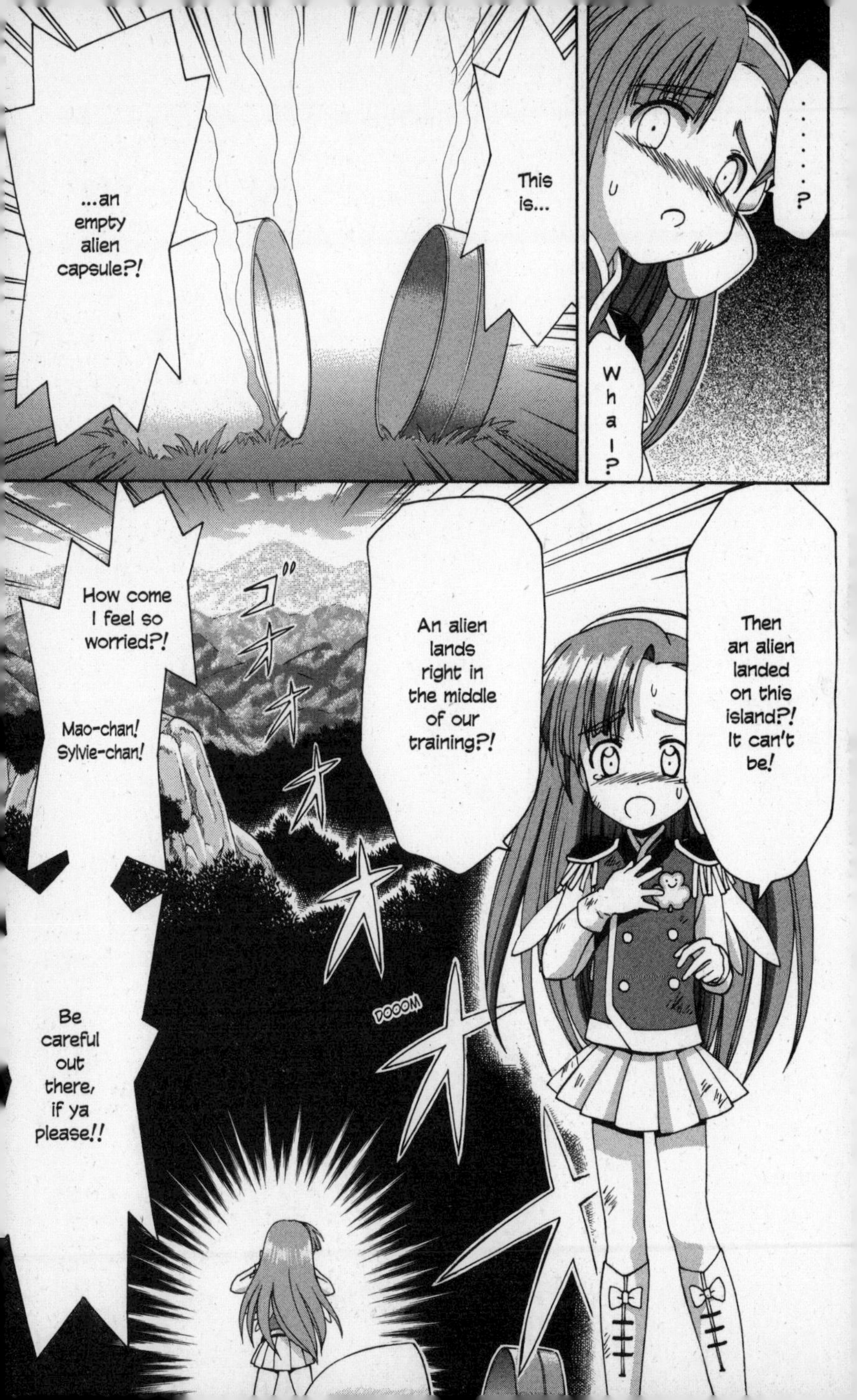
......?
What?
This is...
...an empty alien capsule?!
Then an alien landed on this island?! It can't be!
An alien lands right in the middle of our training?!
ゴォォォ
DOOOM
How come I feel so worried?!
Mao-chan! Sylvie-chan!
Be careful out there, if ya please!!

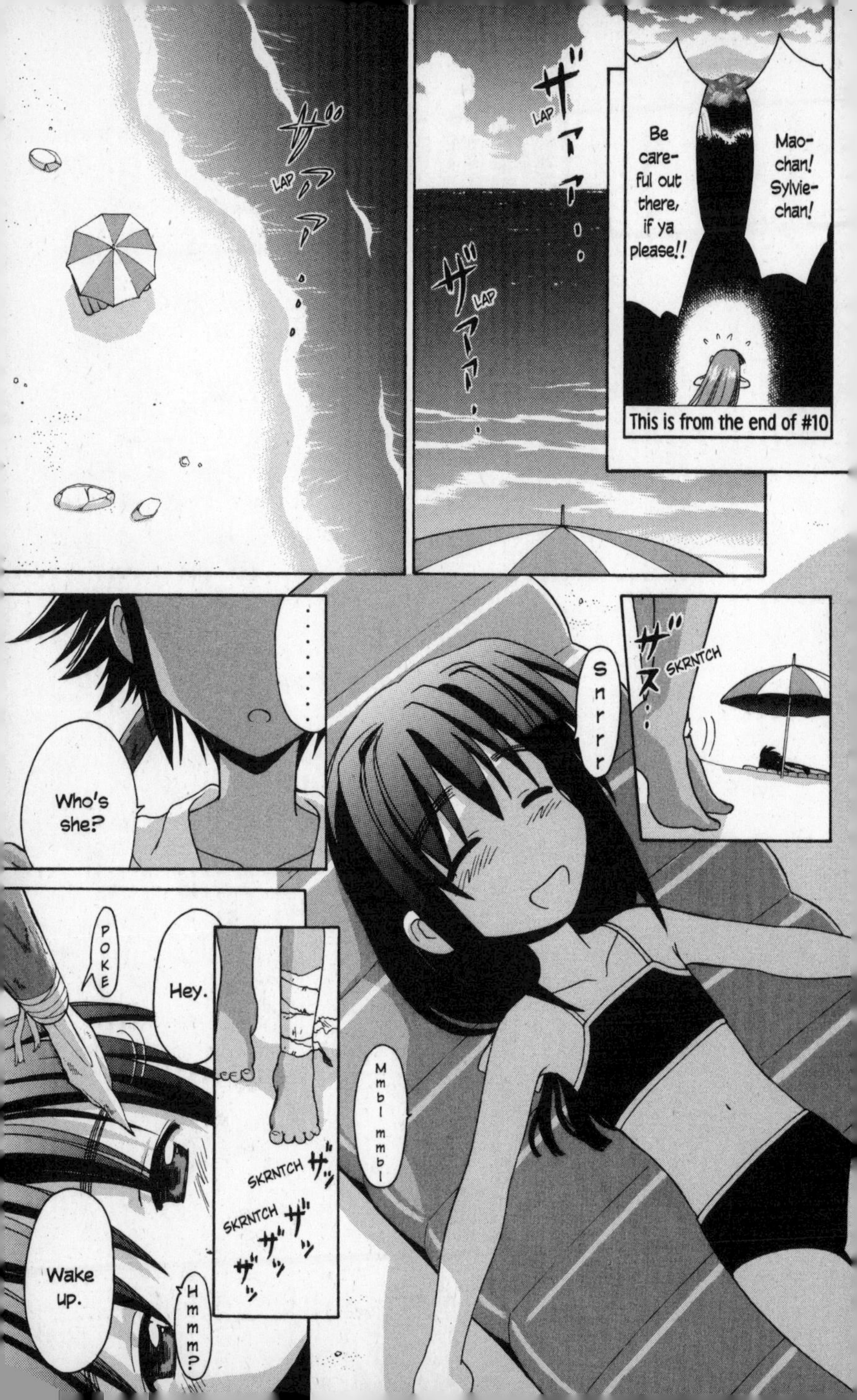
Mao-chan! Sylvie-chan!
Be careful out there, if ya please!!
This is from the end of #10
ザァァ‥
LAP
ザァァ‥
LAP
ザァァ‥
LAP
ザス‥
SKRNTCH
Snrrr
……
Who's she?
Mmbl mmbl
SKRNTCH ザッ
SKRNTCH ザッ ザッ ザッ
Hey.
POKE
Wake up.
Hmmm?

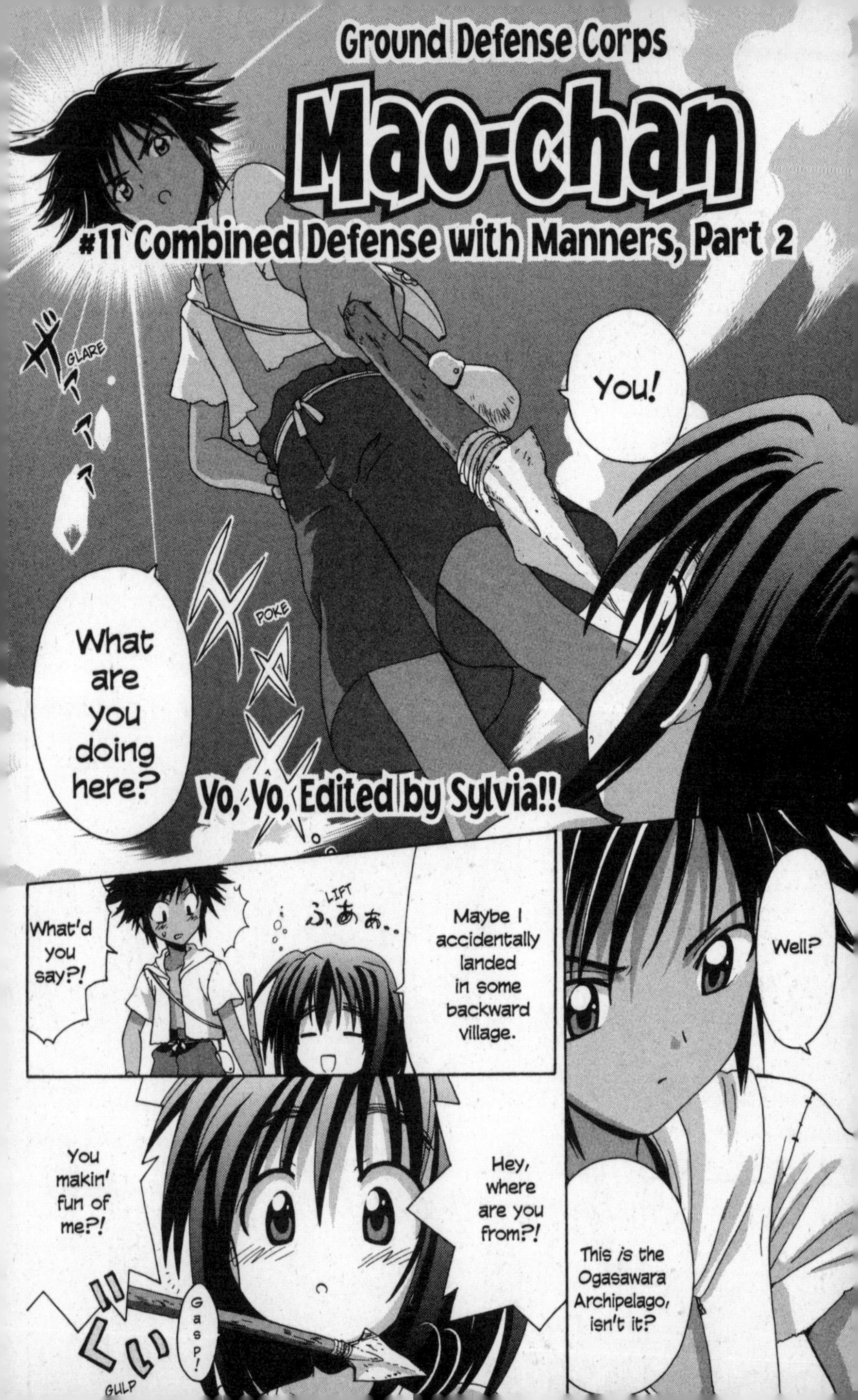
Ground Defense Corps
Mao-chan
#11 Combined Defense with Manners, Part 2
You!
GLARE
POKE
What are you doing here?
Yo, Yo, Edited by Sylvia!!
Well?
This *is* the Ogasawara Archipelago, isn't it?
Maybe I accidentally landed in some backward village.
LIFT
ふあぁ..
What'd you say?!
Hey, where are you from?!
You makin' fun of me?!
Gasp!
GULP

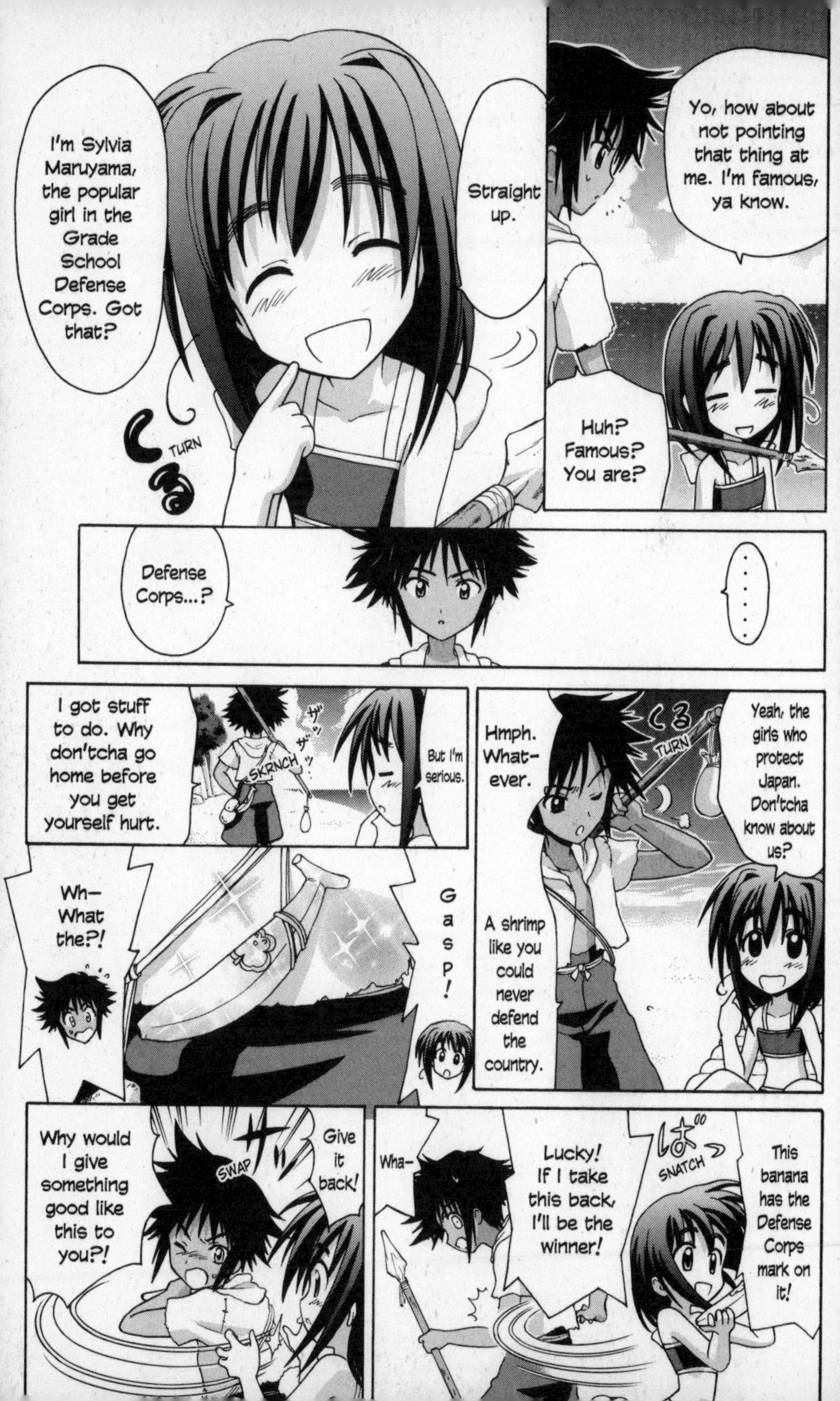

Yo, how about not pointing that thing at me. I'm famous, ya know.
Huh? Famous? You are?
Straight up.
I'm Sylvia Maruyama, the popular girl in the Grade School Defense Corps. Got that?
くる
TURN
......
Defense Corps...?
Yeah, the girls who protect Japan. Don'tcha know about us?
くる
TURN
Hmph. Whatever.
A shrimp like you could never defend the country.
But I'm serious.
ザッ ザッ
SKRNCH
I got stuff to do. Why don'tcha go home before you get yourself hurt.
Gasp!
Wh— What the?!
This banana has the Defense Corps mark on it!
ぱっ
SNATCH
Lucky! If I take this back, I'll be the winner!
Wha-
Give it back!
SWAP
Why would I give something good like this to you?!

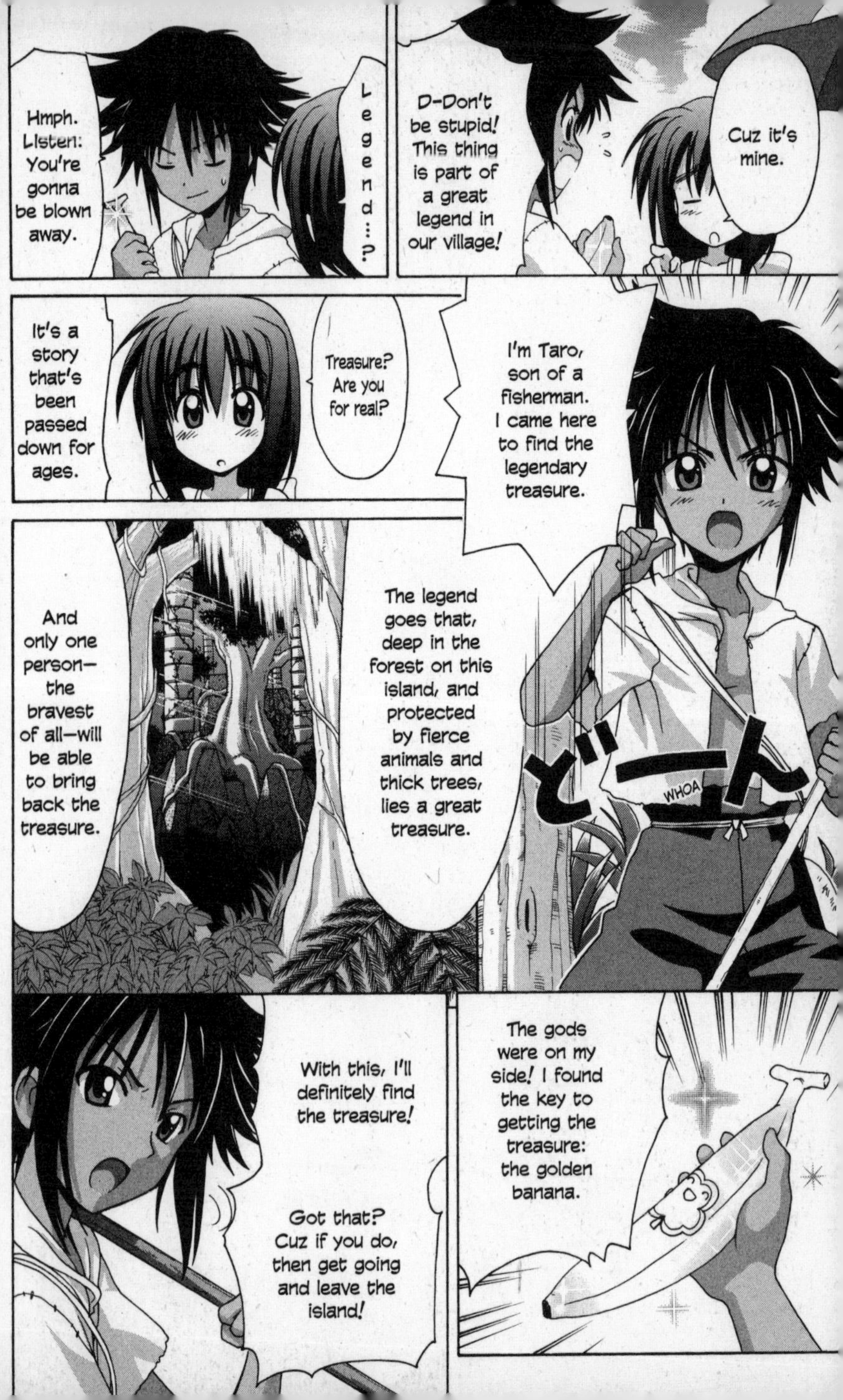
Cuz it's mine.
D-Don't be stupid! This thing is part of a great legend in our village!
Legend...?
Hmph. Listen: You're gonna be blown away.
I'm Taro, son of a fisherman. I came here to find the legendary treasure.
WHOA
Treasure? Are you for real?
It's a story that's been passed down for ages.
The legend goes that, deep in the forest on this island, and protected by fierce animals and thick trees, lies a great treasure.
And only one person—the bravest of all—will be able to bring back the treasure.
The gods were on my side! I found the key to getting the treasure: the golden banana.
With this, I'll definitely find the treasure!
Got that? Cuz if you do, then get going and leave the island!

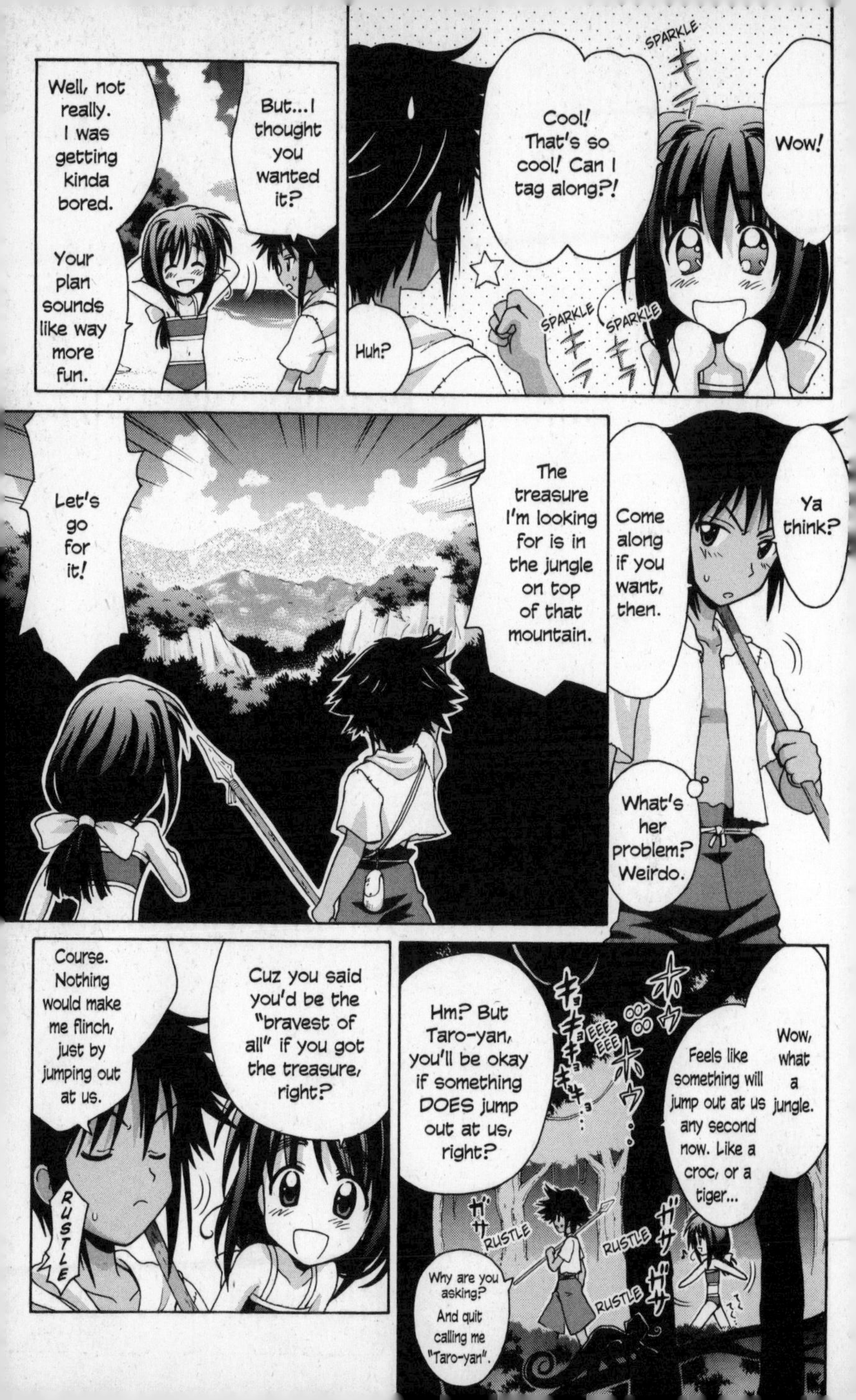
Wow!
SPARKLE
Cool! That's so cool! Can I tag along?!
SPARKLE SPARKLE
Huh?
But...I thought you wanted it?
Well, not really. I was getting kinda bored.
Your plan sounds like way more fun.
Ya think?
Come along if you want, then.
What's her problem? Weirdo.
The treasure I'm looking for is in the jungle on top of that mountain.
Let's go for it!
Wow, what a jungle.
Feels like something will jump out at us any second now. Like a croc, or a tiger...
Hm? But Taro-yan, you'll be okay if something DOES jump out at us, right?
EEE-EEE
OO-OO
RUSTLE
RUSTLE
RUSTLE
Why are you asking? And quit calling me "Taro-yan".
Cuz you said you'd be the "bravest of all" if you got the treasure, right?
Course. Nothing would make me flinch, just by jumping out at us.
RUSTLE

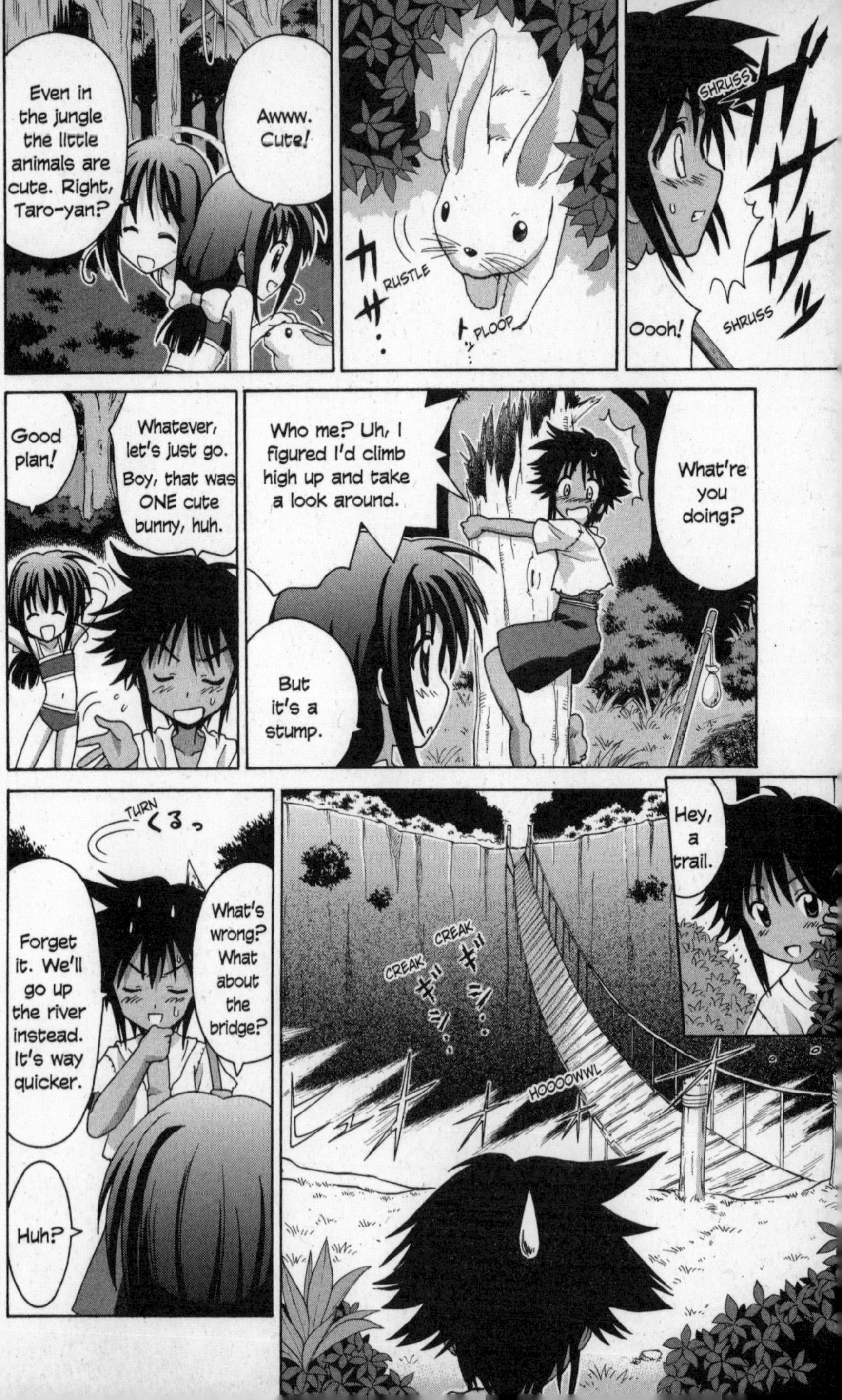
SHRUSS
Oooh!
SHRUSS
RUSTLE
PLOOP
Awww. Cute!
Even in the jungle the little animals are cute. Right, Taro-yan?
What're you doing?
Who me? Uh, I figured I'd climb high up and take a look around.
But it's a stump.
Whatever, let's just go. Boy, that was ONE cute bunny, huh.
Good plan!
Hey, a trail.
CREAK
CREAK
HOOOOWWL
TURN
What's wrong? What about the bridge?
Forget it. We'll go up the river instead. It's way quicker.
Huh?

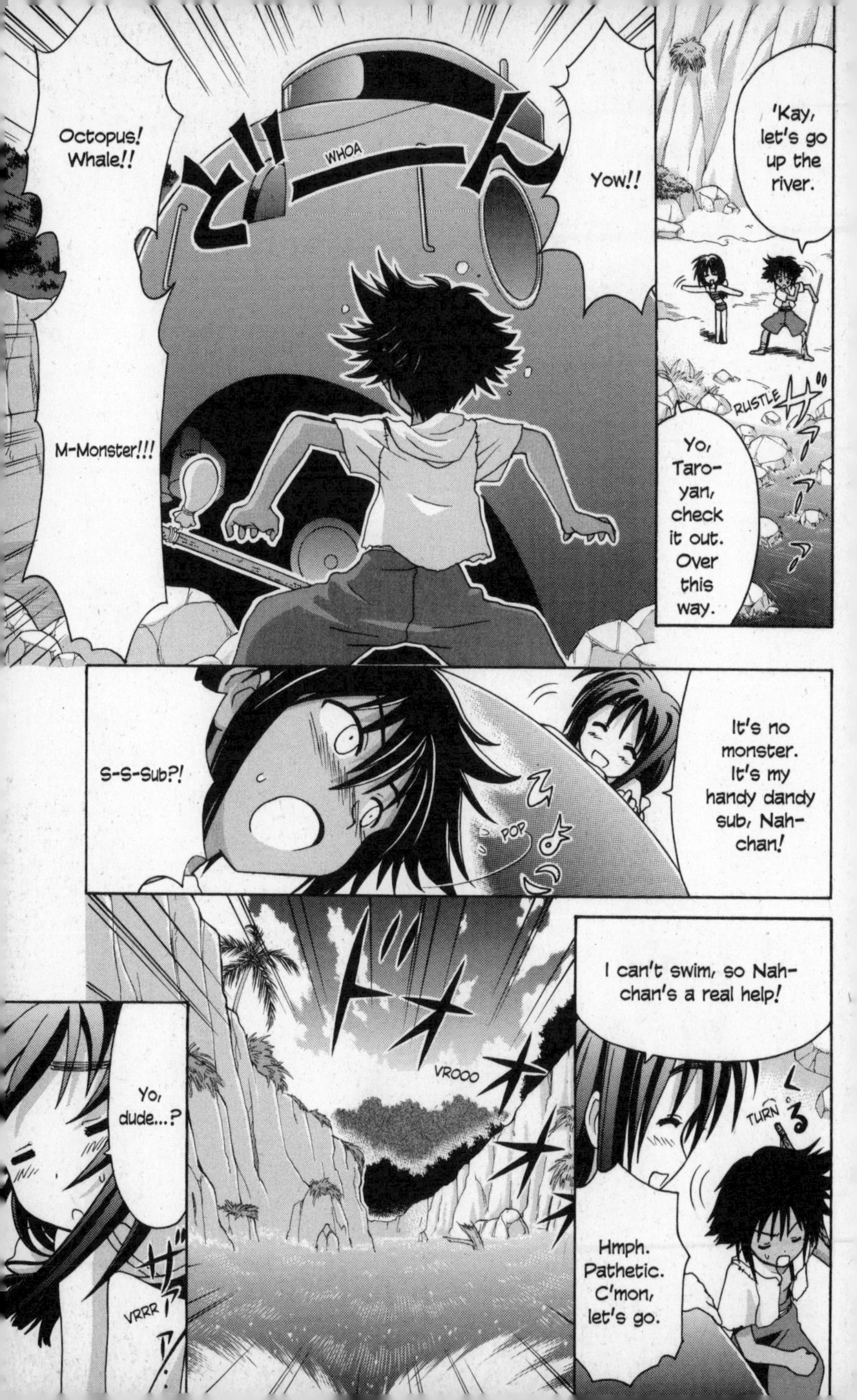
'Kay, let's go up the river.
RUSTLE
Yo, Taro-yan, check it out. Over this way.
Yow!!
WHOA
Octopus! Whale!!
M-Monster!!!
It's no monster. It's my handy dandy sub, Nah-chan!
POP
S-S-Sub?!
I can't swim, so Nah-chan's a real help!
TURN
Hmph. Pathetic. C'mon, let's go.
VROOO
Yo, dude...?
VRRR

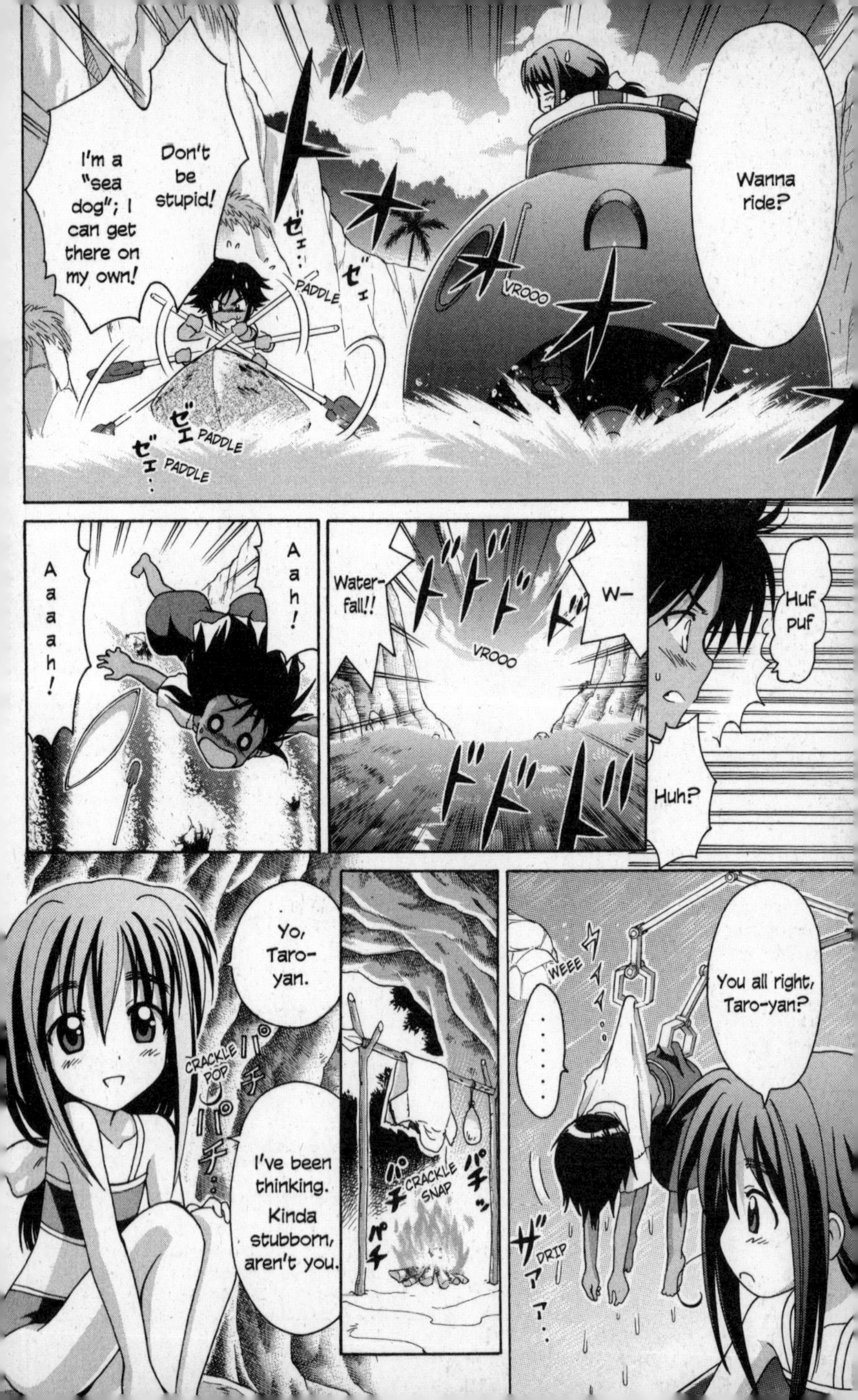

Wanna ride?
VROOO
Don't be stupid!
I'm a "sea dog"; I can get there on my own!
PADDLE
PADDLE
PADDLE
Huf puf
Huh?
W—
VROOO
Water-fall!!
Aah!
Aaaaah!
You all right, Taro-yan?
WEEE
......
DRIP
CRACKLE SNAP
Yo, Taro-yan.
CRACKLE POP
I've been thinking. Kinda stubborn, aren't you.

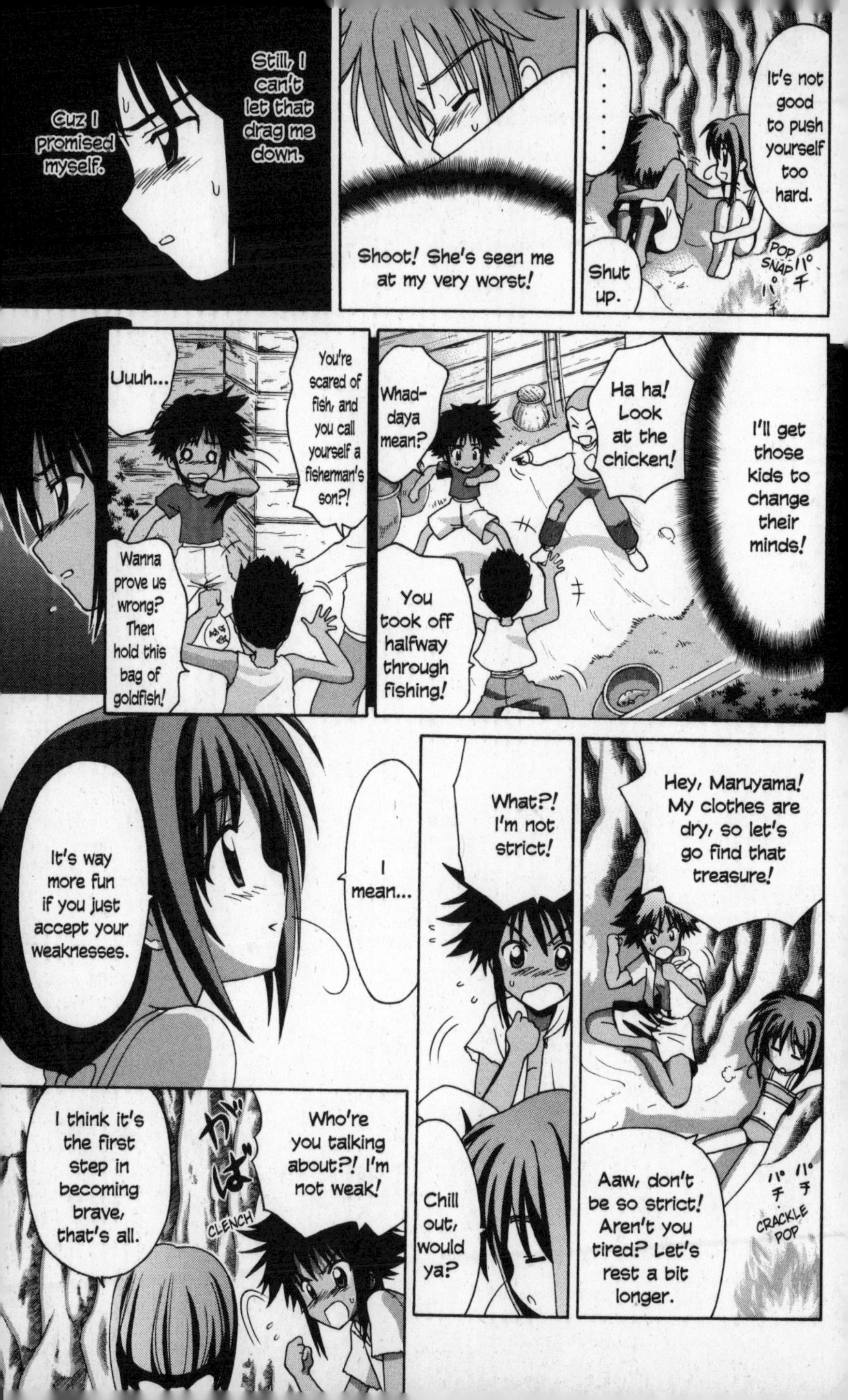
It's not good to push yourself too hard.
......
Shut up.
POP SNAP
Shoot! She's seen me at my very worst!
Still, I can't let that drag me down.
Cuz I promised myself.
I'll get those kids to change their minds!
Ha ha! Look at the chicken!
Whad-daya mean?
You took off halfway through fishing!
You're scared of fish, and you call yourself a fisherman's son?!
Uuuh...
Wanna prove us wrong? Then hold this bag of goldfish!
Hey, Maruyama! My clothes are dry, so let's go find that treasure!
CRACKLE POP
Aaw, don't be so strict! Aren't you tired? Let's rest a bit longer.
What?! I'm not strict!
Chill out, would ya?
I mean...
It's way more fun if you just accept your weaknesses.
Who're you talking about?! I'm not weak!
CLENCH
I think it's the first step in becoming brave, that's all.

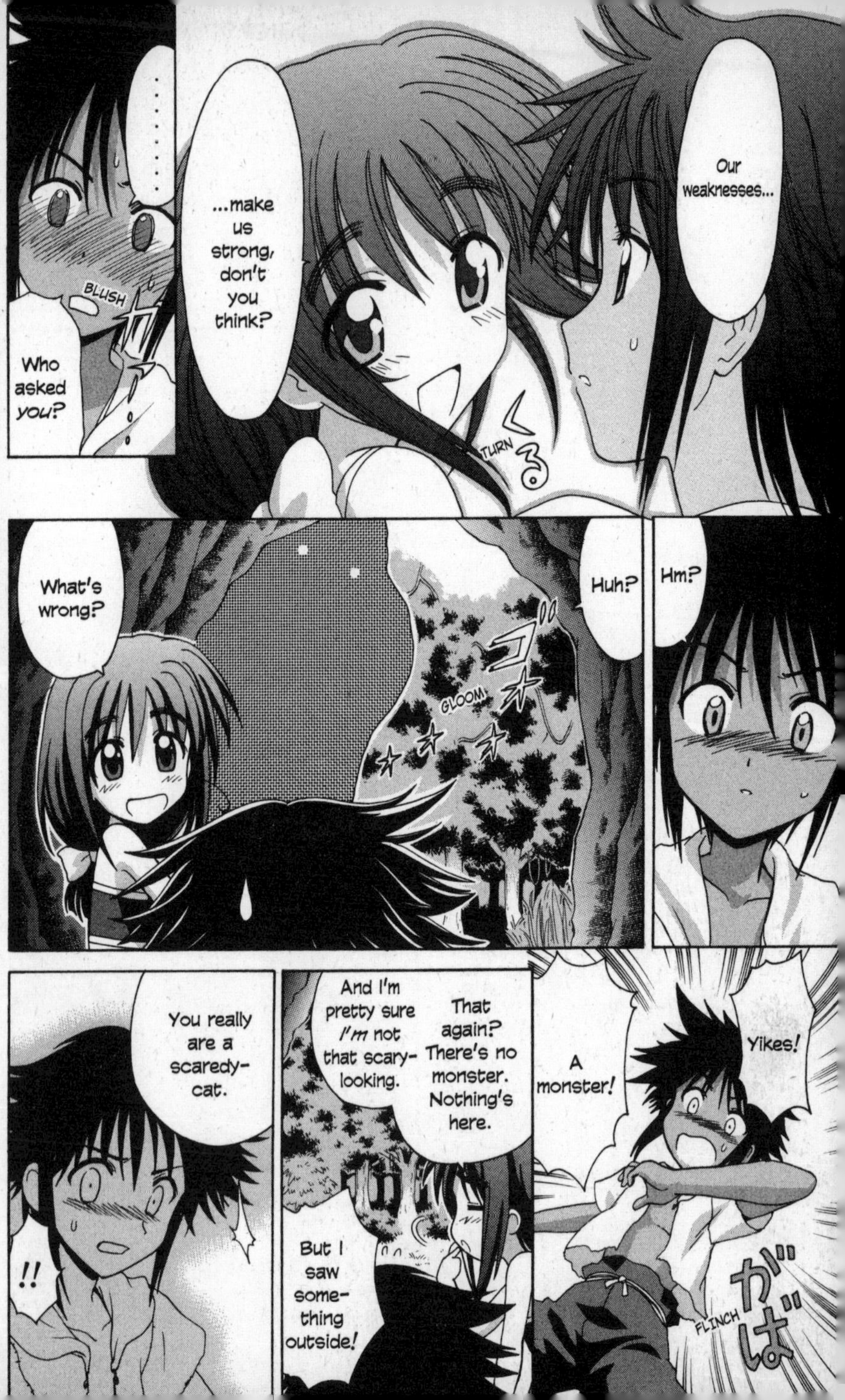
Our weaknesses...
...make us strong, don't you think?
TURN
......
BLUSH
Who asked *you*?
Hm?
Huh?
GLOOM
What's wrong?
Yikes!
A monster!
FLINCH
That again? There's no monster. Nothing's here.
And I'm pretty sure *I'm* not that scary-looking.
But I saw something outside!
You really are a scaredy-cat.
!!

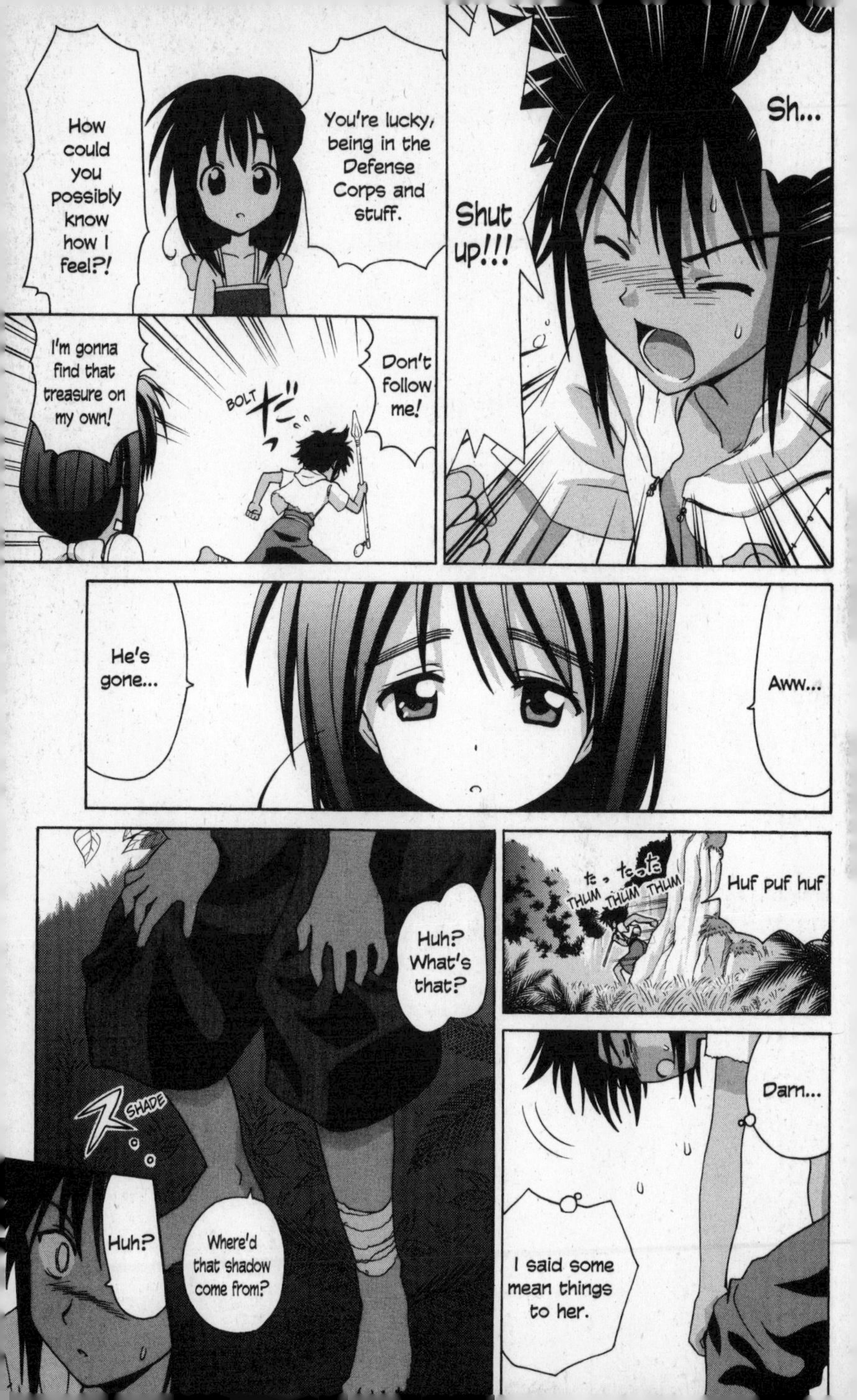
Sh...
Shut up!!!
You're lucky, being in the Defense Corps and stuff.
How could you possibly know how I feel?!
Don't follow me!
BOLT
I'm gonna find that treasure on my own!
Aww...
He's gone...
Huf puf huf
THUM THUM THUM
Darn...
I said some mean things to her.
Huh? What's that?
SHADE
Where'd that shadow come from?
Huh?

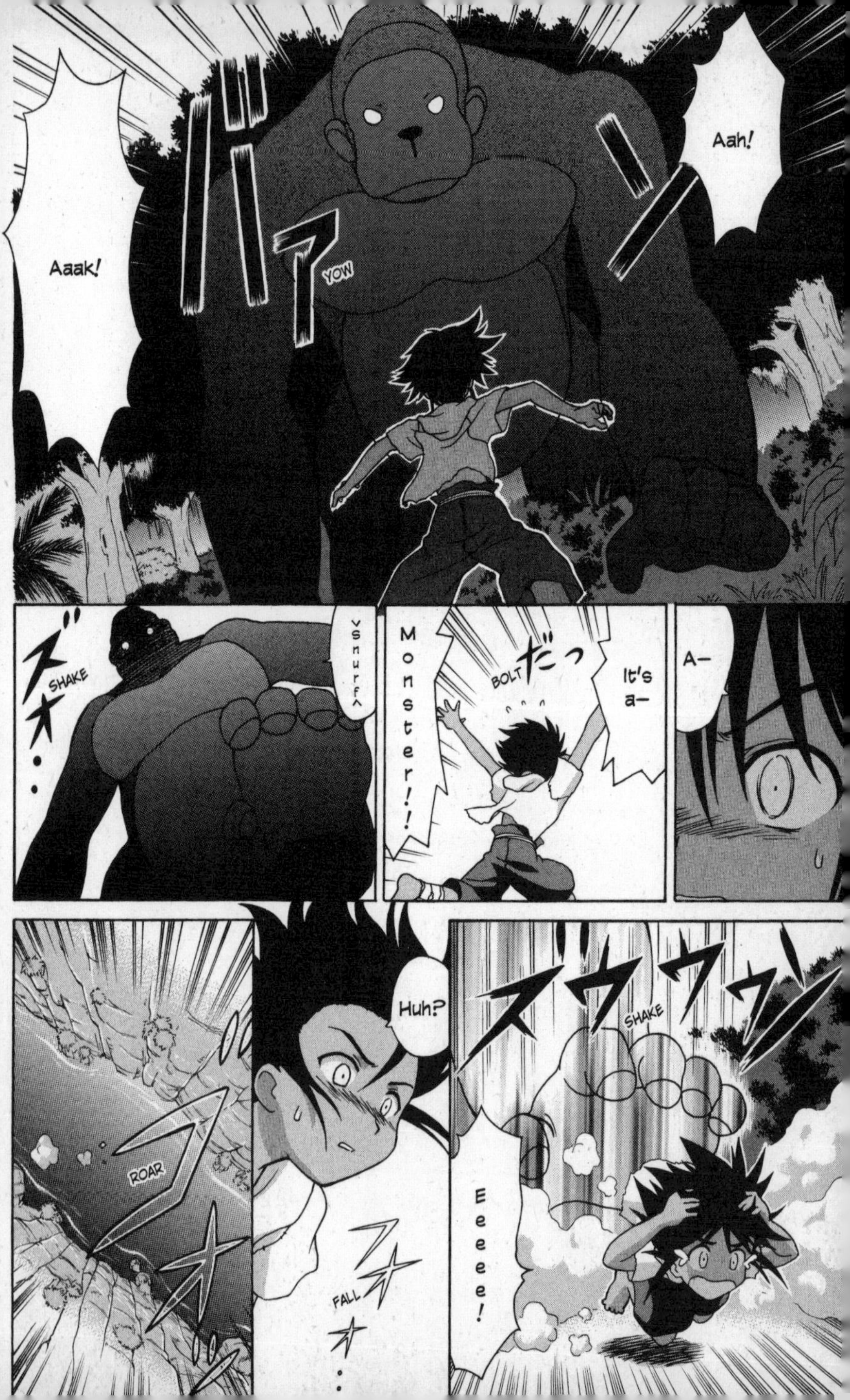
Aah!
YOW
Aaak!
A–
It's a–
BOLT
Monster!!
<Snurf>
SHAKE
SHAKE
Eeeee!
Huh?
FALL
ROAR

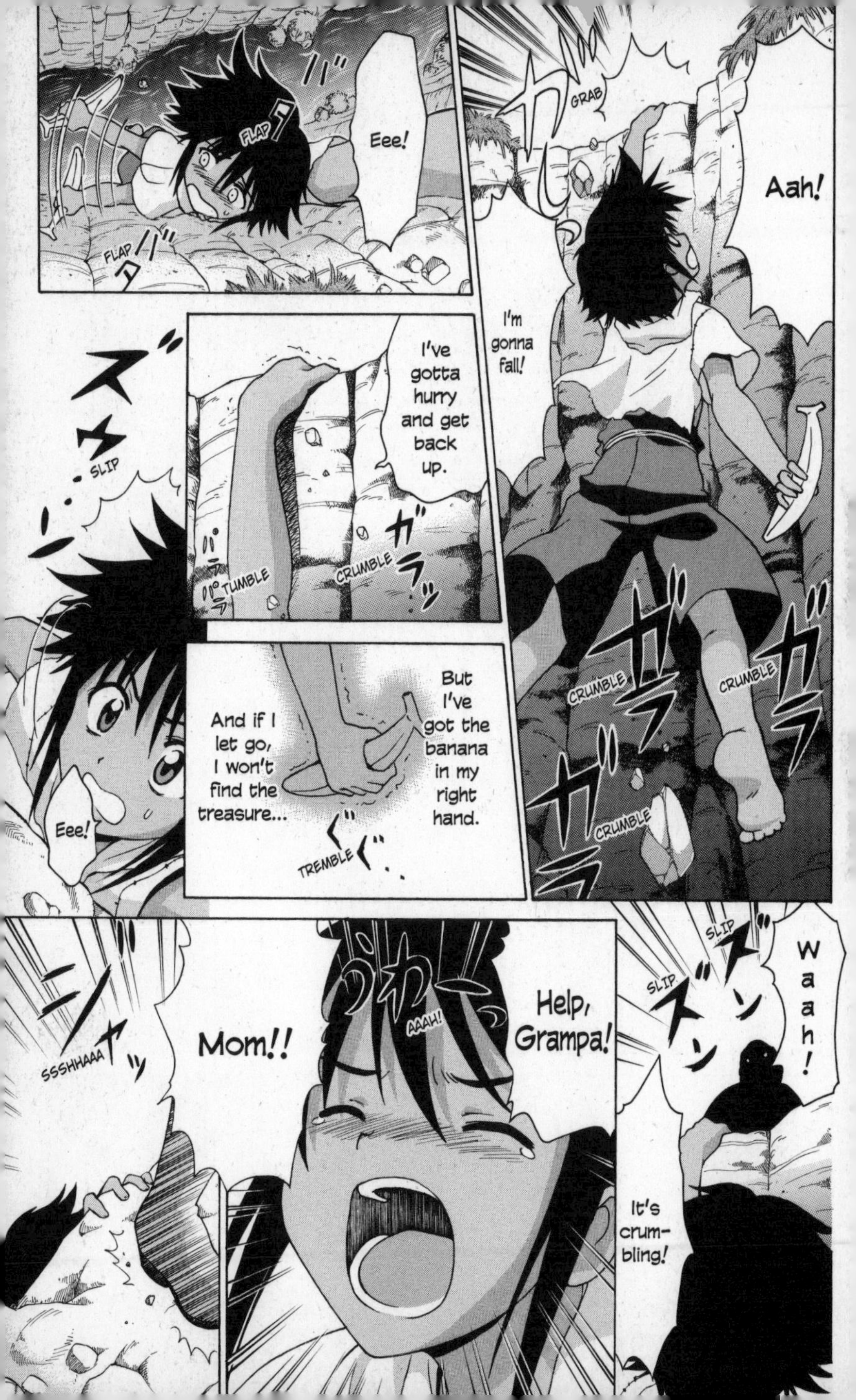
GRAB
Aah!
I'm gonna fall!
CRUMBLE
CRUMBLE
CRUMBLE
Eee!
FLAP
FLAP
I've gotta hurry and get back up.
CRUMBLE
TUMBLE
But I've got the banana in my right hand.
And if I let go, I won't find the treasure...
TREMBLE
SLIP
Eee!
SLIP
SLIP
Waah!
It's crumbling!
Help, Grampa!
AAAH!
Mom!!
SSSHHAAA

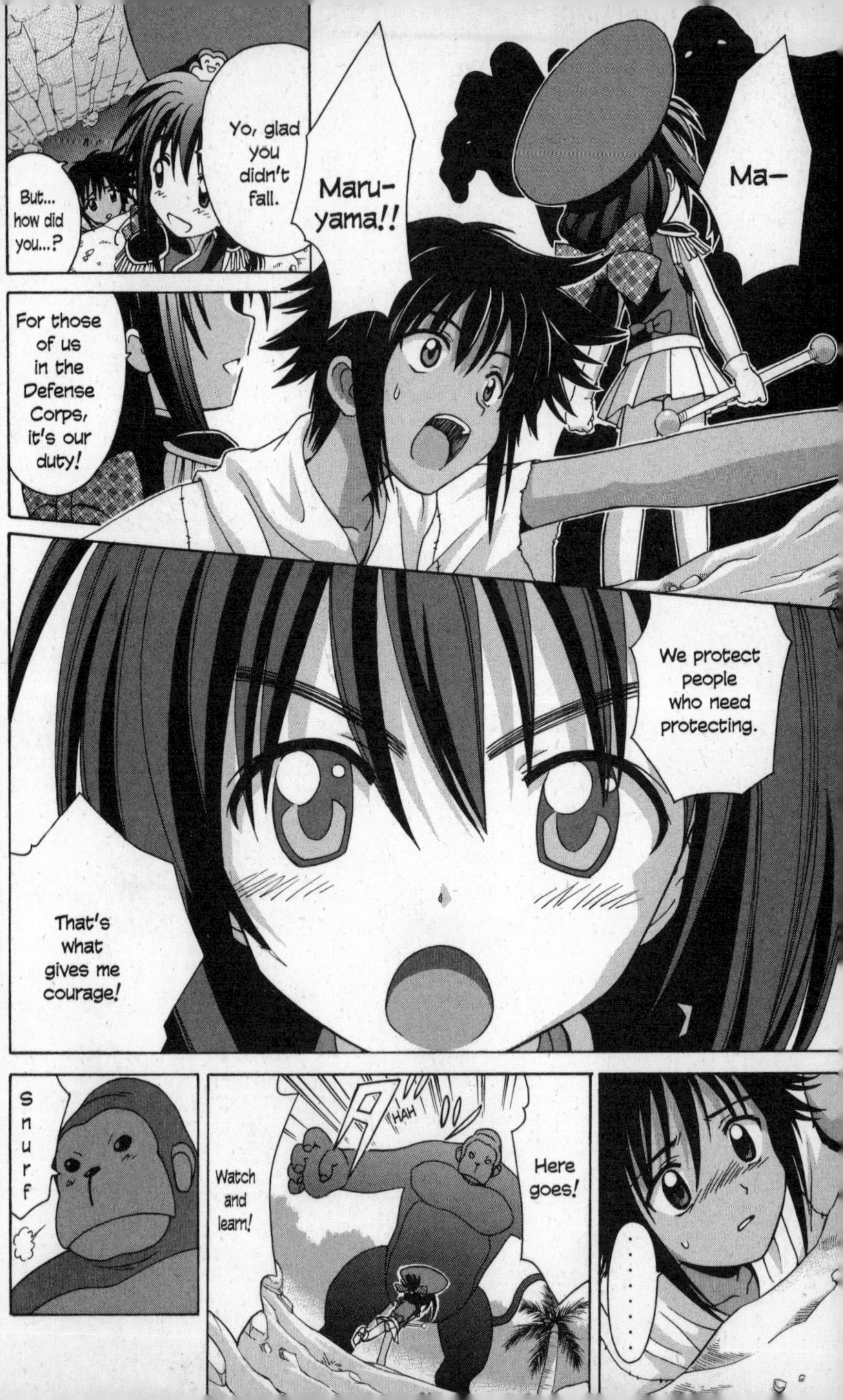
Ma—
Maru-yama!!
Yo, glad you didn't fall.
But... how did you...?
For those of us in the Defense Corps, it's our duty!
We protect people who need protecting.
That's what gives me courage!
......
HAH
Here goes!
Watch and learn!
Snurf

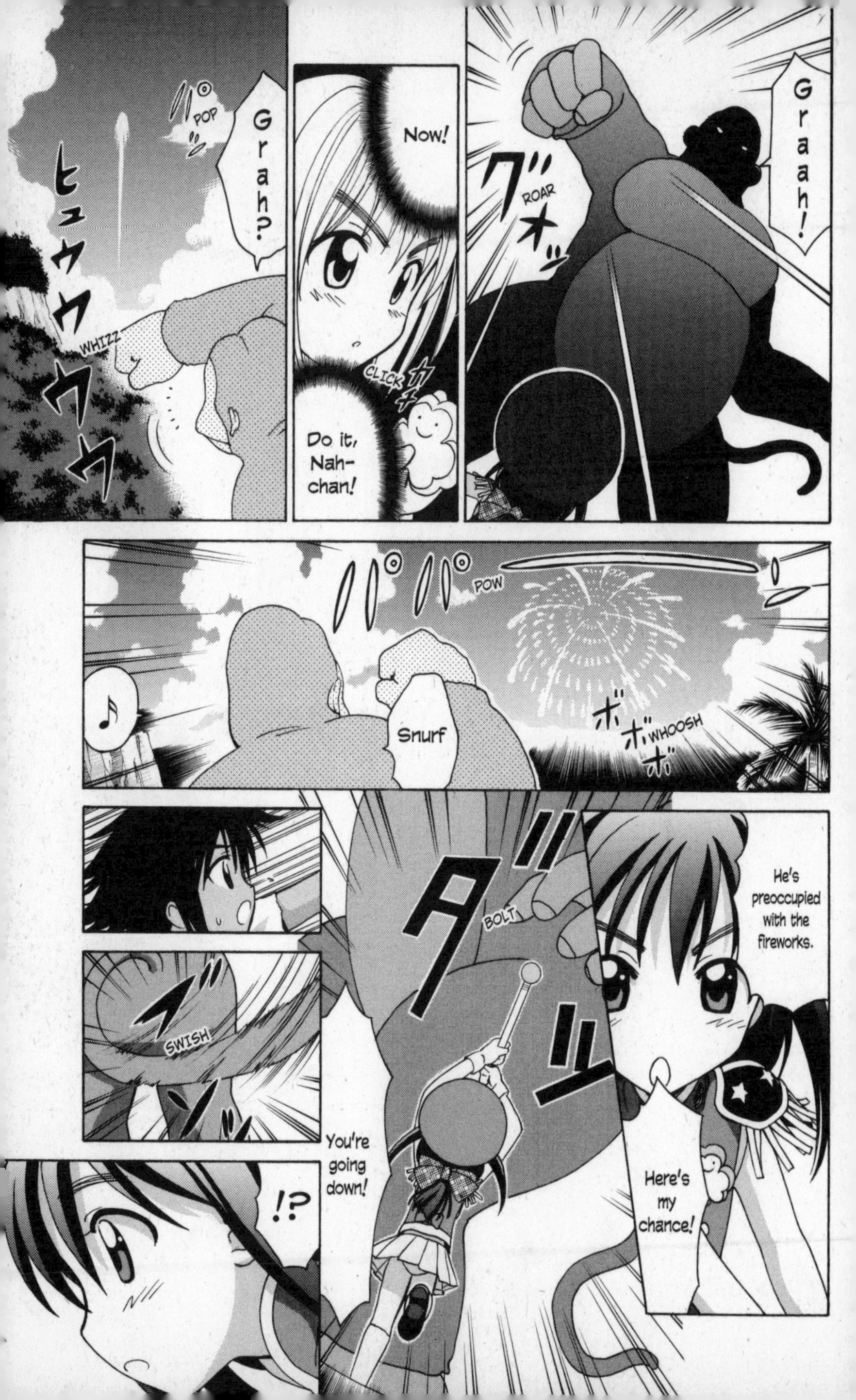
Graah!
グオッ
ROAR
Now!
カチ
CLICK
Do it, Nah-chan!
Grah?
パ
POP
ヒュウウウ
WHIZZ
パパ
POW
ボボボ
WHOOSH
Snurf
♪
He's preoccupied with the fireworks.
Here's my chance!
ダッ
BOLT
You're going down!
SWISH
!?

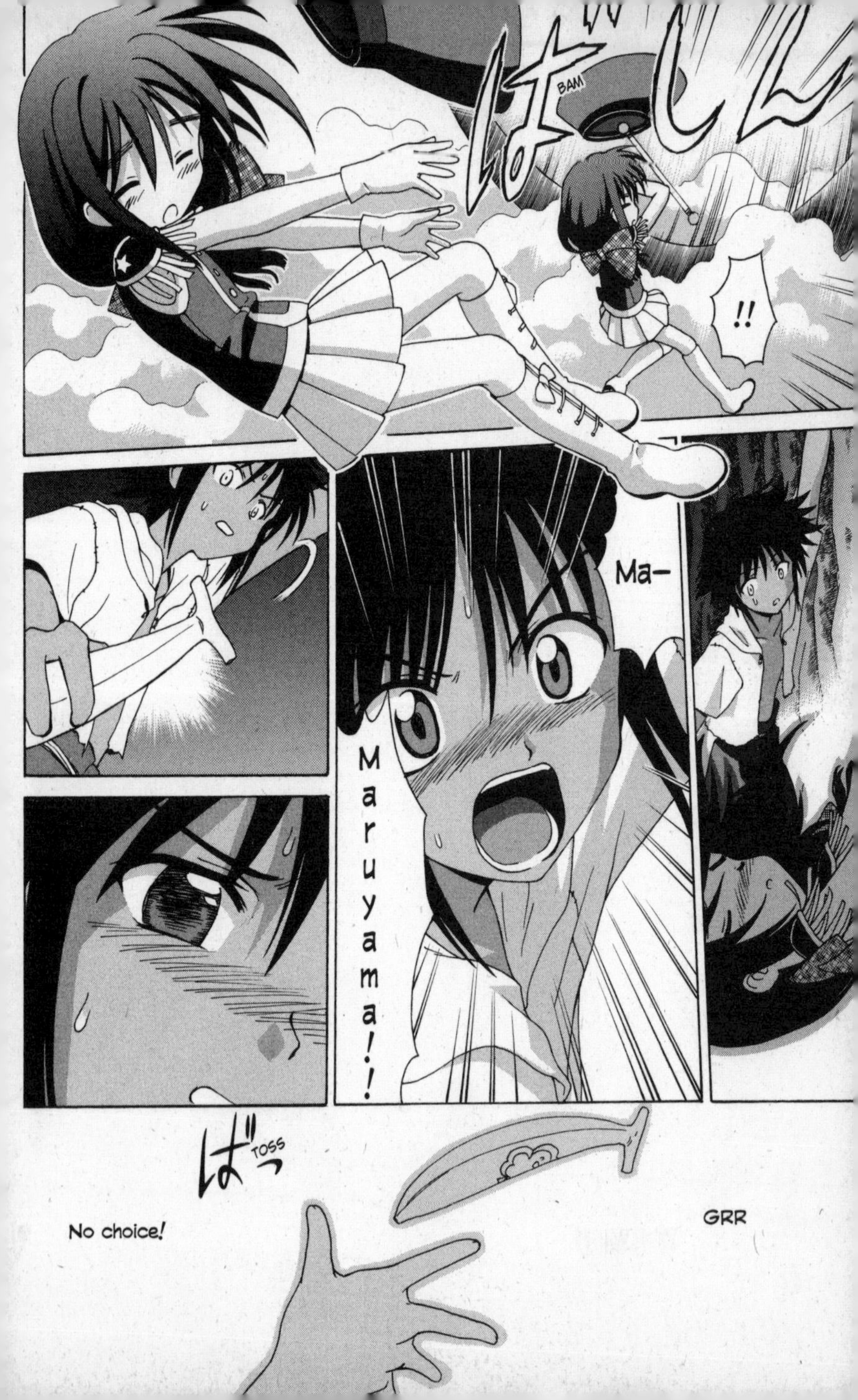
ばしん
BAM
!!
Ma—
Maruyama!!
GRR
ばっ
TOSS
No choice!

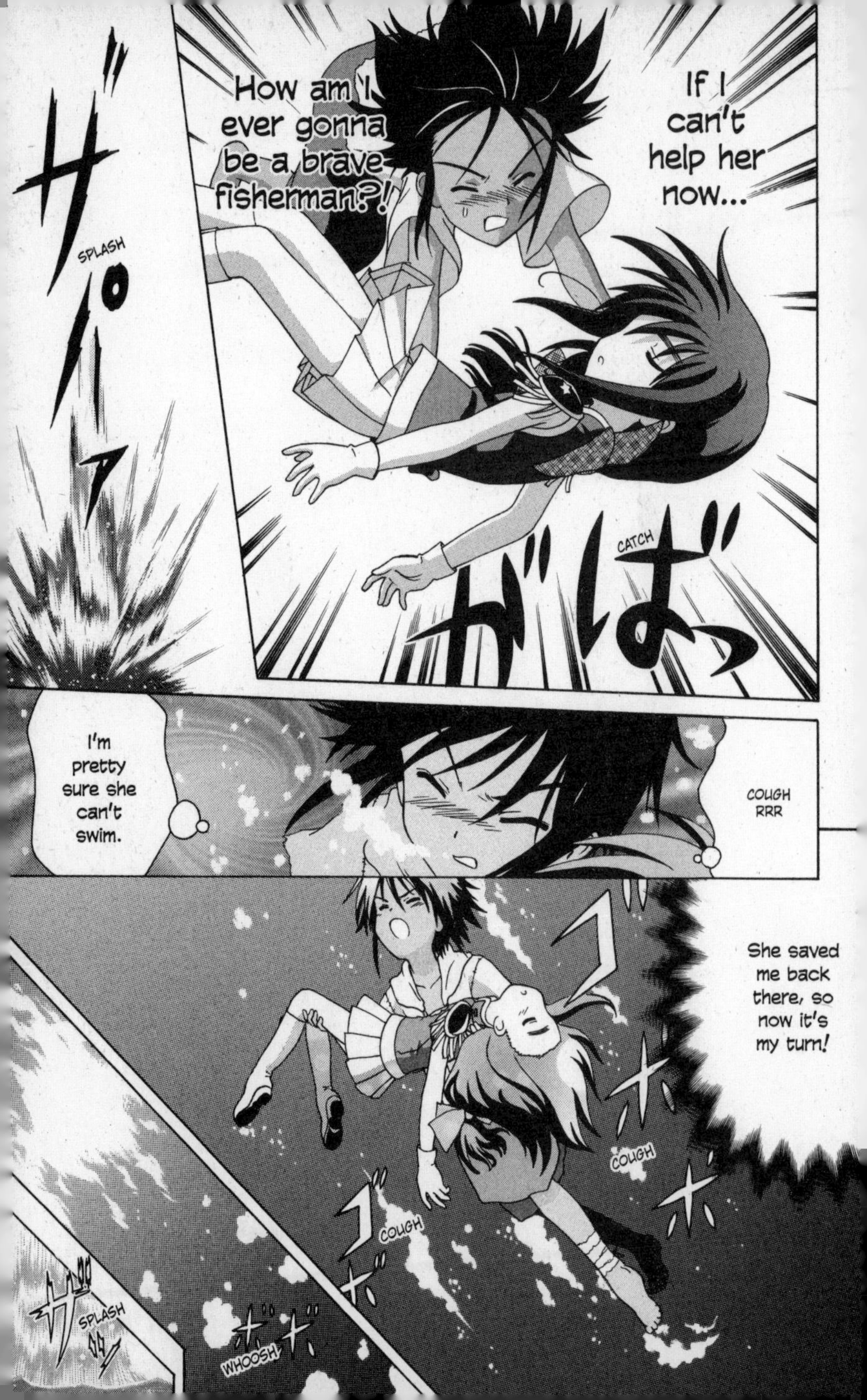
If I can't help her now...
How am I ever gonna be a brave fisherman?!
CATCH
がばっ
SPLASH
COUGH RRR
I'm pretty sure she can't swim.
She saved me back there, so now it's my turn!
COUGH
COUGH
WHOOSH
SPLASH

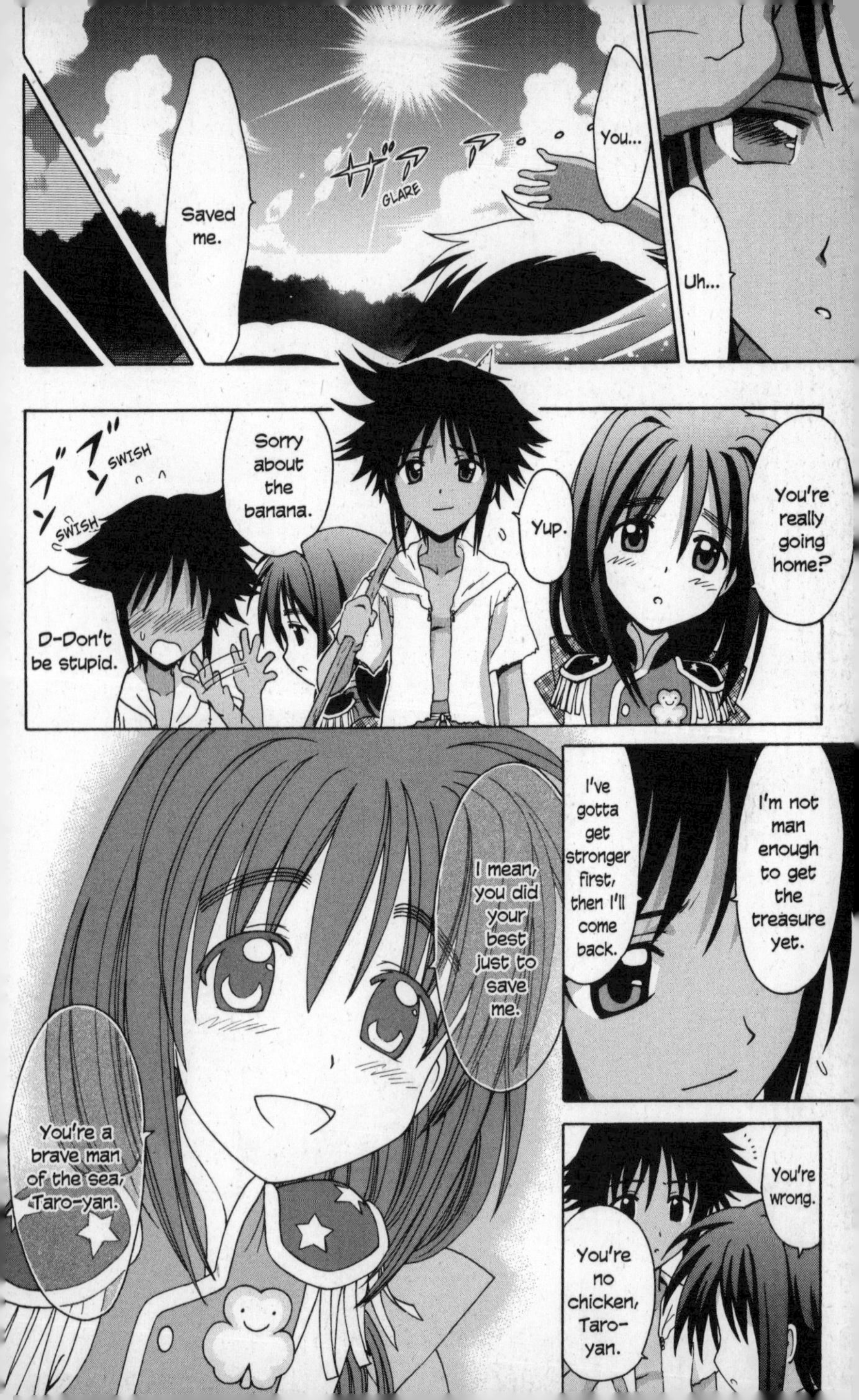
You...
Uh...
GLARE
Saved me.
You're really going home?
Yup.
Sorry about the banana.
SWISH
SWISH
D-Don't be stupid.
I'm not man enough to get the treasure yet.
I've gotta get stronger first, then I'll come back.
You're wrong.
You're no chicken, Taro-yan.
I mean, you did your best just to save me.
You're a brave man of the sea, Taro-yan.

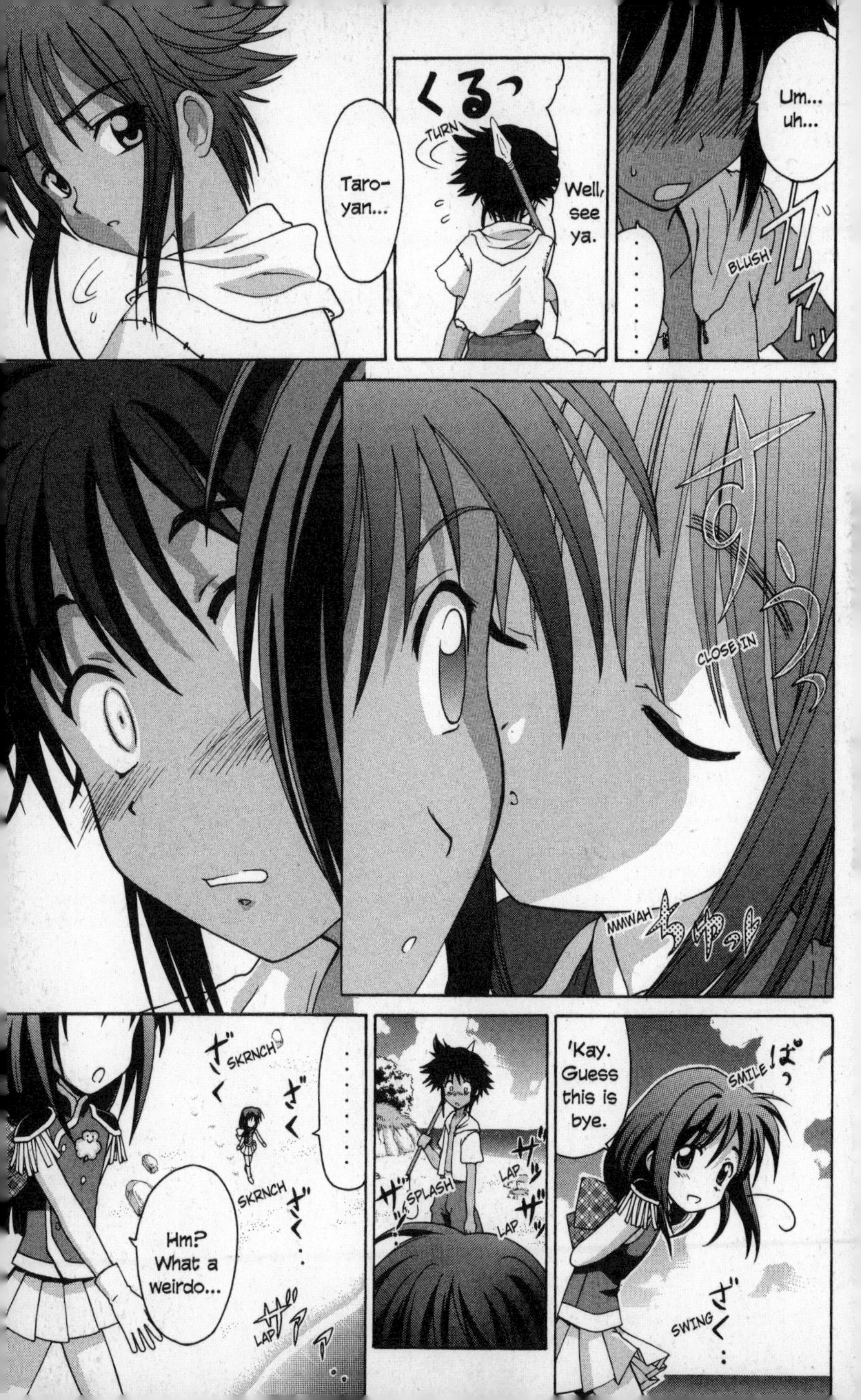
Um... uh...
BLUSH
...
くるっ
TURN
Well, see ya.
Taro-yan...
CLOSE IN
MMWAH
'Kay. Guess this is bye.
SMILE
SWING
SPLASH
LAP
LAP
......
SKRNCH
SKRNCH
Hm? What a weirdo...
LAP

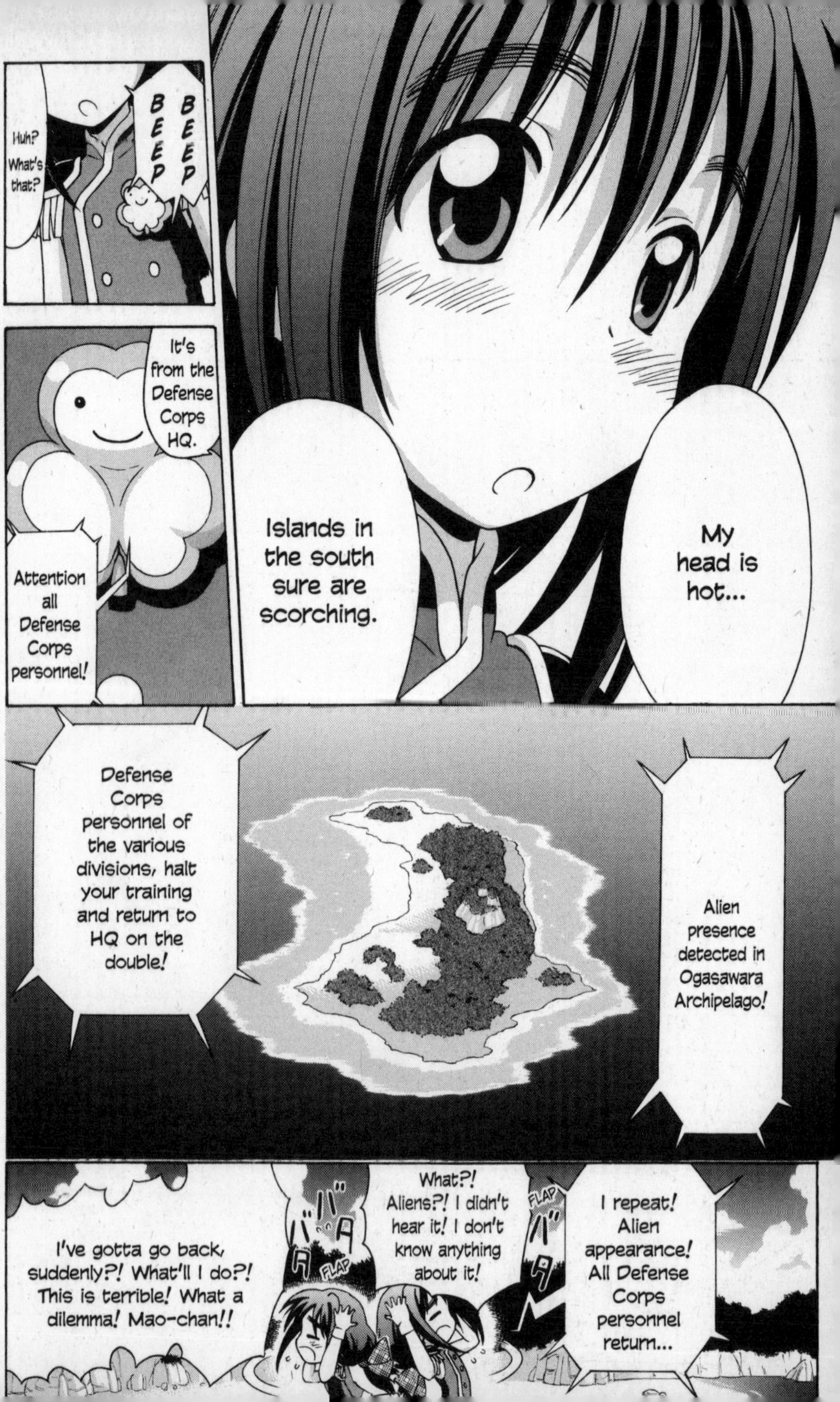

My head is hot...
Islands in the south sure are scorching.
BEEP BEEP
Huh? What's that?
It's from the Defense Corps HQ.
Attention all Defense Corps personnel!
Alien presence detected in Ogasawara Archipelago!
Defense Corps personnel of the various divisions, halt your training and return to HQ on the double!
I repeat! Alien appearance! All Defense Corps personnel return...
FLAP
What?! Aliens?! I didn't hear it! I don't know anything about it!
FLAP
I've gotta go back, suddenly?! What'll I do?! This is terrible! What a dilemma! Mao-chan!!

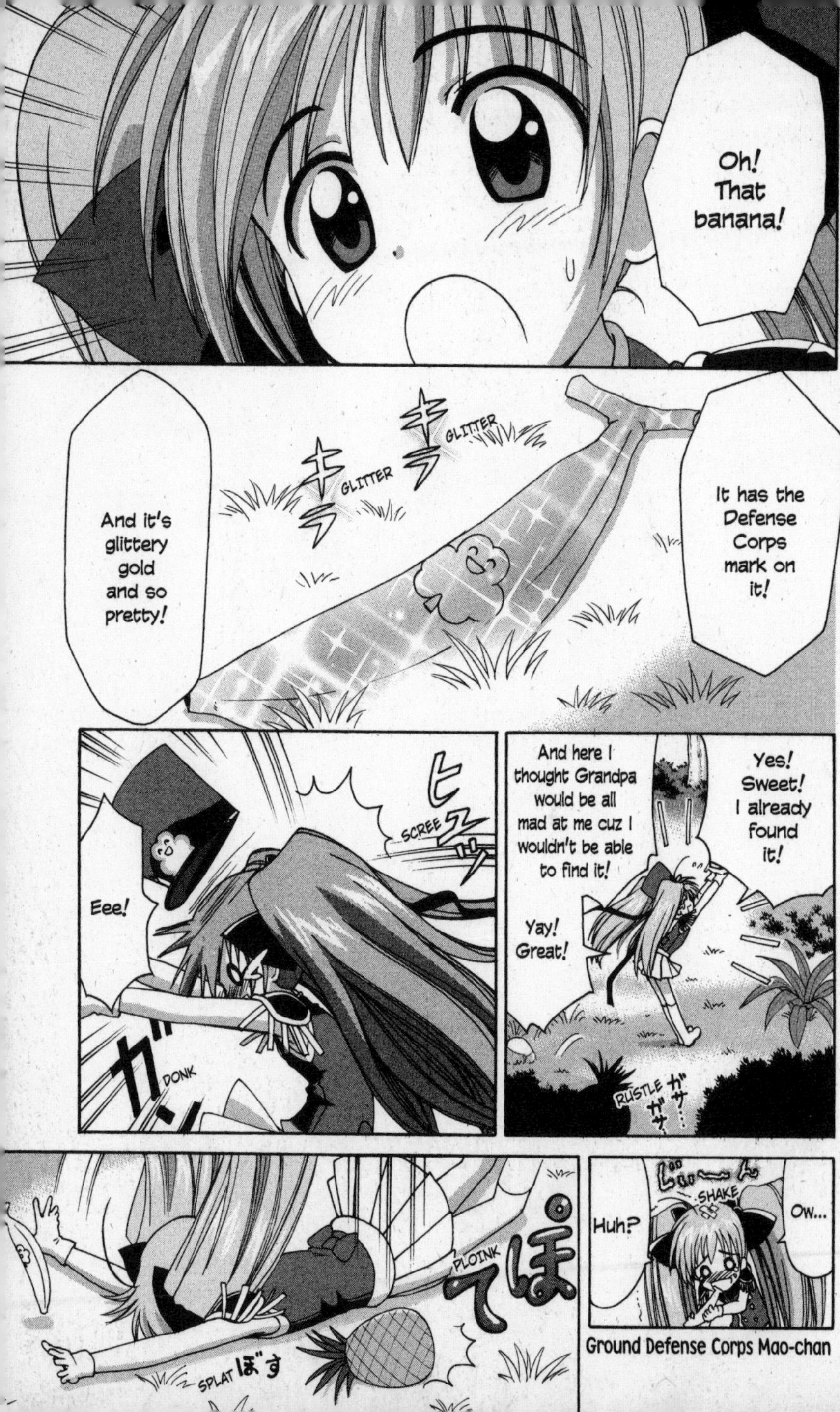
Oh! That banana!
It has the Defense Corps mark on it!
GLITTER
GLITTER
And it's glittery gold and so pretty!
Yes! Sweet! I already found it!
And here I thought Grandpa would be all mad at me cuz I wouldn't be able to find it!
Yay! Great!
RUSTLE
SCREE
Eee!
DONK
SHAKE
Ow...
Huh?
PLOINK
SPLAT

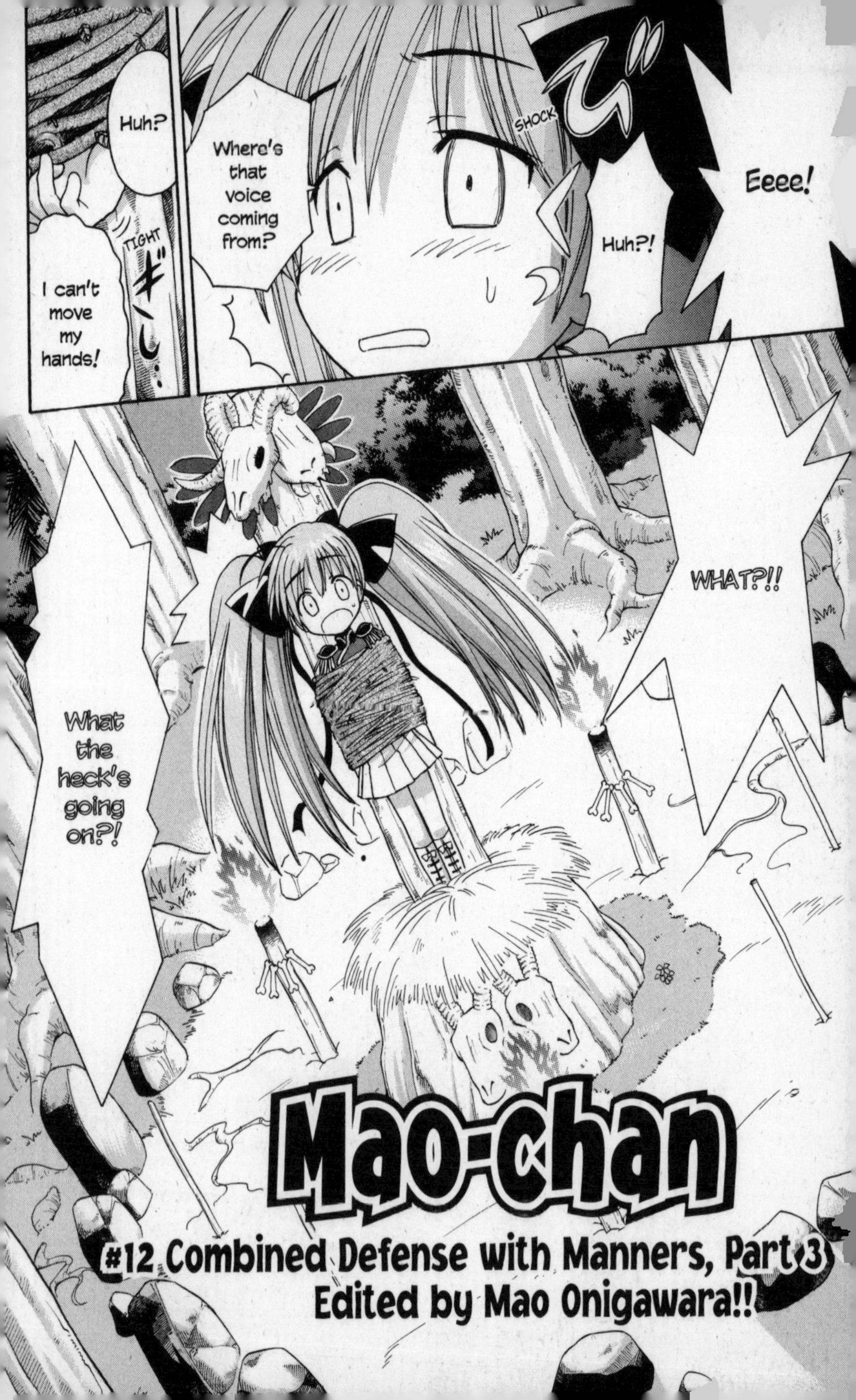
Eeee!
SHOCK
Huh?!
Where's that voice coming from?
Huh?
TIGHT
I can't move my hands!
WHAT?!!
What the heck's going on?!
Mao-chan
#12 Combined Defense with Manners, Part 3
Edited by Mao Onigawara!!

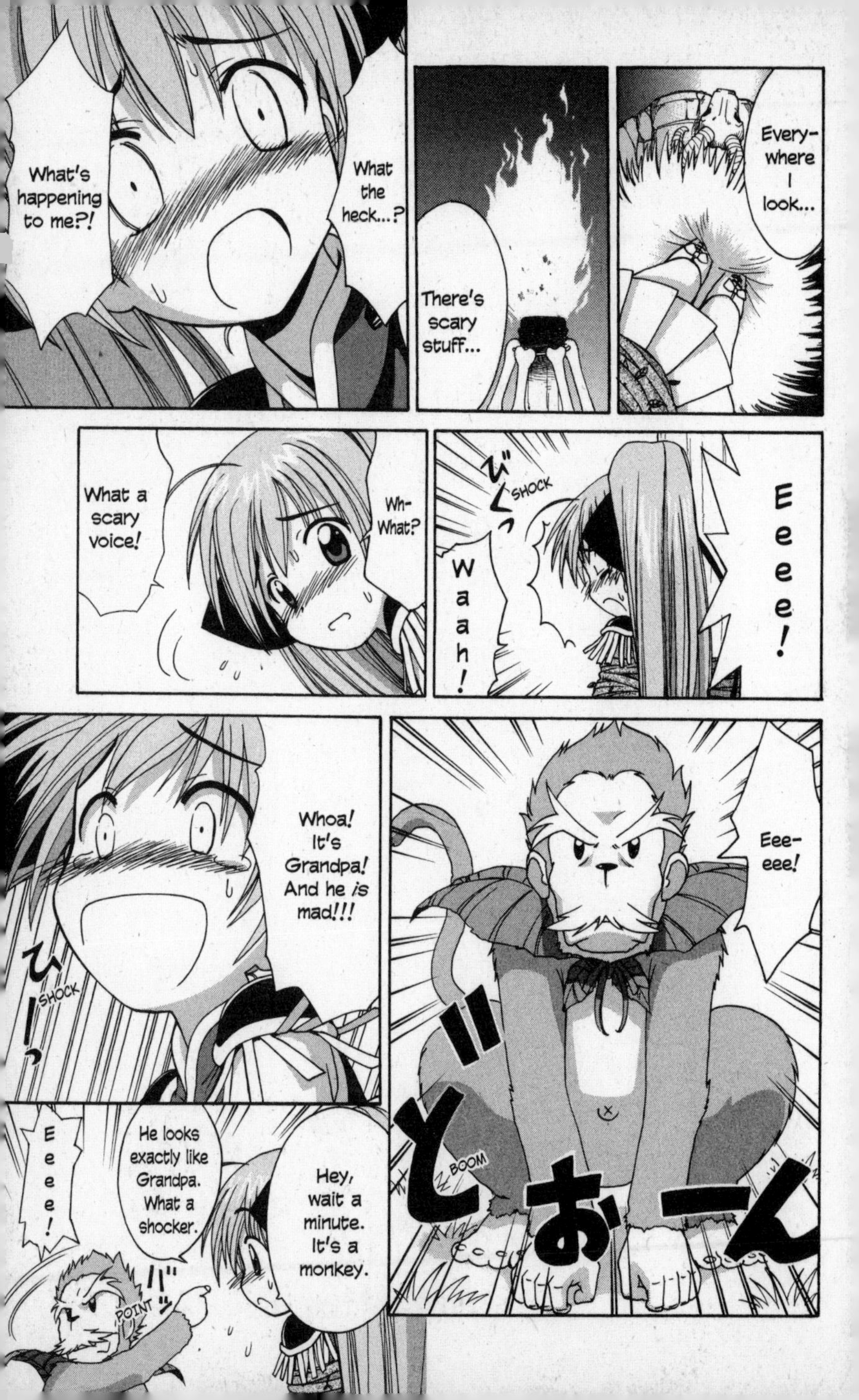

Every-where I look...
There's scary stuff...
What the heck...?
What's happening to me?!
Eeee!
びくっ
SHOCK
Waah!
Wh-What?
What a scary voice!
Eee-eee!
どぉーん
BOOM
Whoa! It's Grandpa! And he *is* mad!!!
ひーっ
SHOCK
Hey, wait a minute. It's a monkey.
He looks exactly like Grandpa. What a shocker.
バッ
POINT
Eeee!

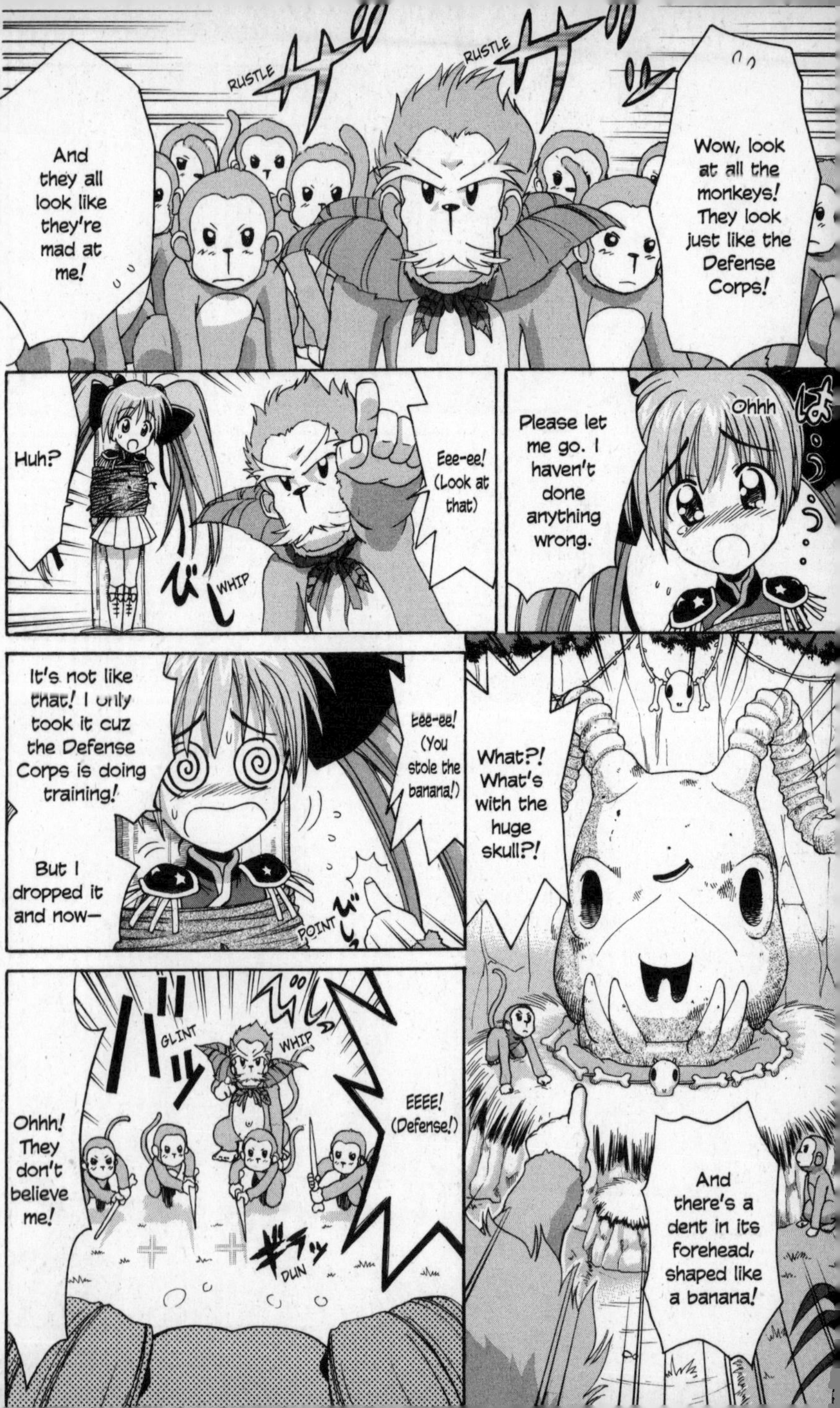
Wow, look at all the monkeys! They look just like the Defense Corps!
RUSTLE
RUSTLE
And they all look like they're mad at me!
Ohhh
Please let me go. I haven't done anything wrong.
Eee-ee! (Look at that)
WHIP
Huh?
What?! What's with the huge skull?!
And there's a dent in its forehead, shaped like a banana!
Eee-ee! (You stole the banana!)
It's not like that! I only took it cuz the Defense Corps is doing training!
But I dropped it and now—
POINT
EEEE! (Defense!)
WHIP
GLINT
Ohhh! They don't believe me!
DUN

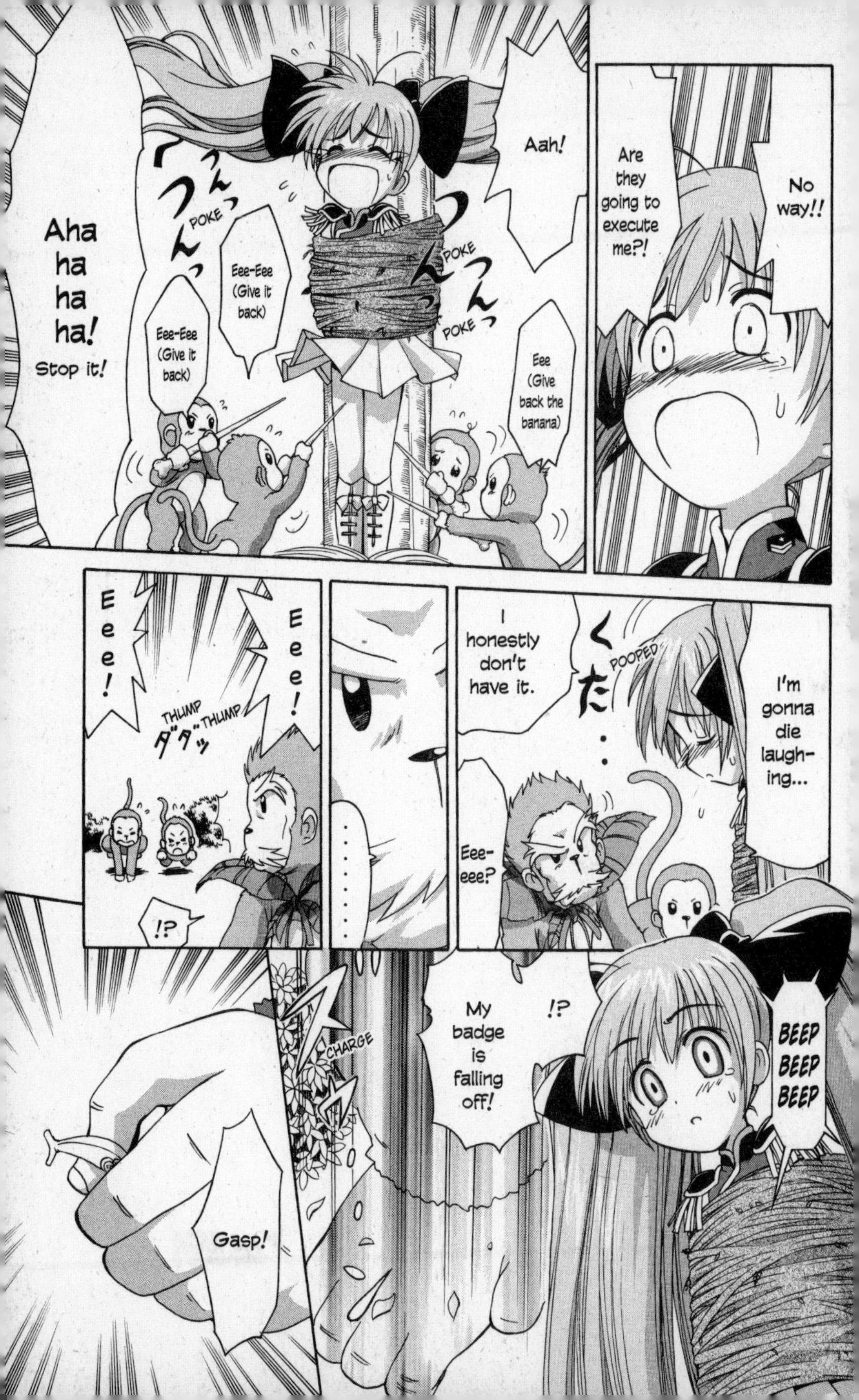
No way!!
Are they going to execute me?!
Aah!
つんっ POKE
つんっ POKE
つんっ POKE
Eee (Give back the banana)
Eee-Eee (Give it back)
Eee-Eee (Give it back)
Aha ha ha ha! Stop it!
I'm gonna die laughing...
くた... POOPED
I honestly don't have it.
Eee-eee?
......
Eee!
Eee!
THUMP ダダッ THUMP
!?
BEEP BEEP BEEP
!?
My badge is falling off!
CHARGE
Gasp!

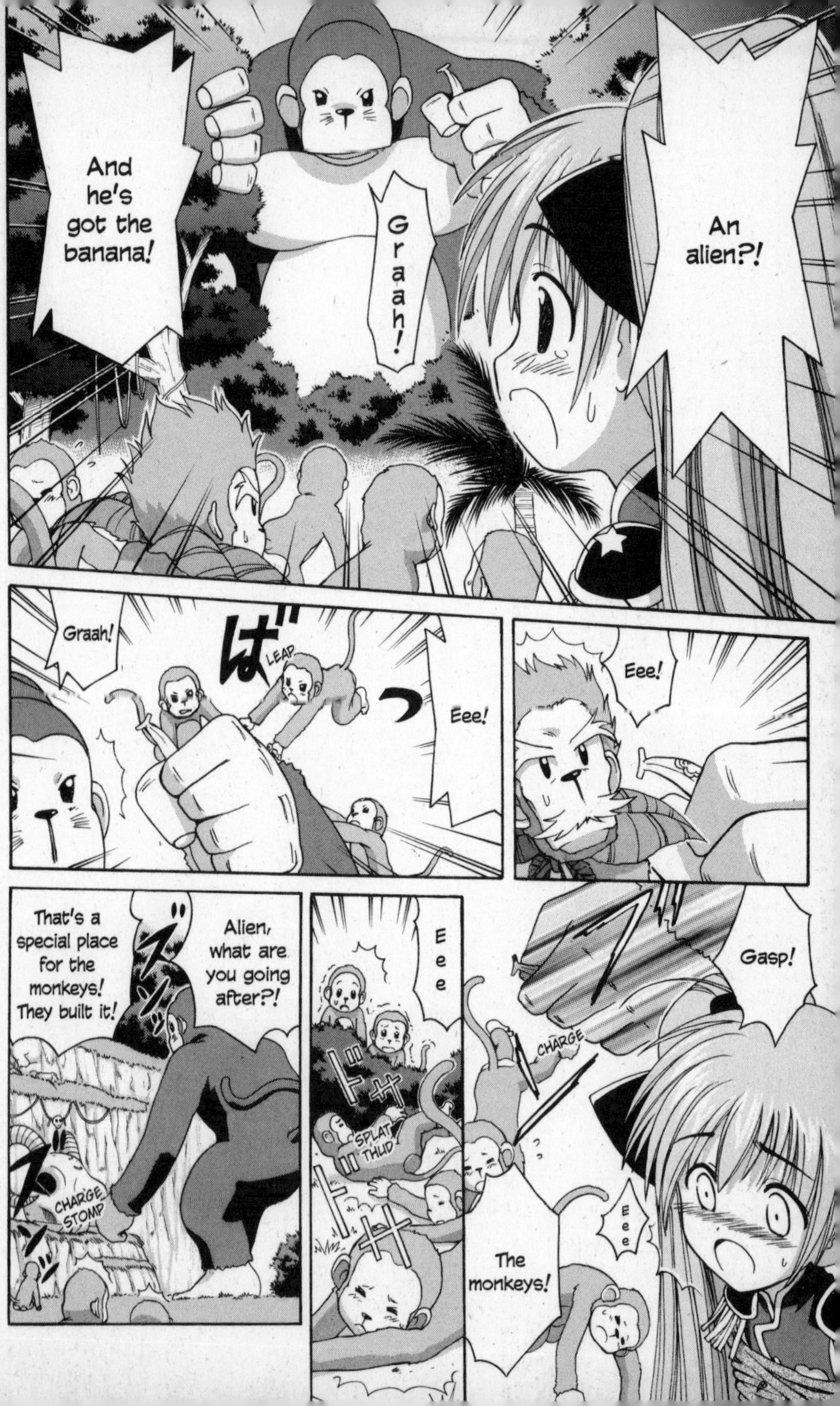
An alien?!
Graah!
And he's got the banana!
Eee!
Eee!
LEAP
ば
Graah!
Gasp!
CHARGE
Eee
The monkeys!
Eee
SPLAT
THUD
Alien, what are you going after?!
That's a special place for the monkeys! They built it!
CHARGE
STOMP

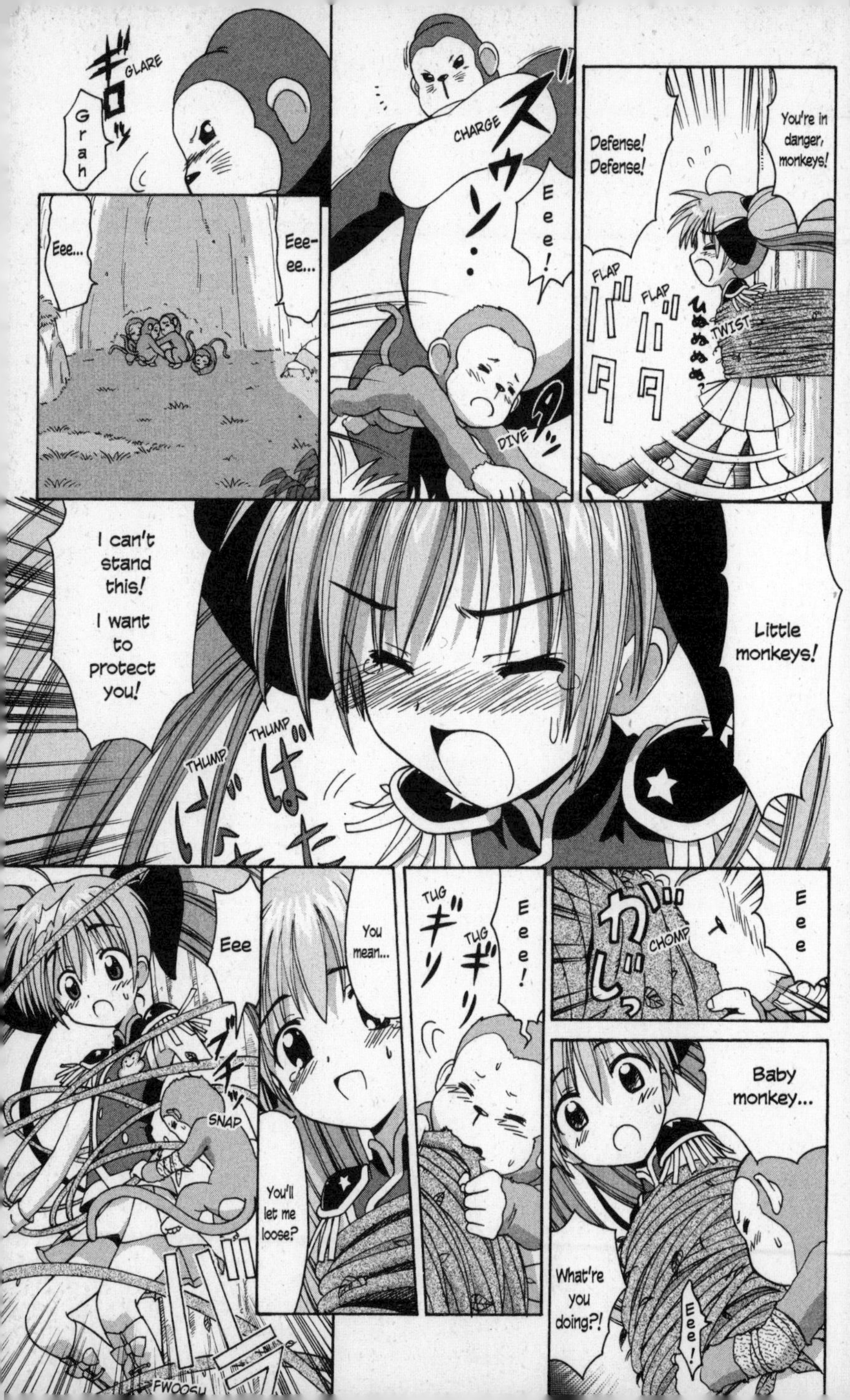

You're in danger, monkeys!
Defense! Defense!
TWIST
FLAP
FLAP
CHARGE
Eee!
DIVE
GLARE
Grah
Eee-ee...
Eee...
Little monkeys!
I can't stand this!
I want to protect you!
THUMP
THUMP
Eee
CHOMP
Baby monkey...
Eee!
What're you doing?!
Eee!
TUG
TUG
You mean...
You'll let me loose?
Eee
SNAP
FWOOSH

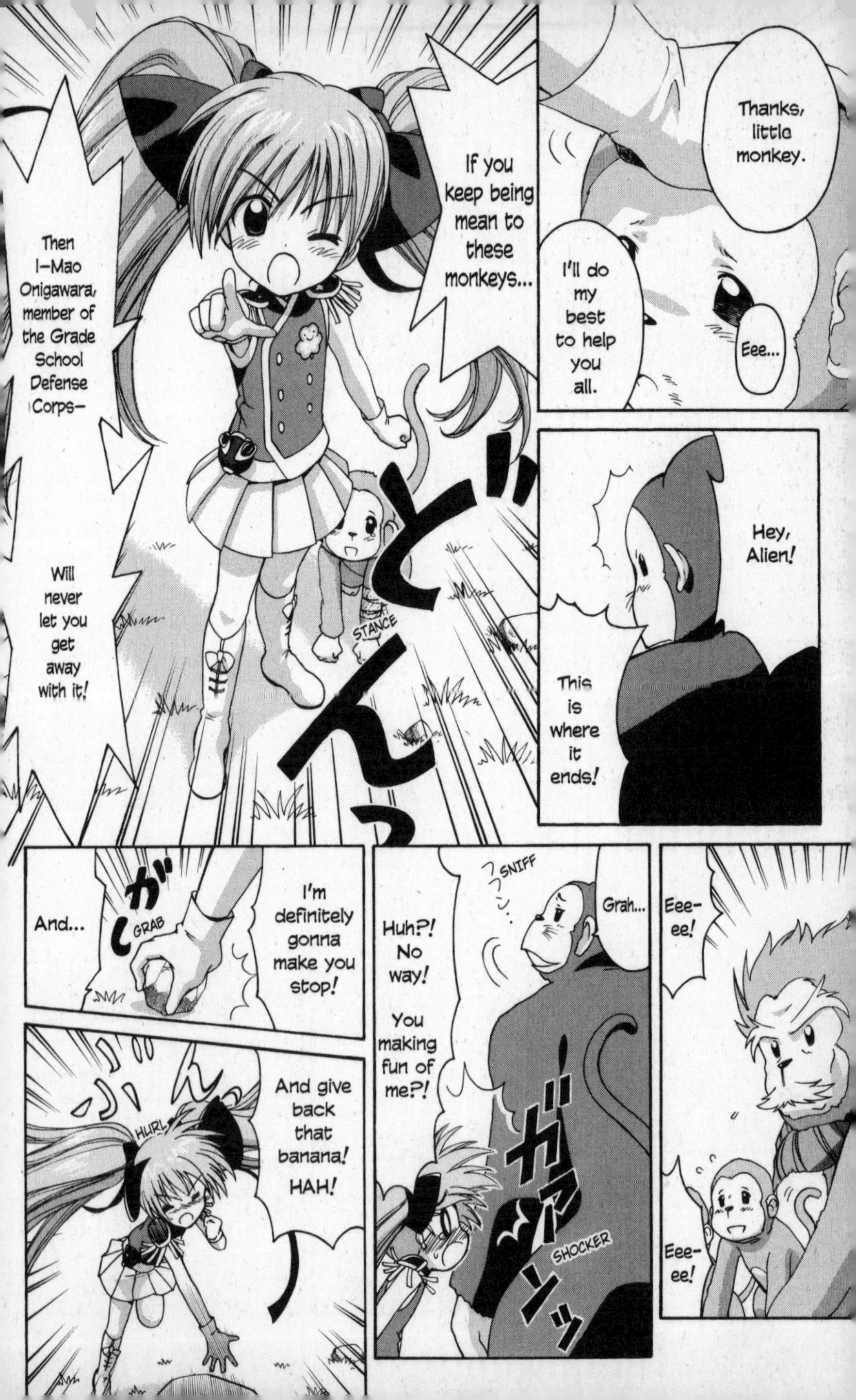
Thanks, little monkey.
I'll do my best to help you all.
Eee...
Hey, Alien!
This is where it ends!
If you keep being mean to these monkeys...
Then I—Mao Onigawara, member of the Grade School Defense Corps—
STANCE
Will never let you get away with it!
Eee-ee!
Eee-ee!
Grah...
SNIFF
Huh?! No way!
You making fun of me?!
SHOCKER
I'm definitely gonna make you stop!
GRAB
And...
And give back that banana! HAH!
HURL

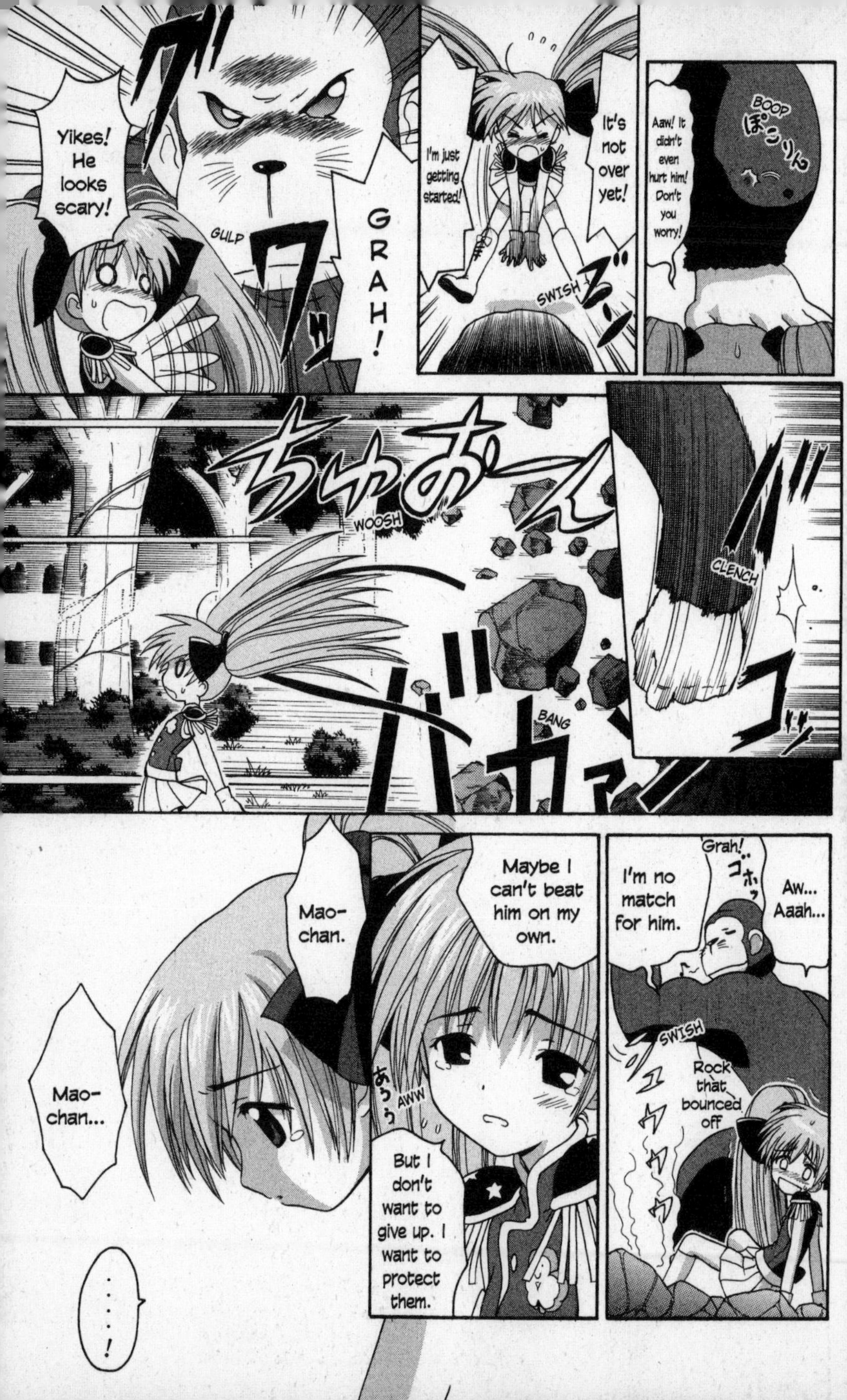
BOOP
ぽこりん
Aaw! It didn't even hurt him! Don't you worry!
It's not over yet!
I'm just getting started!
SWISH
Yikes! He looks scary!
GULP
GRAH!
CLENCH
ちゅおーん
WOOSH
BANG
Grah!
Aw... Aaah...
I'm no match for him.
SWISH
Rock that bounced off
Maybe I can't beat him on my own.
Mao-chan.
AWW
But I don't want to give up. I want to protect them.
Mao-chan...
....!

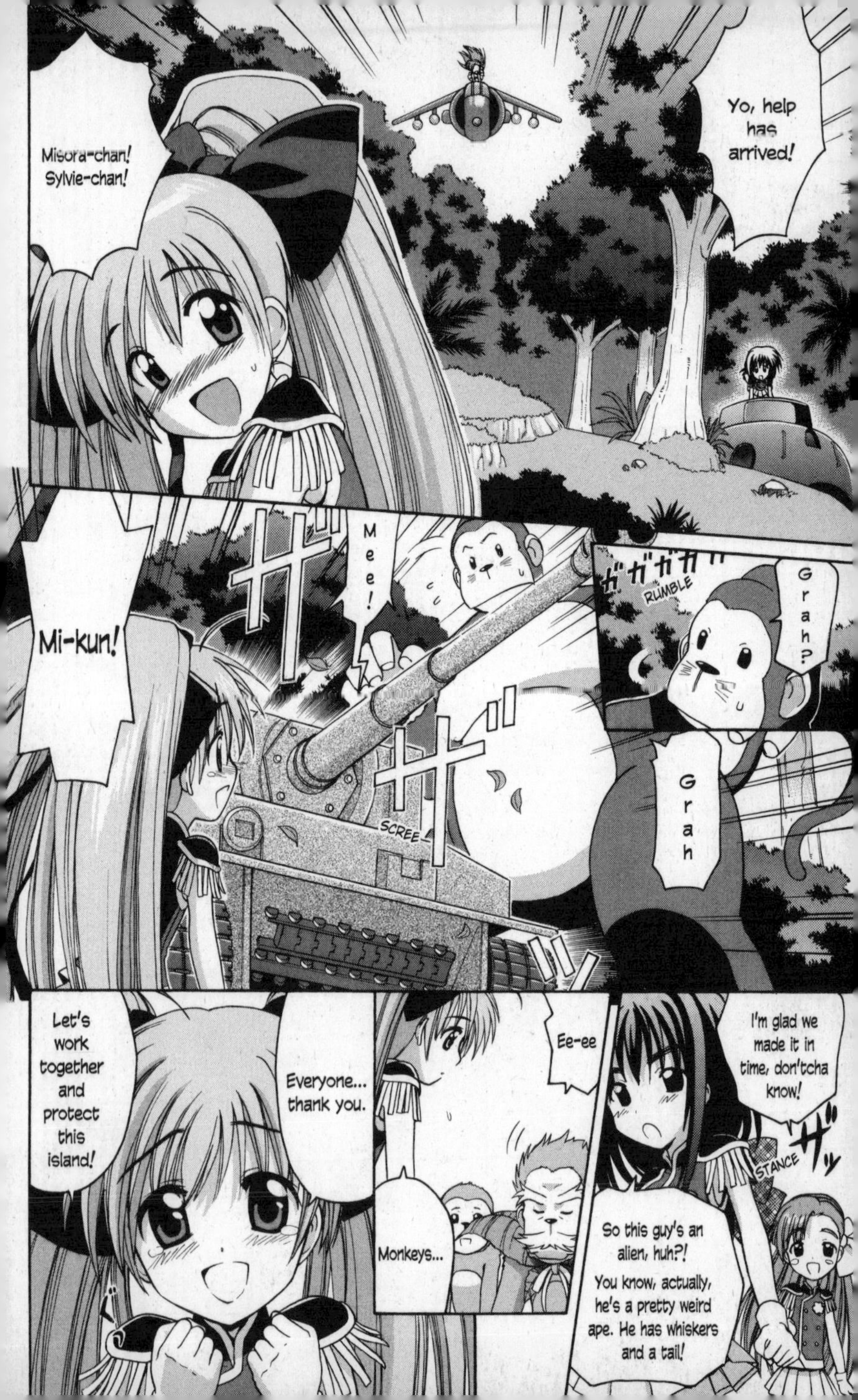

Yo, help has arrived!
Misora-chan! Sylvie-chan!
RUMBLE
Grah?
Grah
Mee!
Mi-kun!
SCREE
I'm glad we made it in time, don'tcha know!
STANCE
So this guy's an alien, huh?!
You know, actually, he's a pretty weird ape. He has whiskers and a tail!
Ee-ee
Monkeys...
Everyone... thank you.
Let's work together and protect this island!

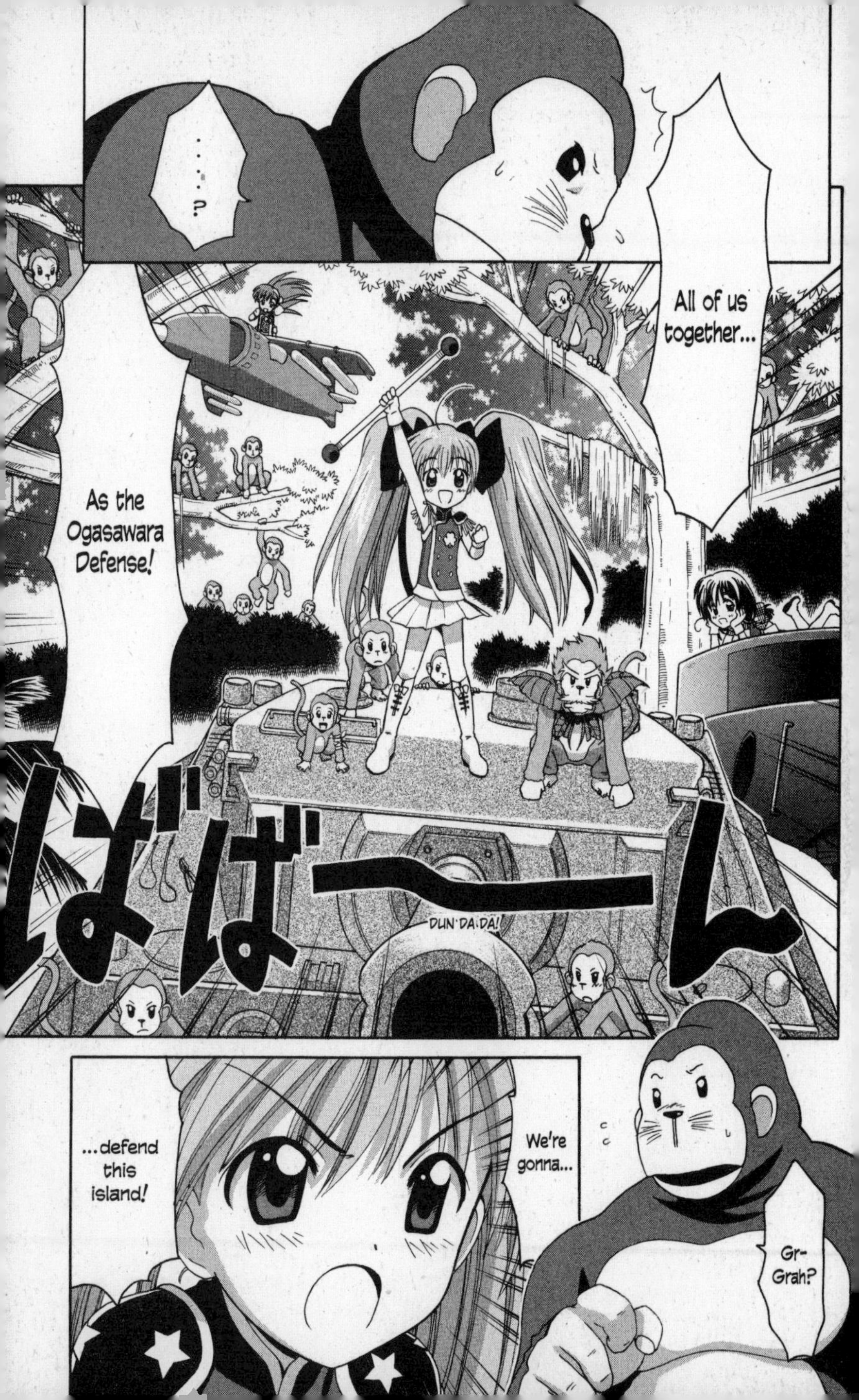
All of us together...
...?
As the Ogasawara Defense!
ばばーーん
DUN DA DA!
Gr-Grah?
We're gonna...
...defend this island!

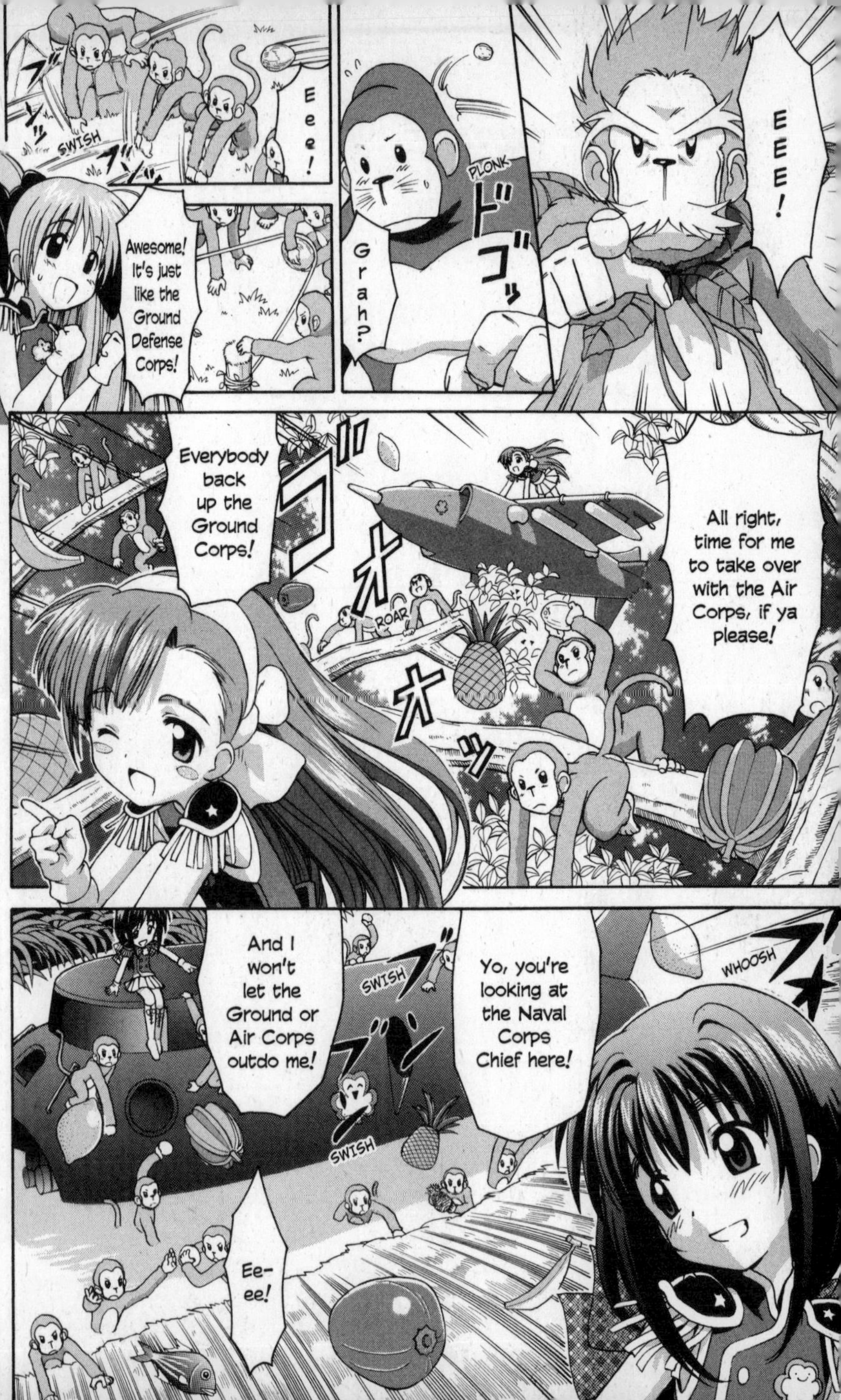
EEE!
PLONK
Grah?
SWISH
Eee!
Awesome! It's just like the Ground Defense Corps!
All right, time for me to take over with the Air Corps, if ya please!
Everybody back up the Ground Corps!
ROAR
WHOOSH
Yo, you're looking at the Naval Corps Chief here!
SWISH
And I won't let the Ground or Air Corps outdo me!
SWISH
Ee-ee!

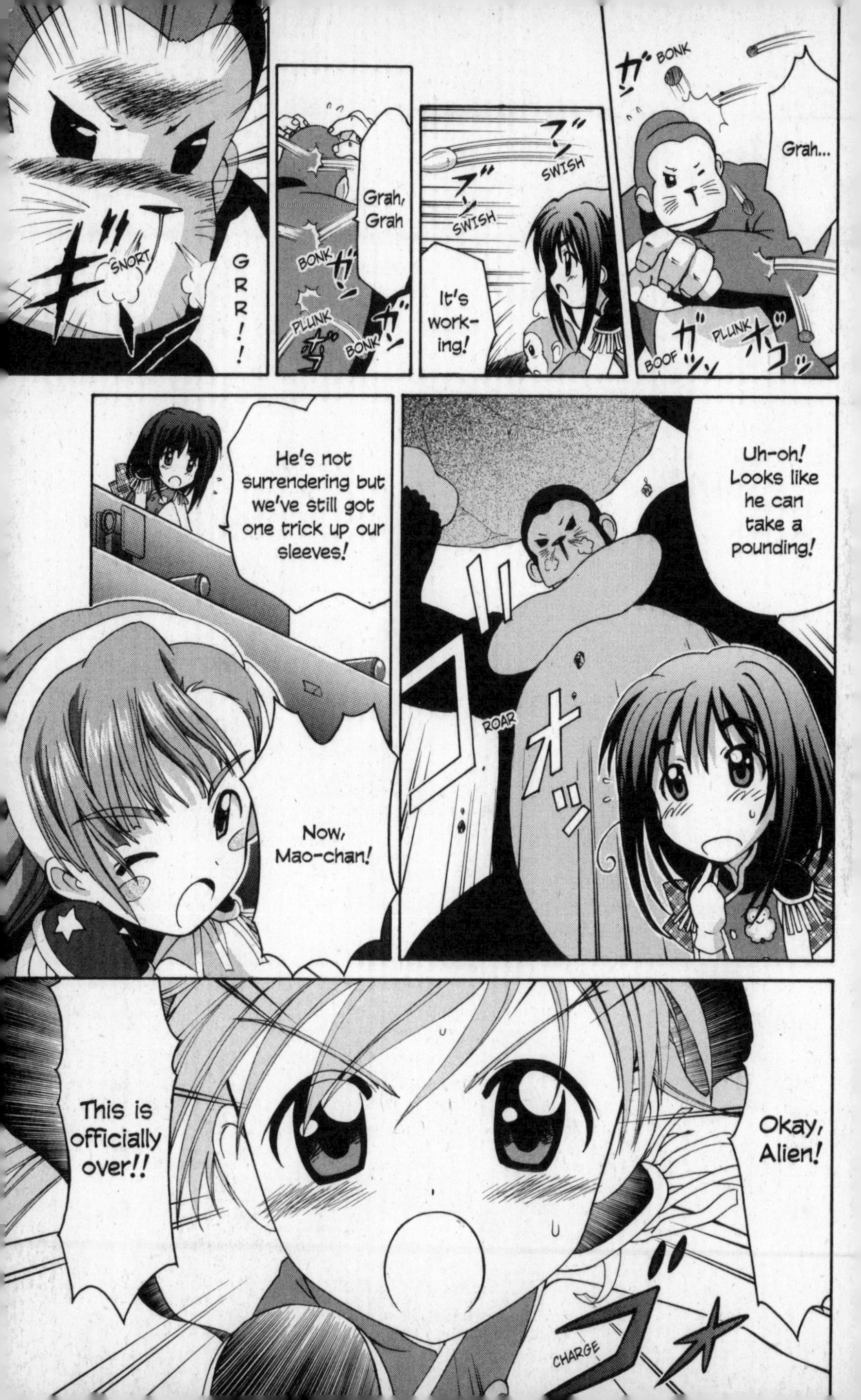

BONK
Grah...
PLUNK
BOOF
SWISH
SWISH
It's working!
Grah, Grah
BONK
PLUNK
BONK
GRR!!
SNORT
Uh-oh! Looks like he can take a pounding!
ROAR
He's not surrendering but we've still got one trick up our sleeves!
Now, Mao-chan!
Okay, Alien!
This is officially over!!
CHARGE

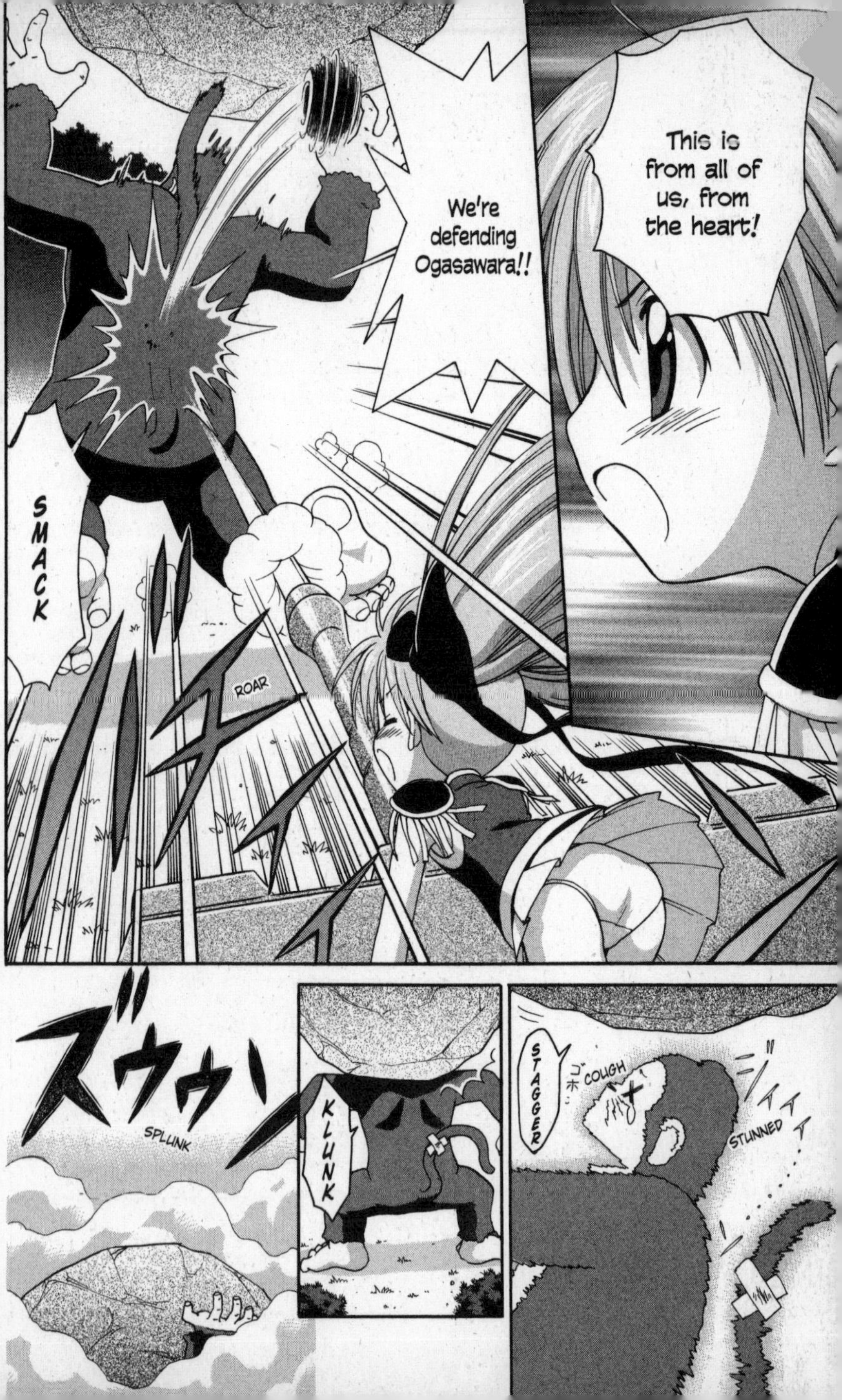
This is from all of us, from the heart!
We're defending Ogasawara!!
SMACK
ROAR
STAGGER
COUGH
STUNNED
KLUNK
SPLUNK

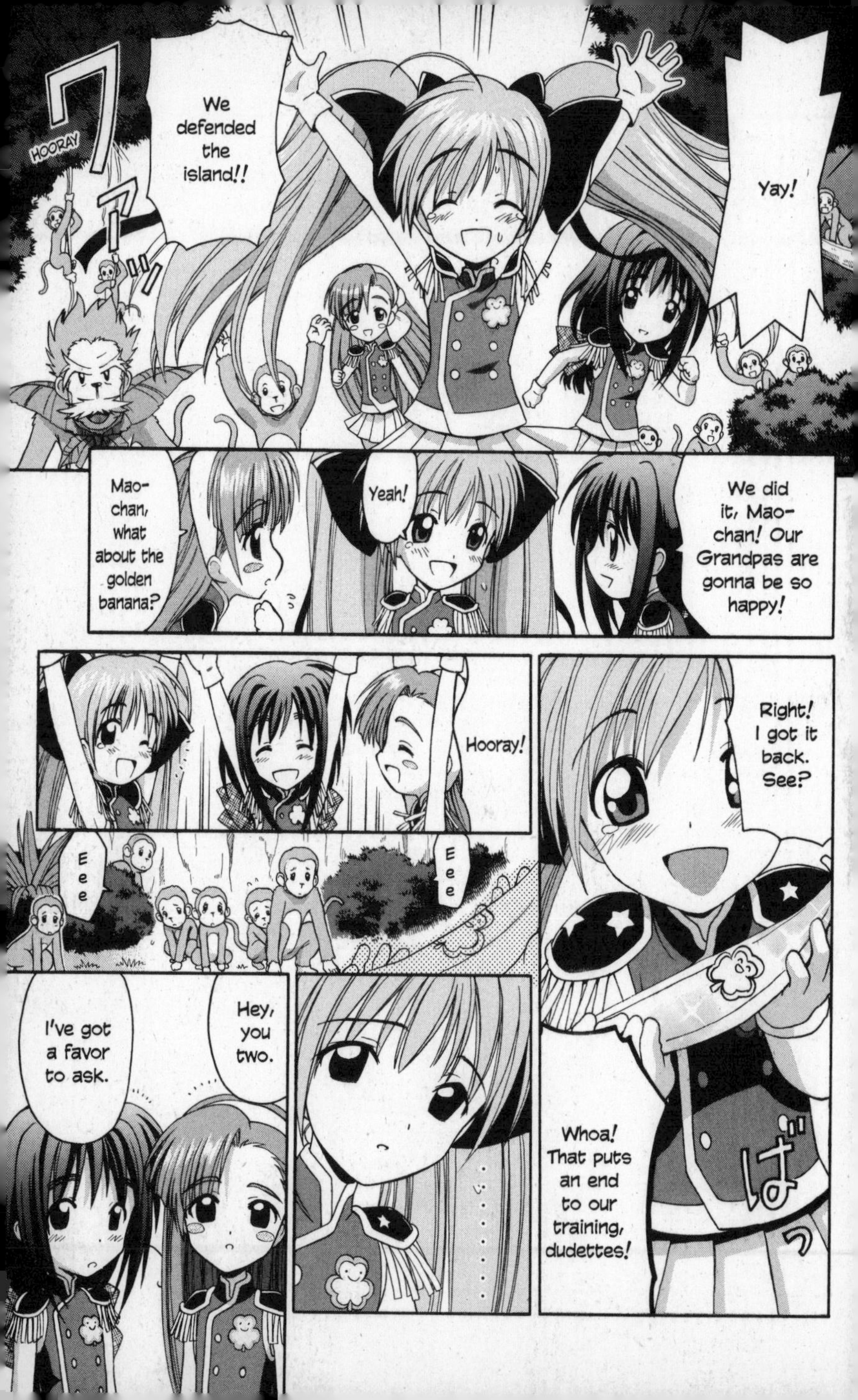
Yay!
We defended the island!!
HOORAY
We did it, Mao-chan! Our Grandpas are gonna be so happy!
Yeah!
Mao-chan, what about the golden banana?
Right! I got it back. See?
Whoa! That puts an end to our training, dudettes!
ばっ
Hooray!
Eee
Eee
Hey, you two.
I've got a favor to ask.

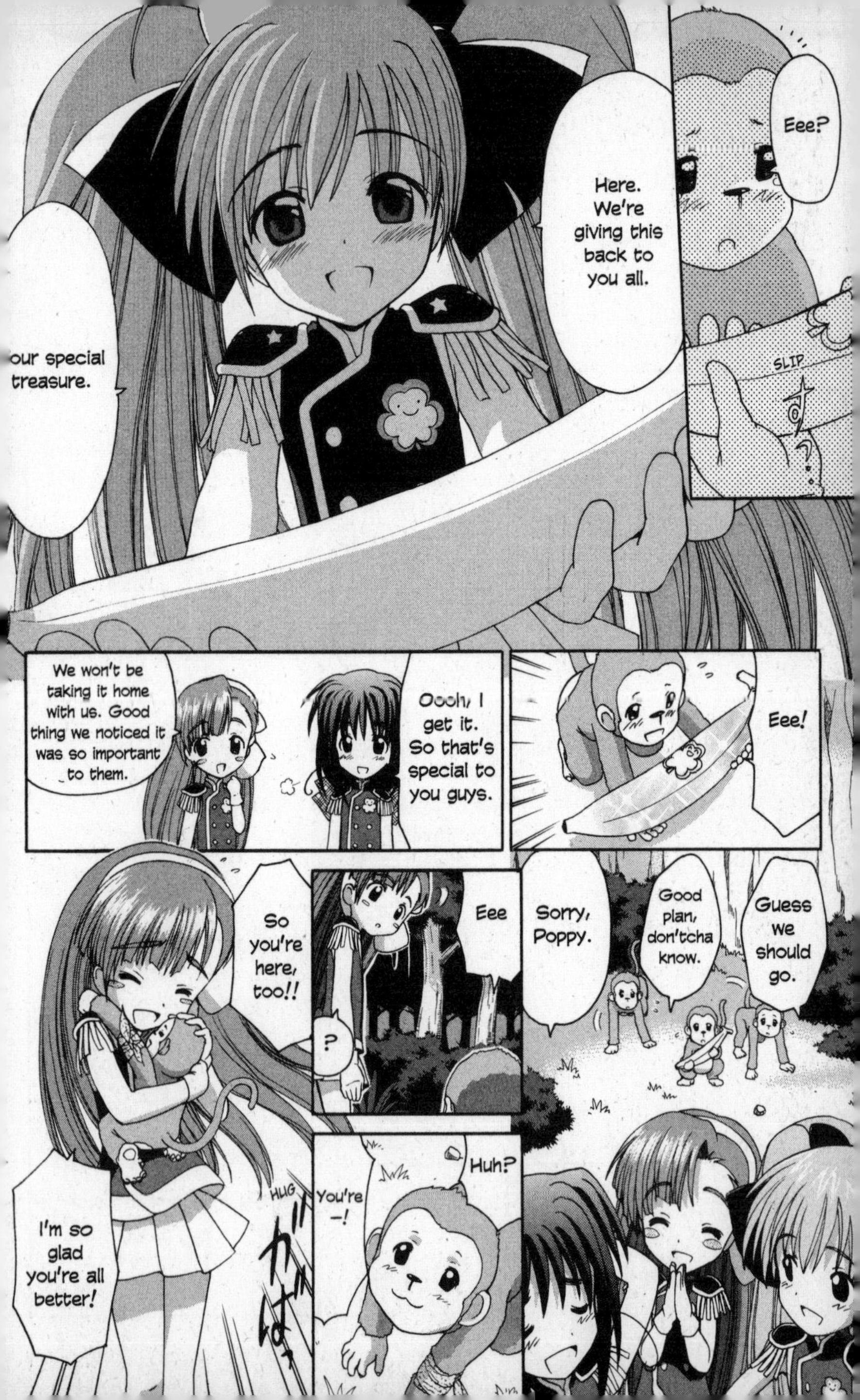
Eee?
SLIP
Here. We're giving this back to you all.
our special treasure.
Eee!
Oooh, I get it. So that's special to you guys.
We won't be taking it home with us. Good thing we noticed it was so important to them.
Guess we should go.
Good plan, don'tcha know.
Sorry, Poppy.
Eee
?
So you're here, too!!
Huh?
You're—!
HUG
I'm so glad you're all better!

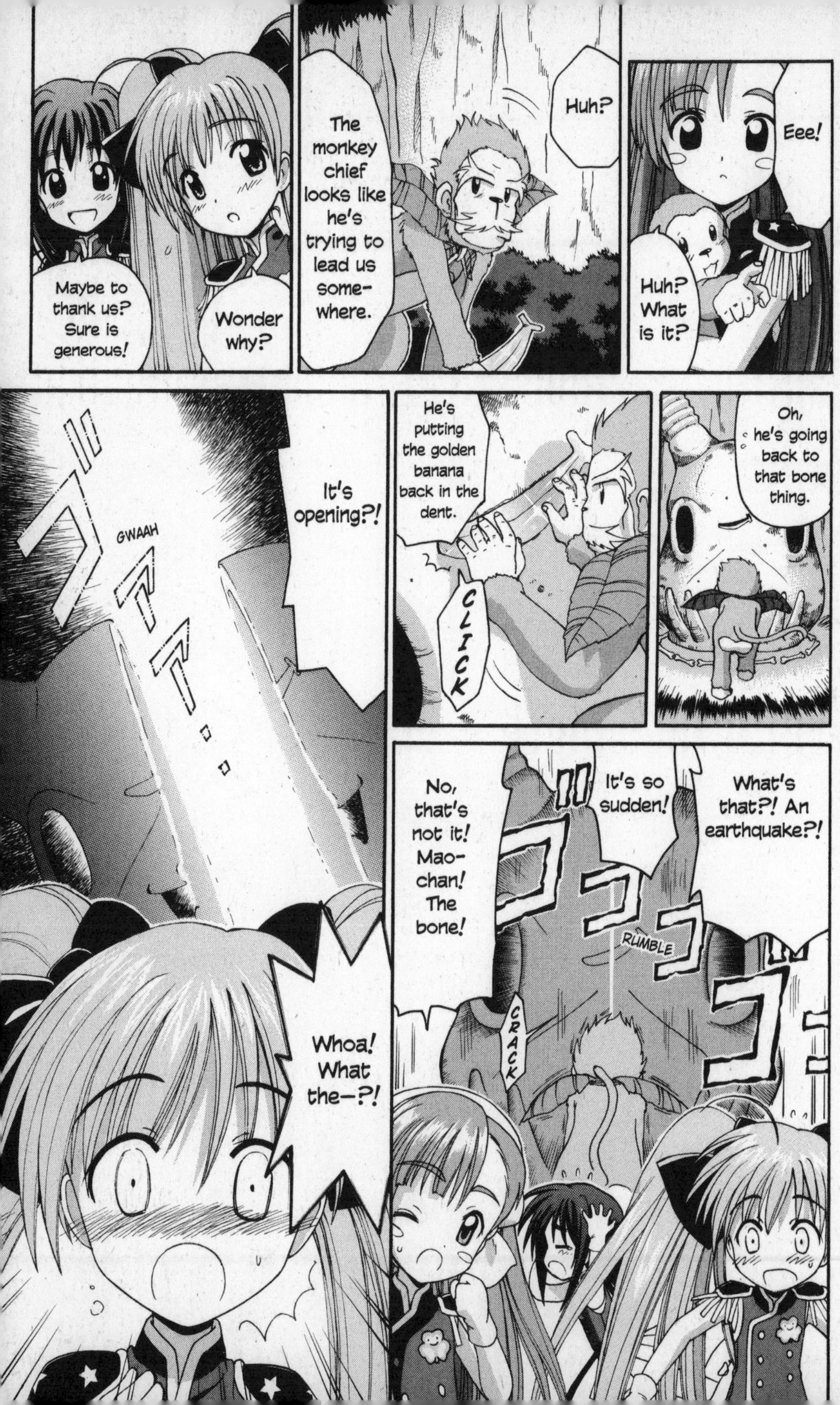
Eee!
Huh? What is it?
Huh?
The monkey chief looks like he's trying to lead us somewhere.
Wonder why?
Maybe to thank us? Sure is generous!
Oh, he's going back to that bone thing.
He's putting the golden banana back in the dent.
CLICK
What's that?! An earthquake?!
It's so sudden!
No, that's not it! Mao-chan! The bone!
RUMBLE
CRACK
It's opening?!
GWAAH
Whoa! What the–?!

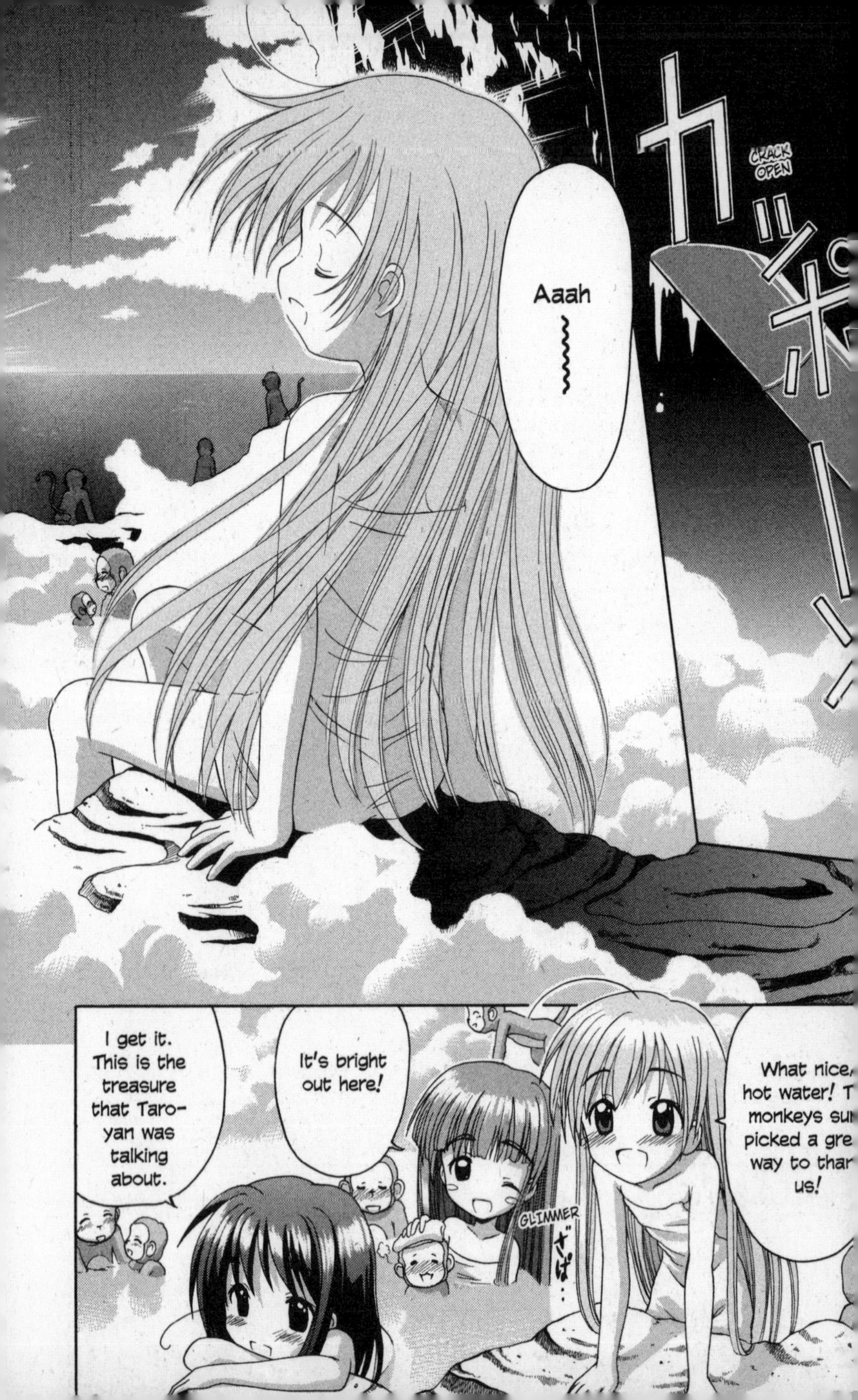

CRACK OPEN
カッポーン
Aaah ~
What nice, hot water! T monkeys su picked a gre way to thar us!
GLIMMER
ざぱ・・
It's bright out here!
I get it. This is the treasure that Taro-yan was talking about.

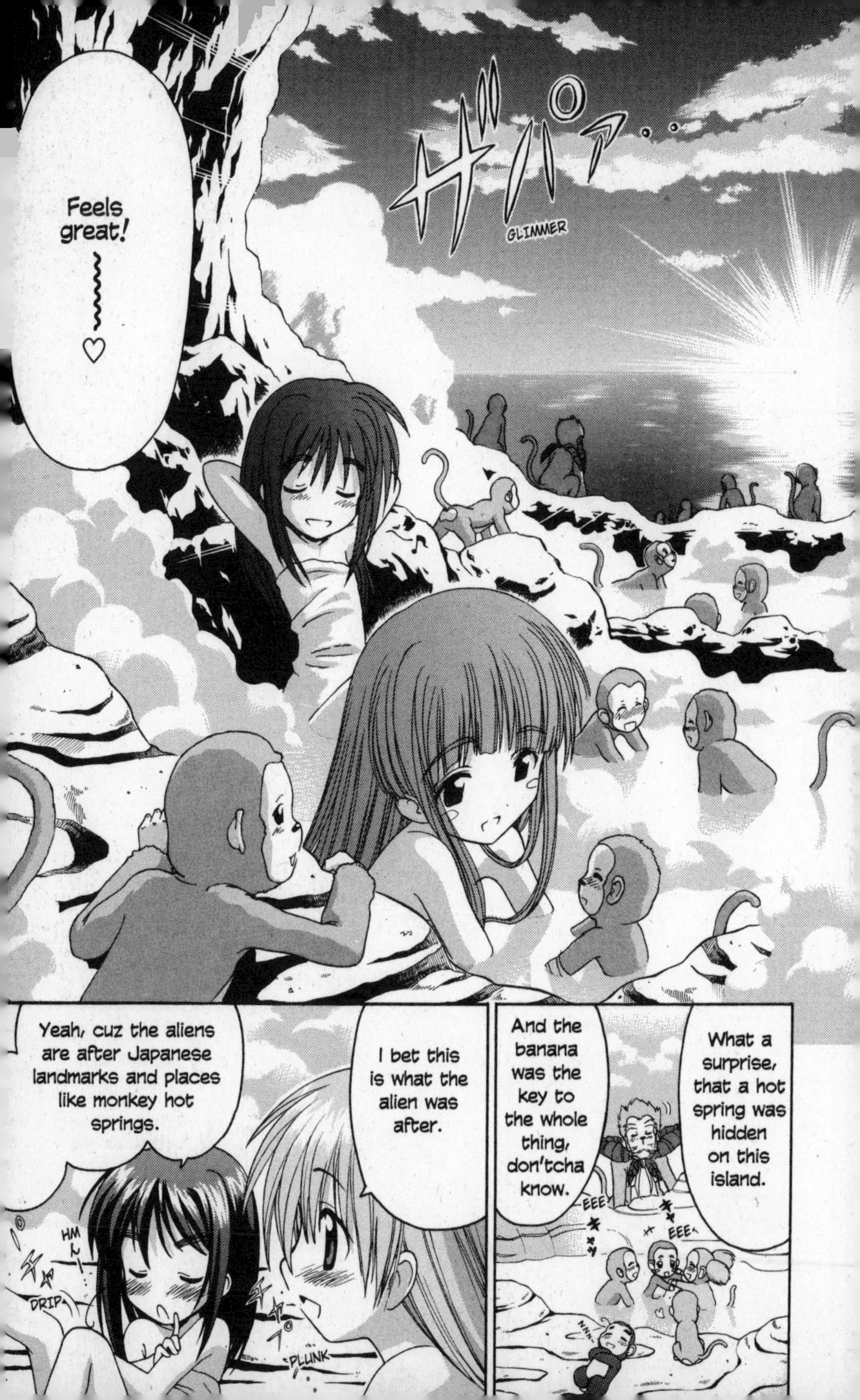
ザパァ..
GLIMMER
Feels great! ~ ♥
What a surprise, that a hot spring was hidden on this island.
And the banana was the key to the whole thing, don'tcha know.
EEE
EEE
NNN
I bet this is what the alien was after.
Yeah, cuz the aliens are after Japanese landmarks and places like monkey hot springs.
HM
DRIP
PLUNK

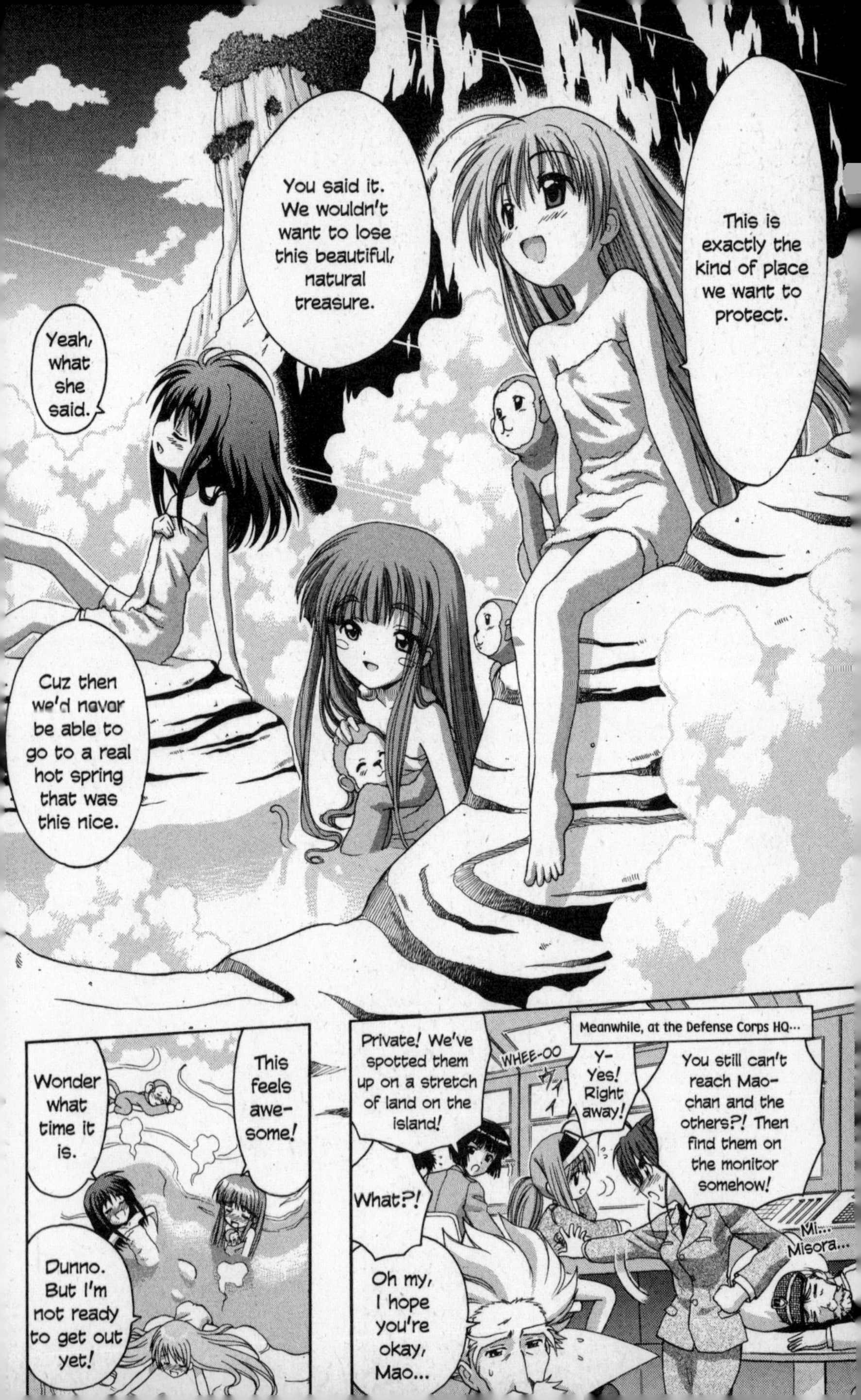
This is exactly the kind of place we want to protect.
You said it. We wouldn't want to lose this beautiful, natural treasure.
Yeah, what she said.
Cuz then we'd never be able to go to a real hot spring that was this nice.
Meanwhile, at the Defense Corps HQ...
You still can't reach Mao-chan and the others?! Then find them on the monitor somehow!
Y- Yes! Right away!
WHEE-OO
Private! We've spotted them up on a stretch of land on the island!
Mi... Misora...
What?!
Oh my, I hope you're okay, Mao...
This feels awe-some!
Wonder what time it is.
Dunno. But I'm not ready to get out yet!

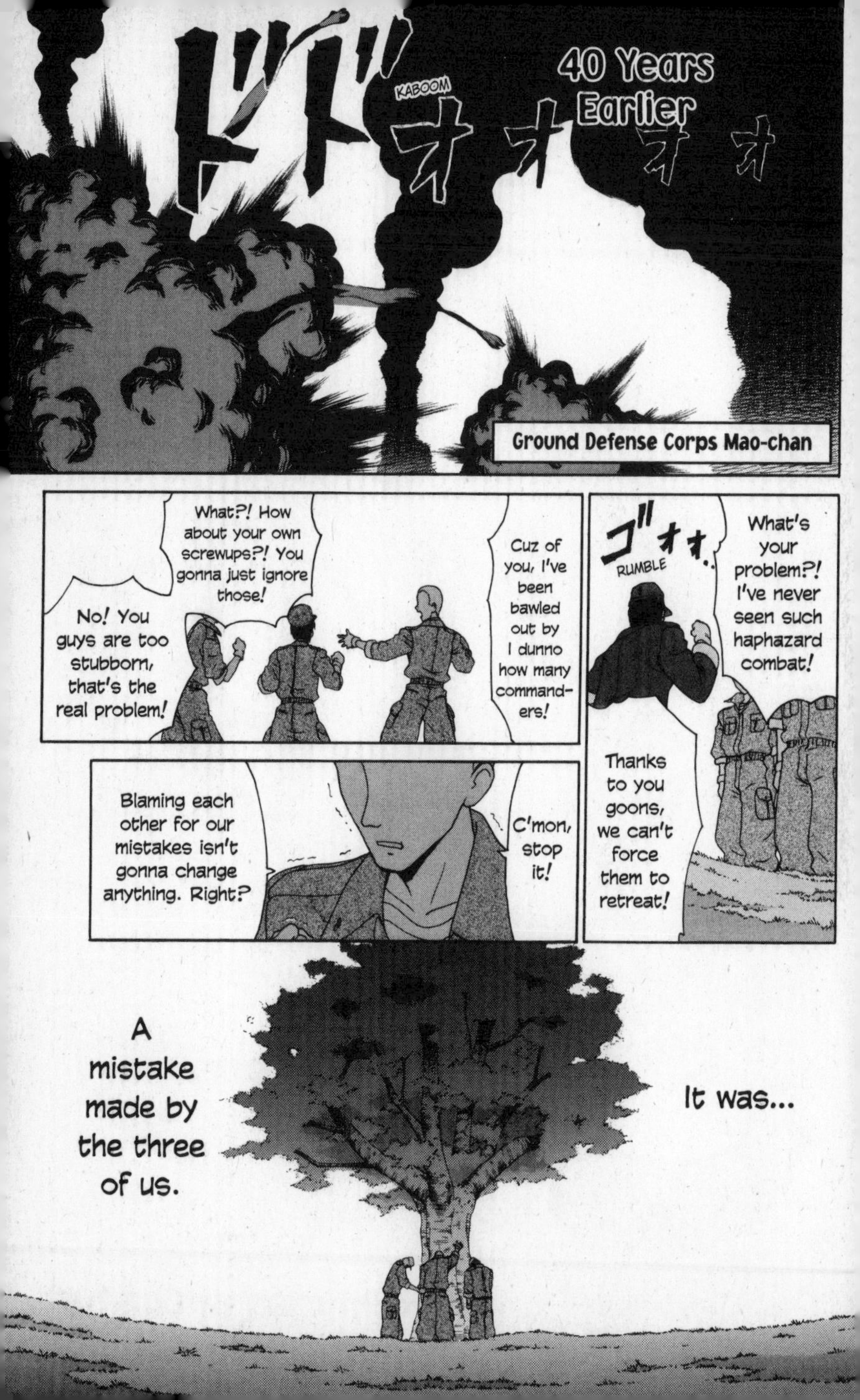
KABOOM
40 Years Earlier
Ground Defense Corps Mao-chan
RUMBLE
What's your problem?! I've never seen such haphazard combat!
Thanks to you goons, we can't force them to retreat!
Cuz of you, I've been bawled out by I dunno how many command-ers!
What?! How about your own screwups?! You gonna just ignore those!
No! You guys are too stubborn, that's the real problem!
C'mon, stop it!
Blaming each other for our mistakes isn't gonna change anything. Right?
It was...
A mistake made by the three of us.

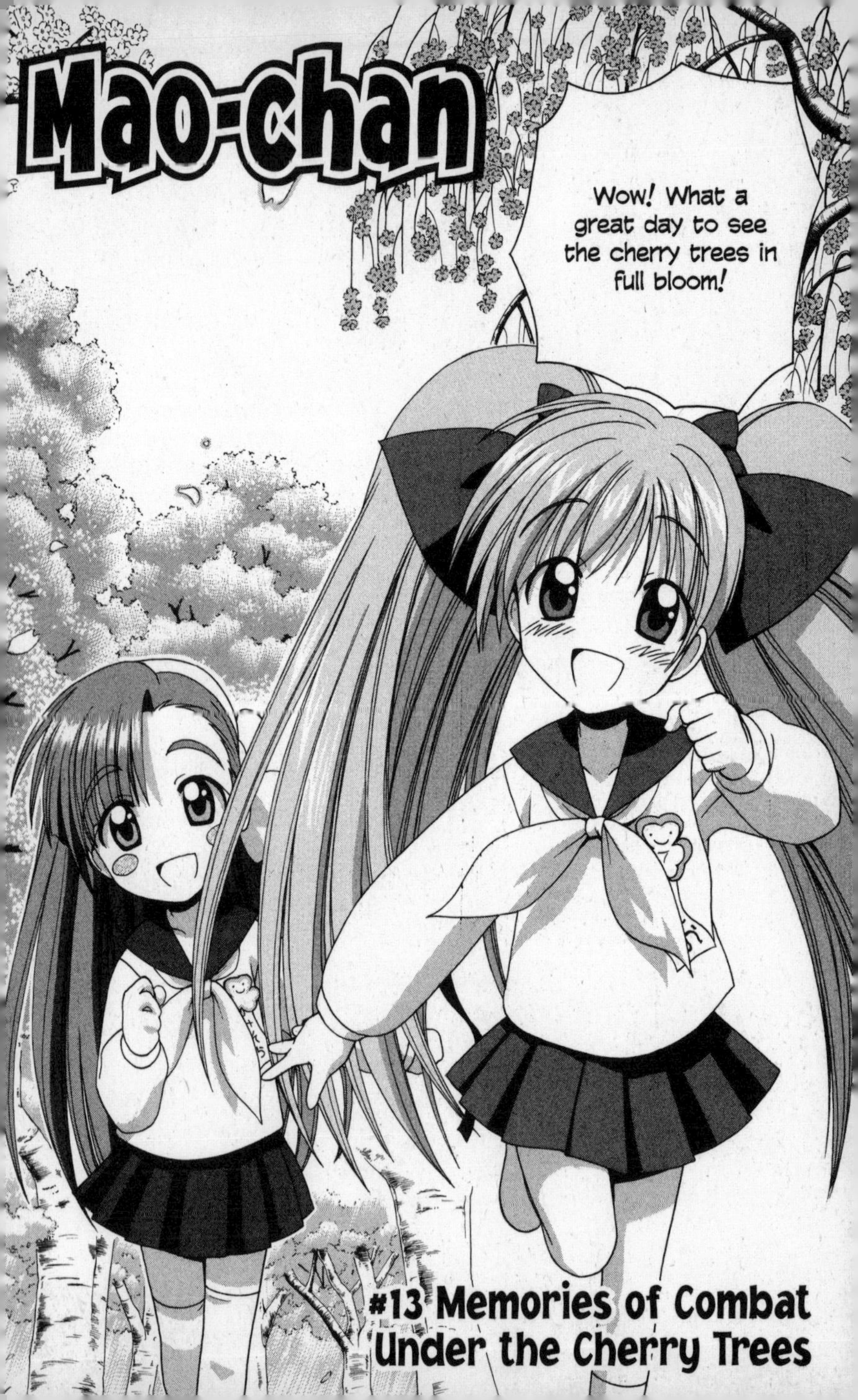
Mao-chan
Wow! What a great day to see the cherry trees in full bloom!
#13 Memories of Combat Under the Cherry Trees

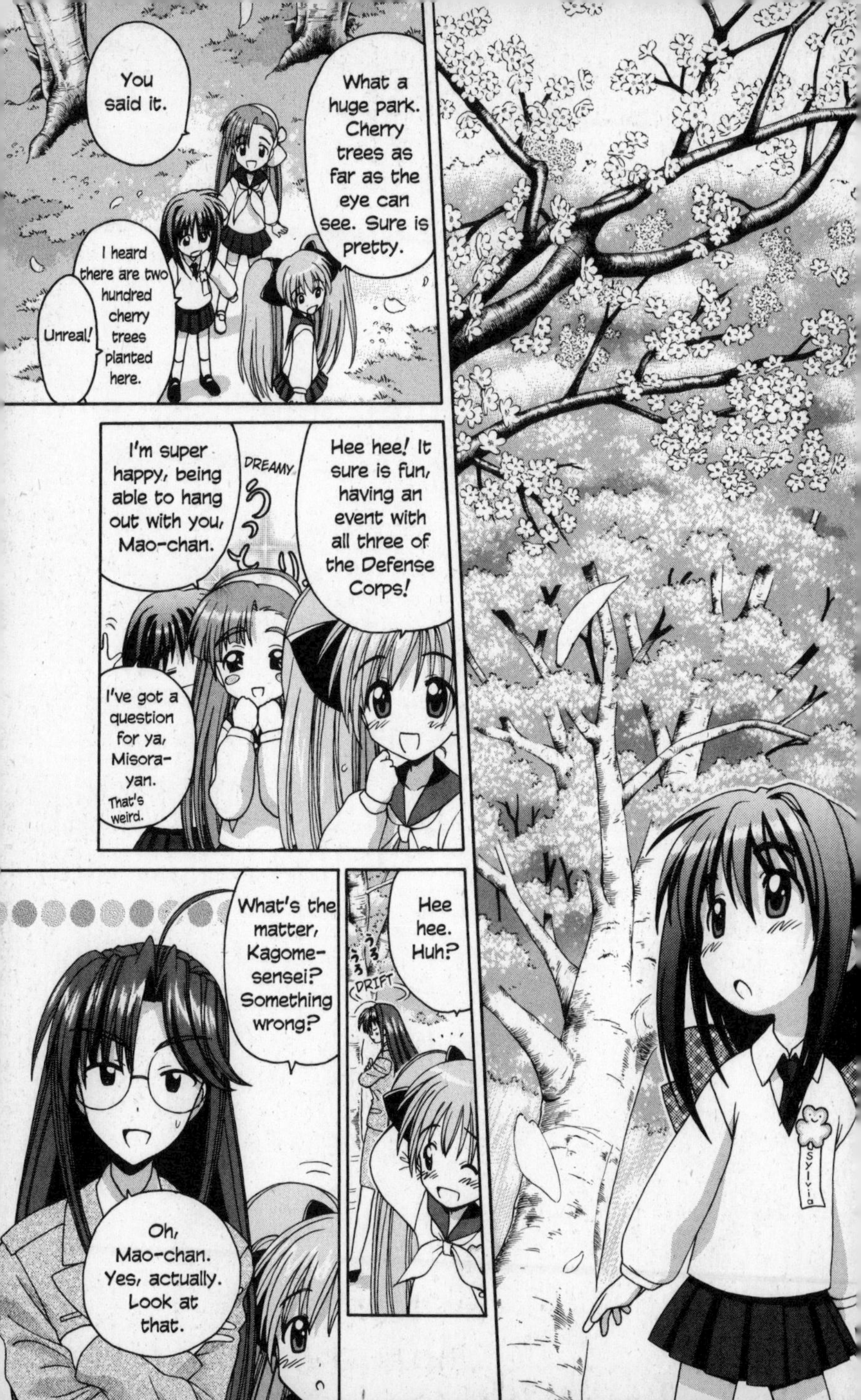
What a huge park. Cherry trees as far as the eye can see. Sure is pretty.
You said it.
I heard there are two hundred cherry trees planted here.
Unreal!
Hee hee! It sure is fun, having an event with all three of the Defense Corps!
DREAMY
I'm super happy, being able to hang out with you, Mao-chan.
I've got a question for ya, Misora-yan.
That's weird.
Hee hee. Huh?
DRIFT
What's the matter, Kagome-sensei? Something wrong?
Oh, Mao-chan. Yes, actually. Look at that.

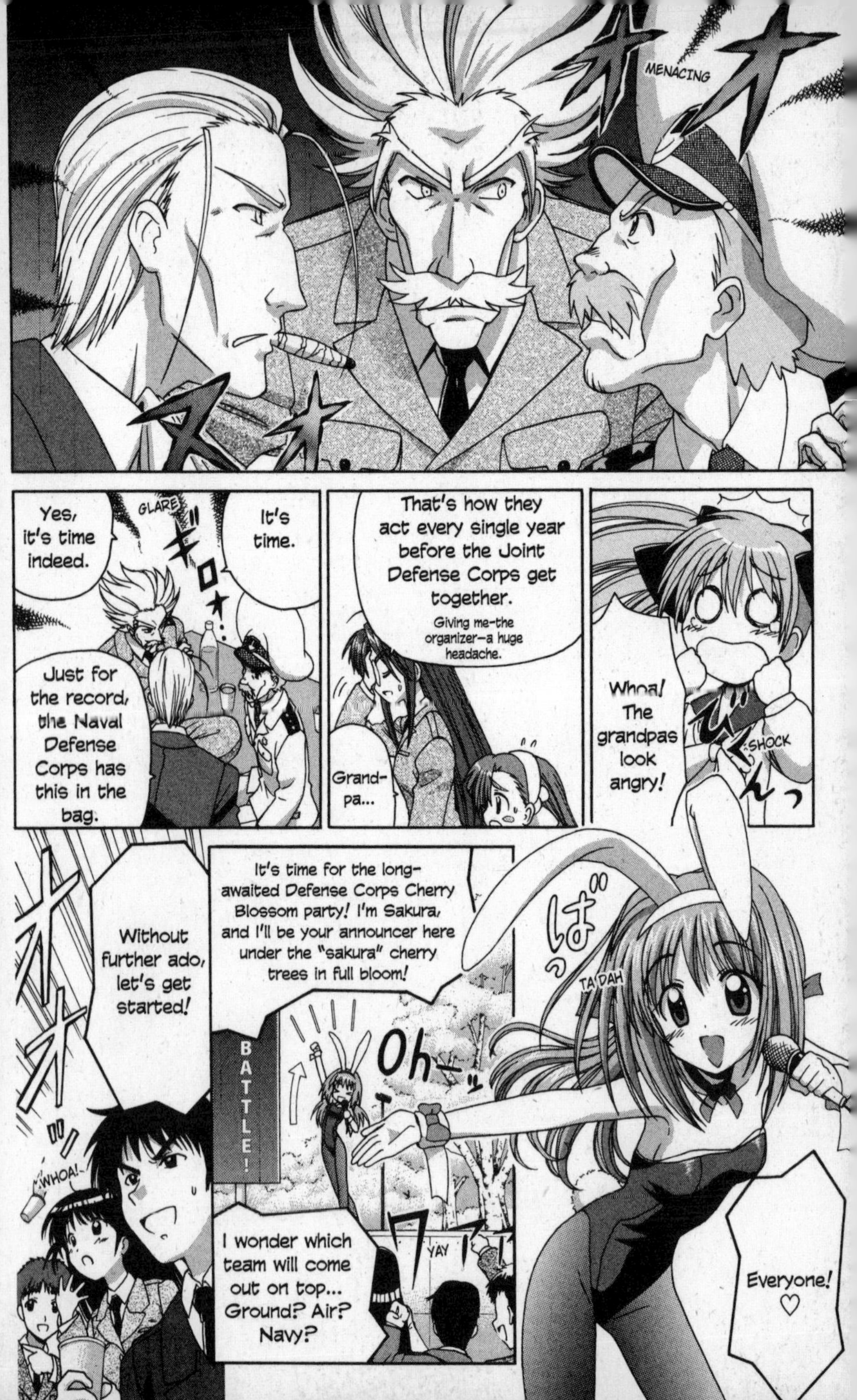
MENACING
Whoa! The grandpas look angry!
SHOCK
That's how they act every single year before the Joint Defense Corps get together.
Giving me—the organizer—a huge headache.
Grand-pa...
It's time.
GLARE
Yes, it's time indeed.
Just for the record, the Naval Defense Corps has this in the bag.
Everyone! ♡
TA DAH
It's time for the long-awaited Defense Corps Cherry Blossom party! I'm Sakura, and I'll be your announcer here under the "sakura" cherry trees in full bloom!
Without further ado, let's get started!
BATTLE!
Oh
YAY
WHOA!
I wonder which team will come out on top... Ground? Air? Navy?

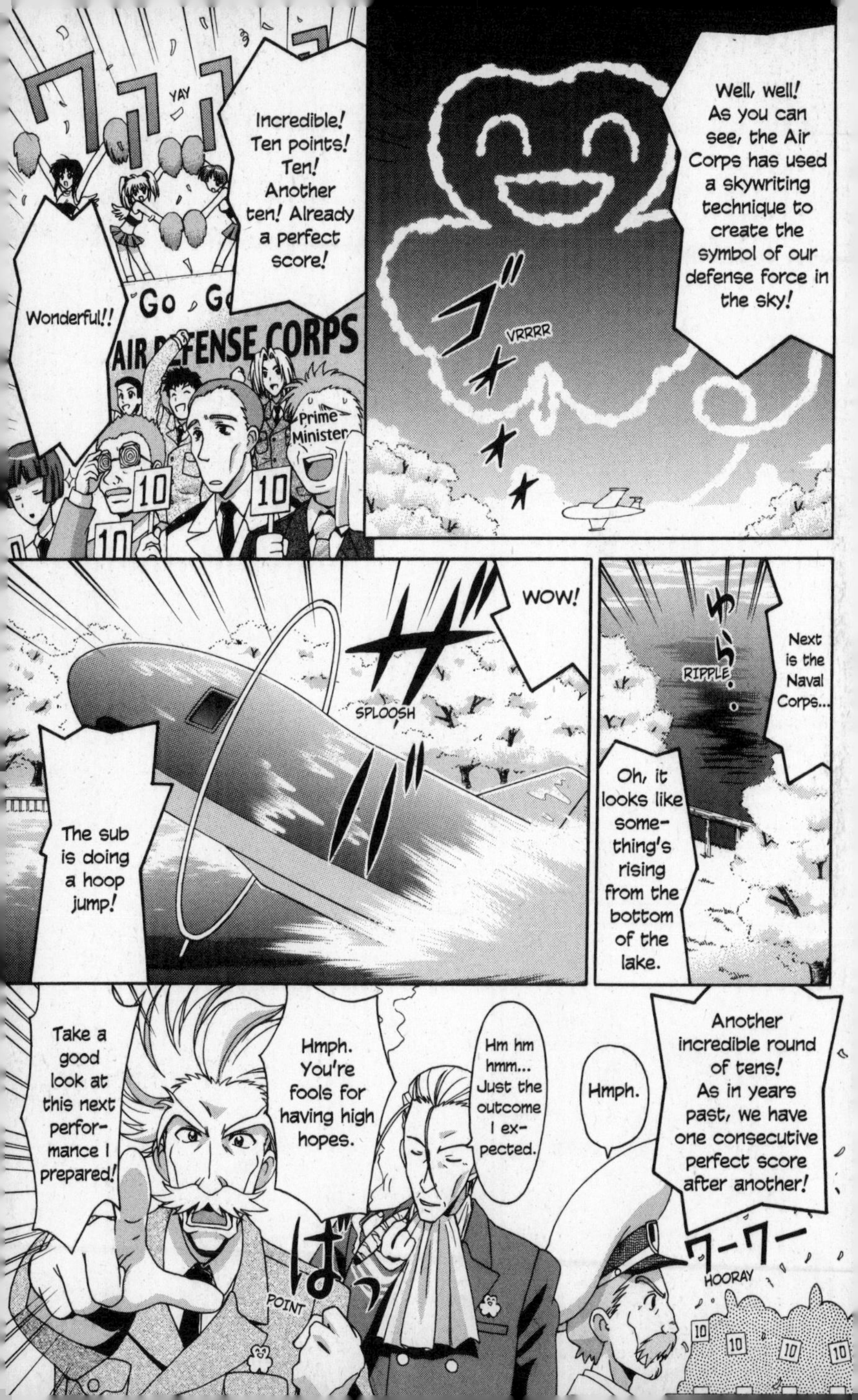
Well, well! As you can see, the Air Corps has used a skywriting technique to create the symbol of our defense force in the sky!
VRRRR
Incredible! Ten points! Ten! Another ten! Already a perfect score!
YAY
Wonderful!!
Go Go
AIR EFENSE CORPS
Prime Minister
10
10
10
Next is the Naval Corps...
RIPPLE
Oh, it looks like something's rising from the bottom of the lake.
WOW!
SPLOOSH
The sub is doing a hoop jump!
Another incredible round of tens! As in years past, we have one consecutive perfect score after another!
Hmph.
Hm hm hmm... Just the outcome I expected.
Hmph. You're fools for having high hopes.
Take a good look at this next performance I prepared!
HOORAY
POINT

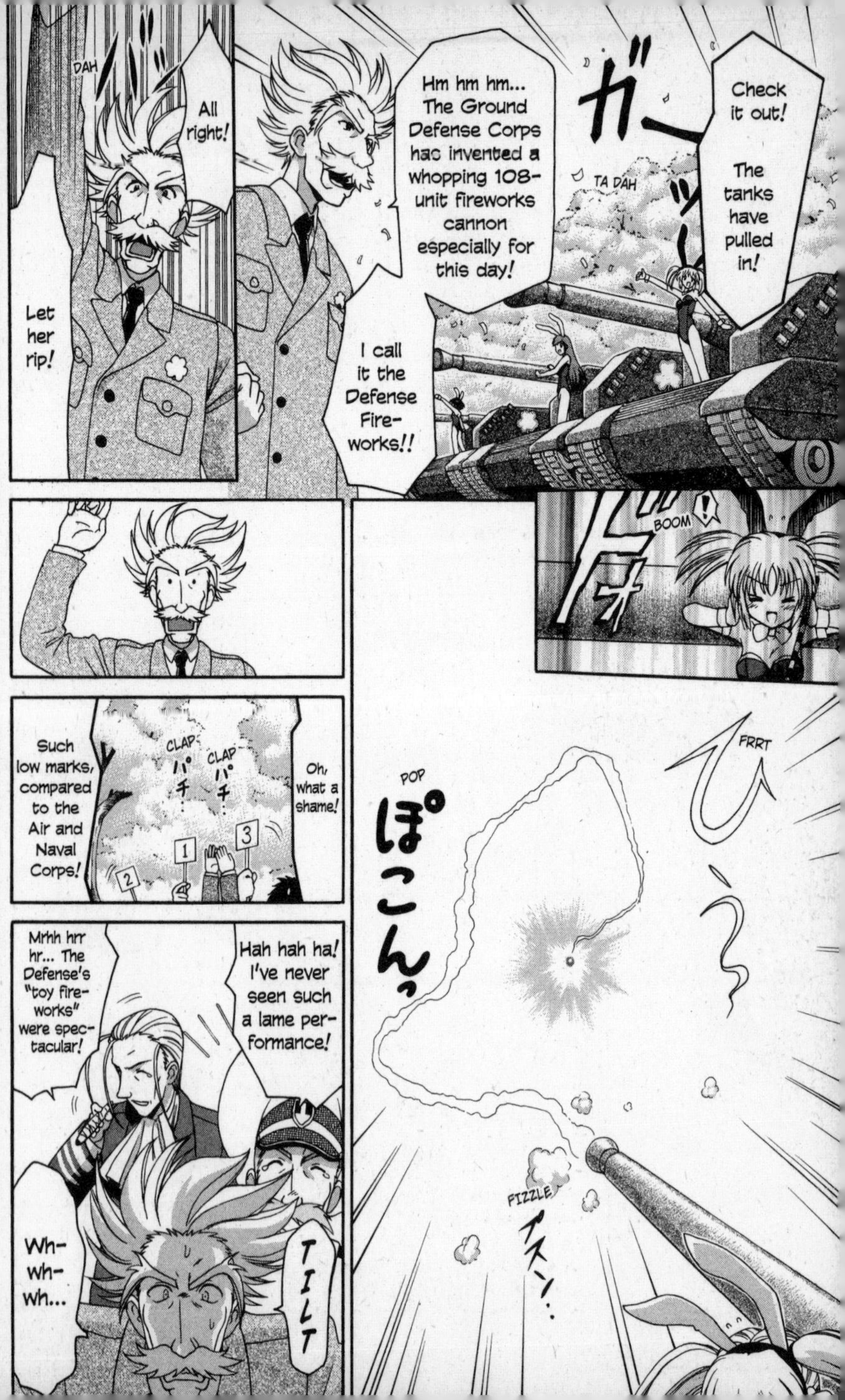
ガーッ
TA DAH
Check it out!
The tanks have pulled in!
Hm hm hm... The Ground Defense Corps has invented a whopping 108-unit fireworks cannon especially for this day!
I call it the Defense Fire-works!!
DAH
All right!
Let her rip!
ドォ
BOOM
!
FRRT
ひゅ～
POP
ぽこん
FIZZLE
ブスン…
Oh, what a shame!
CLAP
パチ
CLAP
パチ
1
2
3
Such low marks, compared to the Air and Naval Corps!
Hah hah ha! I've never seen such a lame per-formance!
Mrhh hrr hr... The Defense's "toy fire-works" were spec-tacular!
TILT
Wh-wh-wh...

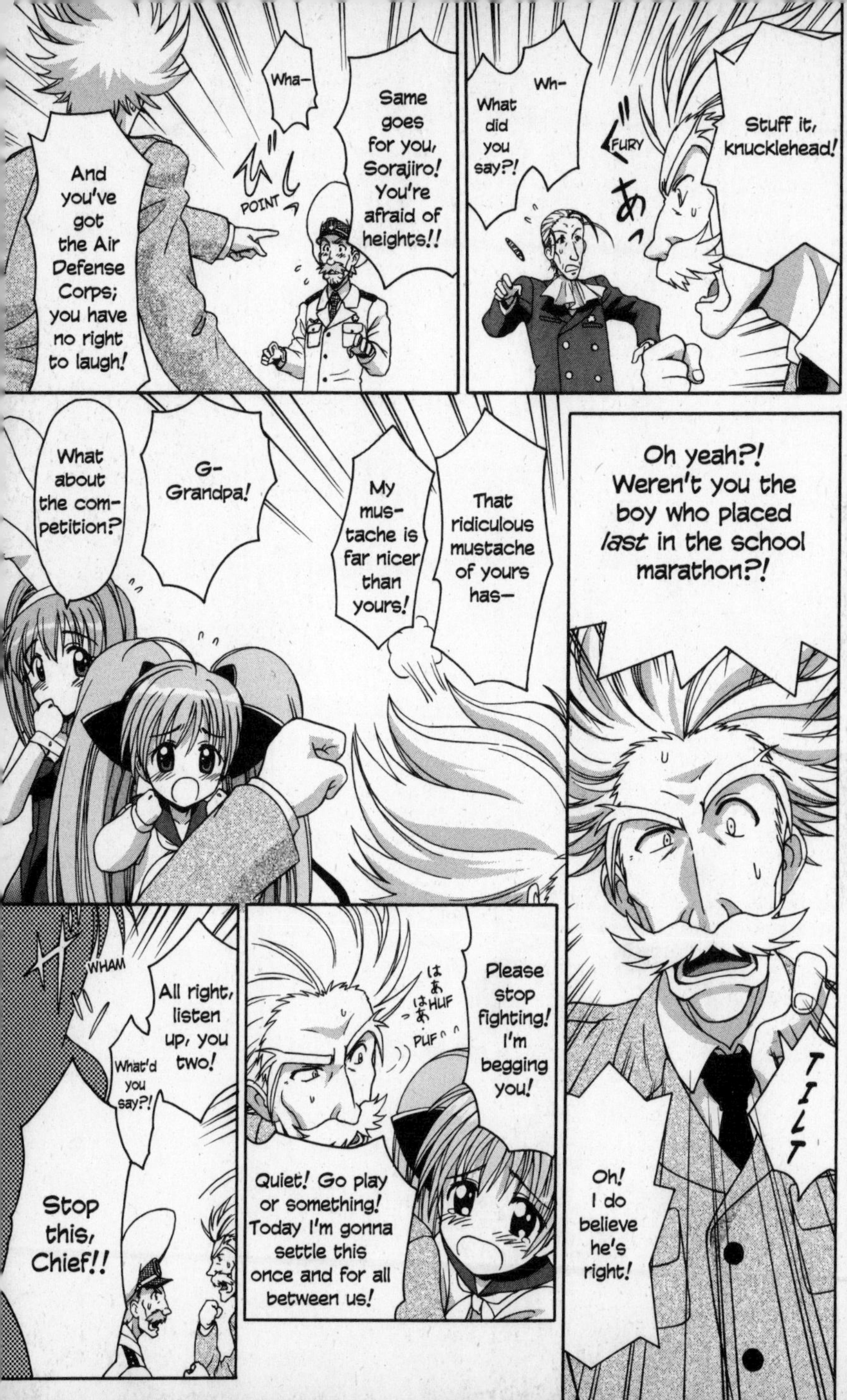
Stuff it, knucklehead!
FURY
あ
Wh-
What did you say?!
Same goes for you, Sorajiro! You're afraid of heights!!
Wha-
POINT
And you've got the Air Defense Corps; you have no right to laugh!
Oh yeah?! Weren't you the boy who placed *last* in the school marathon?!
TILT
Oh! I do believe he's right!
That ridiculous mustache of yours has—
My mustache is far nicer than yours!
G- Grandpa!
What about the competition?
Please stop fighting! I'm begging you!
はあ HUF
はあ PUF
Quiet! Go play or something! Today I'm gonna settle this once and for all between us!
All right, listen up, you two!
WHAM
What'd you say?!
Stop this, Chief!!

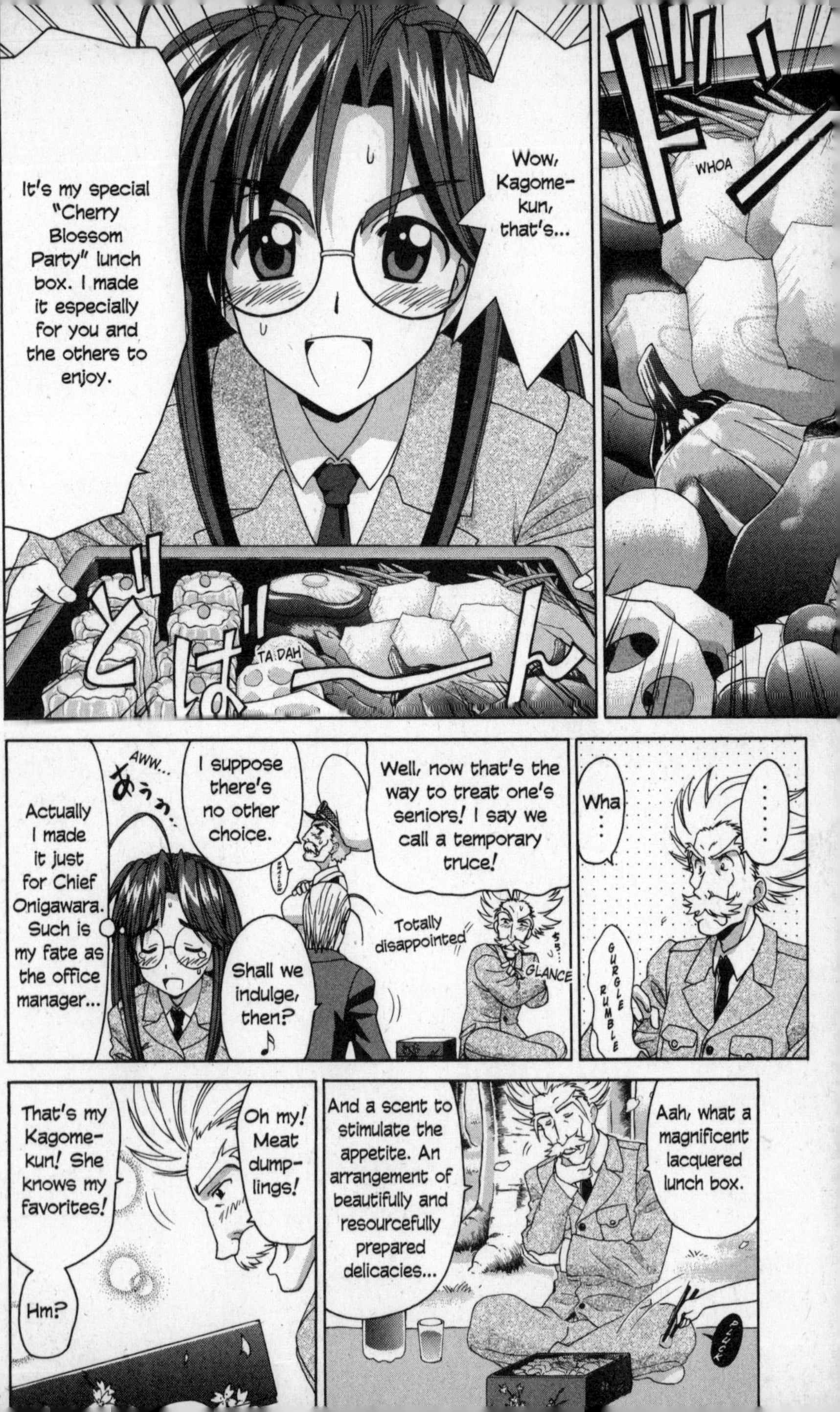
WHOA
Wow, Kagome-kun, that's...
It's my special "Cherry Blossom Party" lunch box. I made it especially for you and the others to enjoy.
TA-DAH
....
Wha...
GURGLE RUMBLE
Well, now that's the way to treat one's seniors! I say we call a temporary truce!
Totally disappointed
GLANCE
I suppose there's no other choice.
AWW...
Actually I made it just for Chief Onigawara. Such is my fate as the office manager...
Shall we indulge, then? ♪
Aah, what a magnificent lacquered lunch box.
And a scent to stimulate the appetite. An arrangement of beautifully and resourcefully prepared delicacies...
PLUCK
Oh my! Meat dumplings!
That's my Kagome-kun! She knows my favorites!
Hm?

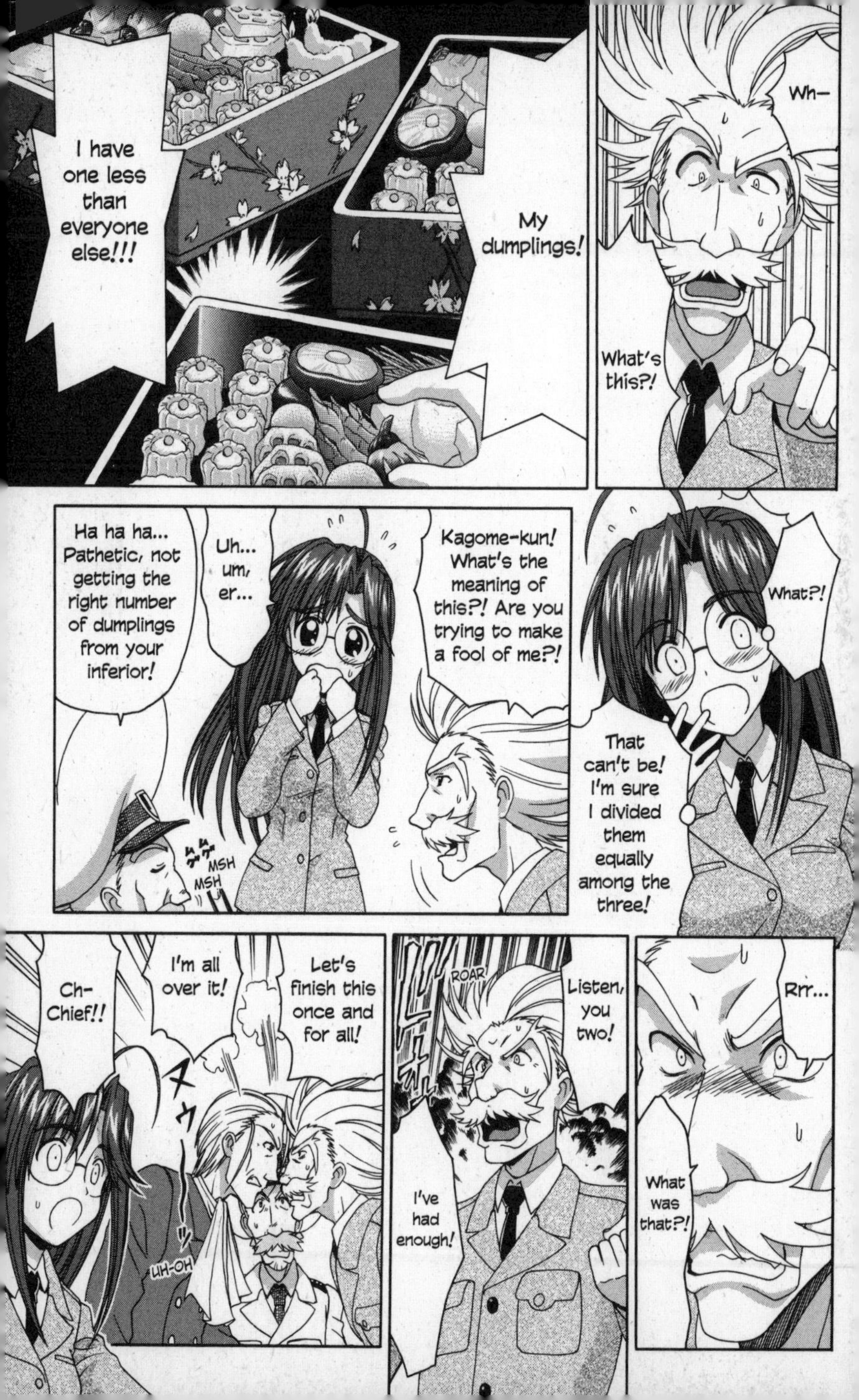
Wh–
What's this?!
My dumplings!
I have one less than everyone else!!!
What?!
That can't be! I'm sure I divided them equally among the three!
Kagome-kun! What's the meaning of this?! Are you trying to make a fool of me?!
Uh... um, er...
Ha ha ha... Pathetic, not getting the right number of dumplings from your inferior!
MSH MSH
Rrr...
What was that?!
ROAR
Listen, you two!
I've had enough!
Let's finish this once and for all!
I'm all over it!
Ch-Chief!!
UH-OH

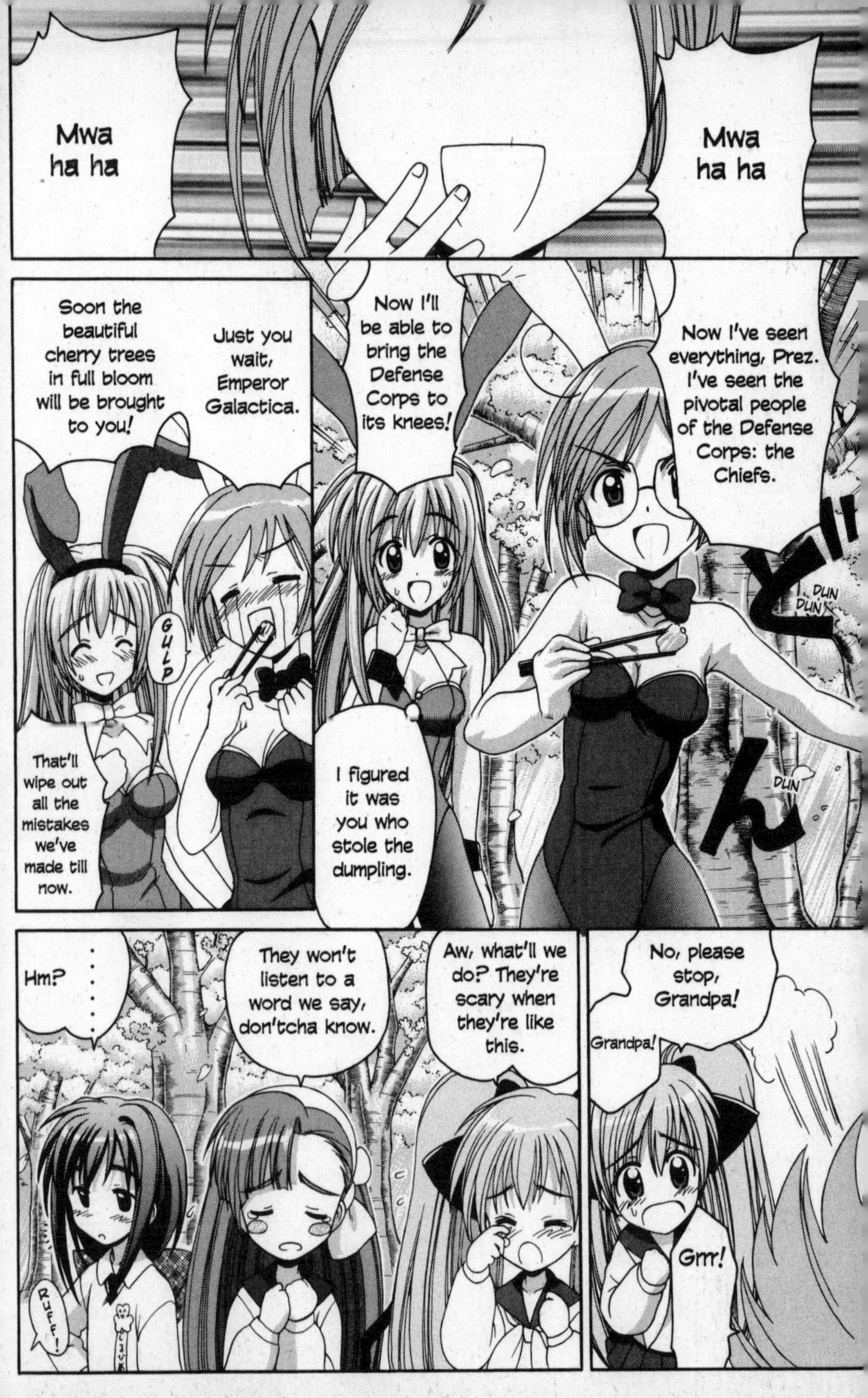
Mwa ha ha
Mwa ha ha
Now I've seen everything, Prez. I've seen the pivotal people of the Defense Corps: the Chiefs.
Now I'll be able to bring the Defense Corps to its knees!
DUN DUN
DUN
I figured it was you who stole the dumpling.
Just you wait, Emperor Galactica.
Soon the beautiful cherry trees in full bloom will be brought to you!
GULP
That'll wipe out all the mistakes we've made till now.
No, please stop, Grandpa!
Grandpa!
Grrr!
Aw, what'll we do? They're scary when they're like this.
They won't listen to a word we say, don'tcha know.
Hm? ......
RUFF!

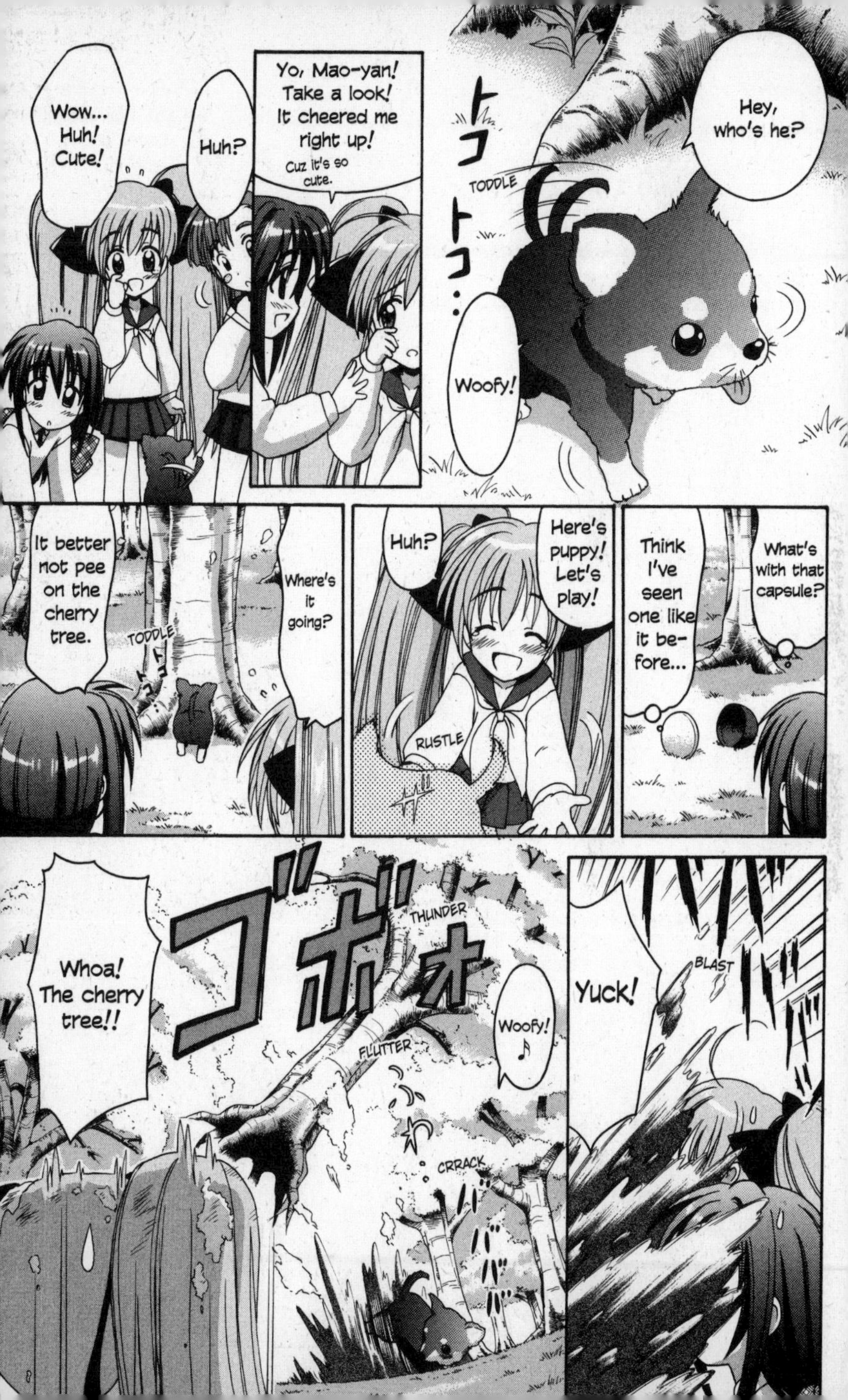
Hey, who's he?
TODDLE
Woofy!
Yo, Mao-yan! Take a look! It cheered me right up!
Cuz it's so cute.
Huh?
Wow... Huh! Cute!
What's with that capsule?
Think I've seen one like it before...
Here's puppy! Let's play!
Huh?
RUSTLE
Where's it going?
It better not pee on the cherry tree.
TODDLE
Yuck!
BLAST
THUNDER
Woofy! ♪
FLUTTER
CRRACK
Whoa! The cherry tree!!

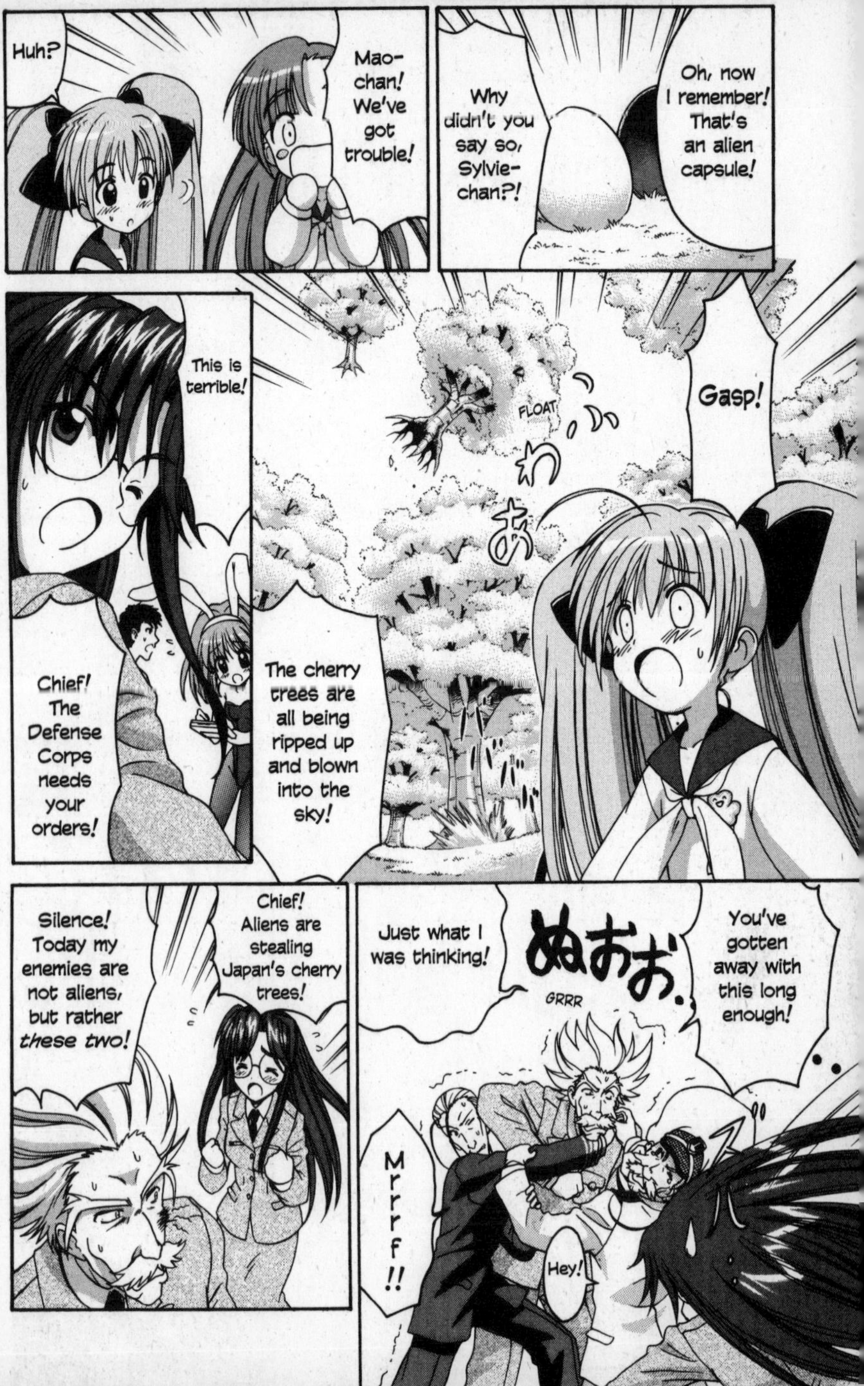
Oh, now I remember! That's an alien capsule!
Why didn't you say so, Sylvie-chan?!
Mao-chan! We've got trouble!
Huh?
Gasp!
FLOAT
わあ
The cherry trees are all being ripped up and blown into the sky!
This is terrible!
Chief! The Defense Corps needs your orders!
You've gotten away with this long enough!
ぬおお
GRRR
Just what I was thinking!
Mrrrf!!
Hey!
Chief! Aliens are stealing Japan's cherry trees!
Silence! Today my enemies are not aliens, but rather *these two*!

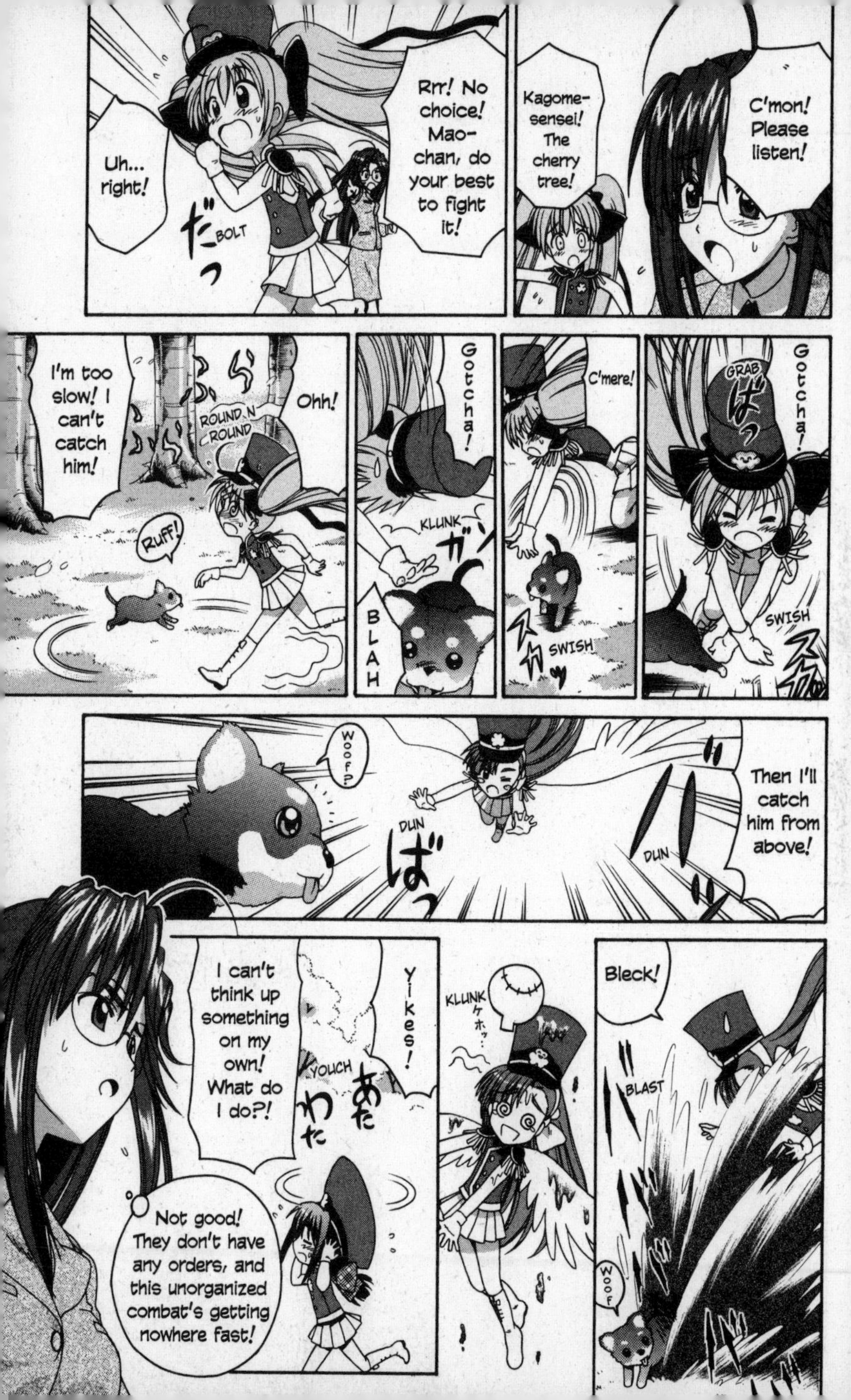
C'mon! Please listen!
Kagome-sensei! The cherry tree!
Rrr! No choice! Mao-chan, do your best to fight it!
Uh... right!
BOLT
GRAB
Gotcha!
SWISH
C'mere!
SWISH
Gotcha!
KLUNK
BLAH
Ohh!
ROUND N ROUND
I'm too slow! I can't catch him!
Ruff!
Then I'll catch him from above!
DUN
DUN
Woof?
Bleck!
BLAST
Woof
KLUNK
Yikes!
YOUCH
I can't think up something on my own! What do I do?!
Not good! They don't have any orders, and this unorganized combat's getting nowhere fast!

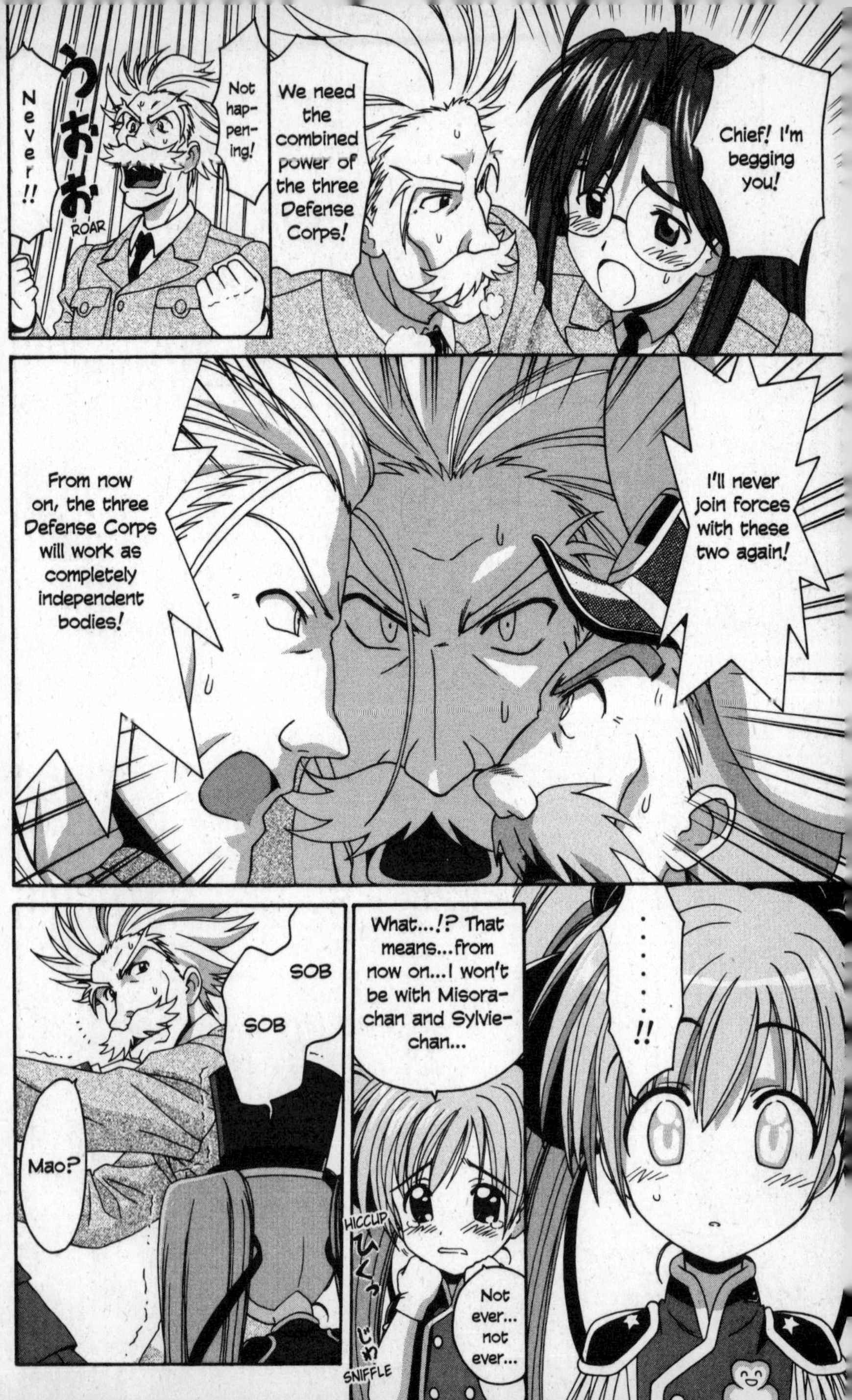
Chief! I'm begging you!
We need the combined power of the three Defense Corps!
Not happen-ing!
うおお
ROAR
Never!!
I'll never join forces with these two again!
From now on, the three Defense Corps will work as completely independent bodies!
......!!
What...!? That means...from now on...I won't be with Misora-chan and Sylvie-chan...
HICCUP
ひくっ
Not ever... not ever...
じわ
SNIFFLE
SOB
SOB
Mao?

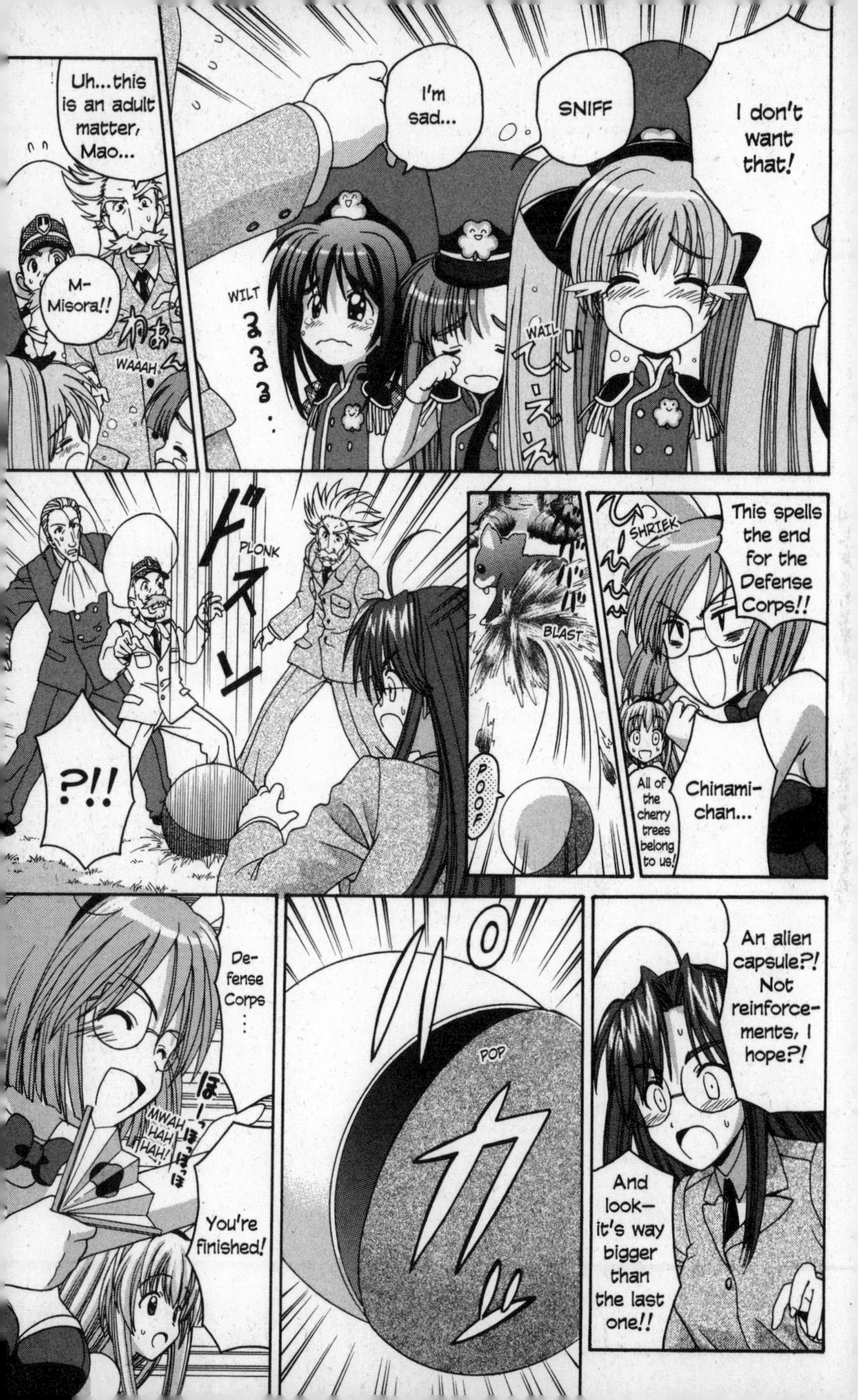
I don't want that!
SNIFF
I'm sad...
WILT
WAIL
Uh...this is an adult matter, Mao...
M-Misora!!
WAAAH
This spells the end for the Defense Corps!!
SHRIEK
Chinami-chan...
All of the cherry trees belong to us!
BLAST
POOF
PLONK
?!!
An alien capsule?! Not reinforcements, I hope?!
And look—it's way bigger than the last one!!
POP
Defense Corps...
MWAH HAH HAH!
You're finished!

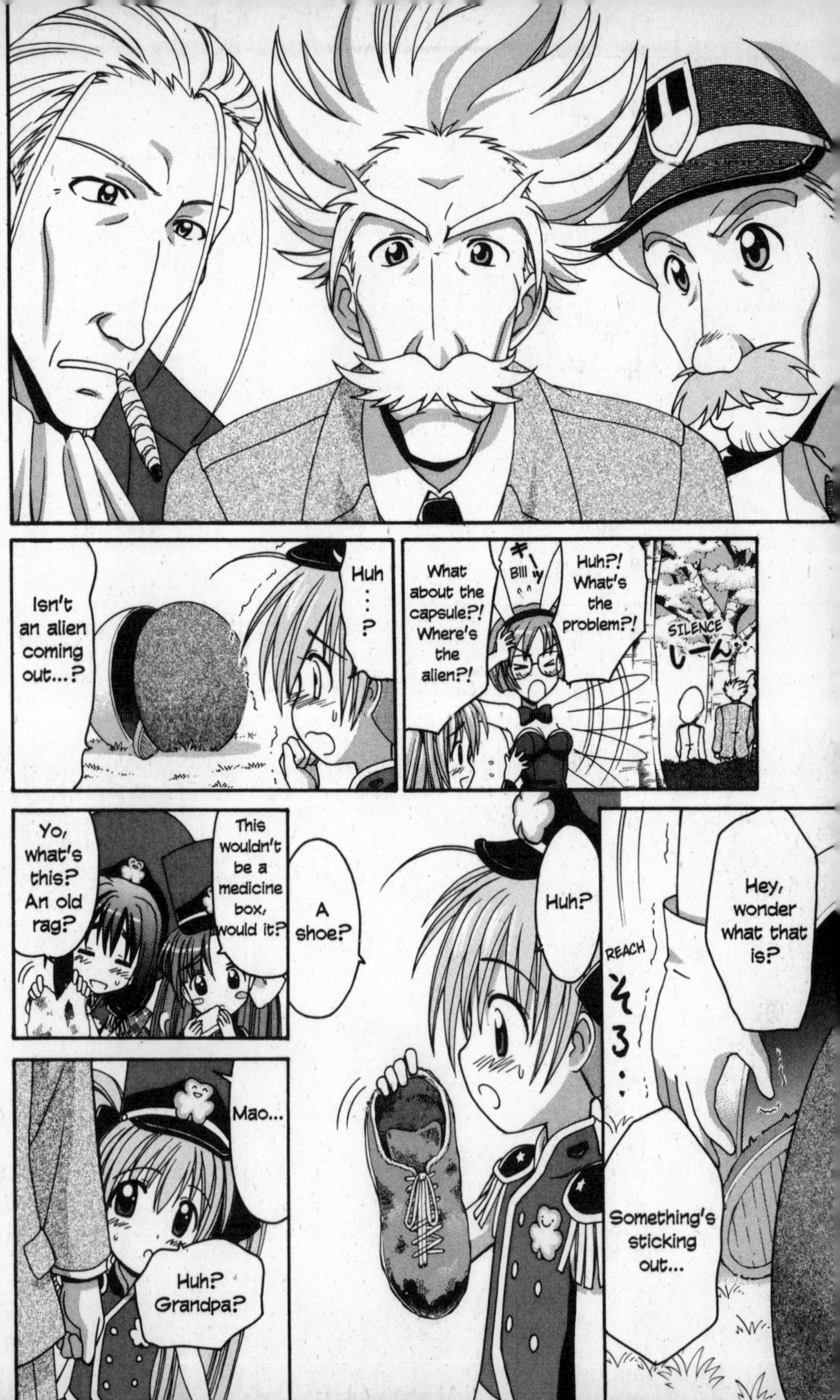
Huh?! What's the problem?!
BIII
What about the capsule?! Where's the alien?!
SILENCE
Huh ...?
Isn't an alien coming out...?
Hey, wonder what that is?
REACH
Something's sticking out...
Huh?
A shoe?
This wouldn't be a medicine box, would it?
Yo, what's this? An old rag?
Mao...
Huh? Grandpa?

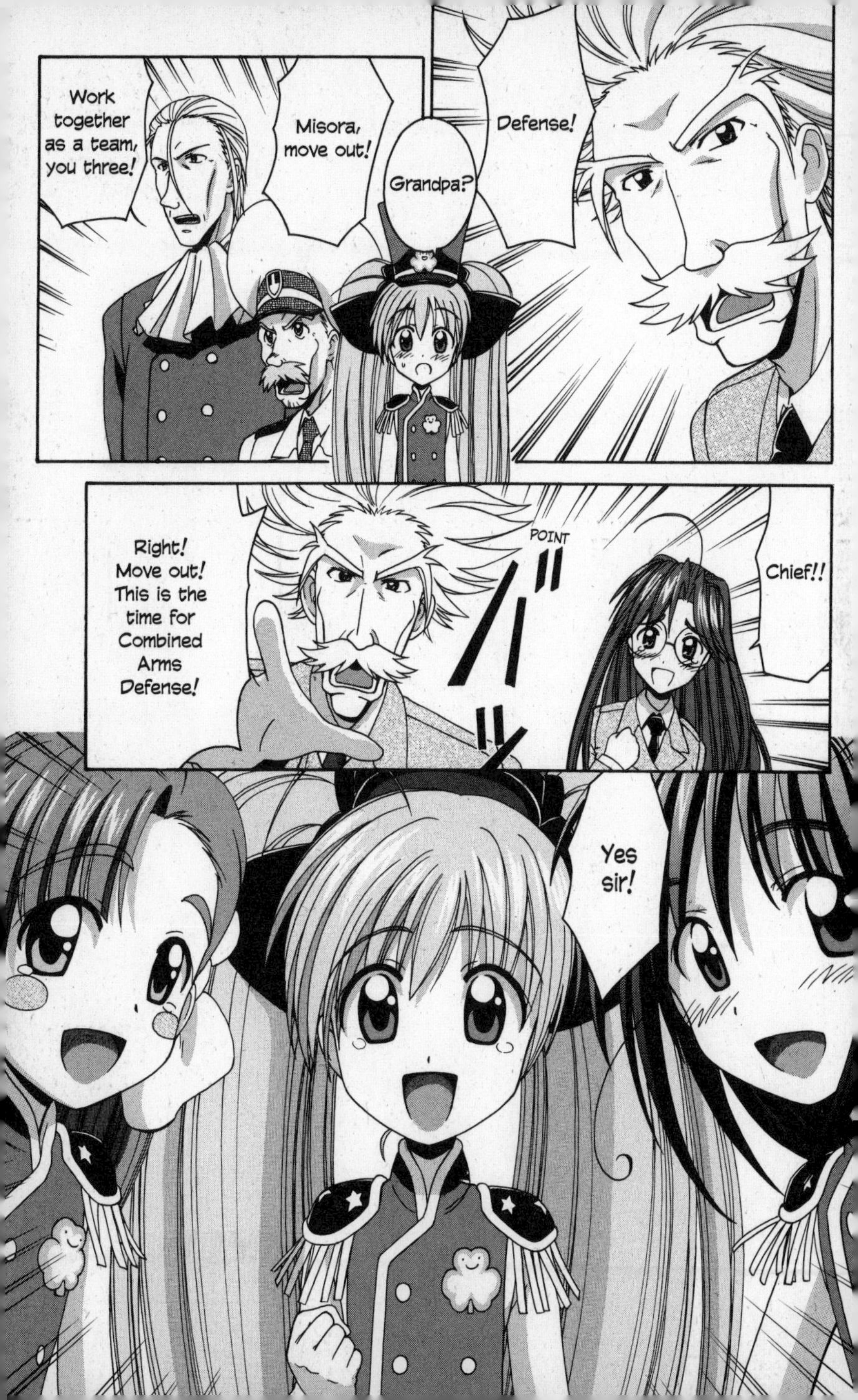
Defense!
Grandpa?
Misora, move out!
Work together as a team, you three!
Chief!!
POINT
Right! Move out! This is the time for Combined Arms Defense!
Yes sir!

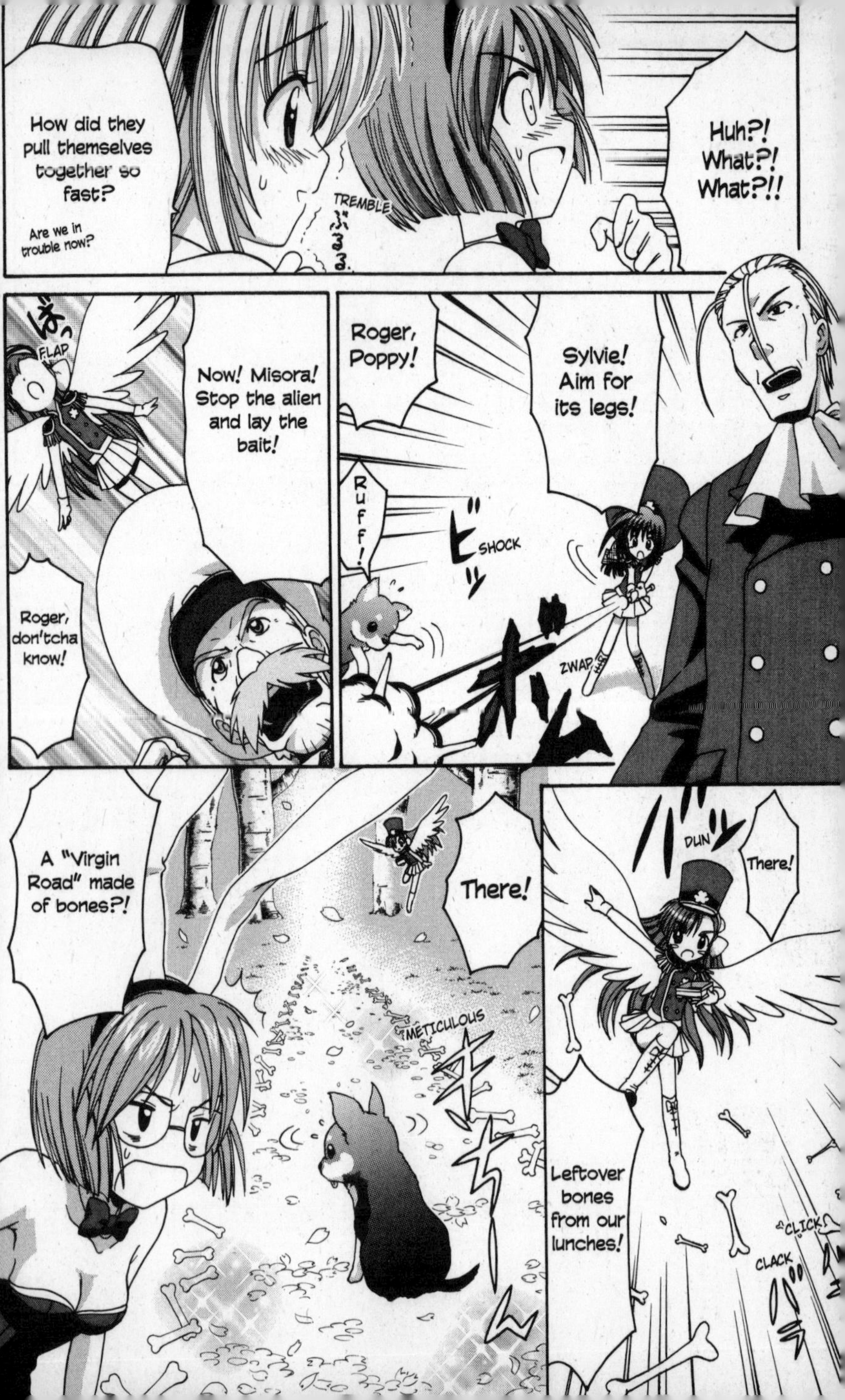
Huh?! What?! What?!!
How did they pull themselves together so fast?
TREMBLE
Are we in trouble now?
Sylvie! Aim for its legs!
Roger, Poppy!
Ruff!
SHOCK
ZWAP
FLAP
Now! Misora! Stop the alien and lay the bait!
Roger, don'tcha know!
DUN
There!
Leftover bones from our lunches!
CLICK
CLACK
There!
A "Virgin Road" made of bones?!
METICULOUS

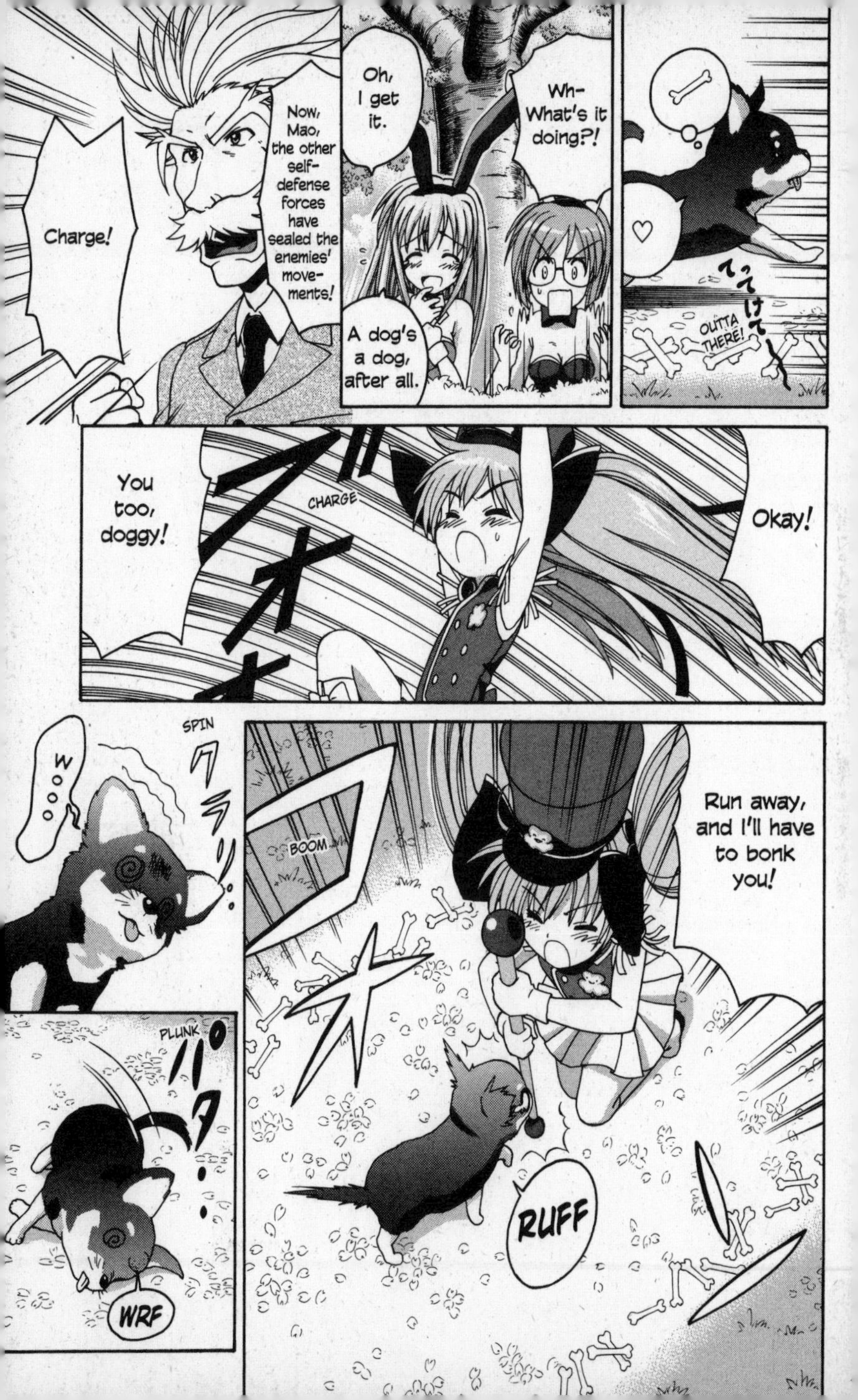
OUTTA THERE!
Wh- What's it doing?!
Oh, I get it.
A dog's a dog, after all.
Now, Mao, the other self-defense forces have sealed the enemies' movements!
Charge!
Okay!
CHARGE
You too, doggy!
Run away, and I'll have to bonk you!
BOOM
RUFF
SPIN
Wooo...
PLUNK
WRF

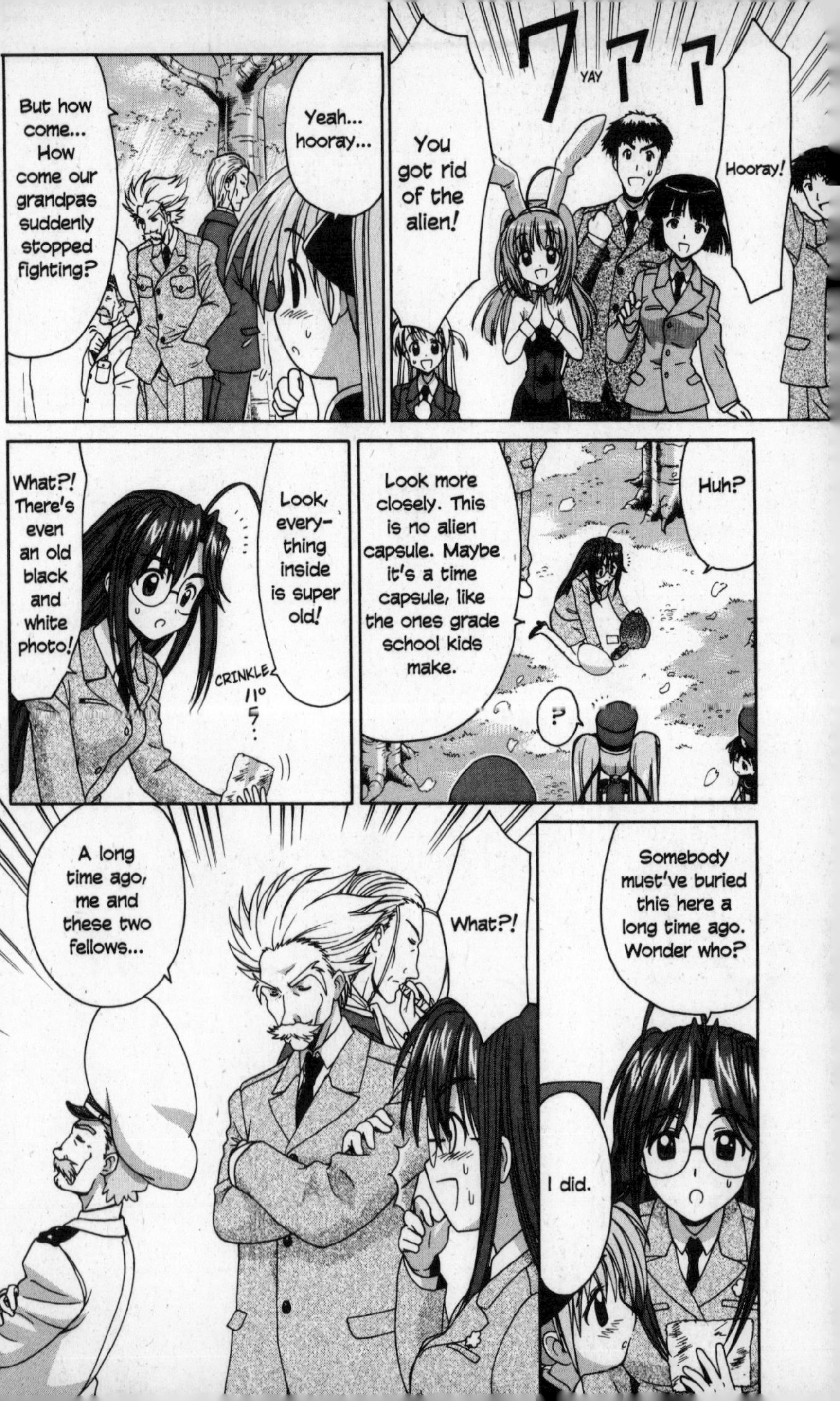

YAY
Hooray!
You got rid of the alien!
Yeah... hooray...
But how come... How come our grandpas suddenly stopped fighting?
Huh?
Look more closely. This is no alien capsule. Maybe it's a time capsule, like the ones grade school kids make.
?
Look, every-thing inside is super old!
CRINKLE
What?! There's even an old black and white photo!
Somebody must've buried this here a long time ago. Wonder who?
I did.
What?!
A long time ago, me and these two fellows...

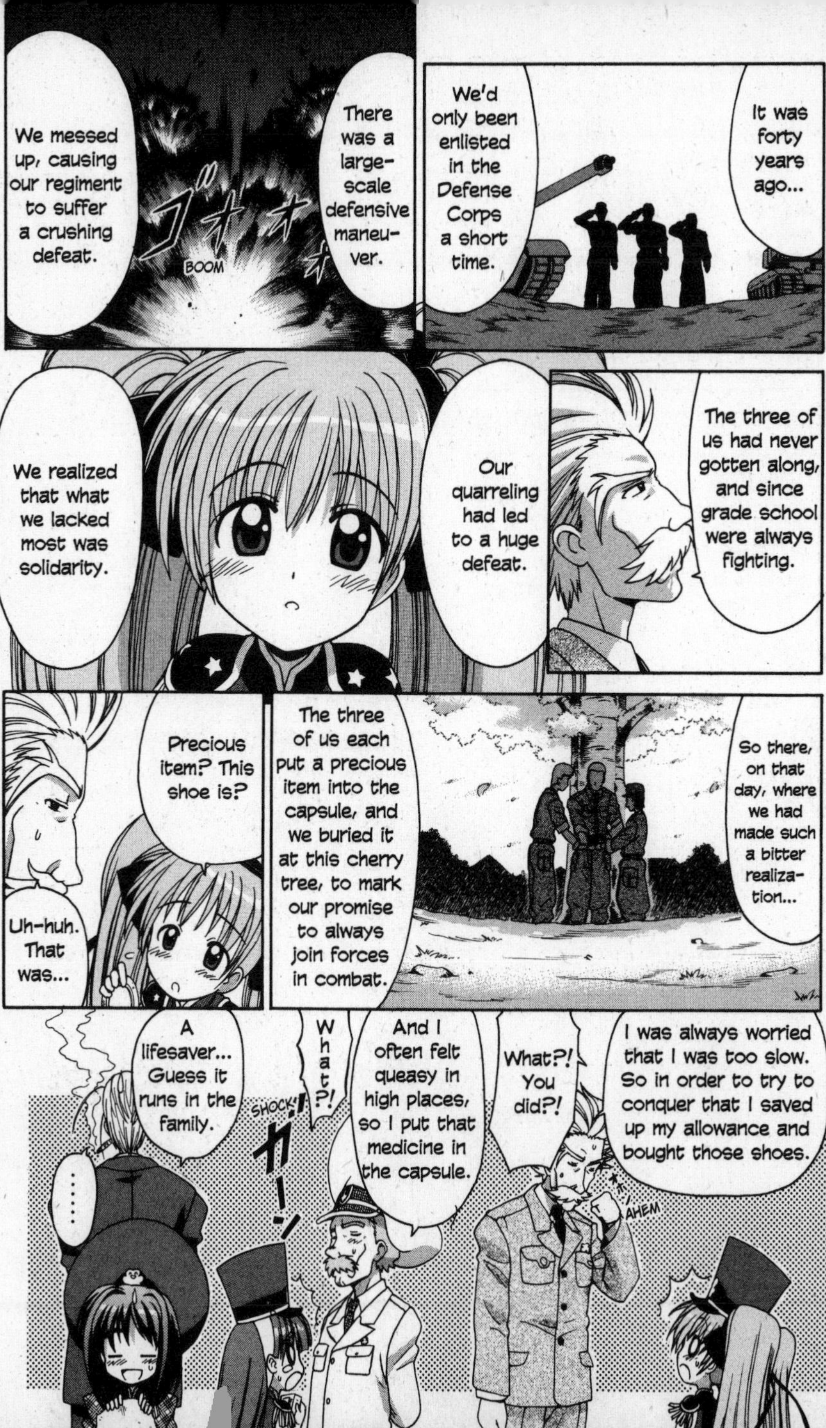
It was forty years ago...
We'd only been enlisted in the Defense Corps a short time.
There was a large-scale defensive maneuver.
BOOM
We messed up, causing our regiment to suffer a crushing defeat.
The three of us had never gotten along, and since grade school were always fighting.
Our quarreling had led to a huge defeat.
We realized that what we lacked most was solidarity.
So there, on that day, where we had made such a bitter realization...
The three of us each put a precious item into the capsule, and we buried it at this cherry tree, to mark our promise to always join forces in combat.
Precious item? This shoe is?
Uh-huh. That was...
I was always worried that I was too slow. So in order to try to conquer that I saved up my allowance and bought those shoes.
AHEM
What?! You did?!
And I often felt queasy in high places, so I put that medicine in the capsule.
What?!
SHOCK
A lifesaver... Guess it runs in the family.
......

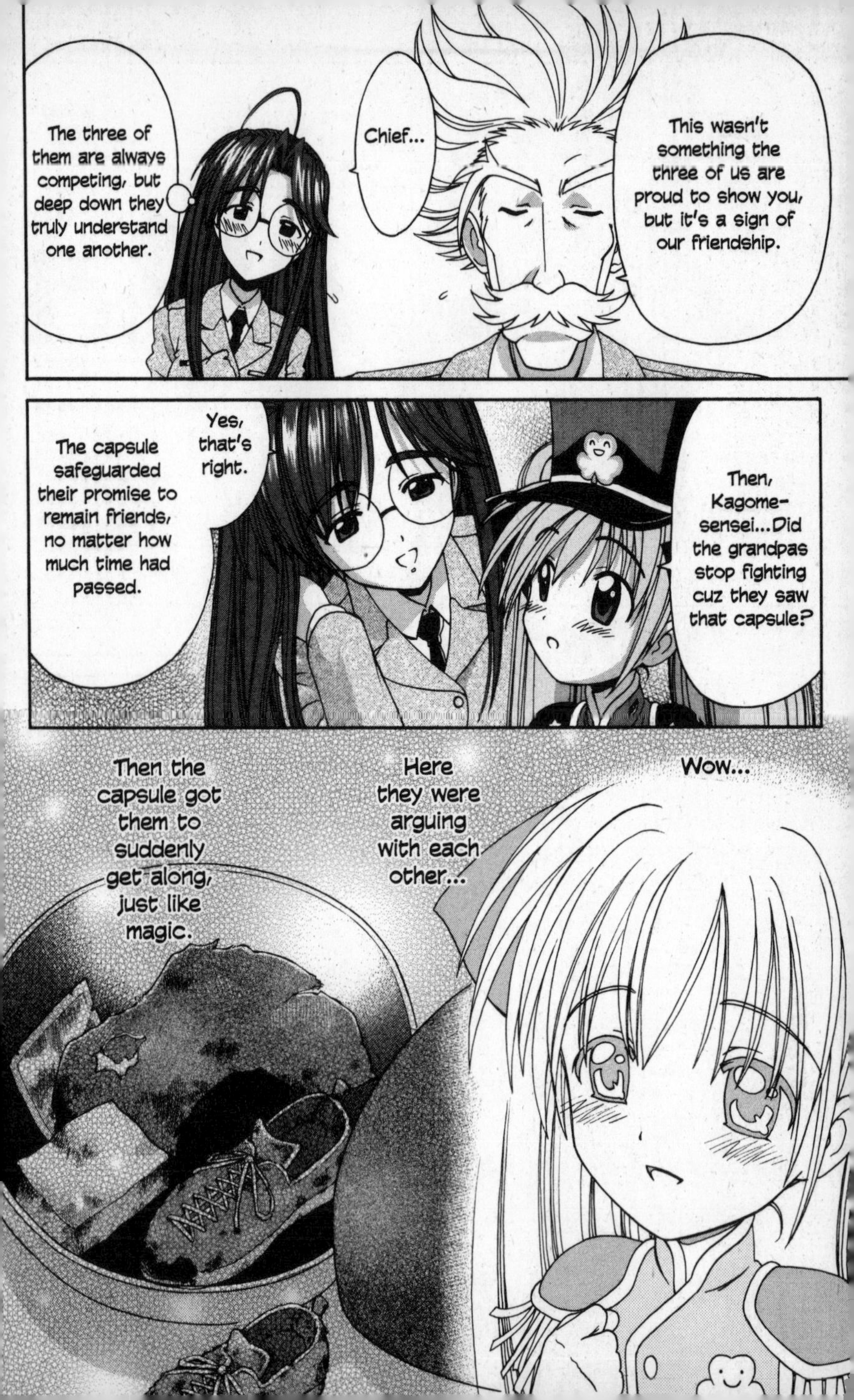
This wasn't something the three of us are proud to show you, but it's a sign of our friendship.
Chief...
The three of them are always competing, but deep down they truly understand one another.
Then, Kagome-sensei...Did the grandpas stop fighting cuz they saw that capsule?
Yes, that's right.
The capsule safeguarded their promise to remain friends, no matter how much time had passed.
Wow...
Here they were arguing with each other...
Then the capsule got them to suddenly get along, just like magic.

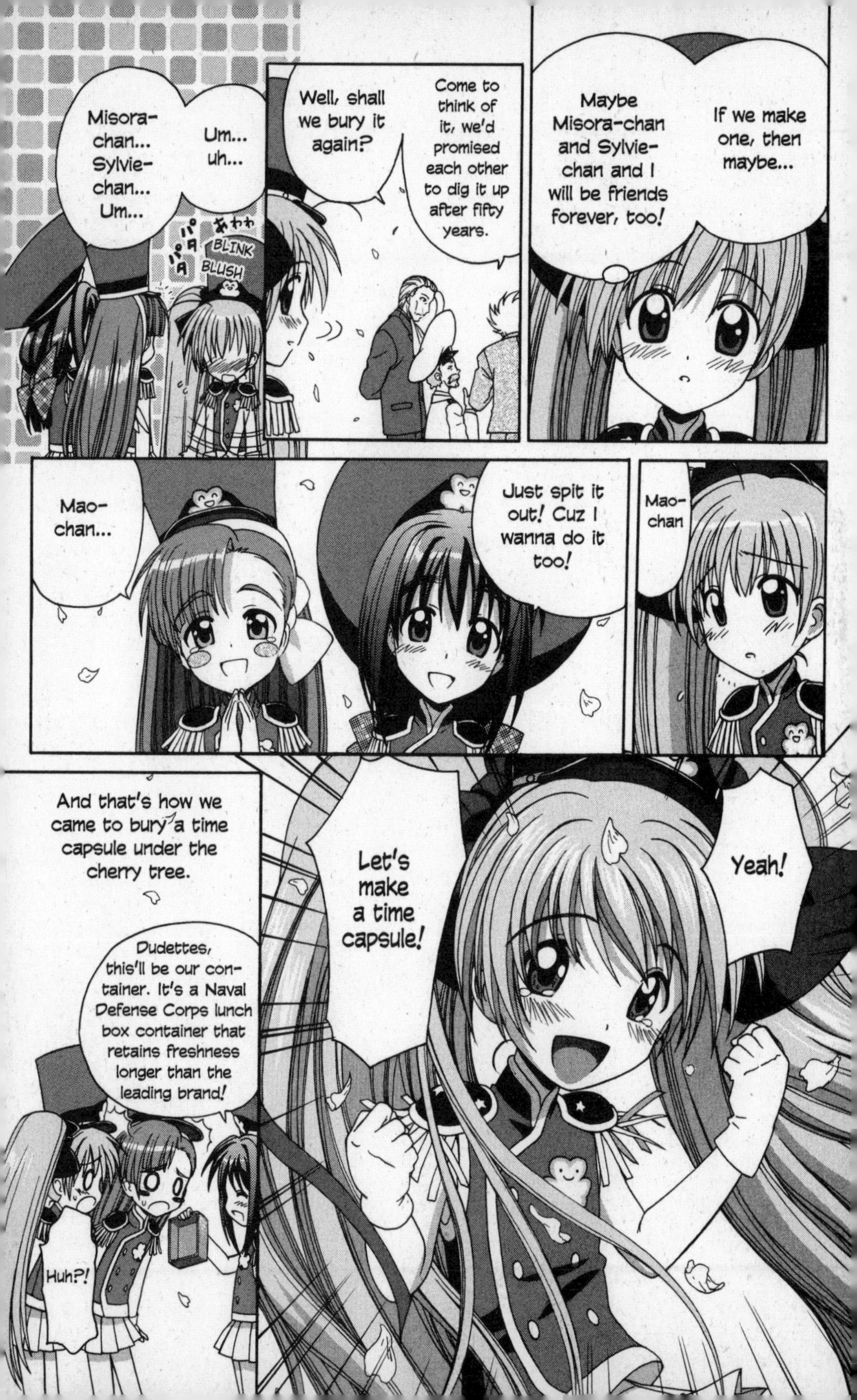
If we make one, then maybe...
Maybe Misora-chan and Sylvie-chan and I will be friends forever, too!
Come to think of it, we'd promised each other to dig it up after fifty years.
Well, shall we bury it again?
Um... uh...
Misora-chan... Sylvie-chan... Um...
あわわ
BLINK
パタパタ
BLUSH
Mao-chan
Just spit it out! Cuz I wanna do it too!
Mao-chan...
Yeah!
Let's make a time capsule!
And that's how we came to bury a time capsule under the cherry tree.
Dudettes, this'll be our container. It's a Naval Defense Corps lunch box container that retains freshness longer than the leading brand!
Huh?!

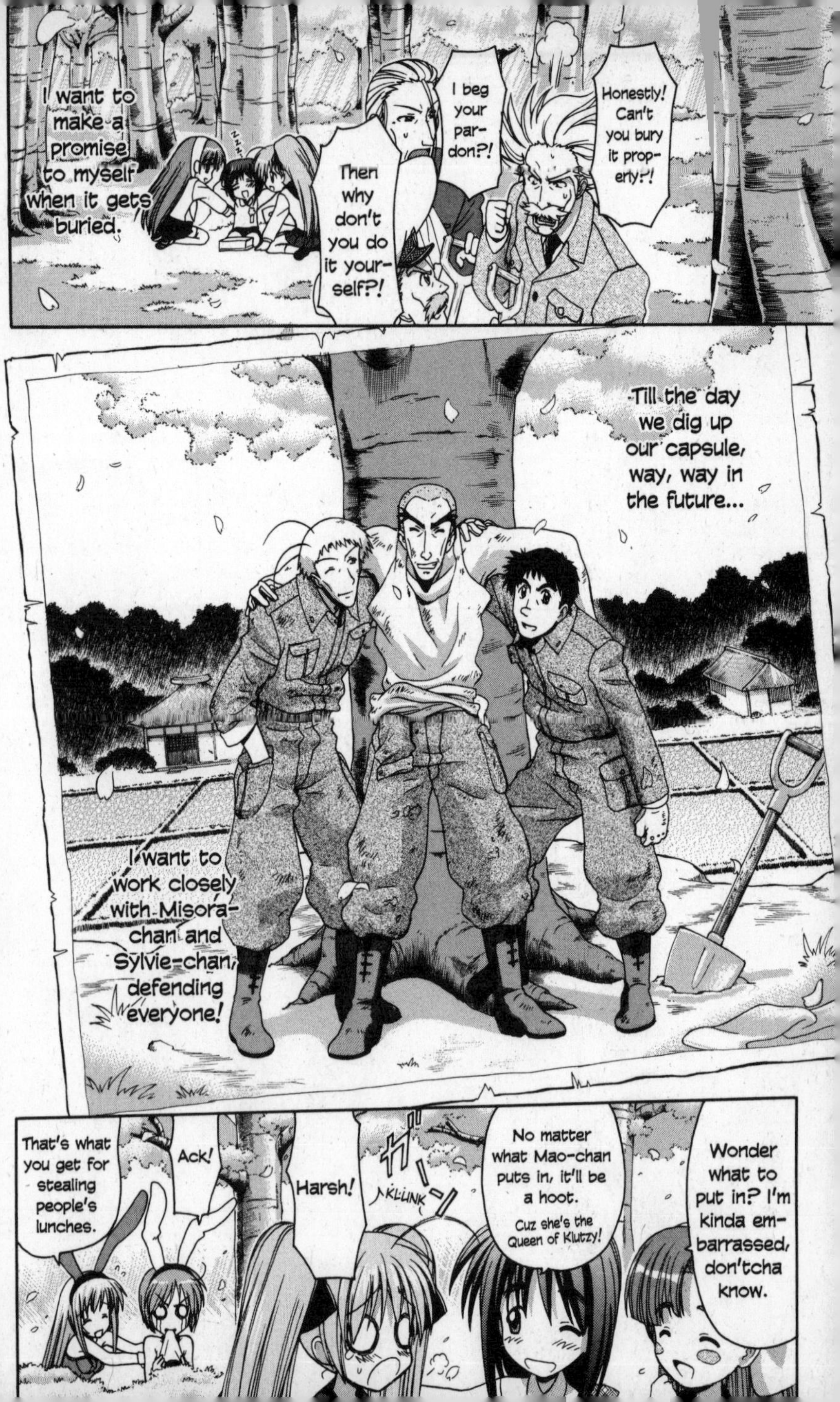
Honestly! Can't you bury it properly?!
I beg your pardon?!
Then why don't you do it yourself?!
I want to make a promise to myself when it gets buried.
Till the day we dig up our capsule, way, way in the future...
I want to work closely with Misora-chan and Sylvie-chan, defending everyone!
Wonder what to put in? I'm kinda embarrassed, don'tcha know.
No matter what Mao-chan puts in, it'll be a hoot.
Cuz she's the Queen of Klutzy!
KLUNK
Harsh!
Ack!
That's what you get for stealing people's lunches.

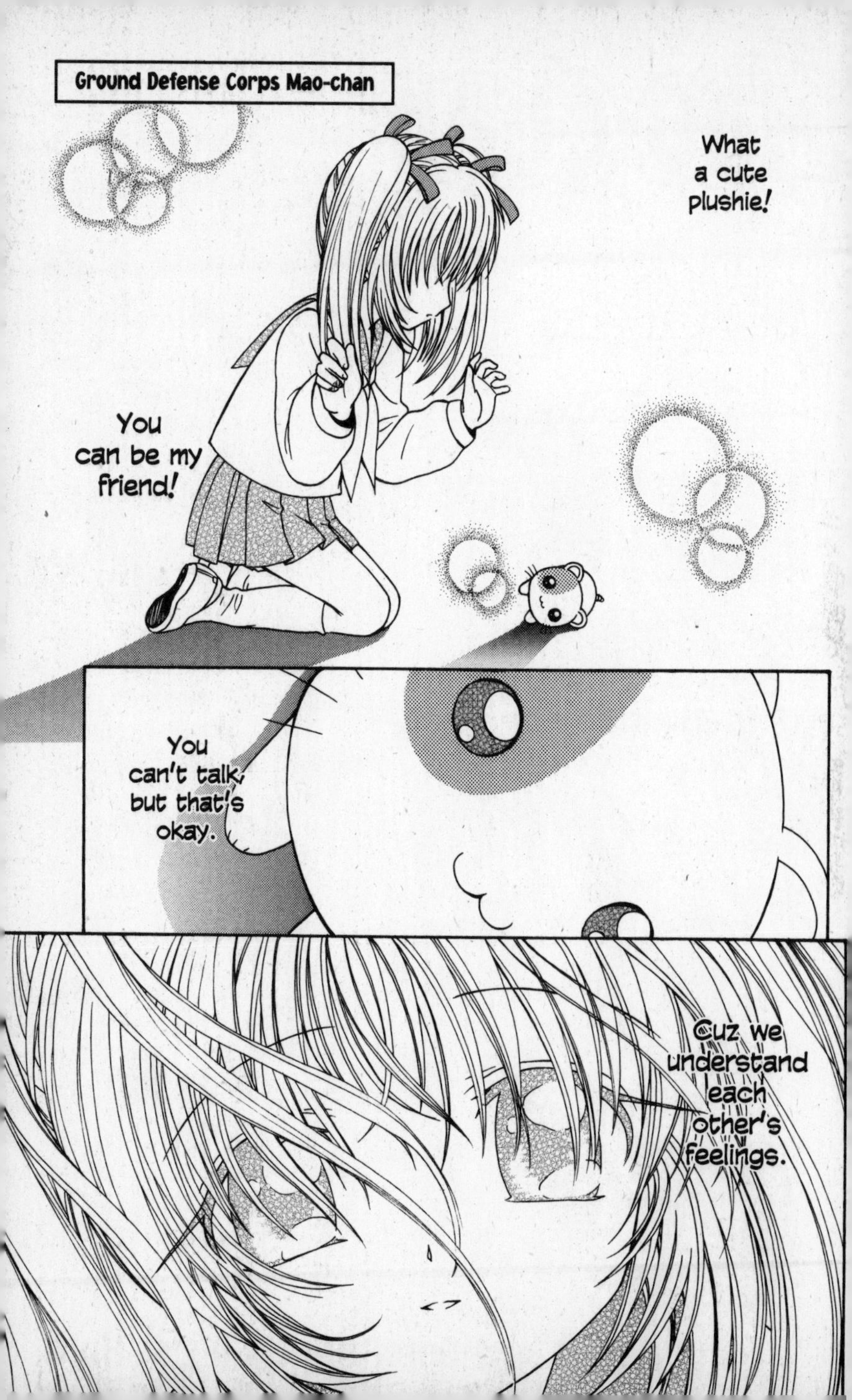
Ground Defense Corps Mao-chan
What a cute plushie!
You can be my friend!
You can't talk, but that's okay.
Cuz we understand each other's feelings.

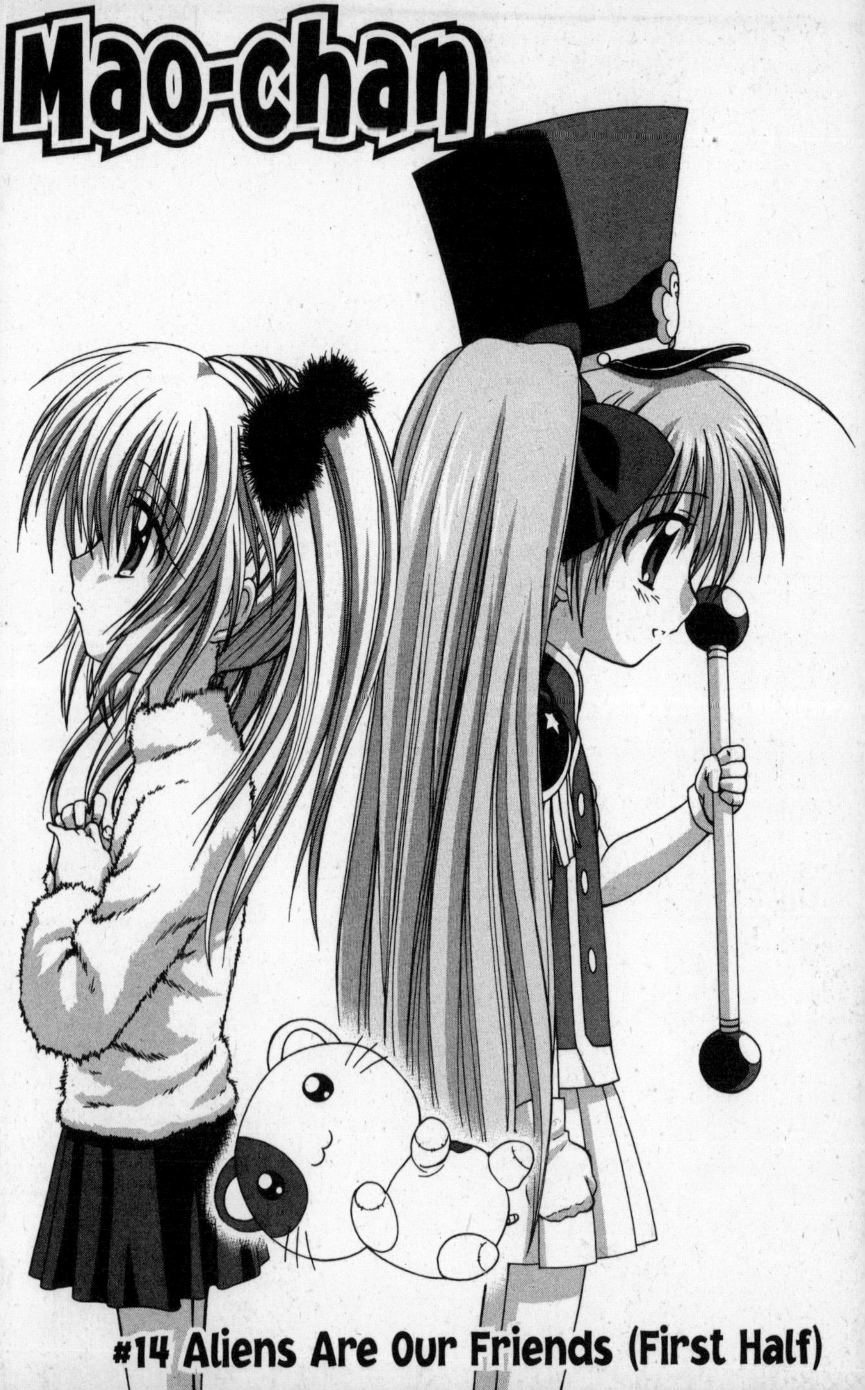
Mao-chan
#14 Aliens Are Our Friends (First Half)

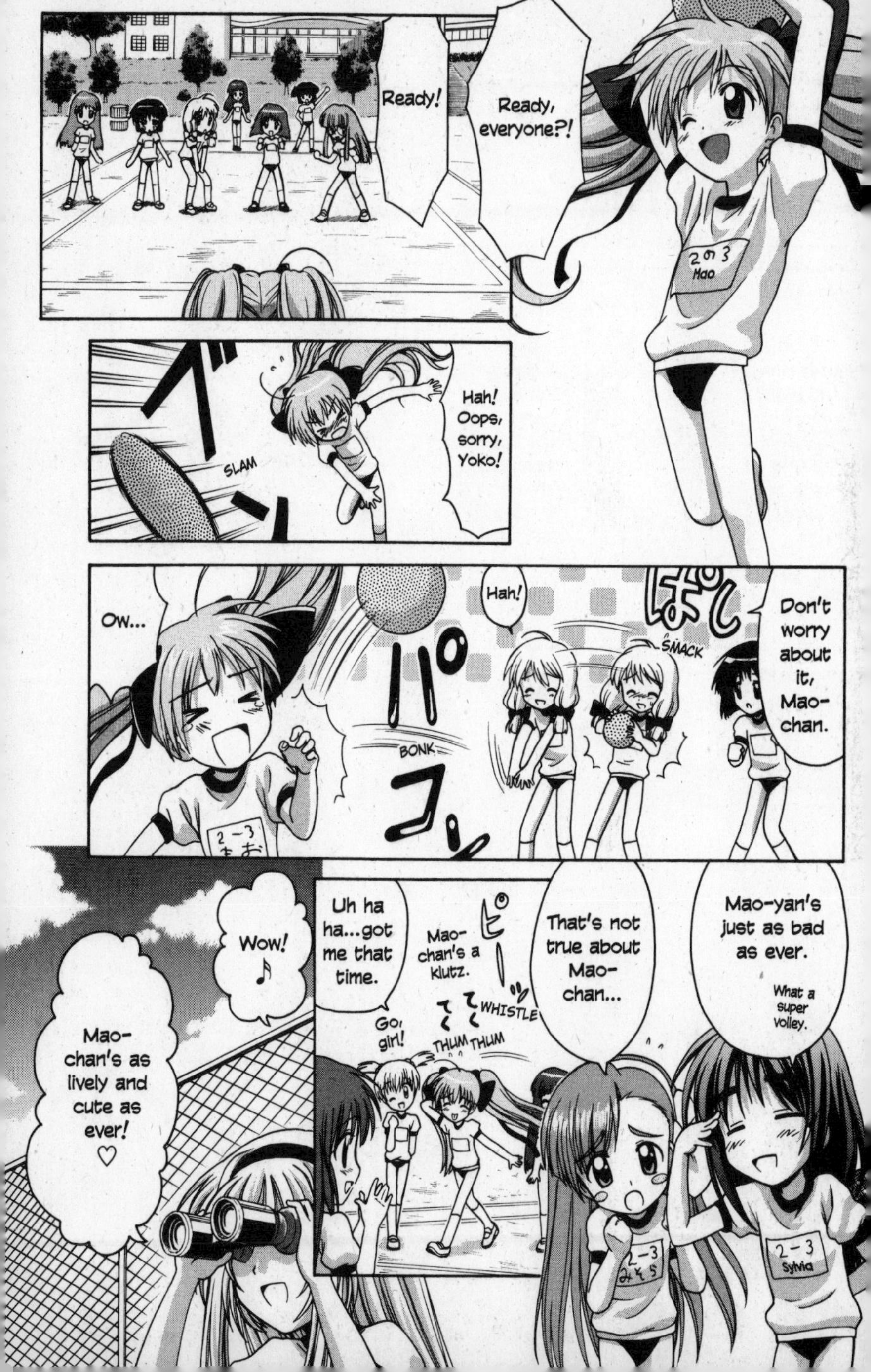

Ready, everyone?!
2の3 Mao
Ready!
Hah! Oops, sorry, Yoko!
SLAM
Don't worry about it, Mao-chan.
SMACK
Hah!
BONK
Ow...
Mao-yan's just as bad as ever.
What a super volley.
2-3 Sylvia
That's not true about Mao-chan...
WHISTLE
Mao-chan's a klutz.
THUM THUM
Uh ha ha...got me that time.
Go, girl!
Wow! ♪
Mao-chan's as lively and cute as ever! ♡

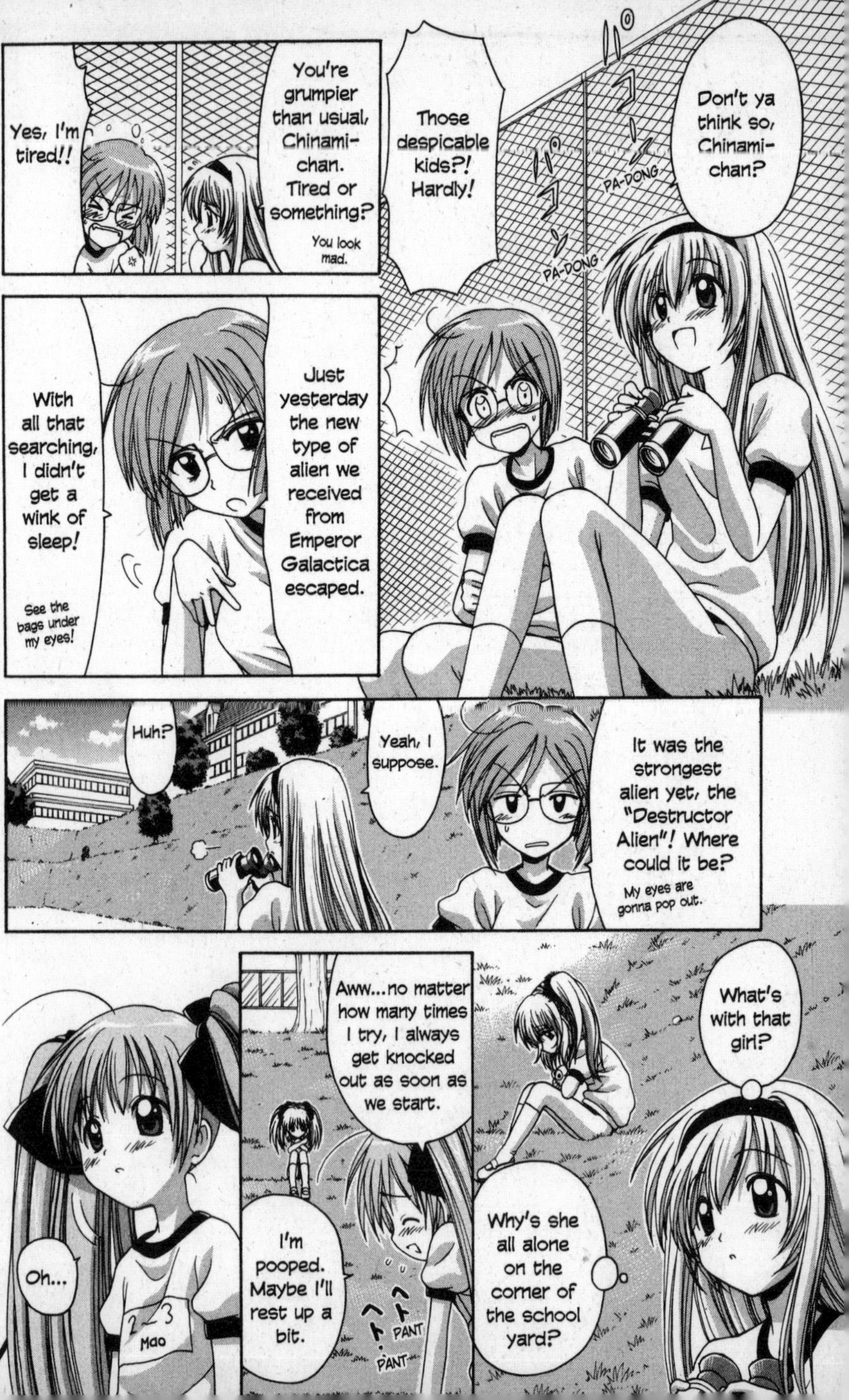
Don't ya think so, Chinami-chan?
PA-DONG
PA-DONG
Those despicable kids?! Hardly!
You're grumpier than usual, Chinami-chan. Tired or something?
You look mad.
Yes, I'm tired!!
Just yesterday the new type of alien we received from Emperor Galactica escaped.
With all that searching, I didn't get a wink of sleep!
See the bags under my eyes!
It was the strongest alien yet, the "Destructor Alien"! Where could it be?
My eyes are gonna pop out.
Yeah, I suppose.
Huh?
What's with that girl?
Why's she all alone on the corner of the school yard?
Aww...no matter how many times I try, I always get knocked out as soon as we start.
I'm pooped. Maybe I'll rest up a bit.
PANT
PANT
Oh...
2-3
Mao

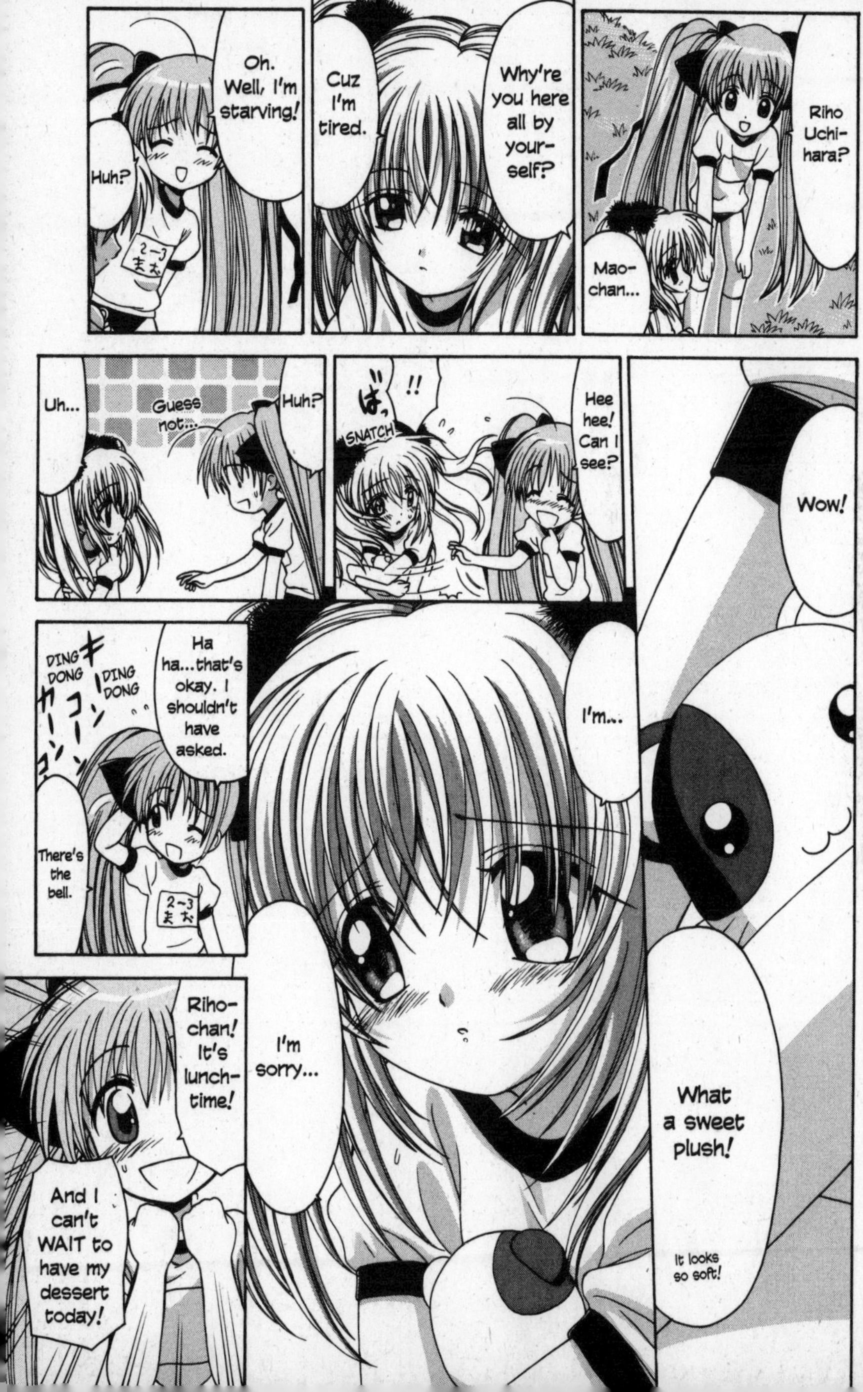
Riho Uchi-hara?
Mao-chan...
Why're you here all by your-self?
Cuz I'm tired.
Oh. Well, I'm starving!
Huh?
Wow!
What a sweet plush!
It looks so soft!
Hee hee! Can I see?
!!
ぱっ
SNATCH
Huh?
Guess not...
Uh...
I'm...
I'm sorry...
Ha ha...that's okay. I shouldn't have asked.
DING DONG
DING DONG
There's the bell.
Riho-chan! It's lunch-time!
And I can't WAIT to have my dessert today!

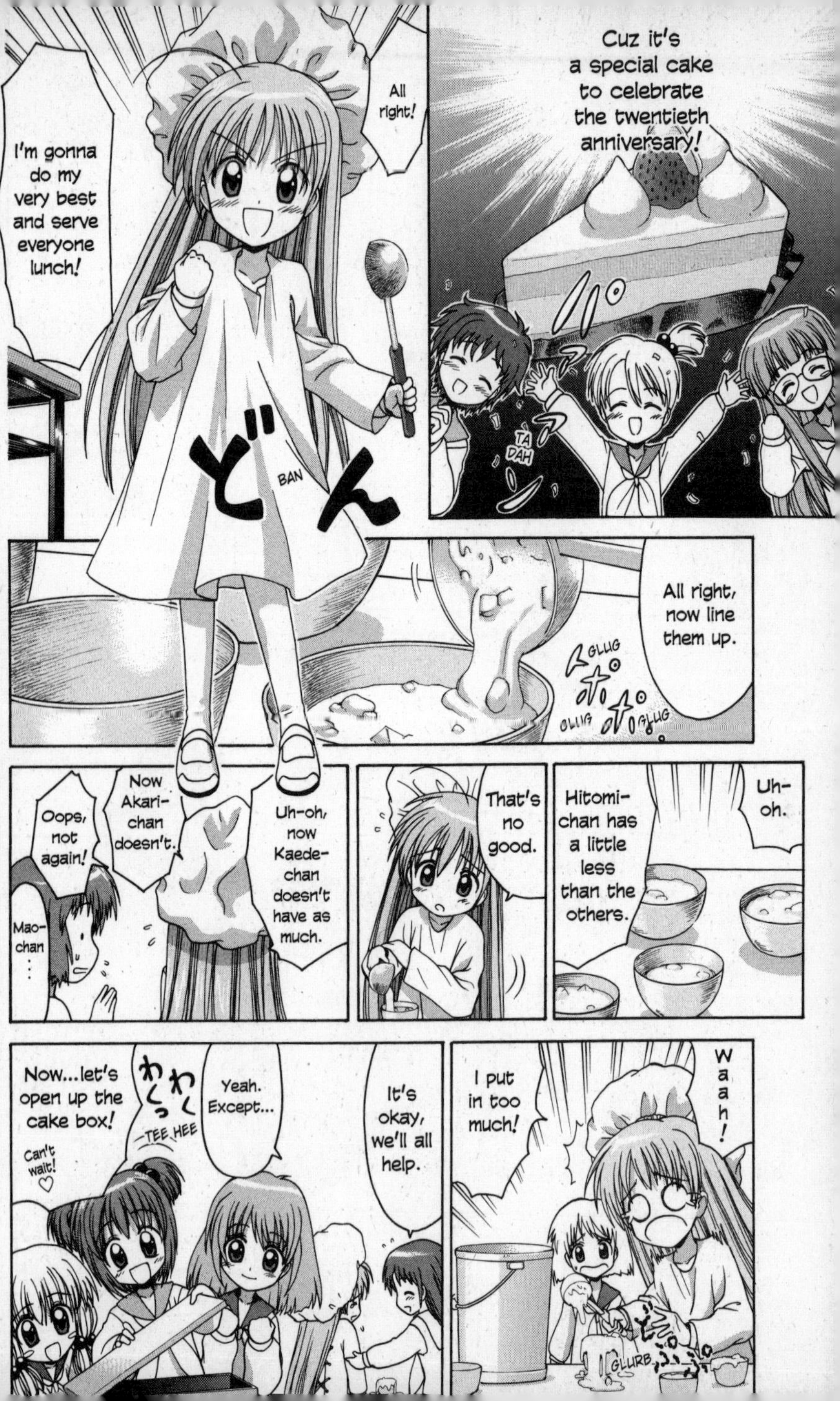
Cuz it's a special cake to celebrate the twentieth anniversary!
TA DAH
All right!
I'm gonna do my very best and serve everyone lunch!
どん
BAN
All right, now line them up.
GLUG
GLUG
GLUG
Uh-oh.
Hitomi-chan has a little less than the others.
That's no good.
Uh-oh, now Kaede-chan doesn't have as much.
Now Akari-chan doesn't.
Oops, not again!
Mao-chan...
Waah!
I put in too much!
GLURB
It's okay, we'll all help.
Yeah. Except...
わくわく
TEE HEE
Now...let's open up the cake box!
Can't wait! ♡

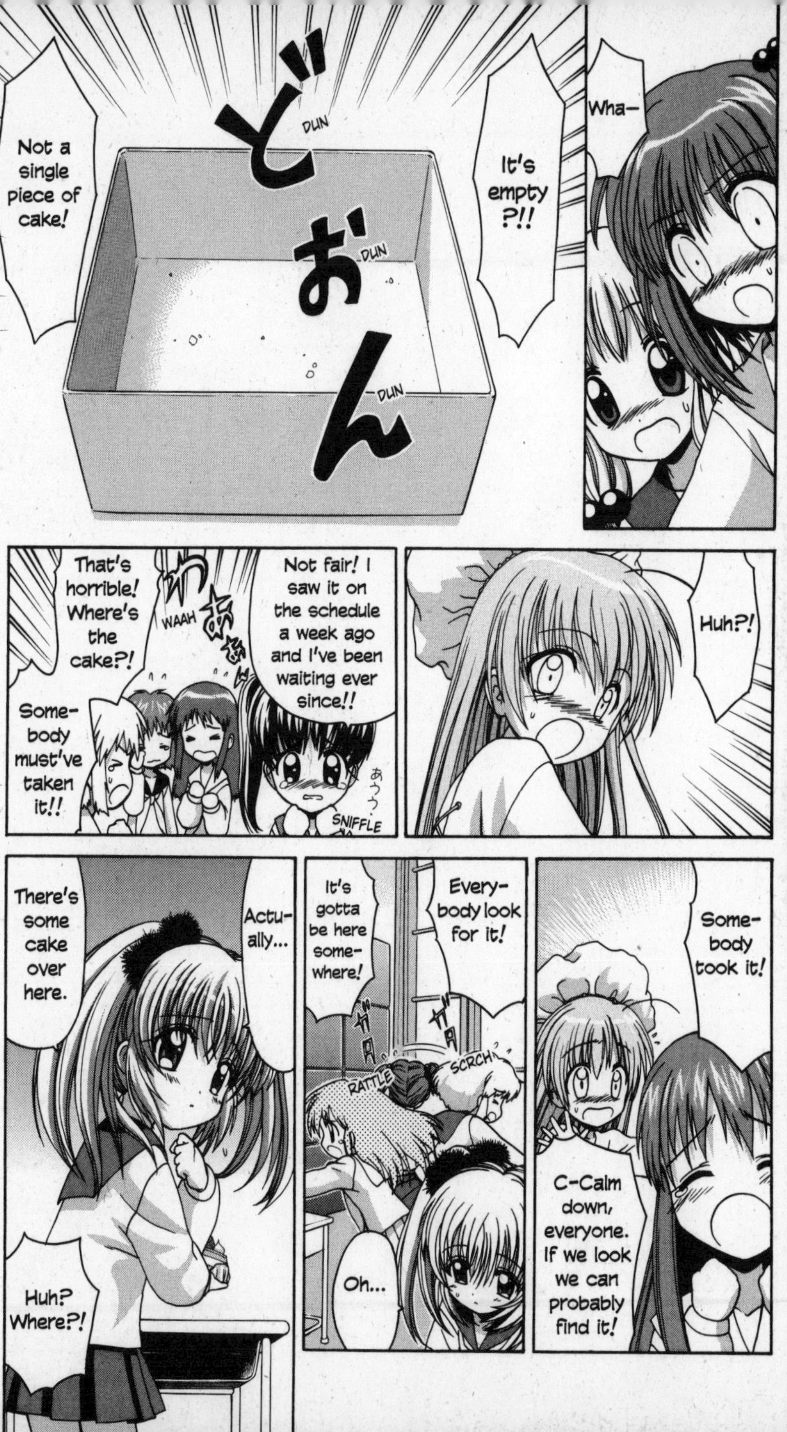
Wha-
It's empty?!!
どおん
DUN
DUN
DUN
Not a single piece of cake!
Huh?!
Not fair! I saw it on the schedule a week ago and I've been waiting ever since!!
That's horrible! Where's the cake?!
WAAH
Some-body must've taken it!!
あうう
SNIFFLE
Some-body took it!
C-Calm down, everyone. If we look we can probably find it!
Every-body look for it!
It's gotta be here some-where!
SCRCH
RATTLE
Oh...
Actu-ally...
There's some cake over here.
Huh? Where?!

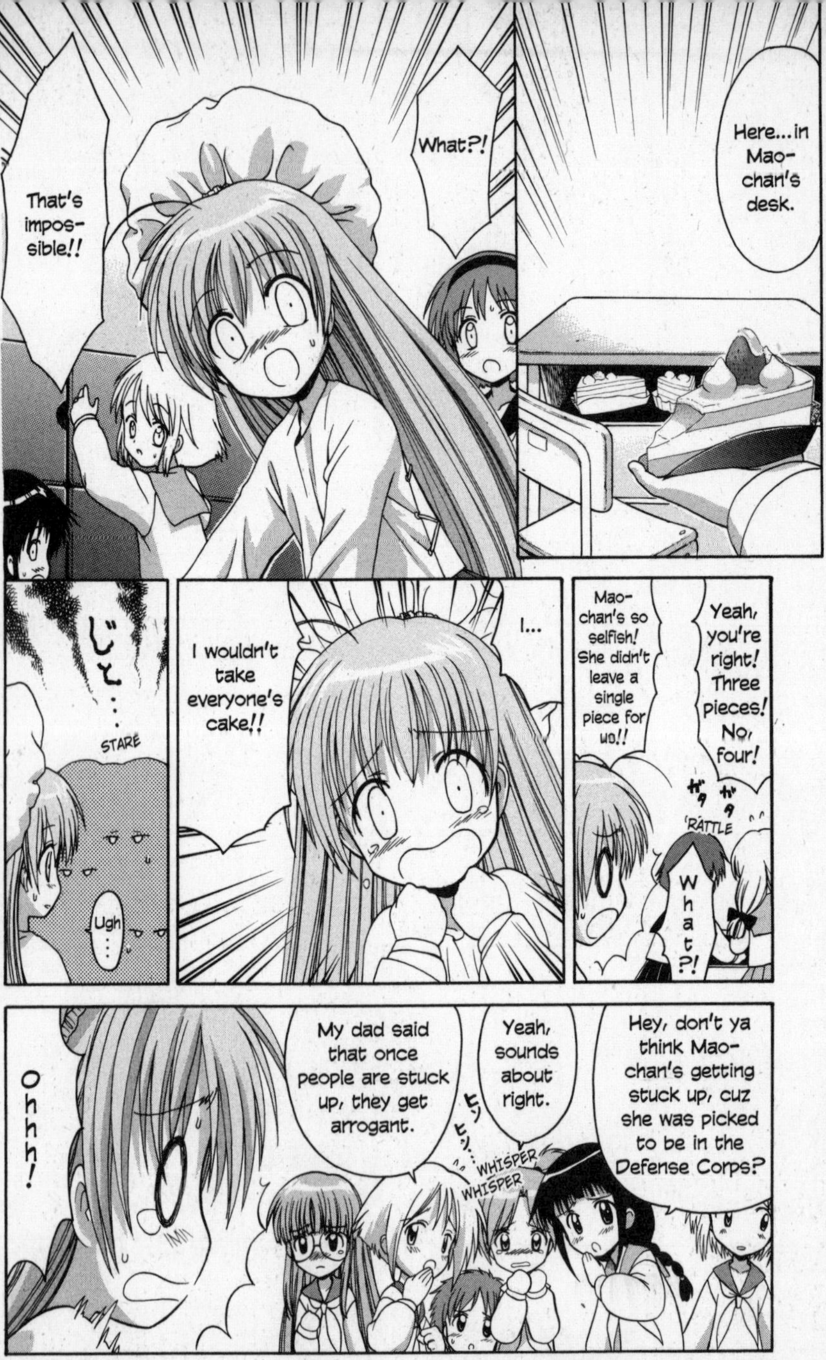
Here...in Mao-chan's desk.
What?!
That's impossible!!
Yeah, you're right! Three pieces! No, four!
Mao-chan's so selfish! She didn't leave a single piece for us!!
ガタガタ
RATTLE
What?!
I...
I wouldn't take everyone's cake!!
じと…
STARE
Ugh…
Hey, don't ya think Mao-chan's getting stuck up, cuz she was picked to be in the Defense Corps?
Yeah, sounds about right.
ヒソヒソ…
WHISPER
WHISPER
My dad said that once people are stuck up, they get arrogant.
Ohhh!

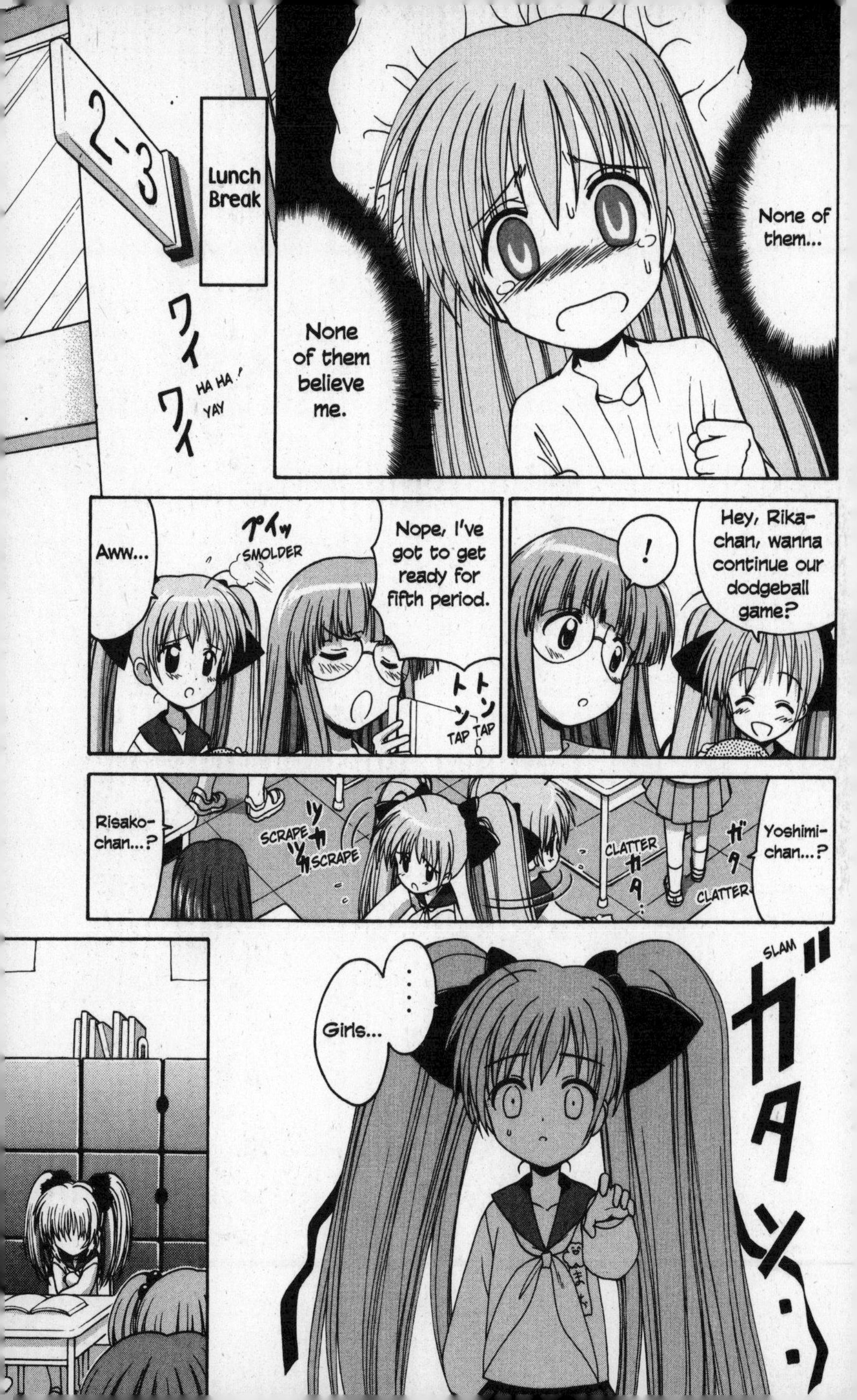
None of them...
None of them believe me.
2-3
Lunch Break
ワイワイ
HA HA! YAY
Hey, Rika-chan, wanna continue our dodgeball game?
!
Nope, I've got to get ready for fifth period.
トトン
TAP TAP
プイッ
SMOLDER
Aww...
Yoshimi-chan...?
ガタ
CLATTER
ガタ
CLATTER
ズリ
SCRAPE
ズリ
SCRAPE
Risako-chan...?
ガタン...
SLAM
....
Girls...

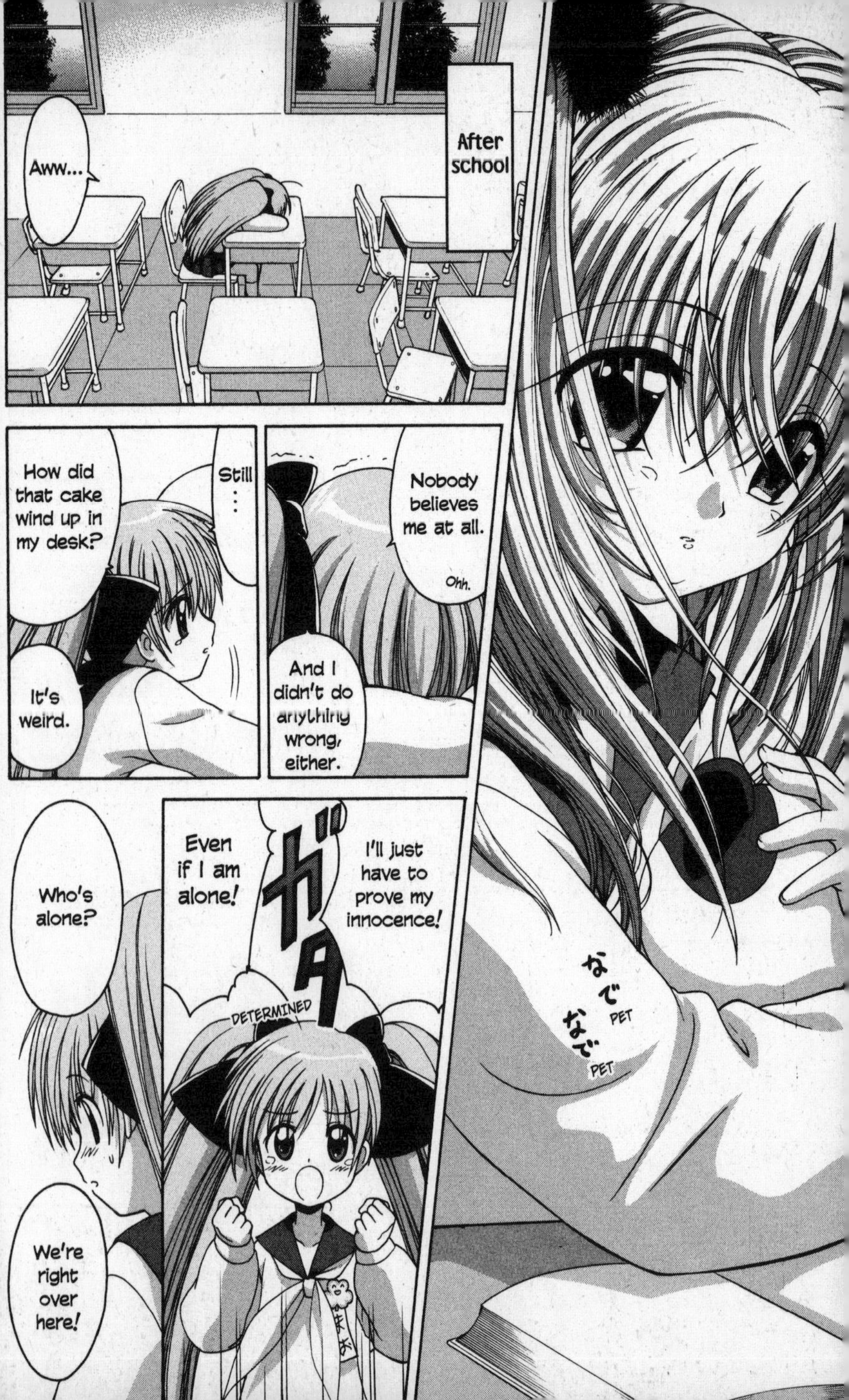
なで PET
なで PET
After school
Aww...
Nobody believes me at all.
Ohh.
And I didn't do anything wrong, either.
Still...
How did that cake wind up in my desk?
It's weird.
I'll just have to prove my innocence!
ガタ
Even if I am alone!
DETERMINED
Who's alone?
We're right over here!

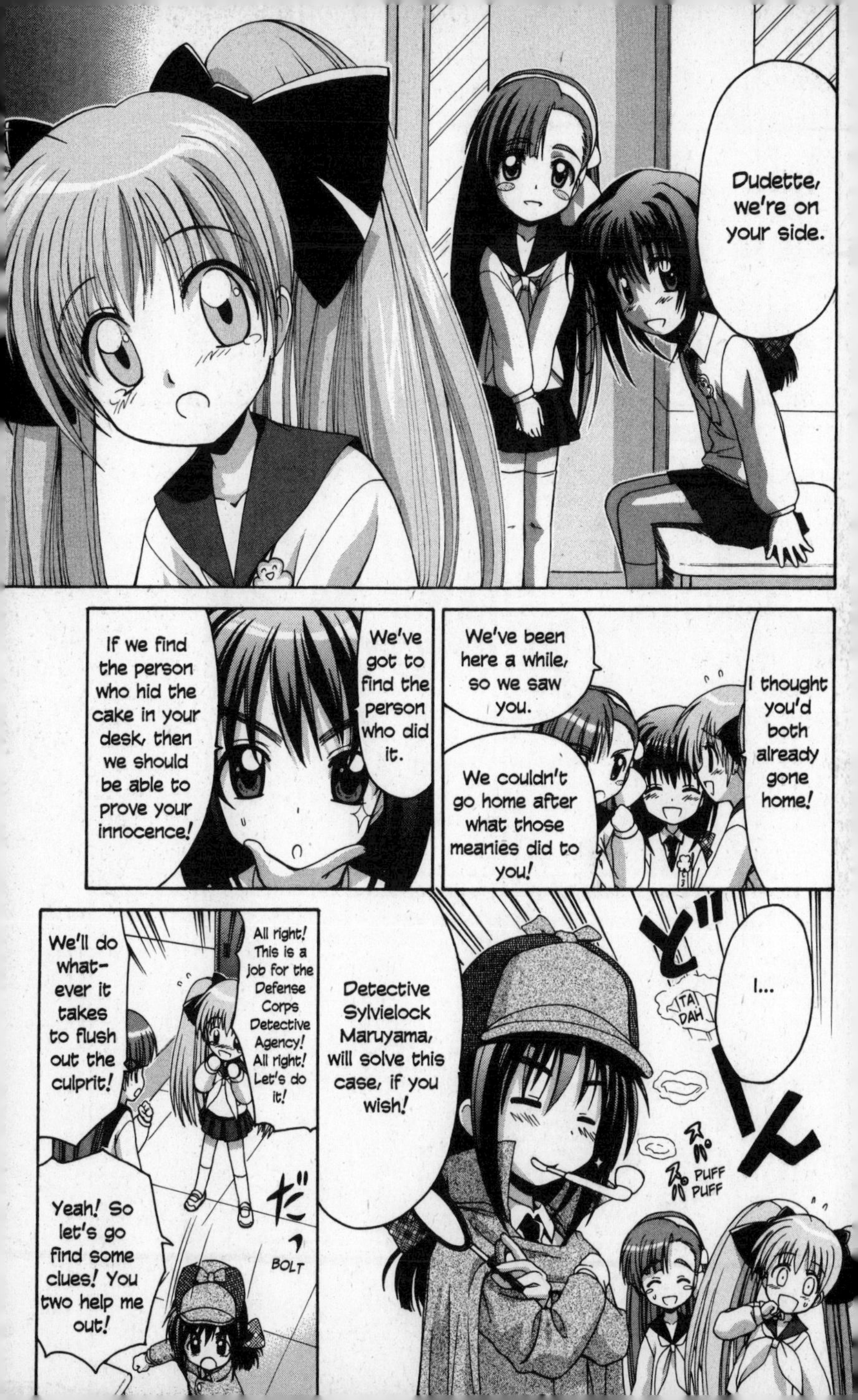
Dudette, we're on your side.
I thought you'd both already gone home!
We've been here a while, so we saw you.
We couldn't go home after what those meanies did to you!
We've got to find the person who did it.
If we find the person who hid the cake in your desk, then we should be able to prove your innocence!
I...
TA DAH
Detective Sylvielock Maruyama, will solve this case, if you wish!
PUFF PUFF
All right! This is a job for the Defense Corps Detective Agency! All right! Let's do it!
We'll do what-ever it takes to flush out the culprit!
BOLT
Yeah! So let's go find some clues! You two help me out!

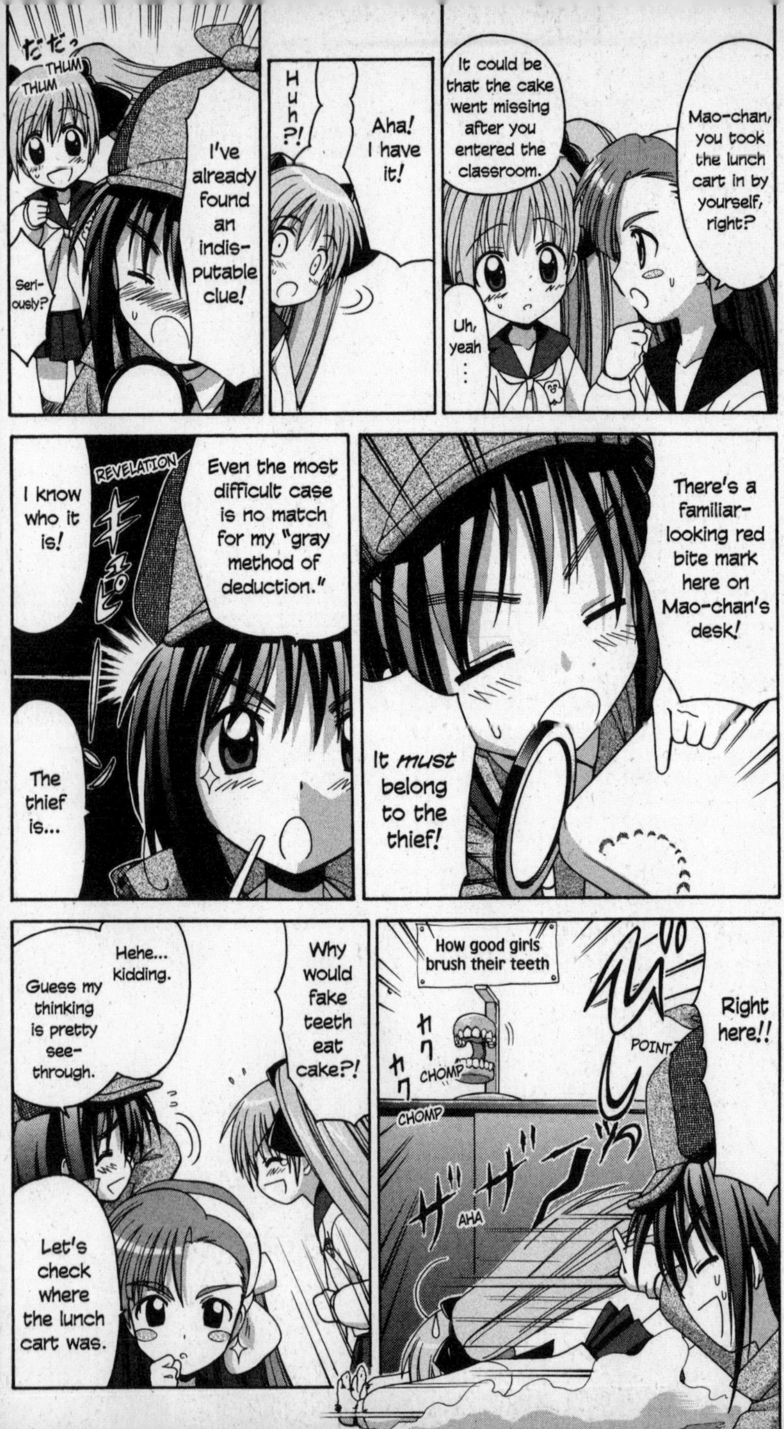

Mao-chan, you took the lunch cart in by yourself, right?
It could be that the cake went missing after you entered the classroom.
Uh, yeah...
Aha! I have it!
Huh?!
I've already found an indisputable clue!
THUM THUM
Seriously?
There's a familiar-looking red bite mark here on Mao-chan's desk!
It *must* belong to the thief!
Even the most difficult case is no match for my "gray method of deduction."
REVELATION
I know who it is!
The thief is...
Right here!!
POINT
How good girls brush their teeth
CHOMP
CHOMP
AHA
Why would fake teeth eat cake?!
Hehe... kidding.
Guess my thinking is pretty see-through.
Let's check where the lunch cart was.

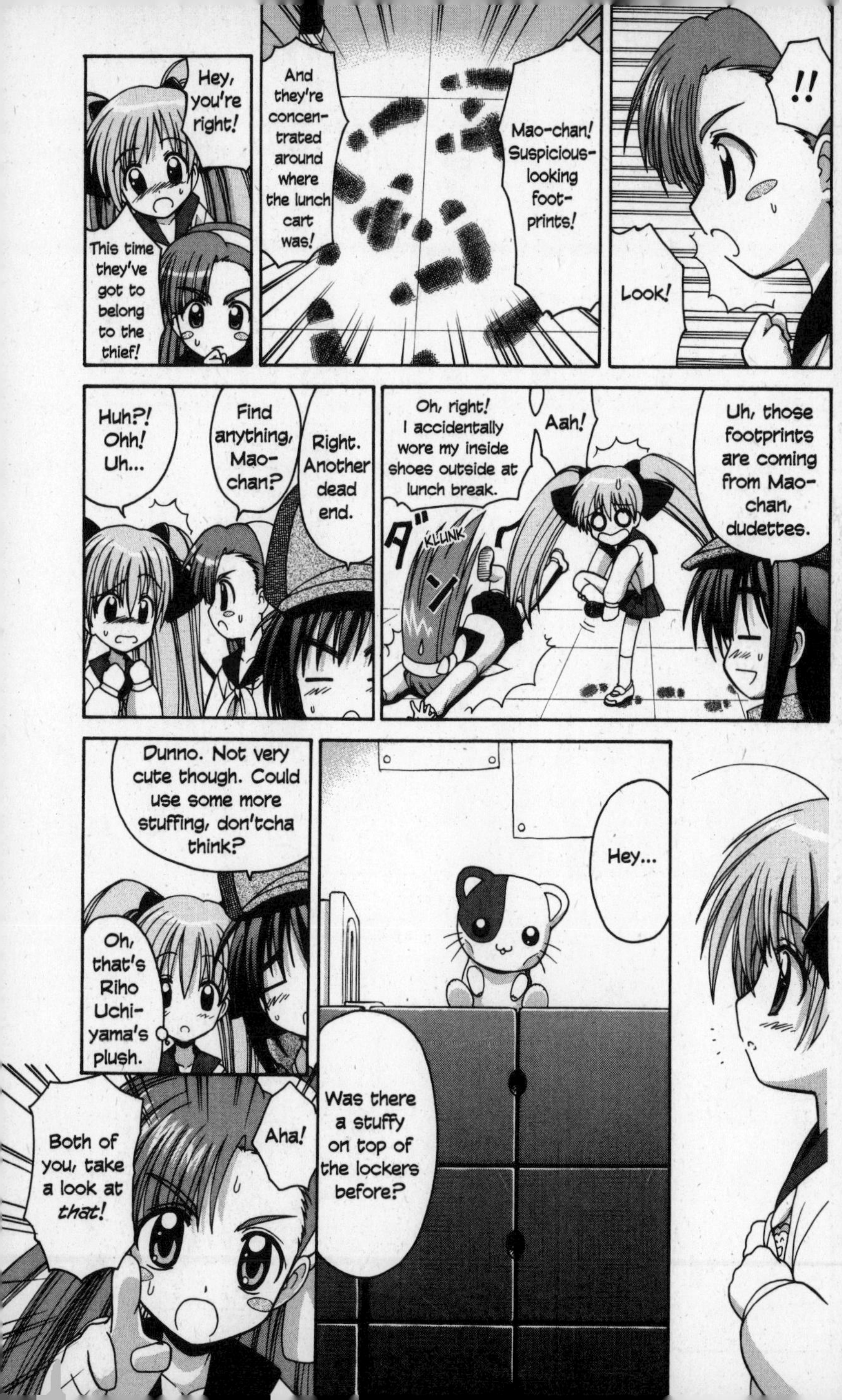
!!
Look!
Mao-chan! Suspicious-looking foot-prints!
And they're concen-trated around where the lunch cart was!
Hey, you're right!
This time they've got to belong to the thief!
Uh, those footprints are coming from Mao-chan, dudettes.
Aah!
Oh, right! I accidentally wore my inside shoes outside at lunch break.
KLUNK
Right. Another dead end.
Find anything, Mao-chan?
Huh?! Ohh! Uh...
Hey...
Was there a stuffy on top of the lockers before?
Dunno. Not very cute though. Could use some more stuffing, don'tcha think?
Oh, that's Riho Uchi-yama's plush.
Aha!
Both of you, take a look at *that*!

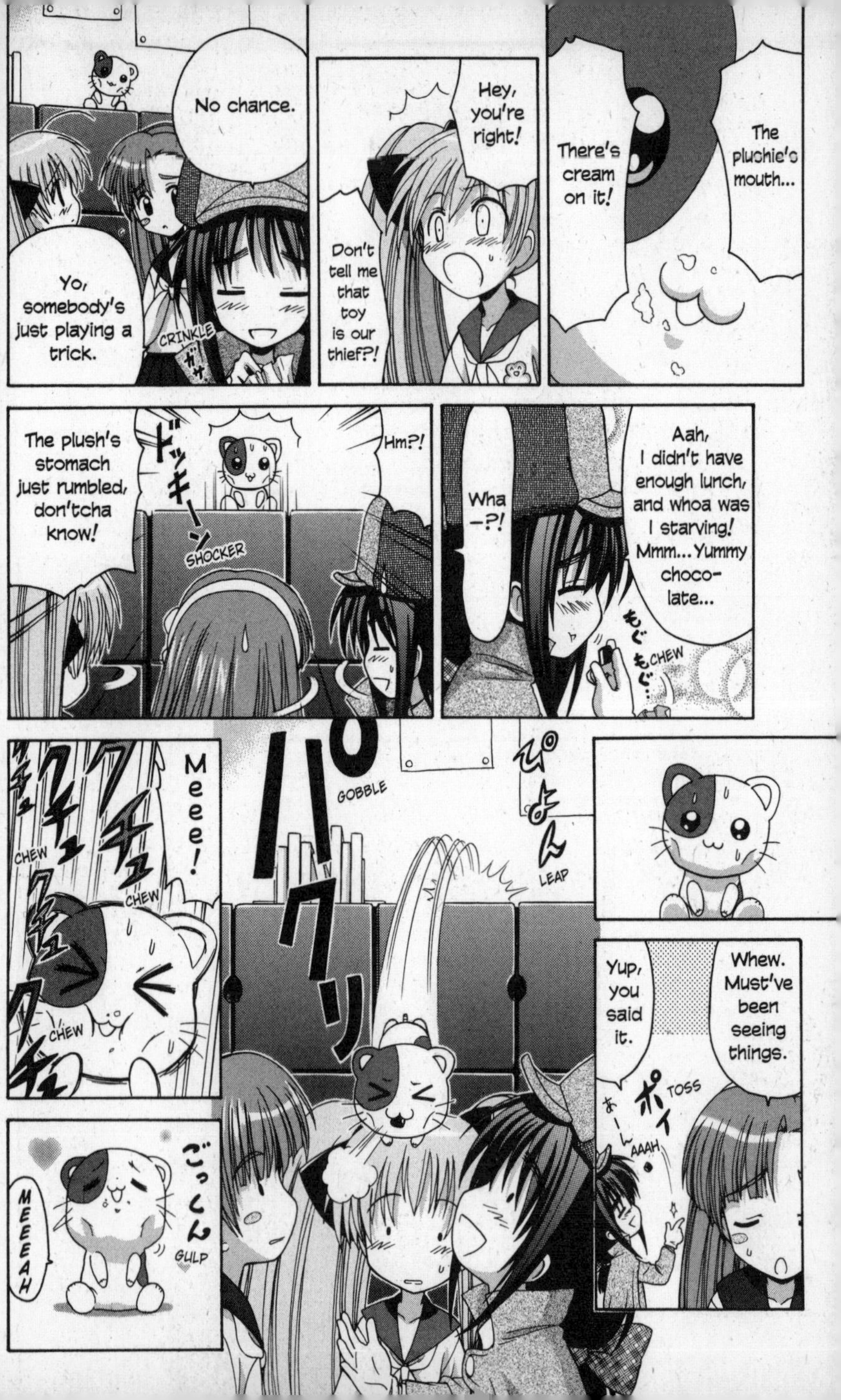
The pluchie's mouth...
There's cream on it!
Hey, you're right!
Don't tell me that toy is our thief?!
No chance.
Yo, somebody's just playing a trick.
CRINKLE
Aah, I didn't have enough lunch, and whoa was I starving! Mmm...Yummy choco-late...
もぐもぐ CHEW
Wha—?!
Hm?!
ドッキーン SHOCKER
The plush's stomach just rumbled, don'tcha know!
Whew. Must've been seeing things.
Yup, you said it.
ポイ TOSS
あ〜ん AAAH
ぴょん LEAP
パクリ GOBBLE
Meee!
CHEW
CHEW
CHEW
ごっくん GULP
MEEEEAH

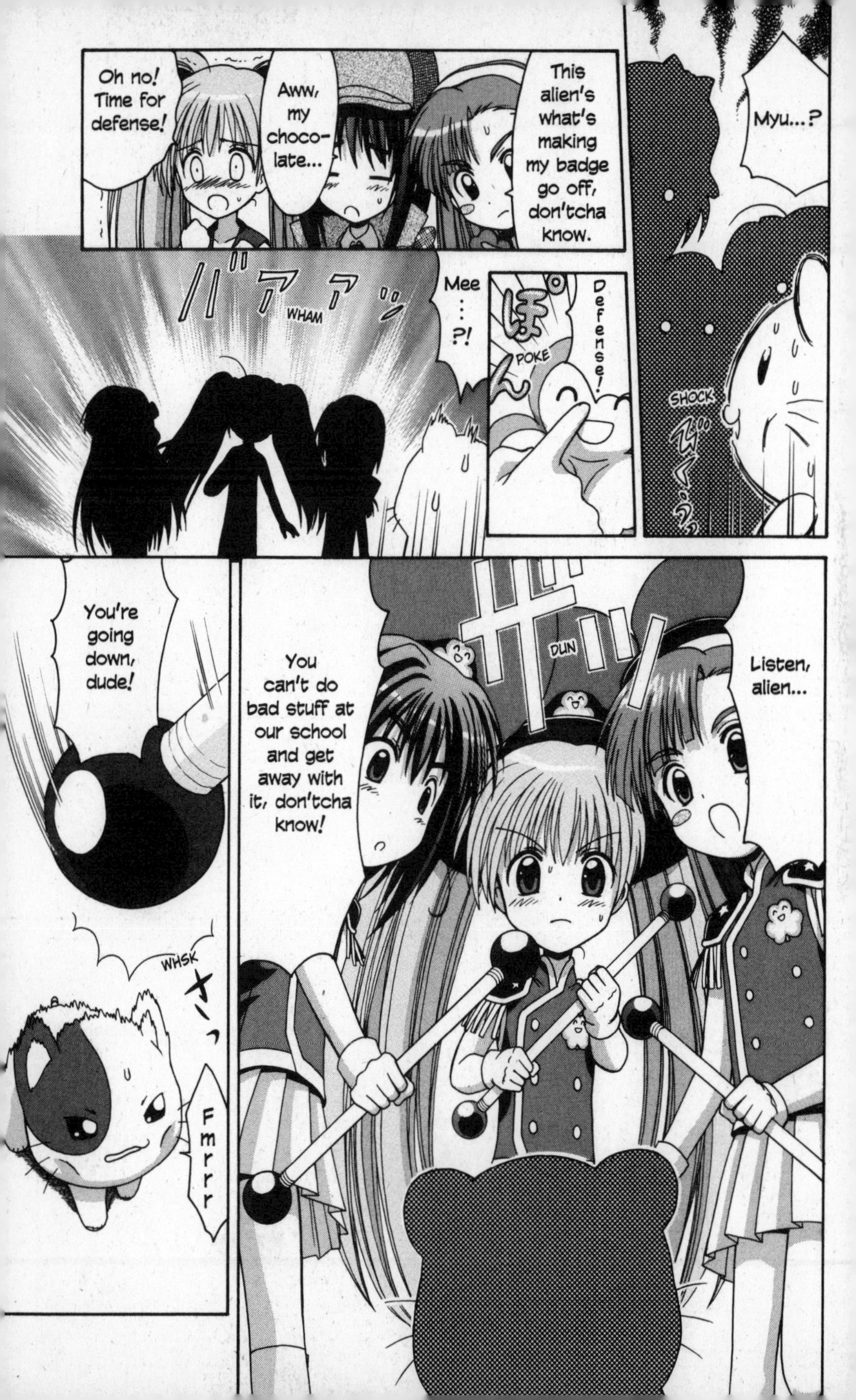
Myu...?
SHOCK
This alien's what's making my badge go off, don'tcha know.
Aww, my choco-late...
Oh no! Time for defense!
Defense!
POKE
Mee...?!
WHAM
Listen, alien...
DUN
You can't do bad stuff at our school and get away with it, don'tcha know!
You're going down, dude!
WHSK
Fmrrr

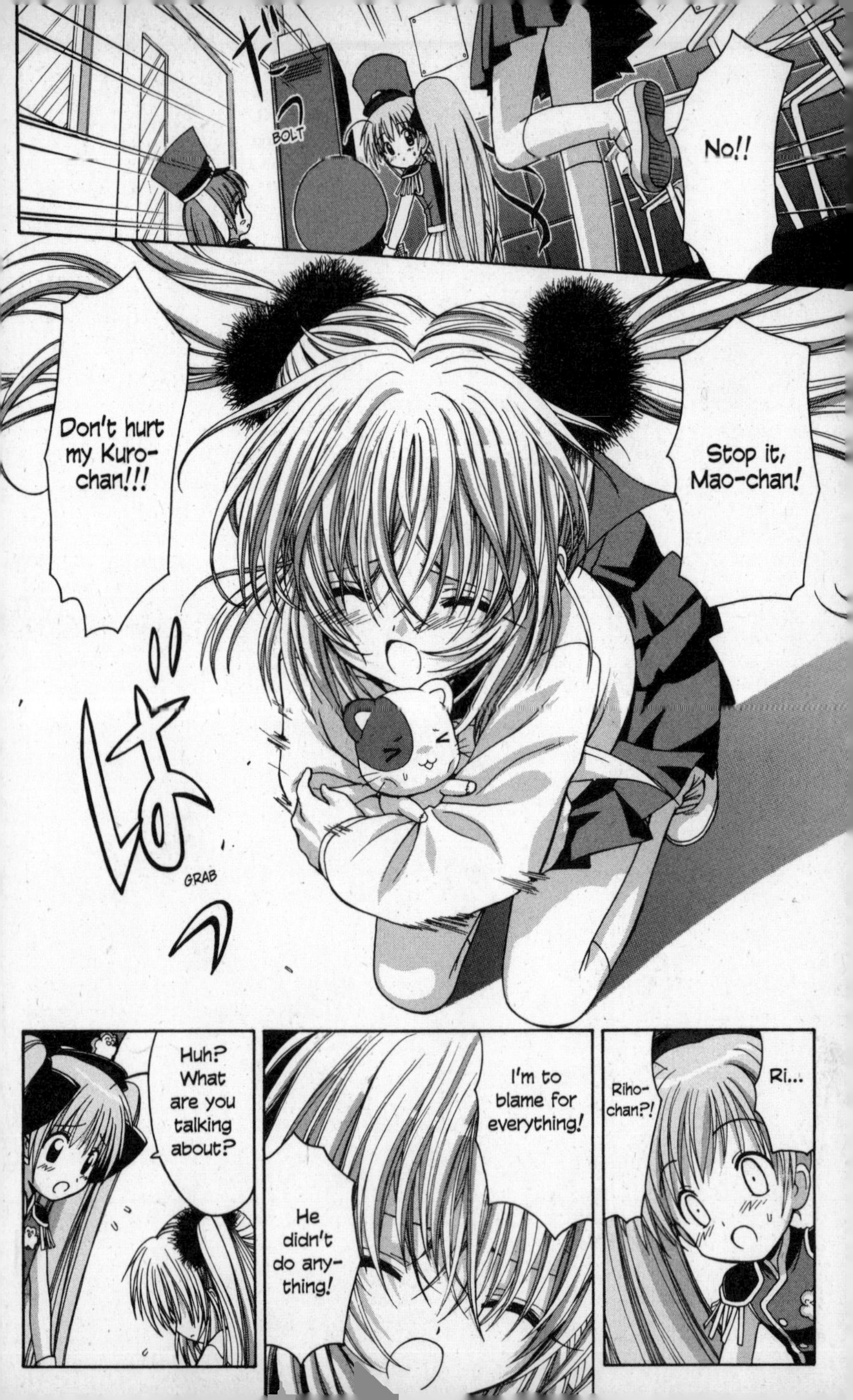
No!!
BOLT
Stop it, Mao-chan!
Don't hurt my Kuro-chan!!!
GRAB
Ri...
Riho-chan?!
I'm to blame for everything!
He didn't do any-thing!
Huh? What are you talking about?

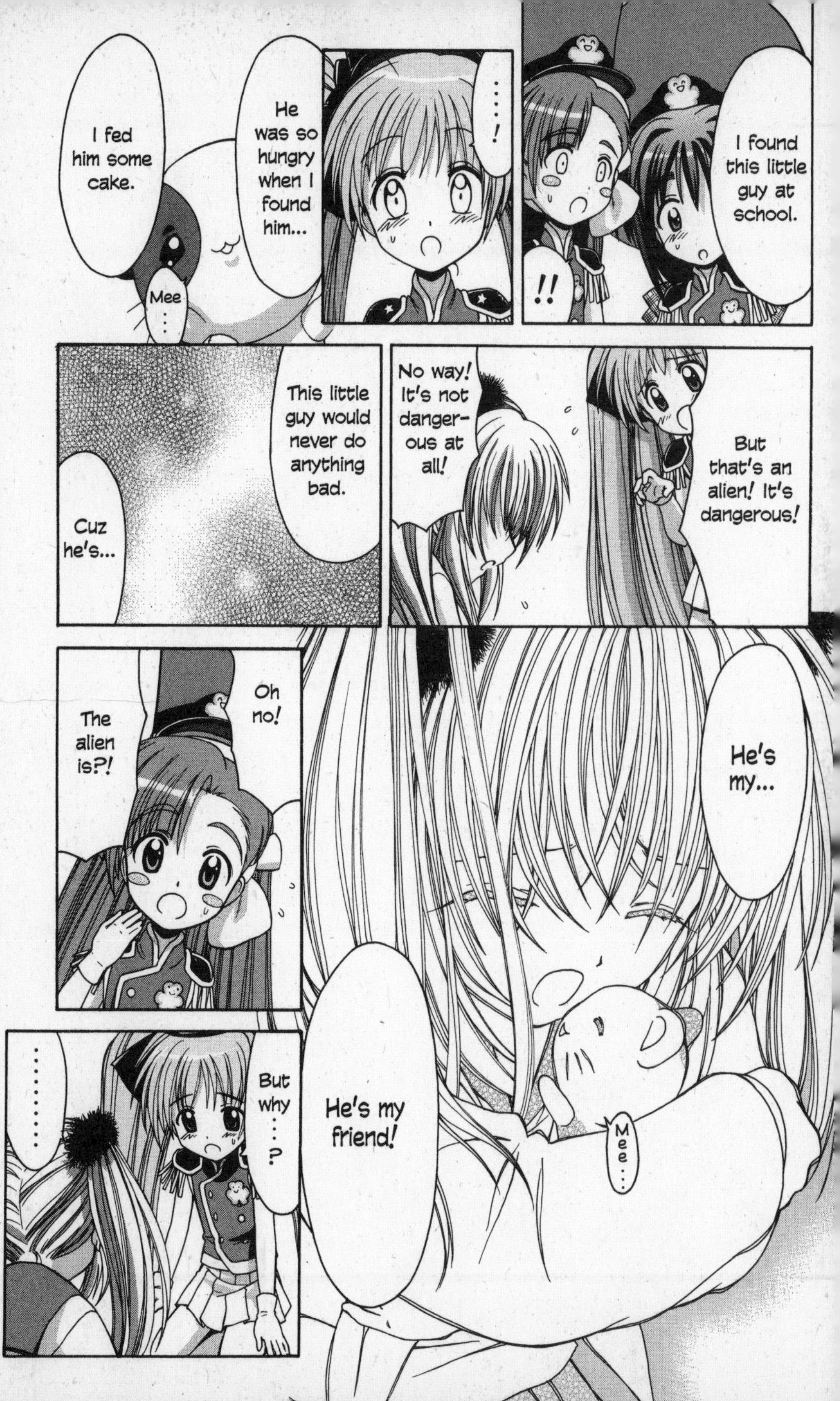
I found this little guy at school.
!!
....!
He was so hungry when I found him...
I fed him some cake.
Mee...
But that's an alien! It's dangerous!
No way! It's not danger-ous at all!
This little guy would never do anything bad.
Cuz he's...
He's my...
Oh no!
The alien is?!
Mee...
He's my friend!
But why...?
....

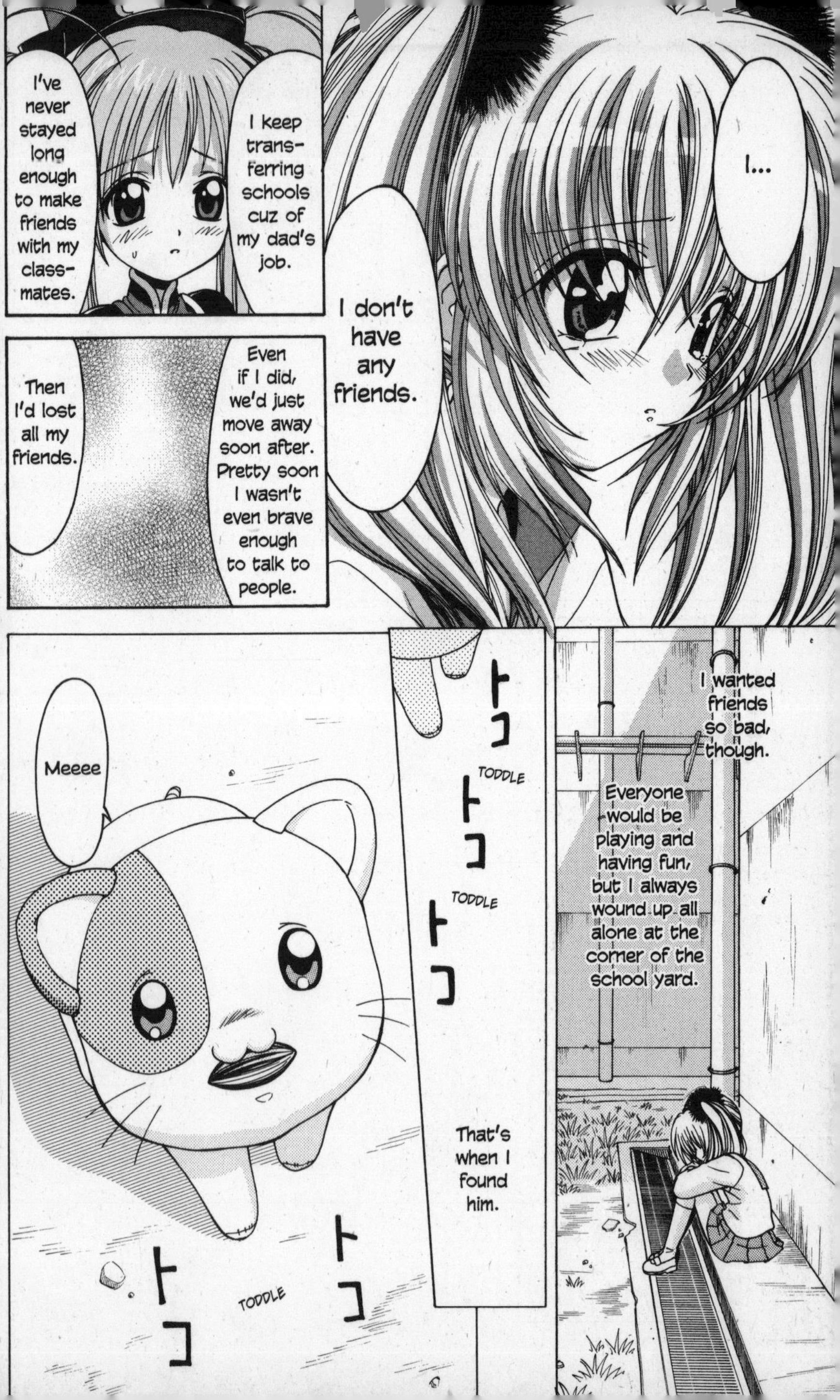

I...
I don't have any friends.
I keep transferring schools cuz of my dad's job.
I've never stayed long enough to make friends with my classmates.
Even if I did, we'd just move away soon after. Pretty soon I wasn't even brave enough to talk to people.
Then I'd lost all my friends.
I wanted friends so bad, though.
Everyone would be playing and having fun, but I always wound up all alone at the corner of the school yard.
トコ
TODDLE
トコ
TODDLE
トコ
That's when I found him.
Meeee
トコ
TODDLE
トコ

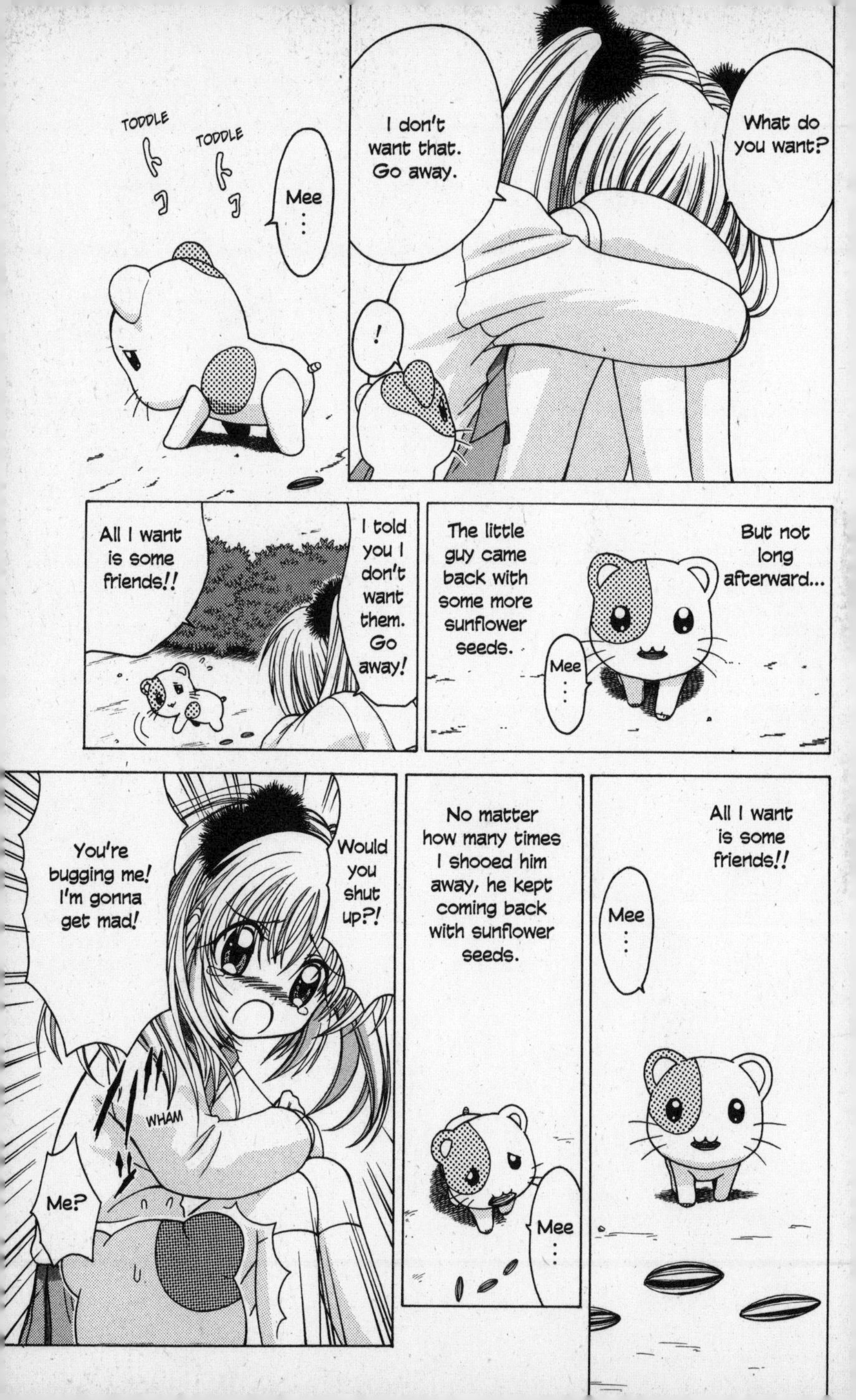
What do you want?
I don't want that. Go away.
!
Mee...
TODDLE
TODDLE
But not long afterward...
The little guy came back with some more sunflower seeds.
Mee...
I told you I don't want them. Go away!
All I want is some friends!!
All I want is some friends!!
Mee...
No matter how many times I shooed him away, he kept coming back with sunflower seeds.
Mee...
Would you shut up?!
You're bugging me! I'm gonna get mad!
WHAM
Me?

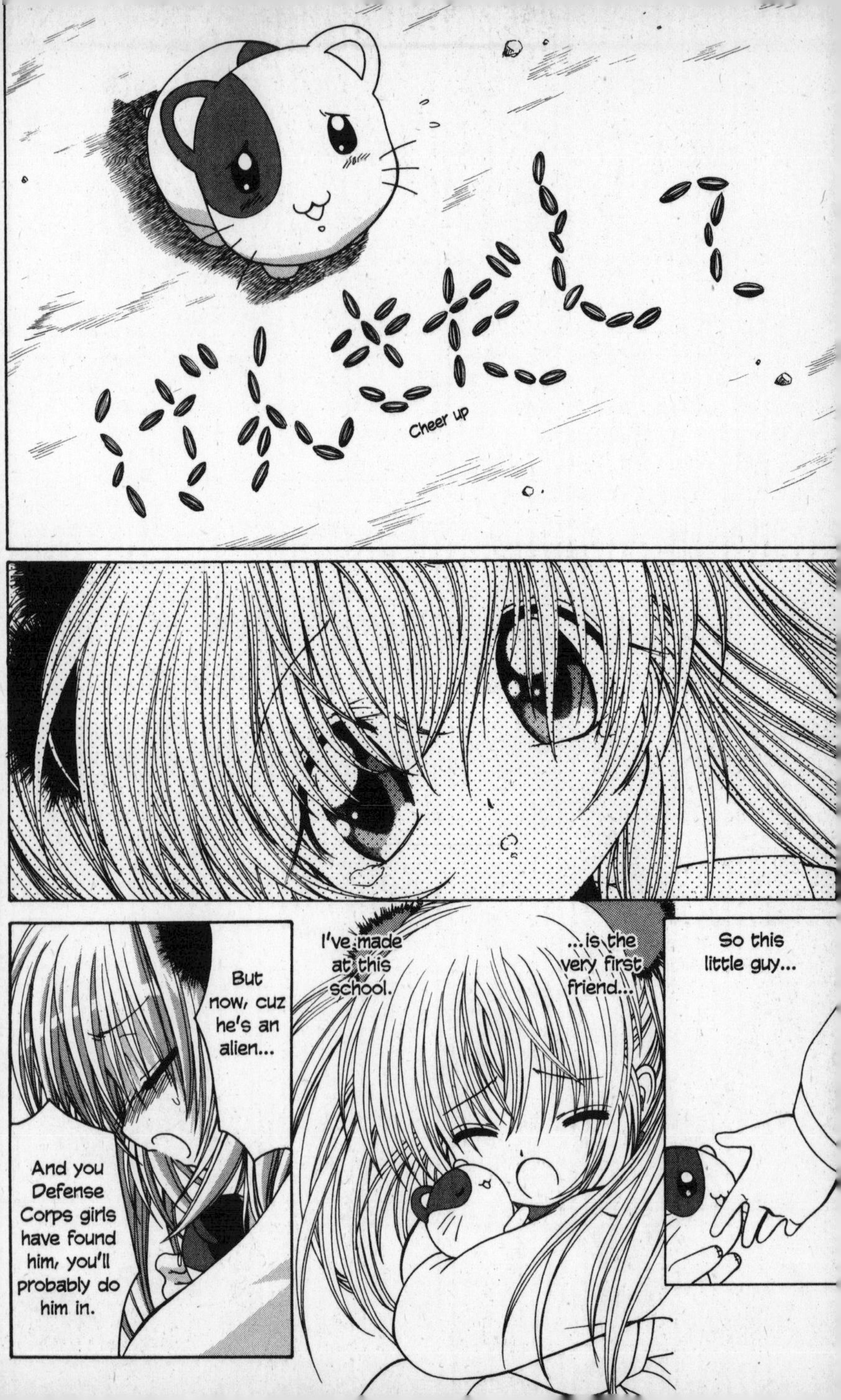
Cheer up
So this little guy...
...is the very first friend...
I've made at this school.
But now, cuz he's an alien...
And you Defense Corps girls have found him, you'll probably do him in.

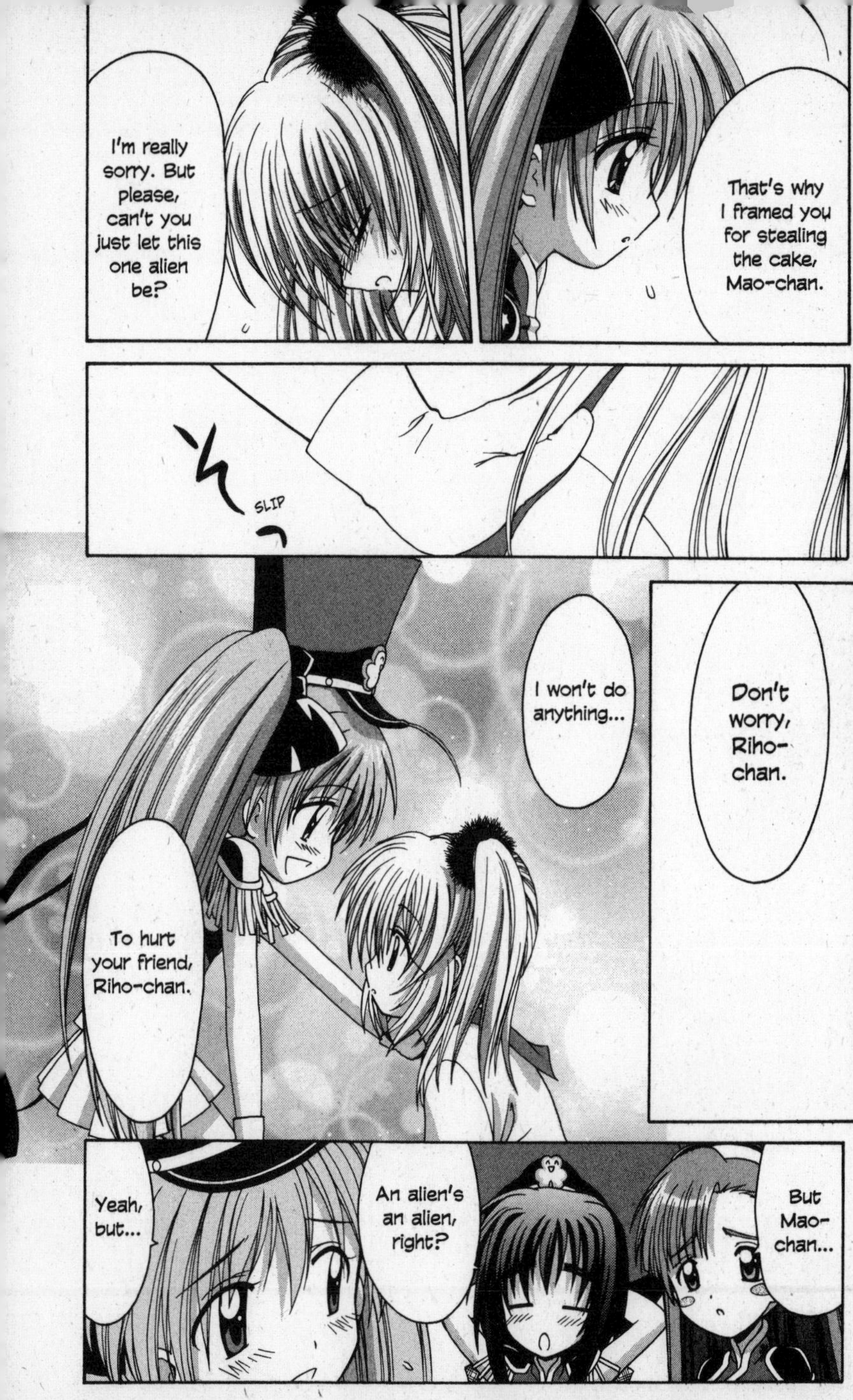
That's why I framed you for stealing the cake, Mao-chan.
I'm really sorry. But please, can't you just let this one alien be?
SLIP
Don't worry, Riho-chan.
I won't do anything...
To hurt your friend, Riho-chan.
But Mao-chan...
An alien's an alien, right?
Yeah, but...

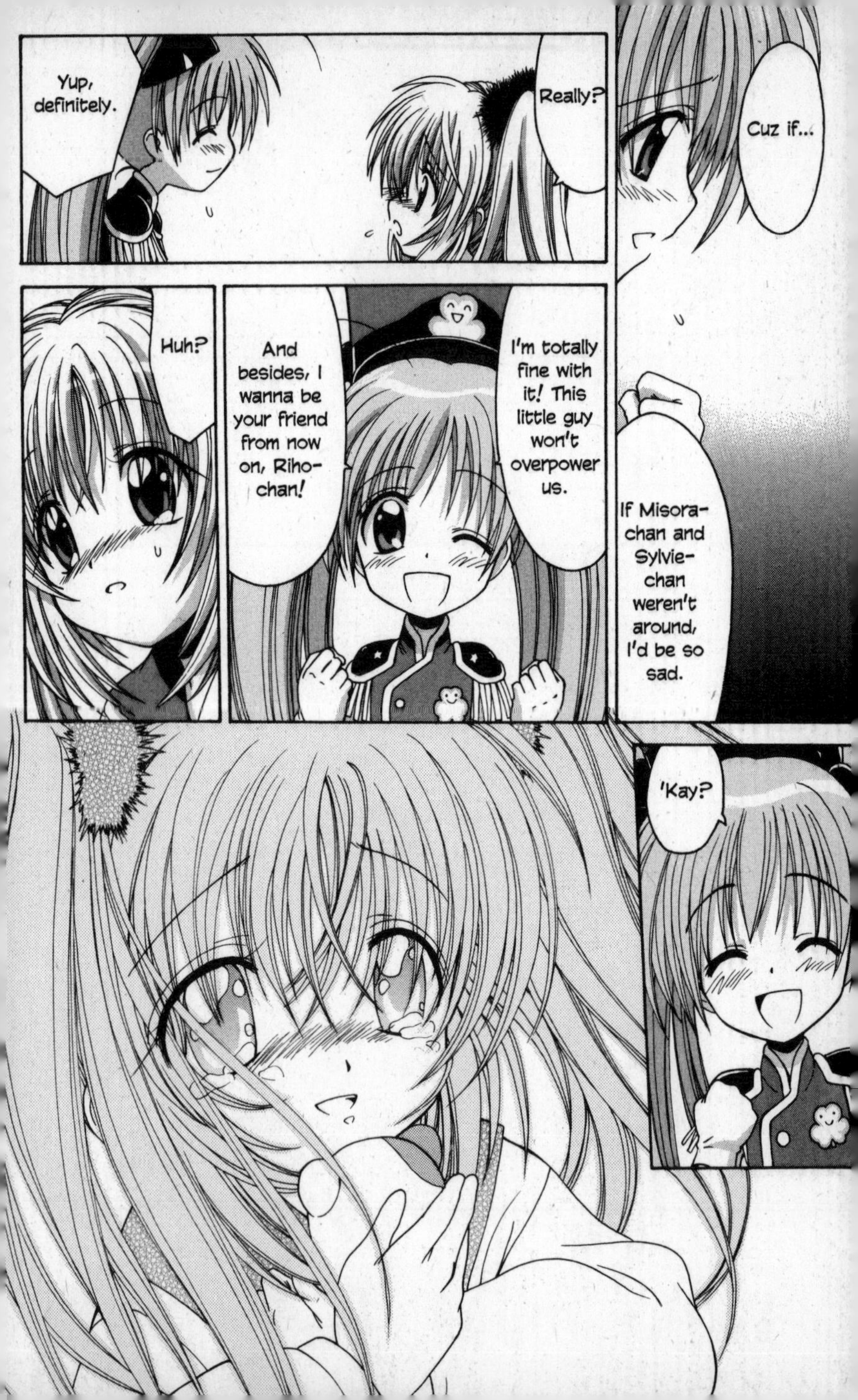
Cuz if...
If Misora-chan and Sylvie-chan weren't around, I'd be so sad.
Really?
Yup, definitely.
I'm totally fine with it! This little guy won't overpower us.
And besides, I wanna be your friend from now on, Riho-chan!
Huh?
'Kay?

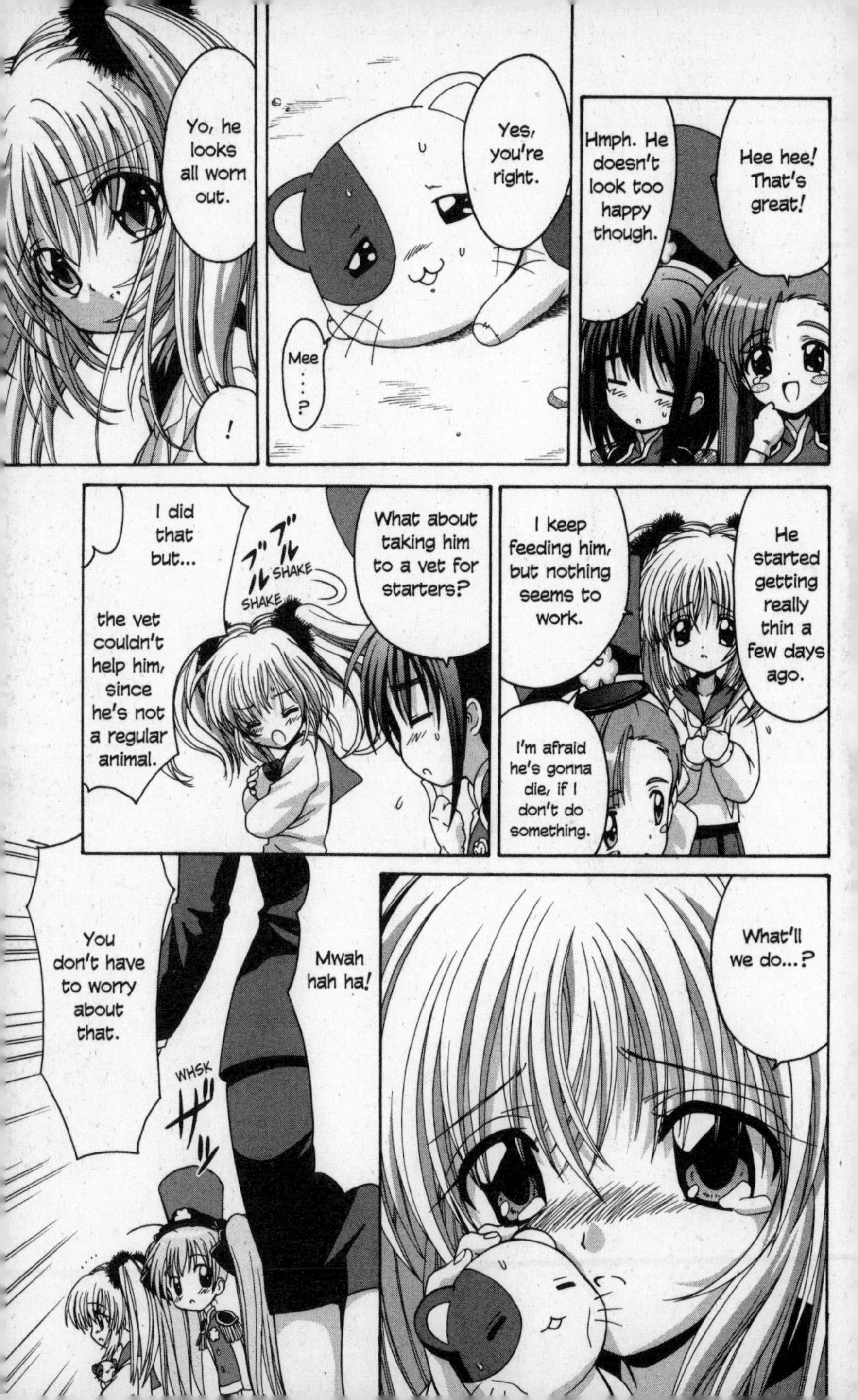
Hee hee! That's great!
Hmph. He doesn't look too happy though.
Yes, you're right.
Mee....?
Yo, he looks all worn out.
!
He started getting really thin a few days ago.
I keep feeding him, but nothing seems to work.
I'm afraid he's gonna die, if I don't do something.
What about taking him to a vet for starters?
ブルブル
SHAKE SHAKE
I did that but...
the vet couldn't help him, since he's not a regular animal.
What'll we do...?
Mwah hah ha!
You don't have to worry about that.
ザッ
WHSK

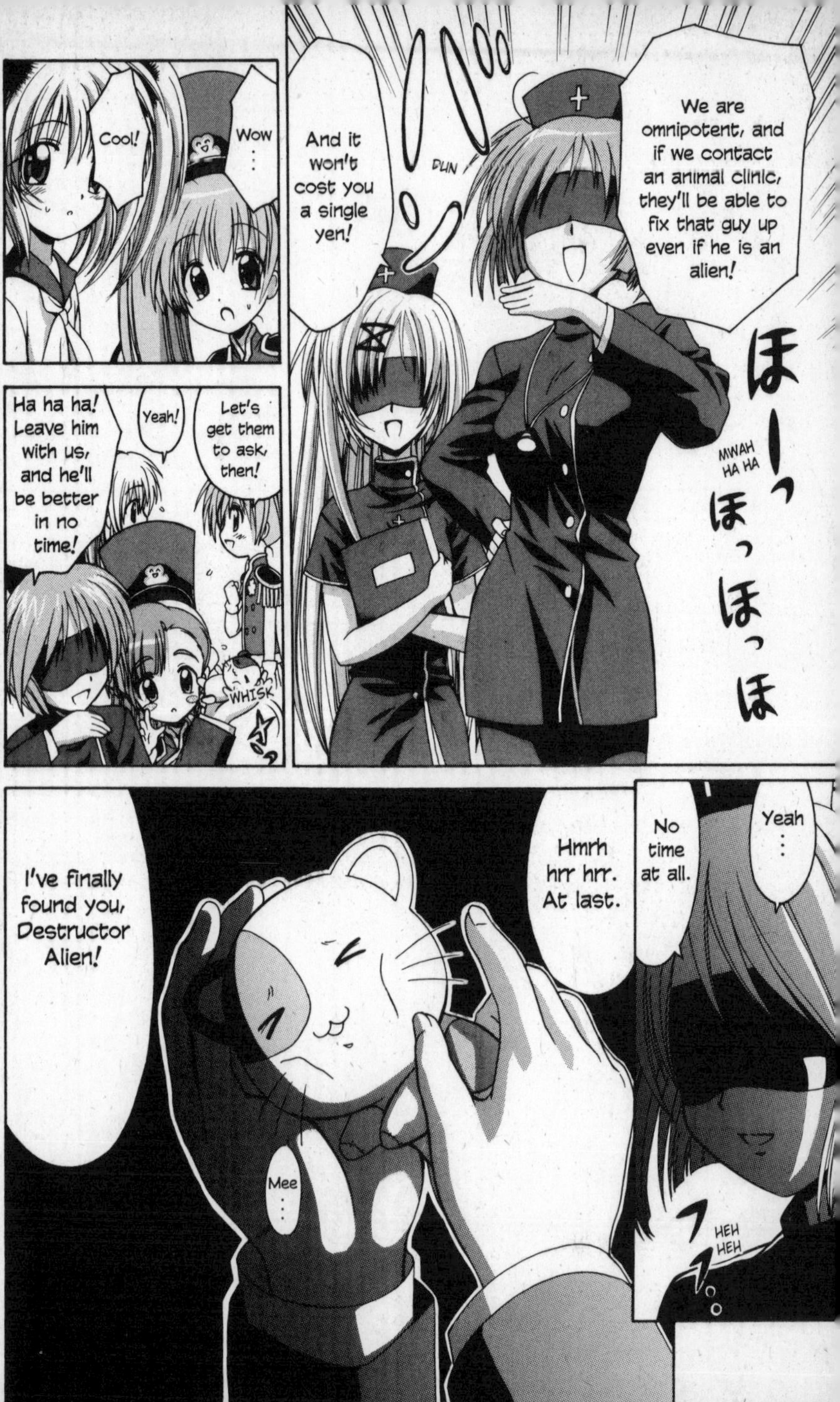
We are omnipotent, and if we contact an animal clinic, they'll be able to fix that guy up even if he is an alien!
And it won't cost you a single yen!
DUN
MWAH HA HA
ほーっほっほっほ
Wow...
Cool!
Let's get them to ask, then!
Yeah!
Ha ha ha! Leave him with us, and he'll be better in no time!
WHISK
Yeah...
No time at all.
Hmrh hrr hrr. At last.
I've finally found you, Destructor Alien!
HEH HEH
Mee...

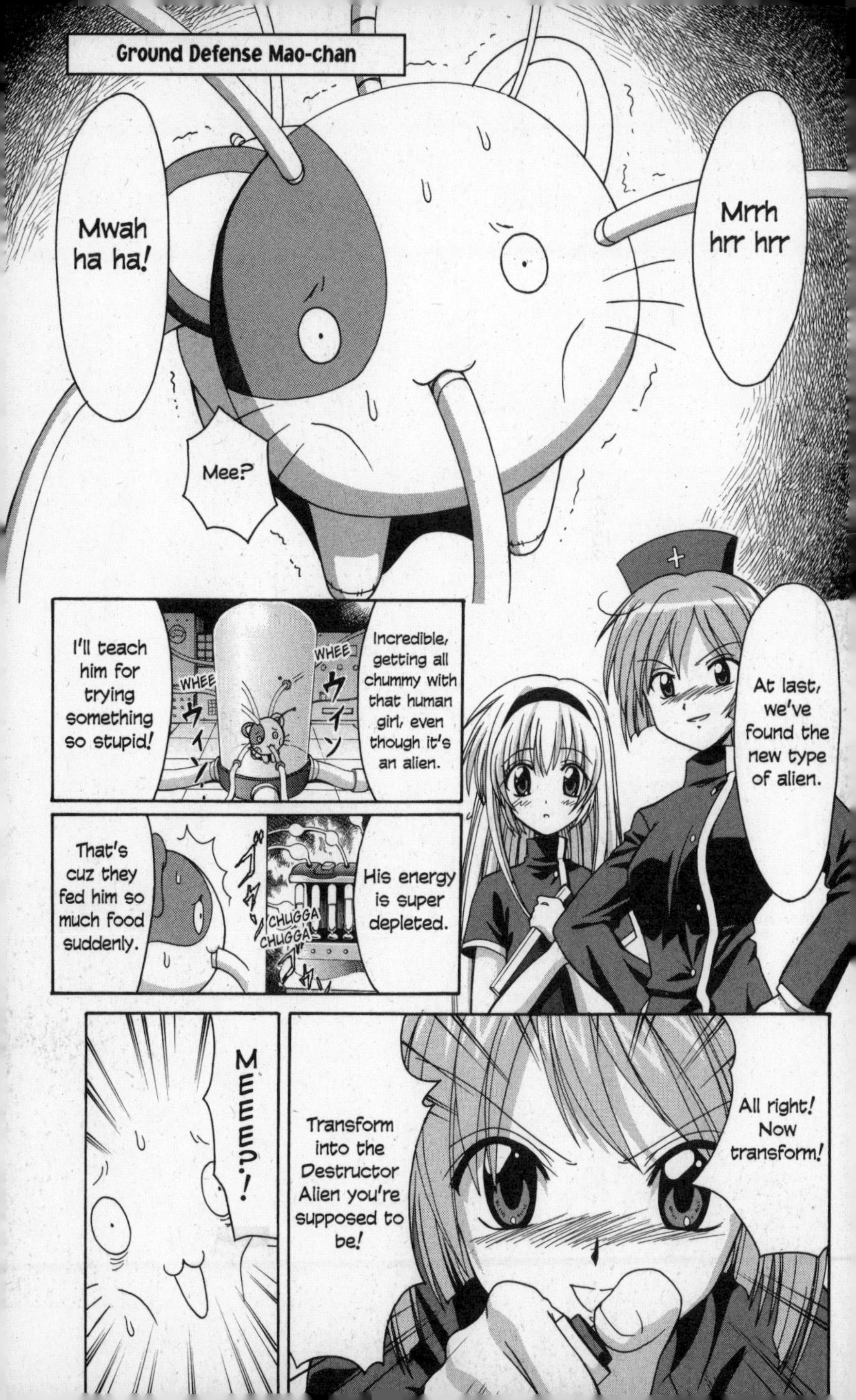
Ground Defense Mao-chan
Mrrh hrr hrr
Mwah ha ha!
Mee?
At last, we've found the new type of alien.
Incredible, getting all chummy with that human girl, even though it's an alien.
WHEE
WHEE
I'll teach him for trying something so stupid!
His energy is super depleted.
CHUGGA CHUGGA
That's cuz they fed him so much food suddenly.
All right! Now transform!
Transform into the Destructor Alien you're supposed to be!
MEEE?!

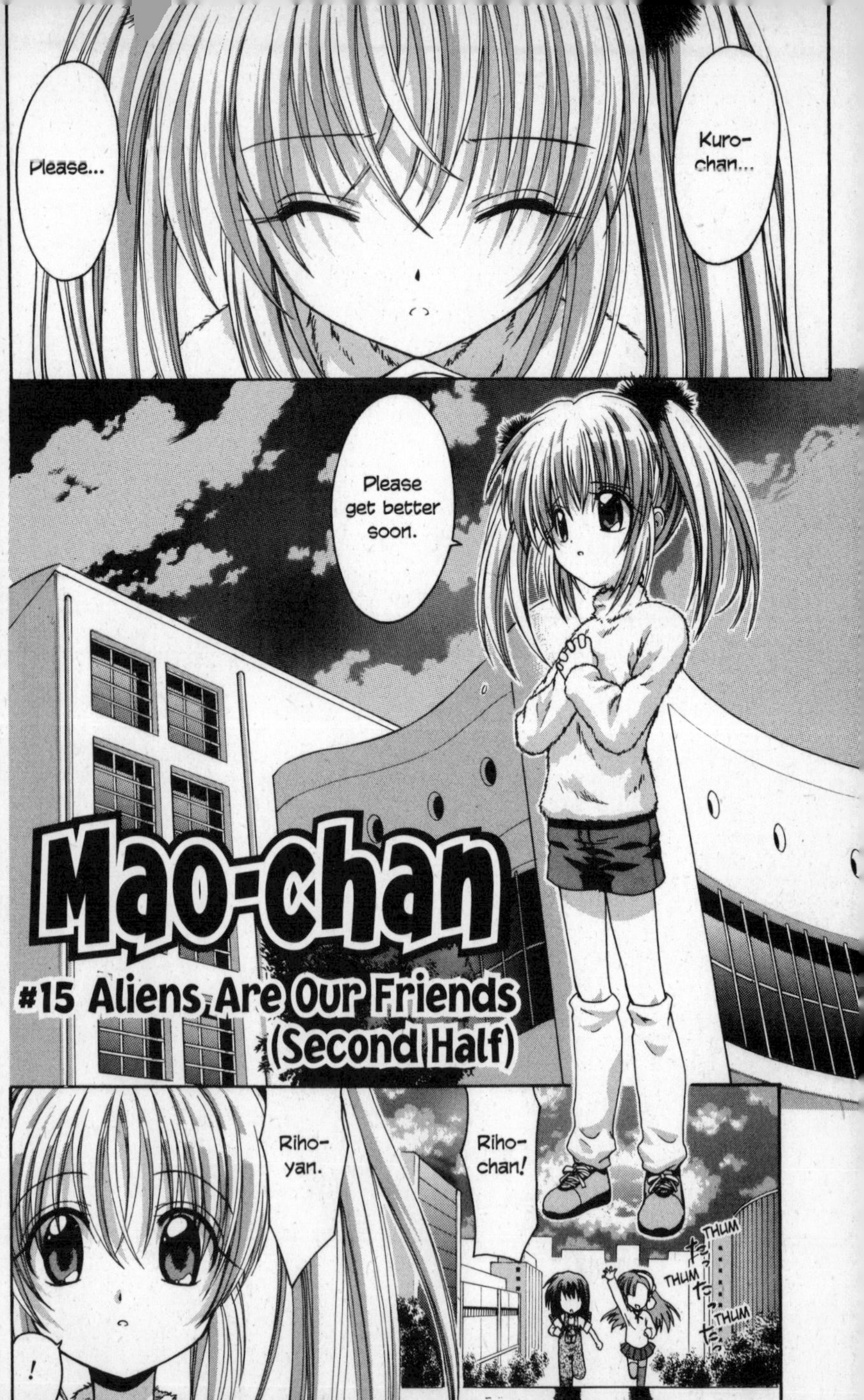
Kuro-chan...
Please...
Please get better soon.
Mao-chan
#15 Aliens Are Our Friends (Second Half)
Riho-chan!
Riho-yan.
THUM
THUM
THUM
!

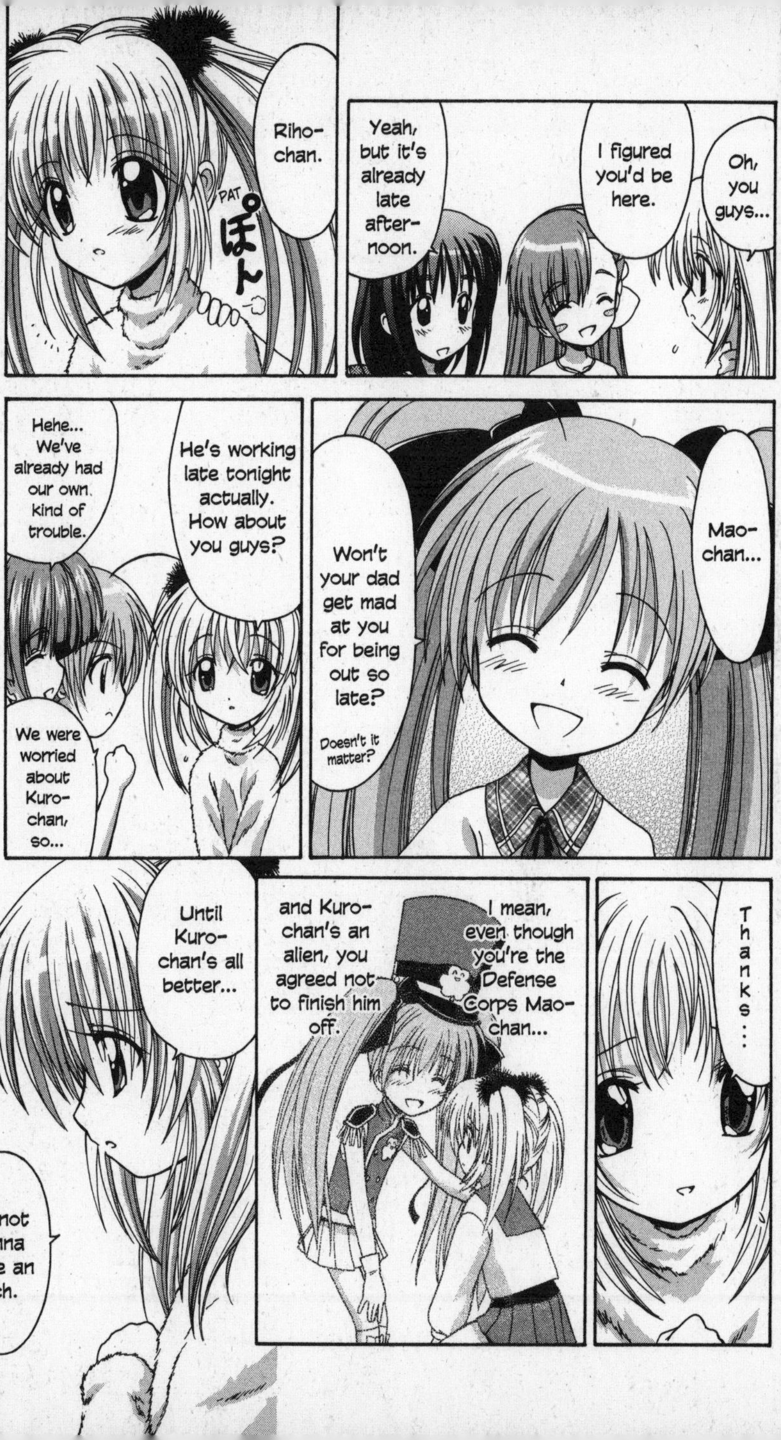
Oh, you guys...
I figured you'd be here.
Yeah, but it's already late after-noon.
Riho-chan.
PAT
ぽん
Mao-chan...
Won't your dad get mad at you for being out so late?
Doesn't it matter?
He's working late tonight actually. How about you guys?
Hehe... We've already had our own kind of trouble.
We were worried about Kuro-chan, so...
Thanks...
I mean, even though you're the Defense Corps Mao-chan...
and Kuro-chan's an alien, you agreed not to finish him off.
Until Kuro-chan's all better...
I'm not gonna move an inch.

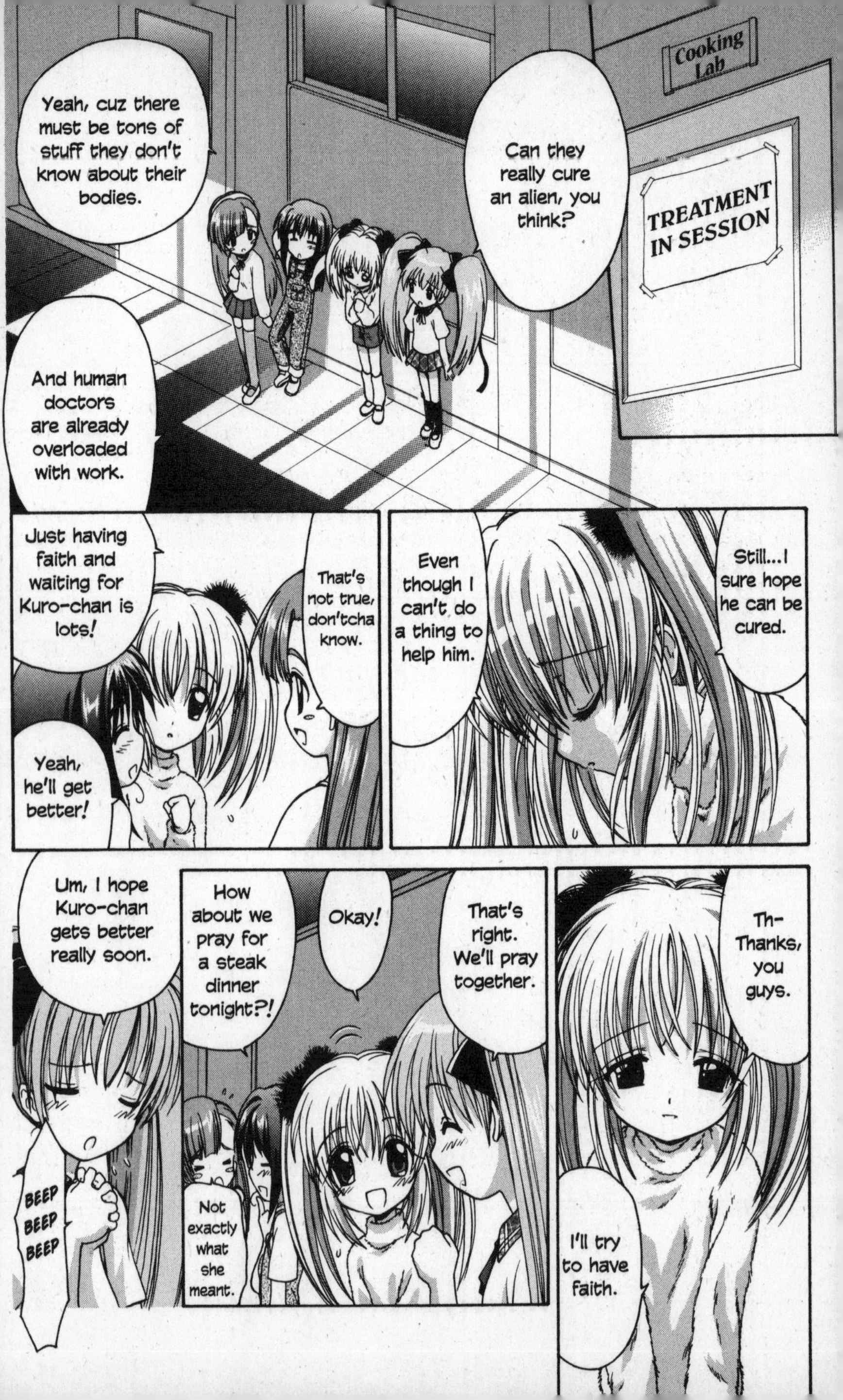
Cooking Lab
TREATMENT IN SESSION
Can they really cure an alien, you think?
Yeah, cuz there must be tons of stuff they don't know about their bodies.
And human doctors are already overloaded with work.
Still...I sure hope he can be cured.
Even though I can't do a thing to help him.
That's not true, don'tcha know.
Just having faith and waiting for Kuro-chan is lots!
Yeah, he'll get better!
Th-Thanks, you guys.
I'll try to have faith.
That's right. We'll pray together.
Okay!
How about we pray for a steak dinner tonight?!
Um, I hope Kuro-chan gets better really soon.
Not exactly what she meant.
BEEP BEEP BEEP

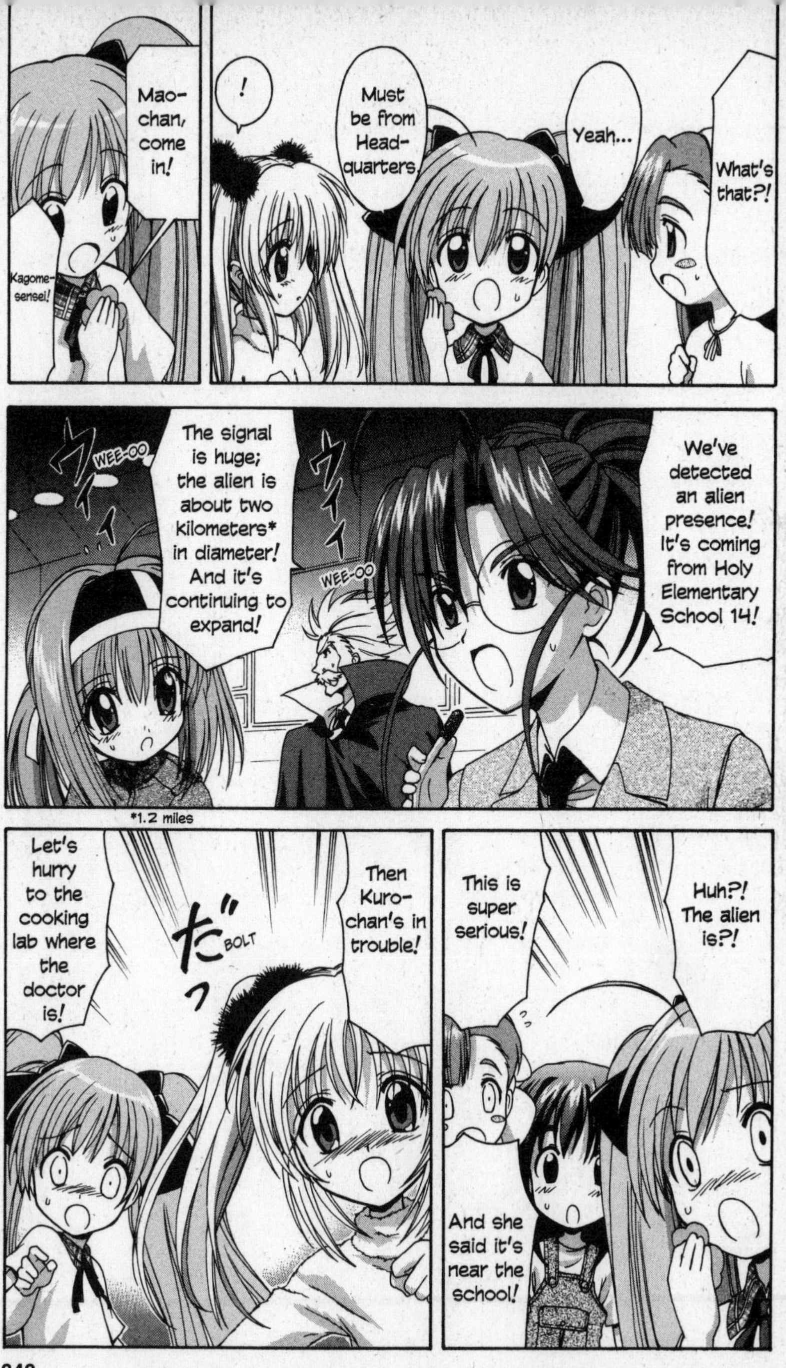
What's that?!
Yeah...
Must be from Headquarters.
!
Mao-chan, come in!
Kagome-sensei!
We've detected an alien presence! It's coming from Holy Elementary School 14!
WEE-OO
The signal is huge; the alien is about two kilometers* in diameter! And it's continuing to expand!
WEE-OO
Huh?! The alien is?!
This is super serious!
And she said it's near the school!
Then Kuro-chan's in trouble!
BOLT
Let's hurry to the cooking lab where the doctor is!

*1.2 miles

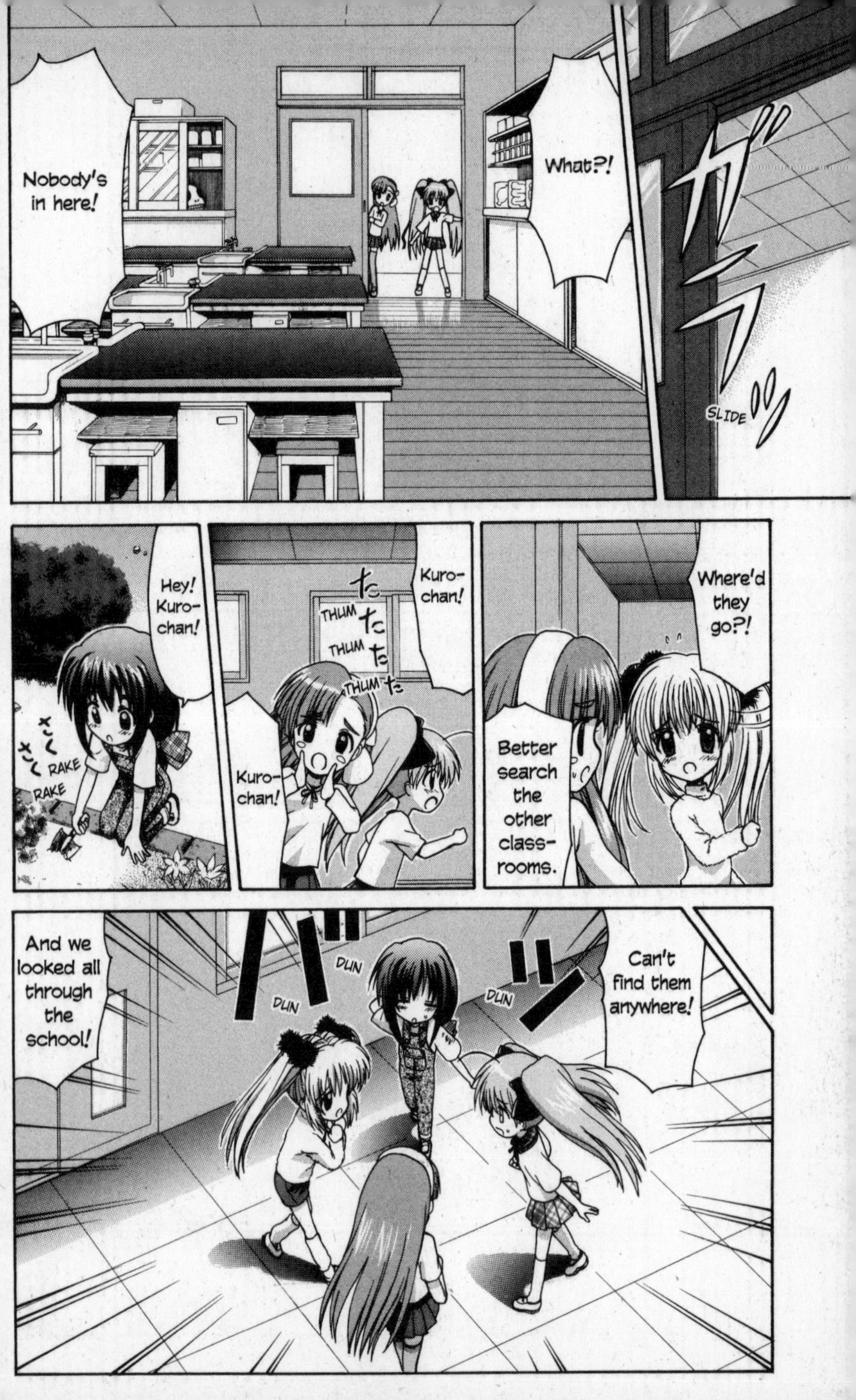
SLIDE
What?!
Nobody's in here!
Where'd they go?!
Better search the other class-rooms.
Kuro-chan!
THUM
THUM
THUM
Kuro-chan!
Hey! Kuro-chan!
RAKE
RAKE
Can't find them anywhere!
DUN
DUN
DUN
And we looked all through the school!

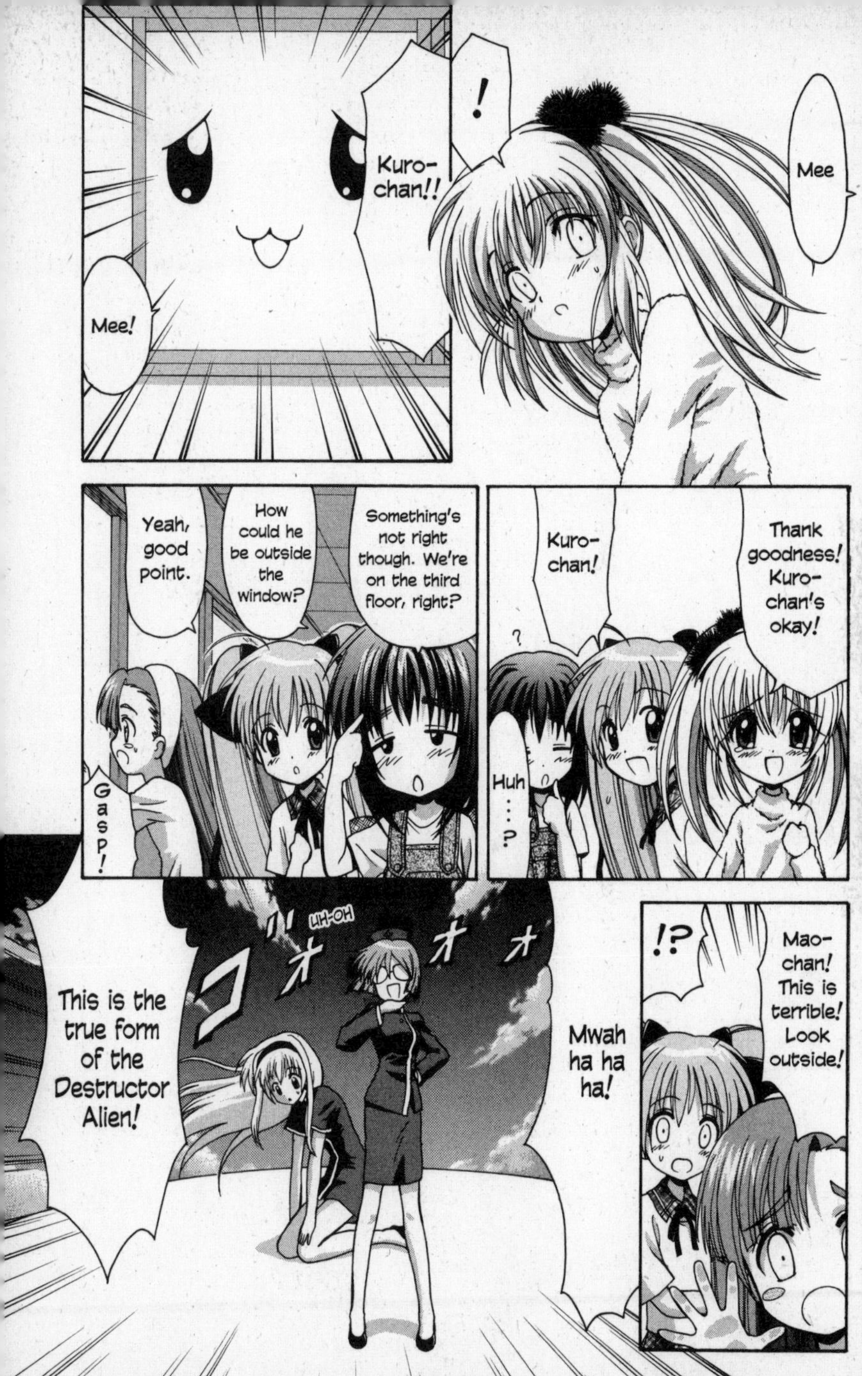
Mee
!
Kuro-chan!!
Mee!
Thank goodness! Kuro-chan's okay!
Kuro-chan!
?
Huh...?
Something's not right though. We're on the third floor, right?
How could he be outside the window?
Yeah, good point.
Gasp!
Mao-chan! This is terrible! Look outside!
!?
Mwah ha ha!
UH-OH
This is the true form of the Destructor Alien!

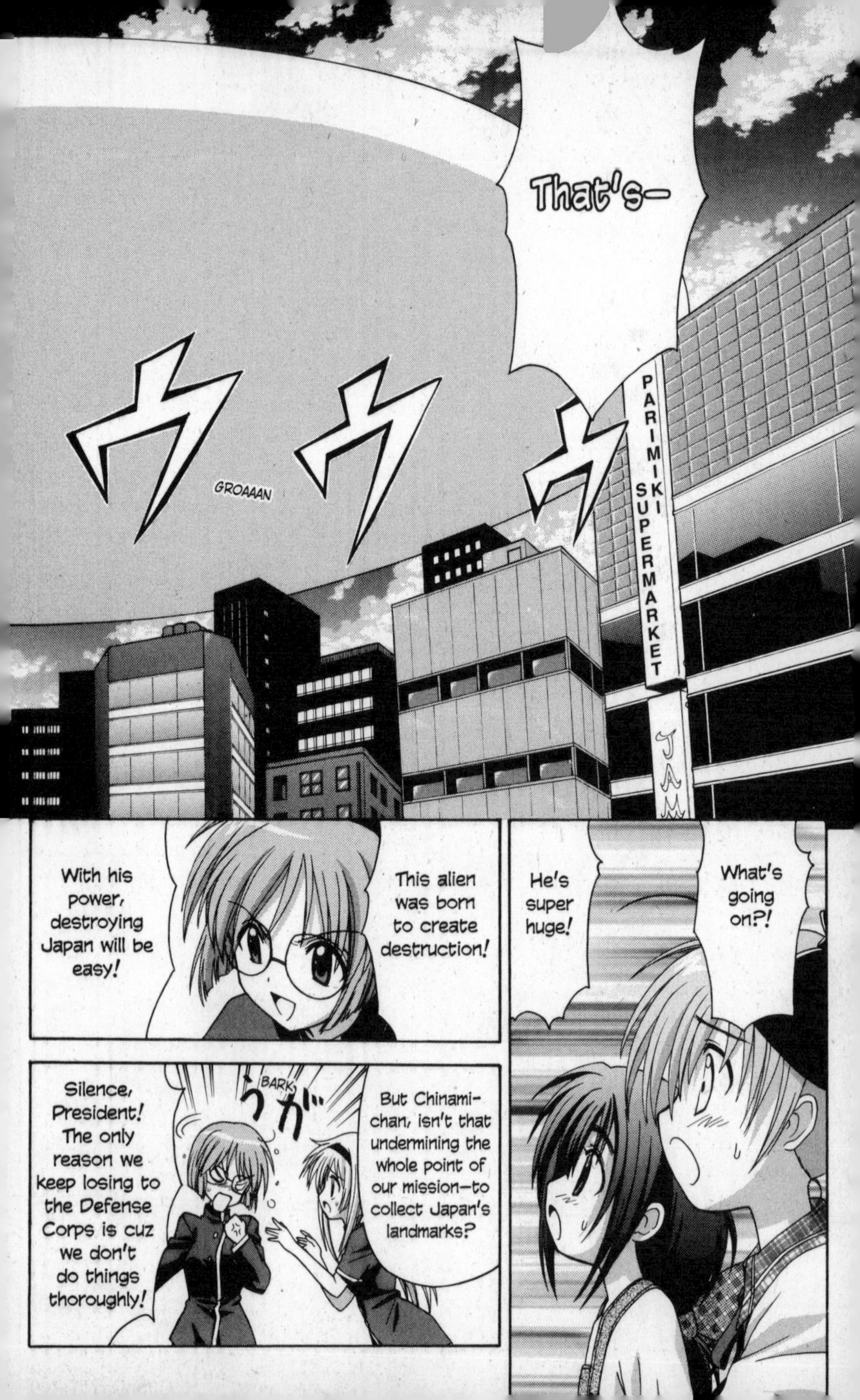
That's-
ウウウ
GROAAAN
PARIMIKI SUPERMARKET
What's going on?!
He's super huge!
This alien was born to create destruction!
With his power, destroying Japan will be easy!
But Chinami-chan, isn't that undermining the whole point of our mission—to collect Japan's landmarks?
BARK
うが
Silence, President! The only reason we keep losing to the Defense Corps is cuz we don't do things thoroughly!

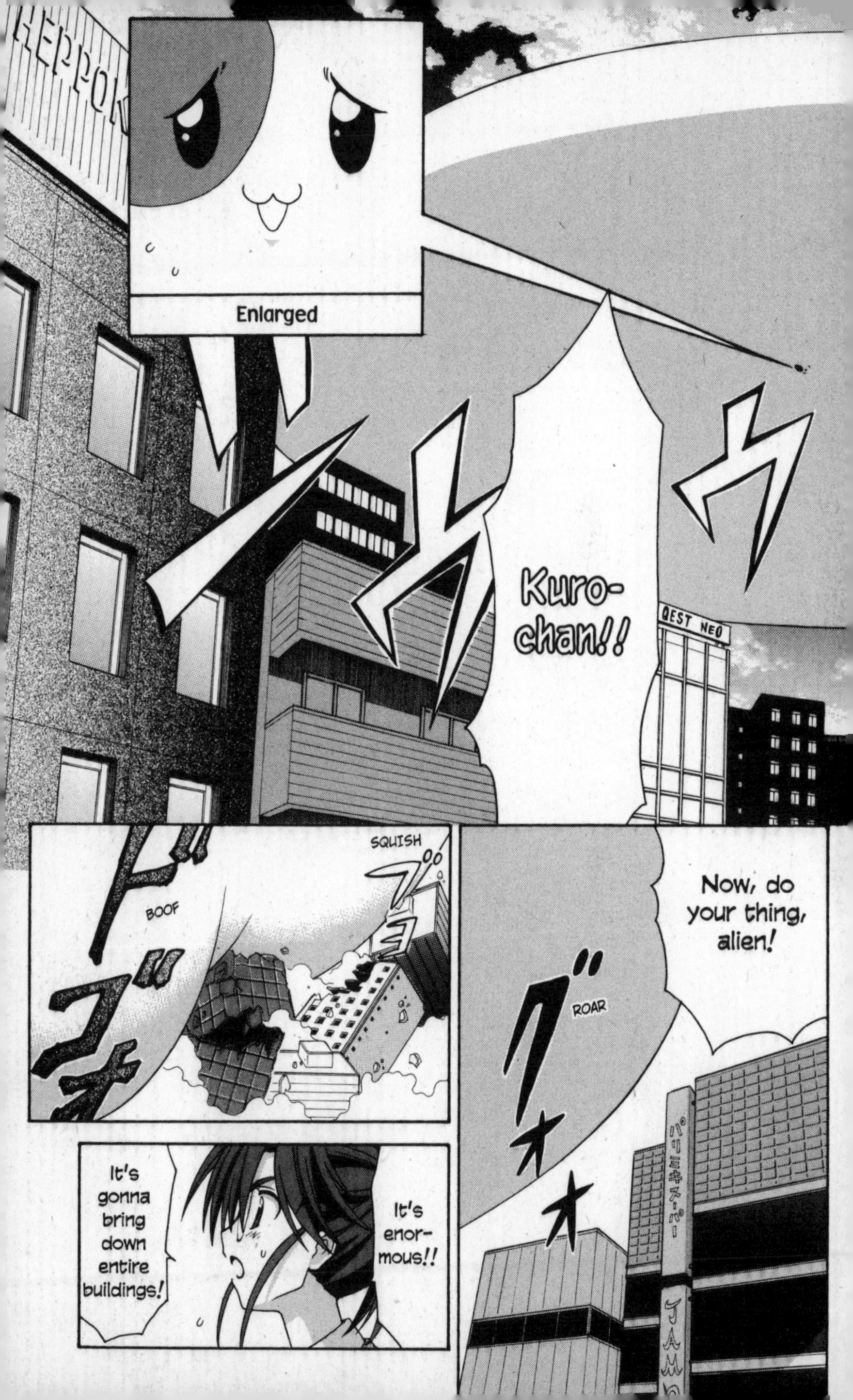
Kuro-chan!!
Enlarged
QEST NEO
Now, do your thing, alien!
ROAR
SQUISH
BOOF
It's enormous!!
It's gonna bring down entire buildings!

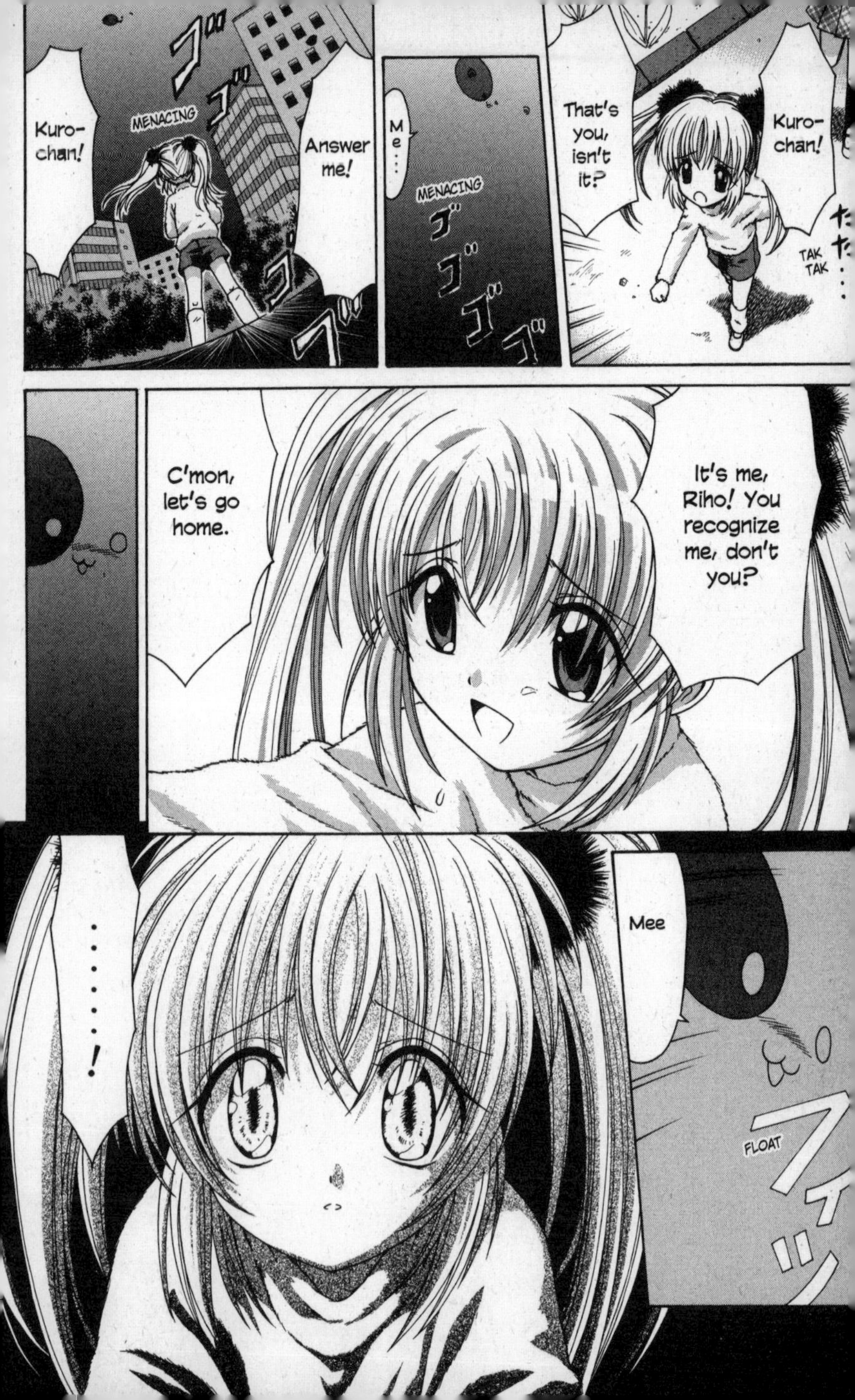
Kuro-chan!
TAK TAK
That's you, isn't it?
Me...
MENACING
Answer me!
MENACING
Kuro-chan!
It's me, Riho! You recognize me, don't you?
C'mon, let's go home.
Mee
FLOAT
......!

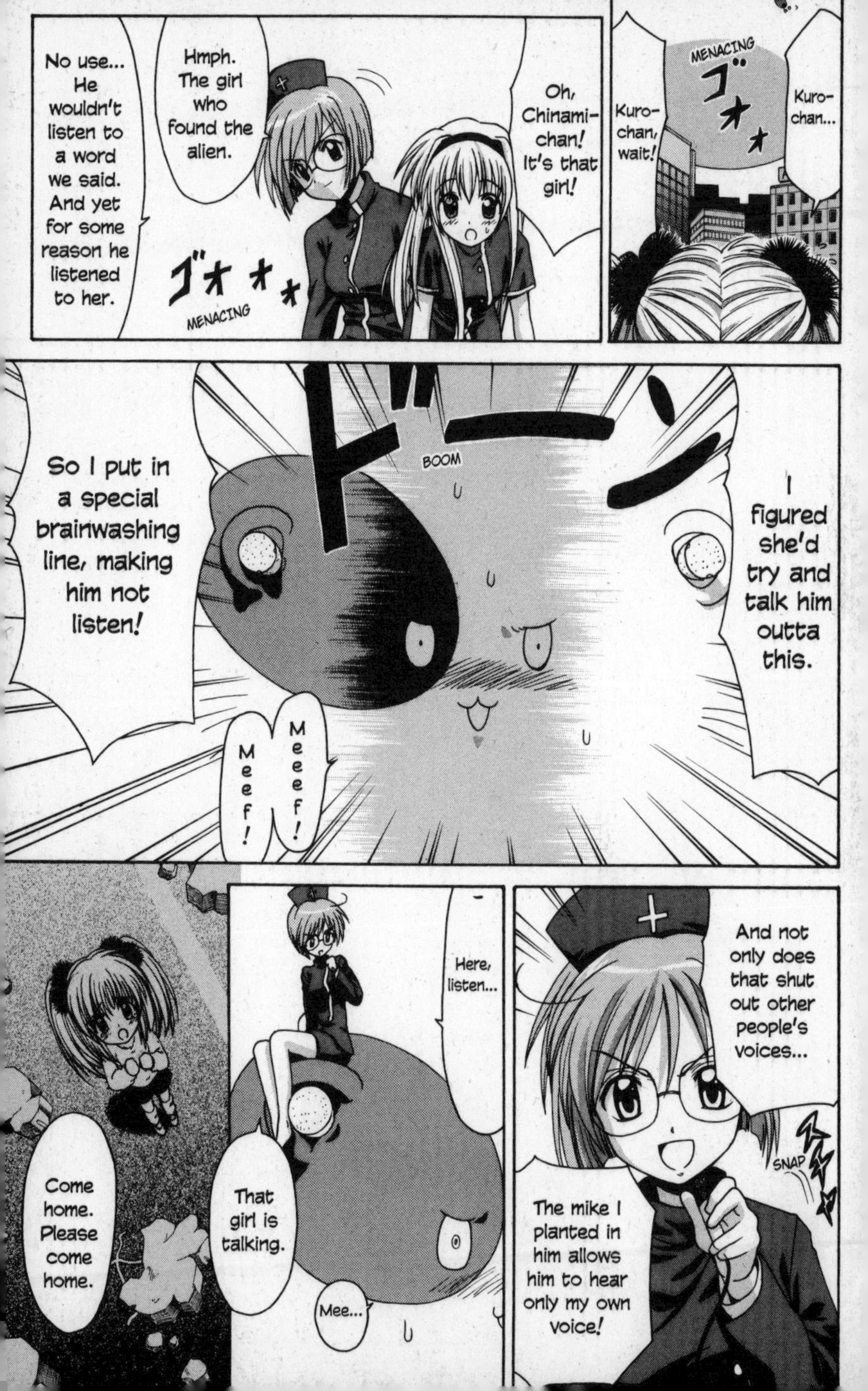
Kuro-chan...
MENACING ゴォォ
Kuro-chan, wait!
Oh, Chinami-chan! It's that girl!
Hmph. The girl who found the alien.
No use... He wouldn't listen to a word we said. And yet for some reason he listened to her.
ゴォォォ
MENACING
I figured she'd try and talk him outta this.
ドーー
BOOM
So I put in a special brainwashing line, making him not listen!
Meeef!
Meef!
And not only does that shut out other people's voices...
SNAP
The mike I planted in him allows him to hear only my own voice!
Here, listen...
That girl is talking.
Mee...
Come home. Please come home.

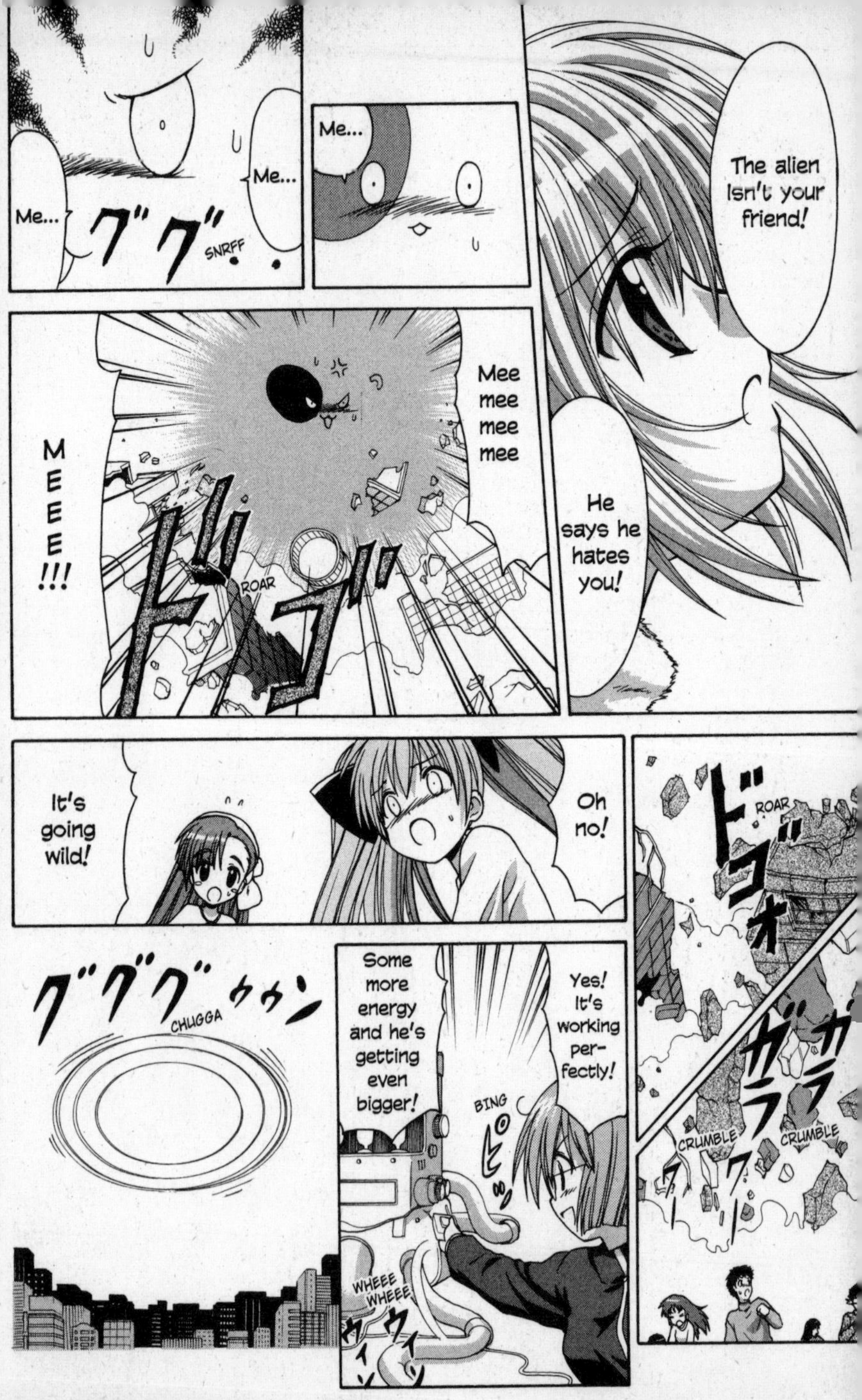
The alien isn't your friend!
He says he hates you!
Me...
Me...
Me...
SNRFF
Mee mee mee mee
MEEE!!!
ROAR
ROAR
CRUMBLE
CRUMBLE
Oh no!
It's going wild!
Yes! It's working perfectly!
Some more energy and he's getting even bigger!
BING
WHEEE WHEEE
CHUGGA

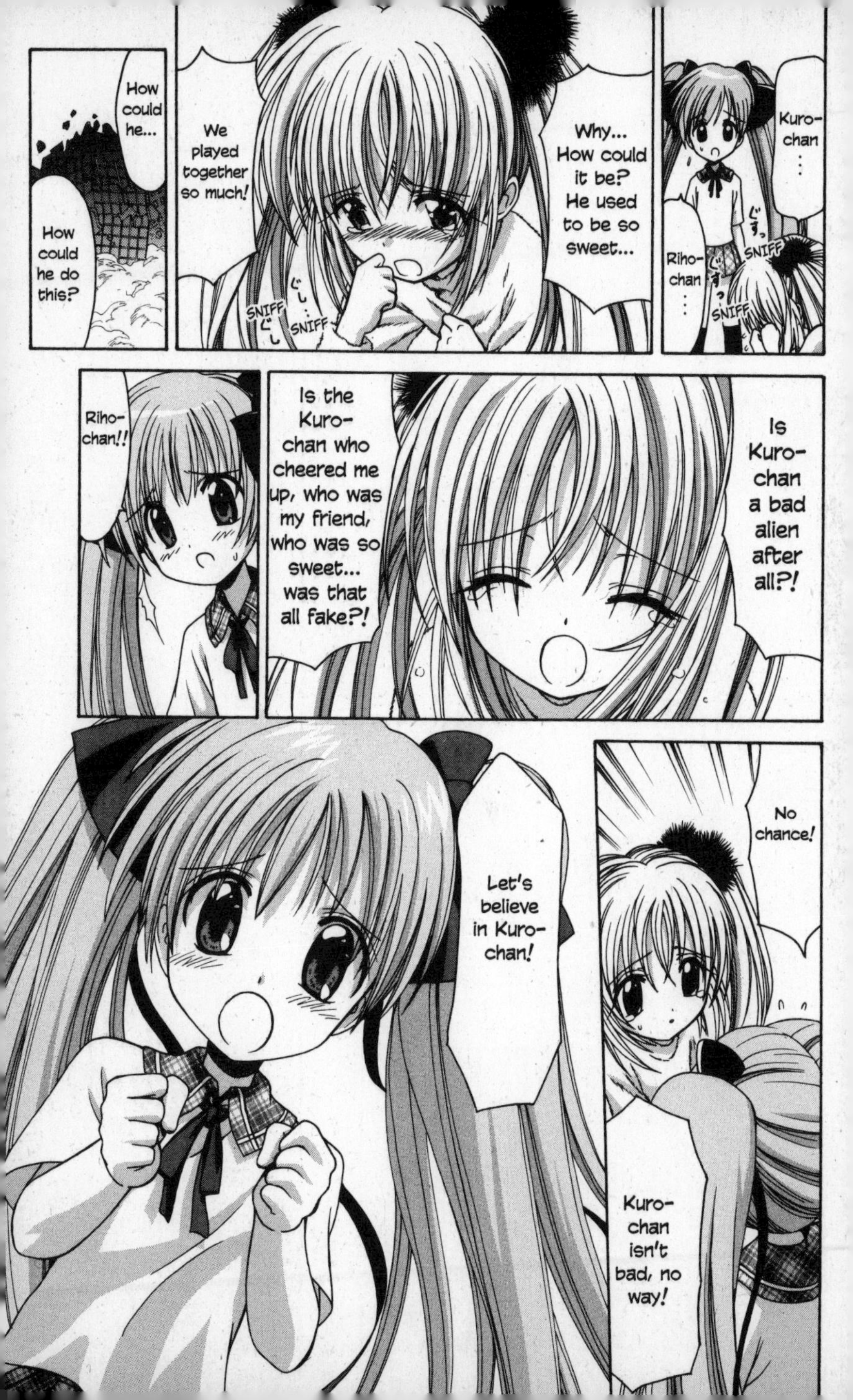
Kuro-chan...
Riho-chan...
SNIFF
SNIFF
Why... How could it be? He used to be so sweet...
We played together so much!
SNIFF
SNIFF
How could he...
How could he do this?
Is Kuro-chan a bad alien after all?!
Is the Kuro-chan who cheered me up, who was my friend, who was so sweet... was that all fake?!
Riho-chan!!
No chance!
Kuro-chan isn't bad, no way!
Let's believe in Kuro-chan!

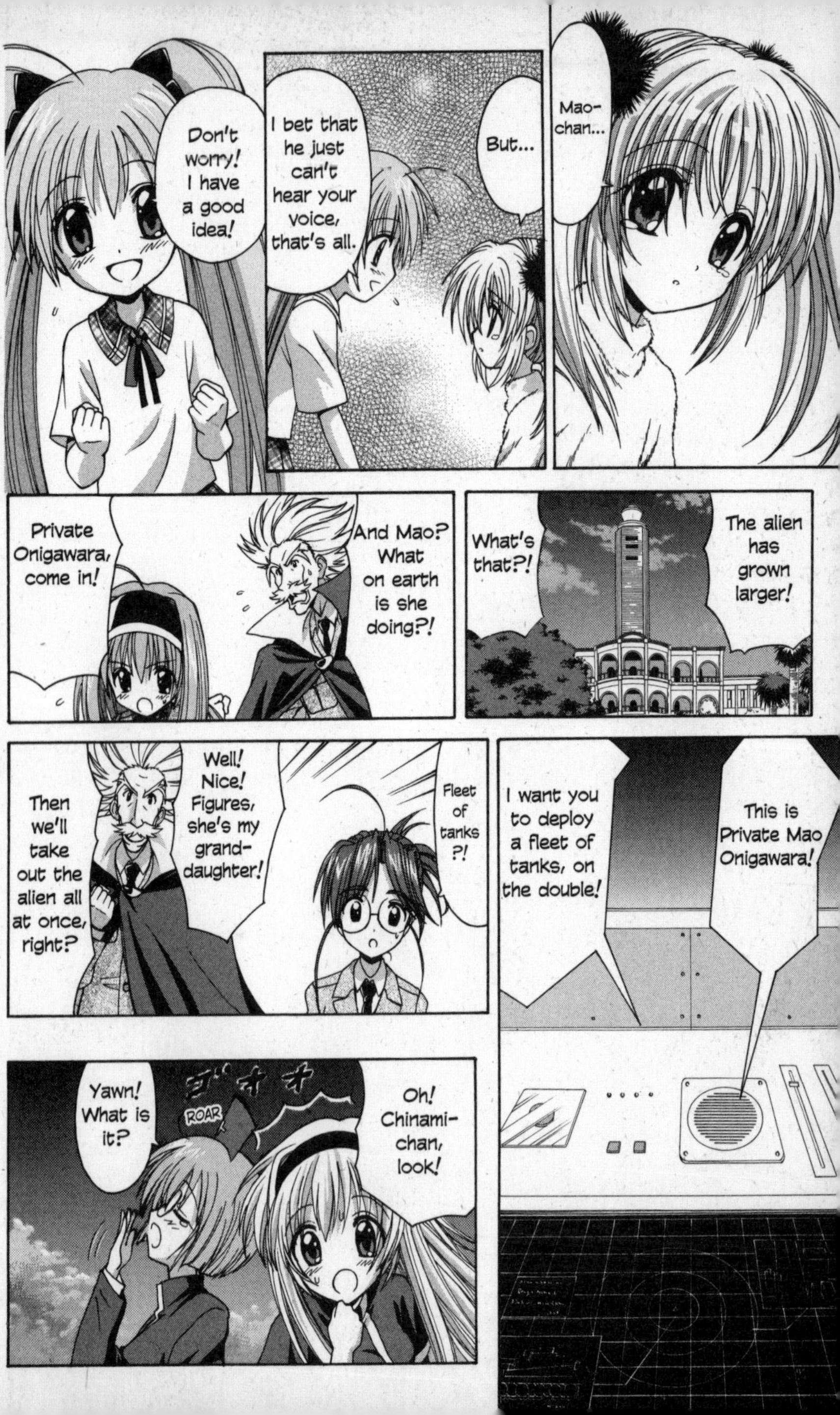
Mao-chan...
But...
I bet that he just can't hear your voice, that's all.
Don't worry! I have a good idea!
The alien has grown larger!
What's that?!
And Mao? What on earth is she doing?!
Private Onigawara, come in!
This is Private Mao Onigawara!
I want you to deploy a fleet of tanks, on the double!
Fleet of tanks?!
Well! Nice! Figures, she's my granddaughter!
Then we'll take out the alien all at once, right?
Oh! Chinami-chan, look!
ROAR
Yawn! What is it?

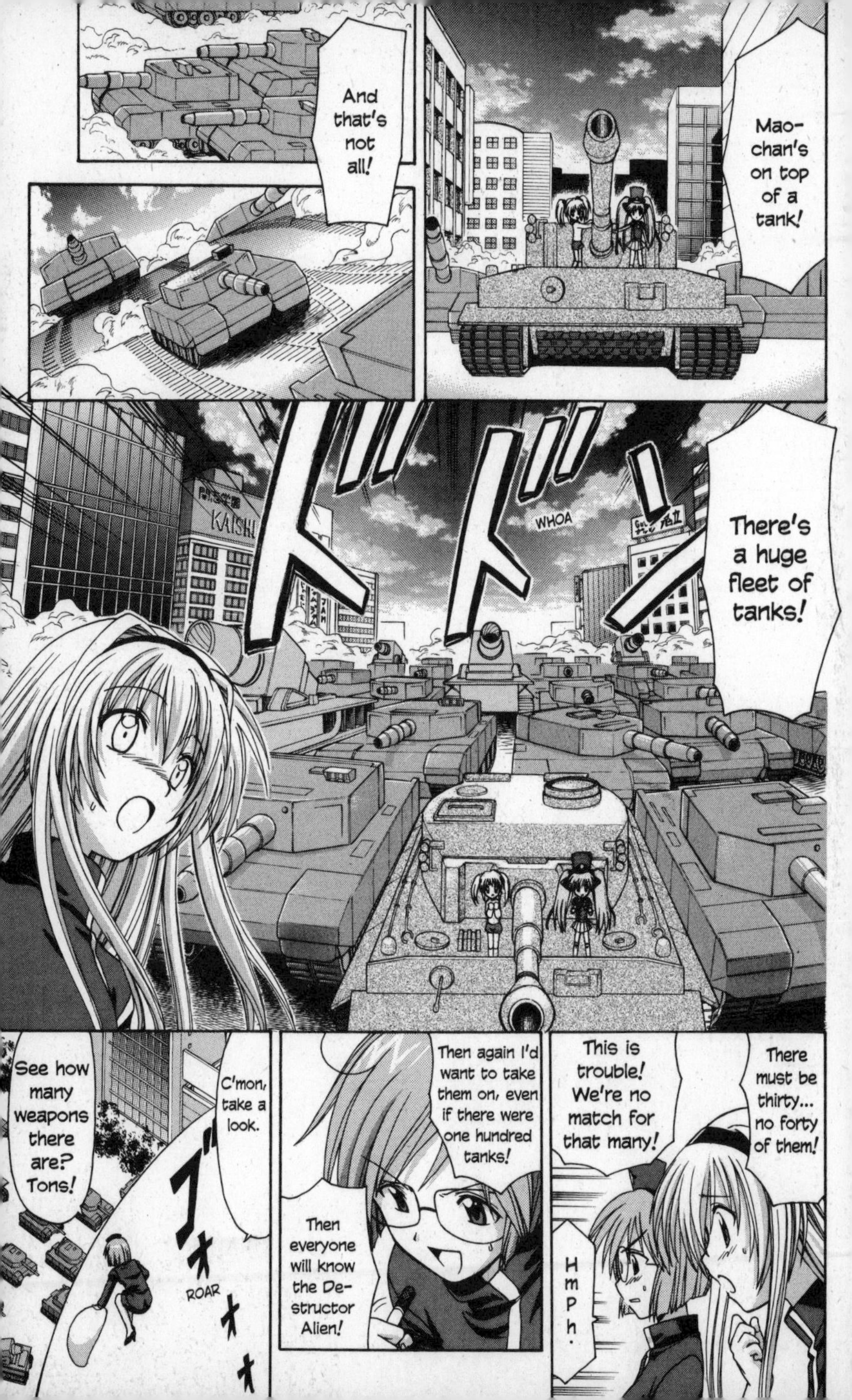

Mao-chan's on top of a tank!
And that's not all!
There's a huge fleet of tanks!
WHOA
KAISHI
There must be thirty... no forty of them!
This is trouble! We're no match for that many!
Hmph.
Then again I'd want to take them on, even if there were one hundred tanks!
Then everyone will know the De-structor Alien!
C'mon, take a look.
See how many weapons there are? Tons!
ROAR

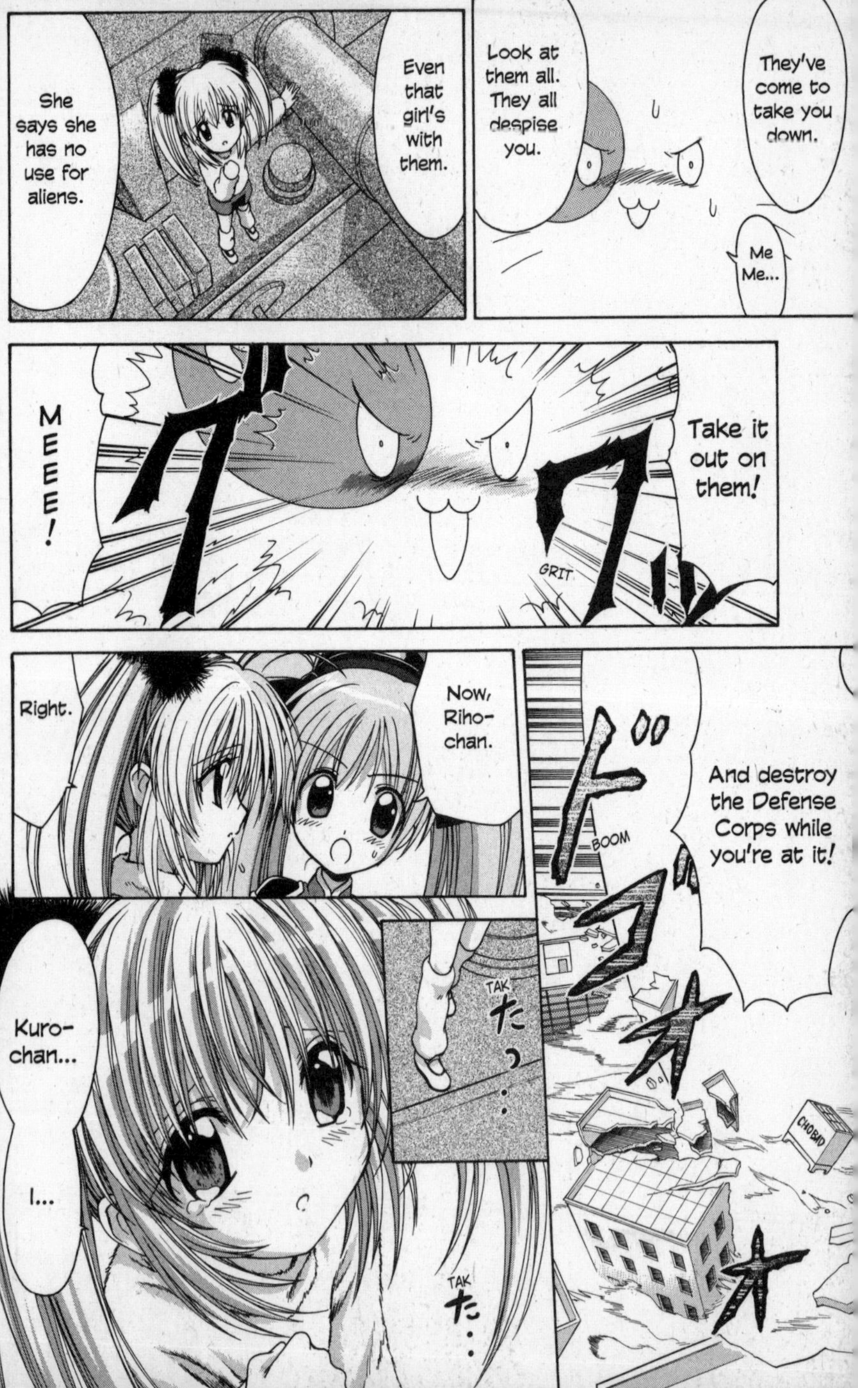
They've come to take you down.
Me Me...
Look at them all. They all despise you.
Even that girl's with them.
She says she has no use for aliens.
Take it out on them!
GRIT
MEEEE!
And destroy the Defense Corps while you're at it!
BOOM
CHOBAD
Now, Riho-chan.
Right.
TAK
TAK
Kuro-chan...
I...

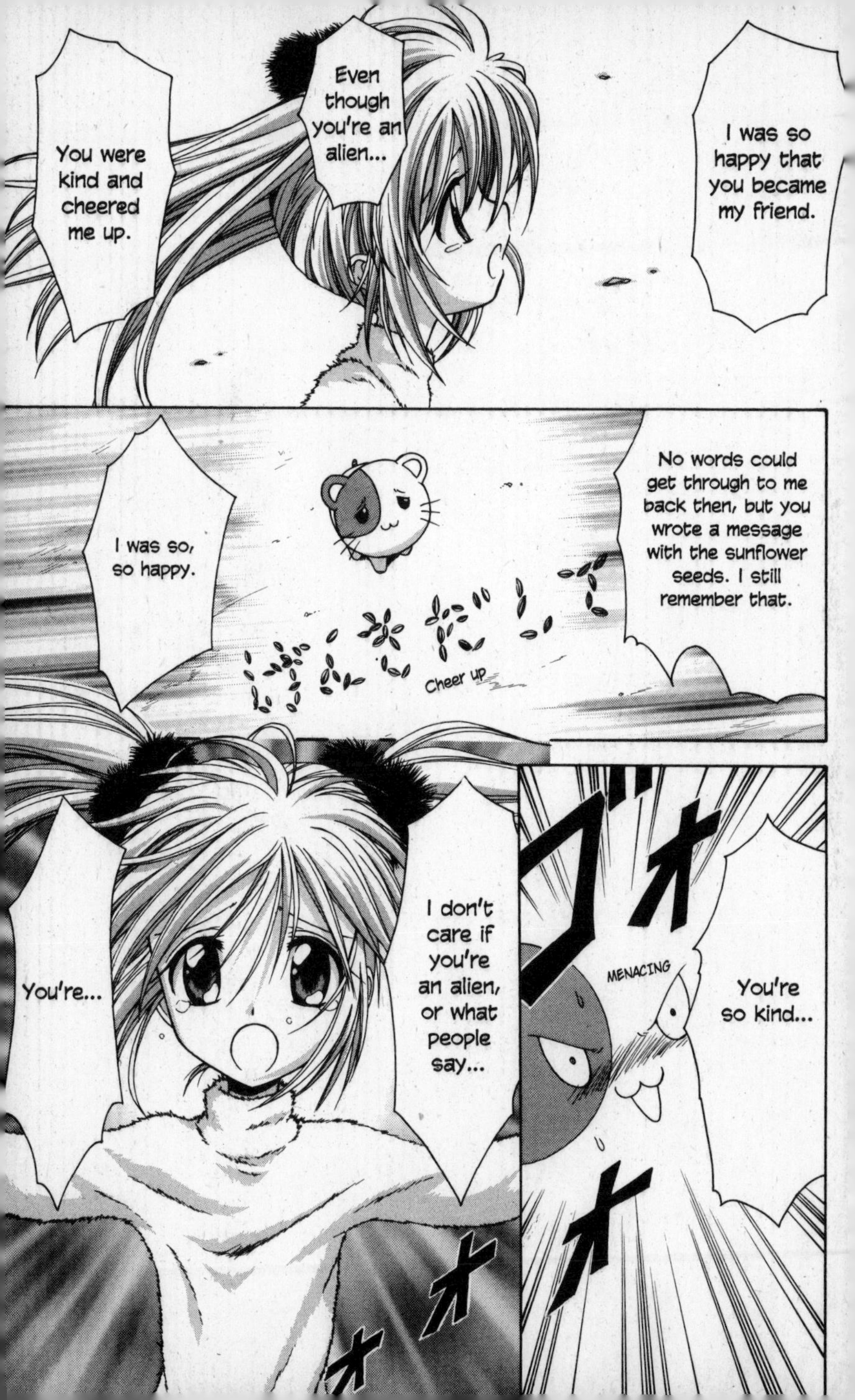

I was so happy that you became my friend.
Even though you're an alien...
You were kind and cheered me up.
No words could get through to me back then, but you wrote a message with the sunflower seeds. I still remember that.
げんきだして
Cheer up
I was so, so happy.
ゴオ
MENACING
You're so kind...
I don't care if you're an alien, or what people say...
You're...

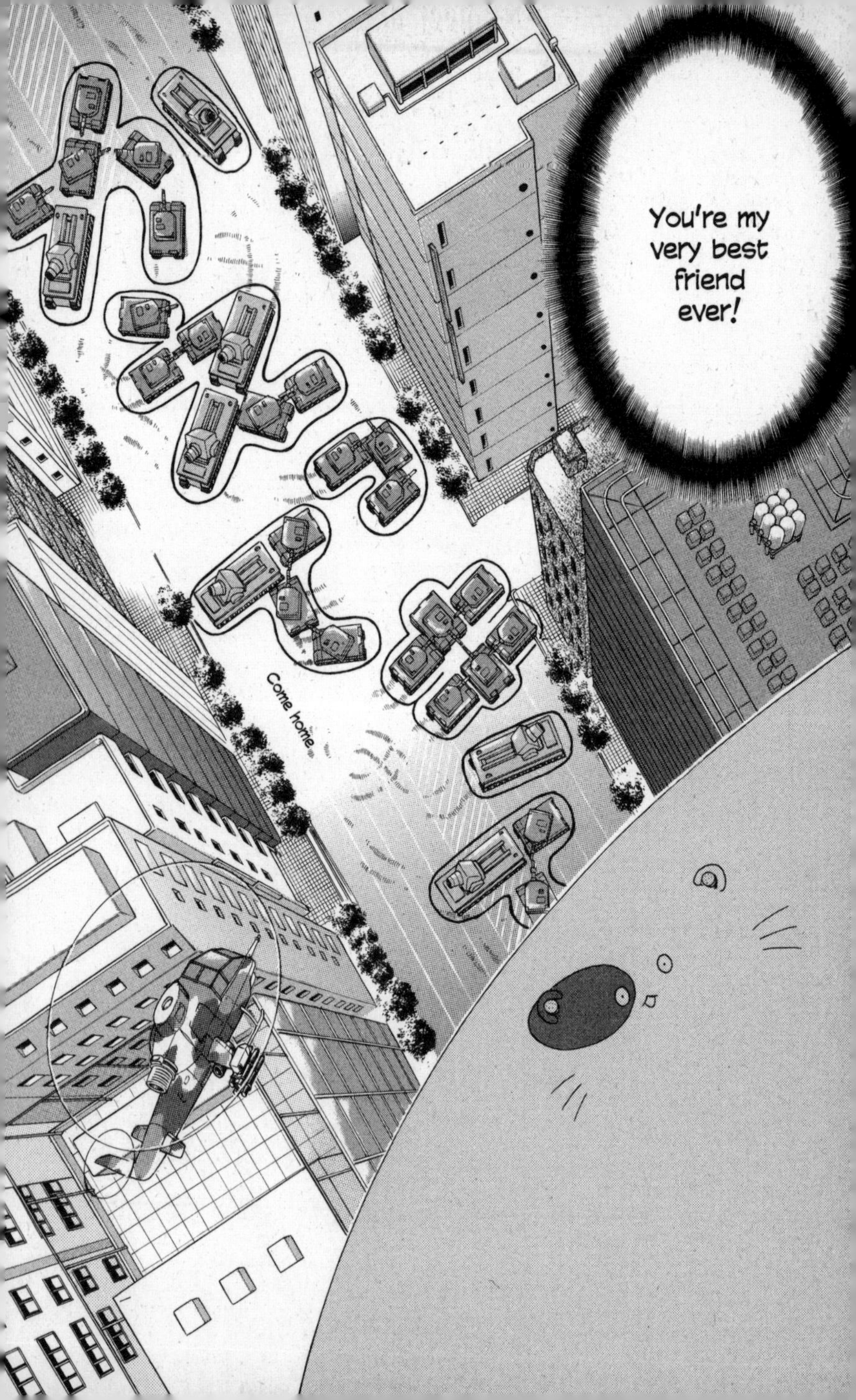
You're my very best friend ever!
Come home

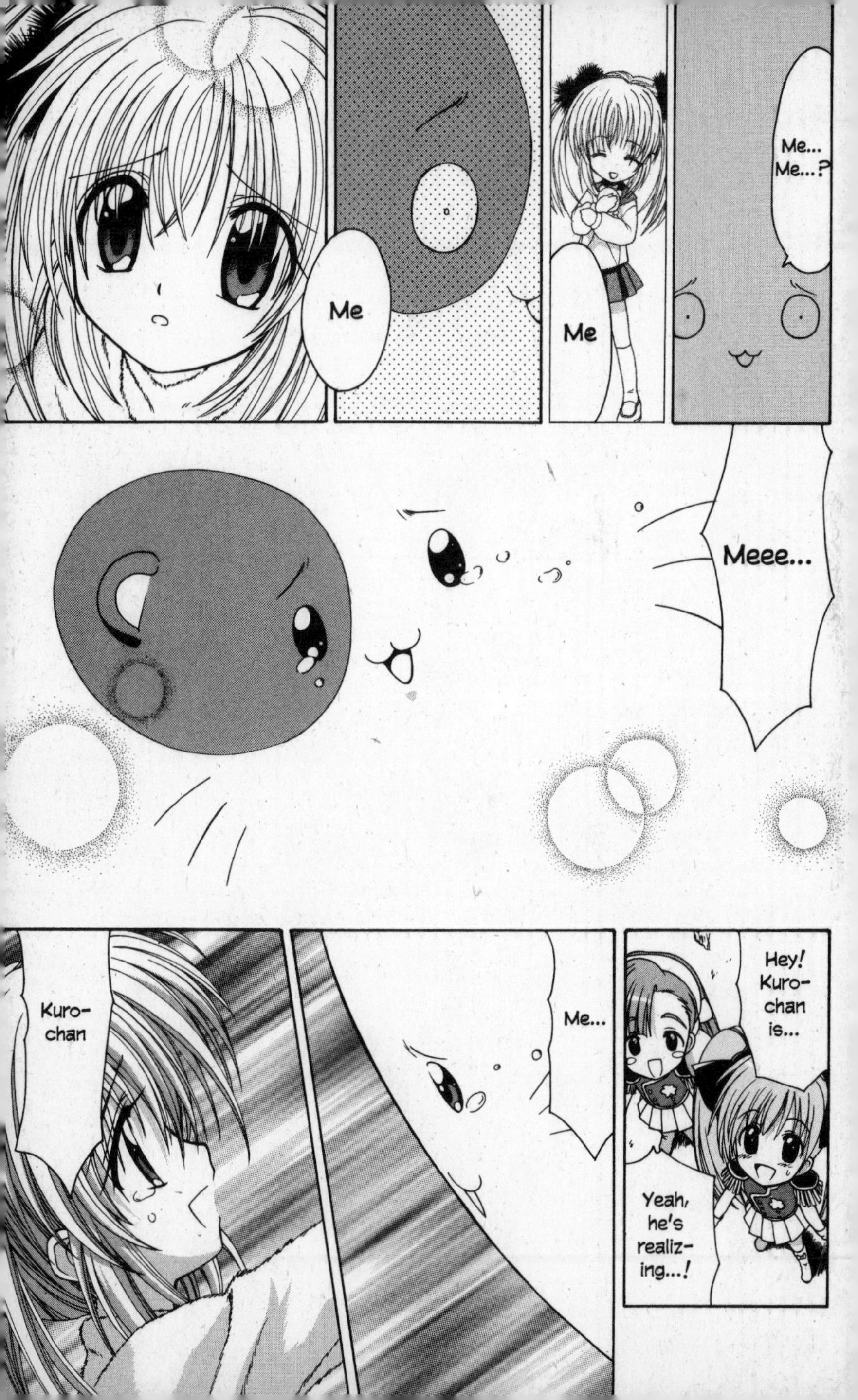

Me... Me...?
Me
Me
Meee...
Hey! Kuro-chan is...
Yeah, he's realiz-ing...!
Me...
Kuro-chan

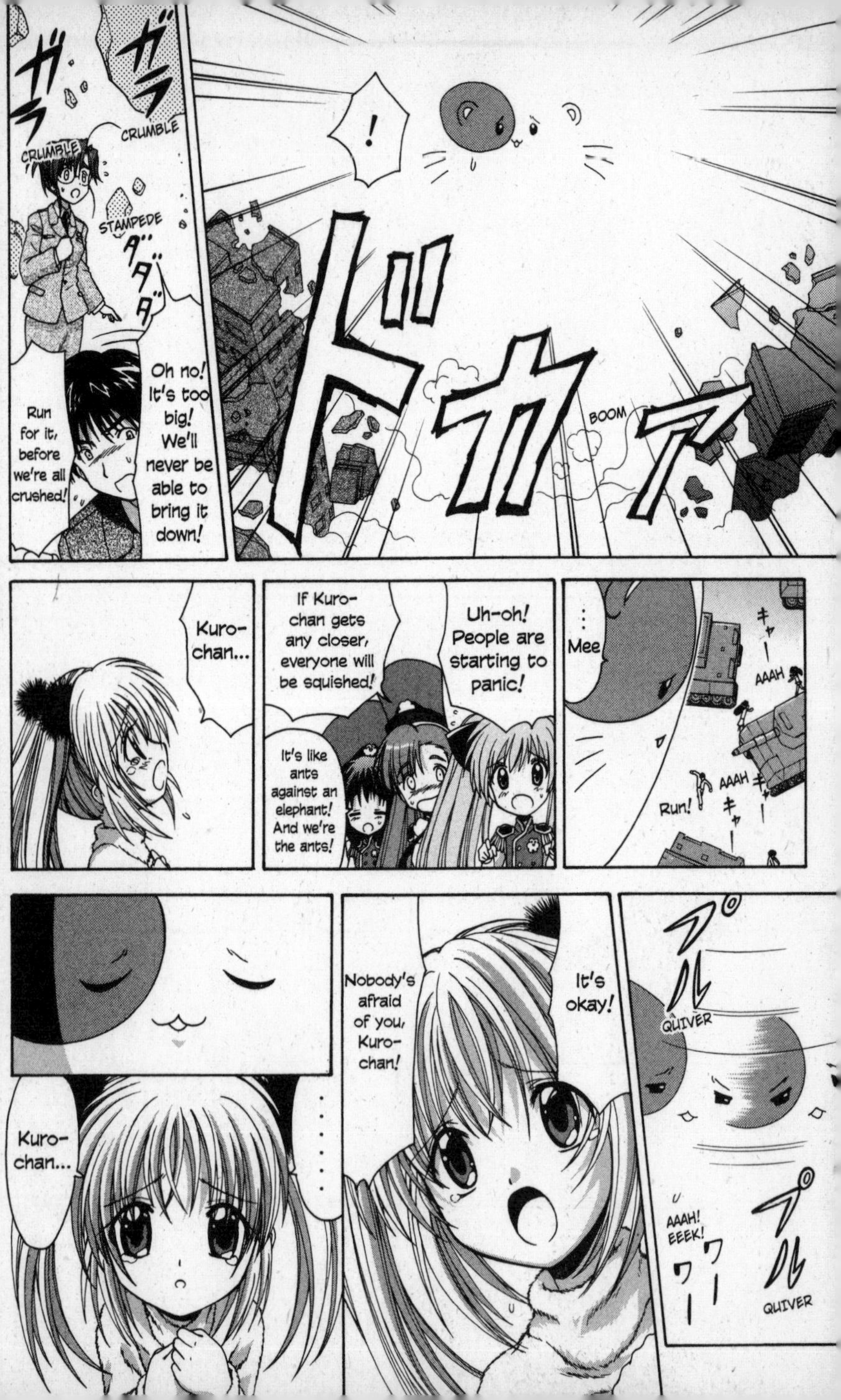
!
ドカァ
BOOM
ガラ
ガラ
CRUMBLE
CRUMBLE
STAMPEDE
ダダダ
Oh no! It's too big! We'll never be able to bring it down!
Run for it, before we're all crushed!
...Mee
キャー
AAAH
Run!
AAAH
キャーキャー
Uh-oh! People are starting to panic!
If Kuro-chan gets any closer, everyone will be squished!
It's like ants against an elephant! And we're the ants!
Kuro-chan...
プル
QUIVER
プル
QUIVER
AAAH! EEEK!
ワーワー
It's okay!
Nobody's afraid of you, Kuro-chan!
......
Kuro-chan...

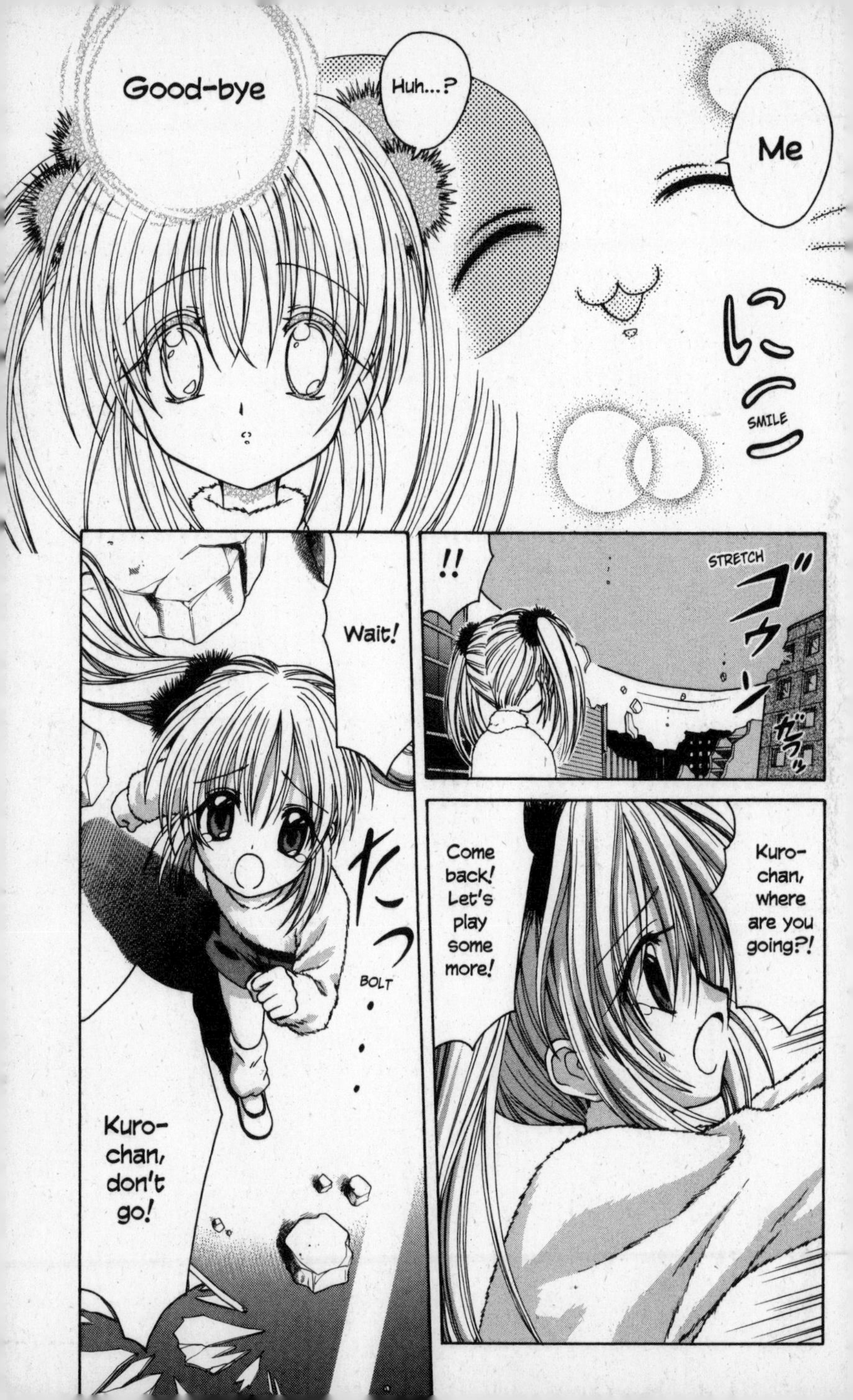
Me
SMILE
Huh...?
Good-bye
STRETCH
!!
Kuro-chan, where are you going?!
Come back! Let's play some more!
Wait!
BOLT
Kuro-chan, don't go!

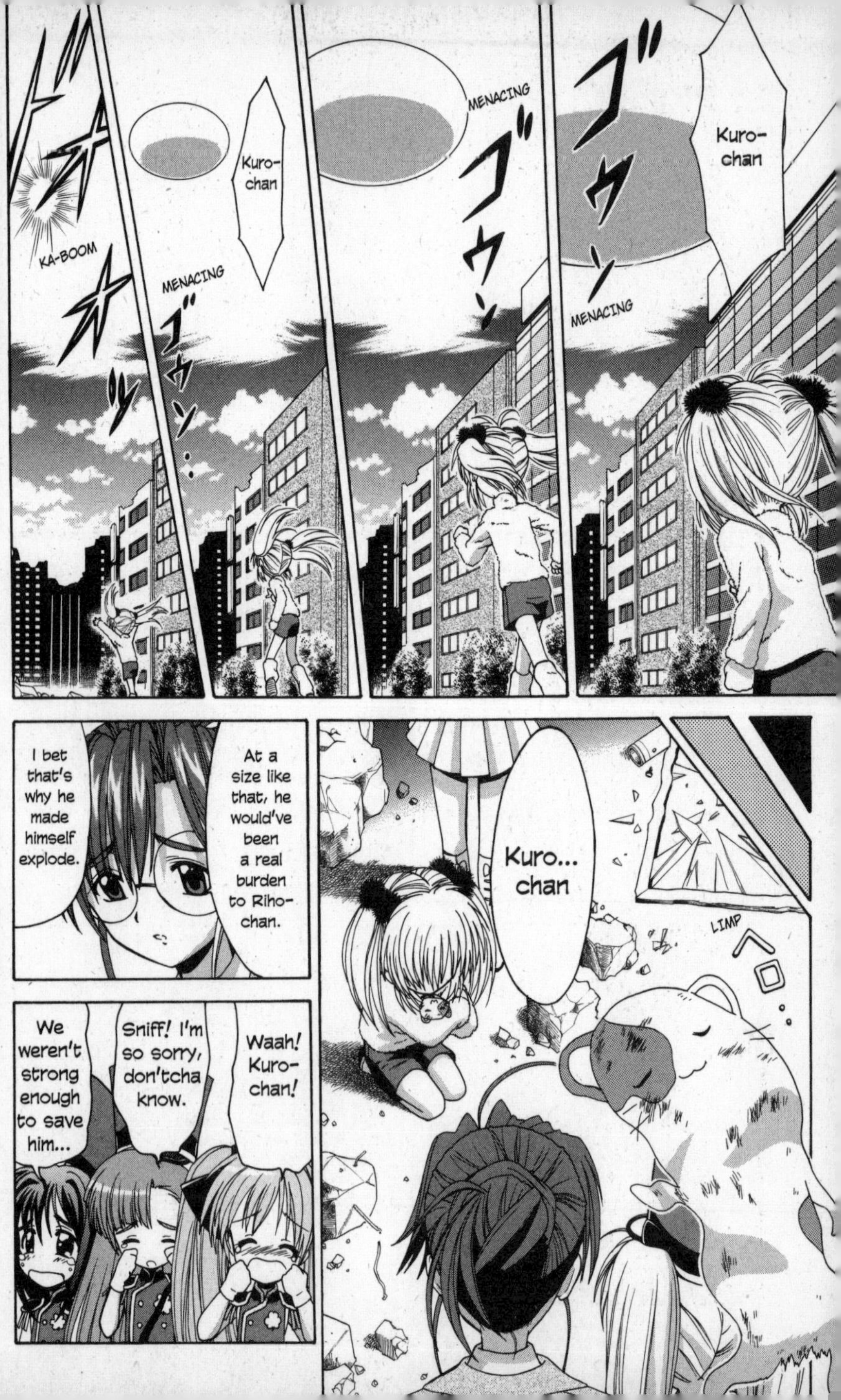

Kuro-chan
MENACING
MENACING
Kuro-chan
MENACING
KA-BOOM
Kuro... chan
LIMP
At a size like that, he would've been a real burden to Riho-chan.
I bet that's why he made himself explode.
Waah! Kuro-chan!
Sniff! I'm so sorry, don'tcha know.
We weren't strong enough to save him...

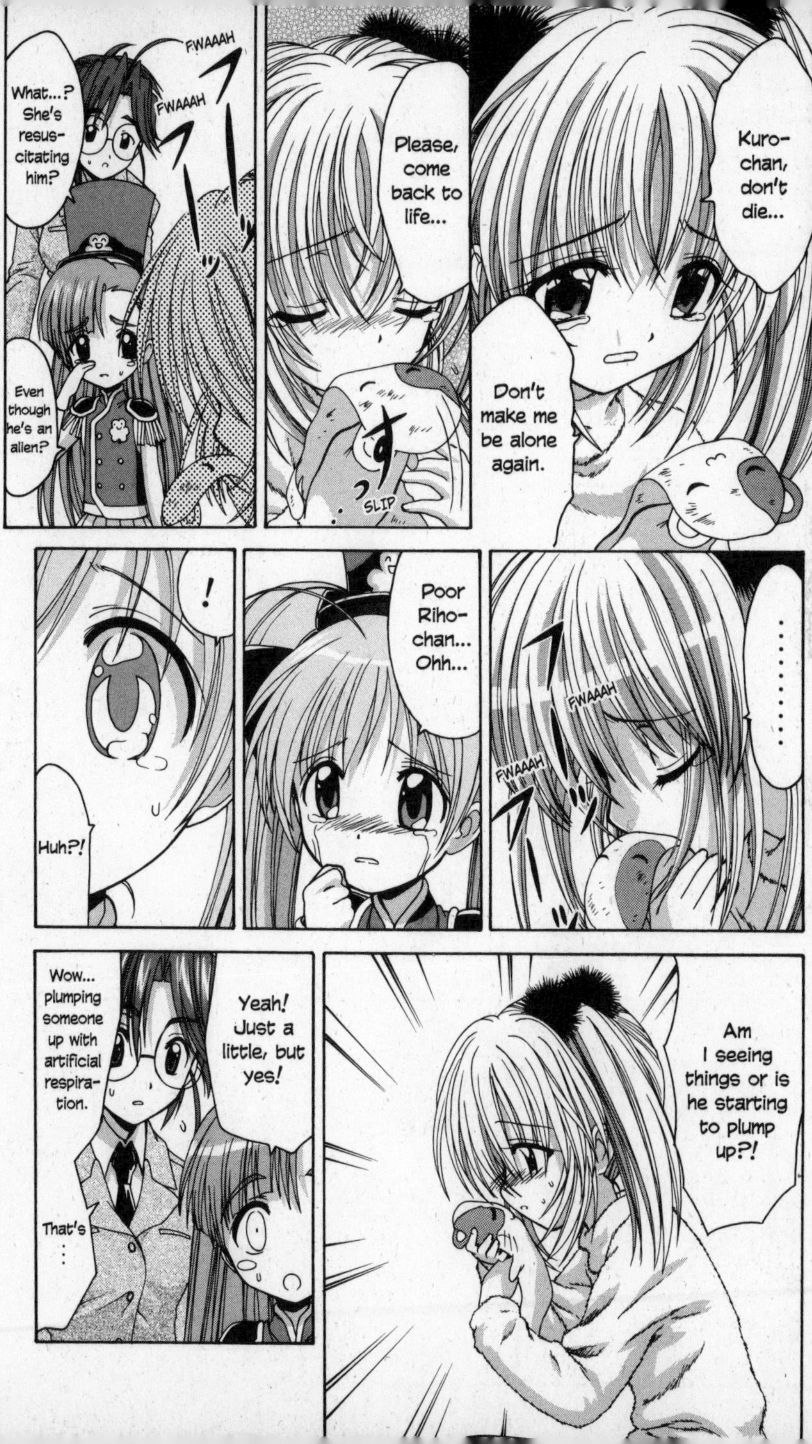
Kuro-chan, don't die...
Don't make me be alone again.
Please, come back to life...
SLIP
FWAAAH
FWAAAH
What...? She's resuscitating him?
Even though he's an alien?
....
FWAAAH
FWAAAH
Poor Riho-chan... Ohh...
!
Huh?!
Am I seeing things or is he starting to plump up?!
Yeah! Just a little, but yes!
Wow... plumping someone up with artificial respiration.
That's...

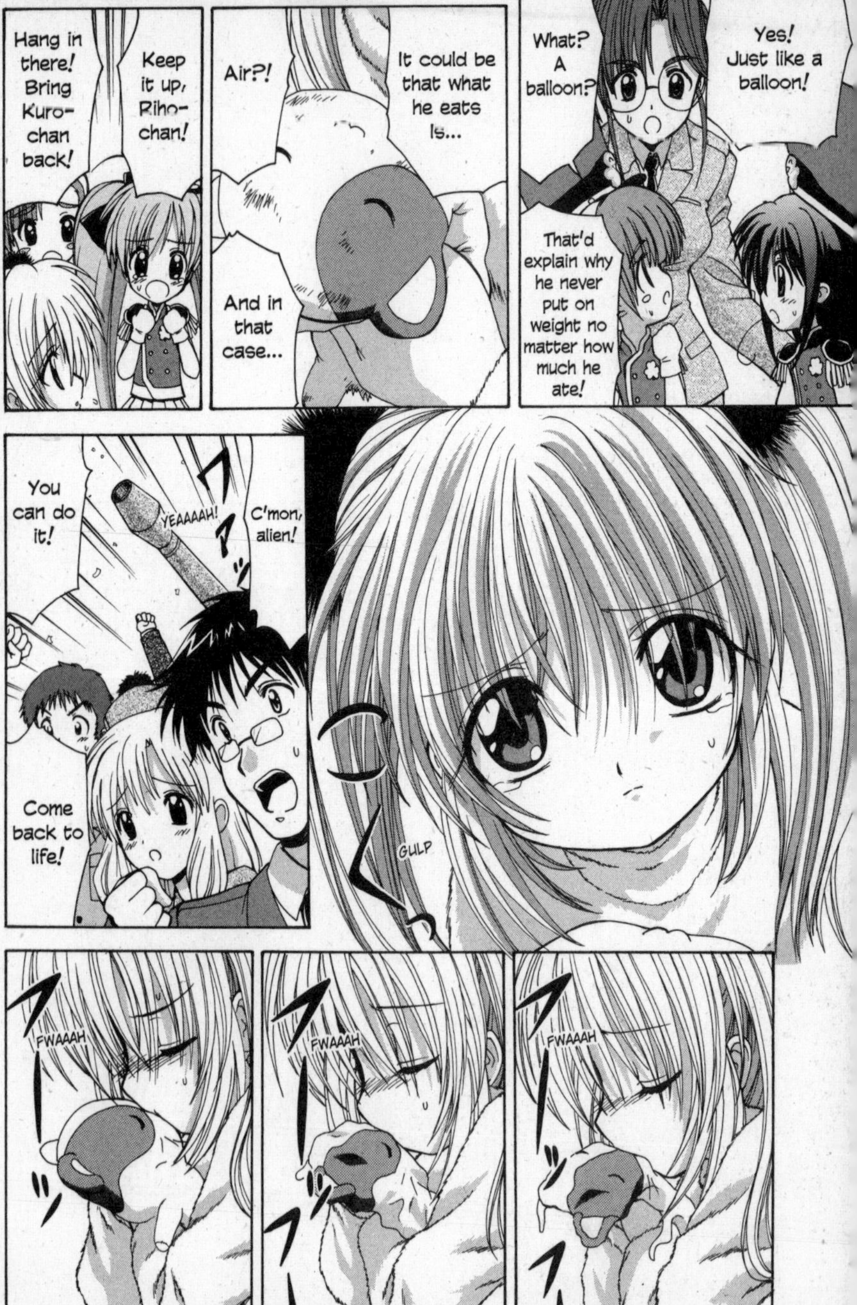
Yes! Just like a balloon!
What? A balloon?
That'd explain why he never put on weight no matter how much he ate!
It could be that what he eats is...
Air?!
And in that case...
Keep it up, Riho-chan!
Hang in there! Bring Kuro-chan back!
GULP
C'mon, alien!
YEAAAAH!
You can do it!
Come back to life!
FWAAAH
FWAAAH
FWAAAH

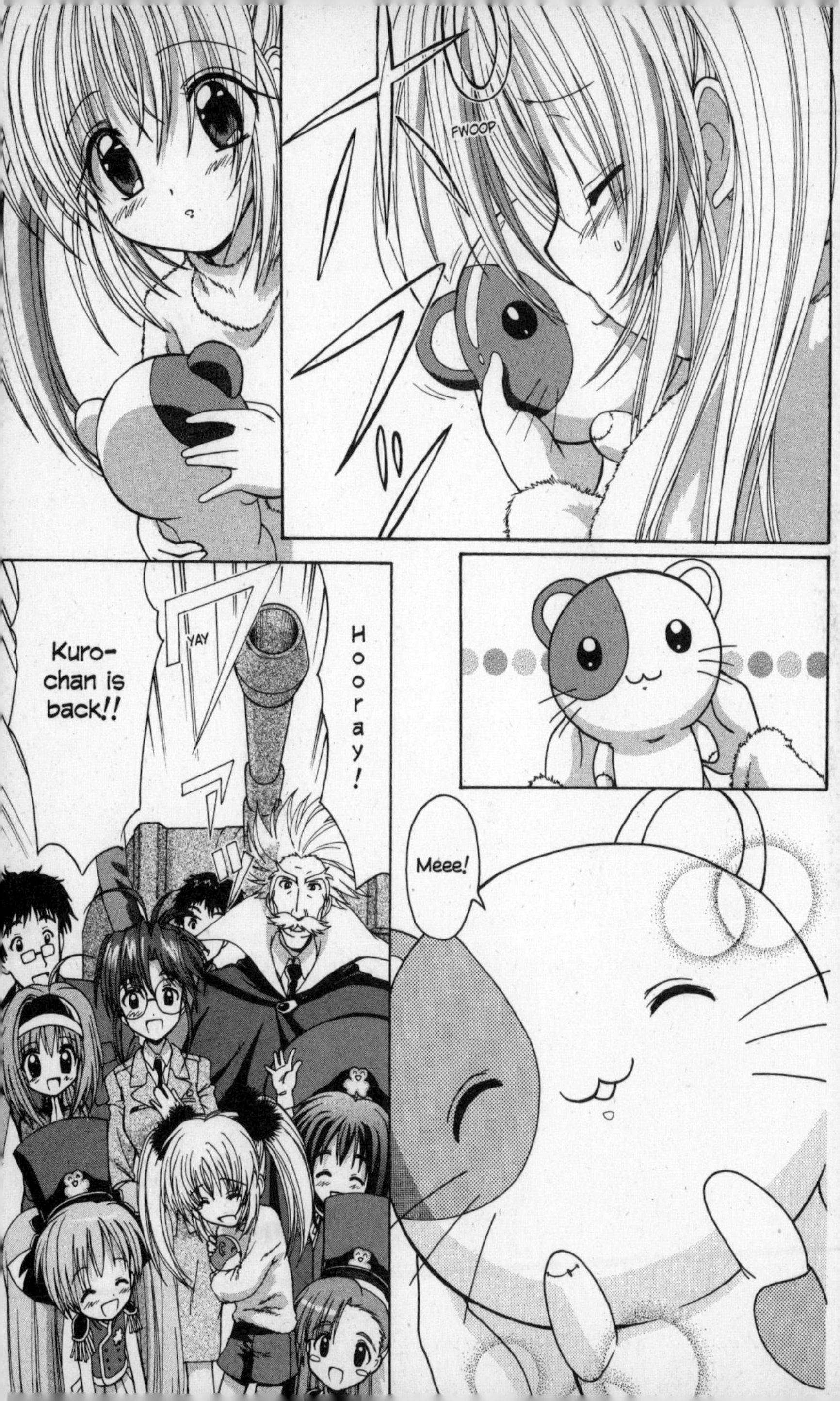
FWOOP
Meee!
Hooray!
YAY
Kuro-chan is back!!

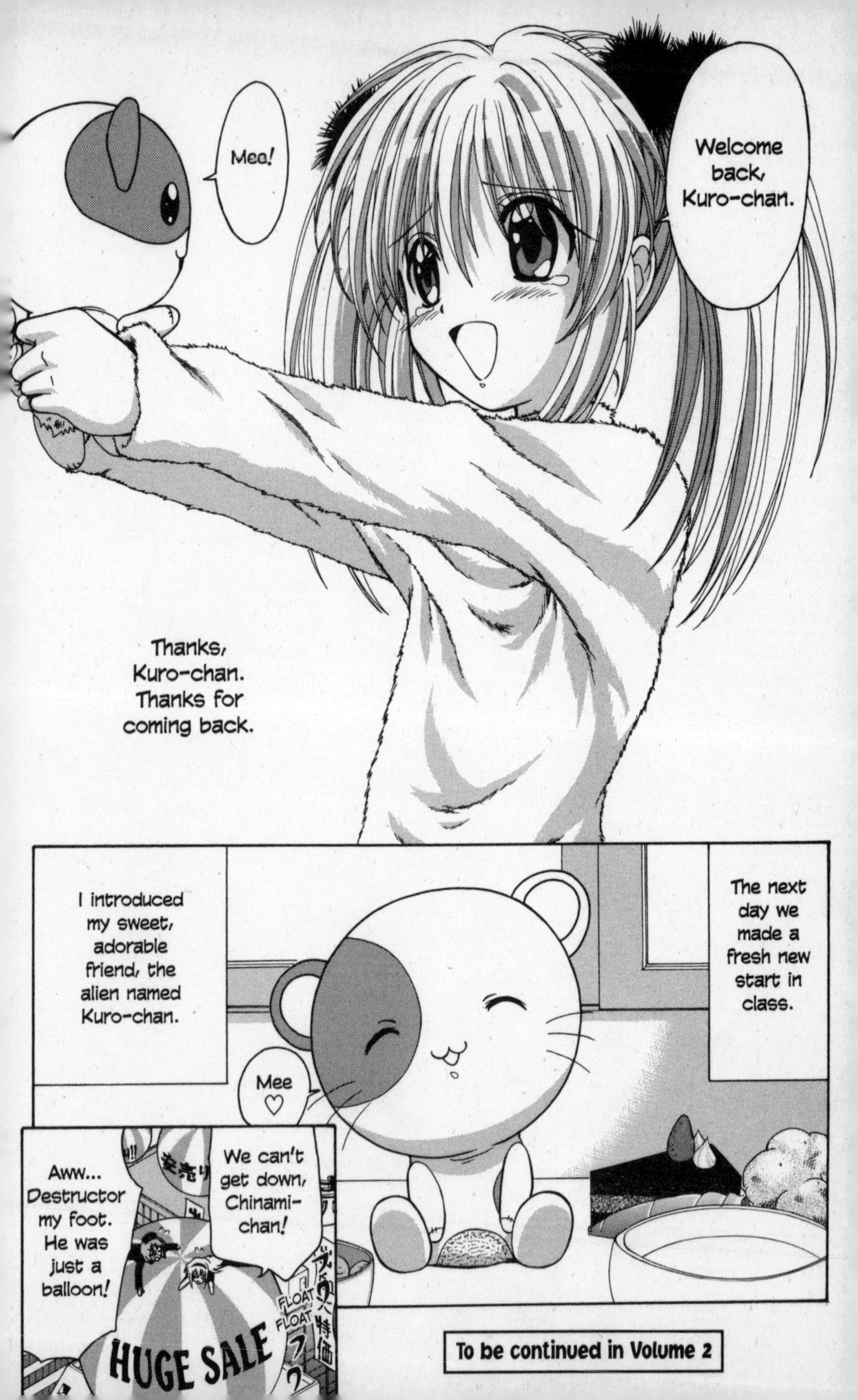
Welcome back, Kuro-chan.
Mee!
Thanks, Kuro-chan. Thanks for coming back.
The next day we made a fresh new start in class.
I introduced my sweet, adorable friend, the alien named Kuro-chan.
Mee ♡
We can't get down, Chinami-chan!
Aww... Destructor my foot. He was just a balloon!
FLOAT FLOAT
HUGE SALE
To be continued in Volume 2

ABOUT THE CREATORS

Ken Akamatsu made his manga debut in 1994 with *AI Ga Tomaranai* (released in the United States with the title *A.I. Love You*). Like all of Akamatsu's work to date, it was published in Kodansha's *Shonen Magazine*. *AI Ga Tomaranai* ran for five years before concluding in 1999. In 1998, however, Akamatsu began the work that would make him one of the most popular manga artists in Japan: *Love Hina*. *Love Hina* ran for four years, and before its conclusion in 2002, it would cause Akamatsu to be granted the prestigious Manga of the Year Award from Kodansha, as well as going on to become one of the best-selling manga in the United States.

RAN took his pen name from his favorite anime character, but his real name is Ryo Sawano. Born in Niigata prefecture, he graduated from Niigata's Anime and Manga Technical School in the Manga Department in 2002. An editor at Kodansha, *Mao-chan*'s Japanese publisher, recruited this outstanding new talent while he was still just a student.

TRANSLATION NOTES

Japanese is a tricky language for most Westerners, and translation is often more an art than a science. For your edification and reading pleasure, here are notes on some of the places where we could have gone in a different direction, or where a Japanese cultural reference is used.

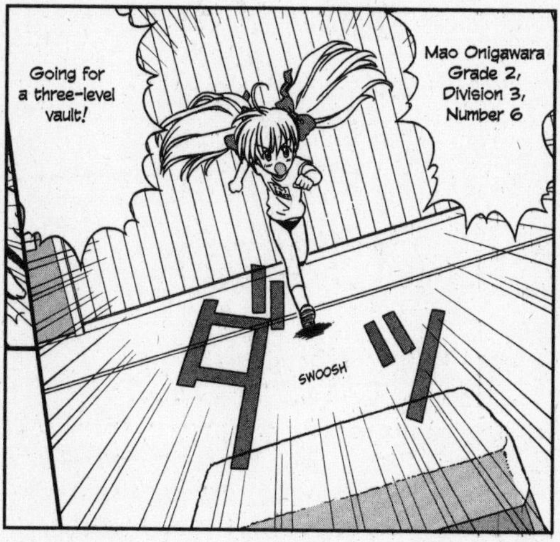
Mao Onigawara Grade 2, Division 3, Number 6
Going for a three-level vault!
SWOOSH

vault, page 5

Vaulting over wooden blocks stacked increasingly higher is a mainstay of P.E. in Japan, and is often seen through students' eyes as a mental hurdle, as much as a physical one. The sport was originally brought over from Europe sometime in the last century, and is noticeably different from the western version of vaulting.

don'tcha know/if ya please, page 8

As with many Japanese characters in manga and anime, Misora has a peculiar way of ending her lines...in her case with arimasu. In English she often ends her lines with "don'tcha know" or "if ya please."

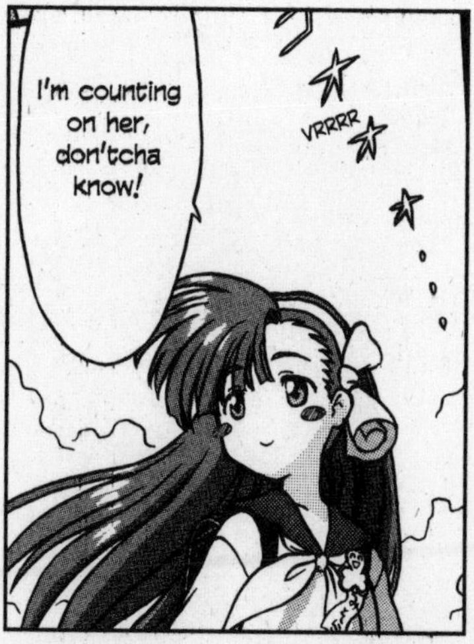
VRRRR
I'm counting on her, don'tcha know!

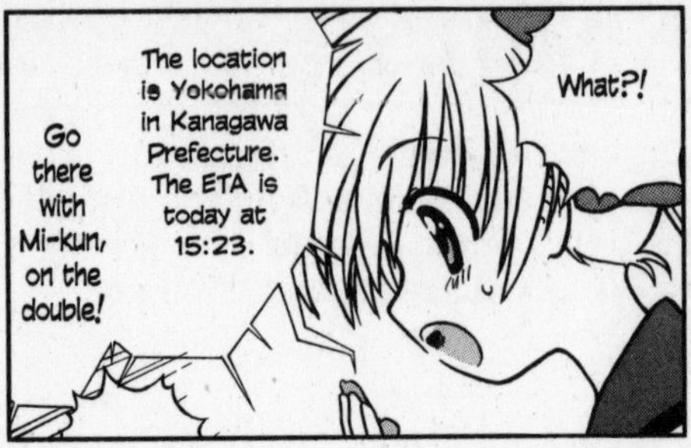
What?!
The location is Yokohama in Kanagawa Prefecture. The ETA is today at 15:23.
Go there with Mi-kun, on the double!

Mi, page 8

As with many nonhuman but animate characters, Mi-kun speaks or replies with only one word, the first part of his name, *Mi*.

Rikushiro, page 13

Rikushiro's name—like that of his competitor—is a play on words, and in his case means "warrior of the land" to reflect his position as Chief of the Ground Defense Corps.

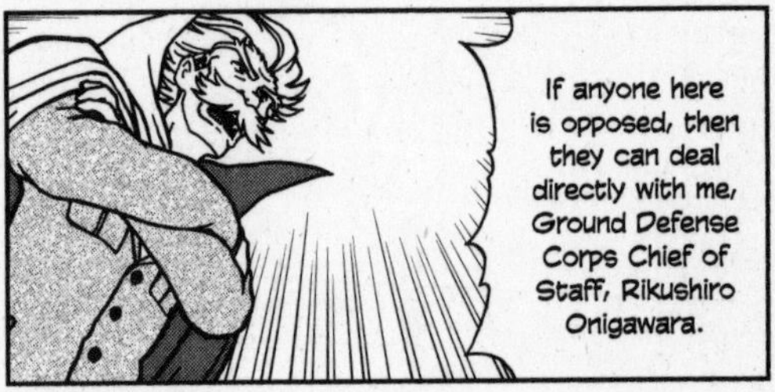
If anyone here is opposed, then they can deal directly with me, Ground Defense Corps Chief of Staff, Rikushiro Onigawara.

Sorajiro, page 38

Sorajiro's name is a play on words, and in his case means "warrior of the sky," to reflect his position as Chief of the Air Defense Corps.

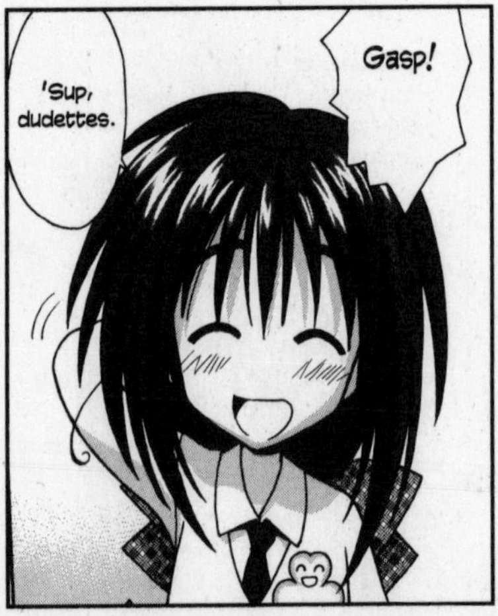
Gasp!
'Sup, dudettes.

dudettes, page 58

Sylvia has, in the same way Misora and indeed many characters in manga and anime have, a peculiar way of speech. Rather than using *chan* for example, she uses *yan*. In English she often uses "yo" and "dudettes" to reflect the casual style of speech she illustrates in the original.

Rain doll, aka *fure fure bozu*, page 81

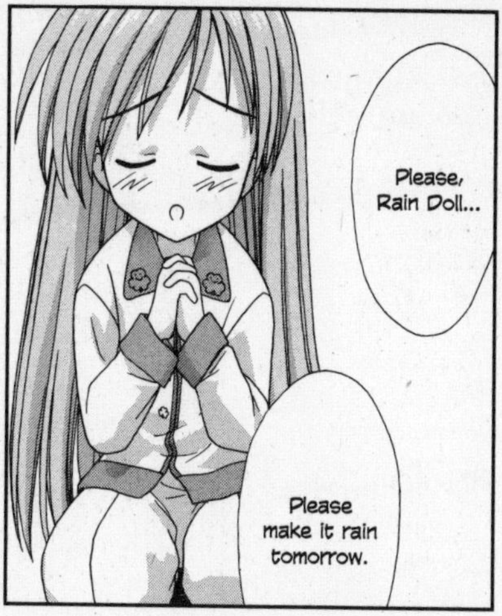
Please, Rain Doll...
Please make it rain tomorrow.

A rain doll, or *teru teru bozu* (literally "shiny shiny priest/baldie"), has been used since the Edo area, originally by farmers and more recently by children. The amulets are made to ward off rain, and the cloth or paper dolls are hung by the window while children chant the equivalent of "fine weather priest, please make it sunny tomorrow." In this case, though, Mao is desperately hoping for rain. So she calls her version a *fure fure bozu* (literally "rain, rain priest/baldie") and hangs it upside down.

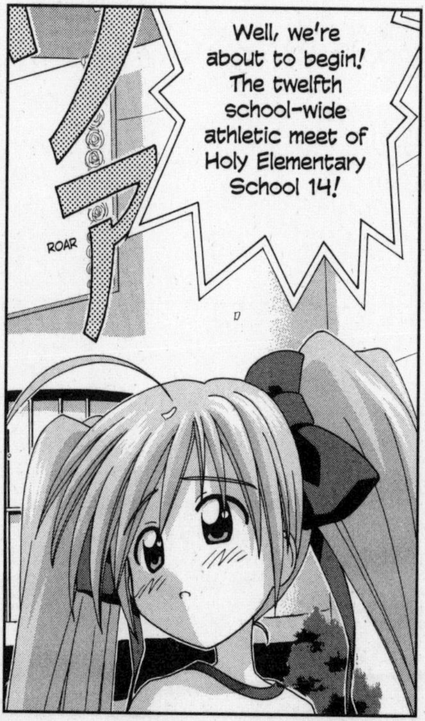
Well, we're about to begin! The twelfth school-wide athletic meet of Holy Elementary School 14!
ROAR

Athletic Meet, page 82

Athletic meets in Japan bare little resemblance to sports days in North America, in that almost all events are team-based and in many cases (such as the event where kids must quickly eat a bun hung on a string, while their hands are tied behind their back) are quite hilarious. The whole school participates, and the cheering, pom-pom-waving students and larger-than-life mascots help create a very festive atmosphere. The athletic meet is one of the rare occasions for entire families to gather at the school, and their boisterousness and specially prepared picnics add to the excitement. Although the team-based aspect of the event might seem as though it creates less pressure than the North American sports day, with its individual events, for a klutz like Mao, it's still a day to dread.

if Mount Fuji caved in, page 90

The equivalent of "if pigs could fly" or "if hell freezes over."

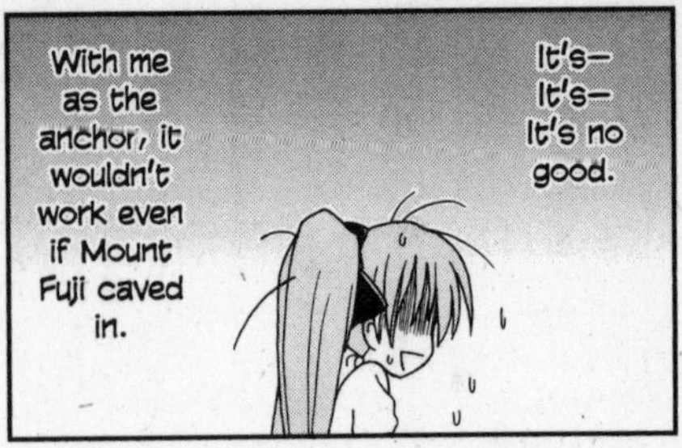
It's—
It's—
It's no good.
With me as the anchor, it wouldn't work even if Mount Fuji caved in.

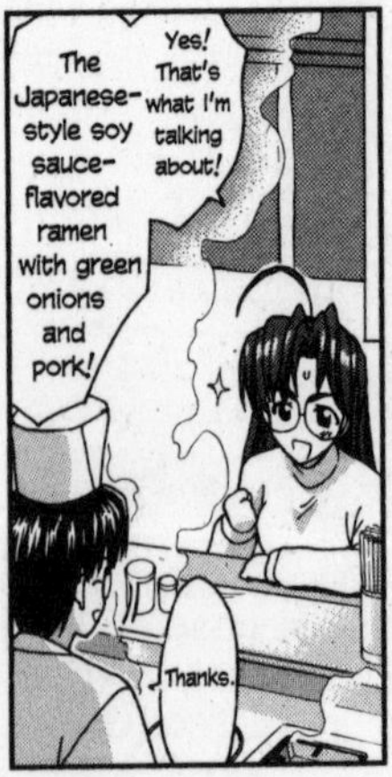
Yes! That's what I'm talking about!
The Japanese-style soy sauce-flavored ramen with green onions and pork!
Thanks.

Ramen, page 110

Ramen is an instant noodle soup dish most North Americans are familiar with, but in Japan ramen usually brings to mind not the instant snack, but its freshly made variation. Many regions are known for their distinct ramen flavors and ingredients, whether it be an added piece of pork, miso flavoring, or handmade noodles, for example. For many citizens travelling within Japan, a highlight of any trip is indulging in a bowl of the region's unique style of noodle soup.

The Great Buddha, page 115

Famous attractions in Kamakura include The Great Buddha (*Daibutsu*), Enkakuji, and Tsurugaoka Hachiman-gun Shrine, all of which attract the attention of the aliens.

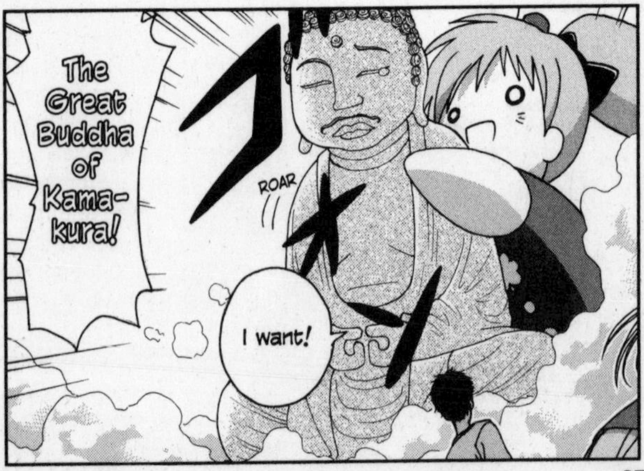
The Great Buddha of Kama-kura!
ROAR
I want!

heated table, page 131

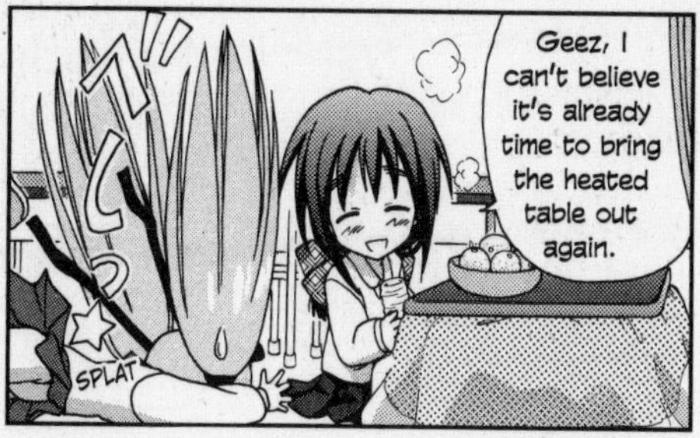
Geez, I can't believe it's already time to bring the heated table out again.
SPLAT

Probably the most telltale sign that winter is approaching is when the family's heated table, or *kotatsu*, is brought out. Technically the table is used year round, but its main function is to keep everyone warm, which is done late fall by plugging in the heat lamp under the table, and putting on the bottom and top futon, or thick, puffy blankets. The bottom blanket goes under the table and is sat upon, and the top one goes between the removable tabletop and the table frame. Thus its users can snuggle up to the table and cover their laps with the top blanket, trapping the warmth inside.

Sticker photo, page 137

Sticker photos, or *puri-kura* (a shortened version of "Print Club"), are a popular phenomenon from the 1990s. Similar to photo booths, the tiny sticker photos can then be personalized with preset graphics and words chosen from the touch screen.

cut the cake, page 158

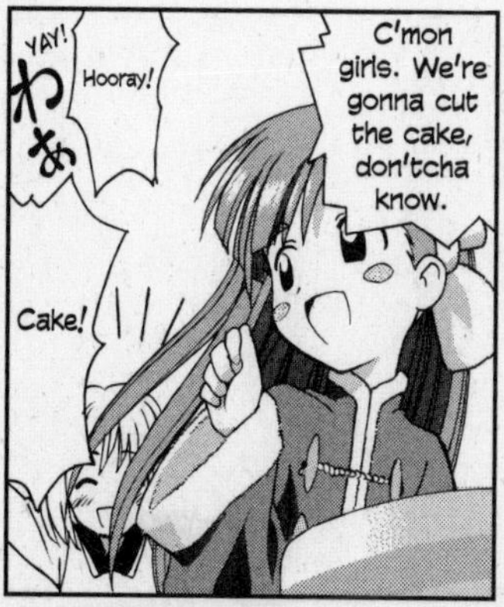
C'mon girls. We're gonna cut the cake, don'tcha know.
YAY!
わぁ
Hooray!
Cake!

Christmas is indeed celebrated in Japan, although for most people it has no religious significance. Christmas trees are virtually nowhere to be seen, and the morning doesn't start off with presents from Santa. Recently people have started exchanging a few small gifts, but typically it's only lovers or kids who observe the new tradition. Young Japanese do love the idea of Santa, a snowy Christmas day and all the associated magic, and in response to this, many stores are decorating more with each passing year. The main event of the day is when everyone gathers around to share a Christmas cake, which is basically a fancy strawberry shortcake.

rice gruel, page 175

Rice gruel is the Japanese version of chicken soup, and is served to people when they have a cold or the flu. Similar to but plainer than *congee*, available in Chinese restaurants.

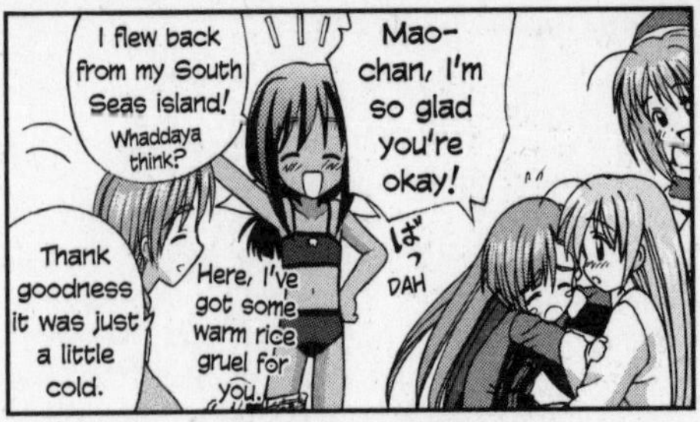
Mao-chan, I'm so glad you're okay!
ばっ DAH
I flew back from my South Seas island!
Whaddaya think?
Here, I've got some warm rice gruel for you.
Thank goodness it was just a little cold.

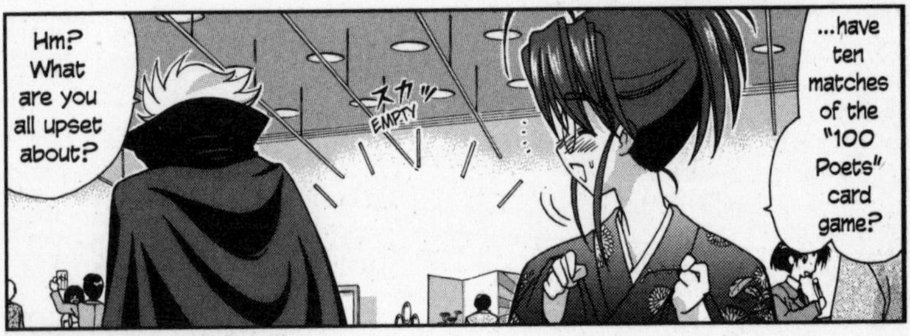
...have ten matches of the "100 Poets" card game?
スカッ EMPTY
Hm? What are you all upset about?

"100 Poets," page 182

A well-known card game, named after the *100 Poems by 100 Poets*, or *Ogura Hyakunin Isshu*, an anthology of *tanka* poetry.

sweet bean buns, page 182

Buns filled with sweetened adzuki beans are one of the most popular treats in Japan, and are readily available in practically any store. Sylvia thinks that because they are so mundane, they don't belong at an *osechi ryori* New Year's feast, which features many delicacies that are typically not served at any other time of the year.

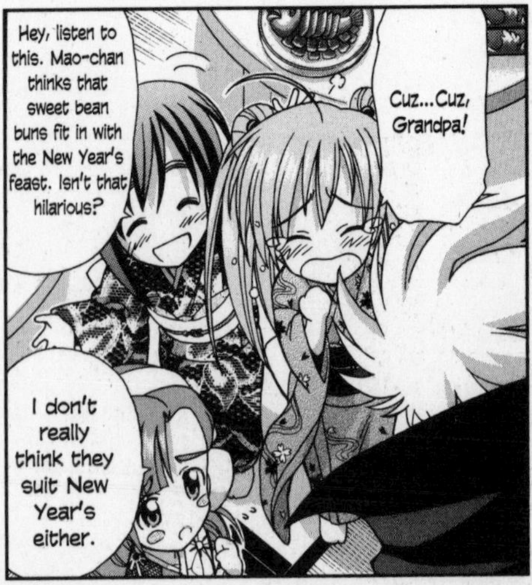
Cuz...Cuz, Grandpa!
Hey, listen to this. Mao-chan thinks that sweet bean buns fit in with the New Year's feast. Isn't that hilarious?
I don't really think they suit New Year's either.

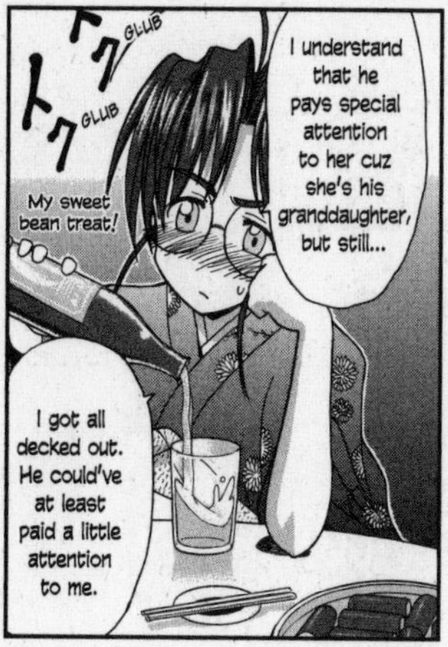
トク
GLUB
トク
GLUB
I understand that he pays special attention to her cuz she's his granddaughter, but still...
My sweet bean treat!
I got all decked out. He could've at least paid a little attention to me.

all decked out, page 183

These days most Japanese only wear kimono on a few occasions a year, one of them being New Year's. Because the kimono is so difficult and time-consuming to don, young ladies and girls dressed in kimono feel very special and dressed up as they bask in the attention and admiration of their peers.

New Year's prayer at the shrine, page 185

Most of the nation kicks off the New Year by dressing up (in kimono or Western clothes) and paying a visit to their local shrine, where they throw some money into a wooden offering box, clap their hands together twice and bow deeply as they say a prayer, then ring a bell or gong to get the attention of the shrine's *kami* or god.

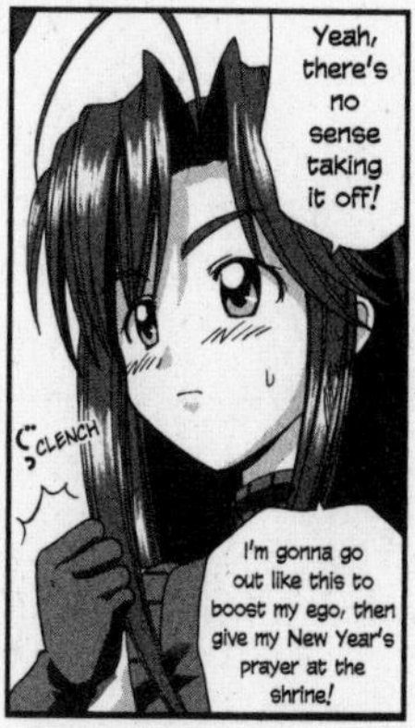
Yeah, there's no sense taking it off!
CLENCH
I'm gonna go out like this to boost my ego, then give my New Year's prayer at the shrine!

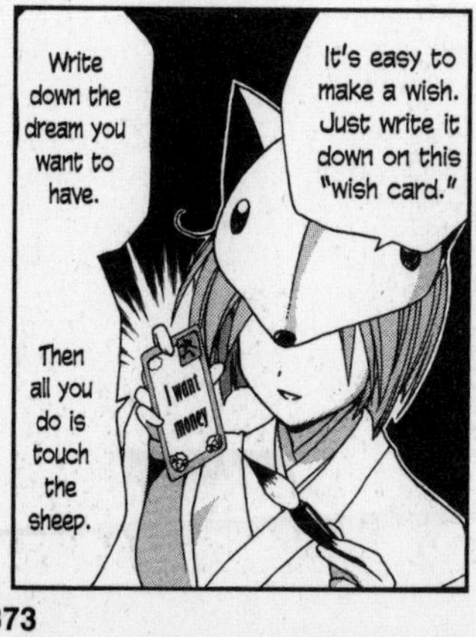
It's easy to make a wish. Just write it down on this "wish card."
Write down the dream you want to have.
I want money
Then all you do is touch the sheep.

wish card, page 187

Often visitors to a shrine will write down their wish and hang or mount it at some designated place on the shrine grounds. Common wishes include passing university entrance exams, success in love or wealth, good health, and so on.

test your forehead, page 211

Just as we in the west use our palms against someone's fever to check for a fever, in Japan they hold their own forehead to that of the sick person.

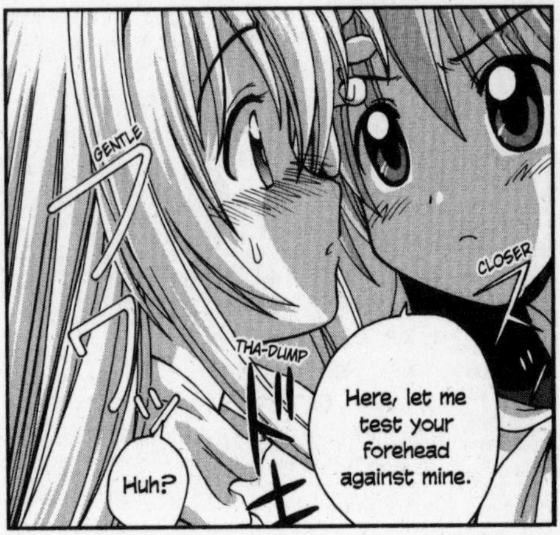
GENTLE
CLOSER
THA-DUMP
Here, let me test your forehead against mine.
Huh?

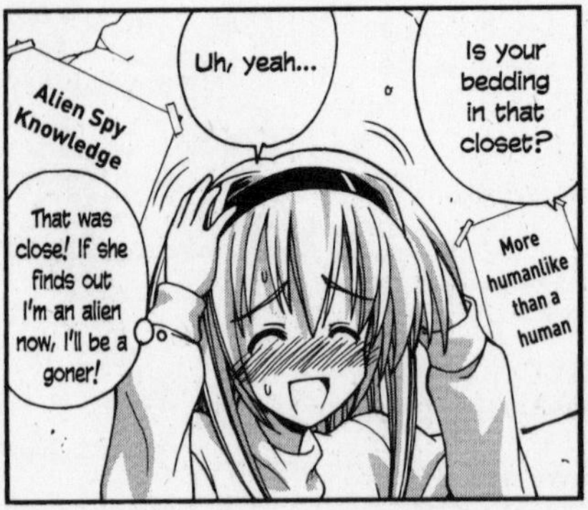
Is your bedding in that closet?
Uh, yeah...
More humanlike than a human
Alien Spy Knowledge
That was close! If she finds out I'm an alien now, I'll be a goner!

bedding in that closet, page 211

Beds are becoming more common in Japan, but futons are still far and away the favorite. Futons in Japan are not the superthick, heavy things we have. Generally they are light cotton-filled mats about 3" in thickness, and are folded away and stored in the closet each morning, unlike a bed which is straightened in the morning but obviously stays put.

hanky's not in my pocket, page 217

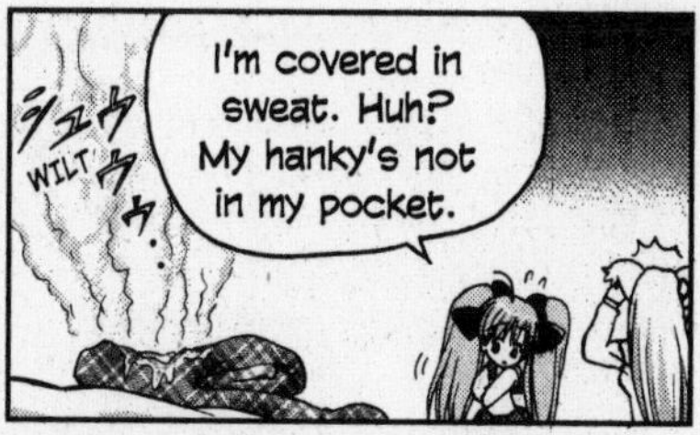
I'm covered in sweat. Huh? My hanky's not in my pocket.
シュウゥ
WILT

Handkerchiefs were commonly used in North American and Europe until the mid-twentieth century, but now it's almost rare to see a person using one. And if they do, it's to blow their nose on. In Japan however, the handkerchief is carried by almost everyone, and it's used for wiping perspiration, to enclose or wrap things (even lunches), to wipe off spills and a host of other uses. Except for blowing the nose. For that, one uses tissue. Use your hanky for the schnozz and you'll attract a lot of negative attention.

hot spring, page 289

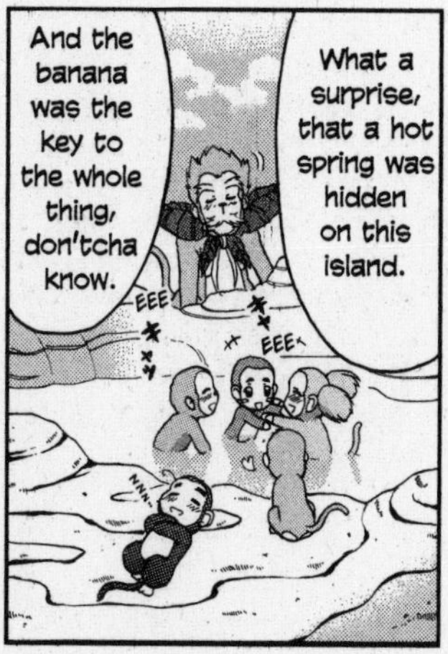
What a surprise, that a hot spring was hidden on this island.
And the banana was the key to the whole thing, don'tcha know.
EEE
EEE
NNN...

Up until the mid-twentieth century, taking a dip in a hot spring was something done almost exclusively by the older generation. Recently though, it has become a favorite pastime of the young and old alike, and indeed many travel plans are based around visits to popular hot springs.

Cherry blossom party, page 294

One of Japan's most popular events in spring is to gather with family, friends or coworkers for *hanami*, or "viewing of the flowers"; specifically cherry tree blossoms. As a casual observer, it might seem as though the drunken, boisterous partiers sprawled out on their tarps under the gorgeous trees are doing anything *except* looking at the cherry blossoms in full bloom. Loud music, singing, drinking, laughter, and delicious home-cooked food are just a few of the things you'll see at any *hanami* across the nation. Oh, and there are the nice cherry trees, too.

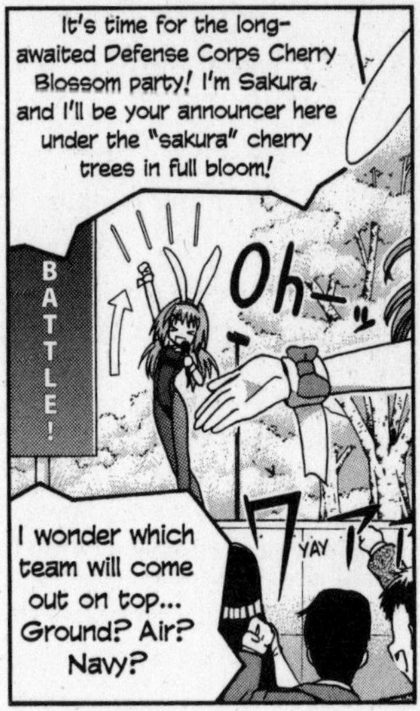
It's time for the long-awaited Defense Corps Cherry Blossom party! I'm Sakura, and I'll be your announcer here under the "sakura" cherry trees in full bloom!
BATTLE!
Oh-
YAY
I wonder which team will come out on top... Ground? Air? Navy?

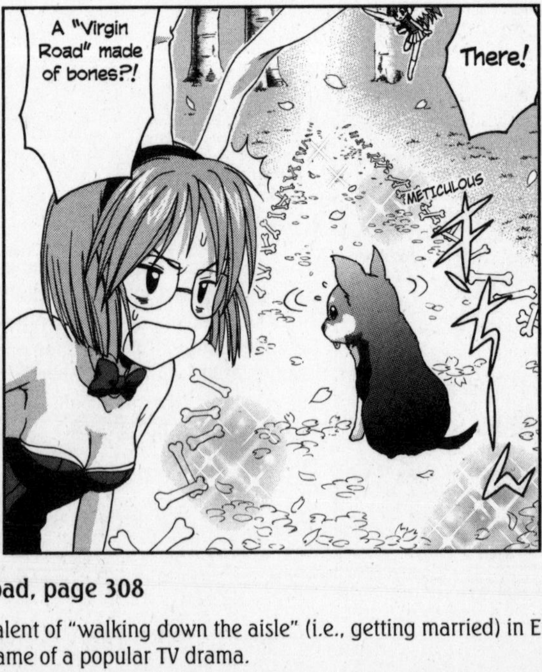
There!
A "Virgin Road" made of bones?!
METICULOUS

Virgin Road, page 308

The equivalent of "walking down the aisle" (i.e., getting married) in English. Also the name of a popular TV drama.

serve everyone lunch, page 320

School lunches are delivered to each classroom on a trolley, then served up by students who take turns being on lunch duty, usually serving in pairs. The lunches are then eaten at each student's own desk.

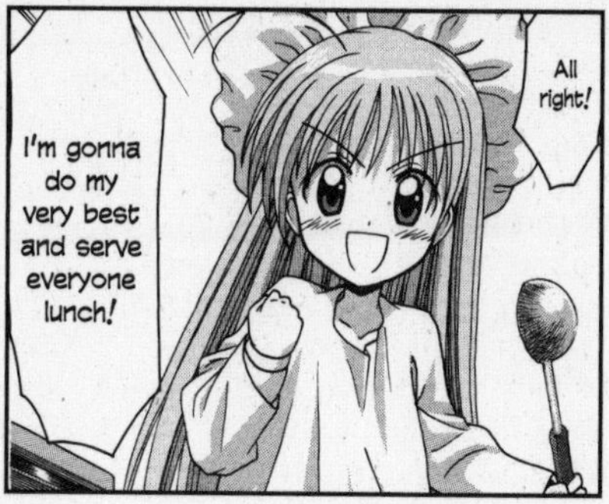
All right!
I'm gonna do my very best and serve everyone lunch!

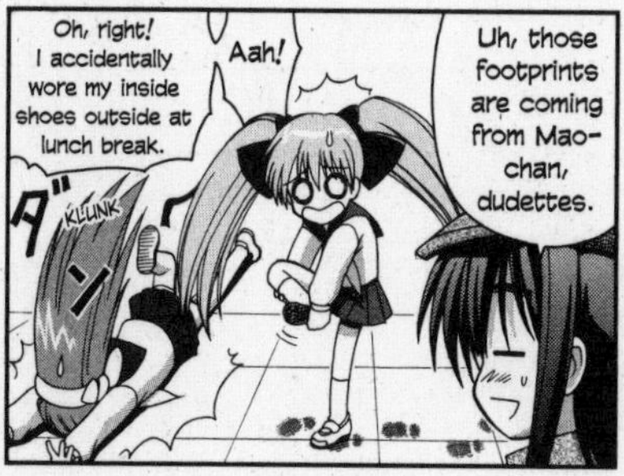
Uh, those footprints are coming from Mao-chan, dudettes.
Aah!
Oh, right! I accidentally wore my inside shoes outside at lunch break.
KLUNK

inside shoes, page 327

All students must take off their "out-door" or regular shoes on entering the school, and shelve them in an open cubby. Only after putting on their *uwabaki* or indoor canvas shoes, can they proceed into the building. *Uwabaki* had its minute of glory in the movie *Tokyo Drift*, in which the American transfer student gets his first lesson in shoe etiquette.

ants against an elephant, page 358

An expression meaning something like our "David versus Goliath."

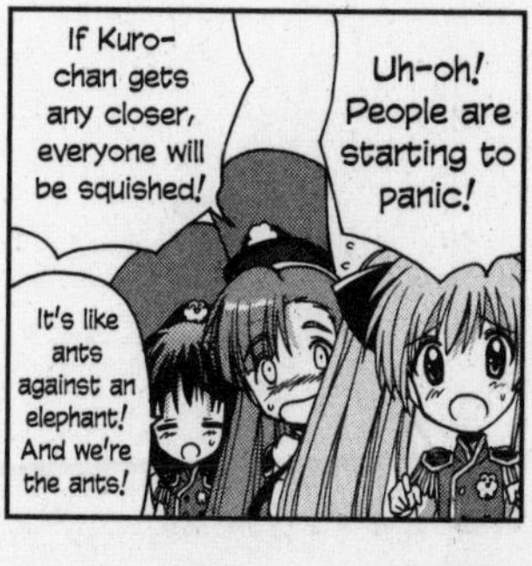
Uh-oh! People are starting to panic!
If Kuro-chan gets any closer, everyone will be squished!
It's like ants against an elephant! And we're the ants!

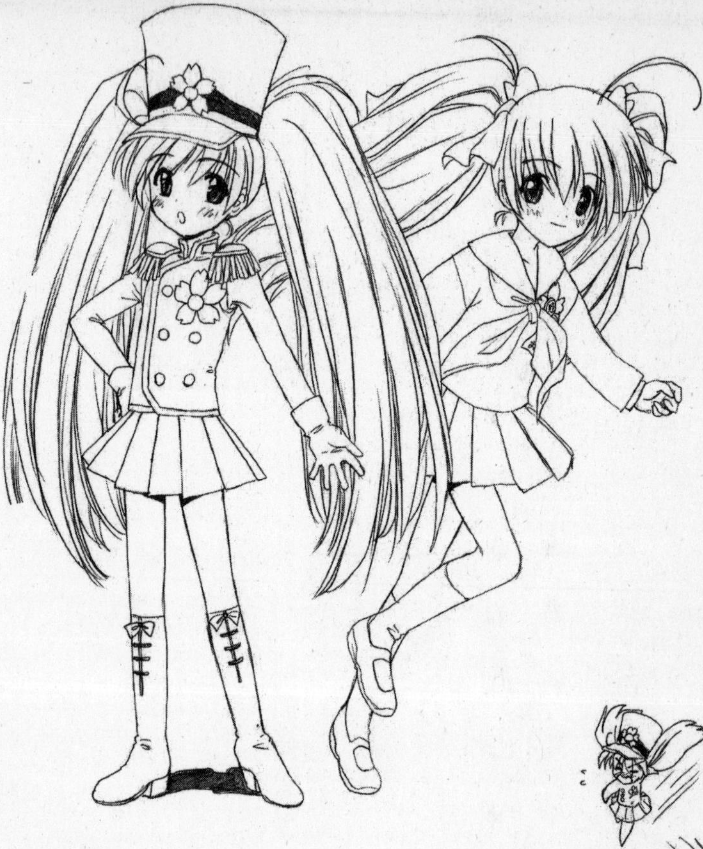

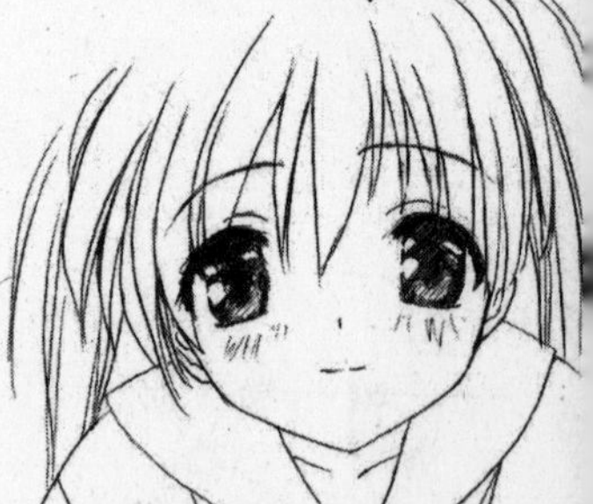

Mao Onigawara

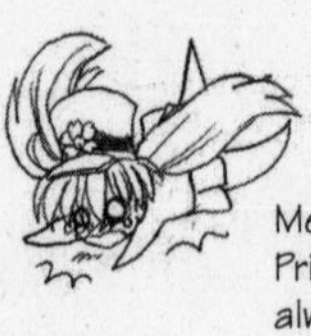

Member of the Ground Defense Corps. Private. This second grader is clumsy, but always tries her hardest. She's a bit of a crybaby, but she is strong when she's on a mission. She has a hard time on the team because she's not athletic. But her friends and family and the defense members love her. Her tenacity also inspires everyone who knows her and gives them courage. In times of trouble, her expression takes on a more mature air.

Intelligence	★★
Physical Ability	★
Seriousness	★★★★

Character Parameter

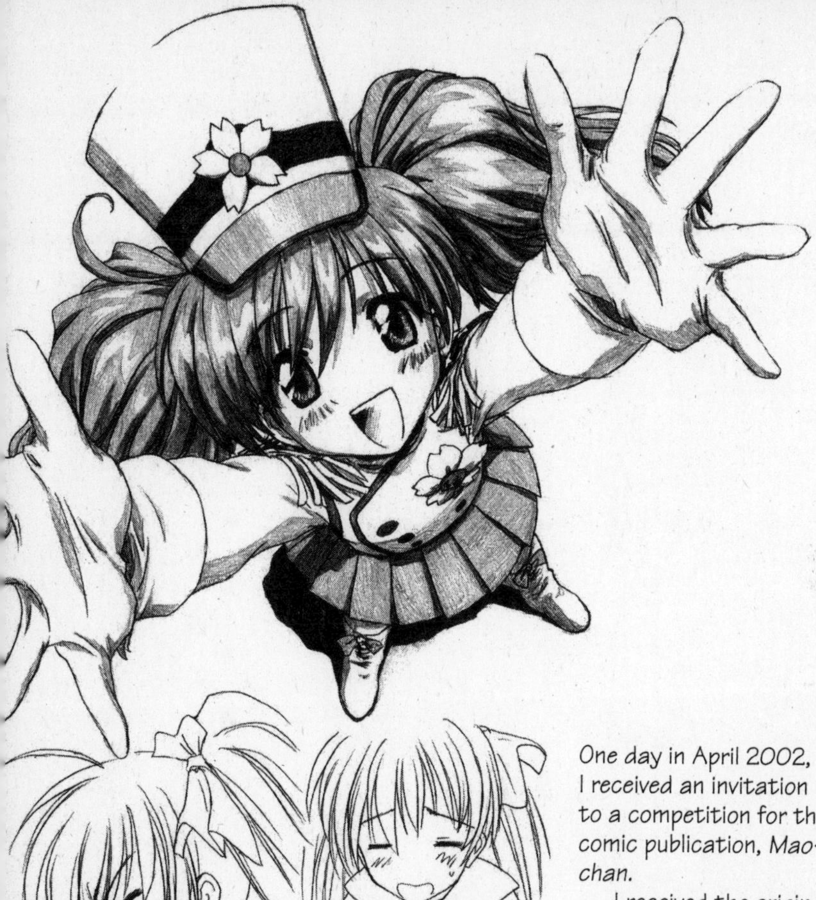

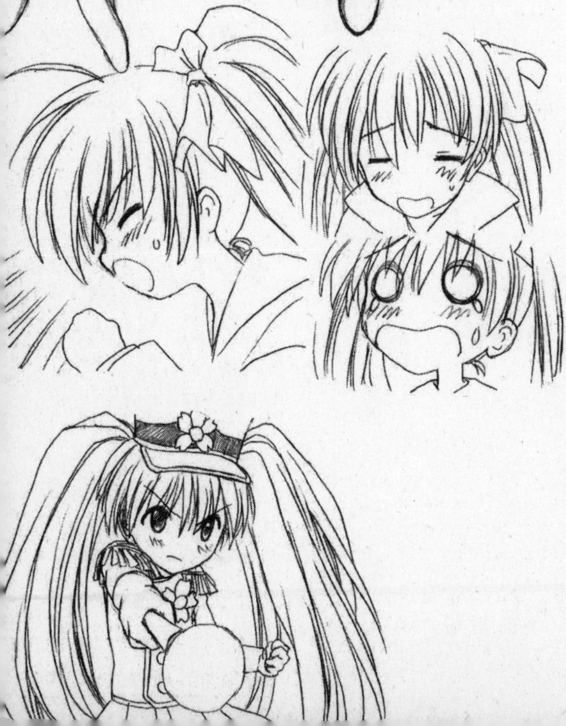

One day in April 2002, I received an invitation to a competition for the comic publication, *Mao-chan.*

I received the original character sketch and did my best to imitate it, and the resulting character is shown here. I was told that my art did not have to resemble Akamatsu-sensei's originals, but in the end this is how it turned out...

The almighty Akamatsu-sensei...!

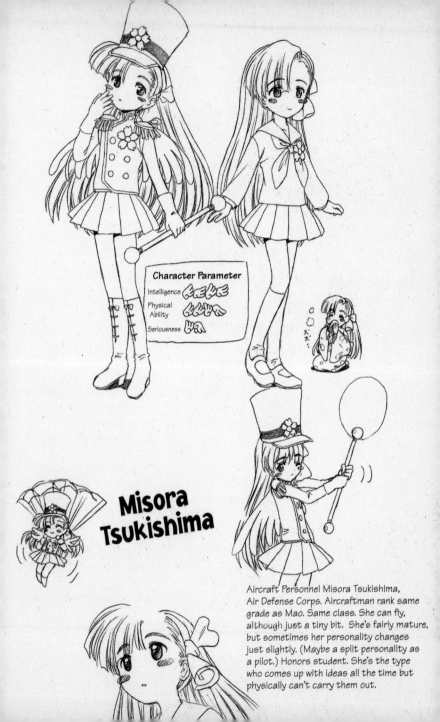

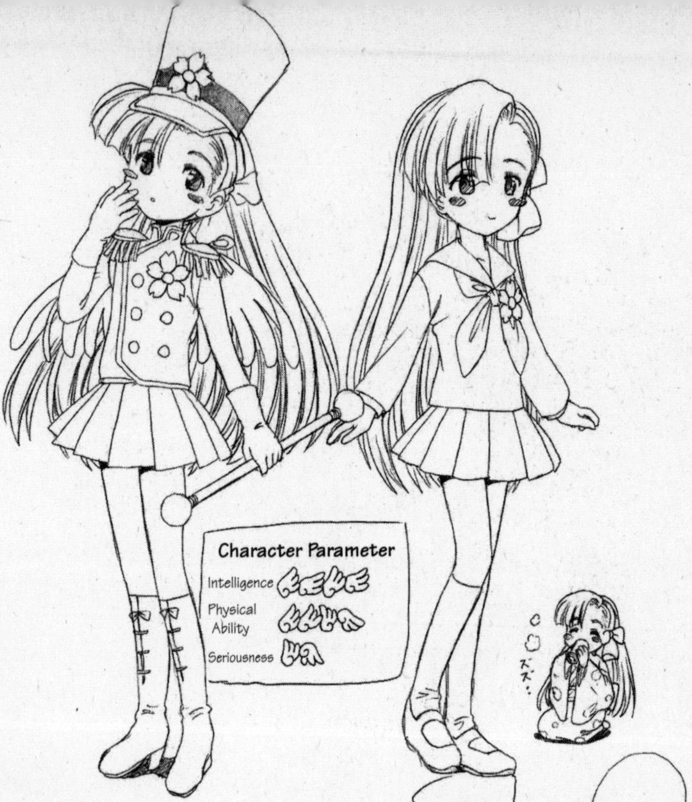
Character Parameter
Intelligence
Physical Ability
Seriousness
ズズ…

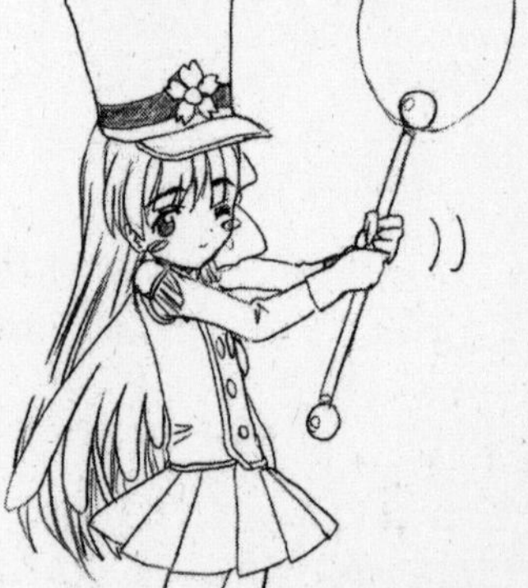

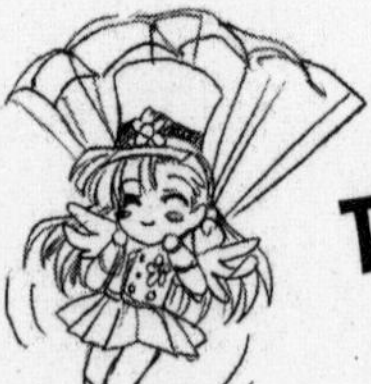

Misora Tsukishima

Aircraft Personnel Misora Tsukishima, Air Defense Corps. Aircraftman rank same grade as Mao. Same class. She can fly, although just a tiny bit. She's fairly mature, but sometimes her personality changes just slightly. (Maybe a split personality as a pilot.) Honors student. She's the type who comes up with ideas all the time but physically can't carry them out.

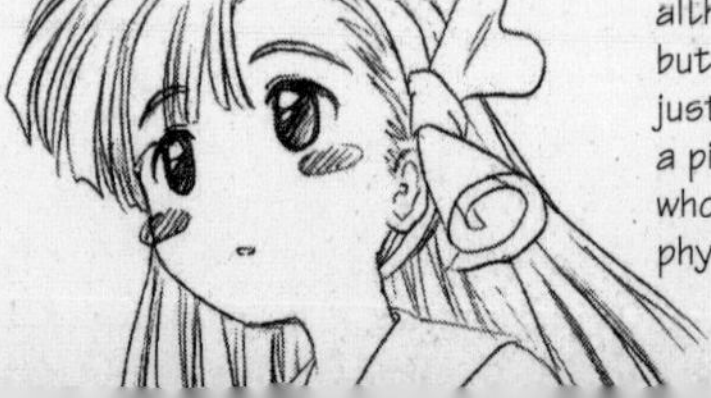

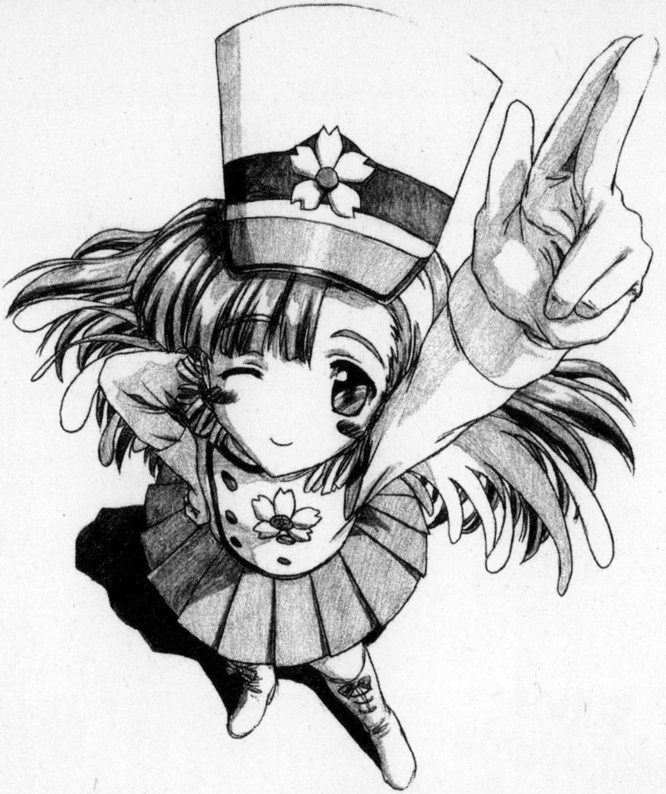

I wanted to show my own flair, too, so I sent in two story ideas. I heard that a number of other people had also entered the competition, so maybe I was a little insecure. In the end, they went with the first version I submitted, which was most faithful to the original. [boo hoo]

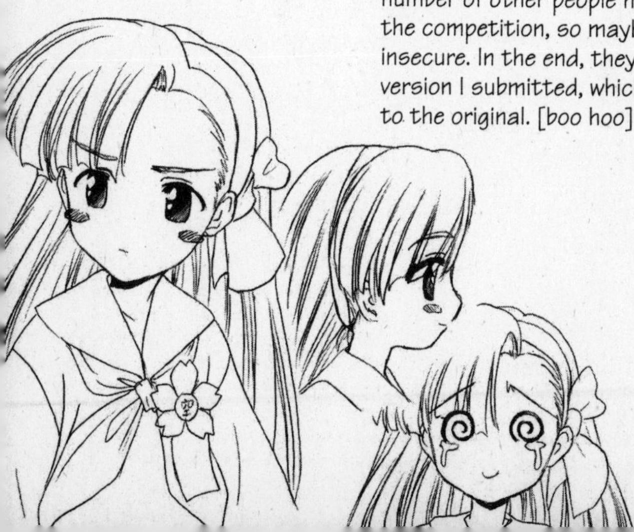

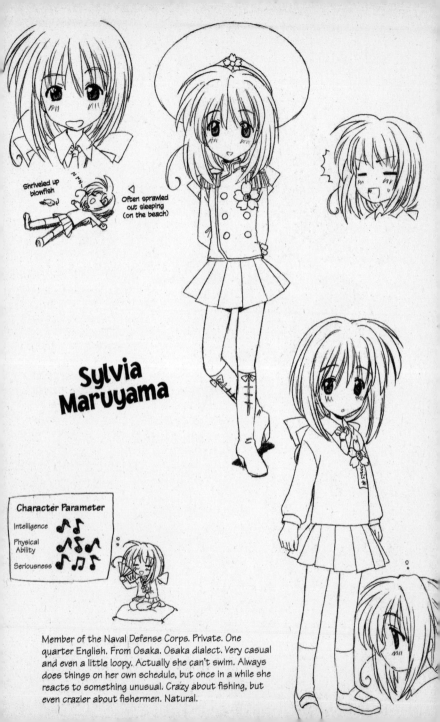

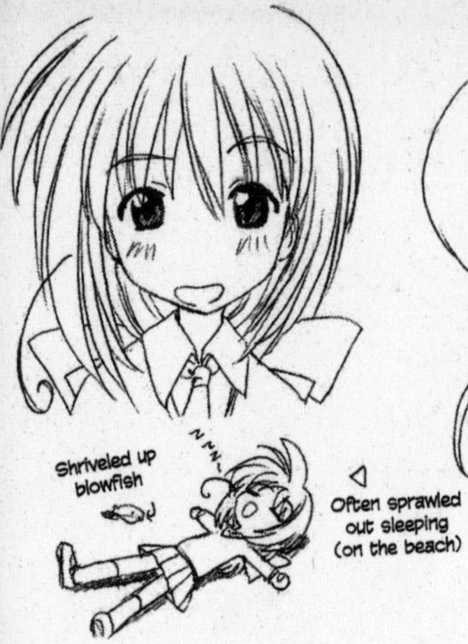
Shriveled up blowfish
Often sprawled out sleeping (on the beach)

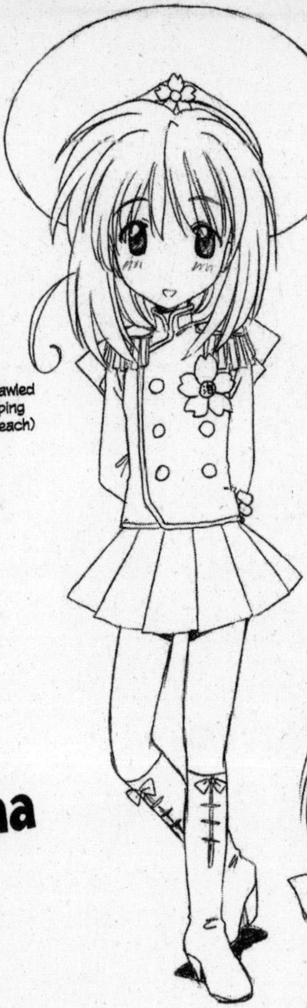

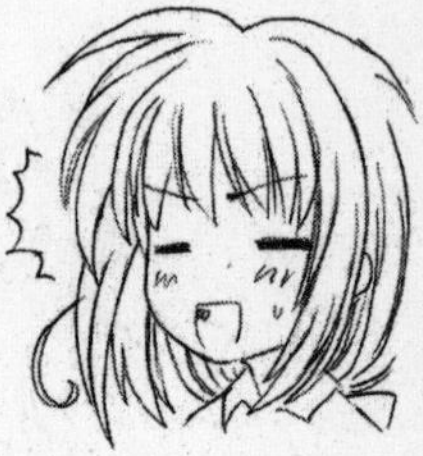

Sylvia Maruyama

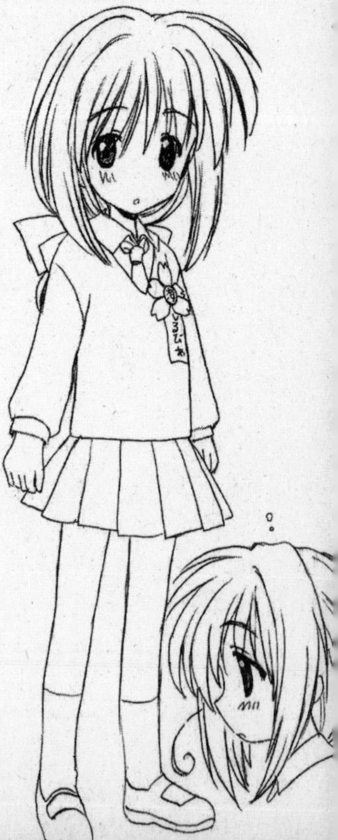

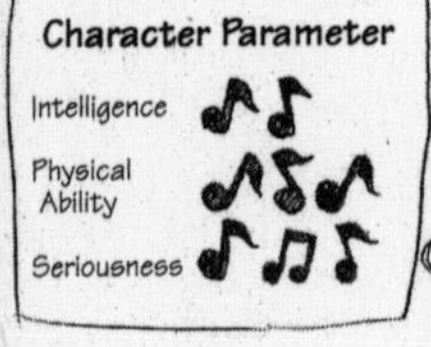
Character Parameter
Intelligence
Physical Ability
Seriousness

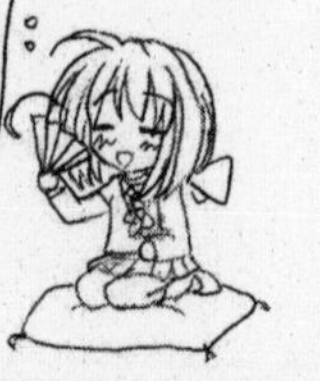

Member of the Naval Defense Corps. Private. One quarter English. From Osaka. Osaka dialect. Very casual and even a little loopy. Actually she can't swim. Always does things on her own schedule, but once in a while she reacts to something unusual. Crazy about fishing, but even crazier about fishermen. Natural.

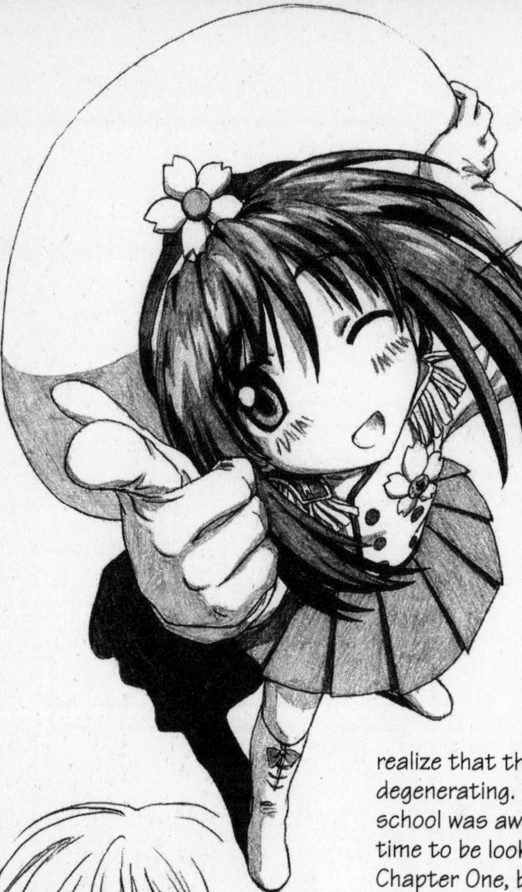

I was thrilled to get the acceptance call and without any delay began production. I was a newbie, and it was more than generous for the editing department to look after the serialization schedule. Not long after we started, I was horrified to realize that the quality of my work was degenerating. The artwork I did in art school was awesome! But I didn't have time to be looking back! Somehow I finished Chapter One, but there's TONS of stuff about the artwork that I'm not happy with. I'm really excited for you to see it...but I'm also afraid that you're going to see it! That's how I feel.

RAN

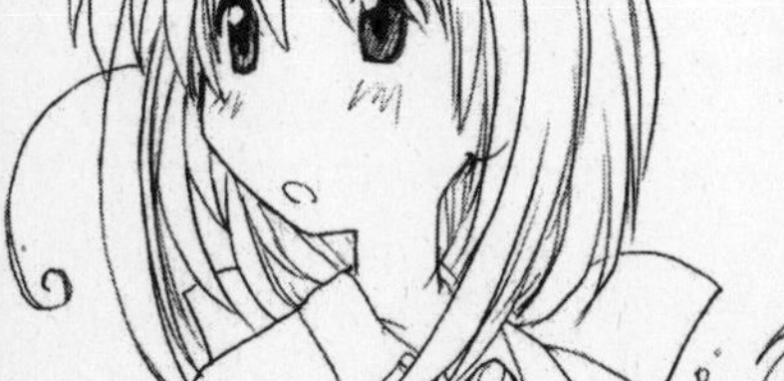

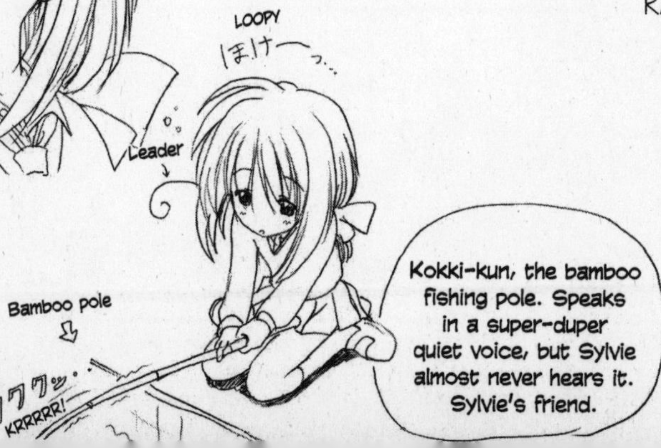
LOOPY
ほけーっ...
Leader
Kokki-kun, the bamboo fishing pole. Speaks in a super-duper quiet voice, but Sylvie almost never hears it. Sylvie's friend.
Bamboo pole
Caught something! Caught something!
ククッ..
KRRRRR!

Yuriko's Sweet Dream

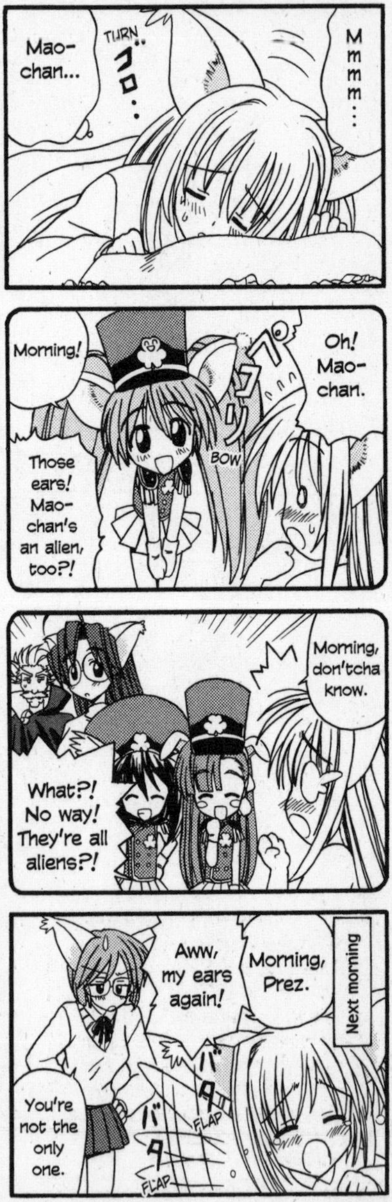
Mmmm...
TURN
Mao-chan...
Oh! Mao-chan.
BOW
Morning!
Those ears! Mao-chan's an alien, too?!
Morning, don'tcha know.
What?! No way! They're all aliens?!
Next morning
Morning, Prez.
Aww, my ears again!
FLAP
FLAP
You're not the only one.

I'll Defend My Country!!

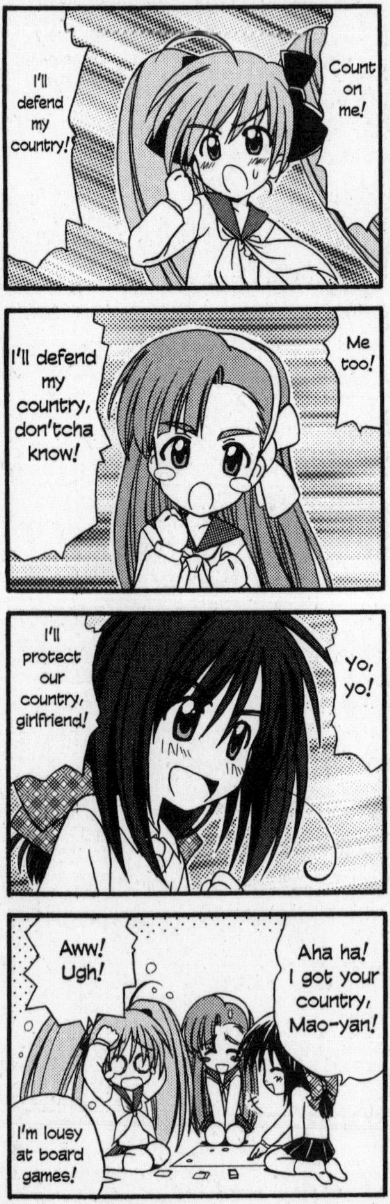
Count on me!
I'll defend my country!
Me too!
I'll defend my country, don'tcha know!
Yo, yo!
I'll protect our country, girlfriend!
Aha ha! I got your country, Mao-yan!
Aww! Ugh!
I'm lousy at board games!

Fair Weather Sketching!

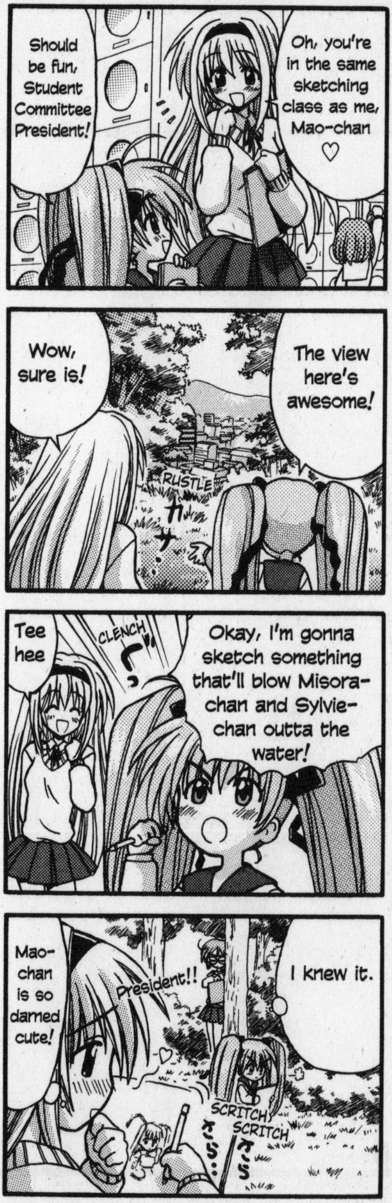

Oh, you're in the same sketching class as me, Mao-chan ♡
Should be fun, Student Committee President!
The view here's awesome!
Wow, sure is!
RUSTLE
Okay, I'm gonna sketch something that'll blow Misora-chan and Sylvie-chan outta the water!
CLENCH
Tee hee
I knew it.
President!!
Mao-chan is so darned cute!
SCRITCH
SCRITCH

When serialization began, in addition to the formal drafts, a lot of "one-off" work fell on my desk. I drew some drafts of these comic strips to use as an "anime storyboard." In the end they weren't published (boo hoo). The stories are simple, so maybe it's okay that you don't get too sucked in . . .? Yeah . . .

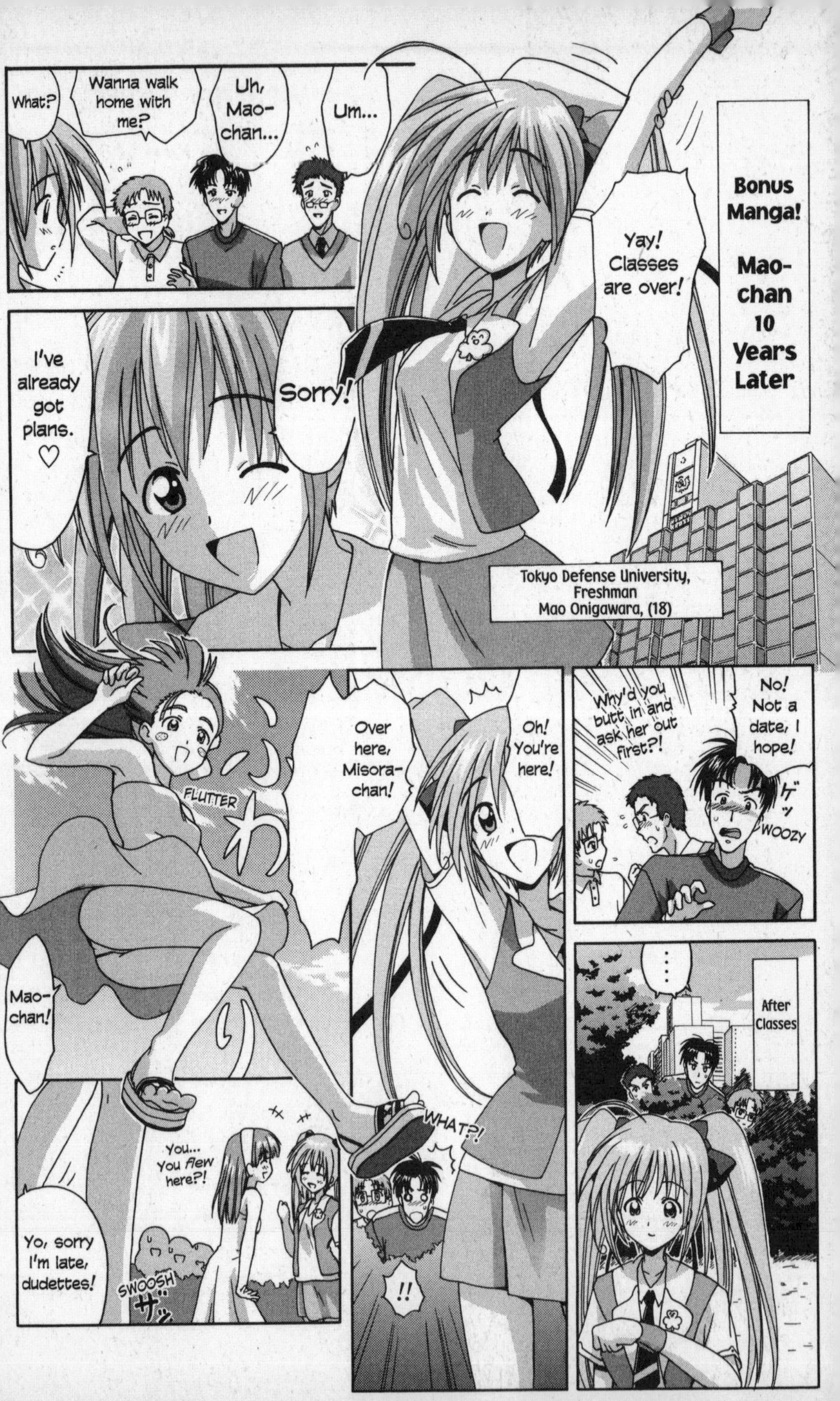
Bonus Manga!
Mao-chan 10 Years Later
Yay! Classes are over!
Tokyo Defense University, Freshman Mao Onigawara, (18)
Um...
Uh, Mao-chan...
Wanna walk home with me?
What?
Sorry!
I've already got plans. ♡
No! Not a date, I hope!
Why'd you butt in and ask her out first?!
WOOZY
After Classes
....
Oh! You're here!
Over here, Misora-chan!
WHAT?!
!!
Mao-chan!
FLUTTER
You... You flew here?!
Yo, sorry I'm late, dudettes!
SWOOSH

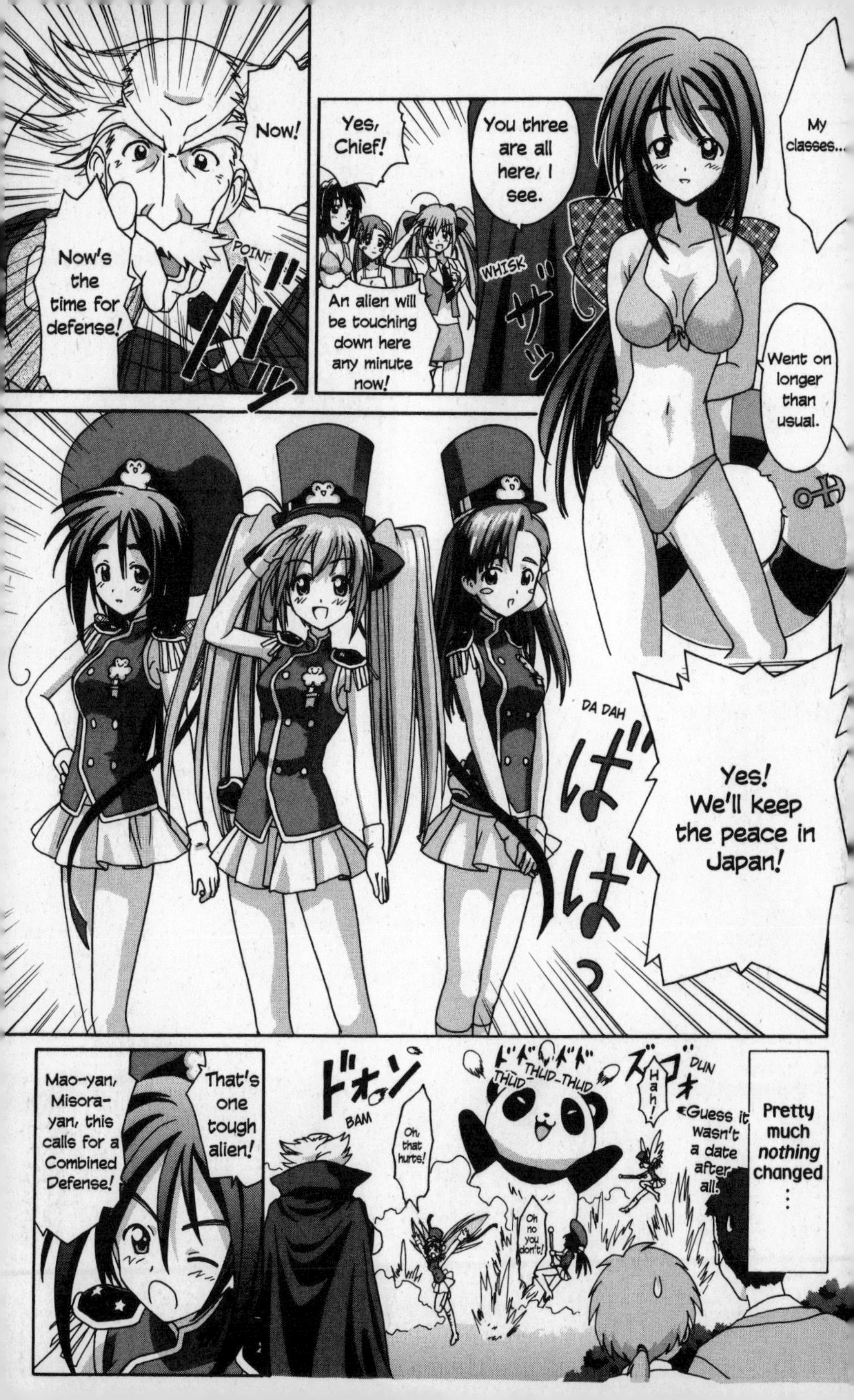

My classes...
Went on longer than usual.
You three are all here, I see.
Yes, Chief!
WHISK
An alien will be touching down here any minute now!
Now!
POINT
Now's the time for defense!
DA DAH
Yes! We'll keep the peace in Japan!
Pretty much *nothing* changed...
Guess it wasn't a date after all.
DUN
Hah!
THUD THUD THUD
Oh no you don't!
Oh, that hurts!
BAM
That's one tough alien!
Mao-yan, Misora-yan, this calls for a Combined Defense!

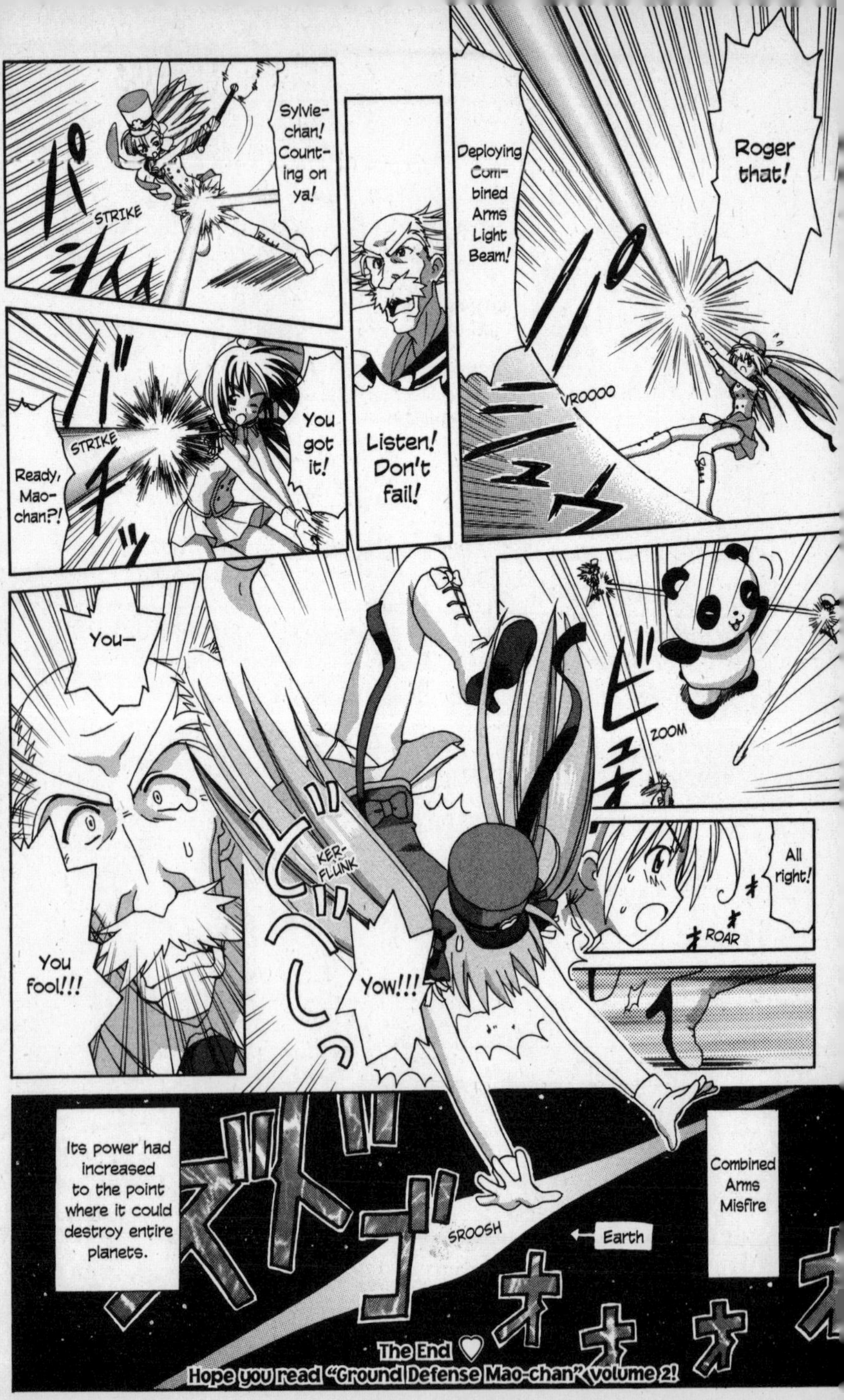
Roger that!
Deploying Combined Arms Light Beam!
VROOOO
Listen! Don't fail!
Sylvie-chan! Counting on ya!
STRIKE
You got it!
STRIKE
Ready, Mao-chan?!
ZOOM
All right!
ROAR
KER-FLUNK
YOW!!!
You—
You fool!!!
Combined Arms Misfire
Earth
SROOSH
Its power had increased to the point where it could destroy entire planets.
The End ♡
Hope you read "Ground Defense Mao-chan" volume 2!

Cute Aliens!

From Chapter One
Alien Tiger
Cute alien from chapter 1. A stuffed animal. Don't his eyes look sweet?

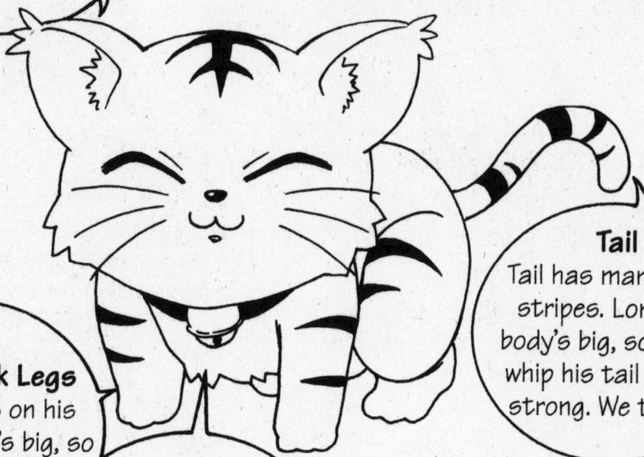

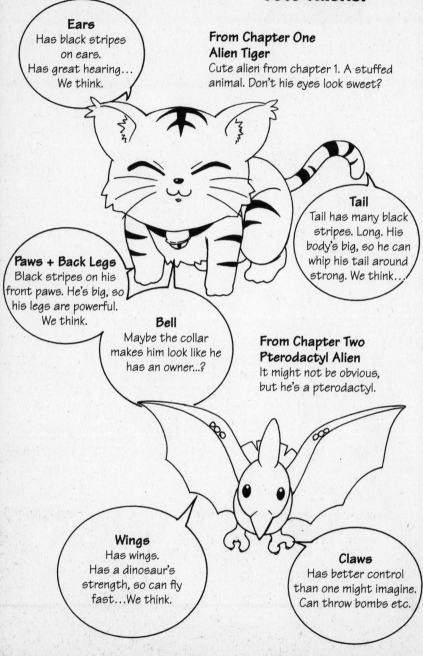

Ears
Has black stripes on ears. Has great hearing… We think.

Tail
Tail has many black stripes. Long. His body's big, so he can whip his tail around strong. We think…

Paws + Back Legs
Black stripes on his front paws. He's big, so his legs are powerful. We think.

Bell
Maybe the collar makes him look like he has an owner...?

From Chapter Two
Pterodactyl Alien
It might not be obvious, but he's a pterodactyl.

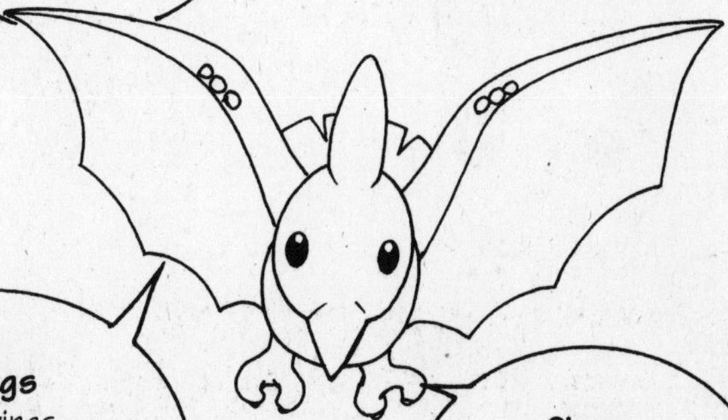

Wings
Has wings. Has a dinosaur's strength, so can fly fast…We think.

Claws
Has better control than one might imagine. Can throw bombs etc.

From Chapter Three
Dolphin Alien
This is a dolphin alien. Mao-chan and the girls take it down before we can see all of its abilities.

Brain
Very intelligent. Can pick up long-distance sonar signals etc.

Tail
The most important instrument in the water. Apparently its body is 100% waterproof!

From Chapter Four
Rabbit-type Alien
Alien that Mao-chan went after during her school Athletic Meet. Since he's small and cute he's not very powerful, but pretty fast on his feet.

Bunny Body
Small. Cute. But weak. Mao-chan took him down with one strike.

Bunny Ears
Big ears, so has good hearing. We think.

From Chapter Four
Grade School Defense Corps Aliens
Specially made to look exactly like Mao-chan and the others. To Chinami-chan they are "Super Aliens," but unfortunately they're such accurate replicas, they were even programmed with Mao-chan's clumsiness!

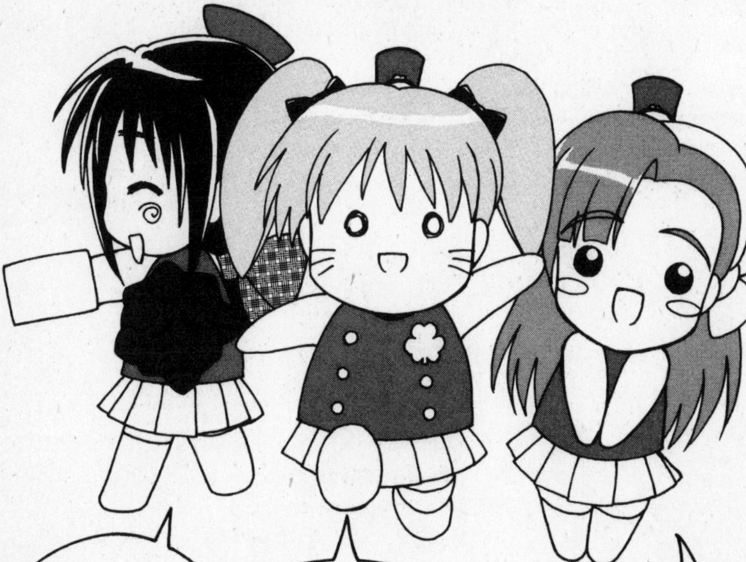

Sylvie-chan
Carries a hammer in her right hand, a club in her left. Capable of doing a lot of damage. Just like the real Sylvie-chan, she smiles all the time so it's hard to figure out what's really going on in her mind.

Mao-chan
Fishlike eyes. And whiskers. Of the three, this one's the least cute. Mao-chan herself is shocked to see it. This alien is super klutzy, just like Mao-chan, and that characteristic is what brings all three aliens down in the end.

Misora-chan
Misora-chan, obedient and polite. Her alien likeness is just the same, and waits patiently at a red light, for example. No other special features to speak of. Unlike the real Misora-chan, the alien can't fly.

At first, *Mao-chan* was just supposed to be a TV anime, so when I heard it would become a comic I was very surprised. I believe that you, RAN, are one of the main reasons we were able to have such great support from readers. Your work is so good, and you have a great way of stretching out the deep nature of the characters and story. You're really like my true successor, so maybe it was simply a matter of time before you leapfrogged me. LOL!

Anyway, work within your limits but don't wear yourself out. After the anime is over, *Mao-chan* will be followed unhurriedly but in earnest by *Negima!*, so I hope you readers will enjoy it!

Ken Akamatsu

The adventures of Mao-chan and her friends will
continue in *Mao-chan*, Volume 2. Please visit our website
(www.delreymanga.com) to find out when this volume will
be available in English!

TOMARE!

[STOP!]

You are going the wrong way!

Manga is a completely different type of reading experience.

To start at the *beginning*, go to the *end*!

That's right! Authentic manga is read the traditional Japanese way—from right to left, exactly the *opposite* of how American books are read. It's easy to follow: Just go to the other end of the book, and read each page—and each panel—from right side to left side, starting at the top right. Now you're experiencing manga as it was meant to be.